W9-CQE-597

IC OP-AMP
COOKBOOK

by

Walter G. Jung

Howard W. Sams & Co., Inc.
4300 WEST 62ND ST. INDIANAPOLIS, INDIANA 46268 USA

Preface

At the time this book was conceived, several texts and handbooks concerning operational amplifiers had already been published. Indeed, many of them are well accepted, and the reader will find them referenced at appropriate points within this one. No attempt is made to detract from these previous efforts; however, it can be said that none addresses itself specifically and wholly to the IC op amp, with an in-depth discussion of applications for specific standard devices. Therein lies the philosophy behind this book and why it is intended to be an appropriate complement to the already existing literature.

Depending on one's particular background, working environment, etc., we each tend to take a slightly different approach to a design problem. There are, however, certain ground rules that the greatest percentage of people will follow in arriving at solutions to these problems. In the use of operational amplifiers, the trend has been toward the IC op amp, and among the numerous types available, there are definite standards that fulfill the greatest percentage of needs. Recognizing the inherent economy and widespread appeal of the IC op amp, this book attempts to address the considerations in applying it with maximum effectiveness in a wide variety of circuits. The name chosen, *IC Op-Amp Cookbook*, is intended to convey this concept. But, as will be seen, the book is more than just a "cookbook"; it involves general applications considerations as well as a substantial amount of theory to support the applications illustrated.

Some insight into the rationale behind the format of the book is helpful in assessing its value to the individual reader. If one is to undertake the task of discussing the uses of IC op amps, there are certain general requirements that must be met. Two of the biggest considerations are style and content—decide what to say and how best to say it. Before getting into the actual contents, a word about the style chosen is appropriate. "Style," as referred to here, is not style in a grammatical sense but is the level on which the book is written. The author firmly believes that practical writing is more useful than pure theory to greater numbers of people. Thus, while there is theory in this book, the main emphasis is on what the theory means in practical applications. The real world of the IC op amp is much more concerned with the details of making a device work as intended rather than making equations balance. So the format chosen is one of "down-to-earth" discussions as viewed from the *user's* standpoint. This is intended to appeal to users on various levels, from student to technician to design engineer, and hopefully to satisfy the needs of all. While a universally appealing book is perhaps somewhat unrealistic, the broadness of applicability can certainly be optimized by keeping everything as clear and understandable as possible while discussing problems meaningful to all users.

The "content" of this book also takes on the prerequisite of broad appeal. Thus, obvious inclusions are such op-amp standards as the 709, 101, and 741. But the scope of the book is not limited to general-purpose devices; it also encompasses other, more-specialized devices —those that are optimized for certain specific performance parameters. The specialized types chosen here are also standard type numbers, as evidenced by broad industry acceptance.

With the complement of devices chosen, a wide range of applications is thus possible, with optimized performance available in terms of virtually any specific criterion. This factor should be of interest to the designer seeking high performance by using op amps. Throughout the book, the discussions are directed to indicate the optimum device for a specific use, and considerations for its application, such as speed, accuracy, dc stability, power consumption, and other performance parameters, are covered.

Given this general format, there is one additional consideration that is generally applicable to circuitry discussions. An applications book may be used in various degrees by different owners. A person new to a particular technique may want to study circuits and theory in some detail. For this type of use, the supportive theoretical background is intended, and appropriate references are listed for further reading in most instances. Others may desire a circuit to fulfill a certain function, and will make minimal use of the text. For this type of use, well-annotated schematics are provided, replete with values and suggestions for modifications if desired. Wherever possible, the pertinent design equations, which summarize the function of the circuit, are also provided.

WALTER G. JUNG

Acknowledgments

No undertaking of this nature can be successful without aid from various sources. The author was most fortunate during the writing of this book to have the benefit of critical review from industry experts. In many cases, these individuals are the designers of the devices discussed.

For an exceptionally thorough critique and innumerable helpful suggestions, special thanks go to Bob Dobkin of National Semiconductor Corporation. Thanks also go to Carl Nelson and Tom Fredriksen of National, to Bob Ricks of Fairchild Semiconductor, to Don Kesner and Don Aldridge of Motorola Semiconductor, to Don Jones of Harris Semiconductor, to Hal Wittlinger of RCA, to Werner Hoeft of Signetics, and to Bob Jones of AAI Corporation.

The author was also fortunate to obtain permission to use portions of manufacturers' technical literature. In this, the aid of the following companies is gratefully acknowledged:

Fairchild Semiconductor
Harris Semiconductor
Motorola Semiconductor Products
National Semiconductor Corp.
RCA Corp.
Signetics Corp.

Finally, and most certainly not least, my sincere thanks to an overworked wife, Anne, for enduring the punishment of literally thousands of pages of "hieroglyphics" and for transforming them into a manuscript. Thanks also go to research assistants Jeannie and Mark.

W. G. J.

To Anne, with my love and appreciation.

Contents

Introduction and Historical Background

Before discussing modern operational amplifiers, we should first review the basics of what an operational amplifier (op amp) is. We will do this in two stages: (1) discuss what an op amp is in the *ideal* sense, and (2) discuss what an op amp *actually* is within the limitations of integrated circuits.

In many applications, the differences between ideal and actual (nonideal) operation will be so small that for all practical purposes they will be negligible. In other applications, the differences will be slight, yet still measurable. Often the overall performance can be enhanced by careful selection of the type of device and by optimizing the parameters that are under our control. This requires an understanding of both the basic concepts of op amps and the specific devices now available.

The original concept of the operational amplifier came from the field of analog computers, where operational techniques were used as early as the 1940s. The name *operational amplifier* derives from the concept of an extremely high gain, differential-input dc amplifier, the operating characteristics of which were determined by the feedback elements used with it. By changing the types and arrangement of the feedback elements, different analog *operations* could be implemented; to a large degree, the overall circuit characteristics were determined *only* by these feedback elements. Thus, the same amplifier was able to perform a variety of operations, and the gradual development of operational amplifiers grew into the beginning of a new era in circuit design concepts.

Early operational amplifiers used the basic hardware of that era—the vacuum tube. Significantly widespread use of op amps did not really begin until the 1960s, when solid-state techniques were applied to op-amp circuit design. This was first evidenced by solid-state op-amp modules, which realized the internal circuitry of the op amp in a discrete solid-state design. Then, in the mid 1960s, the first IC op amps were introduced. Within a few years, IC op amps became a standard design tool encompassing applications far beyond the original scope of analog computer circuits.

With the mass-production capabilities of IC manufacturing techniques, IC op amps became available in large volume, which, in turn, lowered their cost. Today, a general-purpose IC op amp having a gain of 100 dB, an input-offset voltage of 1.0 mV, an input current of 100 nA, and a bandwidth of 1.0 MHz can be purchased for less than a dollar. The amplifier, which was a system comprised of many discrete components in the early days, has evolved into a discrete component itself—a reality that has changed the entire picture of linear circuit design.

With this highly sophisticated parcel of gain available at passive-component prices, discrete active-component designs have become a waste of time and money for most dc and low-frequency applications. Clearly, the IC op amp has redefined the "ground rules" for electronic circuits by placing the emphasis of circuit design more on a systems basis. Intelligent application of these "components that are systems" is what we must now concern ourselves with in order to be ready for the challenges of the future.

I

INTRODUCING THE IC OP AMP

1

Op-Amp Basics

1.1 THE IDEAL OP AMP

The basic fundamentals of the ideal operational amplifier are relatively straightforward. Perhaps the best approach to understanding the ideal op amp is to forget any conventional thinking about amplifier components—transistors, tubes, or whatever. Instead, think only in general terms and consider the amplifier in block form with its input and output terminals. We will then discuss the amplifier in this *ideal* sense and disregard what is inside the block.

Such an idealized amplifier is shown in Fig. 1-1. This amplifier is a direct-coupled device with differential inputs and a single-ended output. The amplifier responds only to the difference voltage between the two input terminals, not to their common potential. A positive-going signal at the inverting ($-$) input produces a negative-going signal at the output, whereas the same signal at the non-inverting ($+$) input produces a positive-going output. With a differential-input voltage, E_{in}, the output voltage, E_o, will be $A_{vo}E_{in}$, where A_{vo} is the gain of the amplifier. Both input terminals of the amplifier will always be used, regardless of the application. The output signal is single-ended and is referred to ground; thus, bipolar ($\pm$) power supplies are used.

With these functions of the input and the output in mind, we can now define the ideal properties of this amplifier, which are:

1. The voltage gain is infinite—$A_{vo} = \infty$.
2. The input resistance is infinite—$r_{in} = \infty$.
3. The output resistance is zero—$r_o = 0$.

4. The bandwidth is infinite—BW $= \infty$.

5. There is zero input offset voltage—$E_o = 0$ if $E_{in} = 0$.

From these ideal characteristics we can deduce two very important additional properties of the operational amplifier. Since the voltage gain is infinite, any output signal developed will be the result of an infinitesimally small input signal. Thus, in essence:

1. *The differential-input voltage is zero.*

Also, if the input resistance is infinite;

2. *There is no current flow into either input terminal.*

These two properties may be regarded as *axioms,* and they will be used repeatedly in op-amp circuit analysis and design. Once these properties are understood, the operation of virtually any op-amp

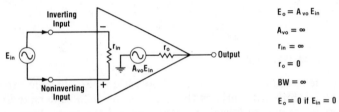

$$E_o = A_{vo} E_{in}$$
$$A_{vo} = \infty$$
$$r_{in} = \infty$$
$$r_o = 0$$
$$BW = \infty$$
$$E_o = 0 \text{ if } E_{in} = 0$$

Fig. 1-1. Equivalent circuit for ideal operational amplifier.

circuit can be logically deduced. The following discussions of basic op-amp circuit configurations will serve to illustrate this point.

1.1.1 Basic Op-Amp Configurations

Operational amplifiers can be connected in two basic amplifying circuits: (1) the *inverting* and (2) the *noninverting* configurations. Virtually all other op-amp circuits are based in some manner on these two basic configurations. In addition, there are closely related variations on the two basic circuits, plus another basic circuit which is a combination of the first two—the *differential amplifier.*

The Inverting Amplifier

Fig. 1-2 illustrates the first basic op-amp configuration—the inverting amplifier. In this circuit, the $(+)$ input is grounded and the signal is applied to the $(-)$ input through R_{in}, with feedback returned from the output through R_f. By applying the ideal op-amp properties previously stated, the distinguishing features of this circuit may be analyzed as follows:

Since the amplifier has infinite gain, it will develop its output voltage, E_o, with zero input voltage. Since the differential input to A is E_s, $E_s = 0$. If E_s is zero, then the full input voltage, E_{in}, must appear across R_{in}, making the current in R_{in}

$$I_{in} = \frac{E_{in}}{R_{in}}.$$

Also, since $I_s = 0$ due to infinite input impedance, the input current, I_{in}, must also flow in R_f; thus,

$$I_f = I_{in}.$$

The output voltage, E_o, appears across R_f and is negative due to a sign inversion in the amplifier. Stating I_f in terms of E_o and R_f, then,

$$I_f = \frac{-E_o}{R_f}.$$

Since I_{in} and I_f are equal, we may state

$$\frac{E_{in}}{R_{in}} = \frac{-E_o}{R_f}.$$

This equality may be restated in terms of gain as

$$\frac{E_o}{E_{in}} = \frac{-R_f}{R_{in}},$$

which is, in fact, the characteristic gain equation for the ideal inverting amplifier.

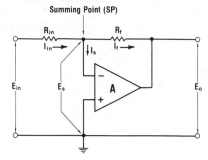

$I_s = 0$, $E_s = 0$, $\therefore$ SP is at zero potential or a virtual ground.

Then, $I_{in} = \dfrac{E_{in}}{R_{in}}$.

Since $I_s = 0$, $I_f = I_{in}$,

and $I_f = \dfrac{-E_o}{R_f}$ (due to inversion),

then $\dfrac{E_{in}}{R_{in}} = \dfrac{-E_o}{R_f}$.

Gain $= \dfrac{E_o}{E_{in}} = \dfrac{-R_f}{R_{in}}$.

Summary of Inverting Amplifier Characteristics:

(1) Gain $= \dfrac{-R_f}{R_{in}}$, unlimited in range (R_f may be 0 for 0 gain).

(2) Input Impedance $= R_{in}$.

(3) $I_f = I_{in}$, regardless of R_f.

(4) Summing point is a virtual ground at the same potential as (+) input.

Fig. 1-2. The op-amp inverting amplifier configuration.

There are additional features of the inverting amplifier which should be noted. The gain can be varied by adjusting either R_f or R_{in}. If R_f is varied from zero to infinity, the gain will also vary from zero to infinity since it is directly proportional to R_f. The input impedance is equal to R_{in}, and E_{in} and R_{in} alone determine I_{in}. Thus, $I_f = I_{in}$ for any value of R_f.

The input to the amplifier, or junction of the input and feedback signals, is a node of zero voltage, regardless of the magnitude of I_{in}. Thus, the junction is a *virtual ground,* a point that will always be at the same potential as the $(+)$ input. Since the input and output signals sum at this junction, it is also known as a *summing point.* This final characteristic leads to a third basic op-amp axiom, which applies to closed-loop operation:

   3. *With the loop closed, the $(-)$ input will be driven to the potential of the $(+)$ or reference input.*

This property may or may not have been obvious already from the theory of zero differential input voltage. It is, however, very helpful in understanding op-amp circuitry to regard the $(+)$ input as a reference terminal which will command the level that *both* inputs assume. Thus, this voltage may be ground (as shown) or any desired potential.

The Noninverting Amplifier

The second basic configuration of the ideal op amp is the noninverting amplifier, shown in Fig. 1-3. This circuit clearly illustrates the validity of Axiom 3. In this circuit, voltage E_{in} is applied to the $(+)$ input, and a fraction of the output signal, E_o, is applied to the

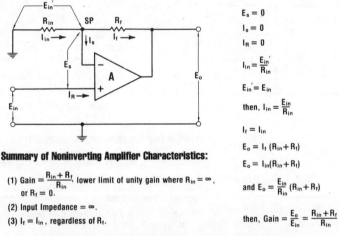

$$E_s = 0$$
$$I_s = 0$$
$$I_R = 0$$
$$I_{in} = \frac{E_{in}'}{R_{in}}$$
$$E_{in}' = E_{in}$$
$$\text{then, } I_{in} = \frac{E_{in}}{R_{in}}$$
$$I_f = I_{in}$$
$$E_o = I_f (R_{in} + R_f)$$
$$E_o = I_{in}(R_{in} + R_f)$$
$$\text{and } E_o = \frac{E_{in}}{R_{in}} (R_{in} + R_f)$$
$$\text{then, Gain} = \frac{E_o}{E_{in}} = \frac{R_{in} + R_f}{R_{in}}$$

Summary of Noninverting Amplifier Characteristics:

(1) Gain $= \frac{R_{in} + R_f}{R_{in}}$, lower limit of unity gain where $R_{in} = \infty$, or $R_f = 0$.

(2) Input Impedance $= \infty$.

(3) $I_f = I_{in}$, regardless of R_f.

Fig. 1-3. The op-amp noninverting amplifier configuration.

(−) input from the R_f-R_{in} voltage divider. Since no input current flows into either input terminal, and since $E_s = 0$, the voltage E_{in}' is equal to E_{in}. Inasmuch as

$$I_{in} = \frac{E_{in}}{R_{in}},$$

then it is also true that

$$I_{in} = \frac{E_{in}'}{R_{in}}.$$

Also, since

$$I_f = I_{in},$$

then

$$E_o = I_f \ (R_{in} + R_f)$$

and

$$E_o = I_{in} \ (R_{in} + R_f).$$

Substituting,

$$E_o = \frac{E_{in}}{R_{in}} \ (R_{in} + R_f).$$

Then, in terms of gain,

$$\frac{E_o}{E_{in}} = \frac{R_{in} + R_f}{R_{in}},$$

which is the characteristic gain equation for the ideal noninverting amplifier.

Additional characteristics of this configuration can also be deduced. The lower limit of gain occurs when $R_f = 0$, which yields a gain of unity. In the inverting amplifier, current I_{in} always determines I_f, which is independent of R_f. (This is also true in the noninverting amplifier.) Thus, R_f may be used as a linear gain control, capable of increasing gain from a minimum of unity to a maximum of infinity. The input impedance is infinite, since an ideal amplifier is assumed.

Configurations Based on the Inverting and Noninverting Circuits

The Differential Amplifier. A third op-amp configuration, known as the differential amplifier, is a combination of the two previous configurations. Although it is based on the other two circuits, the differential amplifier has unique characteristics of its own. This circuit, shown in Fig. 1-4, has signals applied to both input terminals and uses the natural differential amplification of the op amp.

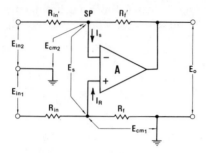

Summary of Differential Amplifier Characteristics:

(1) Differential-Mode Gain ($E_{in_1} \neq E_{in_2}$):

$$\frac{E_o}{E_{in_1} - E_{in_2}} = \frac{R_f}{R_{in}}.$$

(2) Common-Mode Gain ($E_{in_1} \equiv E_{in_2}$):

When,

$$\frac{R_f}{R_{in}} \equiv \frac{R_f'}{R_{in}'}, = 0.$$

When,

$$\frac{R_f}{R_{in}} \neq \frac{R_f'}{R_{in}'}, = \frac{R_f R_{in}' - R_f' R_{in}}{R_{in} R_{in}' + R_{in} R_f}.$$

In terms of resistor match (worst case),

$$= 4\delta \left(\frac{R_f}{R_{in} + R_f}\right),$$

where,

δ = fractional unbalance of resistors (1.0% = 0.01),

and,

R_{in} and R_f are the nominal values.

(3) Input Impedances:

(−) input = R_{in}'
(+) input = $R_{in} + R_f$
differential = $R_{in} + R_{in}'$

$E_s = 0$, $I_s = 0$, $I_R = 0$
$R_f = R_f'$, $R_{in} = R_{in}'$

Let output due to $E_{in_1} = E_{o1}$,

then $E_{o1} = E_{in_1} \left(\dfrac{R_f}{R_{in} + R_f}\right) \left(\dfrac{R_{in}' + R_f'}{R_{in}'}\right)$

$\qquad = E_{in_1} \left(\dfrac{R_f}{R_{in}}\right)$

Let output due to $E_{in_2} = E_{o2}$,

then $E_{o2} = -E_{in_2} \left(\dfrac{R_f'}{R_{in}'}\right) = -E_{in_2} \left(\dfrac{R_f}{R_{in}}\right)$

Total output = $E_o = E_{o1} + E_{o2}$

$E_o = E_{in_1} \left(\dfrac{R_f}{R_{in}}\right) + \left[-E_{in_2} \left(\dfrac{R_f}{R_{in}}\right)\right]$

$\qquad = \left(E_{in_1} - E_{in_2}\right) \dfrac{R_f}{R_{in}}$

Gain $= \dfrac{E_o}{E_{in_1} - E_{in_2}} = \dfrac{R_f}{R_{in}}$

Fig. 1-4. The op-amp differential amplifier configuration.

The circuit may be understood by first considering the two signal inputs separately, then in combination. As before, $E_s = 0$, $I_s = 0$, and $I_R = 0$. In addition, $R_f' = R_f$ and $R_{in}' = R_{in}$.

The output voltage due to E_{in_1} may be termed E_{o_1}. Using the gain equation for the noninverting circuit, and adding the effect of divider R_{in}-R_f, the output, E_{o_1}, will be

$$E_{o_1} = E_{in_1} \left(\frac{R_f}{R_{in} + R_f}\right) \left(\frac{R_{in}' + R_f'}{R_{in}'}\right).$$

Cancelling equal terms and substituting,

$$E_{o_1} = E_{in_1}\left(\frac{R_f}{R_{in}}\right),$$

which is the output due to E_{in_1}.

The output due to E_{in_2} is termed E_{o_2}. Using the gain equation for the inverting circuit, output E_{o_2} will be

$$E_{o_2} = -E_{in_2}\left(\frac{R_f'}{R_{in}'}\right)$$
$$= -E_{in_2}\left(\frac{R_f}{R_{in}}\right).$$

Since the combined output, E_o, will be equal to the sum of E_{o_1} and E_{o_2}, we may write

$$E_o = E_{in_1}\left(\frac{R_f}{R_{in}}\right) + \left[-E_{in_2}\left(\frac{R_f}{R_{in}}\right)\right].$$

By regrouping,

$$E_o = \left(E_{in_1} - E_{in_2}\right)\left(\frac{R_f}{R_{in}}\right).$$

In terms of gain this is

$$\frac{E_o}{E_{in_1} - E_{in_2}} = \frac{R_f}{R_{in}},$$

which is the gain of the stage for differential-mode signals.

This configuration is unique because it can reject a signal common to both inputs. This is due to the property of zero differential input voltage, which is explained as follows:

In the case of identical signals at E_{in_1} and E_{in_2}, the analysis is straightforward. E_{in_1} will be divided by R_{in} and R_f to a smaller voltage, E_{cm_1}, across R_f. Because of infinite amplifier gain and zero differential input voltage, an equal voltage (E_{cm_1}) must appear at SP. Since the network R_{in}'-R_f' is identical to R_{in}-R_f, and since the same voltage is applied to both inputs, it follows that E_o must be at zero potential to maintain E_{cm_2} identical to E_{cm_1}; E_o will be at the same potential as the bottom of R_f, which is, in fact, ground potential. This very useful property of the differential amplifier can be used to discriminate against undesirable common-mode noise components while amplifying signals that appear differentially. If the ratio

$$\frac{R_f'}{R_{in}'}$$

is identical to

$$\frac{R_f}{R_{in}},$$

the gain for common-mode signals is zero since, by definition, the amplifier has no gain for equal signals applied to both inputs.

The two input impedances of the stage are unequal. For the $(+)$ input, the input impedance is $R_{in} + R_f$. The impedance at the $(-)$ input is R_{in}'. The differential-input impedance (for a floating source) is the impedance between the inputs, or $R_{in} + R_{in}'$.

The Summing Inverter. By utilizing the virtual-ground characteristic of the inverting amplifier's summing point, a useful modification is realized—the summing inverter (see Fig. 1-5). In this circuit, as in the inverting amplifier, $E_s = 0$, $I_s = 0$, and $I_f = I_{in}$. However,

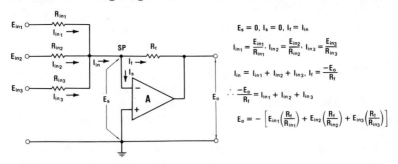

$E_s = 0,\ I_s = 0,\ I_f = I_{in}$

$I_{in1} = \dfrac{E_{in1}}{R_{in1}},\ I_{in2} = \dfrac{E_{in2}}{R_{in2}},\ I_{in3} = \dfrac{E_{in3}}{R_{in3}}$

$I_{in} = I_{in1} + I_{in2} + I_{in3},\ I_f = \dfrac{-E_o}{R_f}$

$\therefore \dfrac{-E_o}{R_f} = I_{in1} + I_{in2} + I_{in3}$

$E_o = -\left[E_{in1}\left(\dfrac{R_f}{R_{in1}}\right) + E_{in2}\left(\dfrac{R_f}{R_{in2}}\right) + E_{in3}\left(\dfrac{R_f}{R_{in3}}\right) \right]$

Summary of Summing-Inverter Characteristics:

(1) Gain (per channel) = $\dfrac{-R_f}{R_{in1}}, \dfrac{-R_f}{R_{in2}}, \dfrac{-R_f}{R_{in3}}$, etc.

(2) R_f varies gain of all inputs; R_{in1}, R_{in2}, R_{in3}, etc., vary individual gains.

(3) Composite output = $E_o = -\left[E_{in1}\left(\dfrac{R_f}{R_{in1}}\right) + E_{in2}\left(\dfrac{R_f}{R_{in2}}\right) + E_{in3}\left(\dfrac{R_f}{R_{in3}}\right) \right]$.

(4) Input impedance = R_{in1}, R_{in2}, R_{in3}, etc.

Fig. 1-5. The op-amp summing inverter.

in the summing inverter I_{in} is the algebraic sum of a number of inputs such as I_{in_1}, I_{in_2}, I_{in_3}, etc. Thus,

$$I_{in_1} = \frac{E_{in_1}}{R_{in_1}},\ I_{in_2} = \frac{E_{in_2}}{R_{in_2}},\ I_{in_3} = \frac{E_{in_3}}{R_{in_3}}$$

and

$$I_{in} = I_{in_1} + I_{in_2} + I_{in_3},\ I_f = \frac{-E_o}{R_f};$$

therefore,

$$\frac{-E_o}{R_f} = I_{in_1} + I_{in_2} + I_{in_3}.$$

Finally, substituting and regrouping gives

$$E_o = -\left[E_{in_1}\left(\frac{R_f}{R_{in_1}}\right) + E_{in_2}\left(\frac{R_f}{R_{in_2}}\right) + E_{in_3}\left(\frac{R_f}{R_{in_3}}\right)\right],$$

which states that the output voltage is the inverted algebraic sum of the input voltages scaled by R_f. Thus, the circuit may be said to be a *scaling adder*.

The overall gain of the circuit is set by R_f, which in this respect behaves as in the basic inverting amplifier. The gains of the individual channels are scaled independently by R_{in_1}, R_{in_2}, R_{in_3}, etc. Similarly, R_{in_1}, R_{in_2}, and R_{in_3} are the input impedances of the respective channels.

Another interesting characteristic of this configuration is the fact that linear signal mixing takes place at the summing point without interaction between inputs, since all signal sources feed into a virtual ground. The circuit can accommodate any number of inputs by adding additional input resistors at the summing point, such as R_{in_4}, R_{in_5}, etc.

Although the preceding circuits have been described in terms of input and feedback resistances, the resistors may be replaced by complex elements, and the basic op-amp axioms will still hold true. Two circuits that demonstrate this are further modifications of the inverting amplifier.

The Integrator. It has been shown that both basic op-amp configurations act to maintain the feedback current, I_f, at all times equal to I_{in}. A modification of the inverting amplifier which takes advantage of this characteristic is the integrator, shown in Fig. 1-6. An input voltage, E_{in}, is applied to R_{in}, thus developing current I_{in}. As in the basic inverter, $E_s = 0$, $I_s = 0$, and $I_f = I_{in}$. The feedback element in the integrator is a capacitor, C_f. Therefore, the constant current, I_f, in C_f builds a linear voltage ramp across C_f. The output voltage is thus an integral of the input current, which is forced to charge C_f by the feedback loop. The change in voltage across C_f is

$$-\Delta E_o = \frac{I_{in}\Delta t}{C_f},$$

which makes the output change per unit of time

$$\frac{\Delta E_o}{\Delta t} = \frac{-E_{in}}{R_{in}C_f}.$$

21

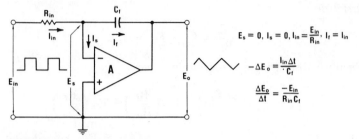

$$E_s = 0,\ I_s = 0,\ I_{in} = \frac{E_{in}}{R_{in}},\ I_f = I_{in}$$

$$-\Delta E_o = \frac{I_{in}\Delta t}{C_f}$$

$$\frac{\Delta E_o}{\Delta t} = \frac{-E_{in}}{R_{in}C_f}$$

Summary of Integrator Characteristics:

(1) Circuit integrates input current, thus

$$\frac{\Delta E_o}{\Delta t} = \frac{-E_{in}}{R_{in}C_f}.$$

(2) Input impedance $= R_{in}$.

Fig. 1-6. The op-amp integrator.

As with the other inverting-amplifier configurations, the input impedance is simply R_{in}.

The Differentiator. A second modification of the inverting amplifier, which also uses the current in a capacitor to advantage, is the differentiator, shown in Fig. 1-7. In this circuit, the positions of R and C are reversed from those in the integrator, placing the capacitive element in the input network. Thus, the input current is made to be proportional to the rate of change of the input voltage:

$$I_{in} = \frac{\Delta E_{in} C_{in}}{\Delta t}.$$

Again,

$$I_f = I_{in},$$

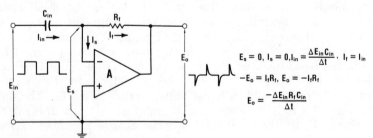

$$E_s = 0,\ I_s = 0, I_{in} = \frac{\Delta E_{in}C_{in}}{\Delta t},\ I_f = I_{in}$$

$$-E_o = I_f R_f,\ E_o = -I_f R_f$$

$$E_o = \frac{-\Delta E_{in} R_f C_{in}}{\Delta t}$$

Summary of Differentiator Characteristics:

(1) Circuit responds to the rate of change of input voltage E_{in}, thus

$$E_o = \frac{-\Delta E_{in} R_f C_{in}}{\Delta t}$$

Fig. 1-7. The op-amp differentiator.

and since

$$-E_o = I_f R_f,$$
$$E_o = -I_f R_f.$$

Substitution gives

$$E_o = \frac{-\Delta E_{in} R_f C_{in}}{\Delta t}.$$

The Voltage Follower. A special modification of the noninverting amplifier is the unity-gain stage shown in Fig. 1-8. In this circuit, R_{in} has increased to infinity, R_f is zero, and the feedback is

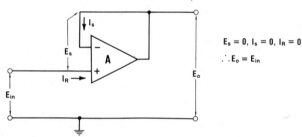

$E_s = 0, \ I_s = 0, \ I_R = 0$

$\therefore E_o = E_{in}$

Summary of Voltage-Follower Characteristics:

(1) Gain = 1.

(2) Input impedance = ∞.

Fig. 1-8. The op-amp voltage follower.

100%. E_o is then exactly equal to E_{in}, since $E_s = 0$. The circuit is known as a "voltage follower" since the output is a unity-gain, in-phase replica of the input voltage. The input impedance of this stage is also infinite.

Summary of the Basic Amplifier Configurations and Their Characteristics

All of the circuit characteristics that have been described are important because they are a basis for the entire foundation of op-amp circuit technology. The five basic criteria that describe the ideal amplifier are fundamental, and from these evolve the three main axioms of op-amp theory, which bear repeating:

1. *The differential-input voltage is zero.*
2. *There is no current flow into either input terminal.*
3. *With the loop closed, the* $(-)$ *input will be driven to the potential of the* $(+)$ *or reference input.*

These three axioms have been illustrated in all of the basic circuits and their variations. In the inverting configuration, the concepts of zero input current and zero differential input voltage give rise to the concepts of the summing point and the virtual ground, where the inverting input is held by feedback to the same potential as the grounded noninverting input. Using the concept of the non-inverting input as a reference terminal, the noninverting amplifier and voltage follower illustrate how an input voltage is indirectly scaled through negative feedback to the inverting input, which is forced to follow at an identical potential. The full differential configuration combines these concepts, illustrating the ideal of simultaneous differential amplification and common-mode signal rejection. The variations of the inverter amplify its principles. In all these circuits, we have also seen how the performance is determined solely by components connected externally to the amplifier.

At this point, we have defined the op amp in an ideal sense and have examined its basic circuit configurations. With one further definition—the symbology of the device—we will move to the real world of practical devices and examine their departures from the ideal and how to cope with them.

1.1.2 The Standard Op-Amp Schematic Symbol and Its Use

One additional basic tool of the op amp is its schematic symbol. This is fundamental, for a correctly drawn schematic transmits a great deal of knowledge about the workings of a circuit. The preferred op-amp symbol is illustrated with annotations in Fig. 1-9.

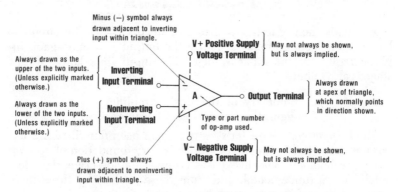

Fig. 1-9. The standard op-amp schematic symbol.

The basic symbol is the triangle, which is generally understood to imply amplification. The inputs are at the base of the triangle, with the output at the apex. In accordance with normal signal-flow convention, the symbol is drawn with the apex (output) to the right, but this may be altered if necessary for clarification of other circuit details.

The two inputs are usually drawn as shown with the noninverting (+) input the lower of the two. Exceptions to this rule occur in special circumstances where it would be awkward to retain the standard arrangement. Furthermore, the two inputs are always clearly identified by (+) and (−) symbols, which are adjacent to their respective leads and are drawn within the body of the triangle.

Supply-voltage leads are preferrably drawn extending above and below the triangle as shown. These may not be shown in all cases (in the interest of simplicity), but they are always implied. Generally, in sketches it is sufficient to use the 3-lead symbol to convey an intent, with power connections understood.

Finally, the type or part number of the device used is centered within the body of the triangle. If the circuit is a general one indicating any op amp, the symbol used is A (or A_1, A_2, etc.).

1.2 THE NONIDEAL OP AMP

So far we have examined the op-amp concept only in a general sense, assuming idealized parameters. In a real-world situation, the ideal amplifier does not exist. However, it is important to stress the idealized line of thinking because in many applications, the differences between ideal and actual are close to negligible. Furthermore, we should always be aware of how closely we actually approach "idealized" performance. We will now examine the factors that determine how small these differences are and learn how to control performance so as to minimize them. As might be expected, these errors arise due to departures from the ideal characteristics set forth in Section 1.1.

1.2.1 Errors Due to Finite Open-Loop Gain

The principal source of error in op-amp applications is the factor contributed by finite open-loop gain. General-purpose IC op amps have a typical dc open-loop gain close to 100 dB, which, while large, is certainly a long way from being infinite. Also, the actual gain figure will vary from unit to unit because of the normal production tolerances associated with IC manufacturing processes. In a given device, the open-loop gain will also vary to some degree with temperature, loading, and supply voltage. In addition to this, the open-loop gain of an op amp decreases with frequency because of the necessity for correcting the overall phase response to ensure stability under closed-loop conditions. As a result, a typical open-loop gain-versus-frequency plot looks something like Fig. 1-10. Thus, in reality, the open-loop gain characteristics of practical IC op amps are nonideal in two of the basic criteria: (1) the dc gain is not infinite and (2) the bandwidth is not infinite.

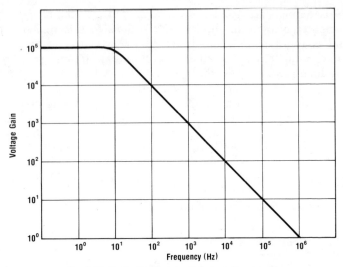

Fig. 1-10. Typical op-amp open-loop gain response.

To express the error factor due to a finite open-loop gain, we must again examine the closed-loop inverting and noninverting configurations and define a few more parameters associated with each. Assume all other characteristics of the amplifier are ideal (for the moment) except for the finite gain, A_{vo}.

Fig. 1-11A illustrates an inverting amplifier which has a finite gain, A_{vo}. R_f and R_{in} are the feedback and input resistors, and the E_{in} generator is assumed to have zero source impedance. If we examine the path of the feedback signal from E_o, we note that it undergoes an attenuation due to the presence of R_f and R_{in}. If we term the attenuated signal that appears at SP as E_e, then E_e is related to E_o by

$$\frac{E_e}{E_o} = \frac{R_{in}}{R_{in} + R_f}.$$

This introduces a new term, β, which is defined as the *feedback attenuation factor* and is expressed as

$$\beta = \frac{R_{in}}{R_{in} + R_f}.$$

By definition, β is the ratio of the feedback signal to the output signal. It can reach a maximum of unity (or zero attenuation) under the condition of 100% feedback. The feedback divider, which determines β, takes into account the total attenuation between the amplifier output and the summing point. This includes frequency-dependent effects due to reactive elements (if any) and, in general, all attenuation. Therefore, to be precise, R_f and R_{in} of Fig. 1-11A symbolize the total equivalent feedback attenuation network. (This will be more evident as we examine other error sources.) The signal, E_e, is amplified by the open-loop gain of the amplifier (A_{vo}) and produces output voltage E_o.

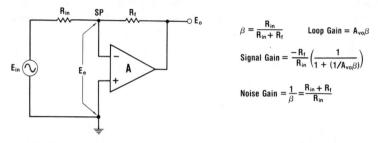

$$\beta = \frac{R_{in}}{R_{in} + R_f} \qquad \text{Loop Gain} = A_{vo}\beta$$

$$\text{Signal Gain} = \frac{-R_f}{R_{in}} \left(\frac{1}{1 + (1/A_{vo}\beta)} \right)$$

$$\text{Noise Gain} = \frac{1}{\beta} = \frac{R_{in} + R_f}{R_{in}}$$

(A) Inverting configuration.

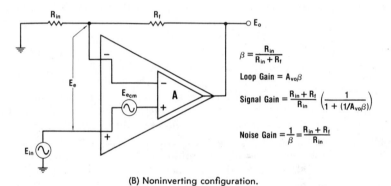

$$\beta = \frac{R_{in}}{R_{in} + R_f}$$

$$\text{Loop Gain} = A_{vo}\beta$$

$$\text{Signal Gain} = \frac{R_{in} + R_f}{R_{in}} \left(\frac{1}{1 + (1/A_{vo}\beta)} \right)$$

$$\text{Noise Gain} = \frac{1}{\beta} = \frac{R_{in} + R_f}{R_{in}}$$

(B) Noninverting configuration.

Fig. 1-11. Gain errors in inverting and noninverting configurations.

At this point, we have traversed the complete path around the feedback loop—through the feedback network, through the amplifier, and back to the output—for reasons which may not yet be obvious. However, if we can momentarily regard the feedback path from E_o with the amplifier disconnected, an interesting observation will ensue. The signal fed back from E_o is attenuated by β, then amplified by A_{vo}. Thus, the total gain of the loop is $A_{vo} \times \beta$, and this expression is known as *loop gain*. Thus,

$$\text{Loop Gain} = A_{vo}\beta.$$

Loop gain is a measure of how closely an amplifying configuration approaches the ideal. If A_{vo} were really infinite, we would not be concerned with the total gain around the feedback loop. This may be intuitively appreciated by visualizing the effects of variations in either A_{vo} or β on the error signal, E_e. Ideally, E_e is zero due to infinite amplifier gain. Any increase of E_e from zero represents a deviation from the ideal. In practice, this can result from either a low A_{vo} or a small β, either of which minimizes their product—loop gain. We have now reached a point where we can relate this to the original ideal gain expression and write a new expression that gives an error factor caused by the finite gain, A_{vo}:

$$A_v = \underbrace{\left(\frac{-R_f}{R_{in}}\right)}_{\substack{\text{Ideal} \\ \text{Expression}}} \quad \underbrace{\left(\frac{1}{1 + (1/A_{vo}\beta)}\right)}_{\substack{\text{Error} \\ \text{Multiplier}}}$$

This equation is separated into two parts to illustrate the modification of the ideal by $A_{vo}\beta$. As the right-hand term of the denominator of the error multiplier approaches zero, the error multiplier approaches unity until $A_{vo} = \infty$, the point at which the equation reduces to the ideal. Thus, the greater $A_{vo}\beta$ is, the closer the amplifier is to ideal performance. In practice, this means that either a greater A_{vo} or a greater β (more feedback) maximizes $A_{vo}\beta$. From this it is obvious that high-gain stages (which require a small β) require more open-loop gain to approach ideal performance.

To examine the effects of loop gain on the noninverting amplifier, we refer to Fig. 1-11B. Although the method of signal amplification is different in this configuration, the feedback path is identical to that of the inverter. Therefore, β is determined in exactly the same manner, and the same general considerations apply concerning $A_{vo}\beta$. There is, however, an additional gain-error term in the noninverting amplifier, which is due to the presence of a common-mode voltage, E_{cm}. In the inverting amplifier, there is no common-mode input voltage, since both inputs are effectively grounded. In a noninverting stage, the inputs see a common-mode voltage equal to the input voltage, or

$$E_{cm} = E_{in}.$$

Since a real amplifier responds to common-mode voltages, this error source must be taken into account. The relationship between the common-mode voltage of an op amp and its common-mode error voltage is expressed as a ratio, termed the *common-mode rejection ratio* (CMRR). The existence of a finite CMRR causes this input common-mode error voltage to be generated, which can be expressed as a fraction of the common-mode input voltage:

$$E_{e_{cm}} = \frac{E_{cm}}{CMRR}.$$

It is convenient to model this error voltage as a separate generator in series with an ideal amplifier and consider its effect on the gain. By expressing the error voltage as a fraction, we can include it with A_{vo} and generate a new expression which includes the effects of common-mode gain:

$$\text{Common-Mode Error} = \frac{E_{e_{cm}}}{E_{cm}}.$$

Since

$$E_{e_{cm}} = \frac{E_{cm}}{\text{CMRR}},$$

we may substitute, leaving

$$\text{Common-Mode Error} = \pm\frac{1}{\text{CMRR}}.$$

We must add the qualifier of $(\pm)$, since common-mode error can be an error in either direction; it can either add to or subtract from the input signal. This uncertainty prevents a simple cancellation of common-mode error by adjusting R_{in} or R_f.

We can now write the modified gain expression for the noninverting amplifier:

$$A_v = \underbrace{\left(\frac{R_{in} + R_f}{R_{in}}\right)}_{\substack{\text{Ideal} \\ \text{Expression}}} \quad \underbrace{\left(\frac{1}{1 + (1/A_{vo}\beta)}\right)}_{\substack{\text{Error} \\ \text{Multiplier}}}.$$

To summarize the gain error for both configurations due to finite or modified A_{vo}, we can express the error as a percentage:

$$\% \text{ Error} = \frac{100}{A_{vo}\beta + 1}.$$

Thus a loop gain of 100 (40 dB), for example, will yield a gain error of approximately 1.0%.

As the reader may already have noted, there is a basic difference between the inverting and noninverting configurations in the method of signal amplification, but no difference in the method of calculating β. As a result, for equivalent signal gains, inverting and noninverting stages will have a different β, and thus will have different loop gains. This is also illustrated in Fig. 1-11.

If we examine a unity-gain condition for both configurations, it will be noted that for the inverting stage,

$$\frac{R_f}{R_{in}} = 1, \text{ or } R_f = R_{in},$$

but for the noninverting stage,

$$\frac{R_{in} + R_f}{R_{in}} = 1, \text{ or } R_{in} = \infty.$$

The β equations for the two configurations are then

$$\beta \text{ (Inverting)} = \frac{R_{in}}{R_{in} + R_f} = \frac{R_{in}}{2R_{in}} = 0.5,$$

and

$$\beta \text{ (Noninverting)} = \frac{\infty}{\infty + R_f} = 1.$$

Thus it can be seen that, for equivalent signal gains, the two stages do not have the same β. This difference is most apparent at the lowest gain that both stages are capable of—unity, where the β of the inverting stage is half that of the noninverting stage. The point of this discussion is that for the two stages, signal gain and β do not have the same relationship. In order to compare the two stages directly in terms of β (and hence, loop gain), we must introduce a new term.

The parameter that is defined identically for both configurations is β. Therefore, a gain defined in terms of β would be a useful basis for comparing the two basic stages. This gain is the reciprocal of β and is termed *noise gain:*

$$\text{Noise Gain} = \frac{1}{\beta} = \frac{R_{in} + R_f}{R_{in}},$$

which is the ideal equation. The term that includes error factors due to nonideal gain is the *true noise gain* or *closed-loop gain:*

$$\text{Closed-Loop Gain} = A_{cl} = \underbrace{\left(\frac{1}{\beta}\right)}_{\substack{\text{Ideal} \\ \text{Expression}}} \underbrace{\left(\frac{1}{1 + (1/A_{vo}\beta)}\right)}_{\substack{\text{Error} \\ \text{Multiplier}}}.$$

Noise gain is the inverse of β. Thus, like β it takes into account all feedback resistance and includes frequency effects. Noise gain is the gain seen by amplifier input referred noise and error (offset and drift) parameters. It is often significantly different from signal gain. It is most important that this point be understood because noise gain —not signal gain—is the parameter used in calculations of closed-loop amplifier performance. To illustrate by means of the unity-gain example, the inverting stage has a noise gain of 2, whereas the noninverting stage has a noise gain of 1. In this example, then, the inverting stage would amplify input error components by a factor of 2.

At this point, it is appropriate to summarize the various gain definitions and bring them all into perspective by means of graphical illustration in Fig. 1-12. The definitions are:

Open-Loop Gain (A_{vo}). The open-loop voltage gain of the basic amplifier without feedback but with loading. This includes frequency dependence.

Signal Gain (A_v). The closed-loop voltage gain of the amplifying circuit for signals applied, as appropriate to the configuration.

Feedback-Loop Attenuation (β). The voltage attenuation of the feedback network including all impedances.

Noise Gain ($1/\beta$). The voltage gain response given by the inverse of feedback-loop attenuation.

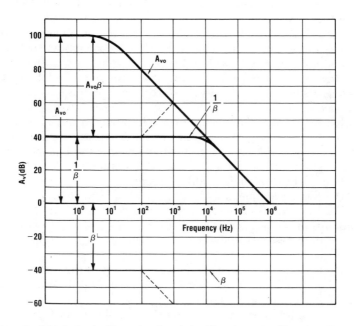

Fig. 1-12. Bode plot illustrating the relationships of A_{vo}, β, $1/\beta$, and $A_{vo}\beta$.

Loop Gain ($A_{vo}\beta$). The net gain around the broken feedback loop as seen from the feedback network input terminal back to the amplifier output. This includes frequency dependence.

Closed-Loop Gain (A_{cl}). The noise gain including the effects of loop gain.

Fig. 1-12 illustrates these definitions on a Bode plot, the basic tool for graphing amplifier gain versus frequency. This is a log-log plot which pictures the entire amplifier response. Gain may be shown either numerically or in dB, but it is conventionally shown in dB;

thus, this terminology is used in Fig. 1-12. With the various gains expressed in dB, they may be added and subtracted, which considerably simplifies the discussion.

The response, A_{vo}, of the basic amplifier is shown as equal to 100 dB at frequencies below 10 Hz. Above 10 Hz, A_{vo} becomes frequency-dependent and reduces 6 dB per octave (or 20 dB per decade) until at 1.0 MHz, $A_{vo} = 0$ dB, or unity. Such a response is typical of many of the general-purpose IC op amps that will be discussed in this book.

To illustrate β and $1/\beta$, a β of 0.01 or -40 dB will be assumed, with no reactive effects for simplicity. Therefore, β is drawn as a flat line (no frequency dependence) at -40 dB on the A_v scale. The reciprocal, $1/\beta$, is drawn as a flat line at $1/\beta = 1/0.01 = 100$, or $+40$ dB on the A_v scale.

Loop gain, or $A_{vo}\beta$, is the resultant of the combination of A_{vo} and β, including frequency dependence. Since A_{vo} is constant below 10 Hz, the product of $A_{vo}\beta$ will also be constant below this frequency. Working in dB, $A_{vo}\beta$ can be arrived at by simply adding A_{vo} and β. Thus, $A_{vo}\beta$ in dB is $+100$, -40, or $+60$ dB (below 10 Hz).

Rather than draw an additional curve referred to the zero-gain axis for $A_{vo}\beta$, we can make use of the information already implicit in the curves. Since $1/\beta$ is the inverse of β, subtracting $1/\beta$ in dB from A_{vo} (dB) will yield $A_{vo}\beta$ in dB. Thus, $A_{vo}\beta$ is that portion of the A_{vo} curve above the $1/\beta$ curve. A careful study of Fig. 1-12 should make the foregoing readily apparent.

With this technique, the loop gain of a configuration can be graphically determined at a glance. In the example shown, loop gain is $+60$ dB up to 10 Hz, but reduces at the rate of 6 dB per octave (due to decreasing A_{vo}) above this frequency, until at 10 kHz, $A_{vo}\beta$ has reduced to zero.

Although a flat β (and $1/\beta$) curve was used in this example, the general consideration regarding the resultant $A_{vo}\beta$ is true for any type of feedback and β. For example, if a slope (greater attenuation) were introduced into β at 100 Hz as indicated in Fig. 1-12 by the dotted-line response, the resultant $1/\beta$ curve would slope in the opposite direction as shown. Note that this reduces the loop gain, $A_{vo}\beta$, even faster at the higher frequencies, since $A_{vo}\beta$ is the difference in dB of A_{vo} and $1/\beta$.

From these relatively limited examples, the reader may already have deduced a salient point: It is β *alone* that determines the overall response of the amplifier. This factor, coupled with $A_{vo}\beta$ (which determines how closely the $1/\beta$ curve is realized), is used to implement feedback configurations.

In an actual design example, the $1/\beta$ curve would be used as a starting point, since it is this curve that represents the final frequency response of the amplifier. Given $1/\beta$ as an objective, the required β may be drawn as its inverse, which defines the characteristics of the feedback network. In practice, a certain requirement for $1/\beta$ will dictate the choice of amplifier to yield a specified loop gain for the required accuracy. This explanation is somewhat simplified, but in sections to follow, we will discuss this and other points in greater detail.

The Curative Properties of Feedback

Operational feedback, as we have discussed, is a means by which the designer can exercise control over total circuit performance. Feedback has a general influence that can be called a "curative" property. This property generally improves such factors as linearity, gain stability, and input and output impedances. In all cases, the degree of improvement is related to loop gain, or the amount of working feedback the amplifier uses in any given situation. Expressions governing the extent of improvement will now be discussed.

Gain Stability. One reason for using a feedback amplifier is to develop a transfer gain that is relatively independent of amplifier characteristics—indeed, the entire reasoning behind the operational amplifier is to render variations in its characteristics negligible, and make the amplifier properties dependent only on the external components.

Variations in open-loop gain for a feedback amplifier may be calculated by

$$\Delta A_v = \frac{\Delta A_{vo}}{1 + A_{vo}\beta}.$$

It can be seen that gain variation is controlled almost entirely by the loop gain if $A_{vo}\beta \gg 1$. This expression is a general one, applicable to any configuration. If A_{vo} and β are modified by other non-ideal terms, the corrected A_{vo}' or β' should be used in calculations. This statement also applies, of course, for the remaining expressions.

Linearity. Feedback reduces open-loop distortion and nonlinearity according to

$$\text{THD}_{cl} = \frac{\text{THD}_{ol}}{1 + A_{vo}\beta},$$

where,

THD is the total harmonic distortion in percent.

Input and Output Impedances. Input and output impedances of op-amp configurations are also transformed (in the positive direction) by feedback. The output resistance (r_o) of any op amp is reduced by feedback to a new resistance, R_o:

$$R_o = \frac{r_o}{1 + A_{vo}\beta} \, .$$

The input impedance is transformed upward or downward, depending on the configuration. In the inverting configuration shown in Fig. 1-13A, the input impedance, R_{in}, seen at the summing point is

$$R_{in} = \frac{r_{in} \| R_f}{1 + A_{vo}\beta} \, .$$

If $R_f \ll r_{in}$ (usually the case) and $A_{vo}\beta \gg 1$, a useful approximation is

$$R_{in} \cong \frac{R_f}{A_{vo}\beta} \, .$$

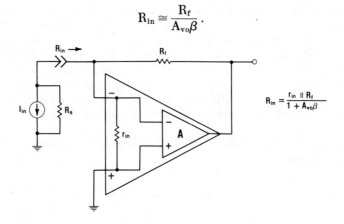

(A) Inverting configuration.

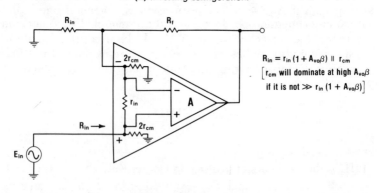

(B) Noninverting configuration.

Fig. 1-13. Effects of feedback on input resistance.

This clearly demonstrates the virtual-ground properties of the inverting configuration, as R_f is "transformed" by feedback to a much lower value. This makes the inverting stage a natural one for processing the output from current generators.

The noninverting configuration is shown in Fig. 1-13B, and its property is to transform the input resistance to a higher value. Since the voltages across both ends of r_{in} are the same (due to zero input-voltage differential), r_{in} is effectively "bootstrapped" by the feedback. The two common-mode resistances, each of value $2r_{cm}$, are not bootstrapped, however, and they appear in parallel with the input terminal. Thus,

$$R_{in} = r_{in}(1 + A_{vo}\beta) \| r_{cm}.$$

At high loop gains, such as with a voltage follower, the common-mode input resistance will usually be the upper limit on the input impedance of the noninverting stage.

From these few observations, it can be seen that loop gain is the primary determinant of feedback performance, and its effect is always positive. Thus, it should be kept in mind that in optimizing feedback, the parameter $A_{vo}\beta$ is the key performance parameter.

1.2.2 Errors Due to Finite Input Resistance

Another factor having definite effects on op-amp circuit performance, in both the inverting and noninverting configurations, is finite input resistance. In this section, we will examine these effects, with all other parameters assumed to be ideal.

Inverting Configuration

Fig. 1-14A illustrates the inverting amplifier connection with the addition of the input resistance, r_{in}. The effect of the input resistance, which appears in parallel with the summing point, is to modify β. R_{in} and r_{in} in parallel form a new β, β', which is lower than in the ideal (unloaded) network. Thus,

$$\beta' = \frac{R_{in} \| r_{in}}{(R_{in} \| r_{in}) + R_f},$$

where,

β' is the β with finite input resistance r_{in}.

The net effect of finite input impedance is therefore a reduction in β and thus a reduction in loop gain.

In practice, the actual loading effects of r_{in} will depend on the feedback impedances and the input impedance of the amplifier used. Generally, as long as the amplifier input resistance is ten or more times greater than the output impedance of the feedback net-

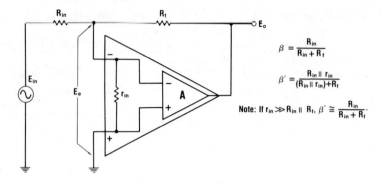

$$\beta = \frac{R_{in}}{R_{in} + R_f}$$

$$\beta' = \frac{R_{in} \| r_{in}}{(R_{in} \| r_{in}) + R_f}$$

Note: If $r_{in} \gg R_{in} \| R_f$, $\beta' \cong \frac{R_{in}}{R_{in} + R_f}$.

(A) Inverting configuration.

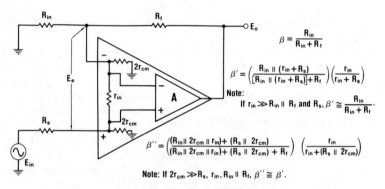

$$\beta = \frac{R_{in}}{R_{in} + R_f}$$

$$\beta' = \left(\frac{R_{in} \| (r_{in} + R_s)}{[R_{in} \| (r_{in} + R_s)] + R_f} \right) \left(\frac{r_{in}}{r_{in} + R_s} \right)$$

Note:
If $r_{in} \gg R_{in} \| R_f$ and R_s, $\beta' \cong \frac{R_{in}}{R_{in} + R_f}$.

$$\beta'' = \left(\frac{(R_{in} \| 2r_{cm} \| r_{in}) + (R_s \| 2r_{cm})}{(R_{in} \| 2r_{cm} \| r_{in}) + (R_s \| 2r_{cm}) + R_f} \right) \left(\frac{r_{in}}{r_{in} + (R_s \| 2r_{cm})} \right)$$

Note: If $2r_{cm} \gg R_s$, r_{in}, $R_{in} \| R_f$, $\beta'' \cong \beta'$.

(B) Noninverting configuration.

Fig. 1-14. Effects of finite input resistance.

work, the error due to input resistance loading will be negligible. General-purpose IC op amps provide input resistances of a few megohms, while FET-input devices achieve input resistances as high as 10^{12} ohms.

Noninverting Configuration

Similar to the inverting configuration, the noninverting configuration can also introduce a reduction in β. In this case, however, there are two potential contributions. This is illustrated in Fig. 1-14B. If the source resistance seen by the $(+)$ input of A is low, then the error due to amplifier input resistance reduces to the same error as in the inverting stage. If the source resistance, R_s, is such that it subtracts significantly from the error voltage, E_e, then the modified equation for β is

$$\beta' = \left(\frac{R_{in} \| (r_{in} + R_s)}{[R_{in} \| (r_{in} + R_s)] + R_f} \right) \left(\frac{r_{in}}{r_{in} + R_s} \right).$$

Also, like the inverting configuration, sufficiently high input impedance in the noninverting configuration can render these error sources negligible and reduce the equation for β to that of the classic form. This is also the case when r_{in} is ten or more times greater than the feedback source resistance, R_s.

Unlike the inverting configuration, the noninverting configuration is subject to errors due to common-mode resistances. The common-mode input resistance is modeled in Fig. 1-14B as two resistances of $2r_{cm}$, one at each input terminal. Taking these resistances into account, the modified equation for β becomes extremely unwieldy:

$$\beta'' = \left(\frac{(R_{in} \parallel 2r_{cm} \parallel r_{in}) + (R_s \parallel 2r_{cm})}{(R_{in} \parallel 2r_{cm} \parallel r_{in}) + (R_s \parallel 2r_{cm}) + R_f} \right) \left(\frac{r_{in}}{r_{in} + (R_s \parallel 2r_{cm})} \right).$$

In practice, this equation is of little more than academic interest, as typical common-mode input impedances of IC op amps are in the hundreds of megohms. Therefore, errors due to common-mode input resistance loading may be neglected in almost all cases; other effects are far more dominant.

1.2.3 Errors Due to Nonzero Output Resistance

The nonzero output resistance of practical op amps also contributes to gain error, having a common effect on either the inverting or noninverting configurations, as illustrated in Fig. 1-15. A real

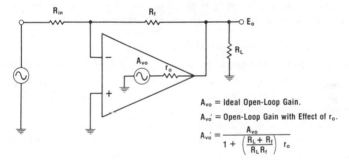

A_{vo} = Ideal Open-Loop Gain.

A_{vo}' = Open-Loop Gain with Effect of r_o.

$$A_{vo}' = \frac{A_{vo}}{1 + \left(\dfrac{R_L + R_f}{R_L R_f} \right) r_o}$$

Fig. 1-15. Effects of nonzero output resistance.

amplifier with output resistance r_o can be modeled as an ideal amplifier with gain A_{vo} in series with output resistance r_o. From this it can be seen that the loading effects of R_L and R_f, combined with r_o, form a voltage divider that reduces the ideal gain to a new gain, A_{vo}'. Including the effects of the r_o-$R_f \parallel R_L$ divider yields a new open-loop gain equation:

$$A_{vo}' = \frac{A_{vo}}{1 + [(R_L + R_f)/R_L R_f] r_o}.$$

From this equation, the greater the open-loop output resistance, r_o, the greater the attenuation of A_{vo}. As a result, loop gain is also attenuated as r_o increases. The attenuation of open-loop gain due to loading can be a significant error in instances where r_o is high in relation to the load resistance. Since there are some IC op amps with output resistances as high as several thousand ohms, this is a factor to be considered when maximizing loop gain. Generally, as long as r_o is $1/10$ or less of the total load resistance, it will not contribute excessive error.

Summary of Gain Errors

The nonideal properties of practical amplifiers discussed thus far all result in deviations from the ideal gain characteristic. This is due to a reduction in loop gain—either from a limited or reduced A_{vo}, or from a reduced β. Loop gain is the key parameter of feedback-amplifier configurations, since it determines the ultimate accuracy.

A complete gain equation that would include all sources of gain error is not given because it would not only be an extremely unwieldy expression but, in practice, the dominant sources of error may often be pinpointed by inspection. As a result, those error factors that warrant exact expression will usually be examined individually to generate modified figures for A_{vo} and β. Quite often the "rule-of-thumb" judgments previously mentioned for such parameters as input and output resistance will give values for $A_{vo}\beta$ to within a few percent, which in most cases is sufficient accuracy.

1.2.4 Effects of Input-Referred Errors

In addition to the static gain errors discussed in the previous sections, there are a number of error sources in practical op amps that are referred to the input terminals. These errors include input voltage and current offsets (with their associated drifts due to temperature changes), and self-generated and power-supply-induced input noise. These nonideal parameters, together with techniques for their minimization, will be covered in this section.

Input Offset Voltage

While the ideal op amp has the property of zero output voltage at zero input voltage, a real amplifier does not. Practical op amps have an input offset voltage, as illustrated in Fig. 1-16. This practical amplifier is modeled as an ideal amplifier, A, with an offset voltage generator, V_{io}, in series with one of its inputs. It does not matter which input is used, since it can be shown that the net effect will be the same for either one. Also, the actual polarity of the offset voltage may be either positive or negative. The input offset voltage, V_{io}, is defined as the voltage applied between the input leads to obtain zero output voltage. Offset voltage is a characteristic independent of operating gain, and it is amplified by the noise gain of the stage. Thus, the output voltage due to V_{io} is:

$$V_o = V_{io}\left(\frac{R_{in} + R_f}{R_{in}}\right).$$

Input offset voltage is due to imperfect matching in the input stage of the op amp. Different op-amp types will exhibit different degrees of matching and so will have better (or worse) input offset

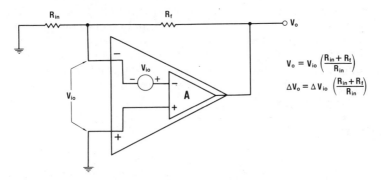

$$V_o = V_{io}\left(\frac{R_{in} + R_f}{R_{in}}\right)$$

$$\Delta V_o = \Delta V_{io}\left(\frac{R_{in} + R_f}{R_{in}}\right)$$

Fig. 1-16. Input offset voltage errors.

voltages. Offset voltage may be nulled by introducing an opposing voltage at one of the input terminals to cancel its effect, or by introducing an imbalance within the amplifier, resulting in an actual input offset of zero. In practice, control of offset voltage can be exercised either by selecting a device which yields an input offset below that required, or by nulling a device to achieve the required offset. Various methods of offset nulling will be discussed in detail in later sections.

Offset Voltage Drift

With input offset voltage adjusted to zero, the remaining voltage offset error is input offset voltage drift. Although input offset may be nulled at room temperature, temperature changes will alter the state of balance in the input stage, inducing an input offset voltage drift. Offset voltage drift, being a component of input offset voltage, is subject to the same considerations; i.e., it is independent of stage gain and is amplified by the noise gain. Thus, output drift is:

$$\Delta V_o = \Delta V_{io}\left(\frac{R_{in} + R_f}{R_{in}}\right).$$

There is no technique for nulling or cancelling offset voltage drift per se, although methods do exist to minimize it. Offset voltage drift will be minimal when the amplifier used is adjusted internally for an input offset voltage of zero. Furthermore, for minimum total drift (after nulling), the amplifier used should have a low offset drift specification.

Input Bias Current

Another parameter of the ideal amplifier, not realized in practice, is zero input current. Real op amps have input currents which may range from as high as 1.0 μA to as low as 1.0 pA. Often the effects of these currents are not negligible and must be compensated. Fig. 1-17 illustrates the effects of input bias current.

The bias current flowing in the input terminals of an op amp can be modeled as a current source in parallel with each lead of an ideal op amp. In Fig. 1-17, these current sources are labeled I_{ib-} and I_{ib+}.

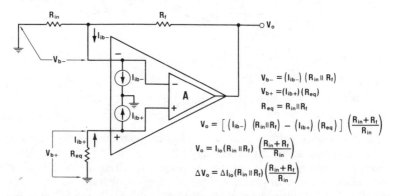

Fig. 1-17. Input bias and input offset current errors.

Although shown as being returned to ground, in actuality these current sources (or sinks) may be referred to the positive or negative supply, depending on the design of the individual amplifier. The currents I_{ib-} and I_{ib+} are independent of the common-mode voltage and flow in a return path (provided externally) at each input.

External to the amplifier, the input currents flow in the source resistances seen at each input and thus develop voltage drops. Current I_{ib-} flows through R_{in} and R_f, thus dropping a voltage

$$V_{b-} = (I_{ib-})(R_{in} \parallel R_f).$$

For the moment we will not consider R_{eq}, but we will assume the (+) input to be grounded directly. Under these conditions, the voltage drop, V_{b-}, due to the (−) input bias current is, in actuality, an input offset voltage (not to be confused with the input offset voltage of the amplifier, V_{io}, which is assumed to be ideal in this discussion).

As with V_{io}, V_{b-} is amplified by the noise gain of the stage. Whether or not V_{b-} is a significant error depends on two factors: (1) the magnitude of I_{ib-} and/or (2) the magnitude of $R_{in} \parallel R_f$. In general, to minimize V_{b-}, either $R_{in} \parallel R_f$ must be small or a very low (<1.0 nA) input current must be used.

Such restrictions on feedback resistance can be lessened considerably, however, by the use of an equivalent resistance, R_{eq}, to the (+) input. R_{eq} is chosen to be equal to $R_{in} \parallel R_f$, then if $I_{ib+} = I_{ib-}$, R_{eq} will drop a voltage, V_{b+}, which will equal V_{b-}. In this manner, the input offset due to V_{b-} is balanced out, and the amplifier sees only the difference in V_{b-} and V_{b+} as an input voltage. If I_{ib-} and I_{ib+} are well matched, this input offset voltage can be quite low.

Input Offset Current

How well the input currents of an op amp match is described in another specification, the input offset current. Input offset current is defined as the difference in the currents into the two input terminals when the output is at zero. Thus, not only is a practical amplifier nonideal from the standpoint that it requires input current, but it is also nonideal from the standpoint that the two input currents it does require are unequal, or offset.

In practice, the offset current is typically 10% or less of the bias current in a well-matched op-amp input, although this figure can vary with different devices. In terms of circuit considerations, the only compensation for bias-current-induced offset voltage that can be provided is a nominally matched set of resistances, such as $R_{eq} = R_{in} \parallel R_f$. Beyond this, an amplifier must be selected for a low and stable characteristic offset current. In general, to minimize bias and offset-current effects, the source resistances seen at both inputs should be matched and maintained as low as is practicable. If the use of high resistances is required, then a low-input-current amplifier should be used. FET-input amplifiers feature initial (room temperature) bias currents in the pA region; however, they also have large temperature coefficients.

Bias and Offset Current Drift

Bias current has a temperature dependence which is variable according to the type of input-stage design used in the op amp. Bipolar-input op amps tend to have relatively stable input bias currents, which also makes their input offset currents relatively stable. Input offset current drift is just as important a specification as input offset voltage drift, because it reduces to an equivalent offset voltage drift in a circuit. Also, like voltage drift, this source of error must be minimized by careful device selection as the final measure of control.

FET-input devices have the lowest bias currents, although on a percentage basis their offset currents are not as low as those of bipolar devices. Their input and offset currents are, however, low enough that in many circuits they do not need offset-current compensation. A disadvantage of FET-input devices is the temperature dependence of bias (and offset) current, which roughly doubles for every 10°C of temperature rise. If very high operating temperatures are required, this characteristic tends to defeat their low-input-current superiority somewhat, although the degree to which this is true depends, of course, on the device.

Summarizing the discussion on input offset voltage and currents, a combined model illustrating both is presented in Fig. 1-18.

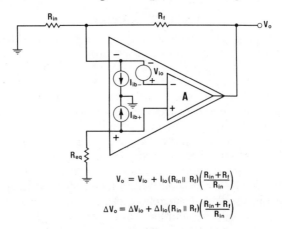

$$V_o = V_{io} + I_{io}(R_{in} \parallel R_f)\left(\frac{R_{in} + R_f}{R_{in}}\right)$$

$$\Delta V_o = \Delta V_{io} + \Delta I_{io}(R_{in} \parallel R_f)\left(\frac{R_{in} + R_f}{R_{in}}\right)$$

Fig. 1-18. Composite input offset voltage and current errors.

Power-Supply-Induced Input Offset Voltage

Due to an incomplete ability to reject power-supply voltage variations, practical op amps have another source of input offset voltage change. This source is termed power-supply rejection or sometimes supply-voltage sensitivity, and is a measure of how much variation appears as an equivalent input offset change for a given amount of variation in the power supplies. This parameter is illustrated in Fig. 1-19.

Inasmuch as this parameter is an input offset change, it may be modeled as an input offset voltage generator in series with one input lead (similar to Fig. 1-16). Since the source of this offset change is either V+ or V−, the supply leads are also shown, labeled with the variations ΔV+ and ΔV−. Thus, the equivalent input offset change is

$$\frac{V_{io}}{\Delta V_S},$$

where ΔV_S implies both supplies varying symmetrically.

Like the previous input offset changes, this parameter is independent of stage gain but is amplified by the noise gain of the stage. Thus, the equivalent output change is

$$\Delta V_o = \left(\frac{\Delta V_{io}}{\Delta V_S}\right)\left(\frac{R_{in} + R_f}{R_{in}}\right).$$

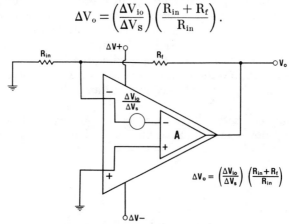

Fig. 1-19. Power-supply-induced errors.

Unlike the previous sources of input offset voltage change, power-supply-induced offset can contain ac components as well as dc. Thus, a complete evaluation of the effects of this error component, as it appears at the output, must include the frequency response of the coupling to the input as well as the frequency response of the amplifier configuration. In general, the power-supply rejection of an op amp will deteriorate at higher frequencies. This will vary according to the op-amp design and is usually given in the form of a graph. Also, the rejection for V+ and V− is not necessarily symmetrical, particularly with respect to frequency. This can be an important factor when operating from supplies having appreciable high-frequency noise components.

The minimization of power-supply noise sensitivity can take one of two general approaches: (1) selection of an op amp for inherently low noise sensitivity, or (2) selection of a standard (general-purpose) op amp and employment of local decoupling where necessary. The evaluation of a specific application to determine which approach is the most appropriate or economical is usually left up to the designer.

Input Noise Sources

Although not specifically stated as one of the primary character-istics of an ideal op amp, it is desirable that noise-free operation be one of its virtues. However, practical amplifiers degrade the input signal by adding noise components. This noise is nearly random in nature and determines the ultimate lower limit of signal-handling capability. It is specified as equivalent input noise and, like the other input error factors, is increased by the noise gain of the stage. Unlike the other input parameters, however, input noise specifica-tion and control is by no means a straightforward process. It in-volves the interpretation of a number of involved specifications, as well as an understanding of the basic physics of its mechanism, to yield maximum performance. Disregarding the basic rules of noise-performance optimization, however, can result in signal-to-noise ratios that may be short of maximum by an order of magnitude or more.

A circuit model for the discussion of input-referred noise com-ponents is shown in Fig. 1-20. Similar to bias current and offset

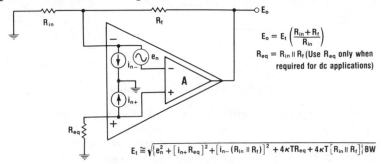

$$E_o = E_t \left(\frac{R_{in} + R_f}{R_{in}} \right)$$

$R_{eq} = R_{in} \| R_f$ (Use R_{eq} only when required for dc applications)

$$E_t \cong \sqrt{\left\{ e_n^2 + \left[i_{n+} R_{eq} \right]^2 + \left[i_{n-} (R_{in} \| R_f) \right]^2 + 4\kappa T R_{eq} + 4\kappa T \left[R_{in} \| R_f \right] \right\} BW}$$

Fig. 1-20. Input current and voltage noise errors.

voltage, the noise generators of an amplifier are modeled as a series voltage-noise generator, e_n, and shunt current-noise generators i_{n+} and i_{n-}. These generators represent the mean values of voltage and current noise referred to the input of the amplifier. They are speci-fied in terms of noise density in volts-squared or amperes-squared per hertz of bandwidth. To these generators must be added two other noise sources—the thermal noise of the source resistances seen by the amplifier, which is R_{eq} and $R_{in} \| R_f$.

Thus, a real amplifier has five potential sources of noise to be con-sidered for minimization. First, there is the thermal noise of the two source resistances seen by the inputs, which is an irreducible mini-mum, existing even with an ideal (noiseless) amplifier. Next, there are the noise-current and noise-voltage generators. For low values of source resistance, the effect of i_n is a minimum. Under these conditions, e_n will dominate as the source of amplifier noise. As the source resistance is increased, the effect of i_n becomes larger until at high source resistances, $i_{n+} R_{eq}$ and $i_{n-} (R_{in} \| R_f)$ are the dominant components of amplifier input noise. Thus, in specifications these two parameters are detailed separately, with e_n specified at a low source resistance and i_n specified at a high source resistance. Both e_n and i_n are given in terms of spectral density, measured with a narrow-bandwidth filter at a series of points across the useful spectrum of the amplifier. Data are given either in terms of e_n (or e_n^2) or i_n (or i_n^2) versus frequency, with typical graphs shown in Figs. 1-21A and B. These particular curves are given in e_n^2/Hz and i_n^2/Hz, but other manufacturers sometimes choose to display the same information in terms of $e_n/\sqrt{\text{Hz}}$ and $i_n/\sqrt{\text{Hz}}$. Conversion between the two may be accomplished by simply squaring or extracting the square root as appropriate. When comparing such data in graphical form, however, it should be noted that variations in terms of e_n^2 will appear

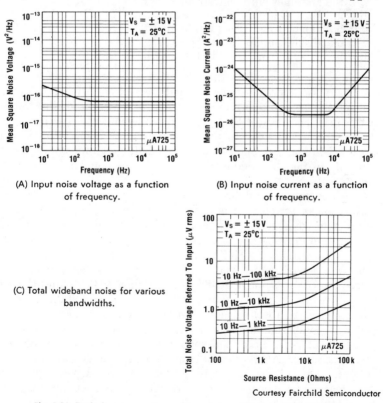

(A) Input noise voltage as a function of frequency.

(B) Input noise current as a function of frequency.

(C) Total wideband noise for various bandwidths.

Courtesy Fairchild Semiconductor

Fig. 1-21. Typical op-amp noise performance specifications—725 amplifier.

exaggerated over the same data expressed in terms of e_n. This clearly emphasizes the need for comparison of data on the same basis.

Although the spectral densities of both e_n and i_n are obviously not flat in the examples given (nor are they in general), it is not unreasonable to select a mean value for e_n and i_n if their total variation across the frequency range of the amplifier is within the same order of magnitude. An accurate calculation of total rms noise would involve integration across the bandwidth of the amplifier. The simplified approach given here will yield order-of-magnitude estimates of noise performance that are adequate for comparison purposes. Thus, given values for e_n, i_n, and bandwidth, the total noise of the circuit can be approximated as follows:

$$E_t \cong \sqrt{\{e_n^2 + [i_{n+}R_{eq}]^2 + [i_{n-}(R_{in} \parallel R_f)]^2 + 4\kappa T R_{eq} + 4\kappa T[R_{in} \parallel R_f]\} BW}$$

where,

E_t is the total circuit noise,
e_n is the amplifier noise voltage in $V/\sqrt{Hz}$,
i_n is the amplifier noise current in $A/\sqrt{Hz}$ (i_{n+} or i_{n-}),
R_{eq} and $R_{in} \parallel R_f$ are the source resistances ($R_{eq} = R_{in} \parallel R_f$),
κ is Boltzmann's constant ($1.38 \times 10^{-23} J/K$),
T is the absolute temperature (Kelvin),
BW is the noise bandwidth in Hz.

It is obvious from this expression that as e_n and i_n are reduced, the total noise approaches the thermal noise of R_s. A further point is that total noise is proportional to R_s and bandwidth. An illustration of this is given in Fig. 1-21C, a plot of wideband noise performance of the same amplifier, with the individual noise components shown in Figs. 1-21A and B. Such a plot is typically given for IC amplifiers and may in fact be adequate information for comparative evaluation.

In choosing an amplifier, the requirements will often dictate a certain source resistance from which the amplifier must work. This will dictate which noise generator is dominant and, therefore, which specification must be minimized—e_n or i_n. In general, low-input-current amplifiers, such as FET types or low-bias-current bipolar types, will have lower current noise, thus tending to be quieter with source impedances above 10,000 ohms. Below 10,000 ohms, the advantage swings to bipolar types, which have lower voltage noise. In any instance, an absolute minimum of resistance should be used so that R_s is composed largely of generator resistance. This means that the feedback resistances used should be low in relation to the generator resistance. Another consideration is that the noninverting configuration has only half the noise gain of the inverting configuration for equal signal gains; therefore, it offers a distinct advantage in signal-to-noise ratio.

In circumstances where it is possible to control source impedance, the characteristic noise resistance, R_n, of the amplifier may be used to advantage; best noise performance for a given amplifier will be obtained when the source resistance is equal to R_n:

$$R_s = R_n = \frac{e_n}{i_n}.$$

Thus, in ac applications, optimum performance may be obtained by using a transformer with a turns ratio selected to transform the actual source impedance to the noise resistance of the amplifier used, as shown in Fig. 1-22. This has the additional bonus of a "noiseless" gain provided by the transformer, allowing the amplifier gain to be reduced and further minimizing the overall noise of the circuit. This technique will be covered in further detail in the applications section (Part II).

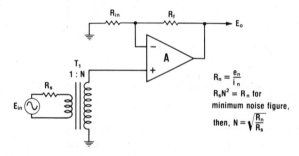

Fig. 1-22. Optimum noise performance by matching noise resistance of amplifier to source impedance with transformer coupling.

In summary, there are a number of considerations that bear on optimum noise performance. The first one is selection of an amplifier appropriate to the application, bearing in mind the source impedance. Second, the external circuit resistance should be minimized, and the noninverting configuration should be used if possible. Finally, the smallest bandwidth necessary should be used, since noise is proportional to bandwidth.

1.2.5 Errors Due to Dynamic Effects

As pointed out in Section 1.2.1, the predominant error factor in most op-amp applications is limited loop gain, due most often to finite open-loop gain. In this section, the Bode plot was introduced with a graphical example of the interrelationship of closed- and open-loop performance parameters. We will now examine some frequency-response considerations of op amps to determine the closed-loop performance characteristics for wide bandwidths.

Gain and Bandwidth Relationships

As discussed previously, a real op amp does not have infinite gain; it also does not have infinite bandwidth. Open-loop bandwidth begins to roll off from the full dc value at some low frequency, generally between 10 Hz and 1.0 kHz but most often near 10 Hz in general-purpose op amps. As is noted in Fig. 1-23, from the open-loop −3-dB point (the point at which the gain is down 3 dB from the full dc value), the rolloff is 6 dB/octave (20 dB/decade) with increasing frequency until the *unity-gain* frequency, f_t, is reached. In a curve such as this, the product of gain and frequency is con-

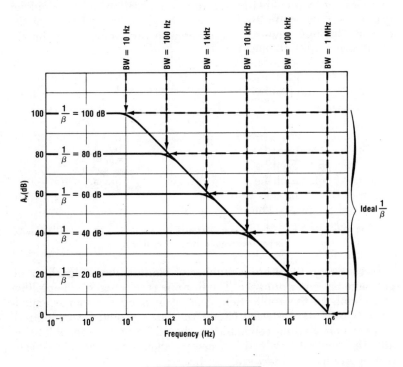

$\frac{1}{\beta}$	BW @ −3-dB
0 dB (1)	1 MHz (10^6)
20 dB (10^1)	100 kHz (10^5)
40 dB (10^2)	10 kHz (10^4)
60 dB (10^3)	1 kHz (10^3)
80 dB (10^4)	100 Hz (10^2)
100 dB (10^5)	10 Hz (10^1)

Fig. 1-23. Illustration of gain and bandwidth interrelationship with constant GBP amplifier open-loop response.

stant at any point on the curve. Thus, the unity-gain frequency also defines the available gain at any point along the curve.

In Fig. 1-23, the example chosen is an amplifier with a unity-gain frequency of 1.0 MHz, typical of a large number of IC op amps. The product of gain and bandwidth (GBP) in an amplifier response such as this is constant; thus,

$$GBP = A_vBW.$$

Graphically, the -3-dB bandwidth point is defined as the point at which the ideal closed-loop gain curve $(1/\beta)$ intersects the open-loop gain curve. An entire family of $1/\beta$ curves is drawn on this plot to illustrate the point, and this relationship is also shown by the table of gains and bandwidths. Thus, for a gain of 10 (20 dB), the bandwidth is 100 kHz and the GBP is 1.0 MHz. Similarly, a gain of 1000 (60 dB) yields a bandwidth of 1.0 kHz, and the GBP is again 1.0 MHz. Although the curves shown are drawn in decade increments of gain and bandwidth for clarity, intermediate values of gain (or bandwidth) will likewise yield a constant gain-bandwidth product.

The conclusion to be drawn from this is a basic mechanism of the feedback process. More feedback (exemplified by the lower gains) allows greater bandwidth, up to the limit imposed by the open-loop response of the amplifier. As far as the amplifier open-loop response is concerned, it remains unchanged regardless of the amount of feedback. Thus, the rationing of gain and bandwidth is an exchange process—if more gain is necessary, reduced bandwidth is the byproduct.

One final conclusion to be drawn from this is perhaps already obvious. With regard to loop gain, there is also an exchange process for various closed-loop gains. Loop gain, as stated previously, may be evaluated graphically as that portion of the response above a given closed-loop curve. For example, loop gain for $1/\beta = 20$ dB is 100 dB, -20 dB, or 80 dB at 1.0 Hz. The loop gain falls to zero at the $1/\beta$ -3-dB point, or 100 kHz. For the $1/\beta = 40$ dB curve, loop gain is 100 dB, -40 dB, or 60 dB at 1.0 Hz. The loop gain falls to zero at 10 kHz, the $1/\beta = 40$ dB, -3-dB point. Thus, the higher the closed-loop gain is, the lower the loop gain is and also (but just as important) the sooner the loop gain diminishes to zero, again due to the fixed gain-bandwidth product. It is sobering to consider these effects at high closed-loop gains—not only does the bandwidth shrink, but even before the -3-dB point is reached, loop gain is falling, diminishing the curative aspects of the feedback. We will now examine methods of optimizing loop gain with frequency, which at this point is obviously a nonideal property.

High GBP Amplifiers

Since the limitation on the available loop gain demonstrated in Fig. 1-23 is due to a limited gain-bandwidth product, it naturally follows that a greater gain-bandwidth product allows proportionally greater loop gain, or greater bandwidth. These factors are demonstrated in Fig. 1-24. For reference, this illustration includes the original 1.0-MHz GBP curve (curve A), as well as a 10-MHz GBP curve (curve B), and a 100-MHz GBP curve (curve C).

The evaluation of this new parameter can be approached from a number of viewpoints. For simplicity, a single $1/\beta$ curve is shown for a gain of 40 dB, but the same general considerations apply for any closed-loop gain. As an example, curve B extends the −3-dB point for the $1/\beta$ curve to 100 kHz, and curve C extends it to 1.0 MHz. This is also apparent from the 10-MHz and 100-MHz gain-bandwidth products, which when divided by a gain of 100 (40 dB), do in fact yield 100 kHz and 1.0 MHz. Moving the frame of reference lower in frequency to observe loop-gain differences, at 10 kHz the 10-MHz open-loop response (curve B) allows 20 dB of loop gain, while the 100-MHz response (curve C) allows 40 dB of loop gain. Moving even lower in frequency, it will also be noted that the higher open-loop −3-dB points allow the full low-frequency loop gain of 60 dB to be extended to 100 Hz and 1.0 kHz for curves B and C respectively. Finally, if the new curves are viewed from the standpoint of a given bandwidth (or loop gain), the higher GBP curves allow more gain to be realized in a given bandwidth. The 10-MHz curve, for example, allows 60 dB of gain in a 10-kHz bandwidth, while the 100-MHz curve allows 80 dB of gain in a 10-kHz bandwidth.

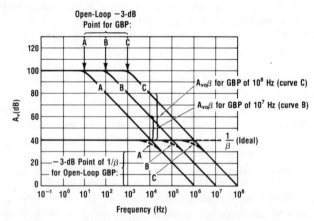

Fig. 1-24. Gain and bandwidth interrelationships with extended gain-bandwidth products.

Figs. 1-23 and 1-24 should be instructive in the interrelationship of gain and bandwidth, and the necessity for a high GBP in achieving high loop gains and subsequent accuracy at high frequencies. The numerical evaluation of gain-bandwidth relationships may be done either mathematically or by using the Bode plot. It is suggested, however, that the reader become familiar with the Bode plot at the earliest opportunity as it yields a large amount of information very quickly, and it is a tool as fundamental to op-amp technology as the op-amp symbol itself.

So far, nothing has been said concerning the methods of achieving the higher gain-bandwidth products represented by curves B and C of Fig. 1-24. High GBP with stability in an op-amp circuit is one of the more "meaty" challenges with which the reader must become familiar, and this subject is discussed in the next section.

Frequency/Phase Compensation

The previous section stressed the characteristics of the 6-db/octave open-loop rolloff rate which is typical of the greatest percentage of op amps. At this point, the reader might justifiably ask: "If more gain is needed at higher frequencies, why not just extend the open-loop bandwidth?" The answer to this question is basic and fundamental to stability in closed-loop feedback systems.

Stability Requirements. The 6-dB/octave rolloff rate is characteristic of a simple RC low-pass lag network such as that shown in Fig. 1-25A. In a network such as this, the maximum phase shift is $-90°$, as illustrated in Fig. 1-25B. At the -3-dB point of

$$f_1 = \frac{1}{2\pi RC},$$

the phase shift is $-45°$. As the frequency is increased, the phase shift reaches a maximum of $-90°$ at approximately

$$f_2 = \frac{10}{2\pi RC},$$

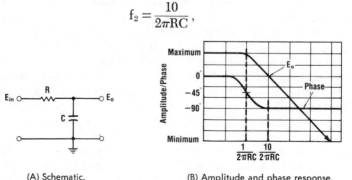

(A) Schematic.   (B) Amplitude and phase response.

Fig. 1-25. Response of a simple RC lag filter.

then remains at $-90°$ for any further increase in frequency. This simple RC network has an important relationship to op-amp frequency response, as we shall see now in Fig. 1-26.

In all the discussions about feedback thus far, no mention of phase shift or its effect on closed-loop performance has been made. The fact is that phase shift and its control are of paramount importance in achieving closed-loop stability in a feedback system. We have been assuming a feedback loop with an inverting sign, which implies a phase shift of $-180°$. Consider now the effects of an ad-

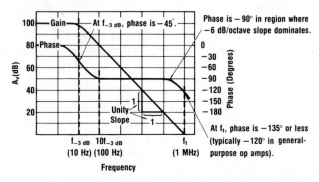

Fig. 1-26. Open-loop gain and phase response for general-purpose op amp.

ditional phase shift. If, in addition to the $-180°$, we were to add more phase shift until we reached an additional $-180°$, we would have achieved $360°$ of phase shift, or an in-phase condition. If the loop gain is greater than unity at the frequency where this additional phase lag is -180, we would also have succeeded in making an oscillator, for these are the two conditions which satisfy the criteria for oscillation. Thus, the control of phase shift and gain in feedback amplifiers is basic to achieving closed-loop stability. However, as there is a criterion for oscillation, there is also a corresponding stability criterion for feedback amplifiers. This fundamental rule can be applied to any feedback amplifier, and a stable system can be graphically determined with the aid of the Bode plot.

As may be deduced from the oscillation conditions just mentioned, the requirements for stability must reduce the total gain to less than unity before the additional $180°$ of phase shift is reached, in order to prevent oscillation. This means that the open-loop gain rolloff of the op amp must be done in such a manner as to prevent its phase from reaching $-180°$ before the gain has dropped below unity. This characteristic is illustrated by the gain and phase plots of Fig. 1-26.

If the entire rolloff range of the amplifier can be made to act like the single RC lag element, then the maximum phase shift it can accumulate is $-90°$, which gives an additional $90°$ of phase margin before the −180° point of potential instability is reached. It is common practice to provide a phase margin in feedback-loop design to allow for component tolerances, capacitive loading, and other effects that can further increase the phase shift.

In Fig. 1-26, the amplifier open-loop rolloff appears as a single lag over most of the range. Such a response is typical of general-purpose op amps with a GBP of 1.0 MHz. At the −3-dB point of 10 Hz, the phase shift is −45°, increasing to −90° at 100 Hz. It then remains at −90° until the frequency nears the unity-gain crossover region, where additional internal phase shifts begin to accumulate, and the phase shifts further toward −180°. At the unity-gain frequency, however, the phase shift is appreciably less than −180°, usually by a phase margin of 60° or more. A phase margin of 45° is considered the minimum acceptable figure for conservative designs.

Such an amplifier as we have just described is said to be *unconditionally stable*, or *unity-gain stable*, because it can be used with any amount of feedback (including 100%) without oscillation or instability problems. The unity-gain condition is the "worst-case" feedback state for stability because under this condition, $\beta = 1$ and $A_{vo}\beta$ is a maximum. With no feedback attenuation, there is a maximum of available gain (the full open-loop gain of the op amp) attempting to satisfy the oscillation criterion. Therefore, control of phase shift is crucial to unity-gain feedback configurations. This is the impetus behind the use of a single, lag-element-type, open-loop response; it affords stable control of open-loop phase characteristics over many decades of gain rolloff, as seen in Fig. 1-26. It was the synthesis of just such a response as appeared in Fig. 1-26 that led to the general-purpose IC op amps we find so useful today.

General Stability Criterion. A more general examination of stability in IC op amps must include conditions other than the specific response shown in Fig. 1-26. These other conditions include multiple-slope rolloffs where the open-loop phase can become −180° and greater, plus special cases of feedback where even the −6 dB/octave slope of Fig. 1-26 can be unstable in special cases.

For any feedback amplifier there exists a stability criterion, which can be stated as follows:

For unconditional stability, the ideal $1/\beta$ curve must intersect the open-loop response with a net slope of less than −12 dB/ octave.

Fig. 1-27 illustrates the open-loop response of a hypothetical op amp with a number of $1/\beta$ curves. The first significant difference to be noted about this open-loop curve is the fact that it has two slopes in its rolloff region. The first section rolls off at a rate of −6 dB/ octave, while the second section rolls off at −12 dB/octave, or twice the rate of the first section. A −12-dB/octave rolloff rate will ultimately reach −180° of phase shift; thus, it is potentially unstable if the loop is closed at or near the point where the phase is −180°. We will now examine the effects of different examples of loop closure (points of intersection shown in Fig. 1-27) on stability.

In the first example, the ideal gain curve, $1/\beta_1$, is a flat gain of 60 dB which clearly intersects the open-loop curve in a −6-dB/octave region. Thus, the net slope (slope between the two curves) is −6 dB/octave (since the $1/\beta_1$ curve has a slope of zero), and the loop is stable. An additional point which indicates stability of this loop closure is that the change in slope to −12 dB/octave is a full decade higher than the intersection of the $1/\beta_1$ curve with the openloop curve. Thus, the phase changes that will be associated with this slope change have not yet begun, so the open-loop phase at this point will be −90°.

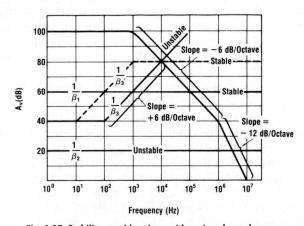

Fig. 1-27. Stability considerations with various loop closures.

In the second example, the ideal gain curve, $1/\beta_2$, is also flat, but it is at a gain of 20 dB. This curve intersects the open-loop curve in the −12-dB/octave region, and since $1/\beta_2$ has zero slope, the net slope at the intersection is −12 dB/octave. Also, since this intersection point is beyond the point of slope change from −6 dB/octave to −12 dB/octave, the open-loop phase shift will have reached −180°. Thus, this loop closure will definitely be unstable and will result in oscillation, because there is still a 20-dB gain at the point where the curves intersect.

So far the examples considered have assumed a flat frequency response for the feedback characteristic, $1/\beta$. However, this is not always the case; $1/\beta$ may include reactive elements. Reactance in the feedback path changes the phase characteristic of $1/\beta$, just as reactance also changes the phase of the open-loop characteristic. For stable closed-loop operation, both reactance effects must be considered.

A reactive feedback characteristic can affect stability even when using the so-called "ideal" 6-dB/octave open-loop rolloff. Such a case is the $1/\beta_3$ curve in Fig. 1-27, which is a "peaked" open-loop response characteristic, typical of a differentiator. This curve intersects the open-loop characteristic with a +6-dB/octave slope, while the open-loop response is −6 dB/octave at the intersection. Therefore, the net slope is −12 dB/octave. The phase of the $1/\beta_3$ characteristic will be 90°, since it is two decades beyond the initial slope change at 100 Hz. The open-loop phase will be −90°, since it is one decade beyond the initial slope change. Thus, the net phase is −180° and the loop closure will be unstable. To restore stability to such a closed loop, the phase characteristic must be modified in order to reduce the net slope difference at the intersection. This may be done by modifying $1/\beta_3$ to the new curve, $1/\beta_3{}'$, which intersects the open-loop characteristic in a region where $1/\beta_3{}'$ is flat. Since this region of $1/\beta_3{}'$ is one decade beyond the last slope change, the phase will be close to zero, so the net phase is reduced to the −90° of the open-loop curve; thus the loop closure will be stable.

There are many other examples that could be used to demonstrate the working of the stability criterion, but they all reduce to control of the net phase between the ideal $1/\beta$ curve and the open-loop characteristic. With a given open-loop gain/phase characteristic, the feedback loop must be controlled in gain and phase so that the stability criterion is satisfied. Generally speaking, the −6-dB/octave slope characteristic of the general-purpose op amp allows freedom of feedback networks without much regard for stability considerations, except in certain special cases such as the $1/\beta_3$ curve in Fig. 1-27.

When gain-bandwidth is to be optimized, it may be more advantageous to exercise control over the open-loop characteristic of the op amp, in order to satisfy loop gain or stability requirements. The reason is that high GBP amplifiers with uniform rolloff rates of 6 dB/octave are rare. In fact, the 100-MHz, −6-dB/octave characteristic alluded to in Fig. 1-24 is not yet a reality in any IC op amp. Such a characteristic is quite difficult to realize because of inevitable high-frequency phase shifts and parasitic effects within the op-amp circuitry. However, over *portions* of the total response, a high gain-bandwidth product can be realized with controlled rolloff rates and controlled phase characteristics. Thus, high-gain, wideband amplifiers can be built using IC op amps with externally adjustable phase/frequency compensation, which allows some shaping of open-loop characteristics.

Effects of Phase/Frequency Compensation

A basic requirement of any op-amp frequency-compensation network is the control of open-loop rolloff so as to guarantee stability under closed-loop conditions. RC networks, placed at appropriate points in the op-amp circuit, cause the open-loop rolloff to assume the characteristic desired.

In general-purpose op amps, rolloff networks cause the open-loop response to assume a single rolloff slope of −6 dB/octave with an associated phase characteristic of −90° lag. This network can be self-contained within the amplifier; then, the amplifier is said to be *internally compensated.* Other op amps require external compensation networks to shape the open-loop response, either to a response similar to a general-purpose type or, with some amplifiers, to a response that may exhibit multiple slopes such as the open-loop characteristic of Fig. 1-27.

It is not the purpose of this discussion to describe the design of these networks, but to impart a useful appreciation of the value of their differences, the basics of what they accomplish, and most importantly, how to interpret different open-loop responses so as to obtain maximum use of various IC amplifiers.

Basically, interpreting an open-loop response is evaluating the gain/phase characteristic in view of a particular application. With the previous background on gain-bandwidth, loop gain, stability requirements, and the general use of the Bode plot as a framework, the reader should now be developing an appreciation for the difference between the dc and ac performance of op amps. We will now examine what frequency-compensation networks accomplish in modifying open-loop response.

In Fig. 1-28, the uncompensated open-loop response of a hypothetical op amp is shown as curve A. This op amp has a number of internal phase shifts associated with it, as is evident from its three different rates of rolloff. The first rolloff begins at 10 kHz, where the open-loop response is 3 dB down and is at a rate of −6 dB/octave. The second rolloff occurs at 1.0 MHz and changes to a rate of −12 dB/octave. The third rolloff occurs at 10 MHz and changes to a final slope of −18 dB/octave. As it stands, this amplifier would be usable only with loop closures of 1.0 MHz or less (from point A2 upward on the curve), which limits it to gains of 60 dB or more. To make this amplifier usable at lower gains, from 60 dB down to unity, compensation must be introduced to synthesize a new rolloff slope of −6 dB/octave.

The most simple and direct method of doing this is to connect a capacitor at an appropriate point within the amplifier to introduce a lag. If the frequency at which this capacitance value reacts is low enough, its rolloff rate will become dominant, thus providing a single rolloff rate. To do this, the natural rolloff effects of the amplifier must be suppressed to a point where they occur at gains less than unity. Curve B demonstrates this effect, which is aptly called a "brute-force" technique. While this type of compensation will work, it ruins practically all the useful high-frequency response of the amplifier.

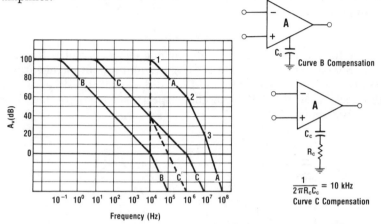

Fig. 1-28. Phase compensation techniques.

A much more desirable technique is to introduce the rolloff at a higher frequency as in curve C. A single capacitor lag introduced at this frequency will also result in a second rolloff due to the unsuppressed amplifier rolloff at 10 kHz. If left as such, curve C′ will result. This makes the amplifier usable with feedback down to 40 dB, but it is still not stable at unity gain because of the phase shift above 10 kHz. If, however, the rolloff due to C_c is removed at the first rolloff frequency (10 kHz), the composite curve can be made to approximate a single rolloff. It will then appear as the complete C curve, which extends to unity gain at 1.0 MHz. Now the amplifier will be stable at unity gain and will have an overall characteristic which resembles a 6-dB/octave rolloff.

Compensation is by nature a rolloff of gain, done in such a manner as to control the overall phase characteristic. Control of phase is the desired objective, and gain rolloff with frequency is the means to this end. As seen in Fig. 1-28, this is costly in terms of high-frequency gain. For example, if the unmodified response (curve A) and the compensated response (curve C) are compared at 10 kHz, the open-loop characteristic (curve A) has 100 dB of gain and can be stabilized at a gain of 60 dB, which will yield a gain accuracy of 1.0%. By contrast, the compensated response (curve C) can only achieve a gain of 40 dB at 10 kHz, the frequency where its loop gain is zero.

From this discussion it is hoped that the reader will be made aware of the tradeoff involved in frequency compensation. While the example chosen is not intended to portray an actual IC amplifier, it is close enough to be representative. Further study of manufacturers' data sheets will be more informative in terms of specific examples.

Slew Rate

The final source of error from dynamic effects is called the *slew rate*. Simply stated, slew rate is the maximum rate of change of the amplifier output voltage. In addition to the small-signal bandwidth discussed previously, it is another aspect of op-amp performance with frequency.

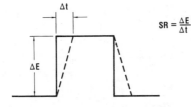

(A) Response (dotted) to pulse or square-wave input.

(B) Response (dotted) to sine-wave input.

Fig. 1-29. Examples of amplifier output waveforms under conditions of slew-rate limiting.

Slew-rate limiting is brought about by a limitation in the internal circuitry of an op amp to drive capacitive loads, either internal or external. The capacitance that limits this slewing ability with a given amplifier is most often the compensation capacitance, either internal or external, although in some instances it is the load capacitance. At high frequencies or high rates of signal change, the current available to charge and discharge the capacitance becomes exhausted, and slew-rate limiting occurs. This is evidenced by distortion in the output, which will appear similar to the waveforms shown in Fig. 1-29. Under these conditions, the amplifier output will change at a maximum slew rate of

$$SR = \frac{\Delta E}{\Delta t}.$$

Since slew rate is a large-signal-performance parameter, a given rate also defines what is called the *power bandwidth*, which is

$$f_p = \frac{SR}{2\pi E_{op}},$$

where,

f_p is the full power frequency,

E_{op} is the peak amplifier output voltage.

Because slew rate is usually related to compensation capacitance, it follows that it is usually a variable for externally compensated amplifiers. One method used to minimize slew-rate problems is the selection of a device that can be optimized externally by adjusting the compensation (where stability requirements allow). If an amplifier is to be used at unity gain, however, a device must be chosen that will meet the slew-rate requirements under the conditions needed for stability.

Summary of Dynamic Effects

Bandwidth, compensation, and slew-rate considerations are some of the most important sources of error that will be encountered in op-amp circuitry. Throughout the remainder of this book, special consideration will be given to optimum ac performance in the circuits discussed. Chapter 6, in particular, explores these areas with regard to specific devices and discusses the optimization of high-frequency amplifiers.

1.3 IC OP-AMP SPECIFICATIONS

IC op-amp specifications can be divided into two general categories: (1) maximum ratings and (2) electrical characteristics. These specifications provide two different kinds of information about an IC op amp, and both are important. Maximum ratings give the maximum operating conditions under which the manufacturer recommends that you operate his device. Exceeding the maximum ratings can lead to immediate destruction of the device at worst, and will almost always result in degradation of the general operating characteristics. Electrical characteristics tell a more detailed story of device performance under typical operating conditions of temperature, supply voltage, loading, etc. These specifications may be defined in terms of certain limits, either minimum or maximum, depending on the particular parameter. A typical value is also given in most cases. This serves as a nominal center for design guidance. In addition to these specification limits, supplementary data is provided in the form of graphs, curves, and test circuits under which specification measurements are made. Data given in the form of curves is not normally guaranteed, whereas "performance limits" are.

This section discusses IC op-amp specifications by first defining the term and identifying its symbol, then clarifying it in the light of practical examples wherever possible.

1.3.1 Maximum Ratings

Supply Voltage (V+ and V−)

The maximum allowable supply voltage that can safely be applied to the amplifier.

Although designed for ±15-volt supplies as standard, most IC op amps will operate over a wide range of potentials, some from as low as ±1.0 volt and some up to ±40 volts.

Power Dissipation (P_D)

The power that a particular device is capable of dissipating safely on a continuous basis while operating within a specified temperature range.

This rating will vary slightly according to the type of package used. Ceramic packages, for example, allow the highest power dissipation. Metal packages allow the next highest, while plastic-encapsulated packages generally allow the lowest. A typical power-dissipation capability for an IC op amp is about 500 milliwatts (up to a specified temperature); the exact figure will vary according to the manufacturer and the device.

Operating Temperature Range (T_{or})

The range of temperature over which the device will perform within the rated specification(s).

Military-grade devices operate from −55°C to +125°C; industrial-grade devices operate from −25°C to +85°C, and commercial-grade devices operate from 0°C to +70°C.

Differential-Input Voltage ($V_{id(max)}$)

The maximum voltage that can safely be applied between the differential-input terminals without excessive current flow.

Some amplifiers have clamping diodes connected back-to-back across the input terminals. These types are limited to a differential-input voltage of ±0.5 volt or less. Other types are limited to ±5.0 volts or less to prevent emitter-base breakdown in the input stage. The highest differential-input-voltage ratings are provided by devices using a combination pnp-npn cascode input, which provides a ±30-volt rating.

Common-Mode Input Voltage ($V_{cm(max)}$)

The maximum voltage that can safely be applied between both input terminals together and circuit common.

There is both a positive and a negative limit to this rating, although typically they are equal.

Output Short-Circuit Duration (t_s)

The length of time that the amplifier can withstand a direct short circuit from the output to ground or to either supply terminal.

Lead Temperature

The lead temperature that the device will withstand during the soldering process for a period of 60 seconds.

This rating is typically 300°C.

1.3.2 Electrical Characteristics

The electrical characteristics of an IC op amp provide a more detailed story of performance by defining the means and limits of behavior, usually in open-loop terms. A device is generally characterized by a range of performance limits, obtained from testing a large number of units on a production run. These limits are defined under standard conditions of room temperature and supply voltage (± 15 volts). Any further conditions are specified in detail with the individual measurements—for example, source resistance, frequency, load, temperature range, etc. Typical performance values are often accompanied by either a minimum or a maximum limit, although sometimes the typical values alone are given.

In the following discussion, the various parameters are grouped into categories such as input, output, dynamic, and general characteristics.

Input Characteristics

Input Offset Voltage (V_{io}). The voltage that must be applied between the input terminals through two equal resistances to obtain zero output voltage.

Ideally, an op amp will have zero input offset voltage. In practice, however, IC amplifiers have low but definite offset voltages. Offset voltage is lowest in bipolar-input op amps because bipolar transistors tend to match extremely well. It is unusual for a bipolar-input IC op amp to have an input offset greater than a few millivolts, and general-purpose types typically have offsets of ± 1.0 millivolt. Special selections of bipolar-input op amps have input offsets lower than ± 0.5 millivolt.

FET-input op amps are relatively poor in terms of input offset voltage because FETs do not tend to match nearly as well as do bipolar transistors. Typically, FET-input offset voltages are in the tens of millivolts region, with some types having worst-case offsets approaching 100 millivolts.

Most IC op amps have provisions for internal offset null adjustment, which allows the input offset to be adjusted to zero.

Depending on the input-bias-current characteristics of the particular device, the specified input offset voltage is guaranteed only up to a certain value of input resistance. In the case of general-purpose types, for example, this value is 10,000 ohms. Such a limitation is generally due to the offset current characteristics (difference in the two bias currents) of the device. With lower bias currents, offset current is also reduced; thus, higher source resistances may be used without offset voltage degradation.

Input Offset Voltage Temperature Coefficient ($\Delta V_{io}/\Delta T$). *The ratio of change in input offset voltage to the change of circuit temperature for a constant output voltage.*

Input offset voltage temperature coefficient, or offset voltage drift, is specified in $\mu V/°C$ of offset voltage change and is an average value over the temperature range of the device. Again, due to the excellent matching characteristics of bipolar-input op amps, these types are best in terms of offset voltage drift. This is one of the more stringent operating parameters of IC op amps and is not specified for all devices.

Input Bias Current (I_{ib}). *The average of the two input currents.*

Input bias current is simply the current that is required at the input terminals of an op amp. It may flow either into or out of the input terminals, depending on the internal design used. In the balanced state, the two input currents are very nearly equal, but the parameter is usually specified as the average of the two input currents. In general, FET-input amplifiers will have lower bias currents, but bipolar amplifiers will have better-matched input currents (in terms of percent).

Input Bias Current Temperature Coefficient ($\Delta I_{ib}/\Delta T$). *The ratio of the change in the input bias current to the change in circuit temperature.* This is an average value for a specified temperature range.

Input bias current temperature coefficient is a measure of how stable the input bias currents remain over the operating temperature range. It is most stable in bipolar-input op amps, usually rising at lower temperature extremes. On the other hand, FET-input op amps have a bias current that doubles (approximately) with every 10°C rise in temperature, because it is essentially a diode leakage current.

Input Offset Current (I_{io}). *The difference in the currents into the two input terminals when the output is at zero.*

Input offset current is a measure of the mismatch between the two bias currents. In general-purpose, bipolar-input op amps, the input offset current is typically 10% of the bias current, but it can be appreciably lower in premium types. FET-input devices do not match as well because there is less control over the bias currents.

Input Offset Current Temperature Coefficient ($\Delta I_{io}/\Delta T$). *The ratio of the change in input offset current to the change in circuit temperature for a constant output voltage.* This is an average value for a specified temperature range.

Input offset current temperature coefficient is a measure of the change in offset voltage over the temperature range of the op amp. Like input offset voltage temperature coefficient, it is an average value. It is one of the more stringent parameters and is not specified for all IC op amps. Also, like input offset voltage temperature coefficient, it is better in bipolar-input devices due to better matching.

Input Resistance (r_{in}). *The resistance seen looking into either input terminal with the other input grounded.*

Input resistance in an IC op amp may be very high, as in the case of FET-input amplifiers; or it may be medium, as in the case of a bipolar-input amplifier. Input resistances for FET-input amplifiers can be as high as 10^{12} ohms at room temperature. General-purpose, bipolar-input op amps have input resistances around 1.0 megohm, but specialized types can be much higher. Ideally, of course, the input resistance is infinite, and this is very closely approximated by FET-input devices.

Input Capacitance (c_{in}). *The capacitance seen looking into either input terminal with the other input grounded.*

Input capacitance is important because of the reduction of input impedance it represents with increasing frequency. At higher frequencies, the input impedance can become limited due to the shunting effect of capacitive reactance. This must be considered when the source resistances seen by the input(s) of the amplifier are large enough to cause appreciable phase shift at the desired operating frequency.

Common-Mode Rejection Ratio (*CMRR*). *The ratio of the input voltage range to the peak-to-peak change in input offset voltage over this range.*

An ideal op amp responds only to differential-input signals and ignores signals common to both inputs. In practice, this is only an approximation; real amplifiers have a small but definite common-mode error. The ratio of the common-mode voltage to the common-mode error voltage is the common-mode rejection ratio, CMRR. It is commonly expressed in dB.

Common-mode rejection is important to noninverting or differential amplifiers because these configurations see a common-mode voltage. It is specified at dc or a very low frequency, and it rolls off with a 6-dB/octave slope starting at the corner frequency. The corner frequency is about 100 Hz for general-purpose op amps, but it is greater in high-speed types. Dc rejection ratios can range from 90 dB to 120 dB, depending on the device. They are generally higher in bipolar-input amplifiers than in FET-input amplifiers, since FETs have inherently poor common-mode rejection.

Power-Supply Rejection Ratio (*PSRR*). *The ratio of change in input offset voltage to the change in supply voltages, with the supplies varied symmetrically.*

The ability of an IC op amp to reject power-supply-induced noise and drift is an important parameter. Voltage changes on the supply lines can be coupled into the amplifier, and they appear as an equivalent input signal, regardless of the configuration used. For low-level, high-gain applications, this noise source must be considered. During measurement, the supply lines are varied equal amounts, and the measured changes are referred to the input. The measured value is noted as

$$\text{PSRR} = \frac{\Delta V_{io}}{\Delta V_s},$$

where ΔV_s is the increment of supply-voltage change.

Typical figures for power-supply rejection may be as low as 2.0 μV/V or as high as 200 μV/V, the performance varying with different designs. In a given type of amplifier, there may also be different limits on the positive- and negative-supply rejection ratios; or the manufacturer may specify the two measurements together, giving a typical value and a maximum limit. This parameter is also frequency-dependent, the exact degree varying with the type of amplifier.

Input Voltage Range (**V**$_{icr}$). *The range of voltage on the input terminals for which the amplifier operates within specifications.*

Input voltage range (also called the *operating common-mode range*) is the maximum range of voltage swing that the input stage can tolerate and still operate within the specification limits of the amplifier. It is applicable to either input since in an actual closed-loop situation, the two inputs will be at or near the same potential. In the case of a unity-gain voltage follower, the inputs are required to swing the full output range of the amplifier because the feedback is 100%. Therefore, it is necessary that the input stage be capable of operating with full specifications over the dynamic range of output swing. If it cannot, the possibility exists that the amplifier may saturate or "latch up" when its input range is exceeded.

Latch-up was a particular problem with early IC amplifiers because the maximum input range could be exceeded with normal output swings. This problem will be discussed in detail in a later section.

The 101, 741, and later amplifiers solved the input-voltage-range problem with typical specifications of ±13 volts or more. The input voltage range is directly related to the supply voltages used since it is the internal biasing potentials which set the input voltage range. Thus, it is reduced for lower supply potentials and increased for higher supply potentials.

Output Characteristics

Output Voltage Swing (V_{op}). *The peak output swing, referred to zero, that can be obtained without clipping.*

Output voltage swing is the ability of an op amp to deliver its rated voltage across a specified value of load resistance. A symmetrical output swing is usually implied, although this is not necessarily true in all cases. The output swing can become limited due to loading effects, power supplies, frequency effects, and source resistance of the amplifier. Generally, IC op amps can supply peak voltage swings to within a few volts of the supply voltages used. There are normally two different load-resistance values into which the rated voltage swing is specified; these are typically 10,000 ohms and 2000 ohms.

With ±15-volt supplies, the 101 and 741 amplifiers are rated for ±14 volts typical swing into a 10,000-ohm load, ±12 volts minimum. Into a 2000-ohm load, the figures are ±13 volts typical and ±10 volts minimum. For supply voltages other than ±15 volts, the output-swing capability will change in proportion.

For load resistances below the rated value of 2000 ohms, the output begins to drop due to the effect of current limiting. This will not damage the amplifier as long as its power-dissipation limits are observed, but it will reduce the open-loop gain due to loading.

Output Short-Circuit Current (I_{osc}). *The maximum output current available from the amplifier with the output shorted to ground or to either supply.*

As a means of self-protection, IC op amps are usually provided with an internal current-limiting feature which prevents output current from rising above a level that would be destructive. This makes operation virtually foolproof from an accident standpoint, since situations will inevitably arise where an output will be short-circuited. Early op-amp types such as the 709 were short-circuit proof only for brief durations and were subject to catastrophic failure if short-circuited for an appreciable length of time. Later op-amp types have incorporated full-time current limiting in the form of active devices which sense load-current flow and limit it to a maximum of 20 to 25 milliamperes in either direction. Since this is not a critical parameter, it is specified only as a typical value. The current is often sensed by a transistor junction voltage; thus the current-limiting level is inversely proportional to temperature.

Output Resistance (r_o). *The resistance seen looking into the output terminal with the output nulled.* This parameter is defined only under small-signal conditions at frequencies above a few hundred hertz, in order to eliminate the influence of drift and thermal feedback.

IC amplifiers vary in output resistance, with resistances from below 100 ohms in general-purpose types up to some designs with output resistances approaching 10,000 ohms. Higher output resistances will result in a loss of gain when the load impedance becomes low in relation to the output resistance because part of the output signal is lost across the output resistance. This must be considered in cases where maximum gain is important. General-purpose op amps with output resistances less than 100 ohms are specified to operate into loads of 2000 ohms or higher, and they suffer little gain loss due to loading.

In all cases, the effective output resistance is reduced by feedback. The degree of reduction is in proportion to loop gain as discussed in the section on nonideal amplifier parameters.

Dynamic Characteristics

Open-Loop Voltage Gain (A_{vo}). *The ratio of the maximum output voltage swing with load to the change in input voltage required to drive the output from zero to this voltage.*

The open-loop voltage gain of an op amp is one of the most important specifications because it has the greatest effect on overall accuracy. General-purpose IC op amps have typical dc open-loop gains of 100 dB when operated with rated loads of 2000 ohms. This gain does not change excessively with operating temperature or variations in the supply voltage, although individual devices will vary in these regards. Special-purpose devices can achieve voltage gains of 130 dB.

Although the high gain available at dc is adequate to provide sufficient accuracy for most applications, the same is not true for ac. Because of the need for a 6-dB/octave rolloff to achieve closed-loop stability, internally compensated, general-purpose op amps typically have an open-loop −3-dB frequency of 10 Hz. Beyond this frequency, gain falls off at a 6-dB/octave (20-dB/decade) rate. An example of such an open-loop gain curve is the 741 response shown in Fig. 1-30A.

Small-Signal, Unity-Gain Frequency (f_t). *The frequency at which the open-loop, small-signal voltage gain is unity with the amplifier compensated for unity-gain stability.*

The small-signal, unity-gain frequency is a very useful amplifier specification because it yields much information about the amplifier frequency response. In many applications, unity-gain stability is required of an op amp. Thus, the most meaningful frequency-response specification for such an amplifier is the unity-gain frequency, as this defines its gain-versus-frequency capability.

For example, with a 6-dB/octave rolloff such as shown in Fig. 1-30A, the frequency where this curve crosses the unity-gain axis defines the entire gain characteristic (since the slope is fixed). Once the f_t of a 6-dB/octave rolloff amplifier is known, its open-loop response can be drawn just by sketching a straight line with a -1 slope through the unity-gain frequency.

For the 741 example shown in Fig. 1-30A, the f_t is 1.0 MHz, which is typical of general-purpose amplifiers. High-speed IC op amps can achieve unity-gain frequencies of 10 to 15 MHz, which extend their high-frequency usefulness considerably.

Gain-Bandwidth Product (*GBP*). *The product of available open-loop gain and bandwidth at a specific frequency.*

Gain-bandwidth product and unity-gain frequency are closely related, and in many instances they are actually the same thing. For example, the 741 gain-bandwidth product may also be stated as 1.0 MHz, since a gain of unity at 1.0 MHz yields a gain-bandwidth product of 1.0 MHz. It should also be noted that this product is constant regardless of frequency (or gain). Thus, a gain of 10^5 at 10 Hz yields a GBP of 10^6, or 1.0 MHz. In a 6-dB/octave rolloff amplifier, the gain at any frequency can be found by dividing the GBP by the bandwidth, since

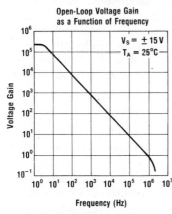

Courtesy Fairchild Semiconductor

(A) Open-loop response of 741 op amp.

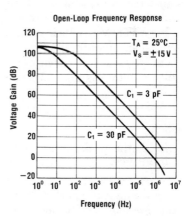

Courtesy National Semiconductor Corp.

(B) Open-loop response of 101 op amp.

Fig. 1-30. Typical open-loop voltage-gain characteristics.

$$GBP = A_vBW.$$

The difference between GBP and f_t becomes apparent with externally compensated amplifiers, which can achieve a higher GBP. This is illustrated in Fig. 1-30B, which shows the open-loop frequency response of a 101 amplifier compensated for two different closed-loop gains. The lower curve is identical to the 741 characteristic in Fig. 1-30A; it has an f_t of 1.0 MHz, which is also its GBP. However, the upper curve has a GBP ten times greater, or 10 MHz, as it yields a gain of 10 at 1.0 MHz. Note that this curve does not allow unity-gain stability as does the lower f_t curve. Therein lies the difference between f_t and GBP—f_t is actually a specific case of GBP, while GBP is a more general type of gain-frequency specification.

Unfortunately, GBP is not always implicit in numerical specifications, whereas f_t usually is. GBP is evident in the performance curves with various compensations, and the higher these curves extend in gain and frequency, the greater is the GBP for a given amplifier. It is true that with externally compensated amplifiers, extremely high GBPs can be achieved only at high gains, but it is also obvious that these are the conditions which require the high GBP for accuracy. Several IC op amps can yield GBPs of 100 MHz or more in some instances.

Slew Rate (*SR*). *The maximum rate of change of output voltage under large-signal conditions.*

Slew rate is the maximum rate of change of the output voltage of an amplifier under large-signal conditions, as opposed to the small-signal rise time. Unless otherwise specified, slew rate is measured and specified for closed-loop conditions, usually for a unity-gain voltage follower, which is the worst case for slew rate. The slewing rate of an amplifier will define a full-power bandwidth, the maximum frequency at which the amplifier will deliver full-rated output voltage with less than 3.0% distortion. The two are interrelated by

$$SR = 2\pi E_{op}f_p,$$

where,

E_{op} is the peak output voltage and f_p is the full-power response frequency.

Slew rate is the parameter normally specified, although full-power response may also be specified. Slew rate is measured in a standard test circuit, using a full-scale input pulse with negligible rise time. The output will then change at a rate limited by the slewing ability of the amplifier.

The slewing rate of an externally compensated amplifier can be proportional to the closed-loop gain if the compensation is adjusted to optimize GBP. This is because more compensation is used at lower gains, and it is the compensation capacitance which determines slew rate. Slew-rate limitations are caused by the limited ability of the internal circuitry of the amplifier to charge and discharge this capacitance. When an operating frequency and output-voltage swing are reached which exceed the ability of the amplifier to charge and discharge the capacitance, the output no longer follows the input linearly but becomes "slew-rate-limited"; the output can then follow only at its rate limit.

In a given type of amplifier, reducing the capacitance that must be charged and discharged (the compensation capacitance) will raise the slewing rate in proportion to the capacitance reduction. Thus, higher-gain stages (which are compensated with less capacitance) have higher slew rates, which, as we stated originally, makes slew rate proportional to closed-loop gain. This, of course, does not hold true for internally compensated amplifiers.

Transient Response (TR). The 10% to 90% closed-loop, step-function response of the amplifier under small-signal conditions.

Like slew rate, the transient response of IC op amps is specified under closed-loop conditions. With a small-signal pulse input, the output will be an exponential function, with a time constant inversely proportional to the bandwidth, according to

$$\text{bandwidth} = \frac{0.35}{\text{rise time}},$$

with bandwidth and rise time normally given in MHz and μs, respectively.

The test circuit used is typically a unity-gain voltage follower, with the amplifier driving its rated values of load resistance and capacitance. The signal level used is generally 0.5 volt or less, to ensure operation well below the slew-rate limits of the device.

Since bandwidth and rise time are interrelated, it follows that devices with high unity-gain frequencies will exhibit proportionally reduced rise times.

General Characteristics

Power Consumption (P_c). The dc power required to operate the amplifier with the output at zero and with no load current.

The power consumption of an IC op amp is the power consumed for biasing purposes. It is not usable output power because none of it is delivered to the load. It should not be confused with power dissipation, which is a measure of the ability of the package to dissipate power.

Power consumption is normally specified numerically at supply voltages of ±15 volts. It may be given in the form of milliwatts of power, or milliamperes of supply current at these voltages from which power may be calculated. In addition, power consumption as a function of temperature and supply potential may be given.

With some IC op amps, power consumption may be controlled externally over an extremely wide range with a master bias terminal. This terminal may be used to switch the IC from completely "off" to "on" by removal or application of the bias current. In addition, the level of the current when "on" may be varied, which, in turn, varies the power consumption of the IC. These types are referred to as *programmable* types and will be covered in more detail in the applications section.

REFERENCES

1. *Applications Manual for Computing Amplifiers.* Philbrick Researches, Inc., Dedham, Mass., 1966.

2. Barna, A. *Operational Amplifiers.* John Wiley & Sons, Inc., New York, 1971.

3. Borlase, W. *An Introduction to Operational Amplifiers.* Analog Devices Application Note, September 1971. Analog Devices, Inc., Norwood, Mass.

4. Clayton, G. B. *Operational Amplifiers.* Butterworth, Inc., Toronto, Ont., Canada, 1971.

5. Giles, J. N. *Fairchild Semiconductor LIC Handbook.* Fairchild Semiconductor, Mountain View, Calif., 1967.

6. Huehne, K. *Getting More Value Out of an Integrated Operational Amplifier Data Sheet.* Motorola Application Note AN-273A, February 1972. Motorola Semiconductor Products, Inc., Phoenix, Ariz.

7. JEDEC Engineering Bulletin No. 1-B, March 1971. *Glossary of Microelectronic Terms, Definitions, and Symbols.* EIA Engineering Dept., Washington, D. C.

8. Microsystems International Applications Bulletin 40001A, 1971. *Basic Principles and Applications of Operational Amplifiers.* Microsystems International Ltd., Ottawa, Ont., Canada.

9. Miler, G. G. *Equivalent Input Noise Measurements on High Gain Monolithic Operational Amplifiers.* Harris Semiconductor Application Note 506, October 1970. Harris Semiconductor, Melbourne, Fla.

10. RCA Application Note ICAN-5290, March 1970. *Integrated Circuit Operational Amplifiers.* RCA Solid State Div., Somerville, N.J.

11. Smith, J. I. *Modern Operational Circuit Design.* John Wiley & Sons, Inc., New York, 1971.

12. Smith, L.; Sheingold, D. "Noise and Operational Amplifier Circuits." *Analog Dialogue,* Vol. 3, No. 1, March 1969.

13. Stata, R. "Operational Amplifiers—Parts I and II." *Electromechanical Design,* September, November 1965. (Available as reprint from Analog Devices, Inc., Norwood, Mass.)

14. Tobey, G. E.; Graeme, J. G.; Huelsman, L. P. *Operational Amplifiers—Design and Applications.* Burr-Brown Research Corp., McGraw-Hill Book Co., New York, 1971.

15. Union Carbide Electronics AN-7, December 1966. *Operational Amplifier Static Gain Errors Analysis and Nomographs.*

16. Vander Kooi, M. K. *Predicting Op Amp Slew Rate Limited Response.* National Semiconductor LB-19, August 1972. National Semiconductor Corp., Santa Clara, Calif.

17. Widlar, R. J. *Drift Compensation Techniques for Integrated DC Amplifiers.* National Semiconductor Application Note AN-3, November 1967. National Semiconductor Corp., Santa Clara, Calif.

2

IC Op Amps: The Evolution of General-Purpose and Specialized Types

2.1 HISTORY AND DEVELOPMENT OF GENERAL-PURPOSE OP AMPS

No discussion of IC op amps would be complete without some historical background to place the different types in perspective. Due to the overwhelming proliferation of op-amp types, this is a challenging task; however, there are distinct evolutionary steps in the development of these devices. From this framework, we can at least lead up to the period of the late 1960s and early 1970s when the diversity of types exploded, so to speak, into the broad spectrum of devices available today.

2.1.1 The μA702

The foundation for IC op-amp design really began with the μA702, the first generally accepted IC op amp, which was introduced by Fairchild Semiconductor in 1963. For a number of reasons, the 702 was not a universally applicable op amp. It had a very limited common-mode input range, relatively low voltage gain (approximately 70 dB), used odd supply voltages (such as +12 and −6 volts), and was susceptible to burnout when the output was temporarily shorted. However, the 702 did set the stage for future trends in IC op-amp design by establishing the practice of using matched-component techniques.

IC Design Philosophy

The design of monolithic integrated circuitry is entirely different from that of discrete-component circuitry, because of inherent limitations in the IC fabrication process. In fabricating ICs, resistors are limited to low values, have very poor tolerances, and exhibit poor performance with changes in temperature. Complementary transistors of equal performance are not feasible without additional processing steps; thus, designs must be either npn-only or worked around the poor-quality pnp transistors that are compatible with the npn process. Capacitors of more than a few picofarads in value are not desirable because they occupy excessive chip area and hence increase the cost per device.

Because conventional discrete-component design techniques were not compatible with monolithic IC processing, new methods had to be devised. The old "ground rules" were discarded in favor of ones which optimized designs based on inherent properties of the monolithic IC process. A brief review of these features is appropriate before we begin to discuss them in the context of actual IC op-amp circuits.

Because of the small size of the transistors used in integrated circuitry, it is possible to lay out and interconnect a large number of them in the space formerly occupied by a single conventional transistor. This is a big advantage, since for a given area (or "chip real estate" as it is termed in the IC world) it is just as economical to create a large number of the smaller IC transistors as it is to create only one discrete transistor. Active components are inexpensive in IC designs; therefore, a larger number of them may be used without materially affecting cost. This is in direct contrast to the reasoning behind discrete-component designs, where the object is to use the minimum number of components that will satisfy the circuit requirements. As a result, an IC schematic will invariably appear to have more transistors and diodes in it than are needed. From the standpoint of cost (which is directly proportional to chip area), it is advantageous to use as many of the smaller active components as possible to accomplish a given function. Since capacitors, resistors, and transistors occupy diminishing amounts of space in that order, designs will lean toward transistors first, resistors next, and capacitors last. Often a transistor may be biased to simulate a large value resistor, because if the resistor were used for the same function, it would occupy a much greater area. Transistors are used in many ways, a few of which are illustrated in Fig. 2-1.

In addition to the substantial use of transistors in various forms, another inherent advantage of the monolithic process is extensively utilized. Due to the very close physical proximity of IC components, and the fact that they are all made simultaneously on the same silicon chip (and thus are subject to identical conditions), all elements tend to match very well. Although the resistors are subject to tolerance variations of up to ±30%, the match between them is much better—within 3%. This matching characteristic not only holds true for resistors but also for transistors. Current gains and base-emitter potentials match up within a few percent, as do breakdown voltages. A pair of IC transistors laid down side by side can be matched to have base-emitter voltages (V_{BE}) within a millivolt of each other. This makes IC transistors naturally suited for balanced-gain stages such as differential amplifiers, which work on the symmetry principle. In addition, diode-connected transistors can be used readily as matched pairs. Since the components on an IC chip are all within a few thousandths of an inch of each other and are an integral part of the chip, these matching characteristics also track very well with temperature changes.

To illustrate the preceding points and to give the discussion some perspective, we will now discuss the 702 circuit, which is an excellent example of the optimum use of matched-component design.

μA702 Circuit Description

A schematic for the Fairfield μA702A is shown in Fig. 2-2. The differential input stage of the 702 is composed of a matched pair of transistors, Q_2 and Q_3, biased by a constant-current transistor, Q_1. Q_1 is an example of a transistor simulating a high value of resistance. Since the idea of an emitter-coupled amplifier, such as Q_2-Q_3, is to respond only to differential signals while ignoring those which are common to ground, it follows that the higher the resistance between the Q_2-Q_3 emitters and $V-$ is, the more nearly constant this current will be. Q_1 serves this function for the circuit by simulating a very high resistance. Q_1 is biased by a matched transistor, Q_9, connected as a diode to temperature-compensate the base-emitter junction of Q_1 and ensure that its emitter current will not drift with changes in temperature. It also serves a similar function for Q_8. The bias divider, R_7-R_9, has a fairly low resistance value (2880 ohms). Note that the ratio would remain the same even if the

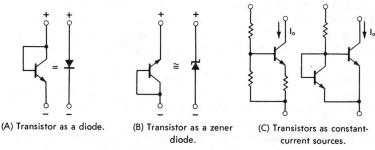

(A) Transistor as a diode.   (B) Transistor as a zener diode.   (C) Transistors as constant-current sources.

Fig. 2-1. Transistors are used to simulate other IC circuit elements.

values of R_7 and R_9 were both to vary by 20% due to tolerances. As long as the ratio is constant, the voltage from the R_7-R_9 divider will be constant, so the bias to Q_1 and Q_8 is relatively unaffected. The use of ratios rather than absolute values is another example of the IC design philosophy of working with the characteristics of the IC fabrication process.

The amplified output current of Q_2 and Q_3 drives the second-stage transistors, Q_4 and Q_5. Here, the differential signal at the bottom of R_1 and R_2 is converted by Q_4 into a single-ended drive to Q_5. Q_4 inverts the signal from Q_2, adding it to that developed by Q_3.

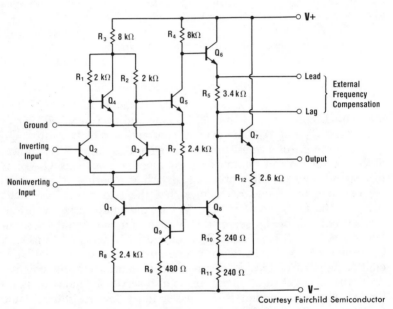

Courtesy Fairchild Semiconductor

Fig. 2-2. Schematic of μA702A op amp.

Q_4 and Q_5 are identical transistors like the input pair (Q_2-Q_3) and are placed close together on the layout. Since the base currents for Q_4 and Q_5 come from a common voltage point through matched resistors (R_1 and R_2), the base voltages of Q_4 and Q_5 will be equal when the currents in Q_2 and Q_3 are equal. With matched base voltages and matched transistors, the currents in Q_4 and Q_5 will be balanced when Q_2 and Q_3 are balanced, making the entire first two stages a completely matched combination. The output from Q_5 is taken single-ended by Q_6, an emitter follower.

An additional balanced design feature of the Q_4-Q_5 circuit is its ability to reject power-supply-induced voltage variations. If the V+ line changes, the current in both Q_4 and Q_5 will change due to the balanced 8000-ohm loads and symmetrical base circuits. The net result is that the collector voltage of Q_5 remains constant, meaning that the power-supply variations are much reduced.

The emitter follower, Q_6, feeds output stage Q_7 through a dropping resistor, R_5. The drop across R_5 allows the signal swing from Q_6 to be shifted downward in dc level and to be centered around zero volts dc. The dc current provided by Q_8 flowing in R_5 creates a constant dc voltage drop, which provides a 5-volt shift in level going from Q_6 to Q_7. However, no signal swing is lost across R_5 because Q_8 appears as a very high resistance for signal variations. The emitter resistor of Q_7 is returned to a tap on the emitter resistance of Q_8 rather than to the V— line. This connection feeds back some of the output signal in such a direction as to enhance the original swing (a form of positive feedback) by a controlled amount. The gain of this output stage is 2.5, again controlled by resistor ratios.

Table 2-1. Typical Electrical Characteristics of the μA702 Operational Amplifier ($T_A = 25\,^{\circ}$C)

Parameter	Value		Unit
	V+ = +12 V V— = −6.0 V	V+ = +6.0 V V— = −3.0 V	
Input Offset Voltage	2.0	2.0	mV
Input Offset Current	0.7	0.5	μA
Input Bias Current	4.0	2.5	μA
Input Impedance	25	40	kΩ
Temperature Coefficient of V_{io}			
$\quad$ 0°C $<$ T$_A$ $<$ +125°C	5.0	5.0	μV/°C
$\quad$ −55°C $<$ T$_A$ $<$ 0°C	10	10	μV/°C
Input Common-Mode Rejection	80	80	dB
Open-Loop Voltage Gain	2600	700	
Open-Loop Bandwidth	1.0	1.0	MHz
Output Impedance	200	300	Ω
Maximum Output Swing	±5.3	±2.7	V
Power Input	70	17	mW
Input-Referred			
$\quad$ V+ Supply Sensitivity	50	100	μV/V
Input-Referred			
$\quad$ V— Supply Sensitivity	100	200	μV/V

The entire circuit of the 702 is based upon the matching of all components and resistor ratios. The absolute values of resistance have little effect on performance. Table 2-1 summarizes the performance characteristics of the μA702A.

Although the 702 is obsolete by present standards, it is historically important because it represents the successful establishment of an IC design philosophy based almost solely on the idea of component matching. This technique set a precedent which still prevails. The 702 is, however, still available from a number of sources.

2.1.2 The μA709

The next major advancement in IC evolution came with the introduction of the Fairchild μA709 in 1965. The 709 improved upon the performance of the 702 in a number of areas; notably, it had higher gain, a larger input and output voltage range, lower input currents, higher output currents, and operation from symmetrical power supplies of ±15 volts. The 709 became a standard type number and is still produced in volume by more sources than any other linear integrated circuit. So universal was the acceptance of the 709 that it must be regarded as a classic among IC op amps. Although many of its individual performance parameters have long since been eclipsed, the 709 remains a unique blend of performance, versatility, and economy—three ingredients that are a hard combination to beat. Therefore, it is fairly safe to assume that the 709 will not only be remembered for its historical value, but will remain valuable for many years to come.

709 Circuit Description

Since the 709 is still widely used and is still an excellent performer in many circuits, its circuit design will be discussed in more detail. The design principles established with the 702 were exercised again in the 709, with some new advances also being introduced. In addition, many of the problems in applying the 702 were eliminated with the 709 design.

Fig. 2-3 is the schematic diagram of a 709 amplifier. Immediately you can see that a large number of transistors are used (15) and that the resistance values are chosen fairly low—R_{15} is the highest at 30,000 ohms. This is in keeping with the basic design philosophy set forth in the 702. Still, this entire circuit does not occupy an excessive chip area—the 709 is a 55-mil square chip of silicon. A photomicrograph of the layout is shown in Fig. 2-4.

Input Stage. In the 709, Q_1 and Q_2 form the input differential-amplifier pair. Each is operated at a collector current of 20 microamperes by the constant-current transistor, Q_{11}. This low current level establishes one important advantage—a big reduction in the input bias current to Q_1 and Q_2. With a typical β of 100 for Q_1-Q_2, this makes the input current 200 nanoamperes or about $1/20$ that of the 702. To obtain a 40-μA current by conventional means would require a very high resistance in the emitter of Q_{11}. In addition, to increase the negative common-mode input range of Q_1 and Q_2, Q_{11} must be biased close to the V− line, otherwise it would saturate as Q_1 and Q_2 swing negative. From this standpoint, Q_{11} should swing to at least -10 volts peak. The solution to the biasing of Q_{11} at 40 μA was a new type of constant-current source made up of Q_{10} and Q_{11}.

In a pair of matched transistors such as those that are readily available in a monolithic IC, the base-emitter voltages that are required for given collector currents form an extremely predictable parameter. Not only will these voltages be within 1 or 2 mV for

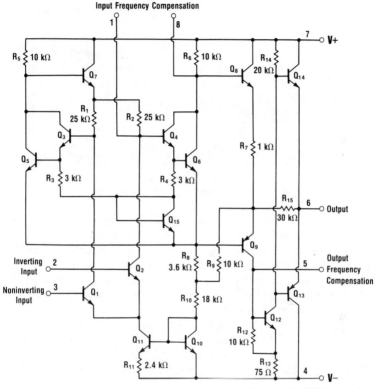

Courtesy Fairchild Semiconductor

Fig. 2-3. Schematic of $\mu A709$ op amp.

equal collector currents, but the *difference* in the two base-emitter voltages for a *ratio* of currents is also very predictable. This is illustrated by Fig. 2-5A. With a current, I_1, flowing in diode-connected Q_1, Q_1 will develop a base-emitter voltage, V_{BE1}, which is proportional to this current. For an identical current to flow in Q_2, Q_2 is connected directly in parallel with the base-emitter junction of Q_1. Since the two transistors are matched, an identical current, I_2, will flow in Q_2 since the V_{BE} of Q_2 equals the V_{BE} of Q_1. This

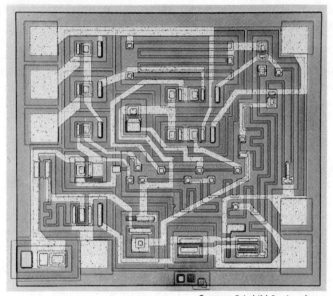

Fig. 2-4. Photomicrograph of μA709 silicon chip.

is a common IC circuit technique for generating a simple constant-current source. By carrying this a step farther, advantage is taken of the fact that transistors Q_1 and Q_2 are well-matched over their entire dynamic range of current flow. In this manner, the ratio of I_1 to I_2 is manipulated by subtracting a portion of the base-emitter voltage of Q_1 from that applied to Q_2, thus causing Q_2 to conduct a smaller current. Transistors are natural logarithmic elements—their base-emitter voltage is the logarithm of the collector current over many decades of current. Typically, for each 10-to-1 change in collector current in a pair of matched transistors, the base-emitter voltage will change by 60 mV. Therefore, to scale I_2 to a level of

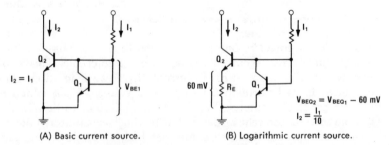

(A) Basic current source. (B) Logarithmic current source.

Fig. 2-5. Matched transistor current sources.

1/10 of I_1, the base-emitter voltage of Q_2 must be reduced to 60 mV below that of Q_1. This is illustrated in Fig. 2-5B. For $I_2 = 1/100$ of I_1, the reduction would be 120 mV. This is accomplished by a simple emitter resistance, R_E, which drops the 60 mV or 120 mV, as the case may be. This allows microampere-level currents from Q_2 to be generated with very small values of resistance for R_E, as the drop across R_E will only be a few tens of millivolts.

Referring to Fig. 2-3, we can see how this is done in the 709 with Q_{10} and Q_{11}. Q_{10} is the reference transistor and R_{11} represents the V_{BE} scaling resistor, R_E (Fig. 2-5A). R_E subtracts a portion of the V_{BE} of Q_{10} from that of Q_{11}, forcing Q_{11} to conduct a much lower current. An additional advantage of this technique is the dynamic range of voltage it allows at the collector of Q_{11}. Since the base of Q_{11} is only 1 V_{BE} above the V− line, the emitters of Q_1 and Q_2 can drop very nearly to the V_{BE} of Q_{11} (or very close to −15 V) before Q_{11} saturates. This maximizes the negative input common-mode range of Q_1-Q_2.

Another interesting feature of the Q_1-Q_2 input stage is its performance with temperature changes. The output current from Q_{11} varies with temperature, but it does so in such a manner that it complements the transconductance variations of Q_1 and Q_2 with temperature changes. As a consequence, the resultant combination of these two opposite effects is a voltage-gain characteristic of the input stage, which stays constant within a few percent over the operating temperature range. In addition, the variations in the operating current of the Q_{11} current source with the supply voltage are reduced due to the relationship of the current in Q_{11} to the current in Q_{10}. The current in Q_{11} is related logarithmically rather than directly to the current in Q_{10}. Although the current in Q_{10} will vary with changes in the supply voltage, the resultant effect on the current in Q_{11} is very much reduced due to this logarithmic relation, so it is practically unaffected by supply-voltage changes.

Second Stage. In essence, the second stage of the 709 is similar to the second stage of the 702 described previously. It is diagrammed in simplified fashion in Fig. 2-6. Note the similarity of this to the 702 schematic shown in Fig. 2-2. R_1 and R_2, the load resistors for the first stage, are higher in value here than in the 702—25 kΩ versus 2 kΩ. The main reason for this is to offset the reduction in first-stage gain which would occur had the lower resistance values been retained. The same balanced biasing features used in the 702 are retained in this portion of the 709 circuit, and it possesses a similar property of immunity to supply-voltage changes. The full circuit is shown in the schematic of Fig. 2-3. Darlington connections are used for Q_5 and Q_6 to minimize loading on R_1 and R_2. An emitter follower, Q_7, is used to feed R_1 and R_2, which is a departure from the basic 702 connection. This removes the input-stage currents flowing in R_1 and R_2 from Q_5 and improves the overall balance. The remaining element of the second stage is diode-connected Q_{15}, which stabilizes the Darlington pairs, Q_3-Q_5 and Q_4-Q_6, by removing excess leakage currents that occur at high temperatures.

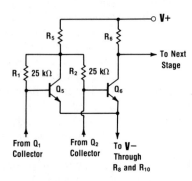

Fig. 2-6. Simplified schematic of 709 second stage.

In the 702, the emitters of the second stage (Q_4 and Q_5 of Fig. 2-2) were connected to a grounded terminal. This placed a serious restriction on the positive range of signal swing that the input stage could tolerate, since input transistors Q_1 and/or Q_2 saturate when the inputs become more positive than $+2 V_{BE}$. This limits this circuit to very low levels of positive common-mode signal swing. In the 709, this situation is improved by returning the emitters of second-stage transistors Q_5 and Q_6 to V− through bias resistors R_8 and R_{10}. In addition, the static voltage on R_1 and R_2 is made high enough so that Q_1 and Q_2 can swing typically to $+10$ volts with $+15$-volt supplies. The second-stage output is developed across R_6 and is buffered by emitter follower Q_8.

Output Stage. The output stage, composed of Q_9, Q_{12}, Q_{13}, and Q_{14}, is entirely different from that of the 702—in fact, this is one of the major differences between the two designs. For a wide range of voltage swing with moderate current output capability, a class-B output stage is highly desirable, as it provides the requisite power with low standby current. The 709 uses a class-B output stage consisting of complementary emitter followers Q_{13} and Q_{14}. This yields an inherently low output impedance with the advantage that both transistors cannot conduct simultaneously due to their direct base connection. A high voltage gain to drive the Q_{13}-Q_{14} pair is provided by common-emitter amplifier Q_{12} and is driven by common-base stage Q_9, which has no current gain. Its primary purpose is to shift the high dc level at Q_8 to a lower dc level compatible with the base-drive requirements of Q_{12}. The entire output stage is, in essence, a single-stage voltage amplifier (Q_{12}) with a buffered output. The voltage gain of the circuit would be essentially the ratio of R_{14}/R_{13}, or $20,000/75 = 260$, were it not for R_{15} and R_7. These resistors provide local feedback around the output stage. R_{15} is the feedback resistor, with R_7 serving as the input resistor. The gain of this local feedback loop from Q_8 to the output is R_{15}/R_7, or $30,000/1000 = 30$. The feedback is used mainly to correct for the "dead zone" of transistors Q_{13} and Q_{14} as the output circuit swings above and below ground level. In addition, it further lowers the output impedance of Q_{13}-Q_{14} by virtue of the negative feedback through R_{15}.

Two new components are introduced into the design in the output stage: Q_9 and Q_{13}, which are pnp transistors. Both of these transistors are made with the same process that is optimized for the remaining transistors, which are all npn. As pnp transistors go, Q_9 and Q_{13} are of poor quality, having current gains of 10 or less. However, this represents no great difficulty since the circuit is designed to allow for these compromises. Q_9 is used only as a level shifter, and thus low current gain does not present a problem since an excess of drive is available from emitter follower Q_8. Q_{13} also has relaxed performance requirements—in reality, it need function only as a diode, since an excess of drive is available from Q_{12}. The gain it may provide, however, can be regarded as a bonus.

A point not obvious from an examination of the circuit is the relative size of Q_{13} and Q_{14}. These transistors, like most of those used in linear ICs, are of small geometry and have a rapid falloff in gain when driven into high-current operation. As a result, the output stage protects itself against short circuits, at least for short durations, by the self-limiting current of the output transistors.

Frequency Compensation. As discussed in the section on basic theory, a prerequisite for stability in a feedback amplifier is the control of phase shift in the amplifier before feedback is applied. Amplifier phase shift must be less than $180°$ at the point where the open-loop and closed-loop gain curves intersect. In the 709, the control of open-loop gain/phase characteristics is accomplished by three frequency-compensation components, as shown in Fig. 2-7A. R_1 and C_1 are called the input compensation, and C_2 is called the output compensation. These three components shape the open-loop response and, with the values noted, yield the family of open-loop responses shown in Fig. 2-7B. These are the networks necessary for stability in configurations of 0-, 20-, 40-, and 60-dB closed-loop gains (see Fig. 2-7C). The impedance at the 709 compensation terminals is high enough that full compensation can be realized with reasonably small capacitors (5000 pF maximum). These networks provide adequate stability with a 709 device under worst-

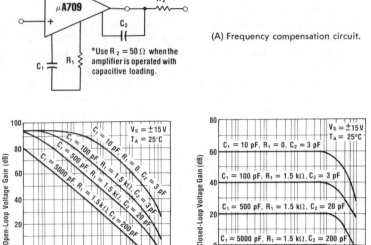

(A) Frequency compensation circuit.

*Use $R_2 = 50\,\Omega$ when the amplifier is operated with capacitive loading.

(B) Open-loop frequency response for various compensation values.

(C) Frequency response for various closed-loop gains.

Courtesy Fairchild Semiconductor

Fig. 2-7. Frequency compensation methods and responses for the 709 op amp.

case conditions of temperature, supply voltage, etc. A summary of the μA709 electrical characteristics is given in Table 2-2.

2.1.3 The 101 and 741 Families

The LM101

Just as the improvements in the 709 over the 702 established a new level of performance and versatility, so also was the LM101 an improvement over the 709. Introduced in 1967 by National Semiconductor Corporation, the LM101 was the next evolutionary step in the history of IC op-amp technology. The 709 devices are regarded as the "first generation" of IC op amps; the arrival of the LM101 began the second generation of IC op amps.

For the same reasons that the 709 has historical and applicational importance, so also does the LM101. It is historically important because it represents the next level of technology. And it is also important conceptually, for it is still the basis for an entire range of general-purpose devices which are variations on its basic design. Like the 709, we will examine the 101 closely because once it is

Table 2-2. Typical Electrical Characteristics of the μA709 Operational Amplifier (T_A = 25°C, V_S = ± 15 V)

Parameter	Value	Unit
Input Offset Voltage	1.0	mV
Input Offset Current	50	nA
Input Bias Current	200	nA
Input Impedance	400	kΩ
Input Common-Mode Range	±10	V
Common-Mode Rejection Ratio	90	dB
Voltage Gain	45,000	
Output Voltage Swing		
R_L = 10 kΩ	±14	V
R_L = 2.0 kΩ	±13	V
Output Impedance	150	Ω
Power Consumption	80	mW
Power-Supply Rejection Ratio	25	μV/V

understood, the entire range of similar devices within the second generation can also be understood. This encompasses the greater percentage of op amps now in general-purpose usage.

LM101 Circuit Description

The objectives of the 101 design were to eliminate the major problem areas associated with the 709. These were:

1. Inadequate short-circuit protection.
2. Complicated frequency-compensation networks.
3. Latch-up when common-mode range was exceeded.
4. Too low differential input voltage.
5. Excessive power dissipation.
6. Sensitivity to capacitive loading and susceptibility to oscillations.
7. Limited supply voltage range.

The 101 design solved all of these problems and also added some additional refinements. Gain was increased to 160,000 over the 45,000 of the 709, and the useful range of supply operation was increased to from ±5 volts to ±20 volts. The device retained the 709 pin configuration for input, output, and power-supply leads. A simplified circuit of the 101 is shown in Fig. 2-8. Although this is a simplified schematic, one thing that is immediately obvious is the absolute minimum use of resistors and the use of a large number of active devices.

To accomplish the primary objective of simple frequency compensation, the 101 uses a two-stage amplifier design; the fewer the number of stages in a device, the fewer the phase shifts with which to contend. However, to meet the high gain required from the de-

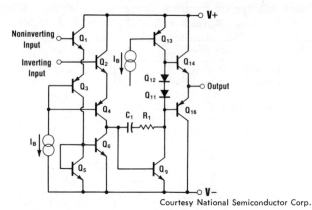

Courtesy National Semiconductor Corp.

Fig. 2-8. Simplified schematic of LM101 op amp.

vice, these two stages must provide the gain previously supplied by three stages in the 709. This means that the gain per stage must be highly optimized to achieve a total gain of 100 dB for the entire amplifier. In the 101, this is done by using active loads, which increase the available gain per stage to a maximum without resorting to undesirable high resistances.

An illustration of this is shown in Fig. 2-9A. A basic common-emitter amplifier will have a gain equal to the ratio of the load resistance (R_L) to the dynamic emitter impedance (R_e). Gain may be optimized by raising R_L to maximum, but a limitation is soon reached. Since high values of resistance are not desirable in an IC, operation with resistance loads at collector currents of 20 μA is prevented because the load resistance required for high gain would be over one megohm. However, with a transistor as a load as in Fig. 2-9B, the situation is different. The output impedance of a transistor biased for a constant collector current is extremely high and can

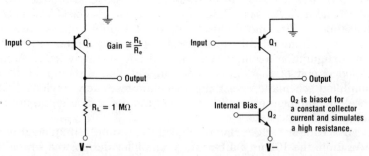

(A) Achieving high gain with high R_L.   (B) Achieving high gain with active loading.

Fig. 2-9. Methods of achieving high single-stage gain in integrated circuitry.

86

easily achieve the required one-megohm level. An additional bonus of this technique is the fact that it requires a minimum of voltage drop across the transistor for operation (as opposed to a resistor), and this extends the dynamic range over which the stage can swing before reaching saturation.

First Stage. Referring to Fig. 2-8, we can see how active loading is utilized in the 101. Q_3 and Q_4 in this stage form an equivalent pnp differential pair. Since monolithic pnp transistors have low gains, their inputs in the 101 are buffered by high-gain emitter followers Q_1 and Q_2. The net equivalent is a composite, high-gain, pnp differential pair. The outputs of Q_3 and Q_4 are loaded by active loads Q_5 and Q_6. This stage also serves as a differential to single-ended converter, transforming the push-pull output from Q_3-Q_4 into an equivalent single-ended drive at the collector of Q_6. One may also note that the common-mode input range of this stage is quite high; Q_1 and Q_2 may swing positive to a limit equal to the V+ line; the negative limit is a level 3 V_{BE} above the V− line. This feature removes any tendencies toward latch-up due to input stage saturation. The gain of this input stage is 60 dB. An additional feature is a very high differential input voltage rating, due to the high base-emitter breakdowns of the pnp transistors. The fact that the input can tolerate differential inputs of ±30 volts removes restrictions on differential input swings.

Second Stage. The second stage of the 101 is composed of a common-emitter amplifier, Q_9, loaded by an active transistor current source, Q_{13}. Again, this is an example of active loading to achieve high gain in a single stage. This high-gain voltage amplifier is buffered to a low impedance level by a class-AB emitter follower composed of Q_{11} and Q_{12}, Q_{14} and Q_{16}. At this point we are ready to consider the composite circuit as a whole, which is shown in Fig. 2-10B. Fig. 2-10A is a two-stage model of the 101.

Frequency compensation of the 101 is accomplished by a single external 30-pF capacitor connected between pins 1 and 8 as shown in Fig. 2-10A. This capacitor makes the second stage a Miller integrator and forces the gain to roll off from its open-loop value of 104 dB. beginning at 10 Hz and continuing at a rate of 6 dB per octave down through the unity-gain frequency of 1.0 MHz. This single-capacitor compensation makes the device stable in any feedback configuration down to the worst-case, noninverting unity gain. This response is shown in Fig. 2-11 for both the unity-gain compensation (30 pF) and the lighter compensation (3.0 pF).

Some further details of the Fig. 2-10B circuit are also worthy of note. In the first stage, buffer transistor Q_7 has been incorporated to minimize the loading on Q_3 and to improve the balance of the input stage differential to single-ended connector. In a similar man-

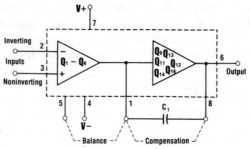

(A) Two-stage model of LM101.

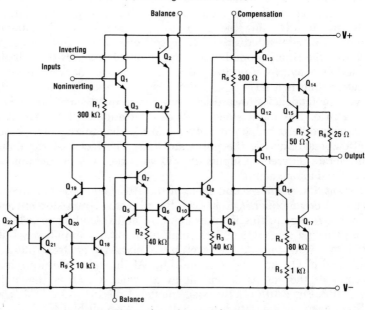

(B) Complete schematic of LM101.

Fig. 2-10. Two-stage model and actual schematic of LM101 op amp.

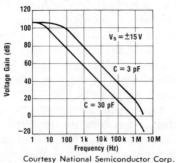

Fig. 2-11. Open-loop frequency response of LM101 for two compensation values.

ner, Q_8 drives Q_9 in Darlington fashion to prevent loading of Q_4-Q_6, thus maximizing the gain of the input stage. In the output stage, Q_{11} and Q_{12} provide a slight forward bias to Q_{14} and Q_{16} to minimize crossover distortion. Current limiting is also added for both directions of output swing. Q_{14} is protected against overcurrent for positive outputs by R_8 and Q_{15}. When an excessive current (about 30 mA) through R_8 creates a drop which exceeds the V_{BE} of Q_{15}, Q_{15} conducts, removing drive from Q_{14} and thus limiting the output current. For negative outputs, overcurrent protection is provided by a combination of effects. When the voltage across R_7 equals 2 V_{BE}, the collector-base junction of Q_{15} conducts and pulls heavy current from Q_{11} through the two series junctions of Q_{15} and Q_{12}. Since Q_{11} is a low-gain pnp, Q_9 must also conduct heavily. This forces a large drop across R_5, which in turn trips Q_{10} on. Finally, Q_{10} limits the drive to Q_8-Q_9 to a safe level, and this limits the negative output current at 30 mA. This rather elaborate negative-swing current limiting not only limits the output current from Q_{16}, but also limits the output from Q_9. The limited output current from Q_9 allows external diodes to be connected to the compensation terminal (pin 8) to clamp the voltage swing of the output stage to defined voltage limits, a valuable feature for comparator applications. The remaining transistors in the circuit (Q_{18}-Q_{22}) are used in providing a self-regulating input bias to the input stage and Q_{13}; they are not part of the signal-flow path.

The 101 again demonstrates the use of a large ratio of active to passive components, containing 22 transistors but only 9 resistors. Performance and applicational ease are both improved from the 709. A summary of LM101 performance is given in Table 2-3. All

Table 2-3. Typical Electrical Characteristics of the LM101 Operational Amplifier (T_A = 25°C, V_S = ± 15 V)

Parameter	Value	Unit
Input Offset Voltage	1.0	mV
Input Offset Current	40	nA
Input Bias Current	120	nA
Input Resistance	0.8	MΩ
Voltage Gain	160,000	
Output Voltage Swing	±14	V
Input Voltage Range	±13	V
Common-Mode Rejection Ratio	90	dB
Power-Supply Rejection Ratio	90	dB
Temperature Range	−55 to +125	°C
Temperature Drift	3.0	μV/°C
Supply-Voltage Range	±5.0 to ±20	V
Power Consumption	50	mW

the intended objectives were accomplished. And, in addition, more open-loop gain, a wider supply-voltage range, and a facility for use as a voltage comparator, were realized.

The LH101

The designers of the 101 intentionally gave the input-stage compensation point (Pin 1 in Fig. 2-10A) a high impedance so that a small compensation capacitance such as 30 pF could be used. They did this not just because a 30-pF capacitor takes up a small amount of board space, but so that ultimately it would be feasible to incorporate this capacitor on the chip itself, thus making a completely self-contained, internally compensated IC op amp. This was accomplished by National Semiconductor in January of 1968 with the introduction of the LH101, a hybrid combination of an LM101 chip and a 30-pF capacitor in a single package. The LH101 has exactly the same specifications as the LM101 compensated externally with 30 pF. Pinout is the same except for the lack of internal offset null and the inaccessibility of the clamp point. A schematic of the LH101 is shown in Fig. 2-12.

The μA741

In May of 1968, Fairchild Semiconductor introduced the μA741, an internally compensated IC op amp with ac and dc performance

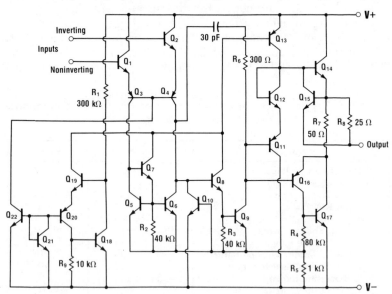

Fig. 2-12. Schematic of LH101 op amp.

characteristics very similar to those of the LM101 compensated for unity gain. A schematic of the μA741 is shown in Fig. 2-13.

Although there are substantial differences in the internal circuitry of the 101 and the 741, these are associated mainly with biasing and the method of short-circuit protection. The 741 may also be modeled as a two-stage amplifier similar to the 101, as shown in Fig. 2-10A and as discussed in the previous section.

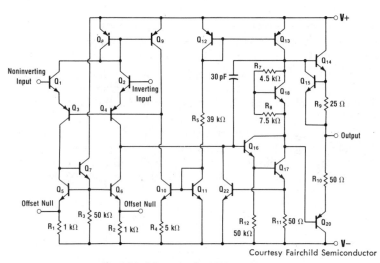

Courtesy Fairchild Semiconductor

Fig. 2-13. Schematic of μA741 op amp.

The main difference between the LM101 and the μA741 is that the 741 accomplishes frequency compensation by means of an on-chip capacitor. This marked the first time that frequency compensation had been accomplished by means of an on-chip capacitor in a monolithic IC op amp. An additional difference in the 741 is the method of offset null. Offset null is accomplished in the 741 by adjusting the differential currents in Q_5 and Q_6 at their emitters, as shown in Fig. 2-13 (pins 1 and 5 in Fig. 2-14A). In the 101, offset null is accomplished by adjusting the currents in Q_5 and Q_6 at their collectors (pins 1 and 5 of Figs. 2-10A and 2-14B). Both methods perform the same function with regard to dc—a slight imbalance of the collector currents of Q_3 and Q_4 to null the input offset voltage. The differences in the actual external connections are shown in Fig. 2-14.

The LM101A

In December, 1968, National Semiconductor introduced the LM101A, an improved version of the LM101. The schematic of

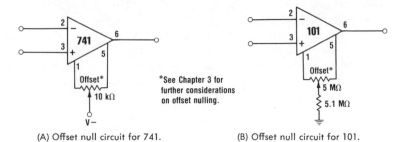

(A) Offset null circuit for 741.   (B) Offset null circuit for 101.

Fig. 2-14. Offset null differences between the 741 and 101 op amps.

the LM101A is shown in Fig. 2-15. As will be noted, there is little difference in the appearance of the circuit from that of the 101. The portion changed is the biasing circuit for the input stage (Q_{18}-Q_{22}), which allows better control of input current characteristics over the operating temperature range. In addition, certain processing refinements for input transistors Q_1 and Q_2 resulted in much lower input and offset currents (typically 30 nA and 1.5 nA, respectively), or about a factor of ten better than the 709. No changes

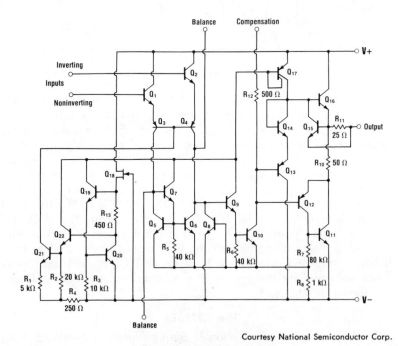

Courtesy National Semiconductor Corp.

Fig. 2-15. Schematic of LM101A op amp.

were made in the other characteristics, and the LM101A is a pin-for-pin replacement for the LM101.

The LM107

National Semiconductor introduced the LM107 and the LM101A at approximately the same time. The LM107 featured the same improved dc performance as the LM101A, except that the 30-pF, frequency-compensation capacitor was built into the silicon chip. The LM107 schematic is shown in Fig. 2-16.

The μA748

In 1969, Fairchild Semiconductor introduced the μA748, an op amp with the dc performance of a 741 but with external frequency compensation. A schematic of the μA748 is shown in Fig. 2-17. The pinout for the 748 is functionally identical to the 101, although the circuit designs are different.

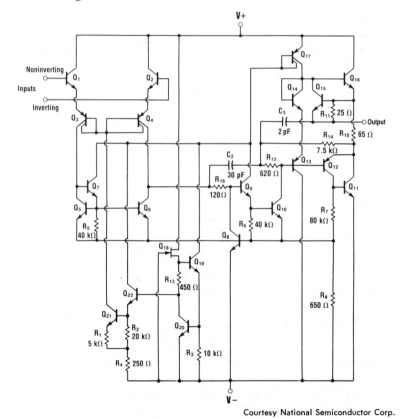

Fig. 2-16. Schematic of LM107 op amp.

Comparison of 101 and 741 Families

At this point, it may already be obvious that there are many similarities between the basic 101 and 741 designs. In fact, if we were to redraw the simplified schematic of the 101, we would find that it applies equally well to all the general-purpose types. By assigning multiple reference designations to the transistors, we can

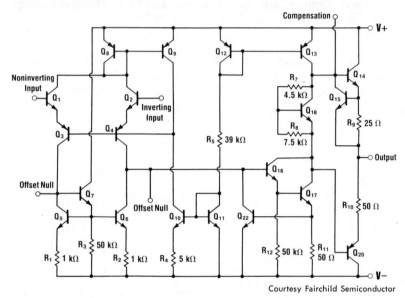

Fig. 2-17. Schematic of μA748 op amp.

further illustrate this basic similarity, as shown in Fig. 2-18. Note that even though there are considerable differences in the 101, 101A, and 741/748 designs, any one of them can be reduced to a functionally equivalent circuit such as that shown in Fig. 2-18. And, as stated previously, all of these amplifiers can be modeled as a basic two-stage design, with frequency compensation accomplished by an integrating capacitor connected around the second stage. This basic design concept is the principle behind the greatest percentage of op amps used today and virtually all of the modern general-purpose types. There are only a few subtleties that really separate the 101 and 741 families. Some important characteristics of the 101 and the 741 families should now be defined.

101 Family. Any "101-type" amplifier can be said to belong to the 101 family. This category includes the basic LM101, the LH101, the LM101A, and the LM107. It also includes corresponding devices of all temperature ranges. For example, LM101 op amps are supplied in three basic temperature ranges: (1) −55°C to +125°C (LM1– series), (2) −25°C to +85°C (LM2– series), and (3) 0°C to +70°C (LM3– series). Thus, an LM301A is the 0°C to +70°C temperature-range equivalent of an LM101A. Both are "101-type" devices, since they belong to the same family. Throughout this book, the numbers used in referring to a device will be the basic part number; e.g., a "101A" amplifier. Thus, to use a 101A amplifier for 0°C to +70°C operation, an LM301A device would be specified. The reader should be cautioned, however, that there are often specification differences between military- and commercial-

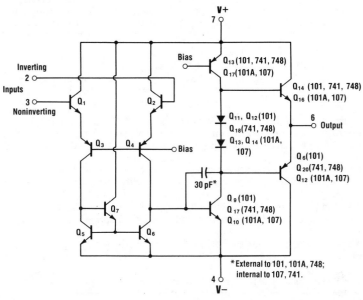

Fig. 2-18. Basic functional circuit diagram of the 101 and 741 op-amp families.

grade devices such as supply voltages, gain, offset, etc. The military-grade devices will almost always have superior ratings and, consequently, higher cost.

741 Family. As with the 101 family, any "741-type" amplifier can be said to belong to the 741 family. This includes the basic 741 device and also multiple versions such as the 747 and 1558 (discussed further in Chapter 3). It also includes the 748, although the 748 may be said to be a "gray-area" device; it comes from the basic 741 design, but has the ac characteristics of a 101 type.

The same general considerations regarding temperature range and part numbers also apply for the 741 family (as well as for any of the other devices to be discussed). If a 741 is mentioned in a circuit, the specifications are assumed to be that of the full-temperature-range (−55°C to +125°C) device. The reader can, however, make the appropriate part number substitution as his requirements dictate.

The salient features of these two general-purpose, op-amp families are summarized in Tables 2-4 and 2-5, and data sheets for the general-purpose types are included in Appendix A.

Table 2-4. The 101 Op-Amp Family*

Military Temperature Range −55°C to +125°C	Industrial Temperature Range −25°C to +85°C	Commercial Temperature Range 0°C to +70°C
LM101 LH101 LM101A LM107	LM201 LH201 LM201A LM207	LM301A LM307

Comments

Basic device of family is the LM101. The LM101 is a general-purpose, externally compensated IC op amp. It is frequency-compensated with a single 30-pF capacitor. It features wide input and output voltage range with freedom from latch-up, output short-circuit protection, controlled power dissipation characteristics, operation from a wide range of supply voltages with little change, and relative immunity to oscillation tendencies.

The LH101 is an LM101 chip with a 30-pF capacitor added to form an internally compensated op amp in hybrid (2-chip) form.

The LM101A is similar to the LM101 but with better dc input characteristics.

The LM107 is an LM101A with internal frequency compensation.

*The designations shown are not intended for ordering purposes. For complete ordering information (package styles, etc.) consult the manufacturer's catalog or individual data sheets.

Summary of General-Purpose Op Amps

General-purpose IC op amps are used in the greatest percentage of applications. A general-purpose type is loosely defined as having a unity-gain bandwidth of approximately 1.0 MHz, operation from power supplies of ±5.0 volts to ±20 volts without serious degradation of performance, and may or may not be internally compensated. This "loose" definition is fulfilled by the 709, 101, and 741 types.

There are, of course, other considerations involved in selecting one particular type over another. Ease of application and amount of necessary peripheral hardware are often considerations, not only from a convenience standpoint but also from the standpoint of board space, the number of parts to be stocked, etc. The 741 will rate favorably in these regards if optimum compensation is not required. If the application requires optimizing speed or overcompensation, then the externally compensated 709 or 101 may be favored. In other situations, dc requirements may dictate a 101A. Although these three types will fulfill virtually all general-purpose applications, no one type is overwhelmingly superior in all situations. Each situation should be evaluated on its own requirements.

For applications that are obviously out of the general-purpose area (high voltage, high speed, low input current, etc.), there are specialized types from which to choose. These types cover a broad range of remaining applications and will round out the devices to be discussed in this book. In the next section, we will briefly discuss each family of special-purpose devices.

Table 2-5. The 741 Op-Amp Family*

Military Temperature Range −55°C to +125°C	Commercial Temperature Range 0°C to +70°C
μA741	μA741C
μA741A	μA741E
μA748	μA748C
μA747	μA747C
μA747A	μA747E
MC1558	MC1458

Comments
Basic device of family is the μA741. The μA741 is a general-purpose, internally compensated IC op amp. It features wide input and output voltage range with freedom from latch-up, output short-circuit protection, operation from a wide range of supply voltages, and relative immunity to oscillation tendencies. The μA741A is similar to the μA741, but with tighter characteristics (to military specifications MIL-M-38510/10101). The μA748 is a μA741 without internal compensation. Compensation and offset null are similar to the LM101. The dc specifications are identical to the μA741. The μA747 is a pair of 741 op amps in a single 14-pin or 10-pin package. The MC1558 is a pair of 741 op amps in a single 14-pin or 8-pin package.

*The designations shown are not intended for ordering purposes. For complete ordering information (package styles, etc.) consult the manufacturer's catalogs or individual data sheets.

2.2 SPECIALIZED GROUPS OF IC OP AMPS AND THEIR CHARACTERISTICS

There are many op-amp applications that cannot be met satisfactorily or optimally by general-purpose types. Special situations may demand very high speed (either wide bandwidth or high slew rate), very low input current, high input impedance, very low offset or offset drift, high voltage or high current output, or a unique type of operation altogether, such as gating or programmability. To complement the general-purpose types discussed in Section 2.1, this section introduces special-purpose types. The array of types presented is broad, but there is a considerable amount of overlap; in fact, several of the ICs could even be categorized in two groups. These types are also standards, representative of the popular version of a particular device type. For reference, the key features which govern the selection of a particular op amp within its group are listed in Table 2-6. The general-purpose types listed in Group I have already been discussed, and that information is also summarized in Table 2-6. We will begin the discussion of special-purpose types with Group II, illustrating typical applications for each device within a group. Commercial and industrial type-number equivalents are noted in parentheses.

2.2.1 Group II Devices (DC and Low-Level Group)

These op amps have one or more of the following features:

1. Very low input currents.
2. Extremely high input resistance.
3. Low offset and/or drift.
4. Low input noise.

Other options within this group include internal or external compensation, high speed, etc. These types include the ICs that are best in terms of dc and low-level performance.

μA725, μA725A (μA725C)

The 725 is an instrumentation op amp intended for highly accurate signal processing and/or high-gain applications. It features the following exceptional characteristics:

1. Very high open-loop gain.
2. Low input current.
3. Low input offset voltage.
4. Low input current/offset voltage drift.
5. Low input noise.
6. Very high common-mode rejection.
7. Very high power-supply rejection.

The 725 is externally compensated and operates over a wide power-supply range. The 725A is a premium version of the 725 with more tightly controlled input parameters.

725 Applications. In general, the 725 is used either for applications which require precise amplification at high gain and moderate bandwidth, or for low-level amplification with low dc error, low dc drift, and low ac noise. These applications include: precision dc regulators, instrumentation amplifiers, low-level audio preamps, high-gain precision amplifiers, and active filters.

LM108, LM108A (LM208, LM208A, LM308, LM308A)

The 108 is a precision IC op amp with very low input currents due to the use of "super-β"* input transistors. It is externally compensated with a single capacitor, has low power consumption, and will operate over a wide power-supply range with low power drain. It is also available in an "A" version with tightened input parameters.

108 Applications. In general, the 108 is used in dc circuits which require low input currents, high input impedance, and very low offset voltage. These applications include: instrumentation amplifiers, low-drift integrators, sample/hold circuits, log amplifiers, and high-impedance transducer amplifiers.

MC1556 (MC1456, MC1456C)

The 1556 is an internally compensated IC op amp with low input currents, again due to the use of a super-β input stage. It has a greater slewing rate than the 741 and a unity-gain frequency (f_t) of 1.0 MHz.

1556 Applications. In general, the 1556 is used as a general-purpose amplifier in the same applications as a 741, but with lower input current and a faster slewing rate. These applications include: sample/hold circuits, bridge amplifiers, log amplifiers, low-drift integrators, and other low-input-current applications.

MC1536 (MC1436, MC1436C)

The 1536 is very similar to the 1556 in its general dc and ac specifications, but it is also designed for high-voltage operation. It has power-supply capability up to ±40 volts.

1536 Applications. In general, the 1536 is used as a general-purpose amplifier in the same applications as a 1556, plus those applications which demand high-voltage capability. These applications include: deflection amplifiers and drivers, audio-output drivers, high-voltage waveform generators, and power-supply regulators.

---

*"Super β" transistors yield current gains of 1000-5000 at low collector currents.

Table 2-6. Op-Amp Groups and Key Specifications

Group	General Characteristics	Device	Key Specifications
I General Purpose	First general-purpose op amp. High gain. Externally compensated. ±10 V input/output range. ±15 V power supplies. 1 MHz unity-gain frequency.	709 Family — 709	$I_{1b} = 200$ nA, $I_{1o} = 50$ nA, $V_{1o} = 1.0$ mV, $A_v = 93$ dB.
		709A	$I_{1b} = 100$ nA, $I_{1o} = 10$ nA, $V_{1o} = 0.6$ mV, $V_{1o}/\Delta T = 1.8\ \mu V/°C$.
		1537, 4709 4709A	Dual 709, 14-pin package, matched characteristics. Dual 709A, 14-pin package, matched characteristics.
	High common-mode range. High differential-input range. Short-circuit protection. Wide supply-voltage range. Simple frequency compensation. Immunity to oscillations. 1 MHz unity-gain frequency.	101 Family — 101	$I_{1b} = 120$ nA, $I_{1o} = 40$ nA, $V_{1o} = 1.0$ mV, $A_v = 104$ dB, externally compensated.
		101A	$I_{1b} = 30$ nA, $I_{1o} = 1.5$ nA, $V_{1o} = 0.7$ mV, $A_v = 104$ dB, externally compensated.
		107	Internally compensated 101A, no offset adjust.
		741 Family — 741	$I_{1b} = 80$ nA, $I_{1o} = 20$ nA, $V_{1o} = 1.0$ mV, internally compensated, offset adjust.
		741A	$I_{1b} = 30$ nA, $I_{1o} = 3.0$ nA, $V_{1o} = 0.8$ mV, $V_{1o}/\Delta T = 15\ \mu V/°C$ (max.).
		748 747 1558	Externally compensated 741. Dual 741, 14-pin package, offset adjust. Dual 741, 8-pin package, no offset adjust.

Category	Characteristics	Device	Specifications
II DC and Low Level	Low bias current. High input impedance. Low drift. Low noise.	725	$V_{1o}/\Delta T = 0.6$ $\mu V/°C$, CMRR $= 120$ dB, PSRR $= 114$ dB, $A_v = 130$ dB, externally compensated.
		725A	$V_{1o} = 0.5$ mV (max.), CMRR $= 120$ dB (min.).
		108	$I_{1b} = 800$ pA, $I_{1o} = 50$ pA, $V_{1o} = 0.7$ mV, $I_s = 300$ μA, $V_s = \pm 2$ V to ± 20 V, externally compensated.
		108A	$V_{1o} = 0.3$ mV, $V_{1o}/\Delta T = 1.0$ $\mu V/°C$, PSRR $= 110$ dB.
		1556	$I_{1b} = 8.0$ nA, $V_{1o} = 2.0$ mV, $f_t = 1.0$ MHz, SR $= 2.5$ V/μs, internally compensated.
		1536	Similar to 1556, but with ± 40 V power supplies.
		8007	$I_{1b} = 2.0$ pA, $r_{1n} = 10^{12}$ Ω, $f_t = 1.0$ MHz, SR $= 6.0$ V/μs, internally compensated.
		110	$I_{1b} = 1.0$ nA, $r_{1n} = 10^{12}$ Ω, BW $= 20$ MHz, SR $= 30$ V/μs.
III AC and High Level	High unity-gain frequency. High gain-bandwidth product. High slewing rate.	8007	SR $= 6.0$ V/μs, $I_{1b} = 2.0$ pA, $r_{1n} = 10^{12}$ Ω, $f_t = 1.0$ MHz, internally compensated.
		531	SR $= 30$ V/μs, $f_t = 1.0$ MHz, externally compensated.
		110	SR $= 30$ V/μs, BW $= 20$ MHz, $I_{1b} = 1.0$ nA, $r_{1n} = 10^{12}$ Ω.
		118	$f_t = 15$ MHz, SR $= 70$ V/μs, internally compensated (with options).
		2620	GBP $= 100$ MHz, $f_t = 10$ MHz, $I_{1b} = 1.0$ nA, $r_{1n} = 500$ MΩ, externally compensated.
		715	GBP $= 3000$ MHz, $f_t = 15$ MHz, SR $= 100$ V/μs, externally compensated.
		540	GBP $= 100$ MHz, SR $= 200$ V/μs, $V_o = \pm 20$ V, $I_o = \pm 150$ mA, externally compensated.

Table 2-6 (cont). Op-Amp Groups and Key Specifications

Group	General Characteristics	Device	Key Specifications
IV High Voltage/Power	High voltage output. High current output.	540 1536	$V_o = \pm 20$ V, $I_o = \pm 150$ mA, GBP = 100 MHz, SR = 200 V/μs, externally compensated. $V_o = \pm 30$ V, $f_t = 1.0$ MHz, SR = 2.0 V/μs, internally compensated.
V Unique Devices		4250, 776 3080 3094 2400 3401, 3900	Programmable I_{1b}, P_c, A_v, SR, and f_t, internally compensated. Programmable I_{1b}, P_c, A_v, SR, and f_t, operates in g_m mode, externally compensated. Similar to 3080, plus npn buffered output, $I_o = 100$ mA, externally compensated. Four digitally selected input channels, one output, $f_t = 8.0$ MHz, SR = 15 V/μs, externally compensated. Quadruple current-differencing amplifiers, single power supply, $f_t = 4.0$ MHz, internally compensated.

8007 (8007C)

The 8007 is a FET-input op amp which features extremely low input current and extremely high input resistance. It is internally compensated, with a unity-gain frequency of 1.0 MHz and a slewing rate of 6.0 V/μs.

8007 Applications. In general, the 8007 is used in all general-purpose applications suitable for a 741, but with the bonus of extremely low input current and extremely high input resistance. These applications include: low-input-current applications such as current-to-voltage conversion, log converters, peak detectors, sample/hold circuits, and other high-input-resistance applications such as buffer amplifiers, voltage followers, and active filters.

LM110 (LM210, LM310)

The 110 is a specialized op amp that is internally connected in the unity-gain, voltage-follower configuration. Its parameters are specifically optimized for this application and include very low input bias currents (due to a super-β input stage), very high input resistance, wide bandwidth, and a fast slewing rate. Also, it is an internally compensated device.

110 Applications. In general, the 110 is used in any application which requires either a fast response or a low-input-current, unity-gain buffer. These applications include: high-speed buffers, active filters, sample/hold circuits, etc.

Because of its wide bandwidth and low attendant phase shift, the 110 can be used within the feedback loop of lower-speed op amps.

2.2.2 Group III Devices (AC and High-Level Group)

These op amps have one or more of the following features:

1. High unity-gain frequency.
2. High gain-bandwidth product.
3. High slewing rate.
4. Low input current.
5. High input resistance.
6. High voltage and/or power.
7. Internal or external compensation.

These types are best in terms of ac and high-level performance.

8007 (8007C)

The 8007 is one of the op amps that bridges the gap between Group II and Group III devices because of its high slewing rate, which allows full power output up to 100 kHz. Typical applications for this device were noted previously in Section 2.2.1.

LM110 (LM210, LM310)

The 110 is another op amp that bridges the gap between Group II and Group III devices. The 110 has a wide bandwidth and a high slewing rate, features that are very useful in high-speed, voltage-follower applications. Typical applications for this device were also noted previously in Section 2.2.1.

SE531 (NE531)

The 531 is a high-slew-rate op amp with dc performance characteristics similar to those of the 741. It is externally compensated with a single capacitor and has a unity-gain frequency of 1.0 MHz. The distinguishing feature of the 531 is a power bandwidth that is nearly equal to the small-signal bandwidth.

531 Applications. In general, the 531 is used as a general-purpose amplifier in applications similar to the 741, but has a much faster slewing rate.

LM118 (LM218, LM318)

The 118 is a wide-bandwidth, high-slew-rate op amp. Although it is internally compensated, external compensation options permit further speed optimization.

118 Applications. In general, the 118 is used in any ac application requiring wide bandwidth with unity-gain stability and high slewing rate. These applications include: analog-to-digital (A/D) and digital-to-analog (D/A) converters, high-frequency active filters, fast sample/hold circuits, fast rectifiers, ac loggers, and fast current-to-voltage converters.

HA-2620 (HA-2622, HA-2625)

The 2620 is an externally compensated, wide-bandwidth, high-slew-rate op amp with low input current. It has a unity-gain frequency of 10 MHz, but gain-bandwidth may be extended with external compensation.

2620 Applications. In general, the 2620 is used in high-gain, wide-bandwidth amplifiers where low input current is required. These applications include: fast integrators, current-to-voltage converters, video amplifiers, A/D and D/A converters, etc.

μA715 (μA715C)

The 715 is an externally compensated, wide-bandwidth, high-slew-rate op amp. It has a unity-gain frequency of 15 MHz, but the bandwidth can be extended with external compensation to allow very high gain-bandwidth products.

715 Applications. In general, the 715 is used in high-gain, wide-bandwidth amplifiers with high slewing rates. These applications include: high-speed inverters and summers, A/D and D/A converters, video amplifiers, fast sample/hold circuits, high-speed integrators, etc.

SE540 (NE540)

The 540 is a special-purpose op amp designed for driving class-B, audio-output transistors. It has a higher current and voltage output than conventional IC op amps, and is externally compensated. It is capable of high gain-bandwidths and high slewing rates with appreciable power output.

540 Applications. Typical applications for the 540 include: audio power drivers, medium-power line drivers, communications amplifiers, power-supply regulators, current regulators, etc., with supply voltages up to ±25 volts and output currents up to ±150 mA.

2.2.3 Group IV Devices (High Voltage/Power Group)

The high voltage/power group is the smallest family of special-purpose op amps. It features devices that are capable of either high voltage output, or a combination of high voltage and high power. This group includes two devices that were previously discussed: the 1536 in Section 2.2.1 (Group II Devices) and the 540 in Section 2.2.2 (Group III Devices).

2.2.4 Group V Devices (Unique Devices Group)

This group consists of op amps that cannot be categorized with any of the others because of certain unique characteristics. These devices include programmable op amps, transconductance op amps, digitally addressable op amps, and current-differencing amplifiers.

LM4250 (LM4250C)

The 4250 is an op amp that has a master bias terminal which controls all key amplifier open-loop parameters. The bias applied to this terminal can be adjusted for optimization of the amplifier characteristics, or the bias can be used to switch the amplifier on and off. The 4250 can be operated with an extremely low standby power consumption and has a wide power-supply voltage range.

4250 Applications. In general, the 4250 is used in any application which demands low power usage, adjustability of amplifier characteristics, and/or on-off amplifier switching capability. These applications include: battery-operated systems and very-low power-drain instrumentation systems, gated amplifiers, sample/hold systems, multiplexers, signal conditioners, etc.

μA776 (μA776C)

The 776 is a programmable op amp similar to the 4250, but with some differences in performance characteristics. It has the capability of low input current, high unity-gain frequency, and fast slewing rate.

776 Applications. In general, the 776 is used in all applications for which the 4250 is suited (battery operation, programmability, etc.) but it has higher speed, lower input current, and a wider range of adjustment.

CA3080, CA3080A

The 3080 is a programmable op amp with a master bias-adjust terminal that is used to establish the operating conditions of the device. The 3080, however, has an entirely different type of output than a conventional op amp, because the output is specified in terms of current. Thus, the device is a *transconductance* (g_m) amplifier; or, since it uses differential inputs, an *operational transconductance amplifier* (OTA). The gain of the device is

$$A_v = g_m R_L,$$

where g_m is established by the master-bias terminal. It is available in an "A" version with tightened parameters.

3080 Applications. In general, the 3080 is used in any application demanding low power consumption, adjustability of amplifier characteristics, gating/switching capabilities, or controlled differential-transconductance characteristics. These applications include: transconductance-controlled multipliers, modulators, multiplexers, gated amplifiers, micropower amplifiers, voltage- or current-controlled amplifiers, etc., as well as conventional operational amplifiers.

CA3094 (CA3094A, CA3094B)

The 3094 is a device similar to the 3080, but it uses an npn output buffer stage with high current capability. This allows the device to be used either as an OTA, a conventional op amp, or a high-current programmable switch. The three basic versions differ in power-supply operating range.

3094 Applications. In general, the 3094 is used in all applications that are possible with the 3080 OTA and in conventional op-amp applications, and it can also be used as a gated power switch. These applications include: low-power audio amplifiers, high-sensitivity power controllers, programmable current and voltage sources, voltage regulators, etc.

HA-2400 (HA-2404, HA-2405)

The 2400 is a different type of programmable op amp with four identical differential input stages, any one of which can be selected by means of digital control. The selected channel and an output buffer stage form the equivalent of a single, high-frequency, high-slew-rate op amp. By using the common output and up to four different feedback networks to the individual inputs, all of the standard op-amp functions can be made electronically programmable.

2400 Applications. In general, the 2400 allows programming between any four functional realizations of standard op-amp configurations by means of digital control. Applications include programmable functions of: gain/attenuation, oscillator frequency, filter characteristics, integrator characteristics, addition/subtraction, power-supply voltage/current, comparator levels, etc.

MC3401, LM3900

The 3401 and 3900 are special types of quadruple internally compensated amplifiers, optimized for single power-supply systems. These amplifiers operate by comparing differential input currents, thus the term *current-differencing amplifier* (CDA). Although they are not op amps in the classical sense, they can be used for many of the standard op-amp functions, as well as functions that are unique to the CDA concept.

CDA Applications. Applications for CDAs include many of the standard, general-purpose op-amp functions. Unique applications are functions that take advantage of the device multiplicity or the current-differencing concept.

Table 2-6 defines the different op-amp groups and lists the key specifications which qualify a device for that group. If a device spans two groups, the parameter(s) of importance to that group headline the listing for the device. For example, the 8007 is listed in Group II because it has an input bias current of 2.0 pA and an input resistance of 10^{12} ohms. However, since the 8007 is a moderately fast slewing device, it is also listed in Group III with its 6.0 V/μs slewing rate as a key parameter. Similar such considerations apply to the 110, 540, and 1536.

When selecting a device for optimum performance in a particular application, the starting point will not always be the same. For example, if dc performance is the key factor, Group II devices would normally be considered. Likewise, if ac performance is the key factor, Group III devices would normally be considered. However, the "ground rules" will not always be this general; sometimes other

Table 2-7. Op-Amp Parameter Optimization Chart

Parameter		Typical Specification	Device
V_{io}		0.3 mV	108A
$V_{io}/\Delta T$		0.6 μV/°C (nulled)	725
I_{io}		0.5 pA*	8007
		50 pA*	108
$I_{io}/\Delta T$		0.5 pA/°C	108
I_{ib}		2.0 pA*	8007
		800 pA*	108
$I_{ib}/\Delta T$	Input	7.0 pA/°C	108
r_{in}		10^{12} Ω	8007
CMRR		120 dB	725
PSRR		114 dB	725
V_{icr}		±14 V (min.)	108
		±14 V (typ.)	725
e_n		9.0 nV/$\sqrt{\text{Hz}}$ @ 100 Hz	725
i_n		0.3 pA/$\sqrt{\text{Hz}}$ @ 100 Hz	725
V_{om}		±13.5 V @ $V_s = \pm15$ V, $R_L = 2$ kΩ	725
		±30 V @ $V_s = \pm36$ V, $R_L = 5$ kΩ	1536
	Output		
I_{om}		±150 mA	540
r_o		75 Ω	741
		0.75 Ω**	110
f_t		15 MHz	118
GBP		3000 MHz***	715
SR	Dynamic	70 V/μs†	118
A_v		130 dB	725
TR		30 ns	715, 118
P_c		9.0 mW	108
		500 nW‡	4250
V_s (min.)		±1.0 V	4250
V_s (max.)	General	±40 V	1536
V_{cm}		±15 V	101, 741
V_{id}		±30 V	101, 741

*Two examples given because of basic difference between FET and bipolar amplifiers.
**A closed-loop parameter.
***At high gain with custom compensation.
†With unity-gain compensation. Others can achieve greater SR with reduced compensation.
‡With programmed current and reduced V_s.

factors such as the required input voltage or some other specific device parameter must also be considered.

Table 2-7 lists the optimum choice of devices in terms of specific parameters. These are divided into input parameters, output parameters, dynamic characteristics, and general considerations. By using this chart, the best device with regard to a specific parameter can be quickly located. All specifications listed are typical and apply to standard operating conditions, except where noted. With these two charts (Tables 2-6 and 2-7) a satisfactory device can be selected for virtually any application.

REFERENCES

1. Dobkin, R. C. *LM118 Op Amp Slews 70 V/μs*. National Semiconductor LB-17, September 1971. National Semiconductor Corp., Santa Clara, Calif.

2. Fairchild Semiconductor Application Bulletin APP-136, July 1969. *A Low Drift, Low Noise Monolithic Operational Amplifier For Low Level Signal Processing*. Fairchild Semiconductor, Mountain View, Calif.

3. Fredriksen, T. M.; Davis, W. F.; Zobel, D. W. "A New Current Differencing Single-Supply Operational Amplifier." *IEEE Journal of Solid State Circuits*, Vol. SC-6, No. 6, December 1971.

4. Fullagar, D. *A New High Performance Monolithic Operational Amplifier*. Fairchild Application Brief, May 1968. Fairchild Semiconductor, Mountain View, Calif.

5. _____. "Better Understanding of FET Operation Yields Viable Monolithic J-FET Op Amp." *Electronics*, November 6, 1972.

6. _____. *The 8007—A High-Performance FET-Input Operational Amplifier*. Intersil Application Bulletin A005, March 1972. Intersil, Inc., Cupertino, Calif.

7. Hoeft, W. *A Monolithic Power Driver For Complementary Power Transistors*. IEEE BTR-18, No. 1, February 1972.

8. Jones, D. *The HA-2400 PRAM Four Channel Operational Amplifier*. Harris Semiconductor Application Note 514, February 1972. Harris Semiconductor, Melbourne, Fla.

9. Kaplan, L.; Wittlinger, H. A. *An IC Operational Transconductance Amplifier (OTA) With Power Capability*. IEEE BTR-18, No. 3, August 1972. (RCA Publication ST-6077, RCA Solid State Div., Somerville, N.J.)

10. Solomon, J. E.; Davis, W. R.; Les, P. L. "A Self-Compensated Monolithic Operational Amplifier With Low Input Current and High Slew Rate." *ISSCC Digest of Technical Papers*, Vol. 12, February 1969, pp. 14-15.

11. Vander Kooi, M. K. *The μA776—An Operational Amplifier With Programmable Gain, Bandwidth, Slew Rate, and Power Dissipation*. Fairchild Application Bulletin APP-218, June 1971. Fairchild Semiconductor, Mountain View, Calif.

12. _____; Cleveland, G. *Micropower Circuits Using the LM4250 Programmable Op Omp*. National Semiconductor Application Note AN-71, July 1972. National Semiconductor Corp., Santa Clara, Calif.

13. _____. *The μA715—A Versatile, High-Speed Operational Amplifier*. Fairchild Semiconductor APP-121, June 1969. Fairchild Semiconductor, Mountain View, Calif.

14. Widlar, R. J. *A Monolithic Operational Amplifier*. Fairchild Application Bulletin APP-105/2, July 1965. Fairchild Semiconductor, Mountain View, Calif.

15. _____. *A New Monolithic Operational Amplifier Design*. National Semiconductor TP-2, June 1967. National Semiconductor Corp., Santa Clara, Calif.

16. _____. "A Unique Circuit Design for a High Performance Operational Amplifier Especially Suited to Monolithic Construction." *Proceedings of the NEC*, Vol. XXI, October 1965, pp. 85-89. (Also available as Fairchild TP-32/2, November 1965. Fairchild Semiconductor, Mountain View, Calif.)

17. _____. *IC Op Amp Beats FETs on Input Current*. National Semiconductor Application Note AN-29, December 1969. National Semiconductor Corp., Santa Clara, Calif.

18. _____. *IC Op Amps Close the Performance Gap on Discretes*. National Semiconductor TP-9, December 1968. National Semiconductor Corp., Santa Clara, Calif.

19. _____. *The Improved μA702 Wideband DC Amplifier*. Fairchild Application Bulletin APP-111/2, July 1965. Fairchild Semiconductor, Mountain View, Calif.

20. _____. *The LM110—An Improved IC Voltage Follower*. National Semiconductor LB-11, March 1970. National Semiconductor Corp., Santa Clara, Calif.

21. Wittlinger, H. A. *Applications of the CA3080 and CA3080A High-Performance Operational Transconductance Amplifiers*. RCA Application Note ICAN-6668, September 1971. RCA Solid State Div., Somerville, N.J.

3

General Operating Procedures and Precautions in Using IC Op Amps

In this final chapter of Part I, we are but one step removed from applying IC op amps in actual circuits. However, in a practical sense, this chapter may be the most important of all the introductory material because it deals with the actual problems involved in using the devices: offset adjustment methods, standard compensation methods, protection against abuses, failure mechanisms, and application pitfalls. It is recommended that this chapter be studied thoroughly before any attempts are made at building op-amp circuits, particularly if the reader has had little previous experience with ICs.

3.1 METHODS OF OFFSET ADJUSTMENT, STANDARD COMPENSATION, AND PINOUTS

In applications that require a high degree of dc accuracy, the residual input offset voltage of the op amp used may be a significant source of error, particularly when operating at high stage gains. These situations require that the input offset voltage be adjusted to zero (nulled) for best performance. Offset nulling can be accomplished either by using a technique recommended by the manufacturer for the particular device (termed *internal* nulling in these discussions), or by using a universally applicable *external* nulling procedure.

3.1.1 Internal Offset Nulling for Individual Devices

In general, the manufacturer's technique for nulling a particular device (709, 101, 741, etc.) is optimum for that device. Unfortunately, the exact method of nulling used varies widely from device to device, and there is no completely standard method of internal offset adjustment (although the 741 technique to be covered later enjoys a fair degree of usage). Other details necessary in the practical application of op amps are methods of frequency compensation and pinout arrangements. In this section we will discuss methods of internal offset nulling, the standard compensation components required for unity gain, and the most popular pinout arrangements for the various op amps covered in this book. Although most op amps are available in a variety of packages, the most popular are the 8-pin packages—the TO-99 metal can and the 8-pin, dual in-line package (MINI-DIP). For dual devices, the 14-pin, dual in-line package (DIP) is the most popular. Alternate pinout arrangements may be arrived at by consulting the manufacturers' data sheets for the particular device.

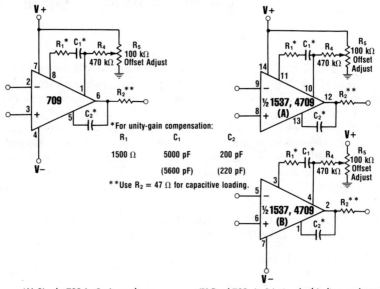

(A) Single 709 in 8-pin package.　　(B) Dual 709s in 14-pin, dual in-line package.

Fig. 3-1. Pinouts and connections for input offset voltage adjustment and frequency compensation for 709-type op amps.

The information provided in this section is sufficient to apply any of the devices in their basic circuit arrangements. Offset adjustments, and even compensation components, are not required in all circumstances and may be deleted where not necessary. Power-supply connections are obviously always required and are shown in this section for reference. Throughout the remainder of the book, however, the power connections are not shown as long as they involve standard

±15-volt supplies. In special circuits or nonstandard power-supply operation, the power connections will be shown in full detail.

Group I Devices (General-Purpose Group)

709 Types. The methods for internal offset voltage adjustment, frequency compensation, and pinout arrangements for 709-type op amps are shown in Fig. 3-1. The hookup for a single 709 in an 8-pin, TO-99 package is shown in Fig. 3-1A, while connections for dual 709 devices (1537, 4709) in a 14-pin dual in-line package are shown in Fig. 3-1B. The three compensation components for the 709 (R_1,

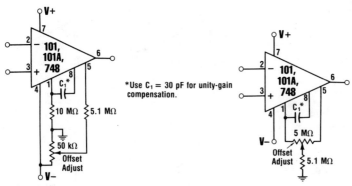

(A) Preferred method of offset nulling for 101/748 types.

(B) Alternate method of offset nulling for 101/748 types.

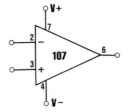

(C) The 107 is equivalent to a 101A with internal frequency compensation and no provision for internal offset nulling.

Fig. 3-2. Pinouts and connections for input offset voltage adjustment and frequency compensation for 101/748-type op amps.

C_1, and C_2) are given for unity-gain operation. R_2 is an optional output resistor which is used for applications that involve capacitive loads.

Offset voltage nulling with the 709 is accomplished by injecting a current into one side of the input stage (pin 1 in Fig. 3-1A). This is done with R_4 and R_5, which unbalance the input stage to the point where the actual input offset voltage is zero. Since R_5 is connected across the power supply, the stability of the null is dependent upon the supply voltage. With this null circuit (and any null circuit in general), short leads should be used on those components that connect to low-level points (in this case, pin 1 in Fig. 3-1A).

101 Types. Uncompensated amplifiers of the 101 family (and the 748) are connected as shown in Fig. 3-2. A 30-pF capacitor is required for unity-gain stability, and there are two methods shown for offset null adjustment. Both methods unbalance the input stage to the point of zero input offset voltage. Method A (shown in Fig. 3-2A) is preferred from a minimum-noise standpoint because it uses

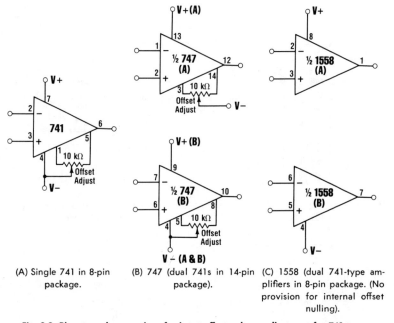

(A) Single 741 in 8-pin package.

(B) 747 (dual 741s in 14-pin package).

(C) 1558 (dual 741-type amplifiers in 8-pin package. (No provision for internal offset nulling).

Fig. 3-3. Pinouts and connections for input offset voltage adjustment for 741-type op amps.

a low-impedance potentiometer, and the fixed resistors can be placed close to the pins of the op amp. However, the stability of method A depends on the V− supply. On the other hand, method B (shown in Fig. 3-2B) is independent of the supply voltage but is more susceptible to noise if the potentiometer is remotely located. The compensation and balance components for 101-type amplifiers should always have short lead lengths because they are connected at nodes of relatively high gain and high impedance. In addition, stray coupling from the output (pin 6) to pin 5 is regenerative and should be controlled so that it is less than the coupling from pin 8 to pin 1. In instances where pin 5 is not needed for nulling purposes, stray coupling can be minimized by clipping off pin 5.

The 748 amplifier operates the same as 101 types insofar as standard compensation and nulling procedures are concerned, although there are differences in the dc specifications.

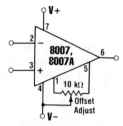

(A) Offset null connections for the 8007 and 8007A amplifiers (internal frequency compensation).

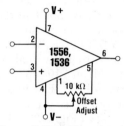

(B) Offset null connections for the 1556 and 1536 amplifiers (internal frequency compensation).

(C) Frequency compensation connections for the 108 and 108A amplifiers (no provision for internal offset nulling).

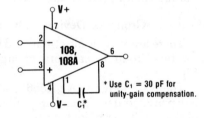

(D) Offset null and frequency compensation connections for the 725 and 725A amplifiers.

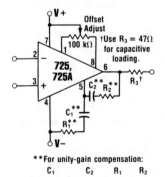

(E) Offset null connections for the 110 voltage follower (internal frequency compensation).

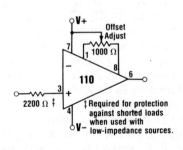

Fig. 3-4. Pinouts and connections for input offset voltage adjustment and frequency compensation for Group II (dc and low-level) devices.

115

The 107 amplifier (Fig. 3-2C) is essentially a 101A with internal compensation. No provision for internal offset nulling is made with this device.

741 Types. Amplifiers of the 741 family are internally compensated devices and are shown in Fig. 3-3. Offset nulling is accomplished with a single 10 kΩ potentiometer with the arm returned to the V− supply. This arrangement has the virtue of appearing at a relatively low impedance point in the circuit, and the null adjustment is not dependent upon the supply voltage.

The 747 (Fig. 3-3B) is a pair of 741 amplifiers in a single 14-pin package with individual offset adjustments. (Some manufacturers offer the 747 in a 10-pin metal can which does not have internal offset null capability.) The two halves of the 747 can be powered independently by using the separate V+ leads.

The 1558 (Fig. 3-3C) is functionally equivalent to two 741-type amplifiers, but is usually supplied only in a single, 8-pin package. This offers the advantage of space economy, but sacrifices the internal offset null capability. (Some manufacturers, however, do offer the 1558 in a 14-pin package having internal offset null capability.)

Group II Devices (DC and Low-Level Group)

There are various offset-null and frequency-compensation methods for the Group II category of amplifiers. These are illustrated in Fig. 3-4.

The 8007 (Fig. 3-4A), 1556, and 1536 (Fig. 3-4B) are internally compensated devices and are nulled with a technique similar to that of the 741. Their pinout arrangements are also identical with the 741.

The 108 (Fig. 3-4C) is frequency compensated by a single external capacitor; it must be nulled externally also.

The 725 (Fig. 3-4D) is frequency compensated with four components: R_1, R_2, C_1, and C_2, with values as shown for unity-gain operation. A series output resistor, R_3, is used for isolation of capacitive loads. Offset nulling of the 725 is accomplished in the V+ supply line as shown. This method is unaffected by supply-voltage changes. The 725 is a low input-voltage-drift amplifier; for best performance in dc applications it should be nulled, because nulling produces a condition of minimum drift in the input offset voltage.

The 110 voltage follower (Fig. 3-4E) is an internally compensated device and is nulled in the V+ supply line. As with the 725, this nulling method is unaffected by supply-voltage variations. For protection against failure due to shorted loads, the source resistance seen by the 110 should be 2000 ohms or higher. If the source resistance is appreciably lower than 2000 ohms, it is good practice to include a series input resistor as shown; this resistor has negligible effect on operation.

Group III Devices (AC and High-Level Group)

The ac and high-level group of amplifiers also have a variety of frequency-compensation and offset-nulling techniques as shown in Fig. 3-5.

The 715 (Fig. 3-5A) is nulled in the V+ supply line with a 50 kΩ potentiometer and a 50 kΩ series resistor. For unity-gain compensation, the 715 requires three capacitors with values as shown in Fig. 3-5A. Latch-up may be a problem with the 715 for use as a high-level voltage follower. For this application, an anti-latch-up diode is recommended (connected as shown). In the next section, we will discuss latch-up problems in more detail. The 715 is usually supplied in a 10-pin package as indicated in Fig. 3-5A.

The 118 (Fig. 3-5B) is an internally compensated, high-speed device. Offset nulling is done in the V+ supply line and is independent of supply voltage.

The 2620 (Fig. 3-5C) is frequency compensated with a single external capacitor. Offset nulling is accomplished in the V+ supply line, similar to the 118, and is also independent of the supply voltage.

The 540 (Fig. 3-5D) has no provision for internal offset null adjustment. It is frequency compensated with a single external capacitor.

The 531 (Fig. 3-5E) is nulled with a method similar to the 741, but is externally compensated with a single capacitor.

Group V Devices (Unique Devices Group)

These specialized devices are covered in detail in a separate chapter of the book (Chapter 8) because of their uniqueness. For the sake of familiarization, however, their pinouts and connections for offset null adjustment and frequency compensation are illustrated in Fig. 3-6.

The 4250 and 776 (Fig. 3-6A) are programmable types with pinouts and offset adjustments similar to the 741. They are internally compensated, and their operating characteristics are adjusted by the current programmed by R_{set}, which is connected either to V− or to ground.

The 3080 and 3094 (Fig. 3-6B) are also programmable types but with external frequency compensation. They are transconductance amplifiers with operating characteristics determined by the programming current (set by an external resistor, which is connected either to V+ or to ground). No internal offset adjustment is provided for either the 3080 or the 3094.

The 2400 (Fig. 3-6C) is an amplifier that consists of four differential-input, op-amp sections, one of which can be selected by means of a digital input and connected to a common output stage. It is

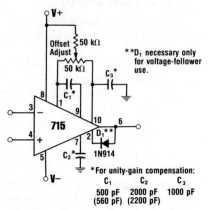

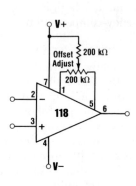

(A) Offset null and frequency compensation connections for the 715 amplifier.

(B) Offset null connections for the 118 amplifier (internal frequency compensation).

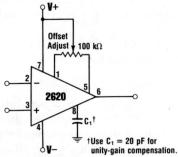

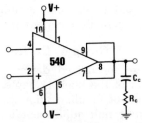

(C) Offset null and frequency compensation connections for the 2620 amplifier.

(D) Frequency compensation connections for the 540 amplifier (no provision for internal offset nulling).

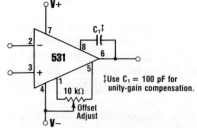

(E) Offset null and frequency compensation connections for the 531 amplifier.

Fig. 3-5. Pinouts and connections for input offset voltage adjustment and frequency compensation for Group III (ac and high-level) devices.

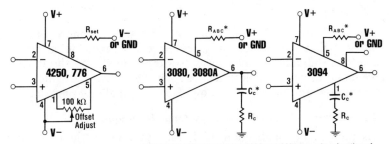

*Unity-gain compensation for 3080 and 3094 types is a function of programming current. See Chapter 8 on special types for details.

(A) Offset null connections for the 4250 and 776 programmable op amps (internal frequency compensation).

(B) Frequency compensation connections for the 3080, 3080A, and 3094 programmable op amps (no provision for internal offset nulling).

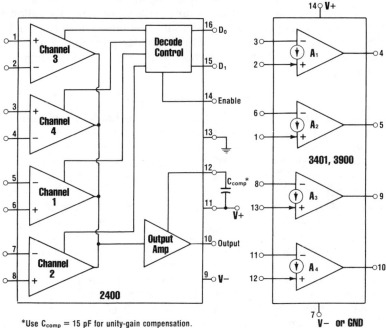

*Use C_{comp} = 15 pF for unity-gain compensation.

(C) Frequency compensation connections for the 2400, four-channel, programmable op amp (no provision for internal offset nulling).

(D) Pinouts for the 3401 and 3900 quadruple op amps (four amplifiers in a single, 14-pin package). These devices are internally compensated and have no provision for internal offset nulling.

Fig. 3-6. Pinouts and connections for input offset voltage adjustment and frequency compensation for Group V devices (unique devices group).

compensated and nulled externally, and is supplied in a 16-pin package.

The 3401 and 3900 (Fig. 3-6D) are not true op amps, but are amplifiers that operate on an input-current-differencing principle. Therefore, differential input currents are provided, and the devices have no offset voltage adjustment as such. The devices are internally compensated and provide four amplifiers in a single, 14-pin package.

3.1.2 Universal External Offset Nulling Techniques

As pointed out in Section 3.1.1, the optimum method of offset adjustment for a particular op amp is the internal method provided for by the manufacturer. This method results in the condition of minimum input offset voltage drift, which occurs when the input offset voltage is zero. Unfortunately, the mechanism for accomplishing this is not available on all op amps, and external methods must be used. This section describes procedures for universal external offset adjustment at the input terminals, allowing any op amp to be nulled for an equivalent input offset voltage of zero. This allows types which do not provide an internal offset adjustment (e.g., 107, 108, 1558, 3080, etc.) to be used with greater precision. The exact method used varies slightly with the type of configuration as detailed in the following:

Inverting Configuration

There are actually two slightly different techniques that can be used with the inverting stage to adjust the input offset voltage. The simpler of the two is shown in Fig. 3-7A. This circuit uses the R_1 and R_2 input and feedback resistors as part of an attenuator network in conjunction with R_3 to generate a variable offset voltage at the inverting input. This voltage is scaled down from the ± 15 volts available from R_4 by the R_3 and $R_1 \parallel R_2$ divider. In this case, the ratio is 1000/1, yielding an offset range of ± 15 mV. For different supply voltages, greater range, or different R_1-R_2 values, R_3 may be re-scaled by use of the equation given in Fig. 3-7A. Note that if more than one input is used, the offset range will be reduced because of the lower equivalent resistance. In this case, the more general equation for multiple inputs should be used to select R_3.

With just one additional resistor, the circuit of Fig. 3-7B accomplishes offset adjustment independent of the feedback elements. This circuit is generally more useful since it injects the offset voltage at the noninverting input terminal, away from the direct signal path. In this circuit, R_3 and R_5 form a simple 1000/1 divider, providing ± 15 mV of offset voltage across R_5 with the values shown. The exact values used for R_3 and R_5 are not critical, but it is good practice to keep R_5 below 1000 ohms.

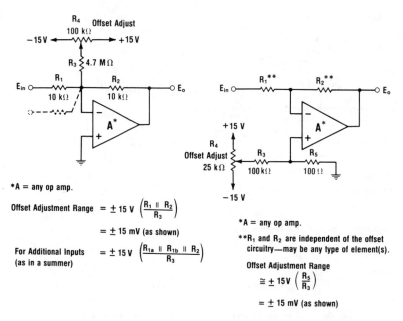

Offset Adjustment Range $= \pm 15 \text{ V} \left(\dfrac{R_1 \parallel R_2}{R_3} \right)$

$= \pm 15 \text{ mV (as shown)}$

For Additional Inputs $= \pm 15 \text{ V} \left(\dfrac{R_{1a} \parallel R_{1b} \parallel R_2}{R_3} \right)$
(as in a summer)

*A = any op amp.

**R_1 and R_2 are independent of the offset circuitry—may be any type of element(s).

Offset Adjustment Range
$\cong \pm 15 \text{ V} \left(\dfrac{R_5}{R_3} \right)$

$= \pm 15 \text{ mV (as shown)}$

(A) Offset voltage applied to the inverting input.

(B) Offset voltage applied to the noninverting input.

Fig. 3-7. Universal external offset null adjustment circuits—inverting amplifier.

Noninverting Configuration

A circuit for external null adjustment for low-gain, noninverting stages is shown in Fig. 3-8A. Here, a low resistance such as R_5 is inserted in the return leg for R_1. The offset voltage is thus developed by the R_3-R_5 voltage divider at this point. Since gain-determining resistors, R_1 and R_2 constitute a voltage divider for the voltage at R_5, the voltage appearing at the inverting input will be reduced by their ratio. This yields a slightly more complicated offset-voltage-range equation. Again, the values shown yield ±15 mV of adjustment voltage.

It should be understood that the gain and offset calculations for this stage are not independent. The presence of R_5 in series with R_1 alters the gain equation as shown; and, with the values shown, the error is 1.0% (ratio of R_1 to R_5).

At high gains, a null may be more simply achieved with what is basically a modification of Fig. 3-8A. This circuit is shown in Fig. 3-8B, which generates the offset voltage directly at the summing junction, using R_1 and R_3 as the offset divider. The reason this technique is not preferred at low gains is that the signal voltage across R_1 (equal to the input voltage by the theory of zero differential

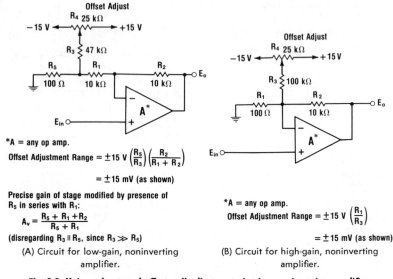

*A = any op amp.

Offset Adjustment Range = $\pm 15 \text{ V} \left(\dfrac{R_5}{R_3}\right)\left(\dfrac{R_2}{R_1 + R_2}\right)$

$$= \pm 15 \text{ mV (as shown)}$$

Precise gain of stage modified by presence of
R_5 in series with R_1:

$$A_v = \frac{R_5 + R_1 + R_2}{R_5 + R_1}$$

(disregarding $R_3 \parallel R_5$, since $R_3 \gg R_5$)

(A) Circuit for low-gain, noninverting
amplifier.

*A = any op amp.

Offset Adjustment Range = $\pm 15 \text{ V} \left(\dfrac{R_1}{R_3}\right)$

$$= \pm 15 \text{ mV (as shown)}$$

(B) Circuit for high-gain, noninverting
amplifier.

Fig. 3-8. Universal external offset null adjustment circuits—noninverting amplifier.

input) is larger at lower gains, which creates a change in the offset voltage generated as the input varies. At high gains, however, this is not as great a problem due to the lower input level.

Voltage Follower

The voltage follower, a special case of the noninverting amplifier, is externally nulled as shown in Fig. 3-9. This circuit introduces a small feedback resistor, R_2, across which the offset voltage is generated. R_1 and R_2 form a voltage divider from the arm of R_3, reducing the ± 15 V to ± 15 mV. The reader will note that the offset of ± 15 mV will appear only when E_{in} is zero. As E_{in} changes from zero, the offset voltage generated will also change. This may not be a

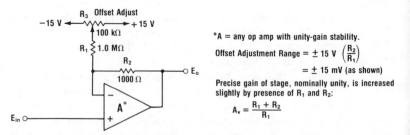

*A = any op amp with unity-gain stability.

Offset Adjustment Range = $\pm 15 \text{ V} \left(\dfrac{R_2}{R_1}\right)$

$$= \pm 15 \text{ mV (as shown)}$$

Precise gain of stage, nominally unity, is increased
slightly by presence of R_1 and R_2:

$$A_v = \frac{R_1 + R_2}{R_1}$$

Fig. 3-9. Universal external offset null adjustment circuit—voltage follower.

serious drawback because the error it does introduce is greatest at full scale, where it is still a small percentage error.

It should be understood that R_1 introduces a small gain error, although the error is only 0.1% for the values shown. Both of the above points should be considered if absolute accuracy is important.

The Differential Amplifier

Fig. 3-10 illustrates a useful technique for balancing a differential-amplifier configuration. The main problem with introducing an offset voltage into a differential circuit is that it must be done without disturbing the differential signal balance.

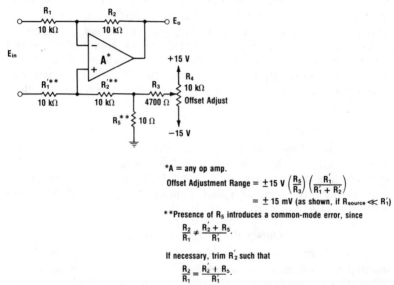

*A = any op amp.

Offset Adjustment Range $= \pm 15 \text{ V} \left(\dfrac{R_5}{R_3}\right)\left(\dfrac{R_1'}{R_1' + R_2'}\right)$

$= \pm 15 \text{ mV (as shown, if } R_{\text{source}} \ll R_1')$

**Presence of R_5 introduces a common-mode error, since

$$\frac{R_2}{R_1} \neq \frac{R_2' + R_5}{R_1'}.$$

If necessary, trim R_2' such that

$$\frac{R_2}{R_1} = \frac{R_2' + R_5}{R_1'}.$$

Fig. 3-10. Universal external offset null adjustment circuit—differential amplifier.

In this circuit, R_5 provides a variable potential at the common end of R_2, which is normally grounded. After being further divided by R_1 and R_2, this voltage serves to null the amplifier. A small R_5 is chosen so that it will be a small percentage of R_2, thereby minimizing the deviation from the ideal bridge ratio. In demanding situations, R_2' may need trimming to ensure that

$$\frac{R_2}{R_1} = \frac{R_2' + R_5}{R_1'}.$$

With the values shown, the offset voltage range is ± 15 mV.

In all of the preceding discussions, it is assumed that the ± 15-V power supplies used to generate the offset voltages are stable potentials. If they are not, it should be obvious that they will introduce noise into the system in proportion to their deviation from perfection. A noisy or relatively unstable power supply may be dealt with by conventional decoupling techniques (see Chapter 4).

In the same light, the stability of the offset adjustment is also proportional to the quality of the components used. For best performance, stable multiturn trimming potentiometers and stable resistors are recommended.

3.2 PROTECTION AGAINST ABUSE AND FAILURE MODES

Monolithic IC op amps have a few idiosyncracies that can cause trouble under certain conditions of operation. Unfortunately, these troubles are not evident by abnormal operation alone; in certain instances a device may fail altogether, possibly causing damage to other components. For the most part, however, these failure modes are predictable, and if taken into account beforehand, there should be no problems in applying the devices. In this section, we will discuss such failure conditions and give positive treatment for their prevention.

3.2.1 Input Limitations

Failure in IC op amps can be induced in the input stage in two general ways: (1) by exceeding the differential input rating, or (2) by exceeding the common-mode rating. Of these two, the differential input rating is the parameter that is most susceptible to abuse; therefore, it will be discussed in some detail.

Differential Input Breakdown

One of the easiest methods of inducing failure in an unprotected op-amp input stage is to exceed its differential input voltage rating. When this happens, one or the other of the differential input transistors (depending on the relative polarity of the input voltage) will go into emitter-to-base zener breakdown. This is shown in Figs. 3-11A and B. An npn input differential pair is actually equivalent to a pair of back-to-back 7-volt zener diodes, as shown in Fig. 3-11B. The anodes of these two diodes are the (+) and (−) input terminals of the op amp.

Whenever the difference between the input terminals exceeds ±7.0 volts, these emitter-base diodes will break down (as will any zener) and conduct a current which will be limited only by the external source resistance. If the source impedance feeding both inputs is low, the current can rise to destructive levels very quickly. Currents greater than 50 mA will cause permanent failure—usually a junction short. Currents lower than this, while not causing junc-

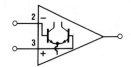

(A) Unprotected differential input stage.

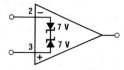

(B) Zener equivalent to differential input stage.

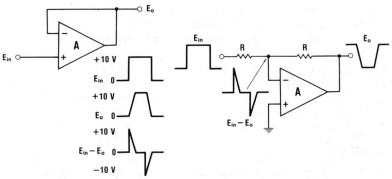

(C) Differential input voltage in a slew-rate limited voltage follower.

(D) Differential input voltage in a slew-rate limited inverter.

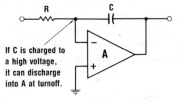

(E) Differential input voltage in a charged integrator at turnoff.

If C is charged to a high voltage, it can discharge into A at turnoff.

Fig. 3-11. Illustration of possible causes of differential input breakdown in unprotected op amps.

tion damage, are still very undesirable because they can cause permanent changes in such dc input parameters as bias, offset current, gain, and noise.

Obviously, in order to prevent this type of breakdown, we must anticipate it beforehand. However, the possible sources of input breakdown can at times be somewhat subtle, as the following examples illustrate.

If a voltage follower (Fig. 3-11C) is driven with a fast step input of +10 volts, the op-amp output will be limited to a rate of rise determined by its slewing ability. During the slewing interval, the amplifier is not operating in a normal closed-loop mode where the differential input voltage is zero; rather, a large differential error voltage exists, as shown by the waveform sketches. These spikes are caused by the fast input rise times which the amplifier cannot follow, so a ±10-volt peak differential exists during the slewing interval(s). In a voltage follower, both inputs can see low source impedance, so this can quickly ruin an input stage due to excessive zener current.

An inverter stage (Fig. 3-11D) can also go into zener breakdown due to slew-rate limiting. Here the problem is not nearly as bad because the resistances limit the zener current during breakdown.

Another problem configuration is the integrator, shown in Fig. 3-11E. In this circuit, input breakdown can result if the supply voltages are turned off while the capacitor is charged to a high potential.

The solution to all of the preceding is quite simple. It involves an input clamping network to limit the differential input voltage and some series resistance to limit the current during clamping. Two methods of accomplishing overvoltage protection are shown in Figs. 3-12A and B. Either method will suffice, but the reverse-connected parallel diodes (Fig. 3-12A) are less expensive. The resistances used with any op amp may range up to 10 kΩ with little degradation of offset voltage. In an actual working configuration, the input ends of the resistors may be considered the inputs of the op amp and used accordingly. Generally for best dc accuracy, equal resistance will be desirable in each leg. However, in many instances it will be possible to eliminate one or possibly both resistors, as long as input or feedback resistances limit the clamping-diode current. Such an example would be the circuit of Fig. 3-11D, which could be protected just by the addition of the diodes, using the input and feedback resistances as current limiters.

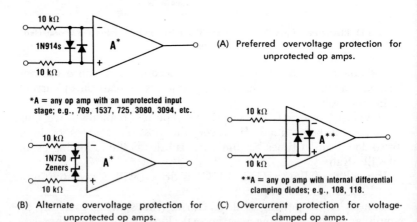

(A) Preferred overvoltage protection for unprotected op amps.

*A = any op amp with an unprotected input stage; e.g., 709, 1537, 725, 3080, 3094, etc.

(B) Alternate overvoltage protection for unprotected op amps.

(C) Overcurrent protection for voltage-clamped op amps.

**A = any op amp with internal differential clamping diodes; e.g., 108, 118.

Fig. 3-12. Differential input overvoltage/overcurrent protection methods.

The reader may wonder if perhaps these points on differential input protection are not belabored, since many IC op amps of newer design than the 709 do not have equally restrictive input voltage limitations. This is certainly true for op amps such as the 101 and 741 families, but it is by no means a universal practice with other designs. The 725 and 3080, for example, have unprotected input stages. It is of prime importance, particularly in high-performance dc amplifiers, to prevent differential input breakdown because it can seriously degrade the dc characteristics.

Other amplifiers, such as the 108 and 118, have the differential clamping diodes built into the device. In the absence of internal resistance, amplifiers such as these must be used with external resistors to prevent possible excessive current in the diodes. This is illustrated in Fig. 3-12C.

Common-Mode Input Breakdown

Another cause of input stage failure is possible destructive input current flow due to exceeding the common-mode input voltage range of the device. Although the 101 and 741 families are notably free of differential input breakdown, they can under certain circumstances fail from common-mode voltage abuse.

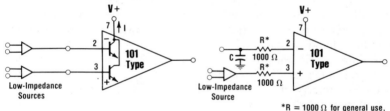

(A) Reason for common-mode input failure in 101-type op amps.

(B) Protection against common-mode input failure in 101-type op amps.

*R = 1000 Ω for general use, but may be as high as 10 kΩ without serious side effects.

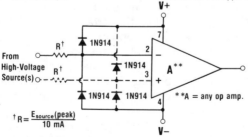

(C) Protection against excessive source-voltage peaks for any op amp.

Fig. 3-13. Common-mode input protection methods.

This failure mechanism is illustrated by Fig. 3-13A, which shows the input stage of a 101-type op amp. In a 101 op amp, both inputs are the base terminals of npn transistors, the collectors of which go to V+. In normal operation, the input terminals will always be negative with respect to V+, so the collector-base junctions of these transistors are never forward biased. If, however, V+ is removed from the op amp with a positive potential remaining on pins 2 and 3, the transistors will then conduct through the collector-base junction into the V+ line. If the source impedance seen at either pin 2 or pin 3 is sufficiently low, the resulting current may be high enough to destroy the input transistors. Such a condition may occur when the input to a system is left connected and the power is removed. Another example is with a capacitive source charged to a high potential at the time of power turnoff. If the capacitance is greater than 0.1 μF, the discharge current from the capacitor can also destroy the input transistors.

The solution to the preceding is also rather simple. It involves series input resistors to limit the worst-case fault current to 10 mA or less (Fig. 3-13B). Since 101 input characteristics are relatively unaffected by input resistances up to 10 kΩ, the resistors may be this high with no side effects. For general use, however, 1000 ohms per side will be adequate. The resistors need only be connected to those inputs which see potentially low impedances or excessive voltage. If it can be guaranteed that neither of these conditions will occur under any combination of input and power, then the resistors can be deleted.

Before concluding, it should be noted that this type of failure mechanism may not be peculiar to only 101-type op amps. The exact internal circuitry of 101 (and 741) types will vary from one manufacturer to another. It is best to check the particular devices you intend to use, either by a simple ohmmeter check (pins 2 and 3 to pin 7) or by measuring fault current in a series resistor under the stress conditions. Also, it is wise in general to be wary of possible power sequencing phenomena in any op-amp circuit, regardless of the device. Finally, when operating from sources of voltage which may have peaks in excess of the op-amp power supplies, the scheme of Fig. 3-13C can be used to protect any op amp. The 1N914 diodes clamp the inputs to a level such that the source-voltage peaks cannot exceed V+ and V− by more than the forward-biased voltage drops of the diodes. The series resistor limits the input current.

Latch-up

A phenomenon that sometimes occurs in op amps is called *latch-up*. Latch-up occurs most often in voltage-follower stages where the output swing is equal to the input and the op amp is driven to a high level. If the bias levels of the input stage are not well in excess of the maximum peak-to-peak voltage swing that the input terminals must undergo, the input stage can saturate on the peaks. When saturation occurs, a normally inverting stage no longer inverts; thus, what was negative feedback becomes positive feedback. With positive feedback the stage will then remain in saturation, and thus it is said to be *latched-up*.

This is illustrated in Fig. 3-14A, an example of an op-amp input stage. To use a specific example, the 709 is subject to latch-up since its minimum common-mode range is +8 V, but its output swing

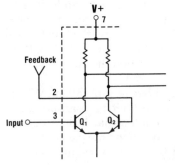

(A) General example illustrating latch-up source in an op-amp input stage.

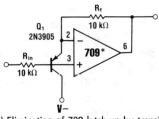

(B) Elimination of 709 latch-up by limiting saturation feedback with high-value resistance (R_f).

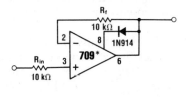

(C) Elimination of 709 latch-up by diode clamping.

(D) Elimination of 709 latch-up by transistor clamping.

(E) Elimination of latch-up (any op amp) by input limiting.

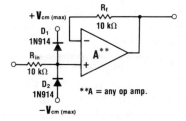

Fig. 3-14. Illustration of latch-up in IC op amps, and methods of elimination.

can be as high as +14 V. If a signal greater than +8 V were applied to a 709 connected as a follower, it is quite possible that it may latch up due to saturation of Q_2. Once latch-up occurs, the positive feedback can usually be broken only by removal of power.

Aside from the "nuisance" disadvantages of latch-up (the necessity of removing power to restore normal operation), there is a more serious potential hazard with the phenomenon. If the circuit of Fig. 3-14A uses a 709 and is driven beyond its common-mode range, it will latch up on the positive peak. If a bipolar input signal from a low-impedance source is assumed, the input signal at pin 3 need go only 7 volts below the saturation level before Q_1 will go into emitter-base zener breakdown. This will almost surely ruin the device because both inputs are connected to low-impedance sources in this stage. Latch-up may not even be triggered by the input signal. Any positive transient on the output line which is fed back to Q_2 can trigger it, and once in the latch-up condition the circuit will stay this way until power is removed.

There are several remedies for the 709 latch-up problem. A 33 kΩ resistor connected in the feedback path to limit the saturation current (R_f in Fig. 3-14B) is perhaps the simplest, but it does degrade the input offset characteristics due to the high resistance seen by the input transistors. Another method is to use a clamping diode as shown in Fig. 3-14C. This prevents the output from rising above the potential on pin 8. A third method is to use a small-signal pnp transistor as in Fig. 3-14D. This transistor prevents permanent latch-up because it will turn on for any positive differential greater than +0.6 V at the (−) input. Under normal closed-loop conditions, the transistor is off and has no effect.

Since latch-up will occur only at the extreme limits of input common-mode range, any method that reduces the common-mode input swing will eliminate (or lessen) the latch-up problem. Therefore latch-up in a 709 (or any amplifier prone to it) will have little likelihood of occurrence when the amplifier is operated at gains higher than unity or in cases when the input levels are safely less than that voltage which triggers latch-up. A circuit that takes advantage of this latter point can be used to prevent latch-up with any op amp and is shown in Fig. 3-14E. Since latch-up will usually occur at only one common-mode limit, only one diode is usually needed. The $V_{cm(max)}$ can be a simple divider across the ±15-V supply.

3.2.2 Output Short-Circuit Protection

Early op amps, such as the 709, did not incorporate full-time current limiting in the output stage. Although a 709 will survive a short of a few seconds duration, a sustained short to ground, V+, or V− will result in destruction of the device.

709 types or any type that does not incorporate current limiting may be protected against short circuits by a low value resistor in series with the output as shown in Fig. 3-15. If this resistor is connected within the feedback loop as shown, its presence will have little effect on performance, except for the obvious drop in output voltage it entails (10% with a 2000-ohm load).

A side benefit of this approach is the extra stability it provides with capacitive loads. For this reason, the series resistor may be helpful even if the amplifier used does have current limiting.

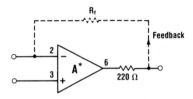

*A = any op amp with an unprotected output stage; e.g., 709, 1537, 715.

In addition to preventing destruction of the amplifier due to shorted loads, the series resistance will enhance stability by isolating capacitive loads.

Fig. 3-15. Output short-circuit protection.

3.2.3 Supply-Voltage Protection

Reversal of Polarity

Because of their internal construction, ICs must always be operated with the specified supply-voltage polarity. If the voltages ever become reversed, even momentarily, destructive currents will flow through the normally reverse-biased isolation diodes of the IC chip. This is a point to be wary of in any IC op amp, with no exceptions. Positive protection against this may be provided by connecting a rectifier diode in the negative supply lead as shown in Fig. 3-16A. Protection for a number of amplifiers in a system or on a printed-circuit card may be provided by connecting a single pair of power diodes in reverse across the supply leads as shown in Fig. 3-16B. The diodes used should have a current capacity greater than the fuse or short-circuit current limit of the supplies used. When a supply reversal or transient condition attempts to force opposite polarity voltages on the amplifiers, D_1 and D_2 clamp the supplies into the limit mode (or blow the fuse) and nothing is damaged. This is a good feature to incorporate into any but the very smallest system.

Overvoltage

Commercial-grade IC op amps are generally specified for a total operating voltage of 36 volts (± 18 V), while full-temperature-range

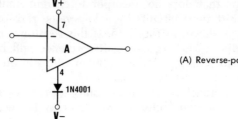

(A) Reverse-polarity protection for a single amplifier.

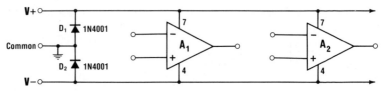

(B) Reverse-polarity protection for a number of amplifiers in a system.

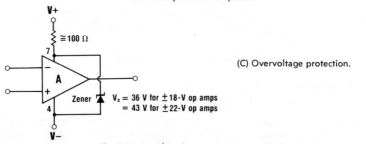

(C) Overvoltage protection.

Fig. 3-16. Supply-voltage protection methods.

devices can operate up to 44 volts (± 22 V). These limits on supply voltage should not be exceeded even for brief durations. If there is a likelihood that the supply may exceed 36 V (or 44 V), a voltage clamp in the form of a zener diode should be used across the terminals as shown in Fig. 3-16C. This zener will be nonconducting with normal ± 15-V (30-V) potentials. For higher maximum-rated supplies, choose the zener voltage closest to but not more than the total maximum— for example, for ± 22 V use a 43-V zener.

3.3 OPTIMUM STABILITY GROUND RULES

In using IC op amps, there are many operating conditions where ac stability becomes a significant problem. Stabilizing a feedback amplifier is no easy task, and it can turn into an impossible situation if good, basic, high-frequency practices are not followed in the layout and circuit arrangement.

3.3.1 Layout and Bypassing

Of utmost importance to stability is a compact, minimum-lead-length layout. The leads to the input and compensation terminals (if used) of any op amp should be as direct as possible with a minimum of conductor length and proximity to other signal leads. Ground paths should have low resistance and low inductance. In wideband circuits, it is good practice (if possible) to use a ground plane on printed-circuit cards to obtain a high-quality ground.

Supply leads to amplifiers should be bypassed at least once for each PC card with good rf capacitors such as $0.1\text{-}\mu\text{F}$ disc ceramics or $1.0\text{-}\mu\text{F}$ tantalums, as shown in Fig. 3-17A. If the amplifiers used

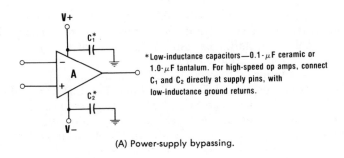

*Low-inductance capacitors—$0.1\text{-}\mu\text{F}$ ceramic or $1.0\text{-}\mu\text{F}$ tantalum. For high-speed op amps, connect C_1 and C_2 directly at supply pins, with low-inductance ground returns.

(A) Power-supply bypassing.

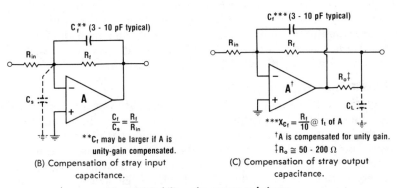

(B) Compensation of stray input capacitance.

$$\frac{C_f}{C_s} = \frac{R_f}{R_{in}}$$

**C_f may be larger if A is unity-gain compensated.

(C) Compensation of stray output capacitance.

$$***X_{C_f} = \frac{R_f}{10} @ \; f_t \; \text{of A}$$

†A is compensated for unity gain.
‡$R_o \cong 50 - 200 \; \Omega$

Fig. 3-17. Stability enhancement techniques.

have a GBP above 10 MHz, more thorough bypassing will be necessary. For example, 715 or 118 amplifiers require a set of local, rf-quality bypasses, such as $0.1\text{-}\mu\text{F}$ disc ceramics, for each amplifier. For good measure, a pair of tantalum bypasses for each PC card (or every five devices) should also be used. General-purpose devices, such as the 101 and 741, are less critical as to bypassing, but cannot be ignored. It is good practice, even with general-purpose devices, to include at least one set of bypasses for every five devices or at least one set per card, regardless of the number of ICs used.

3.3.2 Input Capacitance Compensation

Stray input capacitance in feedback amplifiers can also lead to stability problems. Fig. 3-17B illustrates the nature of input-related capacitance problems. At the input of an op amp there will always be a few pF of stray capacitance, C_s, which consists of the amplifier input capacitance plus wiring capacitance. From the feedback path through R_f, this capacitance represents a potential phase shift at a corner frequency of

$$ f = \frac{1}{2\pi R_f C_s} . $$

The problem is particularly noticeable if R_f is large, since this moves the R_f-C_s frequency downward into a region where it can add to the amplifier phase shift. The result of these cumulative phase shifts may be enough to cause oscillation.

A simple solution is to keep R_f low, which forces the R_f-C_s frequency upward beyond the amplifier limit. But this is not always practical, since R_f may need to be high for gain reasons.

A more general solution is to use a compensation capacitor, C_f, across R_f, which in effect makes C_f-R_f and R_{in}-C_s a frequency-compensated divider. It may not be possible to readily determine the exact value of C_f to satisfy this relation, since C_s is not precisely known. C_f is best determined by experiment; or, if the amplifier used is compensated for unity gain, C_f may be greater than the formula relation to whatever degree desirable. In practice, values of 3-10 pF are typical with feedback resistors of 10 kΩ.

3.3.3 Output Capacitance Compensation

On many IC op amps, the phase shift caused by stray output load capacitance and the amplifier output resistance can be troublesome if the output capacitance is much more than 100 pF. By adding a series output resistance, R_o, the load capacitance is isolated from the amplifier (Fig. 3-17C). Feedback is taken after this resistor, thus compensating for its dc loss. The feedback capacitor, C_f, is then added to reduce the gain of the loop at high frequencies. C_f is chosen so that its reactance is 1/10 (or less) that of R_f at the unity-gain frequency of the amplifier used. The amplifier must be compensated for unity gain, since C_f reduces high-frequency gain to unity. Again, typical values for C_f fall in the 3-10 pF region.

3.3.4 Other Instability Sources

The preceding by no means represents all the sources of possible stability problems in IC op amps, just those that are most likely to occur. Other problem areas are more specific, either in terms of the devices themselves or in terms of circuits in which the devices are used. For example, source resistance may be a problem with some devices. In stubborn cases of instability when other alternatives have been exhausted, amplifier overcompensation may be the solution. If extra bandwidth or optimum slew rate are not necessary, it is usually wise to overcompensate an op amp. For example, this may be accomplished on 709 or 101 amplifiers by increasing the compensation capacitors by a factor of 10 (or by the ratio necessary to obtain stability).

High-current stages can cause instability by feedback through the power supplies. Such stages should be decoupled to localize their circulating currents. Similarly, ground-return paths for high-level and high-gain stages should be kept separate.

In general, many of the stability ground rules simply amount to good practices in layout and construction. These rules should obviously be followed for consistently stable results. Always consult the manufacturer's literature for specific recommendations and for more thorough background on specific op amps.

REFERENCE

1. Dobkin, R. C. *Universal Balancing Techniques.* National Semiconductor LB-9, August 1969. National Semiconductor Corp., Santa Clara, Calif.

II

OP-AMP APPLICATIONS

4

Voltage and Current Regulator Circuits

4.1 VOLTAGE REGULATORS

Voltage regulators using IC operational amplifiers as control elements make very attractive designs in some respects as compared to ICs designed specifically for the purpose of voltage regulation. The advantage of IC op amps is in their inherently high open-loop gain (100,000 typical) which, under closed-loop conditions, can provide regulation percentages as good as 0.01% if sufficient care is taken in layout and construction, and if consideration is given to the significant contributions to error. Compared to an integral IC regulator, an op-amp controlled version will have a larger number of parts, since the op amp is only one of the four basic elements of this type of voltage regulator.

4.1.1 Basic Elements of an Op-Amp Voltage Regulator

The four basic elements of a series-type, op-amp voltage regulator are shown in Fig. 4-1. In this functional diagram, a reference voltage source produces a constant output voltage, V_{ref}, under varying conditions of temperature and input voltage, $+V_{in}$. The reference voltage is applied to the noninverting input of op amp A_1. The output of A_1 drives the series pass transistor, Q_1. The output of Q_1 is the voltage, E_o, which is developed across the load resistance, R_L. Voltage E_o is also fed back through the feedback network, β, causing a fraction of E_o, or βE_o, to appear at the inverting input of A_1. Recalling one of the laws of ideal op-amp behavior, zero differential-input voltage will be present at the inputs of A_1; thus, voltage βE_o will be exactly equal to V_{ref}, since the infinite open-loop gain of A_1 will adjust E_o

until this equality is satisfied. The feedback mechanism of the active components acts to generate an output voltage that is a multiple of the input voltage, V_{ref}. The relationship is simply

$$E_o = \frac{V_{ref}}{\beta},$$

where,

β is the attenuation of the feedback network.

The three active components may be thought of as reference, control, and power, represented by V_{ref}, A_1, and Q_1, respectively. The functions of V_{ref} and A_1 are obvious enough, and Q_1 is necessary to handle load currents beyond the basic output capability of the op amp.

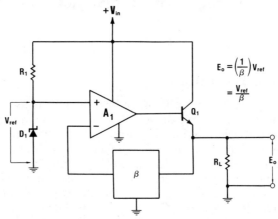

Fig. 4-1. Functional diagram of a series-type voltage regulator.

Within the concept of this basic configuration, voltage regulators of practically any voltage and/or current capability can be constructed by using appropriate elements for V_{ref}, A_1, Q_1, and β. The concept can be extended to include negative voltages by using complementary devices to perform the functions of $+V_{ref}$, $-V_{ref}$, and Q_1. Therefore, to design a regulator using an op amp for A_1, we must have as a minimum the element for V_{ref} and a suitable feedback network, β. In most cases, we will also need a boost transistor, Q_1, to supply additional load current. To begin the discussion of op-amp voltage regulators, we will examine the first element, the reference voltage source.

4.1.2 Requirements of the Reference Voltage Source

The prime requirement of the reference voltage source is that it must maintain a stable output voltage with time and temperature.

A voltage regulator can only be as good as its reference source; there-fore, it is desirable to make the temperature coefficient of the reference as close to zero as possible. Reference sources are commonly made up of a series string of reverse- and forward-biased diode junctions having equal and opposite temperature coefficients of voltage drift. In combination, the opposing effects cancel and the net zero temperature coefficient is usually found only at a specific value of current in the diodes. For a reference diode to maintain the temperature coefficient within its specified limits, a well-maintained current drive is required.

Reference diodes are specified to various degrees of accuracy and, depending on the number of series junctions used, are available in various terminal voltages. One example is the 1N821 series, a 6.2-V, 7.5-mA diode available with temperature coefficients from 0.01%/°C down to 0.0005%/°C. Another example is the 1N935 series, a 9.0-V, 7.5-mA diode available with a range of temperature coefficients comparable to the 1N821. The 1N4611 series is a 6.6-V, 2.0-mA diode available with temperature coefficients from 0.005%/°C down to 0.0005%/°C. The 2.0-mA operating current of this diode is compatible with the output current of a standard IC op amp, thus it will be used as an example in these discussions.

Since the terminal voltage of a reference diode is sensitive to the current flowing in it, one function of the circuitry associated with the diode is to regulate this current against variations in temperature and input voltage. The latter is the more difficult consideration, since in a simple resistor-fed reference diode as shown in Fig. 4-1, the current in R_1 will vary as $+V_{in}$ varies. This will result in variations in the reference voltage, since reference diodes do have a finite impedance. The dynamic impedance of the 1N4611, for example, is 75 ohms. It is also undesirable to load a reference diode to any extent because a varying load will result in a change in the reference voltage due to the nonzero source impedance of the diode. For this reason, reference diodes are usually buffered to minimize loading or, if they are loaded directly, the load is carefully maintained constant.

4.1.3 A Basic Reference Voltage Source

The preceding considerations are illustrated in a simple but effective fashion in the +6.6-V reference voltage source of Fig. 4-2. This circuit uses a combination of negative and positive feedback to maintain the 2.0-mA current in D_1 constant, and it does this independent of variations in both the ambient temperature and the unregulated input. The circuit works as follows:

At the moment of turn-on, the circuit has heavy positive feedback due to the low resistance (R_1) from the output to the noninverting input of A_1, and the fact that D_1 is effectively an open circuit at voltages less than its breakdown voltage. This positive feedback forces the voltage across D_1 to rise in a positive-going direction until the breakdown voltage is reached. D_1 then clamps the noninverting input of A_1 at 6.6 volts, which, in turn, reduces the positive feedback due to the low dynamic impedance of D_1. At this point, the negative feedback through R_3 and R_2 predominates, and a stable condition is established, with A_1 amplifying the 6.6 volts applied from D_1. The 6.6-V reference voltage is scaled upward to a more positive level at the output of A_1. Because a regulated voltage now

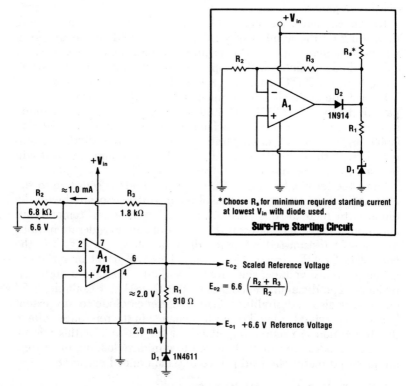

$$E_{o2} = 6.6 \left(\frac{R_2 + R_3}{R_2} \right)$$

Fig. 4-2. Basic reference voltage source—positive output.

exists at either end of R_1, a well-defined and stable voltage drop is created across R_1. Thus, the value of R_1 very effectively establishes the current in D_1. The values of R_2 and R_3 are chosen to set the output level of A_1, then R_1 is chosen for the desired current in D_1.

The unique feature of this circuit is that the reference diode regulates its own current. This current depends primarily on the reference voltage itself and thus will be stable, which lends further overall stability to the circuit. The reference voltage output can be taken directly from D_1 for high-impedance loads, or from the output of A_1 where it is scaled upward by the $(R_2 + R_3)/R_2$ ratio. This output appears at a low impedance and can supply appreciable current without the basic or scaled reference voltages being affected.

The circuit is capable of temperature performance consistent with the diode and op amp used. The temperature coefficient of the 1N4611 diode can be as good as 0.0005%/°C for the higher-quality versions. When these premium diodes are used, a premium op amp should also be used. Also, for a very low overall temperature coefficient, the current-determining resistors used should be stable 1.0% film or wirewound types. This circuit configuration provides exceptional performance in all respects except stability, even with the basic components shown. With a standard 741 op amp and virtually any zener diode in the 5- to 7-volt region, the rejection of line input variations is over 100 dB at 100 Hz.

A word of caution is appropriate at this point with regard to the starting of this circuit. The circuit is definitely *not* guaranteed to start properly if bipolar power supplies are used for A_1—a single-ended supply *must* be used. Although extensive testing with various amplifiers has not as yet revealed a case where the circuit failed to come up to the proper operating state, "Murphy's" law states that somewhere in the world such an amplifier exists and that someone will try to use it without success. Should this happen, the "sure-fire" starting circuit shown in the inset of Fig. 4-2 will make the most stubborn amplifier behave properly.

4.1.4 Error Sources in Op-Amp Voltage Regulators

When a specific degree of output voltage precision must be met in a reference source or regulator, the various error sources that influence the total performance must be separated and analyzed. Among these error sources are the temperature coefficient of the reference diode, diode noise, wiring voltage drops, amplifier input offset voltage and current drift, amplifier noise, and rejection of power-supply and common-mode input changes. These error sources will be discussed briefly in this section, and the reader can apply the basic principles to any of the circuits covered in this chapter.

Input Offset Voltage Drift

Referring again to the basic regulator of Fig. 4-2, if we assume that a stable reference diode is used for D_1, another limitation on overall temperature performance is the input offset voltage drift of A_1. This parameter is not specified for the 741; therefore, it is not a good choice for applications where temperature drift is critical. The average temperature coefficient of input offset voltage ($\Delta V_{io}/°C$) for a 107 or a 101A is specified as 3.0 $\mu V/°C$ (typical), and 15 $\mu V/°C$

(maximum). We will now examine what this means to the overall circuit.

The input offset voltage will change by the average amount specified for each 1.0°C change in chip temperature. This chip temperature change can be due either to self-heating or to the effects of loading. For example, the thermal resistance (θ_{JA}) of a 107 or a 101A is 150°C/W for the TO-99 package, which means that for each watt of dissipation the chip temperature will rise 150°C above the ambient temperature. In the circuit of Fig. 4-2, if we assume a $+V_{in}$ of 30 volts and a V_{out} of 15 volts, then

$$V_{in} - V_{out} = 15 \text{ V.}$$

Therefore, a 3.0-mA load represents a chip power dissipation (P_D) of 45 mW (15 V × 3.0 mA). We then divide the chip dissipation by the thermal resistance to determine the change in chip temperature (Δ°C) due to chip dissipation:

$$\Delta°C = \frac{P_D}{\theta_{JA}}.$$

Knowing in this example that

$$\theta_{JA} = 150° \text{ C/W} = 6.7 \text{ mW/°C,}$$

and

$$P_D = 45 \text{ mW,}$$

then

$$\Delta°C = \frac{45 \text{ mW}}{6.7 \text{ mW/°C}} = 6.7°C.$$

This 6.7°C change in chip temperature due to loading is added directly to the expected variation in ambient temperature to determine the total temperature change that the chip experiences. For example, an ambient temperature change of 70°C would result in a total chip temperature change of 76.7°C. The approximate change in input offset voltage caused by this temperature change would then be:

$$\begin{aligned}
\Delta V_{io} &= (\Delta V_{io}/°C)(\Delta°C) \\
&= (3.0 \text{ } \mu V/°C)(76.7°C) \\
&= 230 \text{ } \mu V.
\end{aligned}$$

This figure of 230 μV is then multiplied by the working voltage gain of A_1 to determine the output drift figure.

An input offset voltage drift of 230 μV is reasonably good; however, it should be remembered that this was based on an average drift of 3.0 μV/°C (typical) for the 107 and 101A. When the maximum figure of 15 μV/°C for the 107 and 101A is considered, the total drift becomes five times greater, or slightly over 1.0 mV referred to the input. Since this is approaching the total drift of a high-quality reference, a better op amp may need to be considered. A good choice would be the 725A, which has an average input offset voltage drift of 2.0 μV/°C (maximum). This figure can be improved to 0.6 μV/°C (typical) by initially adjusting the offset voltage to minimum. Since the 725 requires external compensation and differential-input protection, the components shown in Fig. 4-3 must be added so that the 725 can be used as a pin-for-pin replacement for the 741 or the 107 as a high-stability option in any of the circuits discussed subsequently.

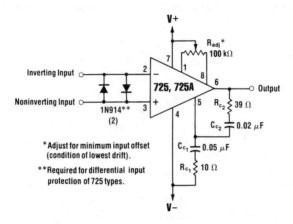

Fig. 4-3. External components required to use the 725 op amp as a high-stability option in precision voltage-regulator circuits.

Input Offset Current Drift

Another error source in op-amp voltage regulators that must be considered in applications where high stability is required is the input offset current drift of the amplifier. The type of op amp used has an important bearing on performance, as was also the case in the preceding discussion of input offset voltage drift. By itself, input offset current does not create much of a problem because this effect can usually be adjusted out. It is the change in input offset current with temperature that creates the major problem.

Referring to the basic regulator circuit of Fig. 4-2 once again, it will be noted that A_1 sees unequal dc input resistances at its two inputs. The noninverting input sees the nominal 75-Ω impedance of D_1, while the inverting input sees the parallel equivalent resistance of R_2 and R_3, or about 1500 Ω. For best stability, these two resistances should be equalized by the addition of a compensating resistor in the lower-impedance input. For this example, a 1500-Ω resistor should be connected between D_1 and the noninverting input of A_1. This equalizes the input bias voltage drops due to source resistance and minimizes the input offset voltage generated by the bias current flowing through these source resistances. The remaining error voltage is due to the bias current offset, which cannot be directly eliminated, but only minimized by careful selection of amplifier type and by lowering the source resistances.

The real problem is due to the change in input offset current with temperature. In order to judge its total significance, offset current drift must be converted to an equivalent input offset voltage drift. Using the typical offset current drift of the 725 (35 pA/$^\circ$C) and a source resistance of 1500 Ω, an equivalent offset voltage drift can be calculated as follows:

$$\Delta V_{io}/^\circ C = (\Delta I_{io}/^\circ C)(R_s)$$
$$= (3.5 \times 10^{-11}V/^\circ C)(1.5 \times 10^3)$$
$$= 5.25 \times 10^{-8}V/^\circ C$$
$$\cong 0.053\mu V/^\circ C$$

Thus, in this example, the input offset voltage drift due to input offset current drift is 0.053 μV/$^\circ$C, which is much less than the pure input offset voltage drift of the 725 (2.0 μV/$^\circ$C typical) and could be disregarded with little consequence.

If, however, the source resistances were on the order of 100 kΩ, the input offset voltage drift due to input offset current drift would be about 67 times higher (the ratio of the resistances), requiring a possible reevaluation of the situation. When working with source resistances in the 1.0-MΩ region, a low-input-current op amp, such as the 108 or 108A, should be chosen. The typical input offset current drift of a 108 is only 0.5 pA/$^\circ$C which, even with a 1.0-MΩ source resistance, creates only a 0.5-μV/$^\circ$C input offset voltage drift.

Noise Filtering

It is an inherent characteristic of zener and reference diodes that they generate an appreciable amount of wideband noise. If a reference source is to be "clean" insofar as spurious ac outputs are concerned, this zener noise must be filtered by some means.

A simple method of filtering the reference source of Fig. 4-2 is to directly bypass D_1 with a capacitor, which lowers the ac shunt impedance and tends to minimize noise output. However, this is not a completely satisfactory solution because the capacitance required to adequately bypass the diode at low frequencies becomes prohibitively large. At 100 Hz, for example, a capacitance of 20 μF is required to equal the diode impedance of 75 Ω. A much more effective solution is shown in Fig. 4-4. This illustration introduces amplifier A_2, which is used as a buffer to minimize loading on reference diode D_1. Since the input impedance of a voltage follower is very high, the point of interface between the reference diode and amplifier A_2 is an ideal place to insert a simple RC low-pass filter such as R_4-C_1. Resistor R_4 increases the output impedance of D_1 a thousandfold, which allows capacitor C_1 to be a small value. The values shown in Fig. 4-4 will provide at least 60 dB of noise attenuation at 100 Hz.

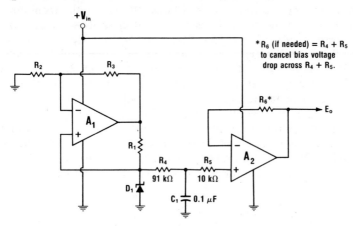

Fig. 4-4. Noise filtering applied to the basic reference source.

Resistor R_5 is included to protect the input of A_2 against the discharge transients of capacitor C_1. If the small voltage drop caused by the bias current of A_2 flowing in R_4 and R_5 is objectionable, resistor R_6 is used and made equal to $R_4 + R_5$ to minimize the dc offset error due to bias current. This noise-filtering technique can be applied whenever required in any of the circuits to be discussed in this chapter.

Wiring Voltage Drops

One of the principal sources of error in a voltage regulator is the wire used between the regulation terminals and the actual circuit load resistance. One foot of No. 20 wire has a resistance of 0.01 Ω; therefore, a 100-mA load current flowing in this wire will create a voltage drop of 1.0 mV between the regulator and the load, which is the total allowable change for a 10-V, 0.01% regulator. Obviously, an actual circuit will have wire lengths much longer than one foot, which will considerably increase the voltage drop due to wire resistance. Wiring voltage drop is a factor that must be considered in any application requiring high currents and/or extremely close regulation tolerances.

To combat wire resistance, first of all use as heavy a wire gauge as is practical and minimize its length. Other than this, a technique known as *remote sensing* should be employed, as illustrated in simplified form in Fig. 4-5. In this illustration, the wiring resistances of the positive and negative regulator output leads are shown as R_W+ and R_W-, respectively. In a conventional hookup, R_3 and D_1-R_2 would be connected to the input (left-hand) side of R_W+ and R_W-, allowing the voltage drops in these resistances to subtract from the voltage across load resistance R_L. Using the technique of remote sensing, however, R_3 is connected *after* R_W+, or directly to the positive side of the load. Likewise, D_1 and R_2 are connected after R_W-, or directly to the negative side of the load. This allows feedback network R_3-R_2 and reference diode D_1 to develop the feedback voltage with respect to the voltage that is directly across load resistance R_L, rather than prior to wire resistances R_W+ and R_W-. In this manner, the feedback loop corrects for the voltage drops in the wiring resistances, and more precise regulation of the load voltage is maintained. In practice, the voltage-sensing leads to R_3 and D_1-R_2 can be relatively small, since the currents in them are small in comparison to the load currents in R_W+ and R_W-.

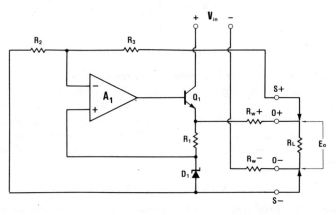

Fig. 4-5. Remote-sensing hookup to cancel the effects of wiring voltage drops.

The effect of wiring voltage drops is the largest source of error that will be encountered in voltage regulator circuits; therefore, remote sensing should be employed in any application requiring close regulation tolerances ($\leq 0.1\%$) or large currents (≥ 100 mA).

Power-Supply and Common-Mode Rejection

Another source of error in precision voltage-regulator applications is the change in op-amp input offset voltage due to changes in the unregulated input supply voltage. The degree of this error is dependent upon two electrical characteristics of the op amp itself: (1) power-supply rejection ratio (PSRR) and (2) common-mode rejection ratio (CMRR). The typical PSRR specification for a 741 is 30 μV/V, but the maximum can be as high as 150 μV/V. The typical PSRR specification for a 107 or a 101A is 16 μV/V. Any of these specifications may be adequate if the input supply-voltage changes are not excessive. Under conditions of widely varying input supply voltage, however, a better choice would be the 725, which has a PSRR specification of 10 μV/V maximum.

Common-mode rejection is a factor because a single varying supply line is equivalent to a constant supply and a varying common-mode input voltage. A given amplifier will show an equivalent change in input offset voltage proportional to its CMRR. For example, the typical CMRR specification for a 741 is 90 dB, which is equivalent to a power-supply change of 31 μV/V. However, the minimum CMRR specification for a 741 is only 70 dB, which equates to a maximum power-supply change of 310 μV/V. The typical CMRR specification for a 107 or a 101A is 96 dB, which is equivalent to a power-supply change of 16 μV/V. The 725 also excels in this category with a minimum CMRR of 110 dB, which equates to a power-supply change of only 3.1 μV/V.

Summary

Voltage regulators using IC op amps make very attractive designs because of the inherently high open-loop gain of the op amp, which allows extremely low regulation impedances. However, there are several sources of error that can easily degrade a theoretical regulation tolerance of 0.005% to over 0.1% if attention is not paid to details. These error sources include temperature drifts, wiring voltage drops, power-supply induced noise and drift, and the quality of the reference source. These basic considerations apply to all subsequent applications in which op-amp regulator circuits are used. The reader will find sufficient information in this chapter to construct voltage regulators to virtually any desired degree of accuracy. A list of references is given at the end of the chapter for readers desiring additional information.

Before proceeding into the discussion of the various regulator circuits, a few additional suggestions are offered which may prove helpful in achieving power-supply stability. These are illustrated in Fig. 4-6.

Boost or current-limiting transistors can create instability if they have very high gain-bandwidth products, as is true for types such as the 2N3904 and 2N3906. Instability can be prevented in these types by the use of a parasitic suppression resistor connected as

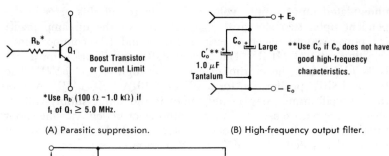

(A) Parasitic suppression.

(B) High-frequency output filter.

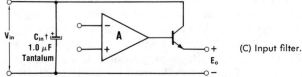

(C) Input filter.

†Use C_{in} close to amplifier if rectifier–filter is remote.

Fig. 4-6. Methods for improving power-supply stability.

shown in Fig. 4-6A. The resistance value of R_b is not critical, and examples are given in the circuits that follow.

The output filter capacitor of the power supply can also create stability problems if it is not a good high-frequency type. Instability can be prevented in these cases by connecting a 1.0-μF tantalum type across the output filter, as shown in Fig. 4-6B. Finally, an input capacitor may be needed, particularly if a number of amplifiers are used and the regulator is some distance away from the power-supply filter. This capacitor should also be a 1.0-μF tantalum type mounted close to the offending amplifier, as shown in Fig. 4-6C.

4.1.5 A Positive Reference Voltage Source With Buffered Output

The basic reference voltage source of Fig. 4-2 is useful as an integral part of larger circuits where the loading on D_1 is very light, such as the noninverting input in a voltage-follower configuration. A generally more useful reference source is the circuit shown in Fig. 4-7, which features a buffered output. (For simplicity, this circuit can use a dual op amp such as the 1558 to accomplish the functions of both voltage reference and buffer within a single IC package.) The buffer stage raises the output current to 5.0 mA and lowers the output impedance to

$$Z_o = \frac{r_o \, (\text{op amp})}{1 + A\beta}$$

$$= \frac{7.5 \times 10^1}{1 + (2 \times 10^5)(1)}$$

$$\cong 3.75 \times 10^{-4} \, \Omega.$$

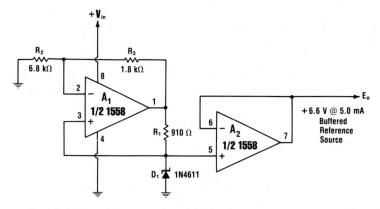

Fig. 4-7. Positive reference source with buffered output (+6.6 V @ 5.0 mA).

For best overall temperature performance, low-drift op amps such as the 107, or the 725 compensated for unity gain, should be used, particularly for A_1. The overall temperature drift can be degraded if the average temperature coefficient of input offset voltage ($\Delta V_{io}/°C$) of A_1 is not lower than the temperature coefficient of reference diode D_1.

4.1.6 A Negative Reference Voltage Source

For applications where a negative reference voltage is required, the basic circuit of Fig. 4-2 can be rearranged to operate from a negative supply, as illustrated in Fig. 4-8. The component values, theory of operation, and considerations for optimum performance are the same as for the circuit of Fig. 4-2. A buffered-output version of the basic negative reference source is illustrated in Fig. 4-9. This circuit is identical in performance to the positive buffered source of Fig. 4-7.

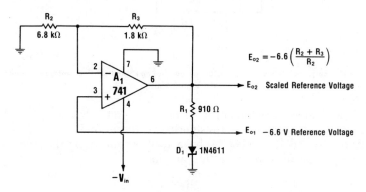

$$E_{o2} = -6.6 \left(\frac{R_2 + R_3}{R_2} \right)$$

Fig. 4-8. Basic reference voltage source—negative output.

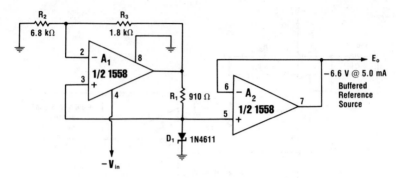

Fig. 4-9. Negative reference source with buffered output (-6.6 V @ 5.0 mA).

4.1.7 Reference Sources With Increased Voltage and Current Outputs

To increase the voltage output of a basic reference source, the R_2-R_3 voltage feedback loop can be designed to provide a specific voltage at the output of A_1, as shown in Fig. 4-10. Although this is still the same basic circuit as that of Fig. 4-2, an important difference is that the output voltage is now taken directly from the output of

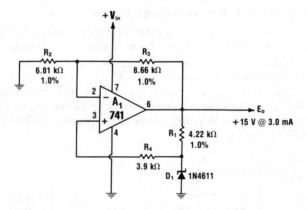

Fig. 4-10. Basic reference source with output voltage greater than reference voltage ($+15$ V @ 3.0 mA).

A_1. The voltage at this point must be more precisely maintained by the use of close-tolerance resistances. In the example of Fig. 4-10, resistors R_2 and R_3 are chosen for a 15-V output, using the standard gain equation for a noninverting amplifier:

$$\frac{E_o}{E_{in}} = \frac{R_2 + R_3}{R_2}.$$

Thus,

$$\frac{15}{6.6} = \frac{R_2 + R_3}{R_2},$$

and with R_2 set at 6.81 kΩ, then

$$2.27 = \frac{6.81 + R_3}{6.81}.$$

Solving for R_3,

$$R_3 = (2.27 \times R_2) - R_2$$
$$= (2.27 \times 6.81) - 6.81$$
$$= 15.46 - 6.81$$
$$= 8.65 \text{ k}\Omega.$$

Thus, the closest 1.0%-tolerance film or wirewound resistance value of 8.66 kΩ is used for R_3. The value for R_1 is chosen to drop the difference between the output voltage and the reference voltage with the reference current of 2.0 mA flowing. In this example,

$$R_1 = \frac{15 - 6.6}{2}$$
$$= \frac{8.4}{2}$$
$$= 4.2 \text{ k}\Omega.$$

Thus, for R_1, a 4.22-kΩ, 1.0% film or wirewound resistor is used for stability of the reference current.

Due to the voltage feedback around Λ_1, this circuit can deliver a regulated output voltage of 15 volts at a low-impedance level. The current capability of the circuit is modest, however, because nearly 3.0 mA of the rated 5.0-mA output of the op amp is used to supply the biasing currents.

For applications that require appreciably more current, a booster transistor may be added inside the feedback loop, as shown in Fig. 4-11. In this circuit, Q_1 amplifies the output current of A_1 to a 100-mA level, and R_4-Q_2 provide protection against short-circuited loads. Resistors R_6 and R_7 are parasitic suppressors, which are necessary when high f_t transistors are used for Q_1 and Q_2.

The regulation percentage possible with this circuit can be estimated by first calculating the output impedance and then calculating the corresponding drop in the output voltage due to loading. The output impedance is,

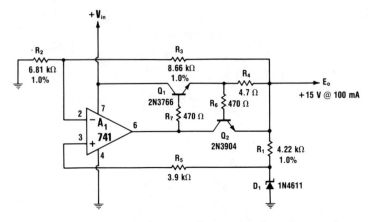

Fig. 4-11. Basic reference source with output voltage greater than reference voltage, and with boost transistor added for increased output current (+15 V @ 100 mA).

$$Z_o = \frac{\left(\dfrac{r_o(A_1)}{h_{FE_{min}}(Q_1)} \right) + R_4}{1 + A\beta}$$

$$= \frac{\left(\dfrac{7.5 \times 10^1}{2 \times 10^1} \right) + 4.7}{1 + (2 \times 10^5)(1/2.27)}$$

$$= \frac{3.75 + 4.7}{1 + (2 \times 10^5)/2.27}$$

$$\cong \frac{8.5}{1 \times 10^5}$$

$$\cong 8.5 \times 10^{-5} \ \Omega.$$

Then,

$$\Delta E_o = \Delta I_o Z_o.$$

For $\Delta I_o = 100$ mA,

$$\Delta E_o = (1 \times 10^{-1})(8.5 \times 10^{-5})$$
$$= 8.5 \times 10^{-6} \ V$$
$$= 8.5 \ \mu V.$$

These infinitesimally small numbers illustrate that an op-amp voltage regulator is theoretically capable of extremely good voltage regulation and very small output impedance. However, this high degree of performance cannot be realized unless all the error sources that were previously discussed are minimized. An example of a high-stability regulator that minimizes these error sources is

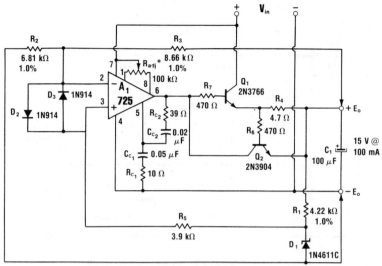

*Adjust for minimum input offset of A_1.

Fig. 4-12. High-stability, 15-V, 100-mA regulator circuit.

shown in Fig. 4-12. A 725 op amp is used in this circuit because of its low offset drift and high common-mode/power-supply rejection capability. A low-drift version of the 1N4611 diode is chosen for D_1, and close-tolerance, low-temperature-coefficient film or wire-wound resistors are used for R_1, R_2, and R_3. Remote sensing is used at the load to correct for wiring voltage drops.

There are many applications that do not require the precision capability of the circuit shown in Fig. 4-12. For such applications, a simplified version of this 15-V, 100-mA regulator (Fig. 4-13), which uses a minimum of components, can be used.

4.1.8 Variable-Output Series Regulators

The examples presented thus far are useful as fixed-level regulators to furnish a precisely constant output voltage. It is often required, however, that a regulated output voltage be variable from zero up to the reference voltage, or from zero to some maximum voltage greater than the reference voltage. These requirements can be fulfilled with but slight modification of the circuits described thus far.

Positive Regulator—Zero to $+V_Z$ (0 V to +6.6 V)

In order to vary the output of a positive reference source from zero up to the level of the reference diode voltage (V_Z), the basic circuit of Fig. 4-2 is modified as shown in Fig. 4-14. Although it is

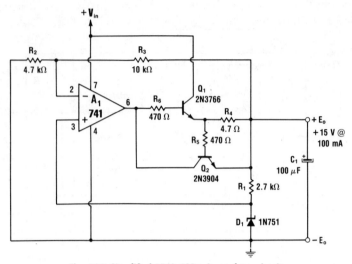

Fig. 4-13. Simplified 15-V, 100-mA regulator circuit.

generally undesirable to load a reference diode, this can be done if the loading is constant or if the loading is negligible, as was true with the buffered reference source of Fig. 4-7.

In the circuit of Fig. 4-14, potentiometer R_4 is connected across reference diode D_1, allowing output voltage adjustment from 0 V to +6.6 V. The loading on D_1 caused by R_4 is made negligible by voltage follower A_2. In order to maintain the current through the

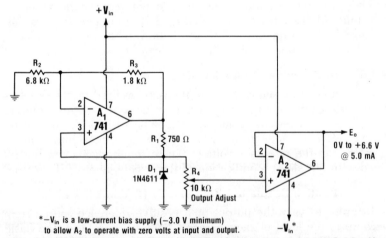

*$-V_{in}$ is a low-current bias supply (-3.0 V minimum)
to allow A_2 to operate with zero volts at input and output.

Fig. 4-14. Positive regulator with variable buffered output (0 V to +6.6 V @ 5.0 mA).

reference diode constant at its specified level of 2.0 mA, the resistance value of R_1 must be lowered from 910 Ω to 750 Ω. This supplies the extra 0.66-mA load current through R_4, making a total current through R_1 of 2.66 mA.

A dual op amp cannot be used for A_1 and A_2 in this circuit because the negative supply terminal of A_2 must be returned to a potential that is slightly more negative than common (-3.0 V) to allow linear output operation down to zero volts. Since the total supply potential on A_2 will be increased by the amount of the $-V_{in}$ supply, the maximum allowable $+V_{in}$ supply must be reduced by the same amount. The output of A_2 will supply 0 V to $+6.6$ V at 5.0 mA, with the level adjusted by R_4. If additional load current is required, an npn booster transistor can be used with A_2, as illustrated in the high-power regulator of Fig. 4-15 to be discussed next.

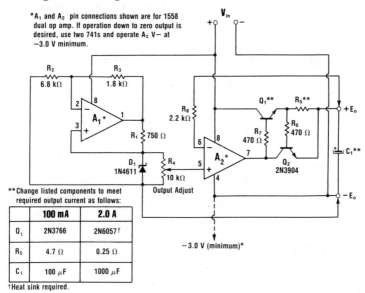

Fig. 4-15. High-power positive regulator with variable buffered output (0 V to +6.6 V @ 100 mA or 2.0 A).

High-Power Positive Regulator—0 V to +6.6 V

A voltage regulator that is variable from 0 V to $+6.6$ V is very useful for powering low-voltage logic devices that require voltages in the range of $+3.0$ or $+6.0$ volts. However, the current demands of these systems can become appreciable; therefore, specific examples of 100-mA and 2.0-A regulators are given in Fig. 4-15. In this circuit, Q_1 is either a single transistor (2N3766) or a Darlington-pair device (2N6057), depending on the output current required. Q_2

provides short-circuit protection for Q_1 by sensing the current flowing in R_5. The output voltage is adjusted by R_4, as in the previous circuit of Fig. 4-14.

Since the circuit of Fig. 4-15 is usually adjusted to some specific level above zero, the negative supply lead of A_2 can be connected to common rather than to a $-V_{in}$ potential. Q_1 must have an adequate heat sink to safely dissipate the heat generated at high output currents and high-input/low-output voltages. Remote sensing is suggested for R_4-D_1 and for pin 6 (through R_8) of A_2 as shown. R_8 is included to protect A_2 from possible discharge of C_1 at turnoff. If desired, a dual op amp (1558 or 747) can be used for A_1 and A_2.

Positive Regulator—Zero to $+KV_Z$ (0 V to +15 V)

By adding an appropriate gain factor "K" to amplifier A_2, the basic regulator of Fig. 4-15 can be made to provide any output voltage

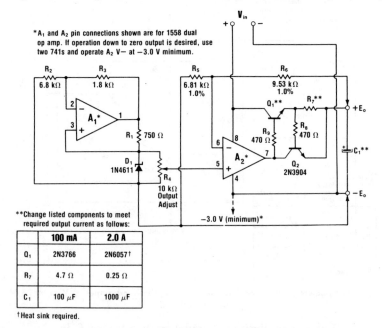

Fig. 4-16. High-power variable positive regulator with increased output voltage (0 V to +15 V @ 100 mA or 2.0 A).

from zero up to a level of $K \times V_Z$, or $K \times 6.6$ V, within the range of A_2 and its power supplies. The circuit is shown in Fig. 4-16 and can be recognized as the basic reference source feeding a buffer stage that has gain due to feedback resistors R_5 and R_6. With an input voltage of E_{in}, the output of buffer stage A_2 will be:

$$E_o = E_{in}\left(\frac{R_5 + R_6}{R_5}\right).$$

Input voltage E_{in} is the variable potential of 0 V to +6.6 V from reference source A_1. The gain factor "K" is represented by $(R_5 + R_6)/R_5$.

For a specified output level such as +15 V, choose a value for K which sets the desired ratio of R_5 to R_6, using a worst-case reference voltage of 6.6 V −5% or 6.27 V. Thus,

$$K = \frac{E_o}{E_{in}}$$

$$= \frac{15}{6.27}$$

$$= 2.4,$$

then,

$$\frac{R_5 + R_6}{R_5} = 2.4.$$

For resistor R_5, a 1.0%-tolerance, 6.81-kΩ value is chosen for stability, and to pass a current of approximately 1.0 mA at an E_{in} of 6.6 V. Then,

$$R_6 = (2.4 \times R_5) - R_5$$

$$= (2.4 \times 6.81) - 6.81$$

$$= 9.534 \text{ kΩ}.$$

Thus, for R_6, a 1.0%-tolerance, 9.53-kΩ value will allow E_o to be adjusted to +15 V with an E_{in} of 6.27 V.

The complete circuit for a 0-V to +15-V, 100-mA or 2-A regulator, which utilizes the foregoing principles, is shown in Fig. 4-16. As in the circuit of Fig. 4-15, the choice of transistor Q_1 determines the output current capability. Short-circuit protection is provided by transistor Q_2, which senses the load current flowing through R_7. A large output capacitor (C_1) is used to maintain a low output impedance at high frequencies, where the gain of A_2 falls off. Remote sensing is also suggested for this circuit, particularly for the higher-current version.

Negative Regulator—Zero to $-V_Z$ (0 V to −6.6 V)

The implementation of a variable-output negative regulator involves a simple modification of the variable-output positive regulator of Fig. 4-14. This is illustrated in Fig. 4-17. The A_1 portion of the circuit is similar to the negative reference source of Fig. 4-8, except that resistor R_1 is lowered in value from 910 Ω to 750 Ω in order to supply the extra 0.66-mA load current through R_4. The output from R_4 is thus variable from 0 V to −6.6 V and is buffered by voltage follower A_2. The positive supply terminal of A_2 must be returned to a potential that is slightly more positive than common (+3.0 V) to allow linear output operation from 0 V to −6.6 V at 5.0 mA. Therefore, a dual op amp cannot be used for A_1 and A_2, as was also true for the circuit of Fig. 4-14.

High-Power Negative Regulator—Zero to −KV$_Z$ (0 V to −15 V)

The calculations involved in designing the circuit of Fig. 4-16 provided a variable-output positive regulator of 0-V to +15-V output at 100 mA or 2.0 A. The same circuit values can be applied to a design that is rearranged to operate from a negative supply. This will provide a circuit with an output variable from 0 V to −15 V with 100-mA or 2-A capability. This circuit is illustrated in Fig. 4-18, which is functionally identical to the circuit of Fig. 4-16, except that the supply potentials are reversed and pnp transistors are substituted for Q_1 and Q_2. Remote sensing is also suggested for this circuit, particularly for the higher-current version.

4.1.9 Tracking Regulators

A tracking regulator is a regulator that has two outputs, with one output "tracking" the other. This usually takes the form of a master/slave combination, wherein the output of one regulator can be varied from zero to some maximum level, and a second regulator creates a mirror image of the first. This is illustrated in Fig. 4-19.

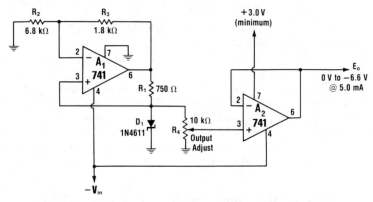

Fig. 4-17. Negative regulator with variable buffered output (0 V to −6.6 V @ 5.0 mA).

In this circuit, amplifiers A_1 and A_2 constitute a variable-output positive regulator, similar to the circuit of Fig. 4-14. It supplies a 0-V to +6.6-V potential at the positive output terminal, +E_o. Amplifier A_3 is connected as a unity-gain inverter, since R_5 and R_6 are equal in value. It produces a voltage that is always equal but opposite in polarity to the output of A_2. As A_2 varies from 0 V to +6.6 V, A_3 will vary from 0 V to −6.6 V. Therefore, potentiometer R_4 controls two outputs that are equal in magnitude but opposite in polarity. If desired, a dual op amp such as the 1558 can be used for A_2 and A_3, since both amplifiers must be capable of operating down to zero volts and thus both require positive and negative supplies.

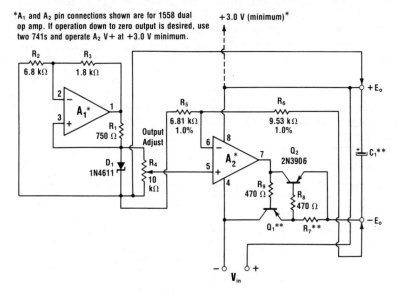

*A_1 and A_2 pin connections shown are for 1558 dual op amp. If operation down to zero output is desired, use two 741s and operate A_2 V+ at +3.0 V minimum.

**Change listed components to meet required output current as follows:

	100 mA	2.0 A
Q_1	2N3740	2N6050†
R_7	4.7 Ω	0.25 Ω
C_1	100 μF	1000 μF

†Heat sink required.

Fig. 4-18. High-power variable negative regulator with increased output voltage (0 V to −15 V @ 100 mA or 2.0 A).

The accuracy of tracking between A_2 (the master) and A_3 (the slave) is determined by the match between R_5 and R_6. Therefore, for accuracy and stability, 1.0% film or wirewound precision resistors should be used here. Resistor R_7 minimizes the effects of bias current in R_5 and R_6.

Dual-Output Tracking Regulator—Zero to $\pm KV_Z$ (0 V to ± 15 V)

A tracking regulator with a single adjustment is a very useful tool as a laboratory power supply. The basic tracking regulator of Fig.

4-19 can be extended to output voltages higher than the reference voltage, and with considerably higher current. Such a circuit is illustrated in Fig. 4-20. This circuit is a combination of previously described subcircuits. A positive 6.6-V reference source (A_1) is used to feed a 0-V to +15-V regulator consisting of A_2, Q_1, and Q_3. A_3, Q_2, and Q_4 comprise a slaved negative regulator, which tracks the voltage from the positive regulator. Both regulators have an output current capability of either 100 mA or 2.0 A, depending on the components used (see the table in Fig. 4-20).

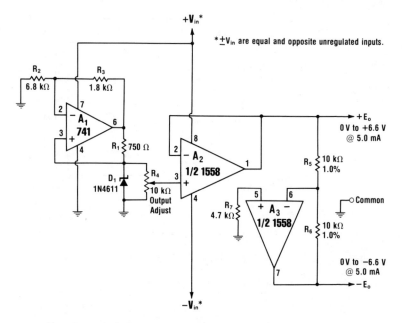

Fig. 4-19. Basic dual-output tracking regulator (0 V to ±6.6 V @ 5.0 mA).

Dual-Output, Independently Variable Regulators—Zero to +KV_Z and Zero to −KV_Z (0 V to +15 V and 0 V to −15 V)

A useful variation of the tracking regulator of Fig. 4-20 is illustrated in Fig. 4-21. This circuit features independently variable positive and negative outputs using a common reference source for both regulators. The reader may recognize this circuit as being a combination of the previously discussed circuits of Figs. 4-16 and 4-18 for the A_2 and A_3 portions. The main difference in this circuit is the method used to derive the positive and negative reference volt- ages. Buffer A_2 uses the positive reference voltage from R_4, while buffer A_3 uses a negative reference voltage developed from the positive voltage across D_1. To develop the negative reference volt-

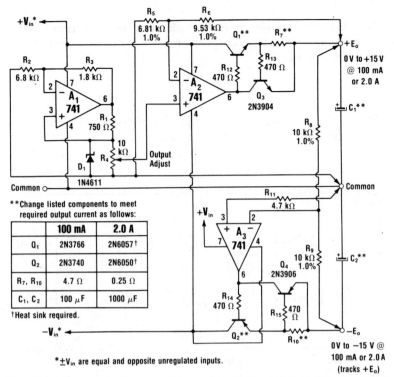

Fig. 4-20. High-power, dual-output tracking regulator (0 V to ±15 V @ 100 mA or 2.0 A).

age, amplifier A_4 is used to invert the +6.6 V across D_1 and produce −6.6 V across R_{11}. R_{12}, the input resistor for A_4, loads D_1 with an additional current of 0.66 mA; therefore, R_1 is decreased to 620 Ω in order to maintain the 2.0-mA current in D_1. Potentiometer R_4 serves as the output adjustment for the positive regulator, while R_{11} serves the same purpose for the negative regulator. Both regulators have an output current capability of either 100 mA or 2.0 A, depending on the components used (see the table in Fig. 4-21).

4.1.10 Shunt Regulators

A shunt voltage regulator is the direct opposite of a series voltage regulator. A shunt regulator controls the output voltage by controlling the conduction of a parallel- (or shunt-) connected transistor, while a series regulator does the same thing by controlling the conduction of a series-connected transistor. The basic configuration of a shunt regulator is shown in Fig. 4-22. In this circuit, the power transistor, Q_1, is the only element changed from the series configuration of Fig. 4-1. There is still a reference voltage, V_{ref}, an amplifier, A_1, and a feedback network, β. Power transistor Q_1 is now connected

163

in parallel with load resistance R_L, rather than in series as in Fig. 4-1. The relationship between output voltage E_o and input voltage V_{ref} remains the same:

$$E_o = \frac{V_{ref}}{\beta}.$$

The same requirements that exist for the series regulator also exist for the shunt regulator: a stable reference voltage, V_{ref}; a high-gain,

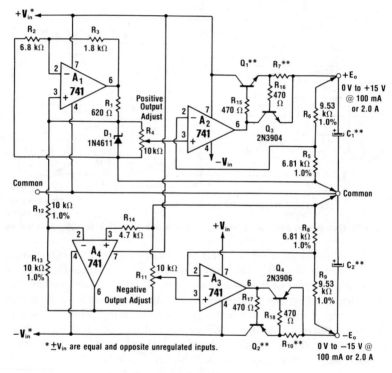

	100 mA	2.0 A
Q_1	2N3766	2N6057†
Q_2	2N3740	2N6050†
R_7, R_{10}	4.7 Ω	0.25 Ω
C_1, C_2	100 μF	1000 μF

**Change listed components to meet required output current as follows:

†Heat sink required.

Fig. 4-21. Dual-output, independently variable regulators (0 V to +15 V and 0 V to −15 V; 100 mA or 2.0 A at each output).

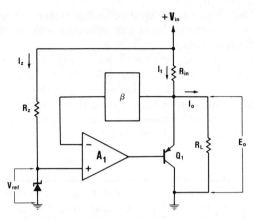

Fig. 4-22. Functional diagram of a shunt-type voltage regulator.

stable op amp, A_1; a power control element, Q_1; and a feedback network, β, which determines the output voltage.

A shunt regulator is inherently inefficient because it achieves regulation by absorbing the current that is not required by the load. Since the maximum available load current is set by R_{in}, Q_1 must shunt this current away from R_L under conditions of small load-current demands. Therefore, the total current consumed in a shunt regulator is constant, since it will pass to either Q_1 or R_L, as required. The circuit can be thought of as an ideal zener diode because it uses the high-gain feedback loop and the variable conduction of Q_1 to simulate perfect zener action. This results in inefficiency because the circuit always consumes the total load current, whereas in a series regulator, only the current demanded by the load (plus unavoidable bias currents) is drawn from the source.

From the standpoint of total power consumption then, the shunt regulator is not as attractive as the series regulator. However, the same properties that make the power drain of a shunt regulator constant, also have positive side effects. Since the total power drain is constant, the use of a shunt regulator in a system reduces the effects of transient disturbances feeding back through the power supplies. Any transients due to load-current changes in R_L will be mostly absorbed by Q_1. Therefore, systems using shunt-regulated (or decoupled) stages tend to be "clean" and noise free.

Also, any changes in the unregulated $+V_{in}$ supply will automatically be smoothed by Q_1 and the feedback loop, and will not be transmitted to the output as changes in E_o. For example, should $+V_{in}$ become more positive and attempt to make E_o more positive, this voltage change will be fed back through β and will be amplified by A_1, thus increasing the conduction of Q_1 and opposing the original voltage change. A shunt-regulator system, therefore, resists any changes in operating level due either to changes in $+V_{in}$ or to changes in load current.

Shunt regulators are best used on a small-scale basis (as one might use zener diodes, for example). This keeps the basic ineffi- ciency of the technique from becoming prohibitive, since a local shunt regulator might represent only a fraction of the total power of a system. Yet, the advantages of the active decoupling can be used to stabilize particularly critical stages where required.

Low-Power Shunt Regulator

IC op amps make just as effective shunt regulators as they do series regulators. The key to their effectiveness is in their class-B out- put stage, which can be either a current sink or a current source. In a shunt regulator, the usual requirement is to absorb the excess load current. An example of a low-power shunt regulator is shown in Fig. 4-23. In this circuit, the output voltage of A_1 is regulated at a value:

$$E_o = V_{ref}\left(\frac{R_2 + R_3}{R_2}\right),$$

where,

V_{ref} is the voltage of zener diode D_1.

The reference current in D_1 is established by R_1 as:

$$I_z = \frac{E_o - V_{ref}}{R_1}.$$

The total current in A_1 is determined by R_4 and output voltage E_o as:

$$I_t = \frac{V_{in} - E_o}{R_4}.$$

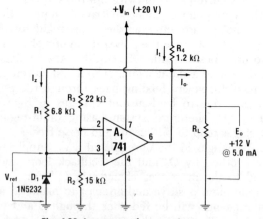

Fig. 4-23. Low-power shunt regulator.

Not all of the current in R_4 is available as load current, however, as part of this current is used to bias D_1, and part is consumed by R_2 and R_3. The reason that D_1 is fed from the output of A_1 rather than from $+V_{in}$ is that the output of A_1 is a regulated voltage, whereas $+V_{in}$ is unregulated. A large increase in the rejection of input-induced noise is gained by this "bootstrapping" technique of feeding the zener from the output of the op amp. The current drawn by D_1 can be compensated for by a small reduction in the value of R_4, with no sacrifice in the overall performance of the circuit.

To design the regulator of Fig. 4-23 for a specified output voltage, start by choosing a voltage for D_1. Since the primary purpose of a shunt regulator is the decoupling of noise from V_{in} to E_o, a nonzero temperature coefficient for D_1 is not a great disadvantage. Therefore, a standard, general-purpose 5.6-V zener such as the 1N5232 can be used, with a zener current (I_Z) of 1.0 mA. This smaller current will minimize the loading on R_4 and lower the diode voltage to approximately 5.1 V, which is closer to the low TC region of the 1N5232.

For a desired output voltage of 12 V, calculate a value for R_1 to produce 1.0 mA of current in D_1:

$$R_1 = \frac{E_o - V_Z}{1 \times 10^{-3}}$$

$$= \frac{12 - 5.1}{1 \times 10^{-3}}$$

$$= 6.9 \times 10^3$$

$$= 6.9 \text{ k}\Omega.$$

The closest standard value of 6.8 kΩ is thus chosen for R_1. Next, select the R_2-R_3 relationship to provide the output voltage of 12 V:

$$12 = 5.1 \left(\frac{R_2 + R_3}{R_2} \right).$$

Since R_2 will have the same voltage across it as does D_1 due to zero differential input voltage, select a value for R_2 that will determine the R_2-R_3 current. This value should be high enough to maintain the R_2-R_3 current at 1.0 mA or less, but the resistance seen by the inverting input (pin 2) of A_1 should be 10 kΩ or less. A nominal value for R_2 would thus be 15 kΩ; then,

$$I_{R_2} = \frac{5.1}{15 \times 10^3}$$

$$= 0.3 \times 10^{-3}$$

$$= 0.3 \text{ mA},$$

and,

$$R_3 = \frac{E_o - 5.1}{I_{R_2}}$$

$$= \frac{12 - 5.1}{3 \times 10^{-4}}$$

$$= \frac{6.9}{3 \times 10^{-4}}$$

$$= 2.3 \times 10^4$$

$$= 23 \text{ k}\Omega.$$

The closest standard value of 22 kΩ is thus chosen for R_3. Next, select a value for R_4 that will provide the required total current of:

$$I_t = I_o + I_z + I_{R_2 - R_3}.$$

Assume a $+V_{in}$ of 20 V and an I_o of 5.0 mA, then

$$R_4 = \frac{V_{in} - E_o}{I_t}$$

$$= \frac{20 - 12}{6.3 \times 10^{-3}}$$

$$= \frac{8}{6.3} \times 10^3$$

$$= 1.26 \text{ k}\Omega.$$

The lower closest standard value of 1.2 kΩ is thus chosen for R_4.

As a supply-voltage decoupler, the regulator of Fig. 4-23 has an effective output impedance of 0.01 Ω at 100 Hz. At the ripple frequency of 120 Hz, therefore, this regulator will have a filtering effect equivalent to a capacitor of 100,000 μF! Obviously, then, it offers an effective, low-cost alternative to bulky RC filters in low-current applications.

High-Power Shunt Regulators

The current-handling capability of a shunt regulator can be extended beyond the 5.0-mA output rating of the basic circuit of Fig. 4-23 by the use of booster transistors, as shown in the circuits of Figs. 4-24A and B. In these circuits, A_1 and its associated components are used as a two-terminal regulator. The op amp regulates its supply (with assistance from Q_1) essentially the same as in the circuit of Fig. 4-23. The output voltage of the regulator is determined in the same manner as for the circuit of Fig. 4-23, and the current capacity is proportional to the gain and power rating of Q_1. For currents up to 100 mA, Q_1 can be a single transistor such as a

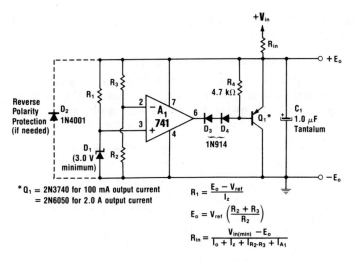

$$R_1 = \frac{E_o - V_{ref}}{I_z}$$

$$E_o = V_{ref}\left(\frac{R_2 + R_3}{R_2}\right)$$

$$R_{in} = \frac{V_{in(min)} - E_o}{I_o + I_z + I_{R_2\text{-}R_3} + I_{A_1}}$$

*Q_1 = 2N3740 for 100 mA output current
    = 2N6050 for 2.0 A output current

(A) Connections for positive regulation.

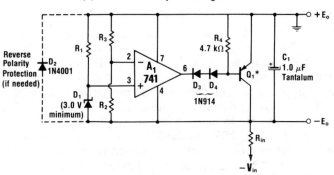

(B) Connections for negative regulation.

Fig. 4-24. High-power shunt regulators.

2N3740; for higher currents, Q_1 should be a Darlington-pair device such as 2N6050.

Since this regulator is a two-terminal device, it can be applied in the same manner that an equivalent zener diode would be applied, using either terminal as common to regulate either positive or negativ voltages. A high-power shunt regulator connected for a positive output voltage is shown in Fig. 4-24A, while the same circuit connected for a negative output voltage is shown in Fig. 4-24B.

Unlike a zener diode, the circuit cannot withstand a reversal of voltage (forward conduction in a zener), because this would reverse the supply polarity to A_1. If a transient condition exists which might reverse the voltage across A_1, a clamping diode (D_2) should be added as shown. A 1.0-μF tantalum capacitor (C_1) connected across the output terminals helps to maintain the output impedance low at high frequencies.

Single-to-Dual Power-Supply Converter

A very useful configuration in which a shunt regulator can be used is a single-to-dual power-supply converter, as illustrated in Fig. 4-25. This circuit is a special type of power supply—it is not really a series regulator and not really a shunt regulator but, rather, a hybrid

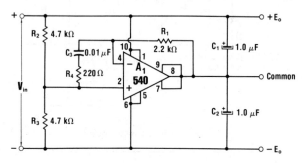

Fig. 4-25. Single-to-dual power-supply converter.

type. It operates between the lines of a single supply, furnishing a floating output that is midway (or some fractional percent) between the two supply lines. This "derived" output terminal is regulated at the voltage set by R_2-R_3 and can either sink or source current, allowing the single supply to be used as two.

The circuit of Fig. 4-25 uses the 540, a power IC having a 1.0-watt dissipation rating and a ±100-mA current output rating. Thus, it can regulate load imbalances of up to 100 mA. The 540 works essentially as a voltage follower in this circuit, with an input voltage set by R_2-R_3. R_1 provides unity-gain feedback from the output (the common terminal), so whatever voltage appears at the input from R_2-R_3 will also appear at the output at a very low impedance. When a load is connected from $+E_o$ to common, the common terminal would tend to rise toward the $+E_o$ potential. However, due to the low output impedance of A_1, the voltage is clamped at the R_2-R_3 potential. A load current from $+E_o$ to common, then, will return to the source through the 540 and the $-V_{in}$ line. A similar reasoning applies for loads from $-E_o$ to common.

In the circuit of Fig. 4-25, R_2 and R_3 are equal; therefore, the V_{in} potential will be equally split. Thus, for a 30-V input, ±15 V will appear at the output. Different output ratios can be selected by scaling R_2 and R_3 for unequal voltage drops. R_2 will drop the positive output voltage and R_3 will drop the negative output voltage since, by definition, their midpoint is at ground (output common).

With the 540, the parallel resistance of R_2 and R_3 should be 2.5 kΩ or less for best stability, and R_1 should be set equal to this value. Capacitors C_1 and C_2 provide frequency compensation for the 540. The 540 will require a heat sink for outputs of 10 mA or more, and its total dissipation should be kept at 1.0 watt or less.

4.2 CURRENT REGULATORS

Current regulators are similar to voltage regulators in that they use the same basic elements of control to accomplish their function. The difference lies in their configuration.

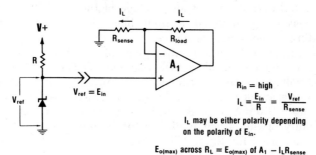

$$R_{in} = \text{high}$$
$$I_L = \frac{E_{in}}{R} = \frac{V_{ref}}{R_{sense}}$$

I_L may be either polarity depending on the polarity of E_{in}.

$E_{o(max)}$ across $R_L = E_{o(max)}$ of $A_1 - I_L R_{sense}$

Fig. 4-26. Basic noninverting VCCS.

The basic elements of a current regulator are illustrated in Fig. 4-26. There is a reference source, V_{ref}; an amplifier, A_1; and a feedback network, β, which consists in this circuit of R_{sense} and R_{load}. At this point, it appears that there is no difference between this circuit and the basic voltage regulator of Fig. 4-1. Actually, with a given value for R_{load}, there would be no difference. R_{load} and R_{sense} would form a feedback network to define some value of β, and the loop would generate an output voltage, E_o. However, the main difference in a current regulator is that it is the current rather than the voltage that we wish to maintain constant. In the circuit of Fig. 4-26, it will be noted that if V_{ref} is constant, if R_{sense} is a fixed value, and if A_1 is an ideal amplifier, the current, I_L, flowing in R_{sense} (and thus R_{load}) will remain constant at a value

$$I_L = \frac{V_{ref}}{R_{sense}}.$$

This is true regardless of the value of R_{load}. The basic concept of a current regulator, then, is the maintenance of a definite value of current flowing in a variable load impedance, with independence from the load variations, temperature changes, and supply-voltage changes.

There are many different types of regulators, which attain various levels of performance. The performance attainable using IC op amps in current regulators can be nearly perfect if sufficient attention is paid to the significant sources of error.

4.2.1 Low-Power, General-Purpose Current Regulators

Basic Noninverting VCCS

With the assignment of component values, the circuit of Fig. 4-26 can serve as a highly useful, general-purpose, low-power current regulator. It can supply current of either polarity through R_{load} up to the rated output current and voltage of the amplifier used. The circuit has a high-impedance input, hence it presents a minimum of loading to the reference source.

If a variable voltage is used in place of V_{ref}, this circuit can be used as a voltage-controlled current source (VCCS). The sensitivity of the voltage-to-current conversion is inversely proportional to R_{sense}. For example, an R_{sense} value of 1.0 kΩ will yield a conversion sensitivity of 1.0 mA/V. It should be readily apparent that the overall stability of the circuit is directly proportional to the quality of the resistor used for R_{sense}. When high accuracy and constancy of load current is required, this resistor should be a precision type.

Basic Inverting VCCS

The inverting op-amp configuration can also be used as a current regulator and a VCCS. This is illustrated in Fig. 4-27. In this circuit, input current I_{in} is equal to load current I_L; therefore,

$$I_L = \frac{E_{in}}{R_s}.$$

Resistor R_s determines the sensitivity of the voltage-to-current conversion as in the previous circuit, but in this circuit it also determines the input resistance, which is equal to R_s. This circuit can also supply current of either polarity up to the rated output current and

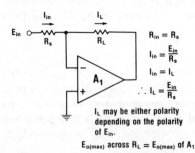

$$R_{in} = R_s$$
$$I_{in} = \frac{E_{in}}{R_s}$$
$$I_{in} = I_L$$
$$\therefore I_L = \frac{E_{in}}{R_s}$$

I_L may be either polarity depending on the polarity of E_{in}.

$E_{o(max)}$ across R_L = $E_{o(max)}$ of A_1

Fig. 4-27. Basic inverting VCCS.

voltage of the amplifier. In addition, it has the advantage that more voltage is available to drive R_L because one end of R_L is at ground potential, whereas in the circuit of Fig. 4-26, one end of R_L is at the same potential as the input voltage, which subtracts from the voltage available to drive R_L.

4.2.2 Boosted-Output Current Regulators

General purpose op amps such as the 741 and 101 are limited to a maximum output current of ± 5.0 mA. This can be boosted to higher currents, however, by adding current-gain transistors within the feedback loop.

Noninverting VCCS With Boosted Output

A circuit illustrating a boosted-output current regulator is shown in Fig. 4-28. This circuit is a 100-mA output, noninverting VCCS

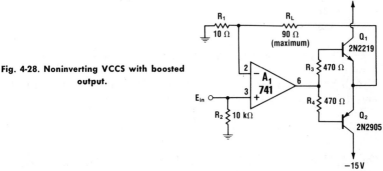

Fig. 4-28. Noninverting VCCS with boosted output.

with bidirectional current capability in load resistance R_L. For positive input voltages, Q_1 conducts, Q_2 is turned off, and current flows from the +15-V supply through Q_1, R_L, and R_1, the 10-Ω sensing resistor. For negative input voltages, Q_2 conducts, Q_1 is turned off, and current flows from the -15-V supply through Q_2, R_L, and R_1. If only single-polarity current flow is required, the opposite polarity transistor can be eliminated. The conversion sensitivity of this circuit is 100 mA/V.

Inverting VCCS With Boosted Output

An inverting VCCS with output boosted to 100 mA is illustrated in Fig. 4-29. One undesirable characteristic of the basic inverting configuration is the fact that the input current is equal to the load current, as diagrammed in Fig. 4-27. This is obviously a drawback for high-current use because the signal or reference might have to supply currents as high as 100 mA! However, there is a method of circumventing this problem known as *current scaling*, which provides an effective gain between the input current, I_{in}, and the load current, I_L.

The circuit of Fig. 4-29 utilizes the current-scaling technique, which works as follows: A voltage of -1.0 V at the input will create a current of 100 μA in R_1 and, because of feedback action, this same current must also flow through R_2. Therefore, the junction of R_2 and

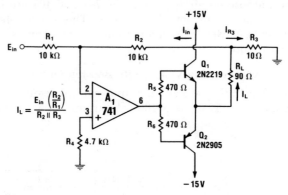

Fig. 4-29. Inverting VCCS with boosted output.

R_3 will be at a potential of $+1.0$ V, which means that R_3 will also have 1.0 V across it. Hence, the current in R_3 will be

$$I_{R_3} = \frac{1.0\ \text{V}}{10\ \Omega} = 100\ \text{mA}.$$

Thus, I_{R_3} has been effectively scaled upward by the ratio of R_2/R_3, which in this case is 10,000/10, or 1000/1.

The total load current, I_L, flowing in R_L consists of the two currents, I_{in} and I_{R_3} so the actual ratio of load current to input current will be

$$\frac{I_L}{I_{in}} = \frac{I_{R_3} + I_{in}}{I_{in}}$$

$$= \frac{100.1}{0.1}$$

$$= \frac{1001}{1},$$

which, to be precise, is 0.1% in error from the R_2/R_3 ratio, but the basic current-scaling technique is illustrated nonetheless. This circuit can also be made bidirectional by the use of complementary buffer transistors for Q_1 and Q_2.

4.2.3 Unidirectional Current Sources With Single Output Terminals

The current sources discussed thus far have been capable of driving loads with both terminals available, or "floating." Often, however, both terminals of a load are not available for this type of connection. For various reasons, it may be necessary that one load terminal be connected to a fixed potential—either supply voltage, for example, or ground. In fact, these applications may be more commonplace than the two-terminal (floating) drives. Also, a large number of applications do not require a bidirectional output current—the current may always remain the same polarity, and even fixed in magnitude. There is a wide range of circuits that fall into these general categories, some with even more subtle options of their own, which will be discussed in this section.

Current Sources With Loads Referred to More-Positive Supply Potentials

Positive-Input VCCS. Fig. 4-30 illustrates a circuit that partially resembles the noninverting buffered VCCS of Fig. 4-28, but with one very important difference. In Fig. 4-30, load resistance R_L has

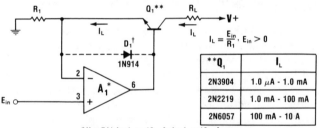

$$I_L = \frac{E_{in}}{R_1}, \; E_{in} > 0$$

**Q_1	I_L
2N3904	1.0 μA - 1.0 mA
2N2219	1.0 mA - 100 mA
2N6057	100 mA - 10 A

*Use 741 for $I_L > 10$ μA; for $I_L < 10$ μA, use low-input-current type such as 8007, 108, or 1556.

†Protection against input polarity reversal.

Fig. 4-30. Basic positive-input VCCS; load referred to V+.

been moved to the collector circuit of Q_1, which places R_L outside the feedback loop for A_1. In operation, this circuit maintains the Q_1 emitter current constant as it passes through R_1 by comparing it to input voltage E_{in}. In this respect, the circuit of Fig. 4-30 is the same as an npn buffered version of the Fig. 4-28 circuit. In Fig. 4-28, however, the total emitter current of Q_1 (collector current plus base current) passes through R_1 and R_L. The situation is slightly different in Fig. 4-30 since R_L is in the collector circuit, but the current that is regulated is the emitter current. Therefore, there is an error due to the base current of Q_1, which does not flow through R_L. This error is caused by the finite h_{FE} of Q_1. (In the example shown in Fig. 4-30, the h_{FE} of a 2N3904 is 100 minimum.) The difference between the current sampled and the current actually flowing in R_L will be $1/h_{FE}$ of the current in R_1, or typically less than 1.0% for currents in the region of 10 mA. The V+ supply to R_L and Q_1 can be either the +15-V line, or it can be as high as the V_{CB} rating of the transistor used, as long as the maximum power dissipation of the transistor is not exceeded. The V+ parameter is not limited by the op amp in this circuit. The circuit responds to positive voltages at E_{in}.

Since this circuit does not load the reference source, E_{in}, it is a very useful type of current regulator. For the reference source, a circuit such as that of Fig. 4-2, or one of its variations, can be used. R_1 and Q_1 are selected for the desired operating current. Q_1 is selected primarily from the standpoint of power and voltage rating. Typical recommendations for Q_1, for different ranges of I_L, are listed in Fig. 4-30.

A 741 is generally adequate for A_1, since A_1 must be a unity-gain-compensated type due to the 100% feedback through Q_1. For very low values of I_L, the input bias current of A_1 (which subtracts from I_L) can become a significant percentage of I_L, thus causing a significant error. For I_L values below about 10 μA then, low-input-current types such as the 8007, 108, or 1556 may be necessary for better accuracy.

One possible trouble with this circuit is failure of Q_1 if the input voltage is reversed from its normal operating polarity. Since Q_1 can conduct only a unidirectional current, a reversal of the input voltage to A_1 will result in an opposite-polarity, saturated output current from A_1. This may be sufficient to cause emitter-base breakdown and possible destruction of Q_1. This situation is easily prevented by diode D_1, which protects Q_1 by reverse clamping the output of A_1.

Negative-Input VCCS. For negative input voltages, the circuit of Fig. 4-31 can be used. This is essentially the same circuit as that of

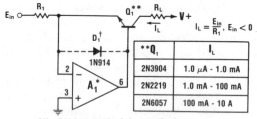

Q₁	I_L
2N3904	1.0 μA - 1.0 mA
2N2219	1.0 mA - 100 mA
2N6057	100 mA - 10 A

*Use 741 for I_L > 10 μA; for I_L < 10 μA, use low-input-current type such as 8007, 108, or 1556.

† Protection against input polarity reversal.

Fig. 4-31. Basic negative-input VCCS; load referred to V+.

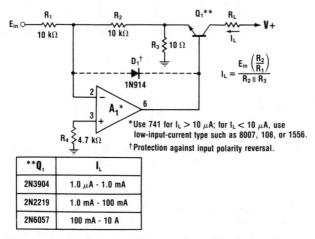

Fig. 4-32. Negative-input VCCS with current gain.

Fig. 4-30 converted to an inverting input. The same general considerations that were true for A_1 and Q_1 in Fig. 4-30 also apply in this circuit. Since Q_1 is biased at near ground potential, this circuit has a larger available output swing to drive R_L. The circuit has the same basic disadvantage as the circuit of Fig. 4-27, however, in that $I_{in} = I_L$, restricting operation to small input currents. This disadvantage can be overcome by using the current-scaling technique, as shown in Fig. 4-32. In this circuit, resistor R_3 forces Q_1 to conduct a much heavier current than the feedback current. The operation is similar to the circuit of Fig. 4-29, with the gain between I_{in} and I_L determined by the R_2/R_3 ratio.

Improving the Accuracy of the Output Current. The circuits discussed thus far are all somewhat imprecise, as was pointed out initially. There are several remedies that can be used to minimize the inaccuracies, and basically all are schemes to minimize that portion of the regulated current which does not reach the load. This problem

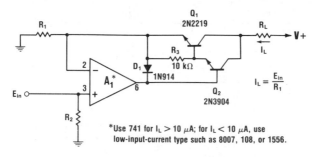

Fig. 4-33. Positive-input Darlington VCCS.

can become rather severe, particularly at high currents where the gain of the transistor falls off, and inaccuracies can reach several percent.

The first remedy that can be used is to substitute a Darlington device for the single transistor used in Fig. 4-30. Such a circuit is shown in Fig. 4-33. In this circuit, Q_1 can be either a single-package Darlington amplifier or it can be two discrete transistors wired as a Darlington pair (shown as Q_1 and Q_2 in Fig. 4-33).

The use of a Darlington amplifier will improve the accuracy by the additional gain, and it will suffice for all but the most stringent applications. For such applications, a FET can be used as shown in Fig. 4-34. This lowers the drive current to the FET (which is, in fact, the error component) to the reverse-bias, gate leakage of the device used. At room temperature, a 2N5459 has a maximum leakage of 1.0 nA, but it rises to a maximum of 200 nA at 100°C. It should be remembered that the gate current of a JFET will double for every 10°C of temperature rise, so for high-temperature use, a Darlington amplifier may still be the better answer.

The FET used must have a minimum zero-bias drain current (I_{DSS}) that is equal to or higher than the desired load current, I_L. For a 2N5459, the minimum I_{DSS} is 4.0 mA, which is also, therefore, the maximum I_L for the device in the circuit of Fig. 4-34. As in previous circuits, the breakdown voltage and power dissipation ratings of Q_1 must be observed.

Some applications may require both a small bias-current error and a high I_L. Such requirements may be satisfied by a FET/power transistor combination, as shown in the circuit of Fig. 4-35. In this circuit, the FET drives the npn transistor as a source follower, and the combination is equivalent to a power FET. The breakdown voltage is limited to that of the device that has the lower rating, which in this circuit is the FET, Q_1. The power rating is determined primarily by Q_2, and the circuit can be used at any current level up to 100 mA with the devices shown.

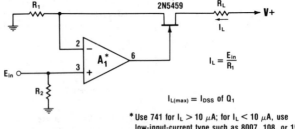

$$I_L = \frac{E_{in}}{R_1}$$

$I_{L(max)} = I_{DSS}$ of Q_1

*Use 741 for $I_L > 10~\mu A$; for $I_L < 10~\mu A$, use low-input-current type such as 8007, 108, or 1556.

Fig. 4-34. Positive-input FET VCCS.

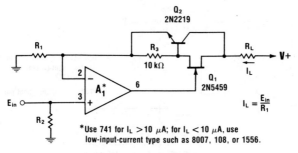

Fig. 4-35. Positive-input, buffered-FET VCCS.

In all of the preceding VCCS circuits with improved accuracy, the general considerations regarding the op amp used should follow the points that were discussed for the circuit of Fig. 4-30, since they are modifications of this basic configuration. In all cases, R_1 is selected to provide the desired output current with a full-scale input voltage in accordance with the equation,

$$I_L = \frac{E_{in}}{R_1}.$$

If desired, the accuracy improvement techniques can also be applied to the inverting configurations of Figs. 4-31 and 4-32. This involves substitution of the appropriate control element (Darlington, FET, or buffered FET) for Q_1 of Figs. 4-31 and 4-32. The equations for I_L remain the same as stated in the respective illustrations.

Current Sources With Loads Referred to More-Negative Supply Potentials

So far, we have discussed a series of circuits which drive loads referred to a positive supply potential. Often, however, the load may be referred to a negative supply potential, with a constant-current source required to drive it, as described previously. In this section, we will discuss an equivalent series of circuits for negative referred loads, together with the types of devices used. Circuit operation is the same as described for the positive counterparts (except for voltage polarities), so a minimum of explanation accompanies these circuits.

Negative-Input VCCS. The basic circuit for a VCCS with a load referred to a more-negative supply potential is shown in Fig. 4-36. This circuit responds to negative voltage inputs to generate an output current,

$$I_L = \frac{E_{in}}{R_1},$$

which, in principle, is exactly the same as the circuit of Fig. 4-30. In

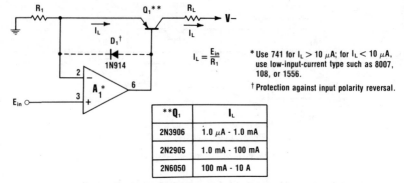

$$I_L = \frac{E_{in}}{R_1}$$

* Use 741 for $I_L > 10\ \mu A$; for $I_L < 10\ \mu A$, use low-input-current type such as 8007, 108, or 1556.

† Protection against input polarity reversal.

**Q$_1$	I$_L$
2N3906	1.0 μA - 1.0 mA
2N2905	1.0 mA - 100 mA
2N6050	100 mA - 10 A

Fig. 4-36. Basic negative-input VCCS; load referred to V−.

the circuit of Fig. 4-36, however, Q_1 is a pnp transistor, which allows R_L to be returned to a V− potential. The same considerations for amplifier selection apply to this circuit as for the circuit of Fig. 4-30, and typical devices suitable for operation at different currents are also listed in Fig. 4-36. Input polarity reversal can be a problem in this circuit also; protection is provided by the reverse-clamping diode, D_1, if needed.

Positive-Input VCCS. A VCCS which responds to positive input voltages to drive a load referred to V− is shown in Fig. 4-37. This circuit is the complement of the circuit of Fig. 4-31 and generates an output current equal to the input current,

$$I_L = \frac{E_{in}}{R_1}.$$

This circuit can be modified to provide a current "gain," as shown in Fig. 4-38.

Improved Accuracy VCCSs for Negative Referred Loads. The three basic configurations of Figs. 4-36, 4-37, and 4-38 are subject to the same inaccuracies as those described for the circuits of Figs. 4-30, 4-31, and 4-32. This problem is solved for the circuits of Figs. 4-36,

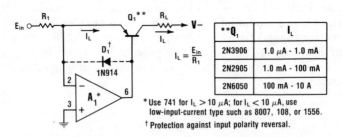

$$I_L = \frac{E_{in}}{R_1}$$

**Q$_1$	I$_L$
2N3906	1.0 μA - 1.0 mA
2N2905	1.0 mA - 100 mA
2N6050	100 mA - 10 A

* Use 741 for $I_L > 10\ \mu A$; for $I_L < 10\ \mu A$, use low-input-current type such as 8007, 108, or 1556.

† Protection against input polarity reversal.

Fig. 4-37. Basic positive-input VCCS; load referred to V−.

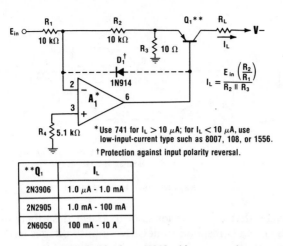

Fig. 4-38. Positive-input VCCS with current gain.

$$I_L = \frac{E_{in}\left(\frac{R_2}{R_1}\right)}{R_2 \parallel R_3}$$

*Use 741 for $I_L > 10\ \mu A$; for $I_L < 10\ \mu A$, use low-input-current type such as 8007, 108, or 1556.

†Protection against input polarity reversal.

**Q_1	I_L
2N3906	1.0 μA - 1.0 mA
2N2905	1.0 mA - 100 mA
2N6050	100 mA - 10 A

4-37, and 4-38 in a similar manner as for the circuits of Figs. 4-30, 4-31, and 4-32—by the use of higher-current-gain control elements, such as Darlington pairs, FETs, and buffered FETs.

Three circuits that eliminate this problem for negative referred loads are shown in Figs. 4-39, 4-40, and 4-41. These circuits operate essentially the same as their counterparts in Figs. 4-33, 4-34, and 4-35,

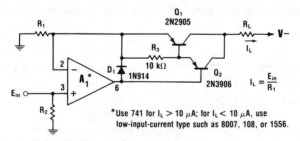

$$I_L = \frac{E_{in}}{R_1}$$

*Use 741 for $I_L > 10\ \mu A$; for $I_L < 10\ \mu A$, use low-input-current type such as 8007, 108, or 1556.

Fig. 4-39. Negative-input Darlington VCCS.

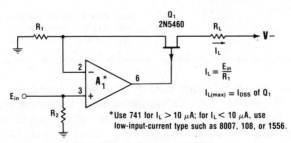

$$I_L = \frac{E_{in}}{R_1}$$

$I_{L(max)} = I_{DSS}$ of Q_1

*Use 741 for $I_L > 10\ \mu A$; for $I_L < 10\ \mu A$, use low-input-current type such as 8007, 108, or 1556.

Fig. 4-40. Negative-input FET VCCS.

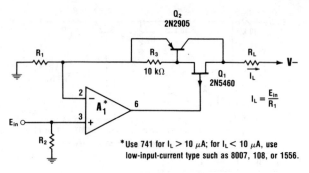

Fig. 4-41. Negative-input, buffered-FET VCCS.

using devices that are complements to those described previously. All of these circuits respond to negative input voltages to develop an output current,

$$I_L = \frac{E_{in}}{R_1}.$$

4.2.4 Bidirectional-Output VCCS

The final category of VCCS is the most general-purpose type of all. It will drive a load referred to ground (or any voltage within its linear output range) with either polarity of output current, and it

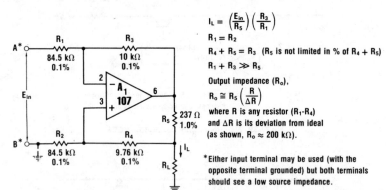

Fig. 4-42. General-purpose, bidirectional-output VCCS with single-terminal load drive.

can be operated from either polarity of input voltage. The circuit is shown in Fig. 4-42. It uses a combination of positive and negative feedback to sense the voltage across R_5, which is proportional to the output current. By maintaining the drop across R_5 constant, the output current is maintained constant regardless of any variations in R_L.

The output current of the circuit is controlled by R_5, R_3, R_1, and E_{in} as,

$$I_L = \left(\frac{E_{in}}{R_5}\right)\left(\frac{R_3}{R_1}\right).$$

In practice, the value for R_5 is selected to drop 1 to 2 volts at the desired load current, in order to minimize the loss of amplifier output. The total resistance of $R_1 + R_3$ is made large in relation to R_5 (100 times or more), and the arms of the bridge formed by R_1-R_3 and R_2-$R_4 + R_5$ are made equal; that is, $R_1 = R_2$, and $R_3 = R_4 + R_5$. Close-tolerance, precision resistors are required for a high output impedance, as indicated in the expression for R_0:

$$R_0 \cong R_5\left(\frac{R}{\Delta R}\right),$$

where,

R is any resistor $(R_1$-$R_4)$,
ΔR is its deviation from ideal.

The circuit responds to negative voltages at input A to generate 5.0 mA of source current for a 10-V input signal. Positive voltages at input A will result in the opposite polarity of output, or sink current. Reversal of input-voltage response may be accomplished by grounding input A and applying the signal to input B. In any case, the source impedance seen at the A and B inputs should be low in relation to R_1 and R_3 so as not to upset the balance.

For very low input voltages, the amplifier should be nulled or an amplifier that has a low V_{io} specification should be chosen. Currents in excess of standard op-amp output currents are possible by using a bipolar booster stage, such as the one shown in Fig. 4-28.

REFERENCES

1. *Applications Manual for Computing Amplifiers.* Philbrick Researches, Inc., Dedham, Mass., 1966.

2. *Applications of OEI Products.* Optical Electronics, Inc., Tucson, Ariz., 1971.

3. Barna, A. *Operational Amplifiers.* John Wiley & Sons, Inc., New York, 1971.

4. Birman, P. *Power Supply Handbook.* Kepco, Inc., Flushing, N. Y.

5. Clayton, G. B. *Operational Amplifiers.* Butterworth, Inc., Toronto, Ont., Canada, 1971.

6. *DC Power Supply Handbook.* Hewlett-Packard Co., Palo Alto, Calif., 1970.

7. Dobkin, R. C. *High Stability Regulators.* National Semiconductor LB-15, January 1971. National Semiconductor Corp., Santa Clara, Calif.

8. Kesner, D. *Regulators Using Operational Amplifiers.* Motorola Application Note AN-480, October 1970. Motorola Semiconductor Products, Inc., Phoenix, Ariz.

9. Miller, W. "Single Amplifier Current Sources." *Analog Dialogue,* Vol. 1, April 1967.

10. Nelson, C. *Monolithic Regulator Specifications.* Teledyne Semiconductor Application Note, 1971. Teledyne Semiconductor, Mountain View, Calif.

11. Scott, M. *Circuit Building Blocks for Voltage Regulators.* Fairchild Application Note, 1968. Fairchild Semiconductor, Mountain View, Calif.

12. Tobey, G. E.; Graeme, J. G.; Huelsman, L. P. *Operational Amplifiers—Design and Applications.* Burr-Brown Research Corp., McGraw-Hill Book Co., New York, 1971.

5

Signal-Processing Circuits

The broadest application area imaginable is one that is ideally suited to IC op amps. This is the general area of signal processing, where a circuit "operates" on an input signal to create a new form of output signal, altered in some manner from the original. Included in this area are such common functions as rectification, clipping, logarithmic or antilogarithmic conversions, phase shifting, filtering, and many others. The basic functions of dc and ac amplification are signal processing in a general sense, but since they are covered elsewhere, they will not be detailed here except in special senses. Signal processing as treated in this chapter encompasses those "specialty" functions which, although common circuit techniques, do not fall into any other category.

Several circuits have been adapted or modified from material supplied by the IC manufacturers. Figs. 5-16, 5-33 through 5-36, 5-54 through 5-57, and 5-59 originate from National Semiconductor data sheets. Figs. 5-70 through 5-75 are adapted from material supplied by Motorola.

5.1 THE PRECISION DIODE

A popular and useful signal-processing circuit is the precision diode circuit shown in Fig. 5-1A. This circuit is basically a voltage follower with a diode inside the feedback loop to confine its operation to half of the input signal swing, thus accomplishing half-wave rectification. D_1 is the rectifier diode, which conducts on input potentials higher than zero, forming a unity-gain replica of the input during the positive half cycle. During the negative half cycle, D_1 switches off and the output is zero.

The nonlinearity and temperature sensitivity of D_1 is not seen in the output waveform, because it is removed by feedback around the op amp. Furthermore, the circuit will not have a minimum forward threshold voltage, as does a conventional diode, because the high amplifier gain will automatically adjust the voltage drive to the diode so that the rectified output is accurately maintained—even at millivolt input levels.

The limitations of the circuit are defined by the op amp used and are speed related. Since the feedback loop is broken when D_1 switches off, the amplifier alternates between half cycles of open- and closed-loop operation. The time it takes for A_1 to settle into a stable output condition after D_1 turns on is limited by the slewing rate and bandwidth of the amplifier, particularly since A_1 must be compensated for unity gain because it operates as a voltage follower when D_1 is on.

In a 101-type amplifier, part of the speed problem can be solved by using an optional "catch" diode, D_2, to clamp the amplifier in the open-loop state so that it cannot saturate. Without saturation, the amplifier recovery time is many times faster. A 101 or 107 will operate in this circuit up to approximately 1 kHz with full output. Beyond this frequency, a faster-slewing type should be used.

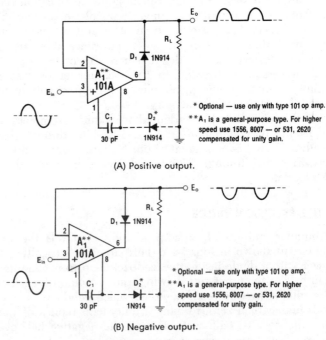

(A) Positive output.

(B) Negative output.

Fig. 5-1. Precision diode circuits.

A lesser problem of the circuit is its high output impedance during the inactive period. The output and D_1 are floating during this time, so a resistive load to ground (R_L) is necessary if it is not provided by succeeding circuitry.

The same general philosophy is also applicable to the sister circuit of Fig. 5-1B, arranged to rectify the negative-going portions of the input signal. This is accomplished merely by reversing D_1 (and D_2, if used).

A word of caution: Do not attempt to use this circuit with low differential-input-voltage op amps such as the 709, 118, or 108, since the input voltage differential is high during the period when the loop is open. High-differential-input devices such as the 101 and 741 families are necessary to prevent input breakdown.

5.2 PRECISION CLIPPERS

Such a basically useful circuit as the precision rectifier, described in Section 5.1, naturally has variations. In this case they are numerous and all are very useful.

5.2.1 Simplified Series Clipper

One very slight variation of the circuits in Figs. 5-1A and B turns them into precision clippers. This is shown in Fig. 5-2. The circuit works by varying the output base line during the period when diode D_1 is off. Since D_1 will conduct whenever the noninverting input is higher than the inverting input, it follows that the input threshold need not necessarily be ground (as in the circuits of Fig. 5-1). By varying the input reference, a clipper (biased rectifier) may be made. This is accomplished merely by returning R_L to a voltage other than ground. In the circuit of Fig. 5-2A, which is a positive-peak clipper, the output will be a replica of those portions lower than the reference voltage. The circuit requires a low-impedance source for reference, particularly if clamp D_2 is used. A negative-peak clipper can be implemented merely by reversing D_1 (and D_2, if used), as shown in Fig. 5-2B. Note that in both cases there is no restraint on the reference voltage as long as it is within the input range of A_1. The output will follow the input whenever the input exceeds V_{ref}. External loading on R_L has the effect of reducing the reference voltage due to voltage division, so the circuit may require an output buffer amplifier, such as a 110 voltage follower.

5.2.2 Self-Buffered Series Clipper (Linear OR Gate)

In situations where the high output impedance of the simple series clipper is a disadvantage, an alternate form of clipper is available (Fig. 5-3). In this circuit the output is always in a low-impedance

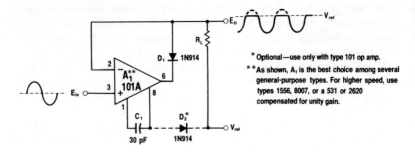

(A) Positive-peak clipper.

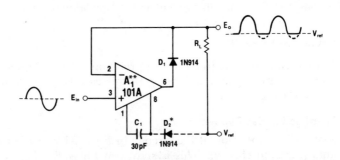

* Optional—use only with type 101 op amp.
** As shown, A₁ is the best choice among several general-purpose types.
For higher speed, use types 1556, 8007, or a 531 or 2620 compensated for unity gain.

(B) Negative-peak clipper.

Fig. 5-2. Precision clippers.

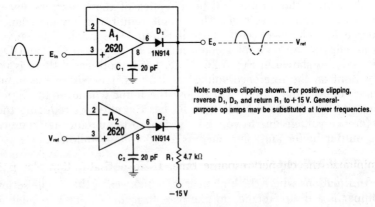

Note: negative clipping shown. For positive clipping, reverse D₁, D₂, and return R₁ to +15 V. General-purpose op amps may be substituted at lower frequencies.

Fig. 5-3. Self-buffered series clipper.

state, because one feedback loop is always closed (around either A_1 or A_2). The two diodes perform a gating function for the input signals, allowing whichever input is greater to pass to the output; thus the terminology, "linear OR." If E_{in} is greater than V_{ref}, A_1-D_1 will be on and E_{in} will appear at the output. When E_{in} falls below V_{ref}, A_1 turns D_1 off and A_2-D_2 provide the output signal, V_{ref}. The inputs are interchangeable, due to the complete symmetry of the circuit.

Because both amplifiers are switching as the input signal goes through threshold, the response time of this circuit is slowed considerably with general-purpose amplifiers, although they may be useful below 100 Hz. The faster 2620, however, gives good performance to above 10 kHz. A positive clipping action can be obtained by reversing D_1 and D_2, and returning R_1 to +15 V. This circuit is useful when the clipping potential must be precise, when a low-impedance reference source is not available, or when a low output impedance is necessary.

5.2.3 Shunt Clipper

A shunt clipper can be formed by yet another variation on the basic precision diode. This is diagrammed in Fig. 5-4. When E_{in} is

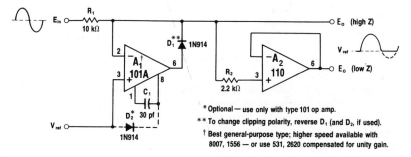

Fig. 5-4. Shunt clipper.

above the reference voltage applied to the noninverting input of A_1, D_1 will be reverse biased and E_{in} will pass unaffected through R_1 to the output. When a negative peak of E_{in} exceeds V_{ref}, A_1 drives D_1 on and absorbs the input current from R_1, clamping the output at the V_{ref} level.

The same considerations for speed apply to this circuit as to the basic one of Fig. 5-1A. An antisaturation clamp (D_2) is useful to minimize the clipper response time. If an antisaturation clamp is used, it requires a low source impedance from V_{ref}. A clipper of opposite polarity can be constructed by reversing D_1 (and D_2, if used).

Due to the high output impedance (essentially the value of R_1), this clipper will usually require a buffer amplifier. A 110 high-speed voltage follower will work well with no additional sacrifice in operating speed.

5.3 DC RESTORER

Yet another useful variation of the ideal rectifier is the dc restorer or peak clamper of Fig. 5-5. This circuit charges C_1 to a voltage that clamps the input waveform peak at V_{ref}. When E_{in} swings negative (below V_{ref}), A_1 drives D_1 on, forming a low-impedance path to charge C_1. After the peak has passed and D_1 is turned off again, the charge on C_1 is retained, since the only bleed paths are the input currents of A_1 and A_2. This gives the circuit a fast-attack, slow-decay response to input level changes. Faster recovery between level

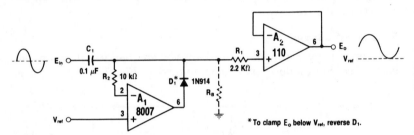

Fig. 5-5. Dc restorer (peak clamper).

changes is accomplished by a shunt resistance to ground (R_B), with some sacrifice in clamping precision. As with the precision diode, this circuit is responsive into the millivolt region, due to the high gain of A_1 driving D_1. The circuit as shown clamps negative peaks to V_{ref}, but positive-peak clamping is possible by reversing D_1. The value of C_1 may be changed to accommodate different input rates and pulse widths.

5.4 HALF-WAVE RECTIFIER

Fig. 5-6 is a half-wave rectifier that produces an inverted half-wave replica of the input signal. For negative input signals at R_1, the output is positive, forward biasing D_1 and closing a negative feedback loop through R_2. This produces an inverted gain of almost exactly one, since R_1 and R_2 are closely matched. For positive input signals, the amplifier output is negative and D_1 is off. D_2 is on in this case, applying negative feedback to the summing point and clamping the op-amp output to −0.6 V. This clamped output swing

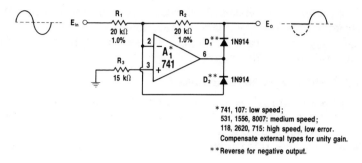

Fig. 5-6. Basic half-wave rectifier.

aids in minimizing response time, because it prevents amplifier saturation.

With a 741, this circuit will be useful at frequencies up to approximately 1 kHz. Again, output impedance is nonuniform—low when D_1 is on and essentially 20 kΩ (or R_2) when D_1 is off. Negative rectified outputs are possible by reversing D_1 and D_2. Operation at higher frequencies is improved by using one of the faster amplifiers listed.

5.4.1 High-Speed Rectifier

Many applications demand a rectifier having good fidelity at frequencies far above a few kilohertz. This may be achieved with fast-slewing, wide-bandwidth amplifier configurations. The general-purpose 101A-type amplifier has an alternate form of compensation, termed *feedforward*, which is very useful in inverting applications; it allows rectification with low errors at frequencies up to 100 kHz. Since this circuit is an inverting configuration, feedforward compensation can be used as shown in Fig. 5-7. In this case C_1 is the compensation capacitor. The circuit can be modified for a negative-

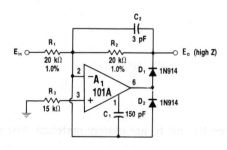

Fig. 5-7. Fast half-wave rectifier.

going output by reversing D_1 and D_2. Due to the higher operating frequencies involved, oscillations are a potential problem. Therefore, a good layout and careful attention to power-supply bypassing are important considerations (see Chapter 3).

5.4.2 Rectifier With Buffered Output

Both of the previous rectifier circuits work in a similar fashion (except for response time), and they both have the slight problem of a nonuniform output impedance between alternations. For applications where this could be troublesome, the circuit of Fig. 5-8

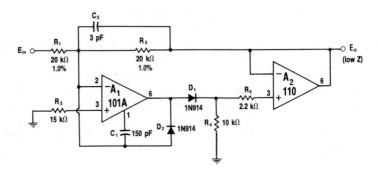

Fig. 5-8. Fast buffered rectifier.

can be used. This circuit contains a 110-type, high-speed voltage follower (A_2) within the feedback loop of A_1; the function of A_2 is to maintain a low output impedance. During positive output alternations, D_1 and R_4 rectify the signal; A_2 "follows" this signal, returning feedback to the input through R_2. On opposite alternations, D_1 is off and the feedback loop of A_2 is closed through D_2. However, the output terminal is maintained at a low impedance by A_2, which sees a ground-level signal from R_4 during this period. As with previous circuits, opposite output polarity is obtainable by reversing D_1 and D_2. Also, the buffering property of A_2 can be applied to either circuit —Fig. 5-6 or Fig. 5-7—with equally good results.

5.5 FULL-WAVE PRECISION RECTIFIER

A full-wave precision rectifier is generally implemented by summing the output of a half-wave rectifier and its input with the proper phase and amplitude relations. Such a circuit is shown in Fig. 5-9.

In this circuit, A_1 is an inverting rectifier similar to that of Fig. 5-6. The output from A_1 is added to the original input signal in A_2 (a summing mixer), with the signal amplitude and phase relations shown. Positive alternations of E_{in} result in no output at E_1 due to the rectification. E_{in} feeds A_2 through a 20-kΩ resistor, and E_1 is fed through a 10-kΩ resistor. The net effect of this scaling is that, for equal amplitudes of E_{in} and E_1, E_1 will produce twice as much current flow into the summing point. This fact is used to advantage here, as the positive alternation of E_1 produces twice the input current of that caused by E_{in}. This causes a current of precisely half the amplitude which E_1 alone would generate due to the subtraction of E_{in}. It is the equivalent of having E_1 feed through a 20-kΩ input resistor and having E_{in} nonexistent during this half cycle, and it results in a negative-going output at A_2. During positive alternations of E_{in}, E_1 is absent and E_{in} produces the alternate output swing which, in summation, produces the desired full-wave rectified response.

As before, operation with the opposite output polarity is possible by reversing D_1 and D_2.

5.5.1 High-Speed Rectifier

In the circuit of Fig. 5-9, faster operation is possible by using the alternate devices listed. Operation up to 100 kHz can be attained with the feedforward circuit in Fig. 5-10, using general-purpose devices.

5.5.2 Filtered Rectifiers

Any of the previous full-wave rectifiers can, with a minimum of complexity, be converted to a version having a dc-averaged output, as shown in Fig. 5-11.

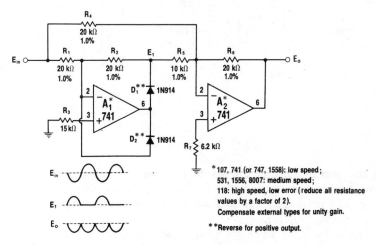

Fig. 5-9. Basic full-wave precision rectifier.

This circuit is nearly identical to the full-wave circuits described before; any one of the half-wave circuits already described (Figs. 5-6, 5-7, and 5-8) can be used as the first stage. The addition of C_1 across R_3-R_5 converts A_1 to a low-pass filter that averages the input signals from R_1 and R_2, thus developing a dc output voltage propor-

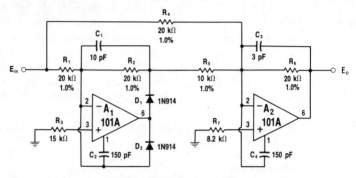

Fig. 5-10. Fast full-wave rectifier.

tional to the full-wave rectified input. Resistor R_5 is added in series with R_3 to make the total feedback resistance greater by the difference between rms and average ac. This allows the output to be calibrated for a dc voltage equal to the rms value of the input. Capacitor C_1 and resistors R_3-R_5 establish the RC time constant of the low-pass filter. This time constant must be appreciably longer than the period

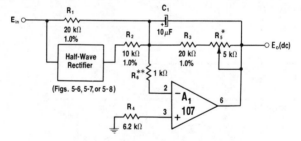

* Adjust to calibrate dc output equal to rms value of E_{in}.
** Use R_6 (≥ 1 kΩ) if $C_1 \geq 0.1$ μF.

Fig. 5-11. Filtered full-wave rectifier.

of the lowest input frequency to be measured. The values shown give 1.0% accuracy down to 20 Hz, and if a feedforward circuit (Fig. 5-7) is used for the half-wave rectifier, this accuracy is maintained up to 100 kHz.

The circuit can be used with either polarity of input rectifier, observing the appropriate polarity for C_1 if it is an electrolytic type.

5.6 PEAK DETECTORS

Peak detectors measure the maximum value of a fluctuating voltage. In this section we will examine three op-amp circuits for accomplishing this function.

5.6.1 Basic Peak Detector

The basic peak detector using an op amp is shown in Fig. 5-12. This circuit operates like an ideal diode, but with the addition of C_1 to store a dc voltage equal to the peak input voltage value. As the input signal crosses zero, A_1 will drive D_1 on and the circuit output will follow the rising signal slope. When the input signal reaches a peak and reverses its slope, C_1 is left in a charged state. In the absence of any bleed resistor to discharge C_1, the only means of discharge is the bias current at the inverting $(-)$ input of A_1.

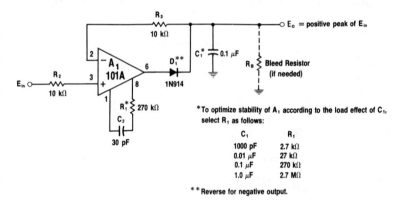

Fig. 5-12. Basic peak detector.

Since the circuit operates with 100% feedback when the loop is closed, unity-gain compensation is necessary for A_1. The rate of voltage rise across C_1 is either I_{max}/C_1 (volts/second, where I_{max} is the short-circuit current of A_1), or the slewing rate of A_1 (volts/second), whichever is smaller.

Unless C_1 is extremely large ($\cong 50$ μF) and used alone (without C_2) for compensation, it will introduce instability (oscillations). The resulting oscillations show up as "chatter"; A_1 tries to drive C_1 to the peak of the input voltage, but the oscillation causes D_1 to switch rapidly on and off. The solution to this problem is to compensate the RC time constant introduced by r_o-C_1 with a resistance in series with C_2. The break frequency of this resistor and C_2 is chosen to occur at the same frequency as $r_o C_1$. This technique restores the 6-dB/octave net slope originally provided by C_2. A table of typical values is given, which can be used with any of the circuits in this section. These values are recommended for optimum stability.

Resistor R_3 (Fig. 5-12) is used to protect the input of A_1 against dangerously large discharge currents from C_1 when the power supply is switched off; R_3 is particularly necessary if C_1 is 0.1 μF or greater. R_2 is included to balance the effect of R_3.

C_1 can be reset with a switch, either manually or electronically via a normally off transistor. Alternately, if a fast-attack, slow-decay response is tolerable, connecting a bleed resistance (R_B) across C_1 will also deplete the charge. Peak reading of negative-polarity signals is possible by reversing D_1.

5.6.2 Buffered Peak Detector

When extremely long holding times are required of a peak detector, the bleed-off leakage of C_1 becomes important. Therefore, to minimize this discharge current, C_1 is usually buffered (Fig. 5-13)

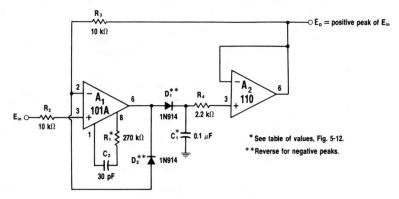

Fig. 5-13. Buffered peak detector.

by a low-input-current voltage follower, A_2. A type-110 used here will require an input current of only about 1 nA (leakage drain current from C_1), so the voltage discharge rate for C_1 will be

$$\frac{\Delta V}{\Delta t} = \frac{I}{C} = \frac{10^{-9}\,A}{10^{-6}\,F} = 1\ mV/s.$$

If discharge rates below this are required, a FET-input amplifier can be used for A_2. However, these have the disadvantage of an input current that nearly doubles in value with every 10°C of temperature rise; thus at high operating temperatures, some FET types may offer little improvement in stability.

Amplifier A_2 in this circuit provides the input bias current for A_1 as well as the output current. R_3 is included here to allow A_1 to be clamped in the off state by D_2, resulting in faster recovery. R_4 is included to protect A_2 from discharge transients. R_2 and R_1-C_2 perform functions here similar to those described for Fig. 5-12. Negative peaks can be measured with this circuit by reversing D_1 and D_2.

5.6.3 Inverting Peak Detector

In some applications it may be necessary to measure the peak value of a signal by using a dc voltage of opposite polarity. This requirement is satisfied by an inverting peak detector such as the one shown in Fig. 5-14. The circuit is similar to Fig. 5-13, but with the

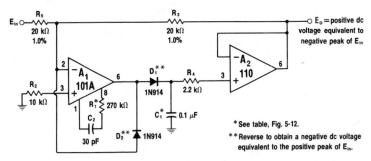

Fig. 5-14. Inverting peak detector.

important difference that the input signal is applied to the inverting input of A_1 rather than to the noninverting input, which is grounded through R_2 in this case. When E_{in} swings negative, A_1-D_1 and the A_2-R_3 feedback loop will follow until the peak value is reached. At the peak negative swing, C_1 will be charged to the corresponding positive voltage. When E_{in} reverses slope after a peak, A_1 switches D_1 off—C_1 now retains the peak voltage. A_2 buffers the voltage across C_1 in a fashion similar to the noninverting circuit, and negative feedback is returned to the summing point through R_3.

The use of a buffer amplifier in this inverting circuit is mandatory, otherwise R_3 would be a direct shunt across C_1; this would shorten the discharge time constant drastically. The rest of the components of Fig. 5-14 perform functions similar to their counterparts in Fig. 5-13. Again, opposite polarity operation is obtained by reversing D_1 and D_2.

5.7 SAMPLE-AND-HOLD CIRCUITS

A sample-and-hold circuit is one having two basic operational states; one in which an input signal is sampled and thus transmitted to the output, and a second in which the last value sampled is held until the input is sampled again.

5.7.1 Basic Operation

The basic circuit operation is diagrammed in Fig. 5-15. In Fig. 5-15A, an input signal (E_{in}) is applied to electronic switch S_1 and, depending on the state of S_1, will be either transmitted to C_1 or blocked. The state of switch S_1 is controlled by the sample/hold control line. When S_1 is closed, the input signal appears across C_1, is buffered by A_1, and also appears at the output. If S_1 is connected

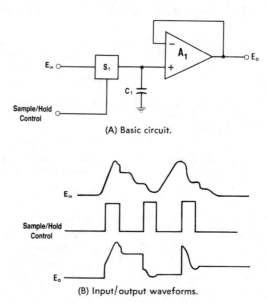

(A) Basic circuit.

(B) Input/output waveforms.

Fig. 5-15. Sample/hold operation.

for a period of time while E_{in} is varying, as with an ac waveform, the operation may also be said to be *tracking* E_{in}; any input changes are transmitted to the output. When S_1 is opened, the latest value of E_{in} is retained on C_1 as a charge, and A_1 continues to read this voltage until the next sample period. This is illustrated by the waveforms in Fig. 5-15B. Sample/hold circuits are used for a wide variety of signal-processing functions, such as data-handling systems, analog/digital interfaces, etc.

5.7.2 Low-Drift Sample/Hold Circuit

The circuit of Fig. 5-16 is an example of a sample/hold design, obviously different from the simplified circuit of Fig. 5-15, but for good reason. The resistance of the switch used in a simple circuit such as the one of Fig. 5-15 can contribute errors due to offset and nonlinearity; also, this finite resistance limits the charging rate of C_1. Another big source of error is "droop," or the discharge rate of C_1, as discussed under peak detectors. This is usually minimized by a feedback configuration using a low-input-current FET (Q_2) as a buffer for holding capacitor C_1 and by placing the switch, Q_1, within the feedback loop. A_1 serves both as an input signal buffer, and as a driver for switch Q_1 and capacitor C_1. When the sample line is raised to +15 V, D_1 is reverse biased and Q_1 is turned on by virtue of a zero gate-source bias. This closes the loop around A_1-C_1; A_1 will now drive Q_1-C_1 until the output terminal reaches equilibrium with the input—that is, A_1 is tracking the input. Any offsets across Q_1 and Q_2 are balanced by the negative feedback, which will force C_1 to assume a charge such that $E_o = E_{in}$. Loop stability is enhanced by resistance R_1, which cancels the RC break frequency formed by C_1 and the minimum resistance of Q_1.

When the sample pulse goes low, D_1 becomes forward biased and pulls the gate of Q_1 toward −15 V. In this state, the channel resistance of Q_1 is extremely high and the feedback loop of A_1 is effectively opened. The output, however, will continue to rest at the voltage last sampled, since C_1 will retain its charge and Q_2 will continue to buffer this voltage and present it to the output. With the low-leakage devices specified for Q_1 and Q_2, the droop in output voltage will be approximately 1 mV/s at room temperature.

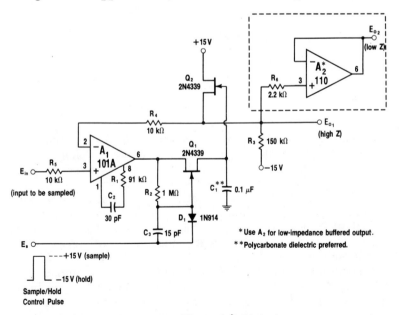

Fig. 5-16. Low-drift sample/hold circuit.

The circuit output current at E_{o_1} is limited by the small current through Q_2, but it can easily be buffered with a voltage follower if needed (shown as an option).

5.8 FEEDBACK LIMITERS

In a signal chain it is often necessary to symmetrically limit or "bound" the peak amplifier output. It is usually desirable to do this before the amplifier reaches saturation voltage, because saturation almost always involves a long recovery time before the amplifier can operate linearly once again. Many applications require peak limiting for other reasons—such as, for example, to interface the op-amp output to digital logic circuits. The positive or negative limit required for digital logic is usually much lower than the typical op-amp voltage swing.

5.8.1 General-Purpose Unipolar Limiter

Fig. 5-17 shows a feedback limiter that is very useful in converting linear input signals to logic levels. This circuit uses a zener diode in

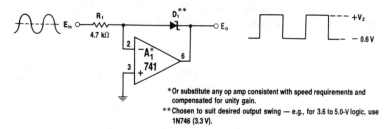

*Or substitute any op amp consistent with speed requirements and compensated for unity gain.
**Chosen to suit desired output swing — e.g., for 3.6 to 5.0-V logic, use 1N746 (3.3 V).

Fig. 5-17. Unipolar feedback limiter.

the feedback loop of an inverter, establishing the limits of the output voltage as equal to the zener forward and reverse voltages. If the input is more positive than ground, the output of A_1 swings negative and forward biases D_1, causing feedback current in D_1 to the summing point. This sets the negative output limit at 0.6 V, equal to the forward voltage drop of D_1. When E_{in} swings negative, the output of A_1 goes positive and the current through D_1 reverses, driving it into the breakdown region and clamping the positive output at the zener voltage, V_Z.

Note that the circuit will have a high gain at low input levels, because D_1 will have a high reverse impedance below the breakdown voltage. This tends to amplify low-level inputs, but only up to the level of V_Z, where the output is clamped by the breakdown of

D_1. As a result, the circuit maintains the output swing at the limit of the diode over a rather wide range of input amplitudes.

The output voltage is equal to that of the diode used and may be reversed by reversing D_1. Due to the essentially 100% feedback through the low impedance of D_1, the op amp used must be compensated for unity gain.

5.8.2 Bipolar Zener Limiter

The unipolar limiter of Fig. 5-17 is actually a special case; the more general form of zener limiter is shown in Fig. 5-18.

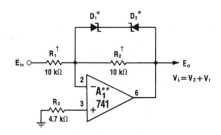

*Matched pair to suit required limit voltage — e.g., 1N758 for $E_o = \pm 10$ V.
** Any op amp compensated for unity gain.
† Selected according to gain requirement.

Fig. 5-18. Bipolar zener limiter.

This circuit limits the op-amp output swing in either direction to the value of $V_Z + V_f$, where V_Z and V_f are the zener- and forward-breakdown voltage of D_1 and D_2. With matched zener voltages, the positive and negative limiting levels will be symmetrical. For example, using 10-V zeners for D_1 and D_2, the output swing of A_1 will be limited at slightly over 10 volts (10.0 + 0.6 volts); this allows a linear ±10-V swing, but still avoids saturation of A_1. Below the breakdown potentials of D_1 and D_2, the amplifier operates as if they were not there, with gain determined by R_1 and R_2 in the conventional fashion. The degree of limiting, or "hardness," is determined by the ratio of the zener network impedance to the resistance of R_2. If the value of R_2 is high in relation to the combined impedances of D_1 and D_2, the limiting will be sharp with little rounding; typical R_2 values of 10 kΩ or above give very sharp limiting.

5.8.3 Bipolar Limiter With Adjustable Level

One drawback in designing symmetrical zener limiters is that zener diodes generally have imprecise breakdown voltages, and hence are difficult to match. If accurate symmetry is desired, one solution is the circuit of Fig. 5-19, which uses a matched pair of monolithic diodes and has an adjustable limit voltage.

A typical pair of monolithic IC transistors will have emitter-base breakdown voltages that match within a few percent or less. Also, the temperature coefficient (TC) of the matched pair will be small, typically less than 1 mV/°C. In Fig. 5-19A, a small fraction (β) of the op-amp output voltage (E_o) is fed to D_1-D_2 through R_4. Resistor

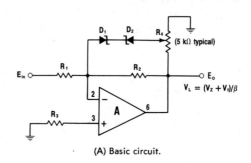

(A) Basic circuit.

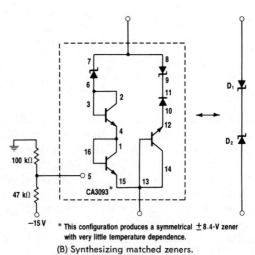

* This configuration produces a symmetrical ± 8.4-V zener
with very little temperature dependence.

(B) Synthesizing matched zeners.

Fig. 5-19. Adjustable bipolar limiter.

R_4 is adjusted to set the limit voltage, which can range from zero to about 10 volts. R_4 should have a relatively low impedance (typically 5 kΩ), so that this resistance will not appreciably affect the output voltage as the output current changes. Fig. 5-19B shows how the matched zener pair can be generated from a CA3093 chip. With the values shown, $V_L \cong \pm 8.4$ V, and the zeners track very well with temperature.

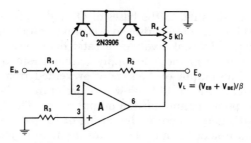

Fig. 5-20. High-speed limiter using transistor junctions.

5.8.4 Transistor Junction Limiter

For very high speed in a general-purpose limiter, transistor emitter-base junctions can be used effectively, because they have a low capacitance. Such a limiter configuration is illustrated in Fig. 5-20. The 2N3906 transistors provide a limit voltage, V_L, of about ± 7 V; again, this value can be varied by adjusting R_4.

5.8.5 Zener Bridge Limiter

A single zener diode is sometimes used for symmetrical limiting by placing it in a diode bridge so that it conducts on both polarities of the output swing. This is illustrated in Fig. 5-21. The diodes can be ordinary general-purpose types such as the 1N914, unless very precise symmetry is required; monolithic diode bridges will provide more accurate symmetry, if needed.

5.8.6 Transistor Feedback Limiter

One circuit that avoids many of the variability problems associated with zener diodes, yet is still a very effective voltage limiter, is diagrammed in Fig. 5-22. This circuit returns current to the op-amp summing point through emitter follower Q_1 and Q_2.

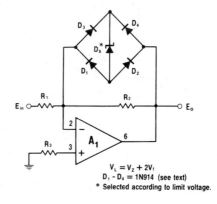

Fig. 5-21. Diode bridge limiter using one zener.

A fraction of E_o is fed to the bases of Q_1 and Q_2 from the tap of divider R_4. When the output rises to a positive voltage high enough so that the tap of R_4 is at a voltage greater than the V_{BE} of Q_1, Q_1 conducts current from the V+ supply terminal into the summing point of A_1. The output of A_1 is now prevented from rising to a higher voltage, as this would result in more current through Q_1 to the summing point, cutting off the output of A_1. The limit voltage of this circuit is determined by the setting of R_4 and the V_{BE} of Q_1. Q_2 performs a function similar to Q_1 for negative signal swings.

Although shown as a variable, symmetrical limiter with a single adjustment (R_4), the circuit can easily be equipped with independent positive and negative limiting. This is done by adding another potentiometer connected between E_o and ground and by operating the two limit transistors from separate controls.

This circuit is capable of high speed due to the low impedances used in the limit circuitry and the moderately fast devices chosen for Q_1 and Q_2. To take advantage of this speed, a type-118 device is used as the amplifier, although general-purpose devices will suffice if speed is not essential. Also, the limit voltage is somewhat temperature-dependent, since it varies directly with the V_{BE} of Q_1 or Q_2.

Whenever single-polarity limiting is intended, it is recommended that a large resistance (R_B) be connected to the base of the remaining transistor; otherwise, this transistor could conduct heavily on opposite voltage swings and become damaged.

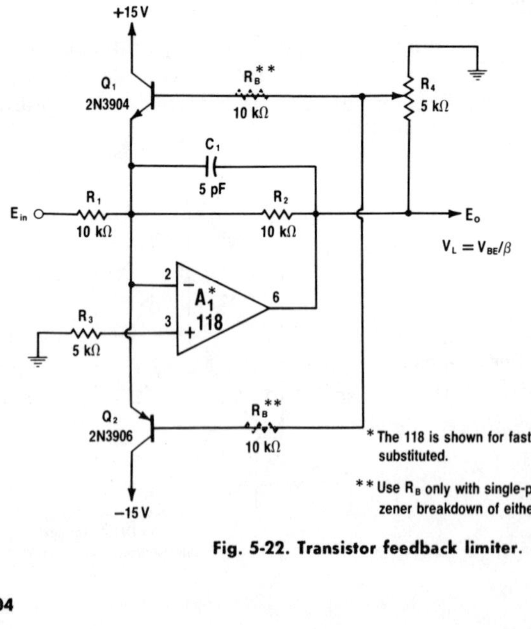

* The 118 is shown for fast response; other types can be substituted.

** Use R_B only with single-polarity limiting, to prevent zener breakdown of either transistor.

Fig. 5-22. Transistor feedback limiter.

5.9 DIODE BRIDGE CIRCUITS

5.9.1 Input Current Limiter

One of the most precise types of signal limiters is formed by passing the signal through a diode bridge, as shown in Fig. 5-23. Here diodes D_1 through D_4 are biased at a continuous current by R_4 and R_5, which are equal-value resistors connected to equal voltages. If D_1 through D_4 are all closely matched in characteristics, the dc potential at the bridge output (D_1-D_3 junction) can be connected directly to the summing point of A_1.

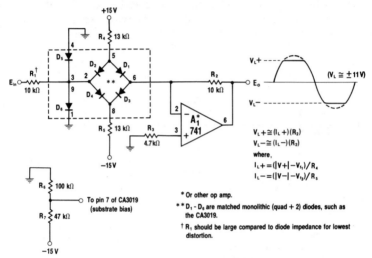

Fig. 5-23. Input current limiter.

Note that there is no direct path for the signal to take through the bridge to the summing point; instead, signal variations are transmitted to A_1 as variations in the currents supplied by R_4 and R_5. Limiting occurs when the input current in R_1 exceeds that capable of being transmitted by the bridge assembly. The bridge "opens," with D_2 and D_3 reverse biased on positive swings and D_1 and D_4 reverse biased on negative swings.

In this state, the entire current available from R_4 or R_5 is diverted through D_1 and D_3 on signal peaks, and the current from the opposite member (R_5 or R_4) is then passed through D_1 or D_3 to the summing point. In this manner, the bridge "peak limits" the input current to A_1 and so controls the output voltage of A_1.

The operation of a current-mode limiter such as this is very smooth and fast, with no "glitches" or overshoots as in voltage-switching limiters. This type is a good choice when the most abrupt limiting possible is desired. Diode nonlinearities do, however, introduce some distortion in the input signal, and this effect can be minimized by making R_1 large in relation to the diode impedance. As an example, the values shown give less than 0.5% distortion. The op amp used should be compensated for unity gain, because when the bridge opens, the feedback is nearly 100%.

The limiting current threshold of the circuit is set by the current in the bridge. With a given value of current flowing in R_4-R_5, the input and output voltages are set by the choices of R_1 and R_2, with the usual considerations for gain. The values shown are for clipping at ±11 volts of output and can, of course, be rescaled if desired. Higher-speed op amps in place of the 741 will take greater advantage of the inherently fast bridge switching capability.

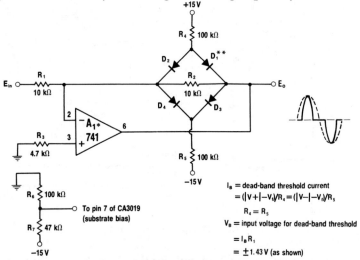

I_B = dead-band threshold current
$= (|V+|-V_t)/R_4 = (|V-|-V_t)/R_5$

$R_4 = R_5$

V_B = input voltage for dead-band threshold
$= I_B R_1$
$= ±1.43\,V$ (as shown)

* Or other op amp compensated for unity gain.

** D_1 – D_4 are matched monolithic diodes, such as the CA3019.
For peak voltage higher than ±7 V, use 1N914s.

Fig. 5-24. Dead-band circuit.

5.9.2 Feedback Circuit With Dead-Band Response

Advantage may be taken of the "current depletion" property of a diode bridge in other unusual circuits. For instance, in Fig. 5-24, the bridge is placed in the feedback loop such that for low-level input signals there is essentially 100% feedback around A_1, and very little voltage output. The only voltage appearing at the output is the relatively small swing required to modulate the current in the bridge as it passes the feedback current.

When the input current in R_1 becomes greater than the allowable current, however, the bridge opens and the output voltage "jumps" to a new level determined by R_2, and the input is amplified by the ratio of R_2/R_1 in a linear manner.

This feature gives the circuit a *dead-band* property for low levels, but when the bridge current is exceeded, the circuit amplifies normally. The current and voltage threshold at the input are determined as before, by selecting R_1 for an input current equal to the bridge current at the threshold level.

5.9.3 Variable Dead-Band Circuit

The previous circuit is easily modified to provide a controlled amount of dead-band response, as shown in Fig. 5-25. With R_2 shorted, this circuit is the same as Fig. 5-24. For low-level input signals, increasing the value of R_2 raises the voltage developed across it, which raises the dead-band level. The circuit gain for small signals is then $(R_2 \parallel R_3)/R_1$. For large signals, the bridge opens and R_2 is effectively removed from the circuit; therefore, the gain becomes R_3/R_1. Note that if R_2 is greater than R_3, the adjustment of R_2 will vary the dead-band level from minimum to nearly the full gain of the circuit. One use for such a circuit is in generating a variable and controlled amount of distortion.

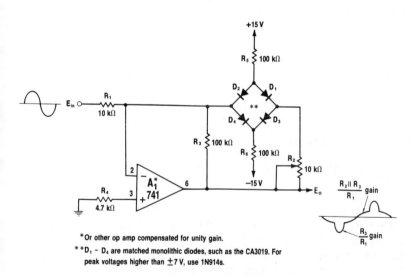

*Or other op amp compensated for unity gain.

**D_1 - D_4 are matched monolithic diodes, such as the CA3019. For peak voltages higher than ± 7 V, use 1N914s.

Fig. 5-25. Variable dead-band circuit.

5.10 VOLTAGE FOLLOWER WITH VARIABLE OFFSET

In some circuits it is necessary to shift the dc operating point between stages without losing signal level or loading the source. A circuit which accomplishes this is the variable-offset voltage follower of Fig. 5-26.

Diodes D_1 and D_2 provide a bias of ± 0.6 V about the output potential of A_1. Since the tap of R_1 is at the same potential as E_{in}, adjustment of R_1 allows the output to be varied by the diode drop of D_1 or D_2 (about ± 0.6 V). D_1 and D_2 have negligibly small impedances by comparison with R_2 and R_3, so there is little dynamic signal loss across this network and the gain is very close to unity. The circuit output will have a temperature coefficient equaling that of either diode, or approximately -2 mV/°C; this can be negligibly small if E_o is large, say several volts.

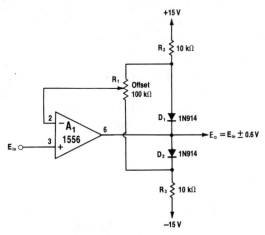

Fig. 5-26. Variable-offset voltage follower.

5.11 SIGN CHANGER

An interesting op-amp configuration is one that allows the choice of 0° or 180° phase reversal. This is the sign-changer circuit of Fig. 5-27.

The circuit can be best understood by visualizing the operational state at various positions of R_3. If the arm of R_3 is at ground, the circuit is an inverter, providing a 180° phase shift. If the arm is at E_{in}, E_{in} will appear at both inputs of A_1; therefore, both ends of R_1 are at the same potential, which implies no current in R_1. If this is true for R_1, it must also be true of R_2; therefore, R_2 will have a potential of E_{in} on both ends, which makes $E_o = E_{in}$. Positions of R_3 at intermediate settings provide gains reduced from these two extremes. For instance, at the midpoint of R_3, the circuit will be recognized as a differential amplifier with a voltage of $E_{in}/2$ at each input. In this case, the output will be zero, because the circuit rejects the common-

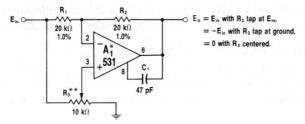

Fig. 5-27. Sign changer with variable output.

mode input signal (in proportion to the CMRR of A_1). R_3 may be calibrated for a linear variation from +1 through zero to −1, if desired.

The circuit can be used with a switch to select the choice of phase, as shown in Fig. 5-28, which allows remote programming.

5.12 LOGARITHMIC CONVERTERS

Some of the most useful circuit techniques with op amps are related to the use of logarithms: dynamic range compression, raising to powers or taking roots, rms conversion, and multiplier/divider circuits are only a few examples. Virtually all these operations de-

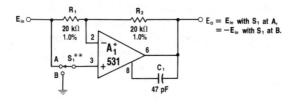

Fig. 5-28. Switch-selectable sign changer.

pend on the conversion of a linear voltage or current into a corresponding logarithmic value.

The heart of the analog logarithmic converter is the simple bipolar transistor. It is a highly useful fact that the base-emitter voltage, V_{BE}, of a silicon transistor is logarithmically related to the collector current over an extremely wide range. Using well-matched, monolothic transistors and IC op amps, it is possible to build log converters with a typical dynamic range of 5 decades (10^5 or 100 dB).

5.12.1 Transistor Logarithmic Characteristics

Since the pn junction is the basis of all the log converters to be discussed, some review of the basic mechanism is in order. The base-emitter voltage of a silicon planar transistor can be expressed as

$$V_{BE} = \frac{\kappa T}{q} \log_e \left(\frac{I_C}{I_o} \right)$$

where,

κ = Boltzman's constant (1.38×10^{-23} J/K),
T = absolute temperature (Kelvin),
q = charge on an electron (1.6×10^{-19} coulomb),
I_C = collector current,
I_o = theoretical reverse saturation current (10^{-13} A @ 27°C).

Stating the equation in terms of $\log_{10}$, it becomes

$$V_{BE} = \frac{2.3 \kappa T}{q} \log_{10} \left(\frac{I_C}{I_o} \right).$$

At T = 27°C the $\kappa T/q$ term is 26 mV, which yields

$$V_{BE} = 60 \text{ mV} \log_{10} \left(\frac{I_C}{I_o} \right).$$

This reduced expression may be stated quite simply: At 27°C, the V_{BE} of a silicon transistor will increase about 60 mV for each decade increase in I_C.

As stated previously, this relationship holds true over a wide range of voltages for low-leakage, high-gain transistors. The lower end of the dynamic range is limited by current gain (minimum I_C), while the upper end departs from logarithmic operation due to ohmic resistance drops above 10^{-2} to 10^{-3} A; exact figures depend upon the specific device.

5.12.2 Basic Transistor Logger

The circuit of Fig. 5-29, called a *transdiode* configuration, is one of the basic logarithmic converters. The collector current of transistor Q_1 is equal to the op-amp input current and, since the base of Q_1 is grounded, the output of A_1 is the V_{BE} of Q_1.

This circuit maintains the collector and base voltages of Q_1 equal through the virtual ground at the input of A_1; thus, the effects of collector-voltage changes on the logging operation are eliminated. Performance limits are governed by the transistor used and—more often—by the op amp; at very low log currents, the input current of A_1 becomes an appreciable factor.

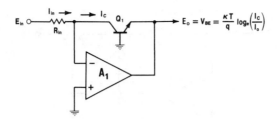

Fig. 5-29. Transdiode logarithmic converter.

The circuit of Fig. 5-29 provides the closest approximation to actual logarithmic operation. In this simple form, however, it has two important drawbacks: first, there are temperature-dependent components that can introduce error. Second, the relatively small (60 mV) output change per decade is inconvenient—some value such as 1.0 V/decade is usually preferred. From the equations of Section 5.12.1, the temperature-affected parameters are seen to be $\kappa T/q$, which is a scaling factor, and I_o, which is an offset factor; both of these may be compensated by additional circuit elements.

The temperature coefficient of $\kappa T/q$ amounts to +0.3%/°C. This can be compensated as shown in Fig. 5-30, by using a thermistor (R_2) to track the changes in output voltage. Resistor R_1 determines the logarithmic scale; with the values shown, the scale factor is about 1.0 V/decade. Thermistor R_2 should be selected to have a TC of +0.3%/°C, to compensate the $\kappa T/q$ factor.

The I_o factor in the equations also changes with temperature. This is compensated by an identical transistor operating at the same temperature and having a constant collector current. The circuit of Fig. 5-31 illustrates this principal, which will be detailed further in actual circuits.

5.12.3 Other Logger Configurations

The transdiode connection is by no means the only transistor circuit useful in log converters. Two alternate feedback configurations are shown in Fig. 5-32. The feedback element can be connected either as a diode (Fig. 5-32A) or as a transistor (Fig. 5-32B).

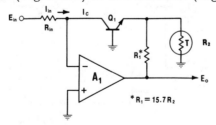

Fig. 5-30. Log converter with temperature compensation of $\kappa T/q$.

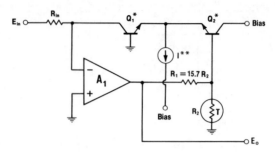

* Matched to track with temperature.

** Current source, typically connected so as to maintain a
  constant collector current for Q_2.

Fig. 5-31. Log converter with temperature compensation of $\kappa T/q$ and V_{BE}.

The diode-connected transistor configuration of Fig. 5-32A is useful from the standpoint that it is a two-terminal device and is therefore easily reversible to accommodate input signals of negative polarity. It becomes limited in accuracy at lower input currents, however. The falloff in transistor gain (β or h_{FE}), creates an increasing error since all of the input current does not flow through the collector as it does in the transdiode. This circuit is useful over about 3 decades of input current, from approximately 1 μA to 1 mA.

The transistor connection of Fig. 5-32B is similar in performance to the diode connection. It does reduce loading on the op amp by virtue of the transistor current gain, but it also introduces some additional bias error due to the higher collector-base voltage. The dynamic range of this circuit is comparable to that of the diode connection, and it has similar errors due to gain falloff. These types of logging elements will not be covered here in any detail; interested readers should consult the references cited for further information.

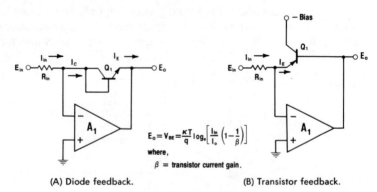

$$E_o = V_{BE} = \frac{\kappa T}{q} \log_e \left[\frac{I_{in}}{I_o} \left(1 - \frac{1}{\beta} \right) \right]$$

where,

β = transistor current gain.

(A) Diode feedback. (B) Transistor feedback.

Fig. 5-32. Alternate log configurations.

Log generators using transdiode connections are notoriously difficult to stabilize, because the feedback network can actually contribute gain, rather than a loss which is usually the case. The gain is in excess of the open-loop gain of the op amp and must be considered in the overall loop. Further complicating matters is the fact that the gain of the transdiode changes with I_C. As a result, circuit stability requires either heavy frequency compensation of the amplifier or a gain reduction within the loop. Both techniques are commonly utilized, as will subsequently be seen.

5.12.4 Log Generator With 100-dB Dynamic Range

A circuit employing many of the design principles set down earlier is the log generator of Fig. 5-33. In this circuit, A_2 supplies a constant reference current (I_{C_2}) to Q_2, which will have a value of

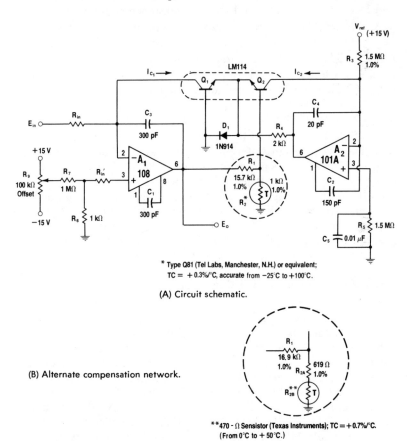

(A) Circuit schematic.

* Type Q81 (Tel Labs, Manchester, N.H.) or equivalent;
TC = + 0.3%/°C, accurate from −25°C to +100°C.

(B) Alternate compensation network.

** 470 - Ω Sensistor (Texas Instruments); TC = +0.7%/°C.
(From 0°C to + 50°C.)

Fig. 5-33. Log generator with 100-dB dynamic range.

V_{ref}/R_3, since the collector of Q_2 is held at virtual ground by the non-inverting input of A_2. A_1 supplies a current (I_{C_1}) through Q_1, which will have a value of E_{in}/R_{in}, since the collector of Q_1 is also maintained at ground potential, in this case by the noninverting input of A_1. Q_1 is being operated here as a transdiode connection, with Q_2 supplying temperature compensation of the offset voltage. The logged output of A_1 is temperature compensated by divider R_1-R_2 and scaled to 1.0 V/decade, as explained in Section 5.12.2. Using either of the thermistor options specified for R_2, temperature compensation is within 1.0% over the range given.

A_1 is frequency compensated with a larger-than-normal capacitance, C_1; feedback capacitor C_3 helps to stabilize the loop gain, as does the loss across divider R_1-R_2. Similarly, R_4 and C_4 stabilize A_2.

This circuit actually generates the log ratio of two currents, I_{C_1} and I_{C_2}. Normally I_{C_2} is fixed at some reference value, which in this case is 10 μA. This reference current determines the value of I_{C_1} for which the log output will be zero, since $\log (I_{C_1}/I_{C_2}) = 0$ when $I_{C_1} = I_{C_2}$. The circuit is accurate within 1.0% over current inputs from 40 nA to 400 μA, a dynamic range of 80 dB. From 10 nA to 1.0 mA (100-dB range), the accuracy of the circuit is within 3.0%.

5.12.5 Fast Log Generator

Fig. 5-34 is a log converter similar in concept to Fig. 5-33, except that the major design criterion here is speed rather than dynamic range. This circuit has a dynamic range of 80 dB, but a settling time of 10 μs. A type-110 voltage follower buffers the base current of Q_1 and the input current to A_1, allowing Q_1 to operate in a diode connection while demanding a minimal input current to A_3. Again the scale factor of this circuit is 1.0 V/decade, and the zero-crossover point of the output swing is controlled by R_3 as before. The logging range is nominally from 100 nA to 1.0 mA with 1.0% accuracy.

5.12.6 Antilog (Exponential) Generator

The generation of an antilog response is a straightforward matter of rearranging the basic log circuitry to perform the inverse operation. An example is the antilog circuit of Fig. 5-35.

In this circuit, Q_2 generates the exponential current, and its output current is summed at the current-to-voltage converter, A_2. Q_1 provides voltage drive to Q_2 such that the collector current of Q_2 is exponentially related to the voltage at the base of Q_1. A temperature-compensating divider scales the input sensitivity to 1.0 V/decade as previously. The feedback of A_1 maintains the collector current of Q_1 constant at 100 μA. This circuit is optimized for speed, using feedforward connections at both A_1 and A_2.

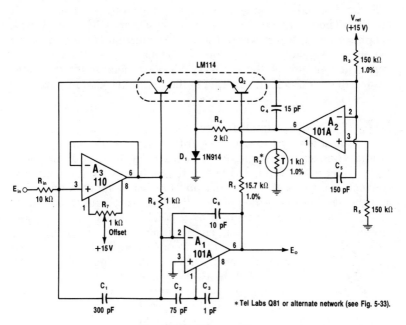

Fig. 5-34. Fast log generator.

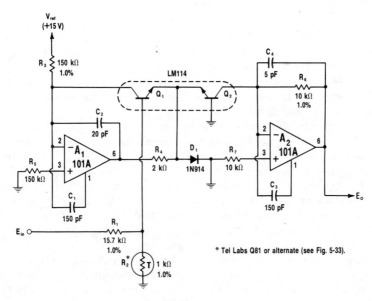

Fig. 5-35. Antilog generator.

215

So far, log and antilog generators have been discussed as separate entities. They may be used together, however, with considerable simplification. In cases where the antilog function is derived immediately, the log/antilog transistors can be matched for thermal tracking, which eliminates the necessity for a temperature-compensated scaling divider. Such an example is the multiplier/divider circuit of Fig. 5-36.

5.12.7 Logarithmic Multiplier/Divider

Multiplication by the use of logarithms is a simple process of addition. Thus, given two numbers in log form, their addition yields the product in log form, and taking the antilog gives the product in conventional form. Similarly, division involves a subtraction of logs and then taking the antilog of this difference to obtain the quotient.

Fig. 5-36 may be recognized as a combination of two previous circuits. The upper half is similar to the log converter of Fig. 5-33, where the output at A_1 is the log ratio of E_1 and E_2. A_3 and Q_3 form another log converter for the E_3 input, and the log output of this converter is added to that of the E_1/E_2 circuit, producing $\log(E_1E_3/E_2)$ at the emitter of Q_4. Q_4 and A_4 take the antilog; this output is $E_1E_3/10E_2$. If just the multiplication process is desired, E_2 can be a reference voltage as in Fig. 5-33, and R_4 will establish the reference current. Matching of transistor pairs should be as shown.

5.12.8 Power Functions of an Input

Just as multiplication and division become processes of addition and subtraction using logarithms, the generation of power functions becomes a process of scaling (multiplying) logarithms. Raising to powers greater than unity (x^2, x^3, etc.) is the scaling upward of the number in log form; taking a root ($x^{1/2}$, $x^{1/3}$, etc.) is the scaling downward of the number in log form. A circuit that will raise the input to a power or take roots is shown in Fig. 5-37.

This circuit is a combination log converter and antilog generator, with a variable scale adjustment between the log/antilog interface. The variable scaling modifies the exponent of the logged input to a value other than unity; therefore, $E_o = (E_{in})^x$ where x is variable.

In this circuit, the divider networks of R_4-R_5 and R_3-R_5 alter the percentage of A_1's output signal fed to Q_2 and Q_3. If the attenuation in the two legs from A_1 is equal, both Q_2 and Q_3 see the same signal and the circuit operates as a straight log/antilog converter. If Q_3 receives a greater percentage of signal than Q_2, this is equivalent to a gain in the exponent, and the output is raised to a power. If Q_3 receives less signal than Q_2, there is a loss in the conversion process, equivalent to the taking of a root. With the values shown, the exponent of E_{in} is variable from $1/2$ to 2. Greater powers or smaller roots

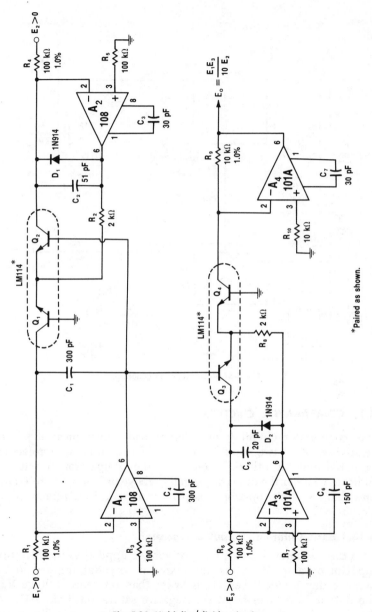

Fig. 5-36. Multiplier/divider circuit.

217

are possible by adjusting the R_3-R_4-R_5 values appropriately, although the span of exponents available will be limited by the dynamic range of the output amplifier, A_4.

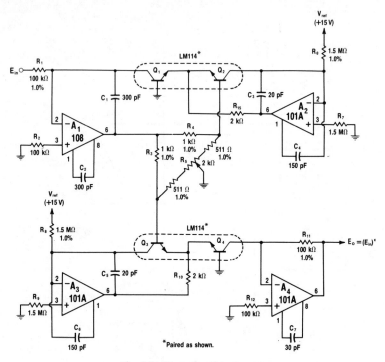

Fig. 5-37. Power-function generator.

5.13 COMPARATOR CIRCUITS

A comparator circuit is one that provides an indication of the relative state of two input potentials. If one input is a reference potential and the other an unknown, the comparator output will indicate whether the unknown signal is above or below the reference potential. A basic op-amp comparator circuit is diagrammed in Fig. 5-38A.

5.13.1 Basic Differential-Input Comparator

In this example, V_{ref} is a positive voltage applied to the inverting input of op amp A_1. E_{in} is the unknown potential, applied to the noninverting input. When E_{in} is lower than reference voltage V_{ref}, the output of A_1 will be at the negative saturation limit, $-E_{o(sat)}$. As soon as E_{in} rises higher than V_{ref}, the amplifier output flips to the positive saturation limit, $+E_{o(sat)}$. A graph of this transfer character-istic is shown in Fig. 5-38B.

In this circuit, the amplifier is operated in an open-loop condition; therefore, the voltage difference required to change the output from one state to the other is quite small, essentially $[+E_{o(sat)} - (-E_{o(sat)})]/A_{vo}$. Since this voltage is but a few hundred microvolts, the dominating factor that determines the exact threshold is the off-set voltage of the amplifier, which may be as great as ±10 mV in some cases. For this reason, precision comparators should be nulled so that the input-differential voltage is as close to zero as practical when the output is zero. Furthermore, any source resistances in the input path should be selected so as to minimize the offset voltage.

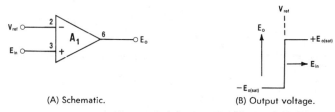

(A) Schematic.   (B) Output voltage.

Fig. 5-38. Basic comparator circuit.

It is generally desired that a comparator be capable of changing output states as rapidly as possible. Since comparator circuits normally operate without negative feedback, there is no necessity for frequency compensation, since there is no closed loop to stabilize. Frequency compensation in a comparator is usually detrimental, because it slows down the open-loop speed of the amplifier. A type 741, for example, with a slew rate of 0.5 V/μs will require 40 μs to swing from -10 V to $+10$ V, due to its slew-rate limitation. By contrast, a 101 type, which has the same (0.5 V/μs) slew rate when compensated, will have a slew rate of 20 V/μs or greater with the compensation removed, so that it can accomplish the -10-V to $+10$-V swing in 1.0 μs or less.

Removal of frequency compensation also increases the high-frequency gain of the op amp as discussed in Chapter 1. This increases the frequency range over which the comparator will have maximum sensitivity, since a high open-loop gain implies that a small input voltage is required to initiate an output transition.

Comparators are subject to wide differential-input voltage swings, since both V_{ref} and E_{in} may be anywhere within the common-mode input range of ±10 V. This requires a differential-input voltage rating of at least ±20 V to accommodate the worst-case limits in a circuit such as Fig. 5-38A. Other comparator configurations can ease this wide voltage-swing requirement as will be seen shortly. Examples of wide differential-input capability in op amps are the 741 and the 101 (±30 V), the 1556 (±22 V), the 531 (±15 V), the 715 (±15 V), and the 2620 (±12 V).

Beyond the basic requirement of input-voltage range, speed is the next criterion in selecting op amps suitable for comparators. Speed has two meanings for comparators: response time and slew rate. Response time is simply the total time required for an output transition to occur once an input trigger has arrived. It is specified both for a positive step input (minus to plus) and a negative step input (plus to minus). Slew rate indicates how rapidly the amplifier output can change during a transition. It can also be different for positive- and negative-going slopes.

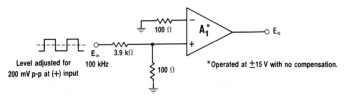

(A) Test circuit.

Device (A$_1$)	Pulse Response Time (μs)		Risetime - Falltime (μs)		Slew Rate (V/μs)	
	Positive Step	Negative Step			Positive Step	Negative Step
715	0.2	0.1	0.3	0.2	90	135
709 **	0.9	0.2	0.25	0.1	108	270
540 **	0.6	1.2	0.2	0.25	125	100
531	1.0	1.0	0.5	0.5	55	45
2620	1.8	1.5	0.7	0.7	35	35
101/748	3.2	4.2	1.5	0.6	18	45

**Differential input protection required for voltages greater than ±5 V (see Chapter 3).

(B) Typical response figures.

Fig. 5-39. Characteristics of op amps as comparators.

Fig. 5-39B is a chart of comparator performance for different op amps, showing response times and slew rates in a standard test circuit (Fig. 5-39A). It is worth noting that devices having the shortest response times and fastest slew rates are those which normally use the *most* frequency compensation—removing this compensation allows greater inherent bandwidth. Some variation in the values shown can be expected, and the chart should be used only for general comparison purposes.

Figs. 5-38 and 5-39 are both examples of noninverting comparators; that is, the output has the same direction of polarity as the input. An inverting comparator may be required in some cases, and this configuration is obtained simply by reversing the inputs so that E_{in} is connected to the inverting $(-)$ op-amp terminal. In either case, the op amp presents a high impedance to both the V_{ref} and E_{in} sources.

5.13.2 Basic Single-Ended-Input Comparator

The differential-input comparator described in the previous section is the most general configuration and the one most often used. Single-ended-input configurations are also possible, however, as illustrated in Fig. 5-40. In this example, both the signal and reference voltages are applied to a common input with the opposite input grounded. R_1 and R_2 form a voltage divider between E_{in} and V_{ref}, and V_{ref} is a voltage of polarity opposite to that of E_{in}. V_{ref} and R_1-R_2 define the threshold value of E_{in} that will cause the voltage at the junction of R_1 and R_2 to cross ground, which changes the state of the comparator. This threshold voltage is $E_{in(th)} = V_{ref}(R_1/R_2)$.

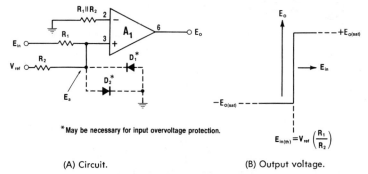

*May be necessary for input overvoltage protection.

(A) Circuit.   (B) Output voltage.

Fig. 5-40. Single-ended comparator.

In practice, the voltage V_{ref} and resistance R_2 will define a current in R_2 for $E_a = 0$ (trip point); thereafter R_1 can be selected for the desired trip level of E_{in}. Although noninverting operation of the comparator is shown, inverting operation is also possible by reversing the inputs, as in the previous example.

This comparator has the advantage of being noncritical as to the specific device used for A_1 in regard to differential-input rating. The voltage between the inputs of A_1 will be smaller than E_{in} and V_{ref} by the division of R_1-R_2, and therefore a smaller input rating is tolerable for A_1. This allows use of such op amps as the 709, which is an unprotected type. E_{in} can be unrestricted in magnitude since R_1 can always be selected to scale down this voltage. It is also good practice to add a pair of back-to-back clamp diodes (D_1 and D_2) to constrain the E_a voltage. They add no error in the threshold point, because when $E_a = 0$ at the trip point, both diodes are nonconducting. The diodes can be connected as diagrammed in Fig. 5-40 or applied directly across the inputs for differential clamping.

5.13.3 Comparators With Hysteresis

The comparators described thus far have been basic open-loop types, which amplify an input signal by comparison to a reference voltage. In situations where the input signal is a slowly varying potential (as with dc or very-low-frequency ac), this can be a disadvantage, for the output will also change slowly. This factor comes into play particularly when the output of the comparator is used to trigger a logic stage requiring fast trigger pulses. One solution is the introduction of positive feedback around the comparator, which alters the output to form a fast "snap" action. Positive feedback is introduced by feeding a portion of the output signal back to the noninverting input.

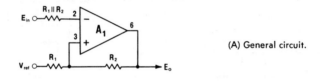

(A) General circuit.

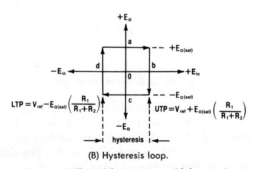

(B) Hysteresis loop.

Fig. 5-41. Differential comparator with hysteresis.

Fig. 5-41A is an inverting differential-input comparator with the reference voltage applied to the noninverting input through R_1. Without R_2, the circuit performs similar to Figs. 5-38 and 5-39. If V_{ref} is +1.0 V, for example, the output would switch as E_{in} goes above or below 1.0 V.

By introducing R_2, however, positive feedback is developed across R_1. If the output is high, R_2 will feed back a signal, which will be added to the reference voltage. This voltage increment will be

$$\Delta V_{ref} = (E_{o(sat)} - V_{ref})\frac{R_1}{R_1 + R_2},$$

making the new reference voltage

$$V_{ref+} = V_{ref} + \Delta V_{ref} = V_{ref} + (E_{o(sat)} - V_{ref})\frac{R_1}{R_1 + R_2}.$$

Therefore, a new trip level is introduced, high by the amount of positive voltage fed back from E_o. As E_{in} crosses this voltage, the output will start to fall. Immediately, the falling condition is sensed across R_1, and the noninverting input is also driven negative. This feedback is regenerative, and the output quickly "snaps" to the opposite state. This effect is prevalent regardless of the rate of change in E_{in}, giving the circuit a constant output transition time for any speed of input variation. Since E_o is now at negative saturation, the voltage fed back to R_1 is

$$\Delta V_{ref} = (-E_{o(sat)} - V_{ref})\frac{R_1}{R_1 + R_2},$$

making a new reference voltage,

$$V_{ref-} = V_{ref} + \Delta V_{ref} = V_{ref} + (-E_{o(sat)} - V_{ref})\frac{R_1}{R_1 + R_2}.$$

Positive feedback has introduced new terms, and there are now two threshold points rather than one; these are called the *upper threshold point* (UTP) and *lower threshold point* (LTP). The difference between these two thresholds is the *hysteresis*.

Graphically, the effect of hysteresis is depicted in Fig. 5-41B. For simplicity, let $V_{ref} = 0$. Assume the output is already in a high state and the input is rising, approaching the UTP. On the figure, this is line *a*. As E_{in} reaches the voltage

$$E_{in} = +E_{o(sat)}\left(\frac{R_1}{R_1 + R_2}\right),$$

the output voltage snaps from $+E_{o(sat)}$ to $-E_{o(sat)}$ (line *b*). As E_{in} decreases toward the LTP (line *c*), E_o will remain at $-E_{o(sat)}$ until

$$E_{in} = -E_{o(sat)}\left(\frac{R_1}{R_1 + R_2}\right).$$

At this point the output voltage snaps back to $+E_{o(sat)}$ (line *d*), thus returning to the original state. The input threshold region is a voltage span determined by the amount of feedback:

$$E_{hys} = V_{ref+} - V_{ref-}$$

$$= V_{ref} + (+E_{o(sat)} - V_{ref})\frac{R_1}{R_1 + R_2}$$

$$- V_{ref} + (-E_{o(sat)} - V_{ref})\frac{R_1}{R_1 + R_2}.$$

If $V_{ref} = 0$, this simplifies to

$$E_{hys} = \frac{R_1}{R_1 + R_2}[+E_{o(sat)} - (-E_{o(sat)})].$$

This threshold region is the hysteresis region shown on the graph as the horizontal span from the LTP to UTP. Hysteresis is always some span about V_{ref}, although the span is not always symmetrical. Note that if V_{ref} is above or below ground, the hysteresis region will not be symmetrical as was the case for $V_{ref} = 0$. If the respective saturation voltages of the op amp are not equal, this will also make the hysteresis region asymmetrical.

Hysteresis is a useful feature in comparators for reasons other than reducing the response time. If the input signal has a low-level noise superimposed on it, an open-loop comparator will "chatter" (switch rapidly back and forth) due to noise fluctuations as the input voltage passes through the threshold region. Also, some open-loop circuits may oscillate during a transition, due to stray capacitive feedback. One cure for either of these difficulties is a small amount of hysteresis, which provides a "dead zone" over which the comparator will not be responsive. Often as little as 10 mV of hysteresis, which can be negligible if the voltage being sensed is large, can eliminate these effects.

5.13.4 Single-Ended Comparator With Hysteresis

Single-ended comparators can also be used with hysteresis; an example is shown in Fig. 5-42A. In this circuit, amplifier A_1 senses

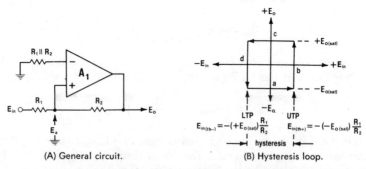

(A) General circuit. (B) Hysteresis loop.

Fig. 5-42. Single-ended comparator with hysteresis.

the difference between ground potential (at the inverting input) and the junction potential of R_1-R_2. In this regard it is similar to Fig. 5-40; in fact, the threshold voltage can be determined the same way by substituting the appropriate voltage representing E_o for V_{ref}. In this case,

$$E_{in(th)} = E_o \left(\frac{R_1}{R_2} \right).$$

The difference is that E_o will not be constant here, whereas previously V_{ref} was constant by definition. The circuit operates as follows: Assuming the output is in a state of negative saturation, a positive voltage applied at E_{in} will raise the potential at E_a until it reaches a potential equal to zero. This is line a in Fig. 5-42B. At this point,

$$E_{in(th+)} = -(-E_{o(sat)}) \frac{R_1}{R_2},$$

the equation for the UTP. The output then snaps positive due to the feedback through R_2 (line b). The voltage at E_a is now positive due to the feedback from $+E_{o(sat)}$. When E_{in} becomes negative, it will reduce the voltage at E_a until E_a again approaches zero. This is represented by line c. When E_{in} has reached a negative value such that

$$E_{in(th-)} = -(+E_{o(sat)}) \frac{R_1}{R_2},$$

the circuit has reached its LTP, and the circuit snaps negative again, tracing section d of the loop and returning it to its original state.

This circuit does not need a separate reference voltage, although a potential may be applied to the inverting input of A_1 as a reference if desired. Using it as in Fig. 5-42A, the output saturation voltages define the trip points in conjunction with R_1 and R_2. This configuration is generally very useful since it does not require a separate reference voltage and can use an unprotected op amp for the same reasons as in Fig. 5-40. The only drawback is the fact that the positive and negative saturation voltages are not stable potentials—they can vary from device to device and also with loading and temperature. Therefore, if the output voltage is used directly as feedback as shown in Fig. 5-42A, the threshold voltage will vary directly with the $\pm E_{o(sat)}$ levels.

5.13.5 Comparators With Clamped Feedback

A solution to the variation in threshold potential is the introduction of a zener clamping network in the positive feedback loop as in Fig. 5-43.

In this circuit, back-to-back zeners D_1 and D_2 clamp the output of A_1 to $\pm V_Z$, and this voltage is used as the feedback voltage. The combination of a single zener junction and two forward-biased diodes in series results in a net TC close to zero, providing temperature-stabilized thresholds.

With the equal-value resistors shown for R_1 and R_2, the input trip level will be equal to the $\pm V_Z$ reference source. Lower or higher input potentials may be realized by scaling R_1 appropriately. Two outputs are available, a direct output from pin 6, which will vary from $-E_{o(sat)}$ to $+E_{o(sat)}$, and the clamped reference $\pm V_Z$ across D_1-D_2. If input voltages beyond the common-mode range of A_1 are used, a pair of input clamp diodes such as D_3 and D_4 should also be used.

5.13.6 Clamped Comparators With 101 Amplifiers

A very useful scheme for defining the output voltage swing of a comparator is possible using 101-type amplifiers. The basic technique is shown in Fig. 5-44.

From the 101 schematic of Chapter 2 (Fig. 2-10), the internal connection on pin 8 of a 101 or 101A is a relatively high-impedance source for either positive or negative swings. The p-p voltage swing at this point is roughly the same value as that at the output, the main difference being the dc offset of the emitter followers between pin 8 and the output. This point, then, is a convenient one to define the range of swing at the output, since it can be clamped either with zener diodes or with biased signal diodes.

Fig. 5-44A illustrates the requirements for clamping positive or negative voltages. Diode D_1 will clamp positive swings to voltage

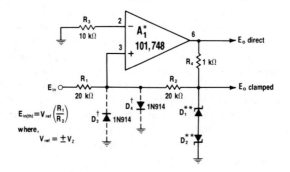

* Substitute to meet circuit requirements —e.g., speed, input
 impedance, input voltage, etc.
** Matched zener diodes—e.g., 1N754 (general purpose), CA3093
 (matched, low TC), 2N3906 (high speed). See also Fig. 5-18.
† Optional—required only if E_{in} can exceed common-mode or
 differential input rating of A_1.

Fig. 5-43. Single-ended comparator with hysteresis and clamped feedback.

$+E_{o(clamp)} \cong +V_{clamp} + 1.2$ V, where $+V_{clamp}$ is the bias voltage applied to the cathode of D_1. The source resistance of $+V_{clamp}$ should be no greater than about 1.0 kΩ for this relationship to apply.

Similarly, diode D_2 may be used to clamp the negative swing to a negative potential, $-V_{clamp}$. The voltage at the output terminal will be $-E_{o(clamp)} \cong -V_{clamp} - 0.5$ V. The source resistance of $-V_{clamp}$ should be no more than about 200 Ω to maintain this relation.

An alternate method of accomplishing the same result uses a zener diode connected to pin 8 (Fig. 5-44B). In this case the zener voltage and ground define the $\pm V_{clamp}$ potentials, and the output swing is the same as in Fig. 5-44A. The zener diode may, of course, be reversed for a predominately negative output swing if desired.

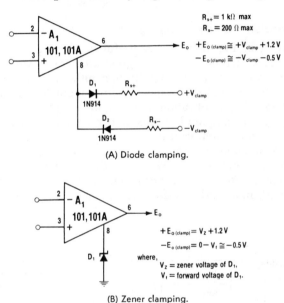

(A) Diode clamping.

(B) Zener clamping.

Fig. 5-44. Clamped comparators.

The advantages of voltage clamping are twofold. First, it makes available the full current output of the op amp by internally clamping at a low-current point. Second, it allows greater operating speed by avoiding saturation of the op-amp voltage-amplification stages.

A circuit for a general-purpose comparator with a clamped 5-V logic output is shown in Fig. 5-45. R_1 and R_2 provide a +3.8-V bias for D_1, clamping the positive output to +5 V; D_2 limits the negative output excursion to −0.5 V. It should be noted that this is still an open-loop circuit, so the output voltage will change in proportion to the load current (the open loop r_o of the op amp is 75 Ω).

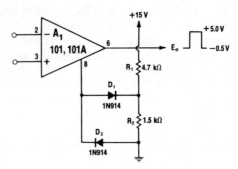

Fig. 5-45. General-purpose comparator with 5-V logic output.

5.13.7 Precision Variable Clamping

The circuit of Fig. 5-45 is very useful for driving DTL or TTL logic devices, which do not require great accuracy in voltage levels. It is entirely adequate for this application, although the output voltage is neither temperature-compensated nor regulated in amplitude.

More demanding applications may require a tight control of positive and negative amplitude limits, and regulation of these amplitudes with load and temperature. A circuit that accomplishes this is Fig. 5-46, a comparator having both output voltage limits regulated independently without a connection to the comparison inputs.

In this circuit, A_2 and A_3 are complementary versions of precision rectifiers with independent reference voltages $+V_{clamp}$ and $-V_{clamp}$,

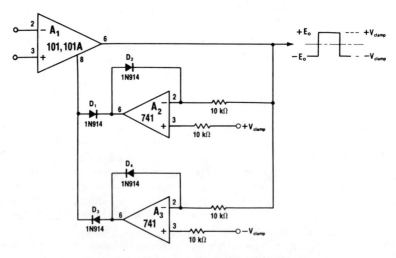

Fig. 5-46. Precision comparator with variable clamping.

both operating in a closed loop through A_1. A_2 senses the positive peak of E_o and maintains it equal to $+V_{clamp}$ by adjusting the voltage applied to D_1. A_3 and D_3 perform a similar function on negative peaks, adjusting $-E_o$ equal to $-V_{clamp}$. D_2 and D_4 minimize response time by preventing saturation of A_2 and A_3.

The feedback network around the output stage of A_1 regulates the output voltage independent of the inputs to A_1. These inputs can be used in any of the previous comparator configurations, with the obvious virtues of a precisely maintained output voltage and stable $\pm V_{clamp}$ potentials. For example, the circuit can be used in a single-ended comparator such as Fig. 5-43 with improved results. Also, the threshold voltages can be made independently variable if desired by separate adjustments for $+V_{clamp}$ and $-V_{clamp}$; operating speed is determined primarily by A_2 and A_3.

5.13.8 Zero-Crossing Detector

One form of comparator finding wide use is the zero-crossing detector. Usually, it takes the form of a high-gain amplifier that changes state each time the input signal changes direction. For an ac signal this occurs when the signal value is zero, hence the name *zero-crossing* detector. The circuit amplifies and "squares" the input signal into a series of rectangular output pulses with rising and falling slopes corresponding to the input zero crossings.

A circuit that derives the zero-crossing information of an ac signal is shown in Fig. 5-47. This is an ac logarithmic amplifier, with feedback current I_f creating a log output voltage due to diodes D_1 and D_2. Amplifier A_1 is connected in the feedforward mode to optimize

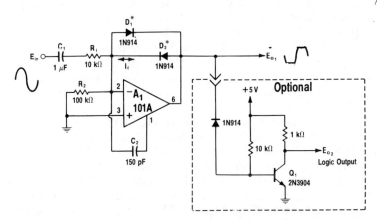

*For greater dynamic range, use a matched, monolithic transistor pair connected as diodes — e.g., CA3018.

Fig. 5-47. Zero-crossing detector.

speed and minimize phase error at high frequencies. The output voltage is nominally $\pm V_f$, where V_f is the forward voltage drop of either diode.

This basic circuit has a dynamic range limited to about 70 dB, which can be increased by using monolithic transistor diodes for D_1-D_2. Should the nominal voltage drop be insufficient as an output or if a constant output is desired, the optional connection in the inset can be used. This is a saturated switch, delivering a 0- to +5-V output at E_{o_2} .

5.13.9 Window Comparators

A window comparator, as its name implies, is a specialized form of comparator designed to detect the presence of a voltage between two prescribed voltage limits—that is, within a voltage "window." This is accomplished by logically combining the outputs of two single-ended comparators, one indicating greater than a lower limit, the other indicating less than an upper limit. If both comparators indicate a "true" condition, the output is true. If either is not true, the output is not true.

Window comparators (also referred to as *double-ended* comparators) are useful in the grading and selection of components or in the production testing of circuits to a specified output tolerance. For these purposes, a variable window voltage position and a variable window voltage width are desirable.

General-Purpose Window Comparator

A simple window comparator is shown in Fig. 5-48A. This circuit gives a high output (+5.0 V in this case) if E_{in} is within the voltage window set by the upper limit (UL) and lower limit (LL) voltages. For example, if UL is +4.0 V and LL is +2.0 V, E_{in} must be greater than +2.0 V and less than +4.0 V for E_o to be high. If E_{in} goes lower than +2.0 V, A_2 turns on Q_1 through D_2. If E_{in} goes higher than +4.0 V, A_1 turns on Q_1 through D_1. As long as E_{in} is within the window, both A_1 and A_2 are low, Q_1 remains off, and E_o remains true (high).

The input/output transfer characteristic of this circuit is shown in Fig. 5-48B, with the voltage examples used illustrated. Note the output is +5.0 V only when $LL \leqq E_{in} \leqq UL$.

A type-1537 (dual 709) op amp is convenient to use for A_1 and A_2 in this circuit if its differential-input rating is observed. The resistor-diode input clamping network is recommended here. For applications not requiring great speed, a 1558 may be substituted and the resistor-diode clamping omitted. R_3 is shown as a fixed load resistor, but may be a relay or a lamp if desired. These types of loads will be covered in the following section.

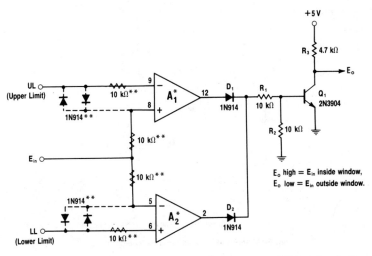

(A) Circuit diagram.

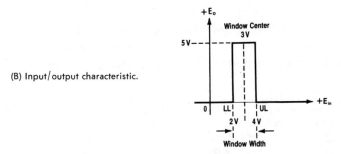

(B) Input/output characteristic.

Fig. 5-48. General-purpose window comparator.

Internally Gated Window Comparator

The circuit of Fig. 5-48A is useful with any op amp if the maximum input voltage restrictions are observed. However, a much simpler overall circuit for a window comparator is feasible, using a pair of 101s with the clamp terminals wired together as shown in Fig. 5-49.

In this circuit, advantage is taken of the fact that the source and sink currents available at pin 8 of a 101 op amp are unequal: the negative-going drive is the greater of the two. Therefore, the voltage at pin 8 will be low if either comparison input (A_1 or A_2) so dictates; for the voltage at pin 8 to be high, *both* A_1 and A_2 must have a high output condition. The outputs of both A_1 and A_2 will follow pin 8,

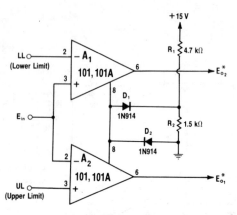

+15 V

$R_1 \lessgtr 4.7\ k\Omega$

LL ○ ── 2
(Lower Limit)

$-A_1$

101, 101A

3 +

6 ──►$E_{o_2}^*$

8   D_1
▶|
1N914

E_{in} ○

$R_2 \lessgtr 1.5\ k\Omega$

D_2
|◀
1N914

8

2 ── $-A_2$

101, 101A

3 +

6 ──►$E_{o_1}^*$

UL ○
(Upper Limit)

*Outputs are identical; either or both can be used.

Fig. 5-49. Internally gated window comparator.

since the op-amp internal circuitry thereafter has unity gain. D_1 and D_2 form a clamp network as in Fig. 5-45. The output from either A_1 or A_2 may be used, with the logic of operation being the same as in Fig. 5-48.

Comparator With Variable Window

As mentioned previously, a variable-width window is very useful, allowing a single comparator to be programmed for a wide variety of

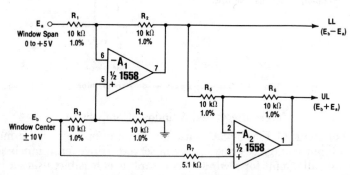

E_a ○
Window Span
0 to +5 V

R_1
10 kΩ
1.0%

R_2
10 kΩ
1.0%

LL
$(E_b - E_a)$

6
$-A_1$
½ **1558**
5 +
7

R_5
10 kΩ
1.0%

R_6
10 kΩ
1.0%

UL
$(E_b + E_a)$

E_b ○
Window Center
± 10 V

R_3
10 kΩ
1.0%

R_4
10 kΩ
1.0%

2
$-A_2$
½ **1558**
3 +
1

R_7
5.1 kΩ

Fig. 5-50. Comparator with variable window.

tasks. Fig. 5-50 is such a circuit, generating variable UL and LL voltages for use with either of the previous comparator circuits.

This circuit combines two variable voltages, E_b (window center) and E_a (window span), such that E_b positions the window and voltage E_a is added to E_b to set the width of the window. A_1 is a subtractor, generating a voltage of $E_b - E_a$, which is used as the LL voltage. This voltage is also added to $2E_b$ at A_2 to derive $E_b + E_a$, the UL voltage. E_b may be any voltage within the comparator common-mode range of ± 10 V. E_a is a positive voltage that is added to E_b at the input; so, the combination of $E_b + E_a$ or $E_b - E_a$ must not exceed ± 10 V for any combination of E_a and E_b. Normally this will not be a restriction, since E_a is commonly a small percentage of E_b —for example, $+5.0$ V $\pm 5\%$.

For applications where E_{in} is much greater than the common-mode range of ± 10 V, it may be scaled with a voltage divider to bring it into the comparison range, allowing window-voltage comparison of much higher voltages.

Staircase Window Comparator

The most basic comparator tells only one thing about an unknown voltage—whether it is above or below a reference voltage. The window comparator tells a little more about the unknown voltage—that it is between two specified voltage limits. But in certain situations, even this may not be enough. A third type of comparator, the staircase detector, tells where (within *which* window) the input voltage lies over a specified range of voltages. An output is indicated only from the comparator closest to the input voltage, generating one voltage from among a rising "staircase" of levels.

Fig. 5-51 is a staircase detector performing such a function. It is actually a series of 101-type window comparators, each similar to Fig. 5-49, but arranged for operation in a sequential fashion. E_{in} is applied in parallel to all comparators (A_1-A_6). If E_{in} is between LL_1 and UL_1, the output from A_2 will be high. When E_{in} rises above UL_1, it moves within the voltage window of the A_3-A_4 comparator (window 2, where LL_2 is the same as UL_1). Under this condition, the output of A_2 drops and A_4 switches high. Should E_{in} rise further (above UL_2, for instance), it moves into window 3, actuating A_6 to a high state with A_4 going low. This "staircase" of windows can be continued indefinitely using as many comparators as necessary to provide the required resolution. An output indicator (lamp, relay, etc.) added to each of the E_{o_1}, E_{o_2}, and E_{o_3} lines will indicate the presence of E_{in} within the corresponding window.

5.13.10 General-Purpose Interfacing Circuits

Fig. 5-52 illustrates a few ways in which any comparator with a bipolar output swing can be used to drive higher-powered loads. Q_1 is a medium-power switching transistor, driven to saturation when the output of A_1 is high. When A_1 is low, Q_1 is off. Clamp diode D_1 prevents possible V_{EB} breakdown of Q_1. When A_1 goes to $+E_{o(sat)}$, this stage can handle voltages up to the Q_1 rating of 30 V, with load currents to 150 mA.

Fig. 5-52B illustrates three specific examples. In the lamp-driver circuit, R_{surge} is added to limit the cold inrush current in Q_1. Lower-voltage lamps of up to the 150-mA current rating may be driven by reducing the lamp supply voltage appropriately. Also shown is a relay driver, using a common 24-V relay. Diode D_2 clamps the back emf of K_1 after turnoff. Again, lower-voltage relays may be driven, as long as I_{max} is 150 mA or less.

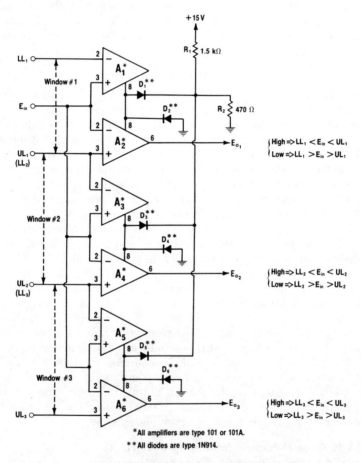

*All amplifiers are type 101 or 101A.
** All diodes are type 1N914.

Fig. 5-51. Staircase window comparator.

Finally, this circuit is easily adapted as an LED indicator driver, using a 2N3904 switch rather than the high-powered 2N2219. Maximum diode current is set by the supply voltage (minus approximately 1.5 V, the LED forward drop) and by R_L; in this case I_{max} is about 20 mA.

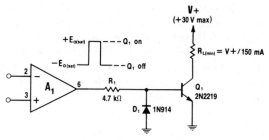

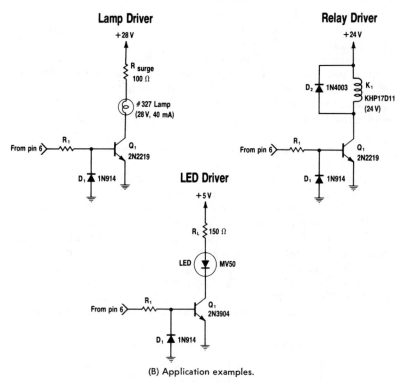

(A) General-purpose circuit.

Lamp Driver

Relay Driver

LED Driver

(B) Application examples.

Fig. 5-52. Comparator output interfaces.

5.14 INSTRUMENTATION AMPLIFIERS

One of the most useful applications of an IC op amp is the differential-input dc amplifier configuration, illustrated in Fig. 5-53. Due to the inherent rejection of common-mode noise (E_{cm}) and the linear amplification of desired signals (E_s) that it provides, this circuit and variations of it find widespread use in signal processing. Dc and low-

235

frequency signals are commonly received from a transducer, amplified, and then transmitted in a single-ended mode. Since the desired signal may have a full-scale amplitude of typically only a few millivolts, while common-mode noise may be several volts, such factors as amplifier input drift and noise are critical to overall accuracy. Equally important is the common-mode rejection of the amplifier configuration. Several instrumentation amplifier circuits are discussed in this section, with the unique and distinquishing features of each highlighted.

5.14.1 Buffered Differential-Input Instrumentation Amplifier

One obvious disadvantage of the basic differential circuit of Fig. 5-53 is the loading effect of R_1 and R_2 on the signal source(s). If a high gain is to be realized from the stage, R_1 and R_2 must necessarily be low. However, this tends to impair common-mode rejection, as there is usually little control over the source resistances of the two inputs. Consequently, even a slight mismatch in these resistances appears as a mismatch between $R_1 + R_{s_1}$ and $R_2 + R_{s_2}$ which degrades the CMRR because the gains for both signals are no longer equal.

The positive cure for impedance mismatch between the differential inputs is a very high impedance at both inputs. This can be accomplished by a voltage follower (input buffer) arrangement as shown in Fig. 5-54. This circuit raises the input impedance to 10^{12} Ω, has a 1.0-nA input current, and the ability to amplify differential signals superimposed on ±11 V of common-mode noise.

The second stage of the circuit, A_3, provides a differential voltage gain of 40 dB while further suppressing the common-mode component. The common-mode rejection properties of this configuration can be realized only when the arms of the differential "bridge" are matched. This requires that $R_2/R_4 = R_3/R_5$, as shown in the figure. The close tolerances indicated are necessary to guarantee this degree

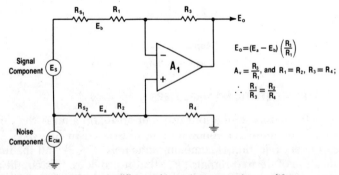

Fig. 5-53. Basic differential-input instrumentation amplifier.

of match without "tweaking" of the circuit. If an adjustment is desired, either ratio may be trimmed for a match. It is usually preferable to trim the noninverting side (R_3-R_5) to avoid upsetting the gain relation of R_4 to R_2. Trimming allows wider tolerances on R_2-R_5. An alternate network is shown which may replace R_5 to allow the CMRR to be trimmed to 100 dB or better, the same as with the 0.1% network.

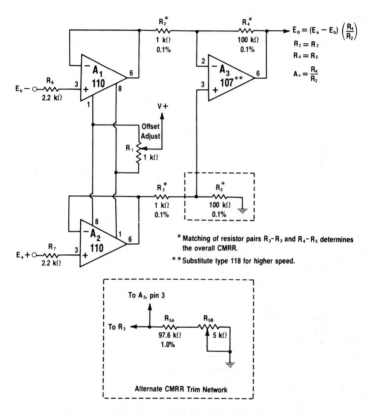

Fig. 5-54. Instrumentation amplifier.

The input offset voltage of the circuit is adjusted by R_1, which provides a differential offset to A_1-A_2. This adjustment (and R_{5B}, if used) should use high quality components for best results, since the voltages it generates appear as equivalent input voltages. Any instability in these components will be amplified by the gain of the circuit. The 107 op amp (A_3) will yield a bandwidth of 10 kHz. A type-118 may be substituted here, if desired, for a bandwidth of 150 kHz.

5.14.2 Differential-Input Amplifier With Variable Gain

While the circuit of Fig. 5-54 is generally very useful, it has one inherent problem—an inability to adjust gain without upsetting the balance. If R_4 of Fig. 5-54 is varied, for example, it will indeed adjust gain, but it will simultaneously ruin the CMRR because of the resulting bridge imbalance. What is needed is a method of varying the differential gain of the circuit with a single adjustment, while retaining a high CMRR.

A modification of Fig. 5-54 allows this and is shown in Fig. 5-55. This circuit varies the gain of stage A_3 by modifying the feedback

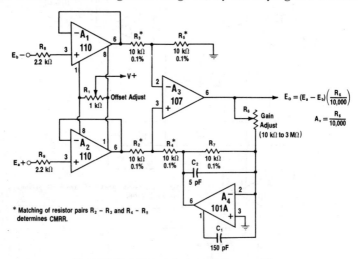

Fig. 5-55. Variable-gain instrumentation amplifier.

returned to R_4, in essence placing a calibrated attenuator within the feedback loop. Since feedback attenuation results in higher gain, this achieves the desired gain variation. An active attenuator (A_4) is used rather than a simple divider because A_4 presents a constant, zero-impedance source to R_4, exactly the condition needed to maintain good balance and a high CMRR. The output impedance of A_4 remains low for any setting of R_6; therefore, gain adjustments do not alter CMRR in this circuit.

An interesting feature of this method of gain adjustment is that the gain is linearly proportional to R_6, which allows R_6 to be a calibrated rheostat for repeatable gain settings. With the values shown, gain can be varied from unity to 300. Offset adjustment R_1 operates here in the same fashion as described for Fig. 5-54, and the same constraints apply. For both these circuits, good layout techniques are recommended—rf bypassing for amplifier supply leads (particularly at A_4), and short, direct signal leads. It is also recommended that the bridge resistances be low-temperature-coefficient types for best dc stability.

5.14.3 Differential-Input Amplifier With High Common-Mode Range

In some situations it may be important that a circuit excel in one regard, even if another parameter is sacrificed. Such an example is the circuit of Fig. 5-56, a differential-input instrumentation amplifier with a common-mode input range of ±100 V.

This circuit trades off input loading in return for a higher common-mode range and reduced common-mode errors. Both A_1 and A_2 are used as inverting stages; thus both have a characteristically low input impedance, in this case the values of R_1 and R_7, or 49.9 kΩ. A virtue of the inverting configuration is the fact that there is no common-mode voltage applied to the amplifier input terminals; therefore, no error can exist due to variations in this parameter.

The circuit is a combination inverting attenuator and scaling adder which rejects common-mode input components while amplifying differential ones. A_1 amplifies signal E_a by a factor of $-R_3/R_1$, or in this case $-1/10$. This signal is combined with E_b at summer A_2. E_b is passed to the output with a gain of $-R_6/R_7$, or -1, while E_a is amplified a second time by $-R_6/R_4$, or -10. The total gain for the E_a signal is then $(-1/10)(-10) = +1$. The resultant gain from both inputs to the output is therefore unity, with signs as shown. A common-mode signal, however, becomes cancelled in stage A_2; it will appear at A_2 as equal and opposite signals, summing to zero. Differential inputs are amplified by the ratio R_6/R_7.

For this circuit to work, the matching of resistor ratios is again critical and should be maintained as shown by the tolerances indi-

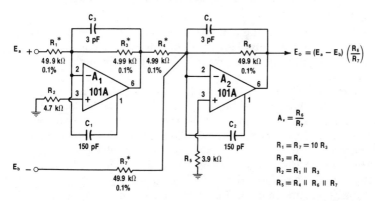

$$E_o = (E_a - E_b)\left(\frac{R_6}{R_7}\right)$$

$$A_v = \frac{R_6}{R_7}$$

$R_1 = R_7 = 10\ R_3$

$R_3 = R_4$

$R_2 = R_1 \parallel R_3$

$R_5 = R_4 \parallel R_6 \parallel R_7$

* Matching of resistor pairs R_1 - R_7 and R_3 - R_4 determines CMRR.

Fig. 5-56. Instrumentation amplifier with common-mode range of ±100 V.

cated. Gain can be adjusted by varying R_6, since the CMRR will not be affected as long as $R_1/R_3 = R_7/R_4$. Low TC resistors should be used for all resistances (except possibly R_2 and R_5), to maintain good thermal stability of gain and CMRR. Due to the wide bandwidth (approximately 1 MHz), rf bypassing of the power supply is also recommended. If wide bandwidth is not required from the circuit, conventional inverters may be used for A_1 and A_2, such as 741 types.

5.14.4 Instrumentation Amplifier With High Input Impedance

A circuit with high input impedance using only two amplifiers is illustrated in Fig. 5-57. Like the previous circuit, it uses a combina-

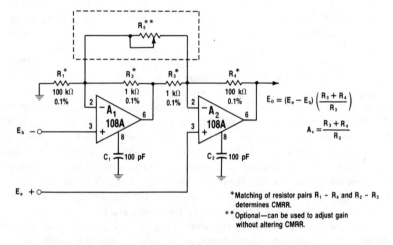

Fig. 5-57. Instrumentation amplifier with high input impedance.

tion of inversion and a summation to cancel the common-mode component at the two inputs. However, in this case a combination of follower configurations also provides an extremely high input impedance.

A_1 amplifies E_b by a factor of $(R_1 + R_2)/R_1$ (in this case, 101/100). The signal is further amplified by A_2, which operates as an inverter for signals from A_1. The stage gain of A_2 is $-R_4/R_3$, in this case $-100/1.0 = -100$. The overall gain to the E_b signal is therefore the product of both stage gains, or $(1.01)(-100) = -101$.

For signals at E_a, A_2 operates as a follower with a gain of $(R_3 + R_4)/R_3 = 101$. Therefore, the overall gain for E_a is +101, exactly equal and opposite that for E_b. If a common-mode signal appears at both inputs, it will be amplified by equal and opposite amounts and cancelled at the output of A_2.

As before, resistor ratio matching is critical to good common-mode rejection. Common-mode rejection is also dependent on the op amp used; therefore, a device with a good characteristic CMRR is desirable, such as the 108A (typically 110 dB). The 108 amplifiers use shunt compensation (C_1 and C_2) to reduce their susceptibility to power-supply-induced noise. The circuit bandwidth is approximately 5 kHz, and this can be extended by reducing the value of C_2.

5.14.5 Instrumentation Amplifier With Differential Preamp

For situations where high input impedance and low offset-voltage drift are required, the configuration of Fig. 5-58 can be used. None of the circuits described previously have been optimized from the standpoint of minimum offset drift. The configuration here is unique in this regard, and a closer examination of how this is accomplished will reveal some attractive properties of the circuit. The circuit consists of two stages—the first consisting of A_1 and A_2, and the second made up by A_3 in a differential configuration. The second stage is similar to many of those already discussed.

A_1 and A_2 constitute a cross-coupled preamp stage with differential input and differential output. If A_1 and A_2 are regarded separately, they will be recognized as modified voltage followers with feedback resistances R_1-R_3 and R_4-R_3, respectively. In a conventional follower with gain, R_3 would be returned to ground. In this case, however, R_3 is shared by A_1 and A_2, and rather than being returned to ground, it is connected to the summing point of the opposite amplifier. This provides a return for R_3 which is at virtual ground for differential signals, but which *follows* common-mode signals. As a result, there is no current flow in R_3 (or in R_1 or R_4) for common-mode signals. This is because there is no difference in voltage across R_3, due to the theory of zero differential-input voltage of A_1 and A_2. By contrast, differential signals at E_a or E_b will result in a voltage drop across R_3; thus the circuit amplifies only differential signals. Common-mode voltages leave the A_1-A_2 stage with unity gain, while differential-input voltages are amplified by a factor of $(R_3 + 2R_1)/R_3$.

Several advantages may be inferred from this fact. One, this stage provides an immediate gain in signal/noise ratio, because the differential signal is raised above the common-mode (noise) component by the ratio of the differential gain of the stage. Two, the gain-determining resistances (R_1, R_3, and R_4) *do not* affect CMRR and are therefore much less critical as to tolerance. Any mismatch in R_1 and R_4 will show up as a mismatch in differential gain between the two outputs, a far less serious condition than a CMRR loss.

Another feature of this circuit is the lack of gain for common-mode input signals. This factor has a bearing not only on actual

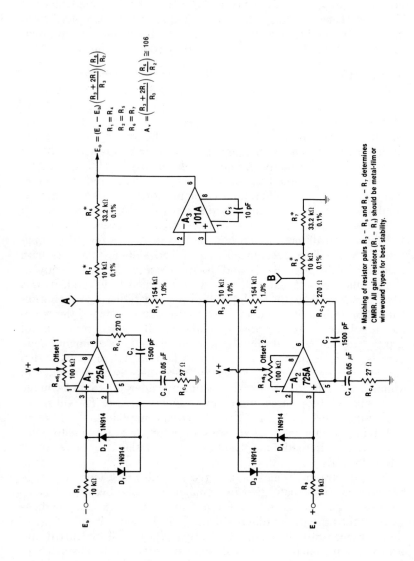

Fig. 5-58. Instrumentation amplifier with differential preamp.

common-mode inputs, but also on the offset drifts of A_1 and A_2. If A_1 and A_2 drift at an equal rate and in the same direction, the drift appears to this stage as a common-mode signal, is not amplified by the first stage, and is rejected by the second stage. This eases the drift requirements of A_1 and A_2, as long as they match. The gain factor of the first preamp stage can be made high enough that the drift and common-mode errors of the second stage become negligible by comparison, also easing the requirements on this amplifier considerably. The total gain of both stages is again the product of the two differential gains, or generally,

$$A_v = \left(\frac{R_3 + 2R_1}{R_3}\right)\left(\frac{R_6}{R_2}\right).$$

The circuit of Fig. 5-58 is optimized for minimum drift by using 725A amplifiers for A_1 and A_2. The total circuit gain is 106, distributed as a gain of 31.8 at A_1-A_2 and a gain of 3.32 at A_3. Nulling is accomplished individually for A_1 and A_2 by Offset 1 and Offset 2. The high common-mode and power-supply rejection ratios (minimum 120 dB and 106 dB, respectively) of the 725A make circuit errors very low as far as contributions from these sources. With the devices shown, the CMRR of the circuit is 120 dB; common-mode input range is ±10 V, and full-scale differential input is ±100 mV. If desired, this configuration can be modified to optimize parameters other than drift. Type-108 amplifiers for A_1 and A_2 will provide lower input current and higher input impedance. Similarly, if speed is the criterion, type 118s can be used for all three op amps.

Low-TC resistors should be used with this circuit to obtain the lowest possible drift, and consideration should be given to thermocouple effects. The circuit should also be shielded from circulating air currents to avoid thermal gradients. Offset voltages on A_1 and A_2 are nulled as follows:

1. Ground the inputs.
2. Ground the junction of R_3-R_4, adjust R_{adj_1} for 0 V dc output at point **A**.
3. Remove the ground at R_3-R_4 and ground the junction of R_1-R_3. Adjust R_{adj_2} for 0 V dc output at Point **B**.

5.14.6 High-Gain, Wide-Bandwidth Instrumentation Amplifier

There are alternate methods of achieving high common-mode rejection that are worth noting. Although not based entirely on op-amp theory, the circuit of Fig. 5-59 is one such example. Q_1 and Q_2 in this circuit are matched monolithic transistors, used as an emitter-coupled pair biased by constant-current sources Q_3 and Q_4. Since the output impedance of a current source such as Q_3 or Q_4 is extremely high, it raises the common-emitter impedance of Q_1 and Q_2. As a result, neither Q_1 nor Q_2 will have significant gain for a signal applied to both bases. Therefore, this stage by itself possesses a fairly high common-mode rejection.

Differential signals applied to Q_1 and Q_2 appear across R_g and are amplified by a factor inversely proportional to the value of R_g, since the signal current flowing in R_g appears doubled in R_8. Common-mode signals are attenuated by the Q_1-Q_2 stage by a factor of 60 dB and appear at the input to A_1 as a common-mode signal from Q_1-Q_2. Since this signal has already undergone a rejection in Q_1-Q_2, the balance of this bridge is not as critical—allowing 1.0% resistor tolerances. R_5 serves to null the output of A_1 when no input is present.

A unique feature is the stable, temperature-independent gain, even though Q_1 and Q_2 are not within a feedback loop. This is provided for by D_1 and Q_3-Q_4, with an output current that varies with temperature, complementing the change in transconductance of Q_1-Q_2 with temperature. The result is a gain characteristic that is flat within 1.0% over a temperature range of $-55°C$ to $+125°C$.

The circuit bandwidth is limited to approximately 2 MHz by the response of A_1. The circuit can handle common-mode input voltages up to $±10$ V, but the differential-input range (or sensitivity) is proportional to R_g. As R_g is lowered, gain is increased and less input

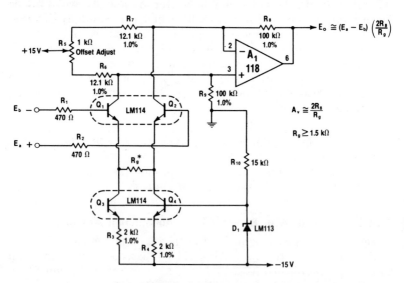

* R_g varied to adjust input sensitivity and gain; can be
greater than 200 kΩ if attenuation desired.

Fig. 5-59. High-gain, wide-bandwidth differential amplifier.

voltage is required for full-scale output. The range of linear gain is slightly over 40 dB—at lower values of R_g, the effect of emitter resistance in Q_1 and Q_2 begins to produce nonlinearities in the full-scale input.

5.15 ANALOG MULTIPLIERS

Earlier in this chapter it was seen how the multiplication of two dc voltages (or currents) is accomplished using logarithmic modules. Generally, logarithmic multiplication is confined to unipolar dc signals rather than bipolar dc or ac signals. When ac signals are to be multiplied, either by a unipolar dc signal or by a bipolar signal, the need arises for a different type of multiplier. This type is what is generally termed an *analog multiplier,* since it processes two analog signals to arrive at their product in analog form. Analog multipliers come in two basic types, two-quadrant and four quadrant. The difference between these two types is in the response to different input polarities.

5.15.1 Two-Quadrant Analog Multiplier

Fig. 5-60 depicts the output response of a two-quadrant multiplier to inputs E_x and E_y. From this may be noted several key features of operation. First, and perhaps most important, is the fact that if either E_x or E_y is zero, the output is zero. This satisfies the mathematical definition of multiplication by zero. Several curves of $E_o = E_x E_y$ are

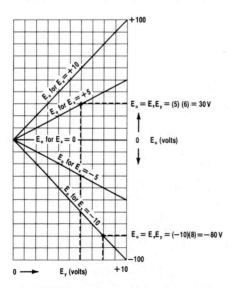

Fig. 5-60. Two-quadrant multiplier characteristic.

drawn for different values of E_x; E_y ranges continuously from 0 V to +10 V. The output resulting for a given E_x and E_y can be determined graphically by locating the intersection of the E_x and E_y curves. For example, if $E_x = +5$ V and $E_y = +6$ V, E_o is +30 V. A second example is $E_x = -10$ V and $E_y = +8$ V; in this case $E_o = -80$ V. These two examples illustrate two-quadrant operation—that is, the output responds to both polarities of E_x but to only one polarity of E_y. The output will follow the sign of E_x, but E_y must always remain in the range of 0 V to +10 V. In circuit terms, this means that E_x can be either a bipolar dc signal or ac signal, but E_y must be a single polarity of dc. This type of multiplier is often used as a linear gain control. Its usefulness can be appreciated by considering a fixed value of E_x as E_y ranges from zero to maximum. With E_x a constant dc value (or steady ac level), the output will be directly and linearly controlled (multiplied) by E_y. Conversely, if operation is viewed from the standpoint of E_y as a signal controlled by E_x, the output will be a varying level as E_x varies, but with the additional capability of sign reversal as E_x goes through zero.

5.15.2 Four-Quadrant Analog Multiplier

Going a step further, the four-quadrant multiplier extends operation of the E_y input into the opposite polarity (Fig. 5-61), allowing unrestricted operation with either E_x or E_y in the range of ±10 V. For operation with E_y from 0 V to +10 V, operation of a four-quadrant multiplier is completely like that of a two-quadrant type. This is

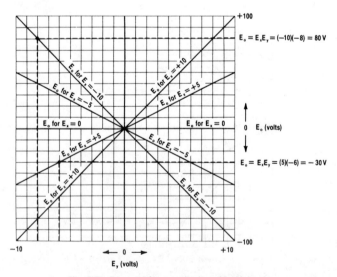

Fig. 5-61. Four-quadrant multiplier characteristic.

shown by the right half of Fig. 5-6. However, for operation with E_y from 0 V to −10 V, the outputs from a four-quadrant type are as shown in the left portion of the graph.

To illustrate four-quadrant operation in E_x and E_y, let $E_x = +5$ V and $E_y = -6$ V. The output is read from the curve of E_o for $E_x = +5$ V in the lower left quadrant. For this example, $E_o = -30$ V. Note that any product obtained in the lower two quadrants will be negative. As a second example, let $E_x = -10$ V, $E_y = -8$ V. The output is in the upper left quadrant on the $E_x = -10$-V line; $E_o = 80$ V. This is the correct mathematical expression for the product of two negative numbers—a positive result. The output of a four-quadrant multiplier will be the product of the two inputs, always with the correct sign. Finally, as with the two-quadrant type, the output will always be zero if either E_x or E_y is zero. In operation, a four-quadrant multiplier may be considered fully symmetrical. Either input offers control of amplitude and sign, and the output is always correct for instantaneous signs(s) and magnitude(s) of E_x and E_y.

So far we have spoken of multipliers in general terms only. To move into practical considerations requires some further definition of multiplier considerations and an understanding of the operation of typical devices. There are a number of circuit techniques for performing analog multiplication. Among these are the logarithmic technique mentioned earlier, the quarter-square technique (piecewise approximation), pulse-width and/or pulse-height modulation techniques, and variable transconductance methods. Of these the variable transconductance multiplier is the simplest and most economical, and it is realizable in a number of IC configurations. This technique is chosen as the foundation for discussion in this section. In the references provided, the interested reader can find material covering other approaches.

The symbolic representation for analog multipliers used in this book is shown in Fig. 5-62. The symbol is largely self-explanatory—like the op-amp symbol, it is not intended to denote circuit details, but simply indicates the function of the device. As will be seen shortly, the inputs may be differential for E_x and E_y, allowing a great

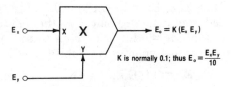

All voltages (E_x, E_y, and E_o) may be single-ended or differential.

Fig. 5-62. Symbolic multiplier representation.

deal of sign and scale-factor flexibility. Also, the output signal from a multiplier is normally scaled to a range of ± 10 V to provide compatibility with standard op-amp signal levels. Typically, the output is scaled by a factor of $K = 0.1$, to allow two full-scale inputs of ± 10 V. This in no way alters the basic multiplication principles; it is a provision for setting the output dynamic range at a practical level. Were this not done, the required output with $E_x = E_y = 10$ V would be ± 100 V, as shown in the theoretical graphs of Figs. 5-60 and 5-61.

5.15.3 Basic Arithmetic Functions Using Multipliers

Division

The process of multiplication is a function upon which many other operations are based. Division can be regarded as multiplication by the reciprocal of the divisor; thus $E_o = E_x/E_y$ can also be written $E_o = (E_x)(1/E_y)$. Since we can generate the reciprocal of a transfer function by placing it within a feedback loop, division is accomplished as shown in Fig. 5-63.

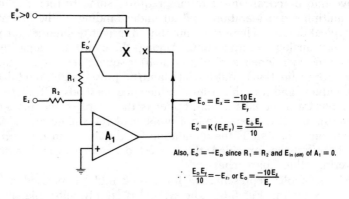

*E_y must be positive to maintain negative feedback around A_1.

Fig. 5-63. Division using a multiplier.

The output of a multiplier is the scaled product of its two inputs (E_x and E_y). In this case, $E_o' = K(E_x E_y) = 0.1 (E_o E_y)$. Since the E_o' voltage also feeds the summing point of A_1 through resistor R_1, it must also be true that $E_o' = -E_z$, since both these voltages must sum to zero at the summing point of A_1. Substituting,

$$E_o' = 0.1(E_o E_y) = -E_z,$$

which yields for E_o,

$$E_o = \frac{-10E_z}{E_y}.$$

It should be noted that, for this circuit to function correctly, E_y must always be a positive voltage. If E_y goes negative, the multiplier feedback becomes positive and a latch-up condition of A_1 occurs.

Squaring and Higher Powers

An obvious use for a multiplier is the multiplication of a signal by itself, or the square function, illustrated in Fig. 5-64A. Since $E_o = E_x E_y/10$ and E_x and E_y are identical signals, the output is then $E_o = E_x^2/10$. In similar fashion, the output of a squaring circuit may be fed into a second multiplier (Fig. 5-64B) along with the original signal to obtain a cube function: $E_o = E_x^2 E_x = E_x^3$. This concept can be extended to generate higher-order functions.

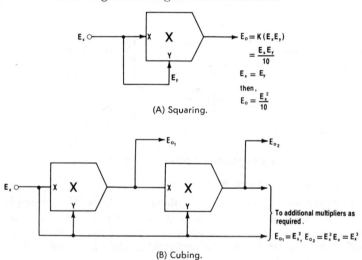

(A) Squaring.

(B) Cubing.

Fig. 5-64. Generating powers with a multiplier.

Square Root

A square-root function can be realized by placing a squarer within the feedback loop of an op amp, as in Fig. 5-65. Since the output of the multiplier is $E_o^2/10$, which will always be positive, the equal values of R_1 and R_2 will cause this value to be equal to $-E_z$. Thus, input E_z must be *negative* to produce a positive output at the amplifier. Finally,

$$\frac{E_o^2}{10} = -E_z,$$

and if $E_z < 0$,

$$E_o^2 = 10\,E_z;$$

so,

$$E_o = \sqrt{\mid 10E_z \mid}.$$

These are the basic arithmetic functions that can be generated using multipliers. There are elaborate variations and combinations of basic arithmetic functions, but they will not be detailed here. The interested reader should consult the references for further information.

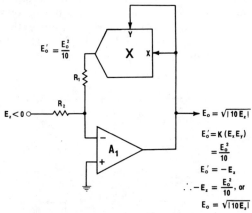

Fig. 5-65. Square-root generator using a multiplier.

5.15.4 Transconductance Multipliers

Virtually all popular IC multipliers operate on the principle of variable transconductance. A very rudimentary circuit that performs two-quadrant multiplication using this technique is shown in Fig. 5-66; it will be used as a developmental model for the more detailed structures to follow.

The circuit works by varying the emitter current of a matched pair of bipolar transistors. If the differential voltage, E_x, applied to Q_1-Q_2 is zero, the output is zero. As E_x varies, the output signal (I_o) from Q_1-Q_2 will be

$$I_o = \frac{q}{2\kappa T} I_E E_x.$$

This differential output is applied to A_1, a differential current-to-voltage converter. (See the section on instrumentation amplifiers.) The output from A_1 will be

$$E_o = I_o R_o = \left(\frac{q}{2\kappa T} I_E E_x \right) R_{10}.$$

Finally, if we vary the emitter currents of Q_1 and Q_2 with a second input, E_y, the value of I_E will be approximately $I_E = E_y/R_3$. This

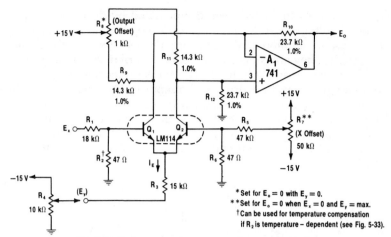

Fig. 5-66. Basic two-quadrant transconductance multiplier.

can be substituted into the equation for E_o and, with some rearrangement,

$$E_o = E_x E_y \left(\frac{q}{2\kappa T}\right)\left(\frac{R_{10}}{R_3}\right).$$

From this it can be seen that the circuit accomplishes multiplication of E_x and E_y if the other terms of the equation are considered constant.

An examination of Fig. 5-66 will reveal that this circuit responds only to single polarities of E_y (negative in this example), but to bipolar signals at E_x. This is (by definition) two-quadrant multiplication. As E_y is varied to change I_E, the collector voltages of both Q_1 and Q_2 rise and fall with the change in common-mode signal. A_1 and the differential bridge resistors (R_9 through R_{12}) reject this common-mode signal while amplifying the desired differential signal (I_o) from E_x. Balance of the bridge is critical to good rejection of the E_y signal at the output; therefore, the bridge should either use close-tolerance (0.1%) resistors or be nulled as shown, with R_8. R_7 zeros the offset voltage of Q_1-Q_2.

An inherent property of this circuit is that linearity holds only for relatively small signal amplitudes of E_x. Directly at Q_1, this limit is ±10 mV for 1.0% linearity; thus, an attenuator network such as R_1-R_2 is necessary to scale the input range up to the standard ±10-V levels. Also, to compensate the TC of gain due to the $\kappa T/q$ factor, R_2 can be made a thermistor with a TC of +0.3%/°C, as in Fig. 5-33.

5.15.5 Improving the Basic Two-Quadrant Multiplier

The circuit of Fig. 5-67 is an improvement on the basic multiplier circuit in two major respects. First, the nonlinearity displayed by

Q_1-Q_2 at the E_x input has been compensated by developing a pre-distorted voltage drive with the feedback loop around A_2 and Q_3-Q_4. Q_3 and Q_4 are a differential transistor pair, operated at a fixed emitter current. They are connected so that the current swing in Q_3 must equal the current swing in R_1. A_2 will force this current to be linear, even though the voltage drive at the input to Q_4 (and Q_1) will be nonlinear. This method ensures a linear current output from the differential pair, Q_3-Q_4; therefore, an identical pair (Q_1-Q_2) can also be driven in parallel, with a similar linear output. R_1 is selected for the desired full-scale input current, I_x; in this case $I_x = \pm 250$ μA at ± 10 V.

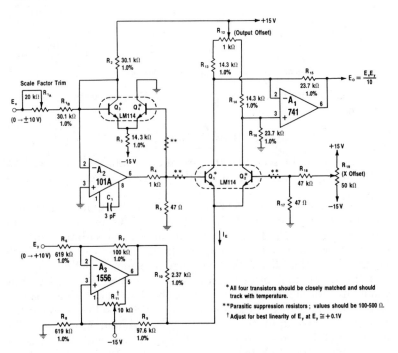

Fig. 5-67. Improved two-quadrant multiplier.

The other improvement is the method of current drive for the controlled pair, Q_1-Q_2. The simple resistive current drive (R_3) used in Fig. 5-66 is not entirely satisfactory in providing a linear variation of I_E as E_y approaches zero. A feedback configuration improves linearity, and this is accomplished by a bilateral VCCS (see Chapter 4), consisting of A_3 and associated components. The VCCS circuit supplies an output current that is linear at any level of E_y, thus extending linearity to cover very small E_y voltages. R_{1_A} trims the overall circuit scale factor by setting the desired value of I_x when E_x is at a maximum. The other trim adjustments perform functions similar to those of Fig. 5-66, except for R_{11}, which nulls the offset voltage of A_3 for best linearity of E_y. Optimum results with this circuit require that the four transistors be matched fairly well to track with temperature.

5.15.6 Monolithic IC Multipliers

The circuitry described so far, while useful, is intended primarily to demonstrate the general principles of variable-transconductance multiplication. This includes not only the basic premise of gain variation by control of emitter current, but also the requirements for linearization and conversion from differential to single-ended operation.

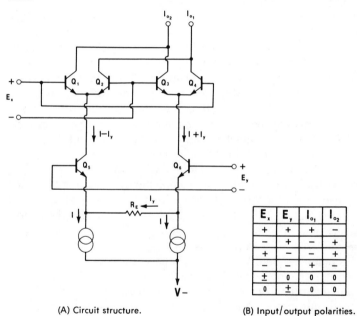

(A) Circuit structure.

(B) Input/output polarities.

E_x	E_y	I_{o_1}	I_{o_2}
+	+	+	−
−	+	−	+
+	−	−	+
−	−	+	−
±	0	0	0
0	±	0	0

Fig. 5-68. Basic operation of a monolithic four-quadrant multiplier.

Commercial IC multipliers are typically four-quadrant extensions of the basic two-quadrant concept. These monolithic units often utilize a circuit structure similar to Fig. 5-68A. The circuit can be viewed as a pair of cross-connected differential pairs (Q_1-Q_2 and Q_3-Q_4), fed by controlled emitter currents (from Q_5-Q_6) and having a common differential base drive (E_x). If the circuit is sectioned between Q_2-Q_3 and Q_5-Q_6, each half is a single differential pair similar to Q_1-Q_2 in Fig. 5-66. In fact, this circuit is actually a pair of two-quadrant multipliers interconnected to form one composite, four-quadrant multiplier. Operation of the circuit is best understood by examining the output current(s) of transistors Q_1 and Q_4.

Current-source transistors Q_5 and Q_6 transform one input voltage (E_y) into complementary currents $I + I_y$ and $I - I_y$. Regarding output terminal I_{o_1} first, we can see how multiplication occurs. If E_x and E_y have the polarities shown (call these positive), Q_4 will be on and receive the current $I + I_y$. When E_x is negative, Q_2 will be on and the I_{o_1} output will be $I - I_y$. This illustrates the control of polarity that E_x exercises over the $I + I_y$ currents. With E_x positive, Q_4 will be on and I_{o_1} will be the current from Q_6. If E_y is also positive at the same instant, this value of I_{o_1} will be $I + I_y$; if E_y is negative instead, the value of I_{o_1} is $I - I_y$. If both E_x and E_y are negative, I_{o_1} becomes the current from Q_5, or $I + I_y$.

When the preceding four cases are summarized, it can be seen that operation is four-quadrant—always with the correct sign for any combination of E_x and E_y. An additional feature of operation occurs when either E_x or E_y is zero. If $E_y = 0$, $I_y = 0$ and $I_{o_1} = I$. As E_x alternates polarity, Q_4 turns on as Q_2 turns off and vice versa. However, the currents in Q_5 and Q_6 remain the same and there is no net change in I_{o_1}. Likewise, if $E_x = 0$, no net change in I_{o_1} will occur as E_y is varied, because the output will contain equal proportions from Q_2 and Q_4. Due to symmetry, the currents $I + I_y$ and $I - I_y$ are equal and opposite, and will therefore cancel each other.

The operation of the circuit for different conditions of E_x and E_y is summarized in Fig. 5-68B. The complementary output (I_{o_2}) will always receive the negative of the current appearing at I_{o_1}. Thus, the output signals at I_{o_1} and I_{o_2} are differentially multiplied *currents*. To convert them back to a voltage requires a differential current-to-voltage converter such as that used in Figs. 5-66 or 5-67.

At this point it should be noted that there is no fundamental guide to the designation of X and Y inputs. The multiplication principle is the same regardless of which input is termed "X" or "Y." This is mentioned only because there is no complete standardization of X and Y designations among manufacturers; however, this should not be a handicap if the fundamental principles are kept in mind.

To complete the multiplier, a diode linearity correction circuit is added to develop a nonlinear voltage drive for the bases of Q_1-Q_4. This linearizes the X input in a fashion similar to the circuit used in Fig. 5-67. Darlington devices are used for the Q_5-Q_6 voltage-to-current converters to minimize error, with similar devices added to the X input. A complete circuit that accomplishes linear four-quadrant multiplication is shown in Fig. 5-69. Both the X and Y inputs are fully differential and are scaled in sensitivity with an external emit-

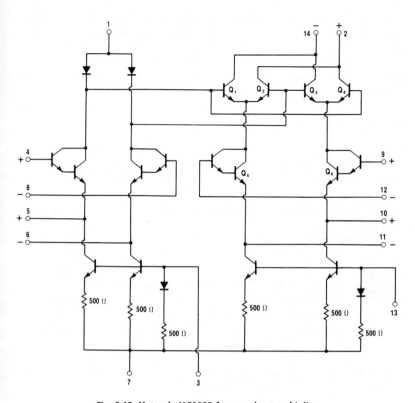

Fig. 5-69. Motorola MC1595 four-quadrant multiplier.

ter resistor. The differential- and common-mode input range is ±10 V. The flexibility of this multiplier block is maximized since virtually all circuit nodes are externally accessible, allowing operation in a variety of modes.

Due to the additional stage in the E_x input of this multiplier, a redefinition of polarities is necessary. This is shown in the block diagram of Fig. 5-70. Pins 4 and 8 are the differential E_x inputs, and pins 9 and 12 are the differential E_y inputs. Current scaling in both inputs is set by resistors R_x and R_y, which set currents I_x and I_y according to $I_x = E_x/R_x$ and $I_y = E_y/R_y$. In using the device, either sign may be realized by applying an input signal to the inverting or noninverting input as desired, with scaling set by R_x and R_y. A summary of input/output relations is also given in Fig. 5-70.

5.15.7 Multiplier Applications

Fig. 5-71 illustrates a four-quadrant multiplier using the basic 1595 multiplier block in conjunction with a 741 current-to-voltage converter. This circuit is useful as either a multiplier or a squarer. Input voltages E_x and E_y are ±10-V bipolar signals, applied in single-ended fashion to the noninverting E_x and E_y inputs (pins 4 and 9). The opposite sides of the two differential inputs (pins 8 and 12) are connected to offset adjustments R_{19} and R_{20} to trim any residual imbalance in the input amplifiers. R_3 and R_7 scale the input signal currents (I_x and I_y), and R_9 is used to set the overall scale factor by adjusting the bias current applied to pin 3. A_1, the output level-shift amplifier, converts the differential currents at pins 2 and 14 into a single-ended output voltage, E_o. Resistors R_{13}-R_{17} form a common-mode rejection bridge similar to those described in Section 5.14. R_{17} is used to trim the bridge for minimum output offset.

There are several points that help clarify the importance of various circuit elements. Generally, the trim adjustments shown are needed for greatest accuracy. If reduced performance is acceptable, they can be eliminated in some cases, although this is not recommended because the cumulative error could exceed 10%. R_4 and R_8, for instance, can be grounded and the entire input offset network eliminated. Similarly, resistors R_9-R_{10} can be replaced with a 15-kΩ fixed value, R_{16}-R_{17} can be fixed at the same value as R_{15}, and the close-tolerance resistors can be replaced with 5% tolerances. Again, however, the loss of accuracy involved in making these alterations is severe and may not be tolerable.

Due to the very wide bandwidth of the 1595, rf instability can be a problem. In situations where the impedance seen at pins 4, 8, 9, and 12 is low, resistors such as R_4 and R_8 are necessary to provide

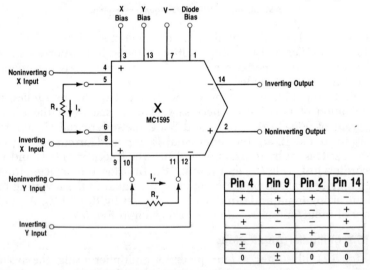

Pin 4	Pin 9	Pin 2	Pin 14
+	+	+	−
−	+	−	+
+	−	−	+
−	−	+	−
±	0	0	0
0	±	0	0

Fig. 5-70. Operational diagram of MC1595 multiplier.

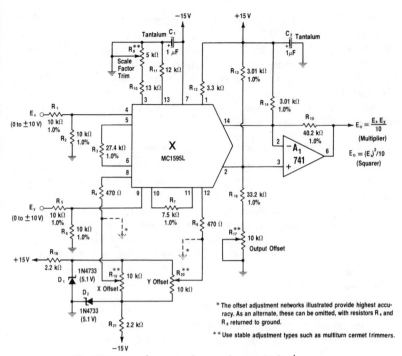

Fig. 5-71. General-purpose, four-quadrant multiplier/squarer.

parasitic suppression. Also, a good rf bypass capacitor (C_1) is needed at the -15-V supply terminal; it is good practice to provide one (C_2) on the $+15$-V line as well. Finally, minimal rf sensitivity requires a direct and compact circuit layout.

With a "multiplying block" such as the 1595, the paramount feature is flexibility, due to the virtually complete accessibility of the internal circuit, and the ability to scale operation as required. For instance, change of input signal polarity at E_x or E_y involves simply interchanging the inverting and noninverting E_x or E_y pins. Similarly, an inverted output sign is possible by interchanging pins 2 and 14. Scale factors are set not only by the overall adjustment of "K" at R_9 but may be set individually for E_x or E_y by adjusting the respective input resistors (R_3, R_7). Operation of the circuit as a squarer of E_x is accomplished by connecting pins 4 and 9, and omitting R_5 and R_6 (at the E_y input).

Divider/Square-Rooter

With only slight modification of the multiplier/squarer, a divider/square-rooter is formed as in Fig. 5-72. This circuit places the multiplier within an op-amp feedback loop, as illustrated earlier in Fig.

5-63. Multiplier bias and operation are similar to Fig. 5-71, with the exception of values. The E_z input is applied to A_1 through R_{15}, and the feedback loop around A_1 is completed through the X input of the multiplier. The E_y input is restricted to positive voltages, as mentioned previously. To convert to a square-rooter for E_x, eliminate R_1 and R_2 (the E_y input) and connect pins 9 and 4.

As previously, 1.0% components and offset adjustments are recommended for highest accuracy.

5.15.8 Communications Circuits Using Multipliers

So far, the multiplier applications discussed have involved arithmetic computation. However, even broader applications are possible using multipliers in the processing of communications signals. These functions include modulation (a-m and dsb), demodulation, electronic gain control, and many others. When operating at high frequencies, the output op amp becomes a limiting factor. Transconductance multipliers such as the 1595 are extremely fast and may be used at frequencies above 10 MHz. This factor is the single greatest advantage to using a "multiplying block" such as the 1595.

Wideband Frequency Doubler

A common communications circuit requirement is a frequency doubler, a circuit that produces an output frequency equal to the

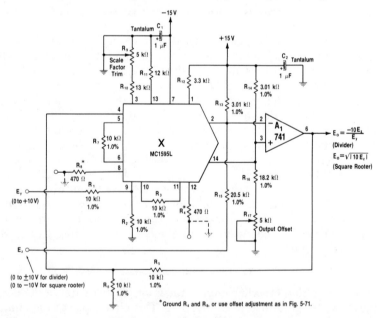

Fig. 5-72. Divide/square-root circuit.

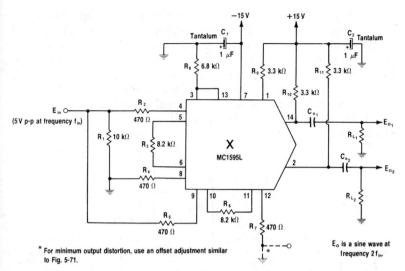

E_0 is a sine wave at frequency $2f_{in}$.

Fig. 5-73. Wideband frequency doubler.

second harmonic of the input. An ac-coupled multiplier connected in the squaring mode can perform this function with no tuned circuits, allowing operation over wide bandwidths with no adjustment. Furthermore, for a sine-wave input waveform, the output will also be a sine wave with low distortion; a THD of 1.0% or less being typically possible.

A circuit that performs the doubling function is shown in Fig. 5-73. Since the X and Y inputs in this example are identical, a common bias setting resistor (R_8) is used. Outputs can be taken from either pin 2 or pin 14, depending on the desired phase. C_{o_1}-C_{o_2} should be chosen for negligible reactance with respect to R_{L_1} and R_{L_2}, the load impedance of the following stage. The circuit will work as shown with R_7 grounded, but an offset adjustment can be utilized for minimum distortion if desired.

The high-frequency performance of this circuit is dependent on the RC time constant at several circuit points. R_{10}-R_{11} and/or R_L may be reduced to decrease the effects of stray capacitance at the output, and buffering with an emitter follower will also help. Similarly, reducing R_3 and R_6 will reduce the effects of stray capacitance at the input. With circuit impedances optimized for hf performance, this basic configuration can operate at frequencies as high as several megahertz.

Balanced Modulation/Demodulation

A circuit very similar to the previous one is the balanced modulator/demodulator shown in Fig. 5-74. This is virtually the same circuit as Fig. 5-73, but with the X and Y inputs separated. If two separate frequencies, f_c and f_m, are applied to the two inputs, the output will contain neither of the two original inputs, only their products, in the form of $f_c \pm f_m$. There is no restriction on which input is used for the carrier or modulation, since they are symmetrical. There is also no limitation on either of the two frequencies, they may be widely separated (as in conventional modulation systems) or nearly identical, because of the untuned, wide-bandwidth method of modulation.

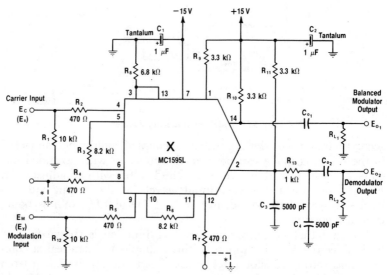

* For greatest accuracy, use offset adjustment (Fig. 5-71) at pins 8 and 12: with a maximum E_{in} at one input, set the opposite input for a null at the output.

Fig. 5-74. Balanced modulator/demodulator.

The circuit will work with R_4 and R_7 grounded as shown, but for optimum suppression of the input signals both channels should be nulled. This is accomplished by applying either input signal and then adjusting the offset control on the opposite channel for minimum output. With nulling, carrier suppression can approach 60 dB. If very wide bandwidth is desired, the time-constant considerations discussed for Fig. 5-73 should be applied.

The modulator/demodulator circuit can be used for a-m or ssb demodulation by applying a modulated carrier to one input and an unmodulated carrier of identical frequency and phase to the second input, and by adding a low-pass filter to the output. The multiplying action of the constant-level carrier and the varying-level modulated wave results in a series of rectified output pulses corresponding to the modulation envelope. The low-pass filter then removes the residual carrier components, leaving only the modulation. This form of demodulation is very linear and has a wide dynamic range, since it does not have the "diode threshold" of standard a-m demodulators. The low-pass filter used to recover the modulation is formed by R_{11} (or R_{10} if taken from pin 14) and C_3 plus R_{13}-C_4. C_{o_2} is a coupling capacitor chosen for low reactance in relation to R_{L_2}. The demodulator circuit, like the modulator, may be used on either output terminal. Offset adjustments are generally not necessary with the demodulator, however, since the output filter rejects any residual carrier which might leak through.

A-M Modulator

Conventional amplitude modulation can also be accomplished with a multiplier as shown in Fig. 5-75. In reality, a-m is a variation

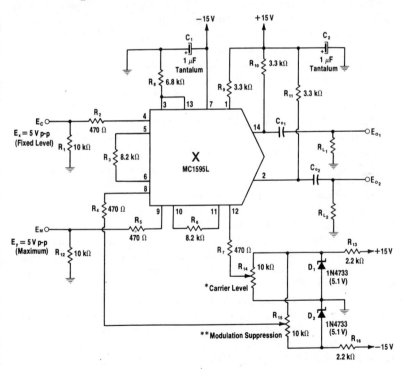

* Set for 100% modulation with input levels at 5 V p-p.

** Adjust for null output with carrier $E_c = 0$.

Fig. 5-75. A-m modulator.

in level of a constant carrier. In this circuit the carrier is applied to one input of the modulator, and a fixed dc level (bias) is applied to the second input. This results in a constant-level carrier output. If modulation is then applied in addition to the bias voltage, with a p-p amplitude of twice the bias level, 100% a-m will result.

In Fig. 5-75, R_{14} inserts a fixed 2.5-V bias at the inverting Y input, producing a constant-level carrier at the output. A 5-V p-p signal at the modulation input will alternately double and cancel the carrier level at the output by summing with this bias. With the values shown, a 5-V p-p signal at the modulation input will result in 100% modulation. The offset adjustment for the Y channel, R_{15}, is used to suppress any direct feedthrough of the modulation signal. The circuit can be optimized for high-frequency carrier operation by reducing the values of R_{10} and R_{11} at the output, and R_3 at the input.

Electronic Gain Control

As was mentioned briefly in the introductory comments on multipliers, both two- and four-quadrant types can be used as electronic gain controls. This allows programmable or remote gain adjustments, agc functions, and a wide variety of special electronic effects. Although either type of multiplier can be used in this manner, the two-quadrant version is more ideally suited, so this type of circuit will be emphasized in the present discussion.

To use a four-quadrant multiplier as a gain control, all that need be done is apply a signal to one input and a variable control voltage to the opposite input. Such a circuit could use, for example, Fig. 5-71 in the multiplying mode. Viewed as a voltage-controlled attenuator, this circuit has an attenuation of 0 dB (unity gain) when the control voltage is maximum. Below this control voltage, the output is attenuated by 20 dB for each 20-dB reduction in control voltage (linear multiplication). However, the drawback is that this relation is valid only over a dynamic range of about 60 dB, and distortion increases rapidly as the gain is reduced, with typical THD figures of 1 to 2%. Neither of these characteristics is satisfactory for a high-quality, audio-signal-processing device. They are due to the basic four-quadrant structure, which relies on a balance between two opposing two-quadrant multipliers.

Actually, an electronic gain control does not require four-quadrant capability at all, since the controlling signal can be defined as unipolar, ranging from some maximum full-scale value down to zero. The basic transconductance multiplier we have been discussing—the 1595—can also be used in a two-quadrant mode, as illustrated in Fig. 5-76.

Conversion of the 1595 to two-quadrant operation involves only the disabling of one of the two-quadrant multipliers shown in Fig.

5-70. In the version shown here (Fig. 5-76), Q_5 is disabled by grounding the base and emitter (pins 11 and 12), and no bias is supplied to pin 13. The remaining two-quadrant multiplier section using Q_6 is biased externally by op-amp A_2, which acts as a positive-input VCCS (see Chapter 4). Operated as shown, the circuit resembles the improved two-quadrant multiplier of Fig. 5-67. Two-quadrant multiplier operation of a differential pair is precisely controllable over an extremely wide dynamic range—100 dB or better of gain control is readily achievable. In addition, the only significant

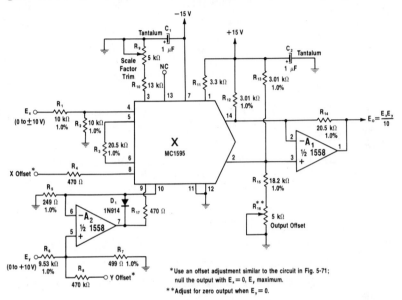

Fig. 5-76. Two-quadrant multiplier using four-quadrant device.

distortion mechanism is "linearization," which comes from the diodes that process the E_x signal internally. This distortion is mostly from the second harmonic; it can be controlled by scaling R_3 (R_x) appropriately, thus limiting the I_x current. For example, in the circuit shown, the THD is below 0.5% at a full-scale input of ±10 V, and it reduces to negligible values at lower input levels, where it would typically be operated in an audio circuit.

A further asset of the two-quadrant multiplier over the four-quadrant is in terms of noise. The two-quadrant transconductance multiplier reduces the output noise level along with the signal, whereas a four-quadrant type does not. This factor is important where good signal-to-noise ratios and wide dynamic range are important.

The circuit is otherwise similar in many regards to previous ones, with the exception of the VCCS, A_2. The accuracy of this voltage-to-current converter will determine the overall dynamic range of attenuation; it is limited at the low end by the residual offset voltage of A_2, which should be nulled for best results. Other variations of the VCCS block can also be used if they are compatible with the bias requirements of the 1595. As shown, the current in R_5 is 2.0 mA for unity gain, and the bias voltage level at pin 10 should be +0.5 V or less.

REFERENCES

1. Analog Devices Application Note, 1970. *Evaluating, Selecting, and Using Multiplier Circuit Modules for Signal Manipulation and Function Generation.* Analog Devices, Inc., Norwood, Mass.

2. *Applications Manual for Computing Amplifiers.* Philbrick Researches, Inc., Dedham, Mass., 1966.

3. Borlase, W. *Application and Analysis of the AD520 Monolithic Data Amplifier.* Analog Devices Application Note, June 1972. Analog Devices, Inc., Norwood, Mass.

4. _____; David, E. *Design of Temperature-Compensated Log Circuits Employing Transistors and Operational Amplifiers.* Analog Devices Application Note E020-10, March 1969. Analog Devices, Inc., Norwood, Mass.

5. Burwen, R. "A Complete Multiplier/Divider on a Single Chip." *Analog Dialogue,* Vol. 5, No. 1, January 1971.

6. _____; Sullivan, D. *AD530 Complete Monolithic MDSSR Technical Bulletin,* July 1971. Analog Devices, Inc., Norwood, Mass.

7. Clayton, G. B. *Operational Amplifiers.* Butterworth, Inc., Toronto, Ont., Canada, 1971.

8. Demrow, R. *Evolution from Operational Amplifier to Data Amplifier.* Analog Devices Application Note, September 1968. Analog Devices, Inc., Norwood, Mass.

9. Dobkin, R. C. *Feedforward Compensation Speeds Op Amp.* National Semiconductor LB-2, April 1969. National Semiconductor Corp., Santa Clara, Calif.

10. _____. *Instrumentation Amplifier.* National Semiconductor LB-1, March 1969. National Semiconductor Corp., Santa Clara, Calif.

11. _____. *Logarithmic Converters.* National Semiconductor Application Note AN-30, November 1969. National Semiconductor Corp., Santa Clara, Calif.

12. _____. *Op Amp Circuit Collection.* National Semiconductor Application Note AN-31, February 1970. National Semiconductor Corp., Santa Clara, Calif.

13. _____. *Precision AC-DC Converters*. National Semiconductor LB-8, August 1969. National Semiconductor Corp., Santa Clara, Calif.

14. Fairchild Semiconductor Application Bulletin APP-138, July 1969. *μA725 Instrumentation Applications*. Fairchild Semiconductor, Mountain View, Calif.

15. Fullagar, D. *The 8007—A High-Performance FET-Input Operational Amplifier*. Intersil Application Bulletin A005, March 1972. Intersil, Inc., Cupertino, Calif.

16. Gilbert, B. "A Precise Four-Quadrant Multiplier With Sub-Nanosecond Response." *IEEE Journal of Solid State Circuits*, December 1968.

17. Giles, J. N. *Fairchild Semiconductor LIC Handbook*. Fairchild Semiconductor, Mountain View, Calif., 1967.

18. Gurski, R. J. "Logarithmic Devices." *The Lightning Empiricist*, Vol. 17, No. 1, March 1969. Philbrick/Nexus Research, Dedham, Mass.

19. Huehne, K. *The MC1556 Operational Amplifier and its Applications*. Motorola Application Note AN-522, 1970. Motorola Semiconductor Products, Inc., Phoenix, Ariz.

20. _____. *Transistor Logarithmic Conversion Using an Integrated Circuit Operational Amplifier*. Motorola Application Note AN-261A, 1971. Motorola Semiconductor Products, Inc., Phoenix, Ariz.

21. National Semiconductor Application Note AN-32, February 1970. *FET Circuit Applications*. National Semiconductor Corp., Santa Clara, Calif.

22. Paterson, W. L. "Multiplication and Logarithmic Conversion by Operational Amplifier-Transistor Circuits." *The Review of Scientific Instruments*, Vol. 34, No. 12, December 1963.

23. Renschler, E. *Analysis and Basic Operation of the MC1595*. Motorola Application Note AN-489, March 1970. Motorola Semiconductor Products, Inc., Phoenix, Ariz.

24. _____. "The Monolithic Multiplier." *Motorola Monitor*, Vol. 7, No. 3, 1969.

25. Rudin, M. *Applying Microvolt/Picoamp Instrumentation Operational Amplifiers*. Precision Monolithics Application Note. Precision Monolithics, Inc., Santa Clara, Calif.

26. Sheingold, D. H. *Analog-Digital Conversion Handbook*. Analog Devices, Inc., Norwood, Mass., 1972.

27. Texas Instruments Application Bulletin CA-149, March 1970. *Logarithmic and Exponential Amplifiers With SN72709*. Texas Instruments, Inc., Dallas, Tex.

28. Tobey, G. E.; Graeme, J. G.; Huelsman, L. P. *Operational Amplifiers—De-*

sign and Applications. Burr-Brown Research Corp., McGraw-Hill Book Co., New York, 1971.

29. Welling, B.; Kinsey, L. *Using the MC1595 Multiplier in Arithmetic Operations.* Motorola Application Note AN-490, October 1970. Motorola Semiconductor Products, Inc., Phoenix, Ariz.

30. Widlar, R. J. "Designing With Super-Beta Transistor Op-Amp ICs." *EEE,* December 1969, February and March 1970.

31. _____. *IC Op Amp Beats FETs on Input Current.* National Semiconductor Application Note AN-29, December 1969. National Semiconductor Corp., Santa Clara, Calif.

32. _____. *Monolithic Operational Amplifiers—The Universal Linear Component.* National Semiconductor Application Note AN-4, April 1968. National Semiconductor Corp., Santa Clara, Calif.

6

Audio Circuits

Some of the most useful IC op-amp applications are in audio-frequency circuits where the inherently high gain of the device elevates the quality of attainable performance to a new high. Distortion can be reduced to extremely low levels; frequency response can be shaped at will by the proper selection of external passive components; and smaller, simpler, and more economical circuits can be built.

However, these obviously attractive virtues cannot be realized by haphazard selection of op-amp types. Although many IC op amps possess excellent dc characteristics, they are not all equally useful at audio frequencies, particularly when operated at high gains and high output levels. The successful designer of quality audio circuits must take these factors into account; therefore, in this chapter the optimization of high-frequency as well as low-frequency performance will be stressed, and methods to circumvent the common pitfalls will be illustrated. Since frequency-response considerations are basic to all audio-frequency circuits regardless of their configuration, it is appropriate to consider the factors that govern correct IC selection prior to the discussion of specific circuits.

6.1 IC OP-AMP PARAMETERS IMPORTANT IN AUDIO APPLICATIONS

The most important dynamic specification of any op amp, including IC op amps, is open-loop gain. Open-loop gain ultimately affects the quality of all closed-loop parameters—distortion, input impedance, output impedance, gain variations, frequency response, and frequency-response variations. The degree of improvement due to feedback is in direct relation to the loop gain—the difference in dB between the open-loop gain and the closed-loop gain in a given circuit configuration. This basic concept is illustrated by the simple inverting amplifier of Fig. 6-1A, which uses a 741 op amp. The open-loop frequency response of the 741 is shown in Fig. 6-1B. If we disregard any nonideal op-amp characteristics for the moment and consider the gain of the circuit for any combination of feedback, the gain is simply $-R_2/R_1$, where R_2 and R_1 are the feedback and input resistances, respectively. Any desired value of gain may be obtained simply by plugging in the appropriate values for R_2 and R_1.

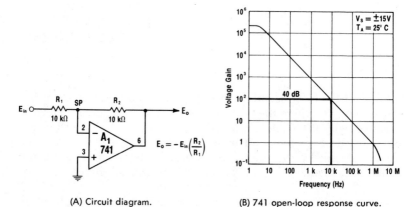

(A) Circuit diagram.   (B) 741 open-loop response curve.

Fig. 6-1. Unity-gain inverter using the 741 general-purpose op amp.

At this point it is appropriate to reiterate the characteristics of an ideal op amp defined in Chapter 1—infinite gain, infinite bandwidth, infinite input impedance, zero output impedance, and zero output with zero differential-input voltage. Also, the reader is advised to review the inverse relationship between gain and bandwidth, referred to as the gain-bandwidth product (GBP), which was discussed at length in Chapter 1. This will be helpful in understanding the following discussion of GBP as it relates to audio circuits.

6.1.1 Gain-Bandwidth Product

With reference to Figs 6-1A and B, and with regard to the effects of a 741 op amp on the simple inverter, it becomes clear that there are definite limitations on the total available open-loop gain. Also, this available gain is reduced as the frequency increases. It is obvious that you can obtain no more gain or bandwidth from a given amplifier than its open-loop response can provide. Inspection of the open-loop response of a 741 (Fig. 6-1B) will show the available gain at a given frequency (heavy vertical line) or, conversely, the available bandwidth for a given closed-loop gain (heavy horizontal line). For example, a gain of 40 dB will yield a maximum frequency response of 10 kHz. This is the absolute best that can be done, and the only way to obtain more bandwidth is to reduce the gain. Also, it should be noted that in a 40-dB, 10-kHz-bandwidth amplifier such as this, there is a decreasing feedback characteristic in the region from 10 Hz and above due to the rolloff in open-loop gain. Therefore, the benefits of the high open-loop gain of the amplifier exist only at 10 Hz and below. In fact, the full dc gain of the amplifier is not realized within the total audio spectrum (approximately 20 Hz to 20 kHz), and the gain decreases at a rate of 6 dB/octave (20 dB/decade) until a point is reached at the upper frequencies (10 kHz in the 40-dB example) where the circuit simply runs out of gain. At this point, the closed-loop gain becomes equal to the open-loop gain. Thus, the 741 would be a poor choice for the 40-dB amplifier of Fig. 6-1, since at the upper frequencies there is no feedback due to the rolloff in loop gain.

For audio-frequency use, the response of a 741 is better suited to lower-gain configurations, such as 0 dB or 20 dB, where the op amp still possesses some feedback at the higher frequencies. Even then, the loop gain resulting with a 0-dB (unity gain), 741 amplifier is only 40 dB at 10 kHz, which is far from the loop gain of 100 dB at 10 Hz. Similarly, a 20-dB, 741 configuration results in only 20 dB of loop gain at 10 kHz. The reader should note that a 0-dB, unity-gain configuration occurs only with the voltage follower, where the feedback attenuation factor (β) is 1, or feedback is 100%. The unity-gain inverter (Fig. 6-1A) has a β of 0.5 due to the noise gain ($1/\beta$) of 2 (6 dB). (The two resistors, R_1 and R_2, reduce the feedback signal by a factor of 2 at the summing point.) Therefore, the loop gain of the inverter will be 6 dB less than that of the follower. From this we can conclude that the open-loop frequency response of a 741-type amplifier represents a real limitation for audio applications, unless the performance requirements are modest.

A 1.0-MHz gain-bandwidth product (GBP), such as represented by Fig. 6-1B, is characteristic of a large number of IC op amps, and the preceding discussion applies in all such types. Some examples are the 741 and its family members (747, 1558); the 709; the 101, 101A, and 748; and the 531, 1556, and 8007.

In order to obtain a higher loop gain at the upper audio frequencies, it is necessary to increase the GBP to significantly above 1.0 MHz, since it has been shown that a 1.0-MHz GBP is only marginally adequate at low gains. This becomes even more important in the cases of high-gain, wide-bandwidth stages. A 60-dB amplifier requires a 10-MHz GBP just to realize a gain of 1000 in a bandwidth of 10 kHz. To provide adequate loop gain in such an amplifier requires a GBP of 100 MHz or better. It should be obvious by now that a high GBP is one factor that is fundamental to high-performance, high-gain ac amplifiers.

A more general picture of the interrelationship between open-loop response, GBP, loop gain, and closed-loop response is shown in Fig. 6-2. With this graph, the requirements for any audio-frequency amplifier can be quickly analyzed in terms of required open-loop gain and GBP. The upper frequency limit of the amplifier being designed is plotted as a vertical line that extends to a height in dB equal to the desired closed-loop gain, plus the loop gain necessary to maintain the accuracy required at this frequency. For example, if a 60-dB-gain amplifier is required to have 1.0% accuracy at a frequency of 10 kHz, a feedback of 40 dB is necessary. Thus, the line would extend to $60 + 40 = 100$ dB at 10 kHz. This is the actual open-loop gain required of the amplifier at this frequency for this amount of feedback.

At this point on the graph of Fig. 6-2 (point A) the frequency-limit line intersects the horizontal line of the required gain (100 dB) and also intersects a line sloping at 20 dB/decade (6 dB/octave), which is the required gain-bandwidth curve. Following this sloping line down to where it intercepts the frequency axis gives the required GBP, which in this case is 1000 MHz.

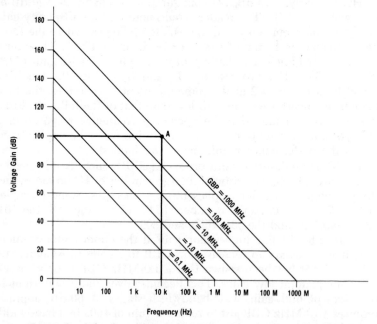

Fig. 6-2. Graph for determining the required gain-bandwidth product (GBP).

The selection of an amplifier can now be made by choosing a device that will provide 100-dB minimum gain at a frequency of 10 kHz. The reader will note that in many cases the low-frequency gain of a particular op amp will exceed 100 dB, then will roll off toward zero at frequencies above some corner frequency. But in terms of providing a required GBP, all that is needed is the computed value of open-loop gain at the highest frequency. Any additional gain at lower frequencies is a bonus—one that serves to increase the low-frequency accuracy of the circuit.

The example given represents an extreme case, since few IC op amps can provide a 1000-MHz GBP. It was chosen specifically to illustrate the importance of GBP, because the requirements used as an example are not unrealistic. A 60-dB, 10-kHz-bandwidth amplifier is a common requirement for a microphone preamplifier. If a single IC type cannot furnish the required GBP (and accuracy), the use of two cascaded stages will ease the specification requirements for each amplifier. In this example, the use of two 30-dB stages with an open-loop gain of 70 dB each (30 + 40) at 10 kHz will reduce the GBP requirement to approximately 32 MHz.

The Benefits of Custom Compensation

Higher effective GBP can be realized by several methods, the most direct being the selection of an IC type that has an inherently high GBP. The 715 and 118, for example, feature a 15-MHz unity-gain frequency, while the 2620 has an 8-MHz unity-gain frequency. But many of the types that have nominal 1.0-MHz GBPs when compensated for unity gain can be custom-compensated for higher effective GBPs at a particular gain chosen for circuit operation. This is true of the 709, 725, 748, 101/101A, 531, and 540. For these amplifiers, the improvement in available gain is almost directly proportional to the reduction in compensation. This option is also available with high-speed types such as the 715 and 2620.

Fig. 6-3 shows the open-loop response curves for the amplifiers listed in the preceding paragraph. These curves illustrate the improvement in gain available with the lowering of compensation values and represent the manufacturer's recommended values for various closed-loop operating gains. The degree of improvement varies from one op-amp type to another. A 748, 101/101A, or 531 will offer a tenfold improvement in GBP from unity-gain compensation to 20-dB compensation. Beyond 20 dB, the effects of stray capacitance will usually reduce the effect of reduced compensation. The GBP of the 709, however, will continue to improve at the same rate because of larger initial compensation capacitors. When compensated as recommended for a closed-loop gain of 60 dB, the 709 has an effective GBP of about 300 MHz—a most respectable figure.

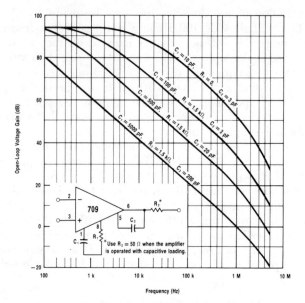

(A) μA709 (Fairchild Semiconductor).

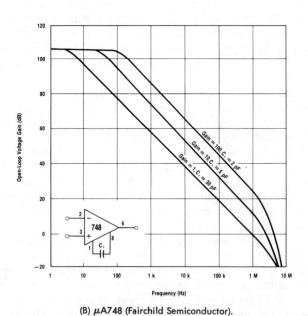

(B) μA748 (Fairchild Semiconductor).

Fig. 6-3. Frequency-response characteristics of

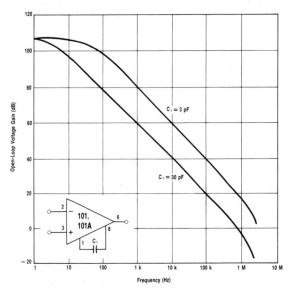

(C) LM101, LM101A (National Semiconductor).

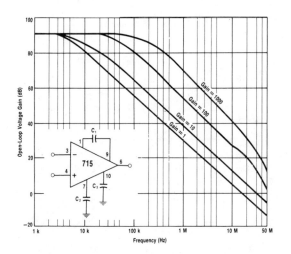

Compensation Component Values

Closed-Loop Gain	C_1	C_2	C_3
1000	10 pF	—	—
100	50 pF	—	250 pF
10	100 pF	500 pF	1000 pF
1	500 pF	2000 pF	1000 pF

(D) μA715 (Fairchild Semiconductor).

various op amps for various compensation values.

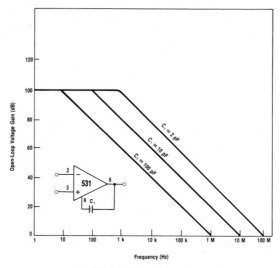

(E) SE/NE531 (Signetics Corp.).

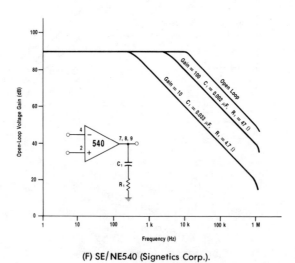

(F) SE/NE540 (Signetics Corp.).

Fig. 6-3 (cont). Frequency-response characteristics of

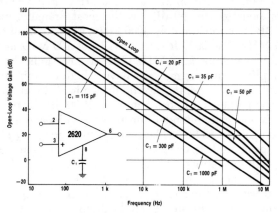

(G) HA-2620 (Harris Semiconductor).

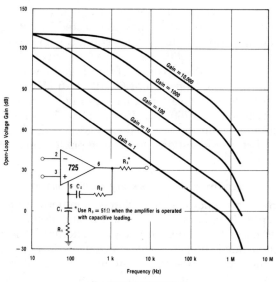

Compensation Component Values

Closed-Loop Gain	R_1	C_1	R_2	C_2
10,000	10 kΩ	50 pF	-	-
1000	470 Ω	0.001 μF	-	-
100	47 Ω	0.01 μF	-	-
10	27 Ω	0.05 μF	270 Ω	0.0015 μF
1	10 Ω	0.05 μF	39 Ω	0.02 μF

(H) μA725 (Fairchild Semiconductor).

various op amps for various compensation values.

The 540 compensated for 40 dB has a 100-MHz effective GBP, while the 715 compensated for 60 dB has the most dramatic increase in effective GBP—to approximately 3000 MHz, with 70 dB of open-loop gain at 1.0 MHz. The 2620 features a GBP of 100 MHz at a gain of 40 dB, and it maintains an 8-MHz GBP at unity gain.

These amplifiers may or may not have a high dc gain in addition to a high GBP. In general, the two do not go hand in hand. The 715, which has the highest GBP, has a dc gain of 90 dB. By contrast, the 725, which is not really intended for use as a wideband audio amplifier, has a dc gain of 130 dB. Therefore, if high accuracy is required at frequencies of 1.0 kHz or less, the 725 is a good choice because it provides 40 dB of loop gain up to 1.0 kHz. This particular requirement cannot be satisfied by any of the other types listed at gains as high as 60 dB due to their lower overall low-frequency gain.

Optimizing loop gain in ac applications is not a completely straightforward matter, since the responses of a number of different amplifiers must be carefully studied to determine the suitability. The graph of Fig. 6-2 is helpful in this respect; it indicates at a glance what gain is required at which frequency. Thereafter, the amplifier that satisfies the requirement is selected by noting the particular gain curve appropriate for the required gain level. To illustrate, suppose that an amplifier is required to have a loop gain of 20 dB at 10 kHz with 1.0% accuracy. From Fig. 6-2 we can see that this represents an open-loop gain of 60 dB at 10 kHz, or a GBP of 10 MHz. Inspection of the various curves in Fig. 6-3 reveals that for 20-dB compensation, the 709, 101/101A, 531, 715, and 2620 are all suitable. Selection from this list is then made on the basis of suitability for other considerations, such as input current, power requirements, cost, etc.

Determining the Necessary Compensation

Since correct frequency compensation is so important for optimum ac performance, it follows that no more compensation should be used than is necessary to ensure adequate stability. The manufacturer's recommended compensation values given in Fig. 6-3 provide ac stability under the worst-case conditions of temperature and supply-voltage variations, so they can be used with confidence for the gains specified. However, there is a difference between the inverting and noninverting configurations in the required compensation values. This should be understood in applying the gain values of Fig. 6-3.

Unless otherwise specified, the manufacturer's compensation values are for noninverting configurations (Fig. 6-4A), where β is unity, or feedback is 100%. This is the worst case insofar as compensation requirements are concerned, since there is no attenuation in the

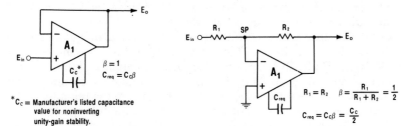

(A) Unity-gain noninverting configuration.

$\beta = 1$
$C_{req} = C_c \beta$

$^*C_c$ = Manufacturer's listed capacitance value for noninverting unity-gain stability.

(B) Unity-gain inverting configuration.

$R_1 = R_2 \quad \beta = \dfrac{R_1}{R_1 + R_2} = \dfrac{1}{2}$

$C_{req} = C_c \beta = \dfrac{C_c}{2}$

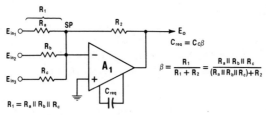

$C_{req} = C_c \beta$

$\beta = \dfrac{R_1}{R_1 + R_2} = \dfrac{R_a \| R_b \| R_c}{(R_a \| R_b \| R_c) + R_2}$

$R_1 = R_a \| R_b \| R_c$

(C) β calculation for multiple-input inverter.

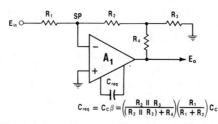

$C_{req} = C_c \beta = \left(\dfrac{R_2 \| R_3}{(R_2 \| R_3) + R_4}\right)\left(\dfrac{R_1}{R_1 + R_2}\right) C_c$

(D) β calculation for inverter with multiple divider feedback.

(E) β calculation for inverter with high-impedance source.

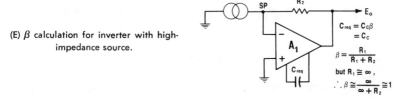

$C_{req} = C_c \beta = C_c$

$\beta = \dfrac{R_1}{R_1 + R_2}$

but $R_1 \cong \infty$,

$\therefore \beta \cong \dfrac{\infty}{\infty + R_2} \cong 1$

Fig. 6-4. Determining optimum compensation capacitances for various amplifier configurations and feedback networks.

feedback path. When the amplifier is stabilized for this condition ($\beta = 1$), it will be stable for all feedback conditions, since there can be no more than 100% feedback. In Fig. 6-4A, C_c represents the capacitance value (or values) recommended by the manufacturer to ensure stability under the condition of 100% feedback. Examples

277

are the 30-pF capacitor used with the 101/101A, and the 5000-pF and 200-pF capacitors used with the 709.

Less compensation is required when β is less than unity, or feedback is less than 100%. This is illustrated in the inverting configuration of Fig. 6-4B, where the feedback situation is different from that of the follower of Fig. 6-4A. The stage gain is still unity since $R_1 = R_2$, but the feedback signal from E_o back to the summing point undergoes an attenuation of 2 to 1 because of the two resistors. This is just another way of saying that for this stage, $\beta = 0.5$. But the compensation requirements of a feedback amplifier are dictated by the value of β regardless of the configuration. In general, the relationship between C_C and C_{req} is:

$$C_{req} = C_C \, \beta,$$

where C_C is the capacitance value for unity-gain stability, C_{req} is the capacitance value for stability for a given β, and

$$\beta = \frac{R_1}{R_1 + R_2} \, .$$

Therefore, the compensation capacitance required for unity-gain stability for the inverting stage of Fig. 6-4B is one-half of that required for the noninverting stage of Fig. 6-4A.

It should be noted that R_1 in the circuit of Fig. 6-4B represents the total resistance seen from the summing point to ground (looking back through the E_{in} source impedance, which is assumed to be low). Thus, when there are multiple inputs as in Fig. 6-4C, an equivalent resistance must be calculated for R_1 before the β calculation is made.

Similarly, the feedback is not always through a single resistance as represented by R_2 in Figs 6-4B and C. In some configurations, the feedback is taken from a voltage divider, as in Fig. 6-4D. In this case, the feedback signal is attenuated twice—once through the divider,

$$\frac{R_2 \parallel R_3}{(R_2 \parallel R_3) + R_4} \, ,$$

and once through the divider,

$$\frac{R_1}{R_1 + R_2} \, .$$

β in this case is the composite attenuation of the two divider networks:

$$\beta_{comp} = \left(\frac{R_2 \parallel R_3}{(R_2 \parallel R_3) + R_4} \right) \left(\frac{R_1}{R_1 + R_2} \right) .$$

A special case of feedback is illustrated by the current-to-voltage converter of Fig. 6-4E. In this configuration, amplifier A_1 is fed from a high-impedance source, such as the collector electrode of a phototransistor. In such cases, the source impedance represented by R_1 is so much greater than R_2 that it offers little divider action with R_2; thus, the feedback becomes essentially 100% and unity-gain compensation is required.

In determining the required compensation for any feedback network, the β divider must be analyzed to determine the loss of feedback signal. This is true for any op-amp configuration—inverter, follower, subtractor, etc. Using this type of analysis, the exact compensation values can be calculated. With reference to the response curves of Fig. 6-3, it can be seen how the feedback effects of β determine the scaling of compensation capacitances. In general, this is a direct 1:10 ratio between unity gain and the first decade (gain of 10), or the ratio of the two β values. Beyond the first decade, this relationship does not hold precisely, because of the effects of stray capacitance.

As stated previously, the manufacturer's compensation values are for the noninverting configuration. The inverting configuration uses lower values, and, in the case of the unity-gain inverter where $\beta = 0.5$ (Fig. 6-4B), the values are halved. However, at higher inverting gains (10 for example) the β scaling may not hold, depending on the particular amplifier used. In these cases, optimum compensation can be verified by experiment, or a conservative approach can be taken by using the compensation values listed for a noninverting gain of 10, which will always ensure stability.

Loop Gain and the Effects of β on Bandwidth

A better appreciation of the importance of optimum frequency compensation in wideband ac amplifiers may be gained by an examination of Figs. 6-5 and 6-6. Fig. 6-5 is a Bode plot for a typical unity-gain inverter using a 1.0-MHz GBP op amp. The β of 0.5 for a unity-gain inverter results in a noise gain $(1/\beta)$ of 2. This is shown on the plot as a dashed line at the +6-dB level. The loop gain is the amount of gain available from the level of the noise gain up to the intersection of the open-loop response curve. Thus, at 10 kHz on the 1.0-MHz GBP curve, the available loop gain is 40 dB − 6 dB, or 34 dB. However, by custom compensating this amplifier for the noise gain of 6 dB, the effective GBP is extended to 2.0 MHz. This restores the available loop gain to 40 dB.

The interplay between noise gain, compensation, and bandwidth is even more effectively illustrated in Fig. 6-6. This is a Bode plot for a 10-input, unity-gain inverter, a very common audio application. Even though the circuit operates with unity gain for each of

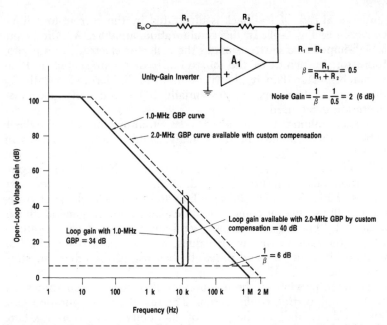

Fig. 6-5. Bode plot illustrating the effects of custom compensation on a simple unity-gain inverter.

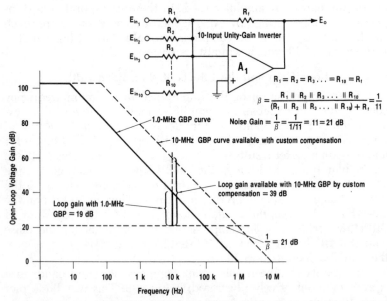

Fig. 6-6. Bode plot illustrating the effects of custom compensation on a 10-input, unity-gain inverter.

the 10 inputs, the noise gain is 11 (21 dB) because of the attenuation of feedback signal by the equivalent resistance of the input (summing) network. The noise gain is sketched on the Bode plot as a dashed line at a gain of 21 dB. With unity-gain compensation, the op amp has a GBP of 1.0 MHz and an open-loop gain of 40 dB at 10 kHz. Since the noise gain is 21 dB, the available loop gain at 10 kHz is only 19 dB—not a very respectable figure. By choosing custom compensation for a gain of 20 dB based on the noise gain, the effective GBP for this amplifier will be increased to 10 MHz, and 39 dB of loop gain will be realized instead of 19 dB—an obviously desirable situation.

The compensation requirements of an op-amp audio stage should be determined with care, particularly when general-purpose types such as the 709, 748, 101/101A, and 531 are used. It has been shown that these types seldom have an excess of gain-bandwidth, a fact that can lead to difficult problems at high frequencies. Also, it is important to remember that compensation requirements are more accurately determined by the noise gain ($1/\beta$) rather than by the closed-loop gain of the circuit—the two are not always the same.

One further point concerning the effects of β on frequency response: There is a "shrinkage" of available bandwidth resulting from the noise gain. The maximum available bandwidth will be no greater than that point where the noise-gain curve intersects the open-loop curve. In Fig. 6-6, the $1/\beta$ curve intersects the 1.0-MHz open-loop curve at 100 kHz, and this will be the bandwidth. This is in sharp contrast to what might be expected from the 1.0-MHz unity-gain frequency. The point is that the noise gain not only determines the loop gain but also determines the resultant bandwidth. Thus, optimizing the loop gain also optimizes the bandwidth at the same time. The 10-MHz custom-compensated case of Fig. 6-6 will have a 1.0-MHz bandwidth.

6.1.2 Slew Rate

Another important factor in the frequency-response performance of an IC op amp is the slewing rate of the amplifier. In the discussion of slew rate in Chapter 1, it was seen that for a sine-wave signal the relationship between slew rate (SR), full-power frequency response (f_p), and peak output voltage (E_{op}) is

$$SR = 2\pi E_{op} f_p.$$

With an output swing of 10 V (peak) and a full-power frequency response of 20 kHz, the required slew rate is

$$SR = 6.28 \times 10^1 \times 2 \times 10^4$$
$$= 1.256 \times 10^6 \text{ V/s}$$
$$= 1.256 \text{ V}/\mu s.$$

This figure is the minimum acceptable slew rate for full-power, distortion-free output at 20 kHz. However, many op-amp types cannot meet this figure, particularly when operated with unity-gain, noninverting compensation.

Slew-rate limiting occurs because of the inability of the internal bias circuits of the amplifier to charge and discharge the compensating capacitance. This is illustrated in Fig. 6-7, which is a simplified schematic of a 101A with its external compensation (C_C) of 30 pF. Q_3 and Q_4 represent the input differential stage, which is fed by a

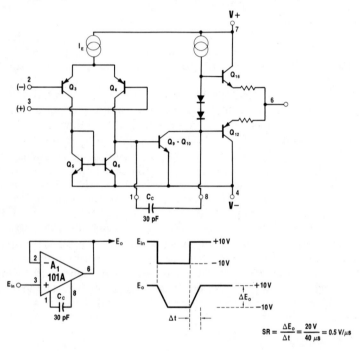

Fig. 6-7. Simplified schematic of a 101A op amp illustrating slew-rate limitations.

constant emitter current (I_E) of approximately 15 μA. In normal operation this stage is balanced, with Q_3 and Q_5 conducting one-half of I_E, and Q_4 and Q_6 conducting the other half. The stage will remain balanced as long as the amplifier is operating linearly. However, when the amplifier is driven at a faster rate than it can respond to, it can no longer operate linearly but can only attempt to follow at its maximum rate of change, or slewing rate. This is illustrated by the input (E_{in}) and output (E_o) waveforms in Fig. 6-7.

Current I_E and compensating capacitance C_C set the slewing rate of the amplifier, since I_E is the maximum current that the input differential pair can deliver to charge C_C. The slewing rate is then given by

$$SR = \left(\frac{I_E}{C_C}\right) V/s.$$

In this example,

$$SR = \frac{1.5 \times 10^{-5}}{3 \times 10^{-11}}$$

$$= 0.5 \times 10^6 \ V/s$$

$$= 0.5 \ V/\mu s.$$

With the current mirror "gain" of Q_5-Q_6 very close to unity, the positive and negative rates of slewing in a 101A will be very nearly equal.

Slew rate can be increased in a number of ways, the most direct way being to reduce the value of compensation capacitance. This is possible at higher operating gains, which is verified by the increased slewing rates for custom-compensated types, such as the 709, 748, 101A, and 108. Internally compensated types, such as the 741, 1556, and 8007, have constant slewing rates because their compensation capacitance is fixed. If the slewing rate of a particular internally compensated amplifier is insufficient for a particular application, then an alternative amplifier must be selected.

Since the slewing rate of an op amp is tied to the value of compensation capacitance, it follows that the worst case of slew rate occurs when the largest compensation capacitance is used—in unity-gain, noninverting configurations. One solution to this problem is to use an amplifier such as the 531, which was designed specifically to circumvent the slewing problems that normally occur with maximum compensation. Although the input stage of the 531 is not exactly the same as that of the 741 or 101, the relationship between charging current and compensation capacitance remains the same. In the 531, however, the slewing rate is not limited by a finite input-stage bias current. The 531 input stage is a unique class-B design, which can supply current peaks up to 40 times the small-signal idling current under large-signal conditions. This results in a full-power response of 500 kHz and a corresponding improvement in the slewing rate to 30 V/μs for a unity-gain follower, and 35 V/μs for a unity-gain inverter.

The use of FET inputs rather than bipolar is another design method of circumventing the input-stage bias-current limitation on slew rate. If Q_3 and Q_4 in Fig. 6-7 were FETs rather than bipolar pnp's, there would be no limitation on current I_E caused by the h_{FE} of Q_3-Q_4. In a FET, there is no direct relationship between the input current and the drain current; therefore, I_E can be increased while the input current is maintained low. Thus, a FET-input amplifier like the 8007 can provide a slewing rate of 6 V/μs—approximately 10 times greater than for the 741.

Other op-amp designs attack the slew-rate problem in various ways with differing degrees of success. The 1556 features a 2.5-V/μs slewing rate, which makes it a good choice for a low-input-current voltage follower where its 1.0-MHz bandwidth is adequate. The 2620 has a slewing rate of 10 V/μs as a unity-gain follower, with higher slewing rates at higher gains. The 715 features an 18-V/μs slewing rate as a follower, and much higher rates at higher gains. The 110, which is connected internally as a voltage follower, has a slewing rate of 30 V/μs and offers a very convenient solution to slew-rate-limited, voltage-follower problems. Finally, the 118 features a 70-V/μs slewing rate in any configuration, since it is an internally compensated type.

In most cases, an adequate slewing rate can be provided by one of the devices listed in Table 6-1. In certain configurations, however, there are additional options with particular devices. The 101A, for example, can be used with *feedforward compensation,* which enables it to slew at 10 V/μs as a unity-gain inverter and extends its unity-gain bandwidth to 10 MHz. And even though the 118 has a fast slewing rate with standard compensation, it can also be used with feedforward compensation, which increases its slewing capability to 120 V/μs as a unity-gain inverter.

**Table 6-1. Slewing Rates of Various
IC Op Amps for Various Compensation Conditions**

Device	Slewing Rate (V/μs)			
	$A_v = +1$	$A_v = -1$	$A_v = 10$	$A_v = 100$
709	0.3	0.6	3.0	15
101, 101A	0.5	10[*]	5.0	15
748	0.5	1.0	5.0	15
107, 741	0.5	0.5	0.5	0.5
725	0.008	0.016	0.08	0.8
108	0.3	1.3[*]	3.0	3.0
1556	2.5	2.5	2.5	2.5
1536	2.0	2.0	2.0	2.0
8007	6.0	6.0	6.0	6.0
110	30	—	—	—
118	70	120[*]	70	70
2620	7.0	14	35	35
715	18	100[*]	38	70
531	30	35	35	35
540	—	30[*]	3.0	30

[*]Achieved by specialized compensation.

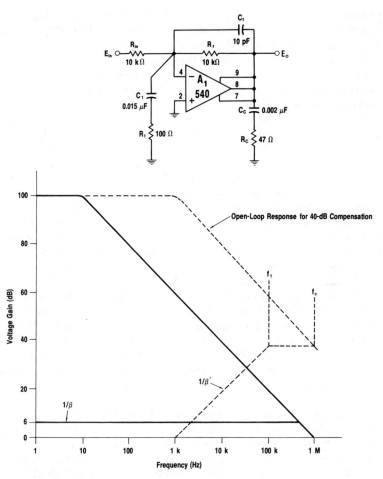

To use input compensation:

(1) Compensate amplifier for a higher gain which yields the desired slewing rate.

(2) Select $\dfrac{R_f}{R_1}$ for this compensation.

(3) Select $C_1 = \dfrac{1}{2 \pi f_1 R_1}$ where, $f_1 = 1/10$ of crossover frequency (f_c) of $1/\beta'$ curve.

(4) Select $C_f = \dfrac{1}{2 \pi f_c R_f}$.

Fig. 6-8. Use of input compensation to achieve a faster slewing rate and greater high-frequency loop gain.

Another useful option is commonly termed *input compensation* and is available with externally compensated op amps (see Fig. 6-8). Input compensation is a technique that allows a low-signal-gain amplifier to be compensated for greater high-frequency gain. This permits a faster slewing rate and a greater loop gain at high frequencies. Since the compensation requirements for stability are governed by the relative phase of the $1/\beta$ curve and the open-loop gain (see Chapter 1), it follows that crossing the $1/\beta$ curve over at higher closed-loop gains (or high frequencies) will allow less compensation and thus a faster slewing rate, as well as greater loop gain if the $1/\beta$ curve is tailored properly.

The relationship is shown by the Bode plot of the simple unity-gain inverter in Fig. 6-8. With a flat $1/\beta$ characteristic, as illustrated by the 6-dB, $1/\beta$ curve, compensation for unity gain (or a gain of 2) will be necessary. However, if a frequency dependence is introduced with a new $1/\beta$ curve (shown as $1/\beta'$), the crossover can be at a higher gain and frequency if the amplifier is compensated for this higher gain. This is shown in Fig. 6-8 by the $1/\beta'$ curve intersecting the 40-dB compensation curve at f_c. Not only does this yield the slewing rate for 40-dB compensation, but it also yields higher loop gain. In the example shown, the loop gain at 1.0 kHz is 94 dB.

In applying input compensation, an amplifier type that lends itself to appreciable increases in slewing rate and GBP with reduced compensation must be used. Some examples are the 540 (as shown in Fig. 6-8), 709, 715, and others to lesser extents. The input network that provides the increased gain consists of R_1 and C_1. R_1 and R_f set the gain of the network between f_1 and f_c. C_1 is chosen to limit the gain of the network beginning at f_1. Frequency f_1 should be $\frac{1}{10}$ or less that of f_c, the crossover frequency. Finally, a small feedback capacitor, C_f, is used to increase the phase margin in the crossover region.

Input compensation is most useful where the highest speed is necessary for a low signal gain, such as the inverter shown in Fig. 6-8. The technique does have a drawback, however, and that is the increase in high-frequency noise due to the higher gain at high frequencies. This effect can be minimized by placing f_1 as high as possible so that the $1/\beta'$ curve breaks upward at as high a signal frequency as possible.

To summarize, the slewing rate of an IC op amp can become a problem in audio circuits whenever high-amplitude signals must be delivered at high frequencies. Slew-rate limiting is caused by the limited ability of an op amp to charge the compensation capacitance used. Internally compensated op amps generally offer no flexibility in slew-rate improvement, but externally compensated types can be custom-compensated for faster slewing at higher frequencies by reducing the compensation capacitance. Slew rate not only varies with the amount of compensation, it also changes with the type of configuration; the worst case being the unity-gain follower. Specialized IC types provide solutions to slew-rate limitations, as do specialized compensation techniques. A summary of the slew-rate capabilities of various IC op amps is presented in Table 6-1. In the circuit discussions that follow, practical examples of slew-rate and bandwidth optimization will be stressed.

6.2 THE BASIC OP-AMP CONFIGURATIONS TRANSLATED TO AUDIO APPLICATIONS

Audio-frequency voltage amplifiers fall into two general categories: (1) low-gain amplifiers such as inverters, followers and buffers, summers, difference amplifiers, etc.; and (2) high-gain amplifiers such as preamps, booster amplifiers, line amplifiers, etc. The approach taken in this discussion is to first illustrate the basic op-amp configurations translated to audio performance (and also for single power-supply operation), and then to illustrate the different options available in more-specialized circuitry.

6.2.1 The Inverting Amplifier

The inverting amplifier applied to audio use is shown in Fig. 6-9. The basic inverter is shown in Fig. 6-9A and can be recognized as

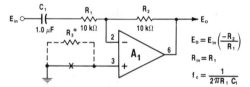

$$E_o = E_{in}\left(\frac{-R_2}{R_1}\right)$$

$$R_{in} = R_1$$

$$f_c = \frac{1}{2\pi R_1 C_1}$$

*To minimize dc output offset, use optional resistor R_3 as shown ($R_3 = R_2$).

(A) Basic inverter.

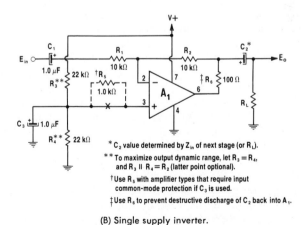

* C_2 value determined by Z_{in} of next stage (or R_L).

** To maximize output dynamic range, let $R_3 = R_4$, and $R_3 \parallel R_4 = R_2$ (latter point optional).

† Use R_5 with amplifier types that require input common-mode protection if C_3 is used.

‡ Use R_6 to prevent destructive discharge of C_2 back into A_1.

(B) Single supply inverter.

Fig. 6-9. The inverting amplifier applied to audio use.

being similar to the standard dc inverter but with C_1 added in series with R_1. This makes the stage responsive to ac input signals at frequencies where $X_{C_1} < R_1$. The lower cutoff frequency is determined by C_1 and R_1 as

$$f_c = \frac{1}{2\pi R_1 C_1}.$$

This is simply the frequency at which $X_{C_1} = R_1$. In the example shown, this frequency is 15.9 Hz. The inclusion of C_1 makes the dc gain of the stage unity, since $R_1 = \infty$ at dc. Gain within the normal passband is simply $-R_2/R_1$. The stage does not amplify offset or low-frequency noise because of the inclusion of C_1.

The direct ground on the noninverting input of A_1 biases the output terminal at a dc potential that is very close to zero. There will be a small offset voltage equal to the unamplified input offset voltage of A_1 plus the dc voltage drop across R_2, cause by the input bias current to A_1. With typical input offset voltages less than ±5.0 mV, the voltage drop due to $I_{bias} R_2$ will become dominant when either R_2 or I_{bias} is high. For example, with an I_{bias} of 100 nA and an R_2 of 1.0 MΩ, the drop across R_2 will be

$$E_{R_2} = I_{bias} R_2$$
$$= 1 \times 10^{-7} \times 10^6$$
$$= 0.1 \text{ V}.$$

This output voltage offset is significant only to the extent that it subtracts from the available peak-to-peak output swing; the offset will not be transmitted to the next stage when capacitive coupling is used. In applications where this offset voltage must be minimized, an optional resistor (R_3) may be added in series with the noninverting input as shown. As a general rule of thumb, R_3 will only be required if $R_2 \geqslant 1.0$ MΩ or $I_{bias} \geqslant 1.0$ μA.

So far, most of the op-amp configurations that have been discussed have utilized symmetrical power supplies of ±15 V, and this is always assumed when the supply connections are not explicitly shown. In many instances, however, it may be desirable to operate the op amp from a single supply potential and ground (common). The inverter of Fig. 6-9A is shown in single supply form in Fig. 6-9B. The feedback and input connections in this circuit are the same as in Fig. 6-9A, and the same relationships apply.

In an op-amp configuration using a single supply, it is desirable to operate the output at one-half the supply potential (½ V+ or ½ V−) for maximum undistorted output. In Fig. 6-9B, divider R_3-R_4 provides a bias that references the noninverting input of A_1 to the ½-V+ potential. Because of C_1, the dc gain of the circuit is unity;

therefore, the output of A_1 is automatically biased to $\frac{1}{2}V+$ for any value of supply voltage. Any noise on the supply line will also be divided by two at the R_3-R_4 junction and will be amplified by the noise gain of A_1. In cases where noise is a problem, an ac bypass (C_3) can be used. To minimize the output offset due to bias current, the value of $R_3 \parallel R_4$ should be made equal to the value of R_2. An output capacitor (C_2) will normally be needed for single supply operation, since the output is biased at a dc level. The value of C_2 is determined by the desired low-frequency rolloff and the input impedance of the next stage. If electrolytic capacitors are used for C_1, C_2, and C_3, proper polarity must, of course, be observed.

Although a positive supply is used in Fig. 6-9B, the circuit could also be operated from a negative supply simply by grounding R_3 and the positive supply terminal of A_1 (pin 7), and then applying a V− potential to R_4 and the negative supply terminal of A_1 (pin 4). Also, the polarity of capacitors C_1, C_2, and C_3 must be reversed when operating the circuit from a negative supply.

The ac inverting configurations of Figs 6-9A and B can be modified into summing inverters simply by connecting additional input networks (same as R_1-C_1) to the inverting input of A_1. The component values shown in Fig. 6-9 are intended only as general examples; they can be used with virtually any op amp for A_1. However, certain op-amp types (such as low-bias-current types) will permit a wider latitude of resistance values.

6.2.2 The Noninverting Amplifier

The noninverting amplifier applied to audio use is shown in Fig. 6-10. Fig. 6-10A is the basic noninverting stage with ac coupling. Stage gain above the lower cutoff frequency is determined in the same manner as for the standard noninverting stage, which is

$$\frac{E_o}{E_{in}} = \frac{R_1 + R_2}{R_1}.$$

There are two low-frequency rolloffs in this stage because of R_1-C_1 and R_3-C_2. The rolloff due to R_1-C_1 acts in a manner identical to the rolloff caused by R_1-C_1 in the inverter of Fig. 6-9, and should be used as the predominant rolloff in order to minimize the low-frequency noise gain of A_1. The R_3-C_2 rolloff frequency can be five to ten times lower than the R_1-C_1 rolloff frequency unless it is desired to have the low-end response roll off more rapidly.

The noninverting amplifier in single supply form is shown in Fig. 6-10B. Resistors R_3 and R_4 bias the noninverting input (and the output) of A_1 to $\frac{1}{2}$ V+ (or $\frac{1}{2}$ V−), and the input signal is applied to this junction. As in the single supply inverter of Fig. 6-9B, proper

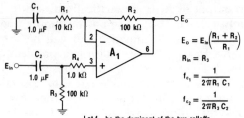

$$E_o = E_{in}\left(\frac{R_1 + R_2}{R_1}\right)$$

$$R_{in} = R_3$$

$$f_{c_1} = \frac{1}{2\pi R_1 C_1}$$

$$f_{c_2} = \frac{1}{2\pi R_3 C_2}$$

Let f_{c_1} be the dominant of the two rolloffs
($f_{c_1} > f_{c_2}$) to minimize low-frequency noise gain of A_1.

(A) Basic noninverting stage.

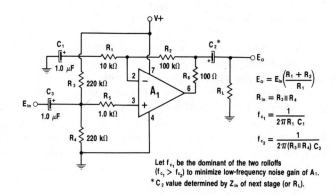

$$E_o = E_{in}\left(\frac{R_1 + R_2}{R_1}\right)$$

$$R_{in} = R_3 \| R_4$$

$$f_{c_1} = \frac{1}{2\pi R_1 C_1}$$

$$f_{c_2} = \frac{1}{2\pi (R_3 \| R_4) C_3}$$

Let f_{c_1} be the dominant of the two rolloffs
($f_{c_1} > f_{c_2}$) to minimize low-frequency noise gain of A_1.
* C_2 value determined by Z_{in} of next stage (or R_L).

(B) Single supply noninverting stage.

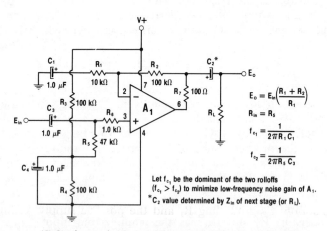

$$E_o = E_{in}\left(\frac{R_1 + R_2}{R_1}\right)$$

$$R_{in} = R_5$$

$$f_{c_1} = \frac{1}{2\pi R_1 C_1}$$

$$f_{c_2} = \frac{1}{2\pi R_5 C_3}$$

Let f_{c_1} be the dominant of the two rolloffs
($f_{c_1} > f_{c_2}$) to minimize low-frequency noise gain of A_1.
* C_2 value determined by Z_{in} of next stage (or R_L).

(C) Single supply noninverting stage with noise decoupling.

Fig. 6-10. The noninverting amplifier applied to audio use.

capacitor polarity must be observed if electrolytic types are used. Operation of this circuit from a negative supply is possible by grounding R_3 and the positive supply terminal of A_1 (pin 7), and then applying a V− potential to R_4 and the negative supply terminal of A_1 (pin 4).

Unlike the inverter of Fig. 6-9B, supply-noise decoupling cannot be applied directly to the noninverting input of A_1 in the circuit of Fig. 6-10B because this would bypass the signal as well as the noise. In order to decouple supply noise in the noninverting amplifier, the circuit of Fig. 6-10C should be used. In this circuit, resistor R_5 is added to isolate R_3 and R_4 from E_{in}, and the supply noise is bypassed by capacitor C_4 without affecting the input signal. For minimum dc output offset, the resistance of $(R_3 \| R_4) + R_5$ should be made equal to R_2.

6.2.3 The Voltage Follower

The voltage follower applied to audio use has some unique considerations of its own; therefore, it is discussed separately in this section and is illustrated in Fig. 6-11. The basic follower with ac coupling is shown in Fig. 6-11A. The output of A_1 is dc referenced at zero potential by the ground connection from R_1 and the input signal ac coupled through C_1. The low-frequency cutoff is determined by C_1 and R_1. The shunting effect of R_1 lowers the input impedance of the stage, which is in contrast to the dc follower, where the input impedance is extremely high. Thus, the naturally high input impedance of the follower configuration can be compromised with ac coupling unless R_1 is high.

If R_1 is made very high (above 1.0 MΩ, for example), it can create an excessive dc output offset unless A_1 has low input-bias current or the offset is compensated. The use of low-bias-current op amps, such as the 110, 1556, or 8007, will minimize dc offset due to bias current and allow bias resistances up to 10 MΩ. Higher-bias-current amplifiers can be used if the drop across R_1 is compensated by including R_2 in the feedback path. If R_2 is large, the input capacitance of A_1 can create a phase shift; therefore, it is best to include a small shunt capacitance ($\cong 0.001 \mu F$) across R_2 if R_2 is much greater than 100 kΩ.

The voltage follower converted to single supply operation is shown in Fig. 6-11B. Resistors R_1 and R_2 bias the noninverting input (and the output) of A_1 to ½ V+ (or ½ V−), and the input signal is applied to this junction. This circuit can also be operated from a negative supply by grounding R_1 and the positive supply terminal of A_1 (pin 7), and then applying a V− potential to R_2 and the negative supply terminal of A_1 (pin 4). Supply-noise decoupling in the voltage follower is accomplished as shown in Fig. 6-11C.

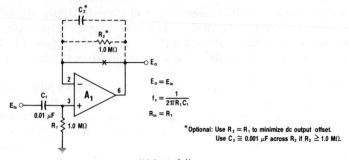

$E_o = E_{in}$

$f_c = \dfrac{1}{2\pi R_1 C_1}$

$R_{in} = R_1$

*Optional: Use $R_2 = R_1$ to minimize dc output offset.
Use $C_2 \cong 0.001\ \mu F$ across R_2 if $R_2 \geq 1.0\ M\Omega$.

(A) Basic follower.

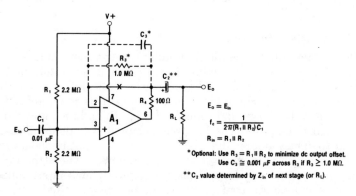

$E_o = E_{in}$

$f_c = \dfrac{1}{2\pi (R_1 \| R_2) C_1}$

$R_{in} = R_1 \| R_2$

*Optional: Use $R_3 = R_1 \| R_2$ to minimize dc output offset.
Use $C_3 \cong 0.001\ \mu F$ across R_3 if $R_3 \geq 1.0\ M\Omega$.

**C_2 value determined by Z_{in} of next stage (or R_L).

(B) Single supply follower.

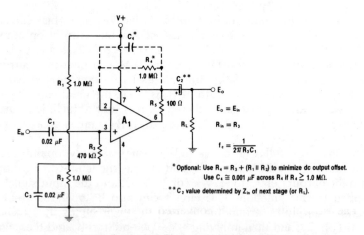

$E_o = E_{in}$

$R_{in} = R_3$

$f_c = \dfrac{1}{2\pi R_3 C_1}$

*Optional: Use $R_4 = R_3 + (R_1 \| R_2)$ to minimize dc output offset.
Use $C_4 \cong 0.001\ \mu F$ across R_4 if $R_4 \geq 1.0\ M\Omega$.

**C_2 value determined by Z_{in} of next stage (or R_L).

(C) Single supply follower with noise decoupling.

Fig. 6-11. The voltage follower applied to audio use.

6.2.4 The Differential Amplifier

The differential amplifier applied to audio use is shown in Fig. 6-12. The basic differential amplifier is shown in Fig. 6-12A and can be recognized as being similar to the standard dc differential amplifier but with coupling capacitors C_1 and C_2 added in series with the two inputs.

This circuit will have two low-frequency rolloffs, f_{c_1} and f_{c_2} determined by the capacitances and resistances seen at the two inputs. For best common-mode rejection, f_{c_1} should be equal to f_{c_2}. The dc output level of this circuit is automatically centered when R_4 is made equal to R_2.

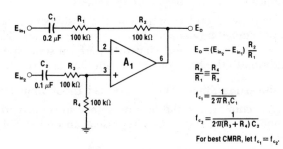

$$E_o = (E_{in_2} - E_{in_1}) \frac{R_2}{R_1}$$

$$\frac{R_2}{R_1} = \frac{R_4}{R_3}$$

$$f_{c_1} = \frac{1}{2\pi R_1 C_1}$$

$$f_{c_2} = \frac{1}{2\pi (R_3 + R_4) C_2}$$

For best CMRR, let $f_{c_1} = f_{c_2}$.

(A) Basic differential amplifier.

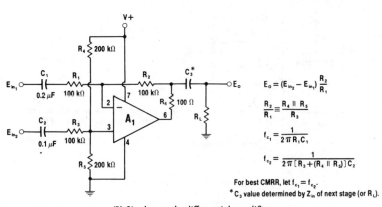

$$E_o = (E_{in_2} - E_{in_1}) \frac{R_2}{R_1}$$

$$\frac{R_2}{R_1} \equiv \frac{R_4 \| R_5}{R_3}$$

$$f_{c_1} = \frac{1}{2\pi R_1 C_1}$$

$$f_{c_2} = \frac{1}{2\pi [R_3 + (R_4 \| R_5)] C_2}$$

For best CMRR, let $f_{c_1} = f_{c_2}$.
*C_3 value determined by Z_{in} of next stage (or R_L).

(B) Single supply differential amplifier.

Fig. 6-12. The differential amplifier applied to audio use.

The differential amplifier converted to single supply operation is shown in Fig. 6-12B. As far as signal considerations are concerned, this circuit is the same as the basic circuit of Fig. 6-12A. Resistors R_4 and R_5 bias the noninverting input (and the output) of A_1 to

½ V+ (or ½ V−). Since these two resistors are of equal value, they also help to preserve the common-mode rejection of the stage.

The basic ac op-amp circuits of Figs. 6-9 to 6-12 are intended primarily to illustrate the configuration differences over the fundamental dc circuits. In essence, the design equations for both the dc and ac circuits are the same except for the differences due to ac coupling and the low-frequency rolloff. The more elaborate audio circuits to follow will in some manner be a variation of the basic ac configurations. Although the component values shown are only intended as examples, they will work well with virtually any op amp if it is properly compensated for the noise gain used.

6.2.5 Modifications of the Basic Configurations

There are many useful variations of the basic configurations that can be implemented as elements of larger-scale circuits. The circuits discussed in this section are designed to perform some specific function in addition to the basic one on which they are based.

Noninverting Stages With Increased Input Impedance

In many circumstances, the bias resistance in shunt with the (+) input of noninverting stages may represent an undesirable load on

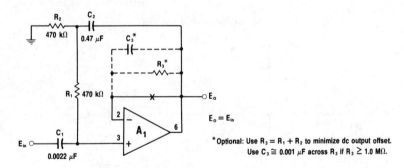

(A) Bootstrapped voltage follower.

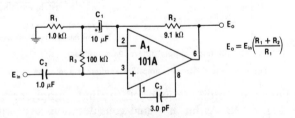

(B) Bootstrapped noninverting amplifier.

Fig. 6-13. High input impedance noninverting stages.

the source. A technique to increase the effective bias resistance is illustrated in Fig. 6-13.

A circuit that increases the input impedance of a voltage follower is shown in Fig. 6-13A. In this circuit, resistor R_1 is bootstrapped for ac signals by the feedback from the output of A_1 through capacitor C_2. C_2 causes the same voltage to appear at both ends of R_1, which drastically lowers the signal current in R_1, thereby effectively increasing the input impedance to many megohms and restoring the high-impedance virtues of the follower configuration.

The same principle applied to a noninverting amplifier is shown in Fig. 6-13B. In this circuit, R_3 is the bias resistance, which is returned to R_1 rather than directly to ground. As far as dc is concerned, this connection has no effect. But for ac signals, the voltage at the junction of R_1, R_3, and C_1 is the same as that at the $(-)$ input (for frequencies where $X_{C_1} \ll R_1$). Thus, for ac, little voltage drop appears across R_3, which effectively raises its value and the input impedance of the stage.

Inverting Amplifier With Increased Input Impedance

One of the fundamental disadvantages of the inverting amplifier is its restriction on input impedance, which is the value of the input resistor used. The only way to raise the input impedance (short of buffering, which requires an extra amplifier) is to raise the value of the input resistor. However, this can create problems when the feedback resistor is raised by the same ratio. Feedback resistances in excess of 1.0 MΩ can cause dc stability problems as well as gain error, due to the shunting effect of the internal input resistance (r_{in}) of the amplifier. In standard configurations, this restricts the use of high feedback resistances to amplifiers having either FET inputs or super-β inputs.

These problems are solved in the inverting amplifier circuit of Fig. 6-14, which provides a 1.0-MΩ input impedance while using a 101A general-purpose op amp. The value of feedback resistor R_2 is

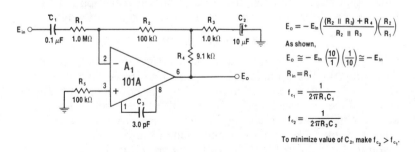

$$E_o = -E_{in}\left(\frac{(R_2 \parallel R_3) + R_4}{R_2 \parallel R_3}\right)\left(\frac{R_2}{R_1}\right)$$

As shown,

$$E_o \cong -E_{in}\left(\frac{10}{1}\right)\left(\frac{1}{10}\right) \cong -E_{in}$$

$$R_{in} = R_1$$

$$f_{c_1} = \frac{1}{2\pi R_1 C_1}$$

$$f_{c_2} = \frac{1}{2\pi R_3 C_2}$$

To minimize value of C_2, make $f_{c_2} > f_{c_1}$.

Fig. 6-14. High input impedance inverting amplifier.

made $\frac{1}{10}$ that of R_1, or 100 kΩ. This attenuates E_{in} by a ratio of 10:1 at the junction of R_2 and R_3; however, the output divider of R_4 and R_3 in parallel with R_2 make up the loss and restore the gain to unity, since E_o will be ten times the voltage at the R_2-R_3 junction.

In this circuit, the 101A op amp operates with a noise gain of 20 dB due to the divider in the feedback loop; therefore, a 3.0-pF compensation capacitor is used to optimize the high-frequency loop gain. If desired, gain can be increased by changing either the R_3-R_4 divider or R_2.

This circuit has two low-frequency rolloffs: f_{c_1} due to R_1-C_1, and f_{c_2} due to R_3-C_2. From the standpoint of component economy, the dominant rolloff should be f_{c_2}. This minimizes the value of capacitor C_2.

6.3 PRACTICAL AUDIO CIRCUITS USING IC OP AMPS

In this section, we will discuss a variety of practical audio circuits in which specific IC op-amp types are utilized. These circuits include: standard voltage amplifiers with optimized frequency and gain performance; power amplifiers; microphone, phono, and tape preamps; equalizers; active filters; and a miscellaneous assortment of specialized circuits, such as mixing amplifiers, load-matching circuits, linear feedback gain-controlled stages, etc.

6.3.1 Standard Audio-Frequency Voltage Amplifiers

The operation of IC op-amp audio voltage amplifiers having stage gains of from 0 dB to 60 dB in both the inverting and noninverting configurations will be considered in this section. With reference to the preliminary discussions on GBP and slewing rate, the circuits presented here will be performance optimized for these parameters. The reader can choose a configuration, then select feedback and compensation values from simple, easy-to-read charts, and use these amplifiers as "gain blocks" in larger systems. Although specific amplifier types are recommended, these charts can be applied to any IC type, provided the compensation is adjusted accordingly.

709 Voltage Amplifiers

The circuits for inverting and noninverting audio voltage amplifiers using the 709 op amp are shown in Figs. 6-15A and B, respectively. It will be noted that these circuits are both general and specific. Components such as C_1, R_1, and R_2 are general and apply to any amplifier used in these applications. Gains from 0 dB to 60 dB are set up by selecting these components from the tabulated values given in the chart in Fig. 6-15. In this chart, C_1 varies as a function of stage gain to keep the low-frequency cutoff point constant. The

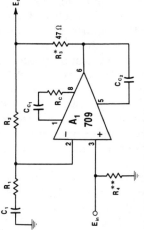

*Use R₃ for capacitive loads ≥100 pF.
**R₄ ≅ R₂.

Table (A) Inverting configuration:

Stage Gain (dB)	Feedback†			Compensation†		
	C_1	R_1	R_2	C_{C_1}	C_{C_2}	R_C
0‡	1.0 μF	10 kΩ	10 kΩ	2500 pF (2700)	100 pF	1.5 kΩ
20	10 μF	1.0 kΩ	10 kΩ	450 pF (470)	18 pF	1.5 kΩ
40	100 μF	100 Ω	10 kΩ	100 pF	3.0 pF	1.5 kΩ
60	100 μF	100 Ω	100 kΩ	10 pF	3.0 pF	0

† See text for detailed discussion of component values.
‡ See text under "Optimum 709 Performance at Unity Gain."

(A) Inverting configuration.

*Use R₃ for capacitive loads ≥100 pF.
**R₄ ≅ R₂.

Table (B) Noninverting configuration:

Feedback†			Compensation†		
C_1	R_1	R_2	C_{C_1}	C_{C_2}	R_C
0	∞	0	5000 pF (5600)	200 pF (220)	1.5 kΩ
10 μF	1.0 kΩ	9.0 kΩ	500 pF (560)	20 pF (22)	1.5 kΩ
100 μF	100 Ω	9.9 kΩ	100 pF	3.0 pF	1.5 kΩ
100 μF	100 Ω	99.9 kΩ	10 pF	3.0 pF	0

(B) Noninverting configuration.

Fig. 6-15. Circuit diagrams and tabulated feedback and compensation values for optimized inverting and noninverting audio voltage amplifiers using the 709 op amp.

C_1 values shown are for a low-frequency rolloff of 15.9 Hz, but the reader can, of course, choose C_1 for any suitable rolloff.

For optimum performance with the 709, values for gain-determining resistors R_1 and R_2 should be as close as possible to the tabulated values. These are precise theoretical values for operating gains from 0 dB to 60 dB in 20-dB steps. For gains intermediate to those listed, R_1 and R_2 can be determined with the appropriate gain equation consistent with the ranges given in the chart. A 30-dB inverting amplifier, for example, would require an R_1 value lower than the 20-dB value of 1.0 kΩ by a factor of 3.16, or 316 Ω. For best stability and accuracy, close-tolerance film or wirewound resistors should be used for R_1 and R_2. In less critical applications, the closest 5% carbon types can be used with proportionately reduced accuracy and stability.

The values specific to the 709 are those for the compensation components, C_{C_1}, C_{C_2}, and R_C, and the optional resistor, R_3. The compensation components are selected from the chart in Fig. 6-15 in accordance with the mode of operation and the gain desired. The reader will note that the values for the inverting configuration are reduced somewhat from the noninverting values, in accordance with the basic difference in the noise gains of the two configurations. These differences are most significant at the lower gains of 0 dB to 20 dB. Mica capacitors are recommended for C_{C_1} and C_{C_2} because of their excellent stability and close tolerance. Although precise values are given, the closest 10% values (shown in parentheses) can be used with no problems.

The optional resistor, R_3, should be used with the 709 to provide ac circuit stability for capacitive loads in excess of 100 pF. Increasing the value of R_3 to 180 Ω will also provide the 709 with short-circuit protection.

The use of bias compensation resistor R_4 is also optional and depends on the gain and the grade of the 709 used. For example, at a gain of 60 dB, R_2 is 100 kΩ and, if a commercial grade of 709 is used, the worst-case bias current could be as high as 2.0 μA. Without the compensation of R_4, the output offset would then be 100 kΩ $\times$ 2.0 μA, or 0.2 V. If this is excessive, R_4 should be used at pin 3 as indicated. In most inverting configurations, pin 3 can be connected directly to ground. In noninverting stages, however, R_4 will almost always be necessary; therefore, its value should be set nominally equal to the feedback resistor, R_2. In either case, the value of R_4 need not be precise; a standard 10% carbon type will be sufficient.

Typical 709 frequency-response curves resulting from using optimized compensation are shown in Fig. 6-16. These curves have essentially constant high-frequency rolloff points, which indicates the effectiveness of the custom compensation in maintaining adequate

GBP as the gain is increased. No low-frequency rolloff is shown since the user selects this by adjusting the value of C_1.

Optimum 709 Performance at Unity Gain

Although the 709 is an excellent performer at high gains, it is not well suited for unity-gain operation with full-power output at high frequencies because of slew-rate limitations. Also, as was discussed in Chapter 3, the 709 has a tendency toward latch-up when used as a voltage follower and is not recommended for such operation unless anti-latch-up precautions are observed (see Fig. 3-14). In situations where there can be no compromise in performance as a unity-gain inverter or a voltage follower, several other IC types make better choices, as was discussed in Section 6.1.

The 709 configurations of Fig. 6-15 are shown as they would be used for bipolar power-supply operation, and the data is valid for supply voltages of ±15 V. Single supply operation is possible with no changes in compensation or feedback values if the biasing connections described in Section 6.2 are applied.

715 Voltage Amplifiers

The 709 amplifier configurations of Fig. 6-15 will perform very well for virtually any audio-frequency application when operated within the ratings of the device. The 709 has a lower dc gain than more recent types such as the 101A, 748, and 531; however, this has little bearing on audio performance because within the audio spectrum, these devices are equal in GBP at unity gain. At higher gains, the 709 is actually superior, as evidenced by its closed-loop frequency response (Fig. 6-16).

There are, however, some applications where a higher unity-gain frequency response is necessary in order to maintain low distortion at the higher frequencies. As has been discussed previously, the only way this can be achieved is by means of a higher GBP. With reference to the open-loop response of the 715 shown in Fig. 6-3D, it can be seen that the higher GBP of this device will provide a loop gain that is virtually flat at any operating gain within the audio-frequency range. Even at the lower gains of 1 and 10, the open-loop response of the 715 is only slightly down at 10-20 kHz. At higher gains, the open-loop response is flat over the entire audio-frequency range, which means that the 715 can maintain more feedback at all audio frequencies at various stage gains than any other IC op-amp type under discussion. It also means that when using the 715 in audio circuits, there will be no measurable deterioration in performance as the frequency is increased.

An undesirable side effect of the increased bandwidth and high-frequency gain of the 715 is that it is more susceptible to oscillations.

In order to minimize this potential problem, good high-frequency construction techniques such as used in video circuitry should be employed. These include: good-quality local rf bypass capacitors on power-supply leads, short direct-signal paths, low-inductance ground paths, and a minimum of capacitive loading. If these considerations are observed, excellent high-frequency performance will be attained with the 715.

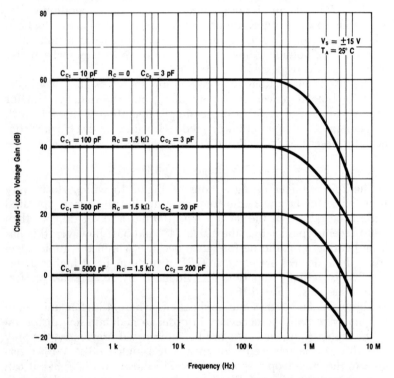

Courtesy Fairchild Semiconductor

Fig. 6-16. Typical 709 frequency-response curves for various closed-loop gains using recommended compensation.

The circuits for inverting and noninverting amplifiers using the 715 are shown in Figs. 6-17A and B, respectively, along with tabulated values for the feedback and compensation components. It will be noted that the feedback components are the same as for the 709 circuits of Fig. 6-15 except for feedback capacitor C_2, which is used to control the phase characteristics in the unity-gain crossover region. The optimum value for C_2 will change according to the value of R_2, so recommended values are listed in the chart. C_2 is always

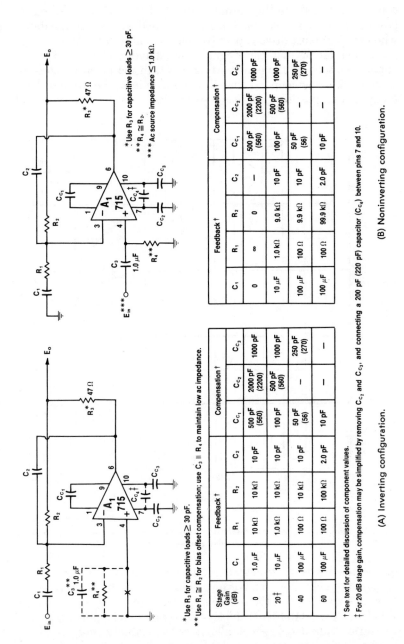

(A) Inverting configuration.

Stage Gain (dB)	Feedback†				Compensation†		
	C_1	R_1	R_2	C_2	C_{C_1}	C_{C_2}	C_{C_3}
0	1.0 μF	10 kΩ	10 kΩ	10 pF	500 pF (560)	2000 pF (2200)	1000 pF
20†	10 μF	1.0 kΩ	10 kΩ	10 pF	100 pF	500 pF (560)	1000 pF
40	100 μF	100 Ω	10 kΩ	10 pF	50 pF (56)	—	250 pF (270)
60	100 μF	100 Ω	100 kΩ	2.0 pF	10 pF	—	—

† See text for detailed discussion of component values.
† For 20 dB stage gain, compensation may be simplified by removing C_{C_2} and C_{C_3}, and connecting a 200 pF (220 pF) capacitor (C_{C_4}) between pins 7 and 10.

* Use R_3 for capacitive loads ≥ 30 pF.
** Use $R_4 \cong R_2$ for bias offset compensation; use $C_3 \parallel R_4$ to maintain low ac impedance.

(B) Noninverting configuration.

	Feedback†				Compensation†		
	C_1	R_1	R_2	C_2	C_{C_1}	C_{C_2}	C_{C_3}
	0	∞	0	—	500 pF (560)	2000 pF (2200)	1000 pF
	10 μF	1.0 kΩ	9.0 kΩ	10 pF	100 pF	500 pF (560)	1000 pF
	100 μF	100 Ω	9.9 kΩ	10 pF	50 pF (56)	—	250 pF (270)
	100 μF	100 Ω	99.9 kΩ	2.0 pF	10 pF	—	—

* Use R_3 for capacitive loads ≥ 30 pF.
** $R_4 \cong R_2$.
*** Ac source impedance ≤ 1.0 kΩ.

Fig. 6-17. Circuit diagrams and tabulated feedback and compensation values for optimized inverting and noninverting audio voltage amplifiers using the 715 op amp.

301

connected directly to the output (pin 6) of the 715, even when R_3 is used. R_3 is a series isolation resistor, used to maintain stability when the 715 must drive capacitive loads of more than 30 pF.

Another factor that can degrade the stability of the 715 is the impedance seen by the noninverting input. In the inverting configuration, it is recommended that this input (pin 4) be grounded directly if at all possible. If a bias resistor (R_4) must be used, it should

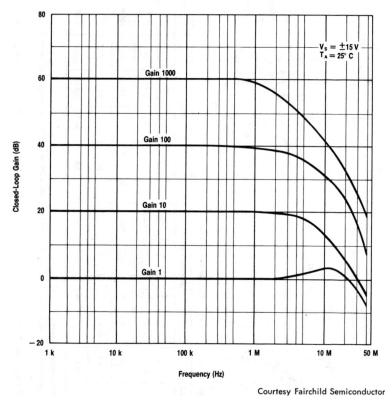

Courtesy Fairchild Semiconductor

Fig. 6-18. Typical 715 frequency-response curves for various closed-loop gains using recommended compensation.

be bypassed with C_3 to maintain an impedance of less than 1.0 kΩ at this input. In the noninverting configuration, R_4 is used as the bias resistance; hence, the source impedance of E_{in} should be below 1.0 kΩ for best stability. If the source has no dc component, R_4 and C_3 can be eliminated, which alleviates the stability problem.

Since the 715 is compensated differently than the 709, correspondingly different values are required for the compensation components,

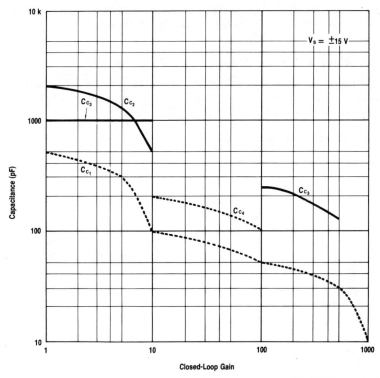

Courtesy Fairchild Semiconductor

Fig. 6-19. Graph of suggested 715 compensation capacitances as a function of the closed-loop gain.

and these are listed in the chart in Fig. 6-17. As was true for the 709, precise values are given in the chart; however, the closest 10% values (shown in parentheses) can be used with no difficulty. Also, stable capacitor types such as dipped mica are recommended.

It will be noted that the compensation values for the 715 are not directly proportional between the different gains as was true for the 709. This is because the open-loop response of the 715 does not have the "idealized" 6-dB/octave (20-dB/decade) rolloff that permits direct proportioning. Hence, direct compensation scaling is not possible with the 715, which is why the same compensation values are listed in the chart for both the inverting and noninverting configurations. However, the 715 has sufficiently adequate gain and bandwidth that this is a relatively unimportant point, which is borne out by the frequency-response curves for various closed-loop gains shown in Fig. 6-18. For intermediate gains between the decade steps of 0 dB to 60 dB, the compensation values may be chosen from the graph of Fig. 6-19. When the 715 is used as a voltage follower, anti-latch-up protection using a clamping diode (D_1) is recommended as shown in Fig. 6-20.

6.3.2 Audio Amplifiers With Increased Power Output

Although IC op amps are extremely useful in audio applications because of their high gain, small size, low cost, and general versatility, most of them are not capable of delivering more than a few milliwatts of power to a load. The standard ±10-V output swing into the rated 2000-Ω load represents only about 25 mW of power, which

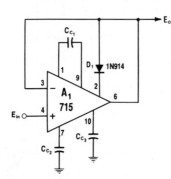

Fig. 6-20. Anti-latch-up protection for the 715 voltage-follower configuration.

is quite modest. Audio applications that require greater power often demand voltages and currents far in excess of what the standard op amp can deliver. For some of these applications, specialized IC types can be used, but, in general, some means of increasing both the output voltage swing and output current capability is necessary in order to take full advantage of the high-gain properties of IC op amps. In this section, we will examine a number of power applications ranging from a simple headphone driver to a high-fidelity power amplifier.

Headphone Drivers

The first power application to be examined involves the use of an IC op amp to drive one or more sets of headphones. Virtually any standard op amp can be used to drive a single set of high-impedance (2000 Ω) phones at a 25-mW level. All that is necessary is to select a suitable configuration and provide the required gain. The IC type can be chosen almost from convenience or personal preference, since most standard types can deliver 25 mW into 2000 Ω.

However, when a number of high-impedance phones (or a smaller number of low-impedance types) are to be driven, the power requirements exceed the output capabilities of the standard op-amp types. One type that is ideally suited for this application is the 540 power driver, which has a 150-mA, 1.0-W output capability. A circuit incorporating the 540 for this application is shown in Fig. 6-21. In this circuit, the 540 is operated as a variable-gain amplifier with maximum gains of either 30 or 40 dB, selected by the user by choosing the appropriate components from the tabulated values given in the illustration. The output level is adjusted with volume control R_3, which controls the input level to the 540.

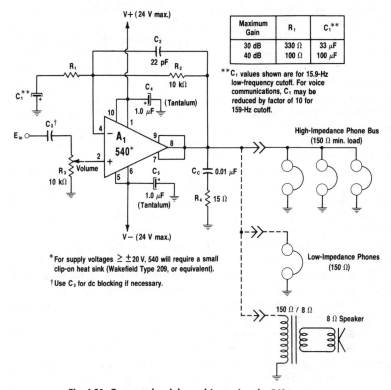

Maximum Gain	R_1	C_1**
30 dB	330 Ω	33 μF
40 dB	100 Ω	100 μF

**C_1 values shown are for 15.9-Hz low-frequency cutoff. For voice communications, C_1 may be reduced by factor of 10 for 159-Hz cutoff.

*For supply voltages ≥ ±20 V, 540 will require a small clip-on heat sink (Wakefield Type 209, or equivalent).

†Use C_3 for dc blocking if necessary.

Fig. 6-21. One-watt headphone driver using the 540 op amp.

Due to the wide power-supply operating capability of the 540, there is a wide range of maximum output levels available from the circuit of Fig. 6-21. With ±24-V supplies, for example, the 540 will deliver 1.0 W into a 150-Ω load, such as might be represented by a set of 150-Ω headphones, a parallel network of high-impedance headphones, or a transformer-driven 8-Ω speaker. This circuit has a variety of uses, such as a multiple-headphone intercom system, high-fidelity headphones, studio cueing amplifier, etc. The total harmonic distortion (THD) is less than 1.0%, even at maximum output. At lower output levels and also with load impedances higher than 150

Ω, the distortion reduces proportionally. If the 540 is operated at supply voltages of ± 20 V or above, a clip-on heat sink such as the Wakefield Type 209 (or equivalent) should be used. Also, since the 540 is a wide-bandwidth device, a compact layout with bypassed power-supply leads is recommended.

Line Amplifiers

A standard audio signal processing circuit is the line or program-distribution amplifier. This is typically a noninverting stage with high input impedance, flat frequency response, voltage gains from 20 to 50 dB, power outputs from +20 to +30 dBm (dB referred to 1.0 mW), and very low distortion and noise characteristics. These requirements are restrictive in terms of standard op-amp performance because the voltage (and current) swing for the power levels quoted is beyond the range of IC power supplies. Therefore, the use of booster techniques becomes necessary in order to satisfy the increased voltage and current demands while maintaining low distortion and noise.

The primary consideration is that of increasing the current output of the op amp to a level that can drive a 600-Ω or 150-Ω load with negligible distortion. Although some op amps with well-designed output stages can come close to delivering a +20-dBm signal into a 600-Ω load just as they stand, it is not good practice to operate them this way; it deteriorates the linearity of the op-amp output stage and also reduces the open-loop gain of the op-amp due to the loading.

A much better solution is to provide an external current-gain buffer stage, which isolates the load currents from the op amp and allows it to operate at maximum gain and deliver its full unloaded output voltage with good linearity.

540 Line Amplifier. The 540 line-amplifier circuit of Fig. 6-22 is a good example of how the performance of an op amp can be improved through the addition of external buffer stages to minimize loading effects. The 540 headphone-driver circuit of Fig. 6-21 will make a good-quality line driver easily capable of +20-dBm levels with less than 0.1% THD, particularly when operated with a stage gain of 30 dB into a 600-Ω load. It is also possible to drive lower load impedances such as 150 Ω with this circuit, but distortion increases with the increased loading because the lower load impedance reduces the open-loop gain of the circuit. In general, the higher the output impedance of an op amp, the more pronounced this effect becomes, until a point is reached where buffer stages must be used to increase the load impedance seen by the amplifier in order to maintain adequate gain.

This effect is very apparent with the 540, since the device has an output impedance of approximately 5 kΩ. Therefore, when loaded with 600 Ω, the open-loop gain of the 540 will drop nearly 20 dB, which can cause a serious loss of loop gain when operated at high stage gains.

In the circuit of Fig. 6-22, the loading problem is circumvented by the addition of class-AB emitter followers Q_1 and Q_2. This stage buffers a 150-Ω load impedance up to a level such that the output of the 540 sees minimal loading and full open-loop gain is realized.

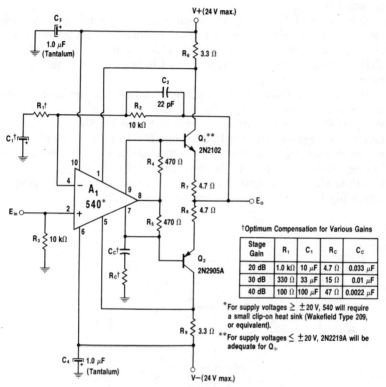

Stage Gain	R_1	C_1	R_C	C_C
20 dB	1.0 kΩ	10 μF	4.7 Ω	0.033 μF
30 dB	330 Ω	33 μF	15 Ω	0.01 μF
40 dB	100 Ω	100 μF	47 Ω	0.0022 μF

†Optimum Compensation for Various Gains

*For supply voltages ≥ ±20 V, 540 will require a small clip-on heat sink (Wakefield Type 209, or equivalent).

**For supply voltages ≤ ±20 V, 2N2219A will be adequate for Q_1.

Fig. 6-22. One-watt line amplifier using the 540 op amp.

Bias for Q_1 and Q_2 is provided by resistors R_4 and R_5, which set the drop across the internal V_{BE} multiplier transistor of the 540 to a value of 2.0 V_{BE}. This bias provides a small idle current in Q_1-Q_2 sufficient to eliminate crossover distortion. Resistors R_6 and R_9, in conjunction with the internal current-limiting transistors of the 540, sense the load current in Q_1-Q_2 and provide short-circuit protection. The current-limiting transistor(s) will be activated when the drop across R_6 or R_9 is only 650 mV; thus, current limiting is accomplished without excessive voltage drops, which allows larger output voltage swings to be developed before clipping occurs.

The power output capability of this circuit is determined by the supply potentials used. For example, ±15-V supplies allow up to +26 dBm into 150 Ω, or +20 dBm into 600 Ω. Increasing the supplies to ±24 V allows up to +30 dBm into 150 Ω, or +26 dBm into 600 Ω. When supplies greater than ±20 V are used, the 540 should be provided with a clip-on heat sink such as the Wakefield Type 209 (or equivalent), since the internal dissipation of the device can approach 1.0 W.

The circuit of Fig. 6-22, when compensated according to the values listed in the chart, has ≅40 dB of feedback at any of the gains shown, due to the output buffering. This is sufficient to maintain a THD of ≤0.1% at any operating level below clipping, and at frequencies up to 10 kHz.

715 Line Amplifier. Another example of how the performance of an op amp can be improved through the addition of external buffer stages is the 715 line amplifier shown in Fig. 6-23. Although the 715 can deliver approximately +18 dBm into 600 Ω without a buffer, this is not guaranteed, and linearity of the output stage suffers at the higher levels. Like the 540, however, the 715 can be operated with a simple class-AB output stage, which greatly enhances its output capability while maintaining high open-loop gain.

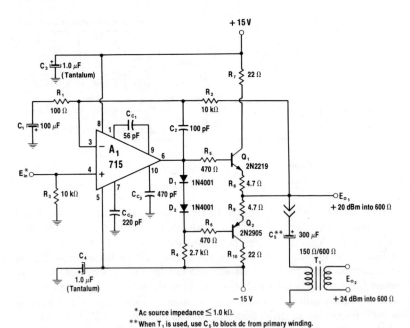

*Ac source impedance ≤ 1.0 kΩ.
**When T₁ is used, use C₅ to block dc from primary winding.

Fig. 6-23. 715 line amplifier.

The circuit of Fig. 6-23 is a noninverting stage with 40 dB of gain, capable of driving 600-Ω or 150-Ω loads directly, or through a transformer. Transistors Q_1 and Q_2 form a complementary-symmetry, class-AB emitter follower, which provides a high current output with minimum loading to the 715. A floating base bias is provided for Q_1 and Q_2 by high-conductance diodes D_1 and D_2. Resistor R_4 provides a negative pull-down current for the 715, which forces its output stage to operate class A for optimum linearity. Resistors R_5 and R_6 prevent parasitic oscillations in Q_1 and Q_2, while R_7 and R_{10} provide short-circuit protection. The stage is compensated slightly heavier than a gain of 40 dB would indicate. This is to provide an extra margin of stability due to the presence of Q_1 and Q_2 within the feedback loop, which gives added insurance against oscillation with capacitive loads.

This circuit will deliver +20 dBm into 600 Ω with standard $\pm$15-V supplies, and by using a 150-Ω/600-Ω line transformer as shown, will deliver +24 dBm into a balanced 600-Ω line. If higher supplies are used for Q_1 and Q_2, the circuit can deliver +26 dBm into 150 Ω, or into 600 Ω by using the 150-Ω/600-Ω step-up transformer.

As with the previous 715 circuits, good high-frequency layout and construction practices are necessary to prevent instability in this circuit. If these precautions are observed, however, the reward will be a THD of less than 0.1% at any level below clipping and at any frequency within the audio range.

709 Line Amplifier. The circuit of Fig. 6-23 illustrates a method of increasing the output voltage swing of a line amplifier through the use of a step-up transformer. However, IC line-driving amplifiers can also be configured to deliver peak-to-peak output voltage swings in excess of their ratings without the use of a step-up transformer. Fig. 6-24 shows such a circuit, a 709 line amplifier with a transformerless, voltage step-up output stage.

This circuit is basically a two-stage amplifier. The first stage is the 709, which provides the bulk of the voltage gain. The second stage consists of transistors Q_1 through Q_4, a complementary-symmetry, push-pull power output stage which increases the output voltage swing of the circuit to over 40 V peak-to-peak. The output stage operates with a voltage gain of 3 and provides local feedback around Q_1-Q_3 and Q_2-Q_4. The two halves of the push-pull output are fed back separately with local feedback dividers R_6-R_{10} and R_7-R_{11}. The separate feedback allows Q_1 and Q_2 to be dc biased individually with R_4 and R_{12}. This controlled dc bias maintains a small quiescent current in Q_3-Q_4 at all times, a factor that is absolutely necessary for positive elimination of crossover distortion.

Using an op-amp with an added voltage-gain stage within the feedback loop means that the compensation necessary will be increased from that implied by the op amp's overall closed-loop gain by the factor of the additional gain. In this case, for example, the overall closed-loop gain is 40 dB, and the output stage (Q_1-Q_4) provides a voltage gain of 10 dB; therefore, the 709 is compensated for a closed-loop gain of 30 dB.

With ±28-V supplies, this circuit is capable of delivering +30 dBm into 150 Ω, or +26 dBm into 600 Ω. Distortion is only noticeable in this circuit above 1.0 kHz and at high levels, rising to 0.2% THD at 10 kHz near full output. Otherwise, the distortion will remain below 0.1% THD at any level below clipping. For extremely critical applications, use a 2620 amplifier for A_1. This device has greater high-frequency loop gain and lower high-frequency distortion. Compensation components C_{C_1}, C_{C_2}, and R_C are omitted for this option. Transistors Q_3 and Q_4 should be provided with clip-on heat sinks such as the Wakefield Type 209 (or equivalent), particularly when the circuit is operated at high-level output over extended periods. The lower supply voltages necessary for A_1 are normally derived from the output-stage supplies with emitter followers Q_5 and Q_6 as shown.

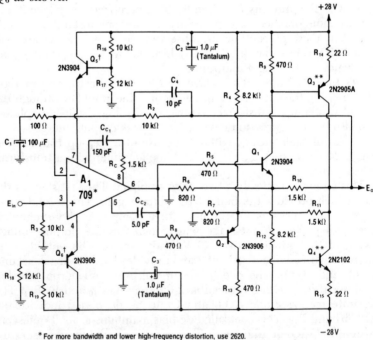

* For more bandwidth and lower high-frequency distortion, use 2620.

** Use clip-on heat sinks (Wakefield Type 209, or equivalent) for Q_3 and Q_4.

† If higher quiescent current is allowed, omit Q_5 and Q_6, and let R_{16}-R_{17} and R_{18}-R_{19} divide ±28 V.

Fig. 6-24. 709 line amplifier.

Single-Supply Mobile Radio Speaker Amplifier

Another audio signal application requiring increased power output is in circuits that are used to drive speaker loads. In such applications, the load currents can reach several amperes, which means that multiple stages of current boost are needed between the op amp and the load.

A unique requirement in this class of amplifier is the output stage of mobile radio equipment. The available supply potential is relatively low (12-16 V), yet the amplifier must deliver several watts of power into the speaker, with a minimum of circuit complexity, good efficiency, and at low overall cost.

An interesting solution to these requirements is shown in Fig. 6-25. This is an op-amp driven, class-B output amplifier that can

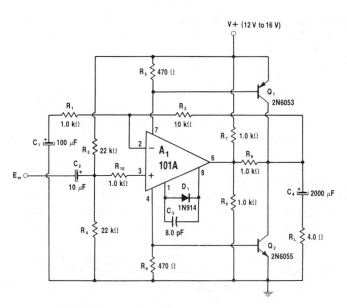

Fig. 6-25. Single-supply mobile radio speaker amplifier.

deliver 3.5 watts into a 4-Ω speaker load at 0.25% THD. In this circuit, A_1 is operated as a noninverting voltage amplifier driving Darlington power transistors Q_1 and Q_2, which are connected in a complementary-symmetry, push-pull output configuration. The circuit has a very low idle current because Q_1 and Q_2 are biased off under no-signal conditions. Q_1 and Q_2 are driven by the current flowing in the supply leads of A_1. This current develops a drive voltage across base resistors R_5 and R_6, which are selected to drop a voltage that is less than the turn-on V_{BE} of Q_1 and Q_2, with no signal input and with the quiescent supply current of A_1 flowing. This maintains a low overall current consumption.

The penalty for operating Q_1 and Q_2 at zero bias is an increase in crossover distortion at low levels, since A_1 must "pulse-on" Q_1 and Q_2 alternately to form an output sine wave. However, this is not a significant factor except at frequencies above 5.0 kHz, since the loop gain of A_1 corrects for the crossover distortion.

The circuit can be viewed as a two-stage amplifier, with the bulk of the voltage gain supplied by the 101A first stage. The second stage, which consists of output transistors Q_1 and Q_2, has a voltage gain of approximately 3, determined by

$$\frac{R_8 + (R_7 \parallel R_9)}{R_7 \parallel R_9} .$$

This is actually local feedback around Q_1-Q_2 and the output stage of the op amp. The purpose of this feedback is to scale the voltage swing seen by the load upward from that at the op-amp output. With the values given, the load voltage swing will be three times the output swing of the op amp. This allows power transistors Q_1 and Q_2 to be driven into saturation, developing nearly the full supply voltage across the load, or 3.5 W into 4.0 Ω with a 14-V supply.

Substitution of other op-amp types for A_1 in this circuit should be done with care. The circuit requires an op amp that has high gain at low supply voltages, which is a design feature of the 101A family. Furthermore, the supply current should be low and independent of temperature and supply-voltage variations, since this current directly affects the bias of Q_1 and Q_2. These factors are also features of the 101A design. Finally, A_1 should be an externally compensated type, since the optimization of high-frequency loop gain in this circuit is important in minimizing crossover distortion.

Circuit components that are provided for safety reasons are resistor R_{10}, which protects the input of A_1 against the discharge of C_2; and diode D_1, an antisaturation clamp which prevents possible latch-up.

540 Power Amplifier (50/100 Watts)

A circuit employing many of the principles described in previous circuits is the 540 power amplifier shown in Fig. 6-26. This circuit is capable of delivering 50 W into 16 Ω, or 100 W into 8 Ω, and features both overcurrent and overvoltage protection for the output transistors.

In block form, this circuit is basically a two-stage amplifier, similar to the 709 circuit of Fig. 6-24. The first stage is the 540, which provides the bulk of the voltage gain. The second stage consists of transistors Q_1-Q_3 and Q_2-Q_4 operating as a class-AB, push-pull power output stage, which provides the necessary voltage gain to increase the output voltage swing of the 540 up to a level approaching the higher ±45-V power supplies. Transistors Q_3 and Q_4 are heavy-duty power devices that are capable of delivering the current necessary to achieve 50-W or 100-W output into 16 Ω or 8 Ω, respectively. The voltage gain of the second stage is set at approximately 4 by resistors R_7-R_8 and R_9-R_{10}. The separate feedback paths to Q_1 and Q_2 allow control over the idle current in the upper (Q_1-Q_3) and lower (Q_2-Q_4) halves of the output stage.

The output stage bias is determined by the voltage presented from base to base of Q_1 and Q_2. This bias voltage is developed by the internal V_{BE} multiplier transistor of the 540, which, in conjunction with R_4 and R_5, develops a multiple of 1.0 V_{BE} between Q_1 and Q_2.

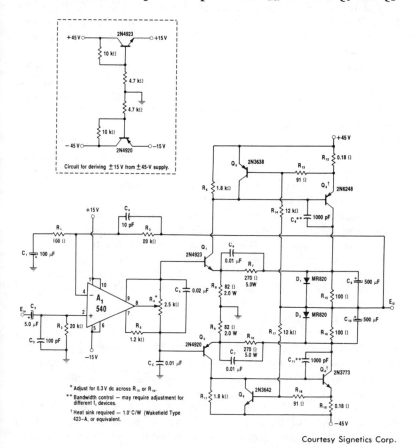

Courtesy Signetics Corp.

Fig. 6-26. 540 power amplifier (50/100 watts).

R_4 is adjusted to set this multiple for the desired bias on Q_1 and Q_2, which, in turn, sets the idle current in the output stage.

A unique biasing system, which is linked with the biasing of Q_1 and Q_2, is used for Q_3 and Q_4. With the feedback loop closed, the output terminal will rest at 0-V dc due to 100% negative feedback around A_1 and the fact that R_3 (reference input) is grounded. Thus, the voltage from the junction of R_{15} and R_7 to ground is a measure of the current in Q_3, since the static current divides between R_{15} and R_7-R_8. (Similarly, the voltage from the junction of R_{16} and R_{10} to ground is a measure of the current in Q_4, since this static current divides between R_{16} and R_{10}-R_9.) The connection of Q_1-Q_3 and R_7-R_8 constitutes a local feedback loop, and it is this loop that sets the current in Q_3. Considering R_7 and R_8 as a β network, it can be seen that this feedback loop will generate a voltage from the junction of R_7 and R_{15} to ground, which is equal to $(R_7 + R_8)/R_8$ times the voltage from the emitter of Q_1 to ground. Since R_{15} is connected to a dc virtual ground, it sets the bulk of the current in Q_3, with some current also flowing through R_7 and R_8.

From this line of reasoning, it can be seen that the bias applied to Q_1 will also set the voltage across R_8, and thus the upper half of the idle current in the output stage. (Similarly, the R_{10}-R_9 divider and Q_2-Q_4 set the idle current in the lower half of the output stage.) In practice, of course, the idle current does not flow to ground but rather flows from V+ to V− through Q_3 and Q_4. Potentiometer R_4 is adjusted so that the voltage drop across R_{15} (or R_{16}) is less than the turn-on voltage of diode D_1 (or D_2), which is approximately 0.9-V dc for the MR820 diodes. Thus, in this circuit, the drop across R_{15} (or R_{16}) is adjusted to 0.3-V dc.

It can be seen from this discussion that the output stage will operate at class A for small signal levels, which prevents crossover distortion. At high signal levels, the current through R_{15} (or R_{16}) will cause the voltage drop to exceed the turn-on voltage of D_1 (or D_2). When either D_1 or D_2 conduct, the circuit will be operating at class B. Capacitors C_9 and C_{10} bypass D_1 and D_2, minimizing the effects of the turn-on transients.

Overload protection for Q_3 is provided by R_{12}, R_{13}, R_{14}, and Q_5. (The same protection for Q_4 is provided by R_{19}, R_{18}, R_{17}, and Q_6.) Resistor R_{12} monitors the emitter current in Q_3, while R_{13} and R_{14} monitor the collector-emitter voltage of Q_3. (Similarly, resistor R_{19} monitors the emitter current in Q_4, while R_{18} and R_{17} monitor the collector-emitter voltage of Q_4.)

When the voltage/current stress limit of Q_3 is exceeded, the 0.6-V turn-on voltage of Q_5 is exceeded, which activates Q_5. Q_5 then clamps Q_3 off, maintaining its operation within safe limits. A similar action takes place between Q_4 and Q_6.

This circuit has a closed-loop gain of 46 dB and, as mentioned previously, can deliver 50 W into a 16-Ω load, or 100 W into an 8-Ω load. Distortion is quite low, being typically below 0.1% THD, as shown in the graph of Fig. 6-27 for 16-Ω, 50-W operation. It is not necessary to have regulated supply voltages; in fact, the only significant effect of supply-voltage variation is a reduction in power output capability. If a separate ±15-V supply is not available to power the 540, these voltages can be derived from the ±45-V supply, as shown in the inset of Fig. 6-26.

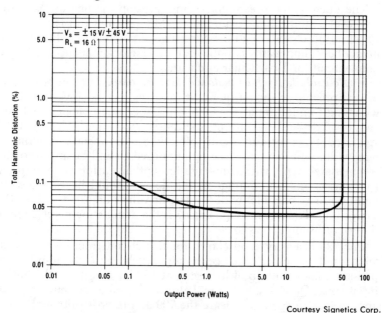

Fig. 6-27. Total harmonic distortion versus output power for the 540 power amplifier of Fig. 6-26.

6.3.3 Audio Preamplifiers

Audio preamplifiers represent the low-level end of the dynamic range of practical audio circuits using IC op amps. In general, amplifying stages that accept input signals at levels of 10 mV or less fall into this category. In this section, we will discuss the three basic types of audio preamps: (1) microphone, (2) tape, and (3) phono.

When working signals reach the level of 1.0 mV, the input noise generated by the first amplifying stage in the system becomes an important consideration if a wide dynamic range and good signal-to-noise ratio are to be preserved. For example, if the internally generated noise voltage of the input stage is 1.0 μV, and the input signal voltage is 1.0 mV, the best signal-to-noise ratio that can be expected is 60 dB. In a given application, it is usually the input voltage level that is fixed; thus, for best signal-to-noise ratio, the input noise generated by the first amplifying stage must be minimized. Minimizing the input noise of an amplifier requires an understanding of the factors that contribute to the total noise, including both the amplifier itself and the external circuit in which it is used, as previously discussed.

Microphone Preamplifiers

The microphone preamplifier (mic preamp) is one of the basic low-level amplification requirements. Mic preamps can have a variety of forms, considering the wide range of possible signal levels and microphone impedances. Both of these factors influence the optimum circuit for a particular application.

Single-Ended, High-Impedance Mic Preamp. The simplest form of mic preamp is shown in Fig. 6-28. This is a noninverting stage with single-ended input for high-impedance microphones. It has a gain of 40 dB and, in concept, could use any op amp. The exact device used, however, can greatly affect the performance. In terms of bandwidth and loop gain, the op amp used should be an externally compensated type, with compensation optimized for the gain used. In terms of noise performance, the device should have as low an input noise as possible, with the circuit values adjusted so that the source impedance (mic impedance) is the dominating percentage of the overall source resistance.

The 725 is a very good choice for this circuit from both a bandwidth and noise-performance standpoint, because its 40-dB compensation allows 40 dB of loop gain at 10 kHz and it has the lowest input noise. Other types that will also work well in this circuit (with appropriate compensation) are the 709 and the 540, although these types are not as well specified in terms of noise performance.

In the circuit of Fig. 6-28, gain-determining resistors R_1 and R_2 are scaled such that the total resistance of $R_1 \parallel R_2$ is less than the lowest expected source impedance, which in this case is 600 Ω. This minimizes the contribution of $R_1 \parallel R_2$ to input noise. Although microphones having impedances less than 600 Ω can be used with this circuit, noise performance will not be optimum. Succeeding circuits will illustrate methods of optimizing noise performance for low-impedance microphones.

The gain of this circuit can be adjusted by changing feedback resistor R_2. Control of microphone signal level should always be exercised after it has undergone a stage of gain, such as in the feedback loop with R_2. Attenuation of the signal level before amplification (such as with resistive pads) should never be done, because it compromises the signal-to-noise ratio.

The circuit of Fig. 6-28 is a good one if modest performance and simplicity are required. For a bandwidth of 10 kHz with a 600-Ω source, the circuit can be expected to have an equivalent input noise of less than 1.0 μV rms, using the 725.

Differential-Input, Low-Impedance Mic Preamp. One problem with using unbalanced microphone lines is noise pickup due to common-mode signals coupled into the cable. The circuit of Fig. 6-29 can minimize such induced noise by cancelling it with a differential-input configuration. This circuit works best when used with low-impedance sources such as 150-Ω (or lower) microphones.

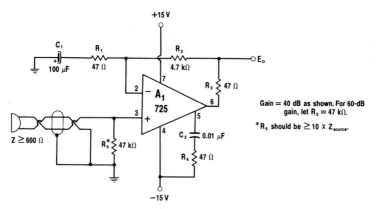

Fig. 6-28. High-impedance microphone preamplifier.

The 725 is also a good choice for this circuit, not only because of its wide bandwidth and good noise performance, but also because of its high CMRR. The ultimate input noise of this circuit will not be quite as low as in the circuit of Fig. 6-28, however, because R_1 and R_2 must be made higher in value. The main advantage of this circuit lies in terms of common-mode noise rejection. The degree of common-mode rejection realized is proportional to the matching of resistor ratios, as indicated in Fig. 6-29. If 0.1% resistors are used, the CMRR can be 100 dB; with 1.0% resistors, the CMRR can be 80 dB. To optimize common-mode noise rejection when 1.0% resistors are used, R_4 can be trimmed with a 10-kΩ potentiometer, as shown.

Transformer-Input, Low-Impedance Mic Preamp. As discussed in Chapter 1, the best noise performance for any op amp is attained when the source resistance (R_s) is equal to the characteristic noise resistance (R_n) of the amplifier. An example of a preamp that takes advantage of this factor, utilizing a matching transformer (T_1), is shown in Fig. 6-30. In order to select an optimum turns ratio to match a given source resistance (R_s) to the characteristic noise resistance (R_n) of the op amp used, R_n must first be calculated from the specified data for e_n and i_n as follows:

$$R_n = \frac{e_n}{i_n},$$

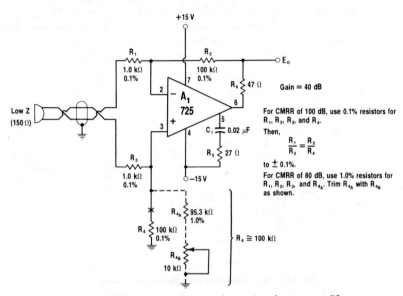

Fig. 6-29. Differential-input, low-impedance microphone preamplifier.

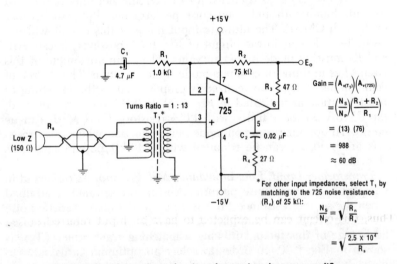

Fig. 6-30. Transformer-input, low-impedance microphone preamplifier.

where e_n is in $V/\sqrt{Hz}$ and i_n is in $A/\sqrt{Hz}$. Then, the turns ratio for T_1 may be calculated as

$$\frac{N_s}{N_p} = \sqrt{\frac{R_n}{R_s}}.$$

For the 725, the values for e_n and i_n are 8.0 $nV/\sqrt{Hz}$ and 0.3 $pA/\sqrt{Hz}$, respectively; thus,

$$R_n = \frac{e_n}{i_n}$$

$$= \frac{8 \times 10^{-9}}{3 \times 10^{-13}}$$

$$= 26.7 \text{ k}\Omega.$$

Since both e_n and i_n vary with frequency, R_n will also vary with frequency. Therefore, an approximate value of 25 kΩ for R_n is used for calculation purposes with little error in cases involving wideband amplifiers. If the amplifier were to be optimized for a specific frequency, then the values for e_n and i_n should be for that frequency. In this example, if R_s is 150 Ω, then the turns ratio for T_1 will be

$$\frac{N_s}{N_p} = \sqrt{\frac{R_n}{R_s}}$$

$$= \sqrt{\frac{2.5 \times 10^4}{1.5 \times 10^2}}$$

$$\approx 13/1.$$

A transformer may now be selected for T_1 which fulfills this requirement. It goes without saying, of course, that T_1 must be adequately shielded and otherwise suitable for operation in low-level environments.

The use of a matching transformer allows the circuit to achieve an equivalent input noise (referred to the transformer input) that is only a few dB above the theoretical limit, or very close to the thermal noise of the source resistance. For example, the thermal noise of a 150-Ω resistor in a 10-kHz bandwidth at room temperature is

$$E_n = \sqrt{4\kappa T \, (150) \, (10^4)}$$

$$\approx 160 \text{ nV}.$$

Thus, this circuit can be expected to have an input referred noise of 200 nV, or less, with a 150-Ω source, using a noise figure of 2 dB (taken from data sheet). A similar procedure may be used in optimizing any amplifier to any given value of source resistance.

An additional advantage of the matching transformer is the voltage gain it provides due to the turns ratio. For a given circuit gain (A_v), this reduces the gain required from the op amp (A) to

$$A = \frac{A_v}{N_s/N_p}.$$

Thus, the composite gain is the product of the transformer gain (N_s/N_p) and $(R_1 + R_2)/R_1$. This has the obvious advantage of allowing more loop gain, hence greater accuracy, lower distortion, etc. In practice, almost the full unloaded voltage gain of the transformer is realized, since it looks into the bootstrapped noninverting input of the op amp, which has an input impedance of many megohms.

In this circuit, the source resistance seen by the op amp is relatively high (25 kΩ); thus, the feedback resistances can be higher than in previous circuits without deterioration of noise performance. This has the additional benefit of allowing a smaller capacitance value for C_1. The 725 stage has a gain of 76, which, in combination with the transformer gain, yields a composite gain of 988, or nearly 60 dB. As always, the op amp is compensated for its noise gain.

Although this circuit has been discussed in terms of a low-impedance source (microphone), the transformer-matching technique is applicable to transducers of any impedance. It is only necessary to know the characteristic noise resistance of the op amp. If this data is not given in terms of e_n and i_n, it is usually implicit from the curves of noise figure versus source resistance. The noise figure is at a minimum when $R_n = R_s$; therefore; it is only necessary to verify the source resistance for minimum noise figure, which will be very close to R_n. This value can then be used in the calculations.

Tape Preamplifier

A typical preamplifier application is in a tape playback system. These circuits often operate at signal levels of 1.0 mV or less, which places stringent requirements on the amplifier if a good signal-to-noise ratio is to be realized. In addition to high average gain, equalized frequency response is necessary, which raises the total low-frequency gain to as high as 80 dB. Few op amps can provide adequate loop gain with low input noise under these conditions. One exception is the 725, which has a low-frequency gain of 130 dB and, as has already been discussed, low input noise.

The general response curve required for tape-playback equalization is shown in Fig. 6-31. Gain is at a maximum below 50 Hz (f_1), which is the lower corner frequency that begins the equalized portion of the curve. Above f_1, the response rolls off at 6 dB/octave until it reaches the upper corner frequency somewhere between f_2 and f_3. This frequency will vary according to tape speed, but a range of 1.0

kHz to 5.0 kHz covers most of the standard frequencies. Frequency f_2 (1.0 kHz) is also the gain reference frequency, and the gain at this frequency may be in the range of 40 to 50 dB. The other frequency of interest is f_0, the low-end rolloff frequency, which is somewhere below 50 Hz. The choice of this frequency is left up to the personal preference of the user.

Rather than attempting to list a number of circuits covering all the possible variations in gain and high-frequency equalization, a universal circuit will be described that will accommodate a range of

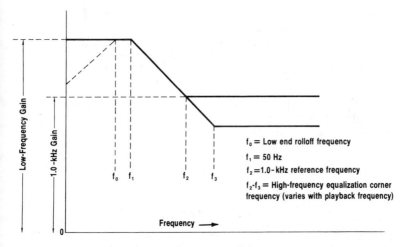

f₀ = Low end rolloff frequency

f₁ = 50 Hz

f₂ = 1.0 - kHz reference frequency

f₂-f₃ = High-frequency equalization corner frequency (varies with playback frequency)

Fig. 6-31. Tape playback equalization curve.

possible conditions. This circuit is shown in Fig. 6-32; it uses a 725 in a low-noise, noninverting configuration. The reader may use this circuit as it stands or substitute fixed resistance values for specific conditions.

The gain and equalization characteristics of this circuit are established by the feedback network consisting of R_1 through R_6, and C_1-C_2. The actions of the various components are best appreciated if analyzed individually. The value of resistor R_1 is low in comparison to the source resistance, as described previously. C_1 and R_1 set the low-end rolloff frequency, which is 33 Hz for the values shown in Fig. 6-32. The ratio of $R_1 + R_2$ to R_1 determines the gain at low frequencies. In a conventional stage, the gain would be simply $(R_1 + R_2)/R_1$, but in this circuit, the divider R_5-R_6 adds an additional gain (variable) of 10 dB. The reason that R_6 is used to vary the gain rather than R_1 is that varying R_1 would also vary the low-end rolloff frequency. R_6 varies the gain without any frequency effects.

The reactance of capacitor C_2 begins reducing the gain from its low-frequency maximum at the frequency where $X_{C_2} = R_2$, or 50 Hz. At frequencies above 50 Hz, the gain rolls off at 6 dB/octave, following the curve of Fig. 6-31. At the frequency where $X_{C_2} = R_3 + R_4$, the high-frequency equalization corner occurs. R_4 is made variable to allow adjustment of this equalization frequency from 1.0 kHz to 5.0 kHz. Above this frequency, the amplifier gain is flat up to the limit of the open-loop bandwidth. R_6 provides an overall gain ad-

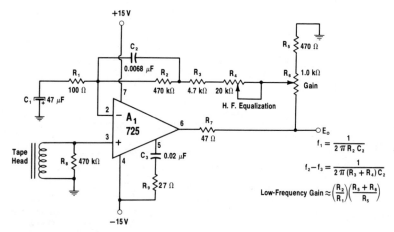

Fig. 6-32. Tape preamplifier.

justment for the circuit, varying low-frequency gain from 70 dB to 80 dB, and varying f_2 reference-frequency (1.0 kHz) gain from 44 dB to 54 dB. R_4 provides high-frequency corner adjustment from 1.0 kHz to 5.0 kHz, which is sufficient to accommodate most playback curves. The 725 must be compensated for the lowest expected gain, which in this circuit is R_3/R_1, or 47. It is not recommended that other op amps be substituted for the 725 in this circuit unless some degradation in performance can be tolerated.

RIAA Phono Preamplifier

Another preamplifier application requiring equalized frequency response is the RIAA phono preamp. The RIAA equalization curve is shown in Fig. 6-33. Like the tape equalization curve of Fig. 6-31, this curve also indicates maximum gain below 50 Hz (f_1). Unlike the tape curve, however, the RIAA curve has two high-frequency breakpoints. Above f_1, the gain rolls off at 6 dB/octave until the first high-frequency breakpoint is reached at 500 Hz (f_2). The gain then remains constant until the second high-frequency breakpoint is reached at 2.1 kHz (f_3), where it again rolls off at 6 dB/octave

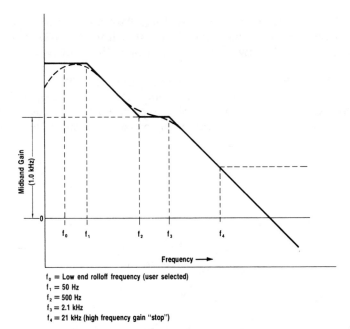

f$_0$ = Low end rolloff frequency (user selected)
f$_1$ = 50 Hz
f$_2$ = 500 Hz
f$_3$ = 2.1 kHz
f$_4$ = 21 kHz (high frequency gain "stop")

Fig. 6-33. RIAA phono playback equalization curve.

through the remainder of the audio region. The low-end rolloff frequency (f_0) is again left up to the personal preference of the user.

The gain of an RIAA preamp is generally specified in terms of the 1.0-kHz reference frequency. Since the shape of the standard curve is fixed, this also defines the gain for all other frequencies. It will be noted from the RIAA curve that the gain characteristic reduces to zero at high frequencies. This implies that an amplifier with unity-gain stability is required, which is indeed true if the standard characteristic is used. In order to illustrate what effect this has on loop gain, a 40-dB gain, RIAA characteristic is shown plotted together with 1.0-MHz and 10-MHz GBP curves in Fig. 6-34. As will be noted from the 1.0-MHz GBP curve and the RIAA curve, a preamp with a 1.0-MHz GBP will have less than 20 dB of feedback at frequencies above 2.1 kHz. The only way to increase the feedback is to lower the gain of this stage and make up the difference in a succeeding stage. By way of contrast, a 10-MHz GBP will allow 34 dB of feedback as a minimum.

However, if a high-frequency gain "stop" is provided above 21 kHz, a modified RIAA characteristic can be made flat at the point of intersection with the open-loop gain curve. This means that an amplifier using external compensation can be compensated for a gain of 20 dB rather than unity gain, which allows the higher loop gain of a 10-MHz GBP curve to be realized. Two versions of an RIAA phono preamp using this principle are shown in Fig. 6-35. The circuit is presented in two versions for reasons that will be explained shortly.

A 40-dB-gain, RIAA phono preamp using the 725 is shown in Fig. 6-35A. This circuit is compensated for a closed-loop gain of 20 dB, which allows it to achieve a 10-MHz GBP as discussed previously. In a 40-dB RIAA preamp, the gain at low frequencies is only

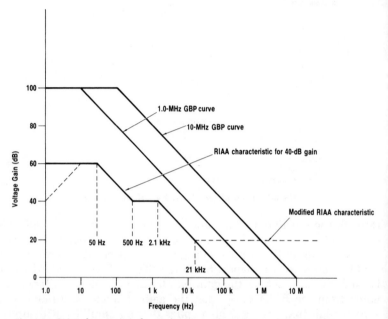

Fig. 6-34. RIAA characteristic for 40-dB gain, with 1.0-MHz and 10-MHz GBP curves.

60 dB, as contrasted to the tape preamp where low-frequency gain can be as high as 80 dB. In Fig. 6-35A, the low-frequency gain is set at 60 dB by R_2/R_1. The 50-Hz lower corner frequency (f_1) is set by C_2 and R_2 at the point where $X_{C_2} = R_2$. At frequencies above this point, the gain rolls off at 6 dB/octave until the 500-Hz breakpoint (f_2) is reached, where $X_{C_2} = R_3$. The gain then flattens out to 40 dB at the midband reference frequency of 1.0 kHz. At the 2.1-kHz breakpoint (f_3), $X_{C_3} = R_3$ and the gain again rolls off at 6 dB/octave until it reaches the high-frequency gain "stop" point at 21 kHz (f_4), where $X_{C_3} = R_4$. At this point, the circuit is at its minimum gain of 20 dB.

The 725 is an excellent performer in this circuit in terms of bandwidth and noise. However, it does have one drawback, and that is

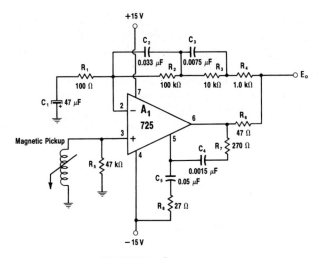

(A) 725 RIAA phono preamp.

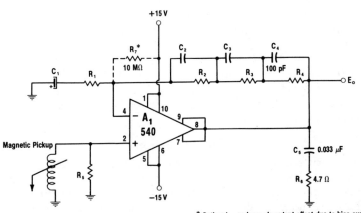

* Optional — reduces dc output offset due to bias current.

(B) 540 RIAA phono preamp.

Fig. 6-35. RIAA magnetic-pickup phono preamplifiers.

its slewing rate. When compensated for a gain of 20 dB, the slewing rate of the 725 is about 0.1 V/μs, which limits the output level at high frequencies. At 20 kHz, for example, this slewing rate will allow only 1.59 V p-p of output. The slew-rate problem can be eased somewhat by operating the 725 at a higher gain, but the increased sensitivity may create overload problems. In addition, many professional applications require full power (± 10 V) at 20 kHz.

For the reasons given in the preceding paragraph, an alternate version of the 40-dB RIAA phono preamp using the 540 is shown in

Fig. 6-35B. The 540 also has low input noise and, when compensated for a gain of 20 dB as shown, can slew at 3.0 V/μs, which allows full power output at frequencies above 20 kHz. In this circuit, only those components that are unique to the 540 are shown with values; the remaining components are identical to those in the 725 circuit of Fig. 6-35A. In Fig. 6-35B, C_5 and R_6 provide frequency compensation, and C_4 corrects the feedback phase in the gain crossover region. If minimum dc output level is required, the 1.5-μA bias current flowing in R_2, R_3, and R_4 may be a drawback, since this can cause about 0.2 V of offset. However, the offset can easily be compensated by R_7, which supplies a nominal 1.5 μA from the +15-V line. In all other circuit details, the 540 stage is identical to the 725 configuration.

The 540 RIAA preamp is capable of full power output with low distortion across the entire audio range. It also has the capability of driving 600-Ω loads, if necessary, although loading should not be less than 10 kΩ for distortion figures on the order of 0.1% or lower.

6.3.4 Equalized Amplifiers

With frequency-dependent feedback around an operational amplifier, virtually any desired gain-versus-frequency characteristic can be synthesized, generally to an accuracy limited only by the passive components used. Specific examples of equalized amplifiers have been covered in the previous section; namely, the tape and RIAA phono preamps. In this section, we will cover more general examples of equalized amplifiers that are suitable for high-level audio signal processing.

Shelving Equalizers

One very common audio-equalizer application is the *shelving* equalizer, so named because of the shape of its frequency response characteristic, as shown in Fig. 6-36. This is a graph of both high- and low-frequency shelving. Such a response is typical of the familiar hi-fi "tone" controls, where the low-frequency end is controlled

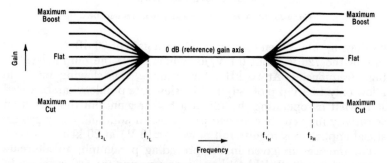

Fig. 6-36. Shelving equalizer characteristics.

by the "bass" control and the high-frequency end is controlled by the "treble" control. In general, "boost" (and "cut") capability is symmetrical, with a maximum capability of ±20 dB or less. The frequencies at which the equalization begins (f_{1_H} and f_{1_L}) are generally centered within the audio spectrum so that maximum boost (or cut) is available only at the extreme ends of the frequency range, above f_{2_H} (20 kHz) and below f_{2_L} (20 Hz). Fig. 6-37 illustrates two circuits that accomplish the shelving-equalizer function with simplicity, predictability, and symmetry.

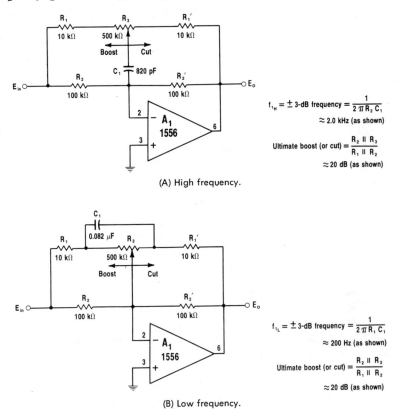

$$f_{1_H} = \pm\,3\text{-dB frequency} = \frac{1}{2\pi R_2 C_1}$$
$$\approx 2.0 \text{ kHz (as shown)}$$

$$\text{Ultimate boost (or cut)} = \frac{R_2 \parallel R_3}{R_1 \parallel R_2}$$
$$\approx 20 \text{ dB (as shown)}$$

(A) High frequency.

$$f_{1_L} = \pm\,3\text{-dB frequency} = \frac{1}{2\pi R_1 C_1}$$
$$\approx 200 \text{ Hz (as shown)}$$

$$\text{Ultimate boost (or cut)} = \frac{R_2 \parallel R_3}{R_1 \parallel R_2}$$
$$\approx 20 \text{ dB (as shown)}$$

(B) Low frequency.

Fig. 6-37. Shelving equalizers.

High-Frequency Shelving Equalizer. The schematic for a high-frequency shelving equalizer is shown in Fig. 6-37A. It will be noted that in the absence of R_1, R_1', R_3, and C_1, this circuit is a simple unity-gain inverting stage. By building upon the basic symmetry of this inverting configuration, different types of equalizers are possible. In the circuit of Fig. 6-37A, when R_3 is at its electrical center, there will be no voltage across C_1 and thus no current flow into the summing point. When R_3 is rotated toward R_1, the input current will increase by virtue of the lowered input impedance, $R_1 + X_{C_1}$. Similarly, when R_3 is rotated toward R_1', the feedback impedance is lowered by virtue of $R_1' - X_{C_1}$. The frequency at which the shunting of R_1-C_1 and R_1'-C_1 comes into play is determined by R_2 and C_1, as

$$f_{1_H} = \frac{1}{2\pi R_2 C_1}.$$

On the graph of Fig. 6-36, this is the frequency at which the high-frequency shelving curves have departed from the flat response by 3 dB. The total amount of boost (or cut) is determined by the ratio of input and feedback impedances, as in the standard inverter. In this case it is

$$\text{boost (or cut)} = \frac{R_2 \parallel R_3}{R_1 \parallel R_2}.$$

It will be noted that the final ratio is limited by R_3 if R_3 is not $\gg R_2$, which is the case in this circuit.

With the values shown in Fig. 6-37A, the total boost (or cut) is within a decibel of 20 dB, but is limited by the value of R_3. The value of R_3 can be increased, if desired, but this introduces a drawback in that nearly all the total change in boost (or cut) occurs in the last few degrees of control rotation. This effect is evident to some extent with the 500-kΩ value, but it is deemed desirable because it makes the "flat" setting easily repeatable. The actual value chosen for R_3 is largely a matter of user preference, but in any case it should be a linear control.

If desired, the degree of boost (or cut) can be altered by varying the ratio of R_2 to R_1. In the circuit of Fig. 6-37A, the shunting effect of C_1 introduces a slope in the response curve of ± 6 dB/octave, thus the total dB change determines the f_{1_H}-f_{2_H} frequency difference. With the values shown, $f_{1_H} = 2.0$ kHz, and full boost (or cut) is realized at $f_{2_H} = 20$ kHz.

Low-Frequency Shelving Equalizer. The schematic for a low-frequency shelving equalizer is shown in Fig. 6-37B. It will be noted that the only difference between this circuit and the high-frequency circuit of Fig. 6-37A is the value of C_1 and its connection to R_3. The rotation of R_3 in this circuit has the same effect as previously—a decrease in either the input impedance or the feedback impedance. In this case, however, the frequency range is at the low end. At high frequencies, the rotation of R_3 has no effect, since C_1 causes both ends of R_3 to assume the same potential. The point at which low-frequency equalization begins is given by

$$f_{1_L} = \frac{1}{2\pi R_1 C_1}$$

and is the frequency where the reactance of C_1 becomes equal to R_1. Below this frequency, the slope of the response curve is 6 dB/octave, as in the high-frequency circuit. Also, the total amount of boost (or cut) is determined by the ratio of R_2 to R_1, and it is limited by R_3 if R_3 is not $\gg R_2$, as previously. With the values shown in Fig. 6-37B, f_{1_L} occurs at 200 Hz, and full boost (or cut) is realized at $f_{2_L} = 20$ Hz.

In applying either of the two shelving equalizers of Fig. 6-37, some general considerations are in order. First of all, the 1556 op amp was chosen because of its fast slewing rate (2.5 V/μs), which allows full power output over the entire audio range. Also, the low input current of the 1556 (15 nA maximum) allows high resistances to be used without serious bias current offsets. In general, the op amp used should be compensated for unity gain. Since the greatest percentage of applications for these circuits will be in hi-fi stereo amplifiers, two of each will be required. Thus, dual devices such as the 747 or 1558 can be used and will perform satisfactorily, except that the slewing rate of these devices (0.5 V/μs) will limit high-frequency output to low levels. Both circuits require low source impedances such as another op amp to work properly. Also, they should not be ac coupled, if possible, since this introduces additional variables into the total response.

Resonant Equalizers

Another common equalizer application is the *resonant* equalizer, so named because it resonates at a certain frequency. This effect may be applied either in the form of a response peak or a dip at the frequency of resonance. Conceptually, the circuit of Fig. 6-37A can be converted to a resonant equalizer simply by placing an inductor in series with the capacitor, as shown in Fig. 6-38. No other circuit elements need be changed, and this very simple circuit will peak or dip at the LC resonant frequency. In practice, however, inductors often introduce more problems than they solve. They tend to be bulky, expensive, sensitive to external fields, and, in general, a circuit element to be avoided whenever possible. By using op-amp techniques, however, it is possible to synthesize an inductor response without having to endure its pitfalls.

If the characteristics already described for the high-frequency and low-frequency shelving equalizers are combined in such a manner as to make their response slopes overlap, the composite response will be a resonance, as illustrated in Fig. 6-39. To achieve the resonance effect, f_{1_L} and f_{1_H} are placed symmetrically above and below the

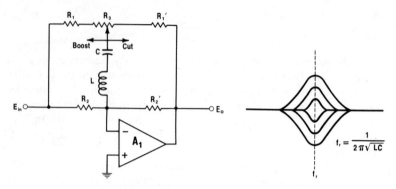

Fig. 6-38. Resonant equalizer using LC network.

The resonant frequency equation in the figure:

$$f_r = \frac{1}{2\pi\sqrt{LC}}$$

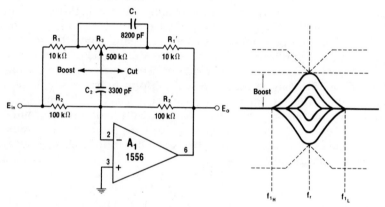

(1) Select resonance boost or cut in dB:

$$\frac{f_r}{f_{1_H}} = \frac{f_{1_L}}{f_r} = \text{"n" octaves}$$

$$\text{total} = (n)\ (6\ dB/octave)$$

(2) Select f_{1_H} and f_{1_L} to be "n" octaves removed from f_r:

$$f_r = 2\,n\,f_{1_H} = \frac{f_{1_L}}{2\,n}$$

(3) Calculate C_1 and C_2 values:

$$C_1 = \frac{1}{4\,n\pi R_1 f_r}$$

$$C_2 = \frac{n}{\pi R_2 f_r}$$

(4) Example for $f_r = 1.0$ kHz, $n = 1$:

$$C_1 = \frac{1}{4\,n\pi R_1 f_r} = \frac{1}{1.26 \times 10^8} = 0.794 \times 10^{-8}$$

$$= 7940\ pF\ (\text{use 8200 pF})$$

$$C_2 = \frac{n}{\pi R_2 f_r} = \frac{1}{3.1416 \times 10^8} = 0.318 \times 10^{-8}$$

$$= 3180\ pF\ (\text{use 3300 pF})$$

Fig. 6-39. Resonant equalizer using RC networks.

desired resonant frequency, f_r. The effect is as if the two individual circuits were placed in series, but it is accomplished within one circuit.

The actual circuit used in Fig. 6-39 is a combination of the two circuits of Fig. 6-37, and R_1, R_2, and R_3 perform similar functions. By varying the percentage of "overlap" of the two circuits, the resonance boost (or cut) can be made a percentage of the total available boost (or cut) implied by R_2/R_1.

In designing this circuit, the starting point is the minimum boost (or cut) required, which determines the frequency difference. If $f_r = f_{1_L} = f_{1_H}$, the boost (or cut) will be 3 dB, and as f_r, f_{1_L}, and f_{1_H} separate, the response curve rises (or falls) at approximately 6 dB/octave of frequency difference. Thus, the separation of f_r, f_{1_L}, and f_{1_H} determines the total boost (or cut). Once the value for "n" octaves of frequency separation is known, values for C_1 and C_2 are calculated using the modified equations given in Fig. 6-39. The total boost (or cut) will be in excess of that predicted by "n" because of the 3-dB effect at $f_r = f_{1_L} = f_{1_H}$. However, this is not normally a drawback, since infinite control is available for boost (or cut) by virtue of the infinite resolution of R_3. The example shown in Fig. 6-39 is for a 1.0-kHz, ±6-dB equalizer.

The circuit of Fig. 6-39 can actually be called a *universal* equalizer, because if C_1 and C_2 are switched in and out in various combinations, any of the three equalizer responses can be achieved by the same circuit. Because of its basic simplicity and ease of adaptation, this configuration can be a very useful circuit building block.

6.3.5 General-Purpose Active Filters

A large number of second-order active filter networks can be synthesized using op amps as active elements and only resistors and capacitors as passive elements. All the standard filter functions—low-pass, high-pass, and bandpass—can be realized with cutoff slopes of 12 dB/octave in a single stage. In this section, we will discuss several of the more commonly used active filter designs.

VCVS Filters

The simplest active filter design is based on the voltage-controlled voltage source (VCVS) configuration, which can be either a unity-gain voltage follower or a voltage follower with gain. The most basic VCVS filters are the low- and high-pass, unity-gain voltage-follower types illustrated in Figs. 6-40A and B. These circuits implicitly have a gain of unity (within the passband), which is independent of resistor values. Thus, they can easily be used for filtering functions without any concern for scaling error due to resistor tolerances. The most useful version of this type of filter occurs when the response is "maximally flat," or when $Q = \sqrt{2}/2$. These conditions are illustrated in the examples chosen.

In the low-pass filter of Fig. 6-40A, when $C_1 = 2C_2$ and $R_1 = R_2$, the high cutoff frequency, f_{c_H}, is

$$f_{c_H} = \frac{1}{2\pi R_1 \sqrt{C_1 C_2}}.$$

In the example shown, $f_{c_H} = 100$ kHz.

The high-pass filter of Fig. 6-40B is similar to the low-pass circuit but with the resistor and capacitor elements interchanged. In this circuit, when $C_1 = C_2$ and $R_1 = R_2/2$, the low cutoff frequency, f_{c_L}, is

$$f_{c_L} = \frac{1}{2\pi C_1 \sqrt{R_1 R_2}}.$$

In the example shown, $f_{c_L} = 10$ Hz.

For accuracy and stability in both circuits, the resistors used should be good quality film types, and the capacitors should be mica

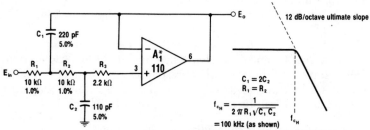

*Selection guidelines for A_1: high input resistance, low input current, high speed. Examples: 110, 1556, 8007.

(A) Low-pass.

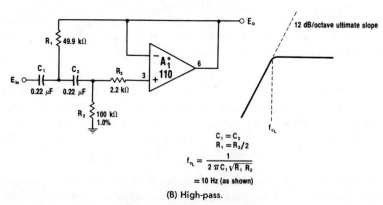

(B) High-pass.

Fig. 6-40. Unity-gain VCVS filters.

or plastic dielectric types. The general requirements for the op amp used are those that are optimum for voltage follower use—low input current, high input resistance, and high speed. The 110 is a good choice here because of its good input parameters and wide bandwidth. When necessary, the tuning of either circuit can be accomplished by simultaneously adjusting the values of the resistors and capacitors. For example, use a rotary switch for selecting different capacitance values in steps, and use a ganged potentiometer for simultaneously varying both resistors.

Another useful version of the VCVS filter occurs when the passband gain of the circuit is scaled upward, with the object being to make the R and C tuning elements equal. For a maximally flat response, this occurs when the gain (set by R_a and R_b) is made equal to $3 - \sqrt{2}$ (nominally 1.586). In order to satisfy this, the R_a to R_b ratio is set at 1 to 0.59. The actual values used for R_a and R_b are then selected so that $R_a \parallel R_b$ is nominally equal to the dc resistance seen at the noninverting input. For both the low-pass and high-pass circuits, shown in Figs. 6-41A and B, respectively, $R_1 = R_2$, $C_1 = C_2$, and the cutoff frequencies are

$$f_{c_L} \text{ (or } f_{c_H}) = \frac{1}{2\pi R_1 C_1}.$$

Tuning is accomplished as in the unity-gain circuits but is simplified because the R and C tuning elements are equal.

Multiple Feedback Filters

Another useful family of active filters is the multiple feedback type. Although not as straightforward or as easily tunable as the VCVS filters, multiple feedback filters are useful in certain situations. Since they operate in the inverting mode, they remove common-mode errors and thus the choice of amplifier type is less critical. The gain of these filters is not as easily controlled as the VCVS type, however, because it depends on component ratios, and sometimes capacitor ratios. This type of circuit is best suited to fixed parameter applications; that is, constant frequency, constant Q, or constant gain. The high-pass and low-pass cutoff slopes are 12 dB/octave.

The low-pass version of the multiple feedback filter is shown in Fig. 6-42. In this circuit, R_1 and R_2 set the passband gain, H_o. The higher cutoff frequency is set by R_2-R_3 and C_1-C_2 as

$$f_{c_H} = \frac{1}{2\pi} \sqrt{\frac{1}{R_2 R_3 C_1 C_2}}.$$

In the design of this filter, some simplifications are helpful. For maximally flat response, the Q will normally be $\sqrt{2}/2$. The ratio of C_1 to C_2 is a constant, K, which, when $K = 4Q^2(H_o + 1)$, yields simple

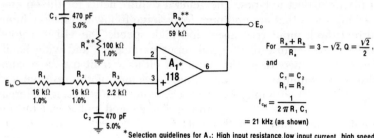

For $\dfrac{R_a + R_b}{R_a} = 3 - \sqrt{2}$, $Q = \dfrac{\sqrt{2}}{2}$,

and

$C_1 = C_2$
$R_1 = R_2$

$f_{c_H} = \dfrac{1}{2\pi R_1 C_1}$

$= 21$ kHz (as shown)

* Selection guidelines for A_1: High input resistance, low input current, high speed.
Examples: 118, 1556, 8007.

** For $Q = \sqrt{2}/2$ (maximally flat), ratio of R_a / R_b is as
shown; but in general, $R_a \parallel R_b$ should be $\cong R_1 + R_2$ (or R_2).

(A) Low-pass.

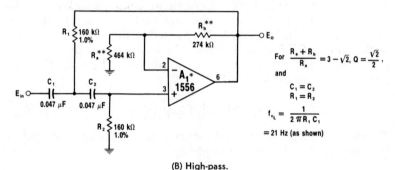

For $\dfrac{R_a + R_b}{R_a} = 3 - \sqrt{2}$, $Q = \dfrac{\sqrt{2}}{2}$,

and

$C_1 = C_2$
$R_1 = R_2$

$f_{c_L} = \dfrac{1}{2\pi R_1 C_1}$

$= 21$ Hz (as shown)

(B) High-pass.

Fig. 6-41. VCVS filters with gain.

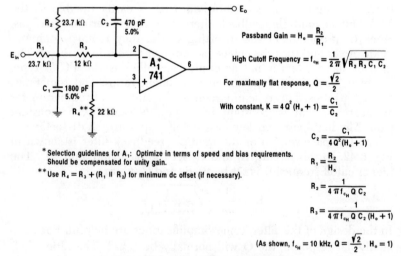

Passband Gain $= H_o = \dfrac{R_2}{R_1}$

High Cutoff Frequency $= f_{c_H} = \dfrac{1}{2\pi} \sqrt{\dfrac{1}{R_2 R_3 C_1 C_2}}$

For maximally flat response, $Q = \dfrac{\sqrt{2}}{2}$

With constant, $K = 4Q^2 (H_o + 1) = \dfrac{C_1}{C_2}$

$C_2 = \dfrac{C_1}{4Q^2 (H_o + 1)}$

$R_1 = \dfrac{R_2}{H_o}$

$R_2 = \dfrac{1}{4\pi f_{c_H} Q C_2}$

$R_3 = \dfrac{1}{4\pi f_{c_H} Q C_2 (H_o + 1)}$

* Selection guidelines for A_1: Optimize in terms of speed and bias requirements.
Should be compensated for unity gain.

** Use $R_4 = R_3 + (R_1 \parallel R_2)$ for minimum dc offset (if necessary).

(As shown, $f_{c_H} = 10$ kHz, $Q = \dfrac{\sqrt{2}}{2}$, $H_o = 1$)

Fig. 6-42. Low-pass, multiple feedback filter.

value expressions. The design process is begun with the selection of C_1 and C_2, then R_1, R_2, and R_3, in that order. R_4 is an optional bias resistor that is used to minimize dc output offset when necessary. Selection of the amplifier type will generally be in terms of the speed or dc error required, and it must be compensated for unity gain. A 741 is usually adequate, but other types may be required for high-gain, high-frequency applications or very low dc errors.

The high-pass version of the multiple feedback filter is shown in Fig. 6-43. In this circuit, C_1 and C_2 set the passband gain, H_o. For

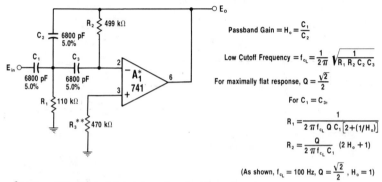

$$\text{Passband Gain} = H_o = \frac{C_1}{C_2}$$

$$\text{Low Cutoff Frequency} = f_{c_L} = \frac{1}{2\pi} \sqrt{\frac{1}{R_1 R_2 C_2 C_3}}$$

For maximally flat response, $Q = \frac{\sqrt{2}}{2}$

For $C_1 = C_3$,

$$R_1 = \frac{1}{2\pi f_{c_L} Q C_1 \left[2 + (1/H_o)\right]}$$

$$R_2 = \frac{Q}{2\pi f_{c_L} C_1} \quad (2 H_o + 1)$$

(As shown, $f_{c_L} = 100$ Hz, $Q = \frac{\sqrt{2}}{2}$, $H_o = 1$)

*Selection guidelines for A_1: Optimize in terms of speed and bias requirements. Should be compensated for unity gain.

**Use $R_3 = R_2$ for minimum dc offset (if necessary).

Fig. 6-43. High-pass, multiple feedback filter.

maximally flat response and for $C_1 = C_3$, the lower cutoff frequency is set by C_2-C_3 and R_1-R_2 as

$$f_{c_L} = \frac{1}{2\pi} \sqrt{\frac{1}{R_1 R_2 C_2 C_3}} \cdot$$

The design is begun with the selection of C_1, C_2, and C_3, then R_1 and R_2. R_3 is an optional bias resistor that is used to minimize dc output offset when necessary. Selection guidelines for the amplifier are generally the same as for the low-pass filter.

A bandpass version of the multiple feedback filter is shown in Fig. 6-44. This circuit is generally useful with Qs up to 10 with moderate gains. The design process is begun by selecting C_1. For simplification, $C_2 = C_1$, so this also sets C_2. The center frequency of the passband is

$$f_{cf} = \frac{1}{2\pi C_1} \sqrt{\frac{R_1 + R_2}{R_1 R_2 R_3}} \cdot$$

R_1, R_2, and R_3 are then selected to satisfy the design requirements.

The selection guidelines for the amplifier are somewhat more restrictive in this circuit because in addition to the general considerations for speed and bias, high Qs, frequencies, and gain will cause a loss of accuracy unless a high gain-bandwidth device is used. For example, if gains of greater than 1 with Qs approaching 10 are desired at frequencies above a few kilohertz, a high f_t device such as the 118 should be chosen.

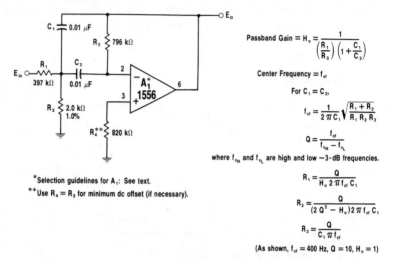

Passband Gain $= H_o = \dfrac{1}{\left(\dfrac{R_1}{R_3}\right)\left(1 + \dfrac{C_1}{C_2}\right)}$

Center Frequency $= f_{cf}$

For $C_1 = C_2$,

$$f_{cf} = \frac{1}{2\pi C_1}\sqrt{\frac{R_1 + R_2}{R_1\,R_2\,R_3}}$$

$$Q = \frac{f_{cf}}{f_{c_H} - f_{c_L}}$$

where f_{c_H} and f_{c_L} are high and low −3-dB frequencies.

$$R_1 = \frac{Q}{H_o\,2\pi f_{cf}\,C_1}$$

$$R_2 = \frac{Q}{(2Q^2 - H_o)2\pi f_{cf}\,C_1}$$

$$R_3 = \frac{Q}{C_1\,\pi f_{cf}}$$

(As shown, $f_{cf} = 400$ Hz, $Q = 10$, $H_o = 1$)

*Selection guidelines for A_1: See text.
**Use $R_4 = R_3$ for minimum dc offset (if necessary).

Fig. 6-44. Bandpass, multiple feedback filter.

State Variable Filter

An excellent combination of filtering capability is provided by the "state variable filter" shown in Fig. 6-45. This filter uses three op amps and simultaneously provides high-pass, low-pass, and band-pass outputs. It is relatively insensitive to Q variations due to change in its elements and is capable of Qs up to 100. Furthermore, center frequency and Q are independently variable. This circuit is useful as a general-purpose building block and is often termed a *universal* active filter.

Simplification is also helpful in reducing this filter to an easily used form. If $R_2 = R_3$, $R_5 = R_7$, and $C_1 = C_2$, it becomes easily tunable and adjustable. The center frequency is then determined as

$$f_{cf} = \frac{1}{2\pi R_5 C_1}.$$

The Q is set by R_1 and R_4 as

$$Q = \frac{R_1 + R_4}{2R_1}.$$

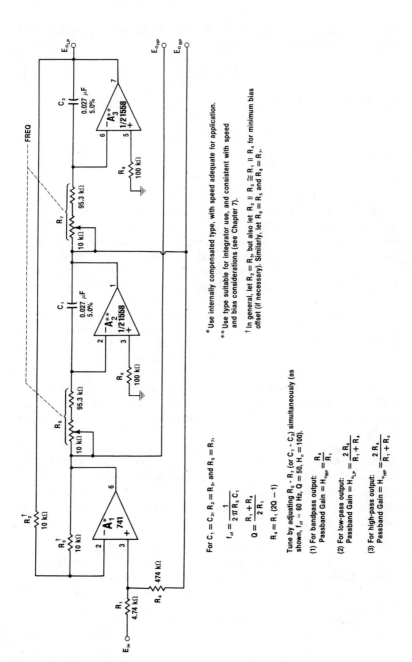

For $C_1 = C_2$, $R_2 = R_3$, and $R_5 = R_7$:

$$f_{cf} = \frac{1}{2\pi R_5 C_1}$$

$$Q = \frac{R_1 + R_4}{2 R_1}$$

$$R_4 = R_1 (2Q - 1)$$

Tune by adjusting $R_5 - R_7$ (or $C_1 - C_2$) simultaneously (as shown, $f_{cf} = 60$ Hz, $Q = 50$, $H_o = 100$).

(1) For bandpass output:
Passband Gain = $H_{oBP} = \dfrac{R_4}{R_1}$

(2) For low-pass output:
Passband Gain = $H_{oLP} = \dfrac{2 R_4}{R_1 + R_4}$

(3) For high-pass output:
Passband Gain = $H_{oHP} = \dfrac{2 R_4}{R_1 + R_4}$

*Use internally compensated type, with speed adequate for application.

**Use type suitable for integrator use, and consistent with speed and bias considerations (see Chapter 7).

†In general, let $R_2 = R_3$, but also let $R_2 \| R_3 \cong R_1 \| R_4$ for minimum bias offset (if necessary). Similarly, let $R_6 = R_5$ and $R_8 = R_7$.

Fig. 6-45. State variable filter.

337

The passband gain equations for the three outputs differ only slightly. For the bandpass output,

$$H_{O_{BP}} = \frac{R_4}{R_1} .$$

For the low-pass output,

$$H_{O_{LP}} = \frac{2R_4}{R_1 + R_4} .$$

For the high-pass output,

$$H_{O_{HP}} = \frac{2R_4}{R_1 + R_4} .$$

This circuit offers a second-order response for the low-pass and high-pass outputs, but it should be noted that maximally flat response cannot be realized with a high Q, such as will often be desired from the bandpass output. If desired, a fourth output in the form of a notch at the center frequency may be obtained by summing to the low-pass and high-pass outputs through equal value resistors.

All three op-amps used in this circuit must be unity-gain stable, but only A_1 must respond to differential signals. By controlling the R_2-R_3 and R_1-R_4 absolute values, the dc errors of the circuit can be kept low. A_2 and A_3 are integrators and ideally have very low bias currents. The use of low-input-current devices, such as FET or super-β types, will permit high resistance values for R_5 and R_7 and will minimize capacitance values in achieving very low frequencies. Tuning is accomplished by the simultaneous variation of C_1-C_2 or R_5-R_7.

In the circuit shown in Fig. 6-45, operation is tailored for the bandpass response, yielding a Q of 50 at a frequency of 60 Hz and with a gain of 100. R_5 and R_7 are made variable by a small percentage to allow for the initial tolerance of C_1 and C_2. This allows tuning the filter exactly to the prescribed frequency, which is a virtual necessity with a high-Q circuit.

Twin-T Notch Filter

A well-known frequency rejection filter is the twin-T configuration of Fig. 6-46. Theoretically this circuit is capable of infinite rejection at its frequency, f_o, if the components are well matched and if the source impedance is low and the load impedance is high. Buffering the output with a voltage follower will satisfy the requirement for high load impedance, and driving the input from an op-amp output will normally satisfy the requirement for low source impedance.

In terms of Q or notch width, the response of the basic twin-T network can be enhanced appreciably by bootstrapping the normally

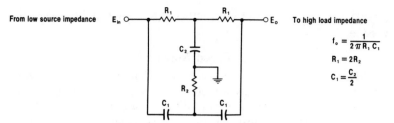

Fig. 6-46. Basic twin-T filter configuration.

$$f_o = \frac{1}{2\pi R_1 C_1}$$
$$R_1 = 2R_2$$
$$C_1 = \frac{C_2}{2}$$

grounded node of R_2-C_2 from the follower output, as shown in Fig. 6-47. This allows extremely narrow bandwidth notches to be realized even at low frequencies, with Q values of up to 50. Such a characteristic is very useful in removing 60-Hz hum components, for example, with a minimum of degradation to the bordering frequency response. If a variable-Q characteristic is desired, the loop can be broken at "X" and the A_2 circuit inserted, as shown in Fig. 6-47. The Q control (R_3) serves to continuously vary the effective performance between the normal and the bootstrapped condition. In either case, the R_2-C_2 node of the twin-T network should see a low source impedance in order to minimize null depth or frequency variations.

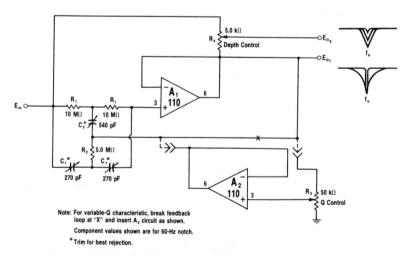

Note: For variable-Q characteristic, break feedback loop at "X" and insert A_2 circuit as shown.

Component values shown are for 60-Hz notch.

*Trim for best rejection.

Fig. 6-47. High-Q, twin-T filter with buffered output and variable-Q option.

The depth of the notch provided by the twin-T network can be effectively varied by connecting a potentiometer (R_4) from the input to the output and taking the output from the arm of the control as shown. This provides continuously variable control of notch depth, and it can be used with either the normal or the variable-Q version.

Easily Tuned Notch Filter

Although the twin-T filter provides excellent rejection at a specific frequency, it is not readily adapted to the requirements of tuning. The circuit of Fig. 6-48, however, allows tuning by varying either a single capacitor or a resistor. The circuit is actually a bridge consisting of R_4-R_5, and R_3 plus the C_1-R_1-R_2 network. A_2, C_2, and R_1-R_2

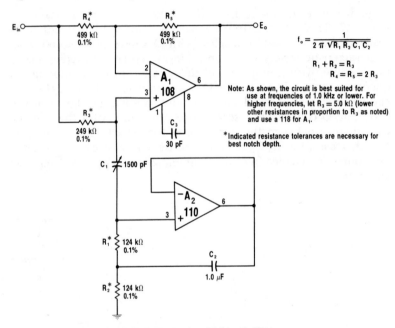

$$f_o = \frac{1}{2\pi \sqrt{R_1 R_2 C_1 C_2}}$$

$$R_1 + R_2 = R_3$$
$$R_4 = R_5 = 2 R_3$$

Note: As shown, the circuit is best suited for use at frequencies of 1.0 kHz or lower. For higher frequencies, let $R_3 = 5.0$ kΩ (lower other resistances in proportion to R_3 as noted) and use a 118 for A_1.

*Indicated resistance tolerances are necessary for best notch depth.

Fig. 6-48. Easily tuned notch filter.

form an equivalent circuit inductance, which at some frequency resonates with C_1, forming a notch in the response. The notch frequency, f_o, is

$$f_o = \frac{1}{2\pi \sqrt{R_1 R_2 C_1 C_2}}.$$

Thus, either R_1, R_2, C_1, or C_2 can be used to tune the circuit. It is convenient to make C_2 a large fixed value and use C_1 as a trimmer, as shown in the schematic. An alternate method is to use a potentiometer for R_1-R_2 equal in value to R_3 and trim the circuit in this manner. The close tolerances indicated for the resistances are necessary for best notch depth. These resistances can be realized either by using high-quality precision resistors or by trimming.

When the 108 is used for A_1, the circuit of Fig. 6-48 is best suited for high-performance applications at frequencies of 1.0 kHz or lower. For higher-frequency use, the 118 can be substituted for A_1, with a general lowering of resistance values as indicated. Both of these amplifiers have good common-mode rejection. For less critical applications, a dual 741 device, such as the 747 or 1558, can be used for both A_1 and A_2. In such cases, it is best to keep R_3 in the range of 100 kΩ or less.

6.3.6 Miscellaneous Audio Circuits

This final section of the audio chapter concerns miscellaneous circuits that do not fit into any of the other distinct categories.

Summing Amplifier

A standard audio-signal processing function is the linear combination of a number of individual signals into a common output with-

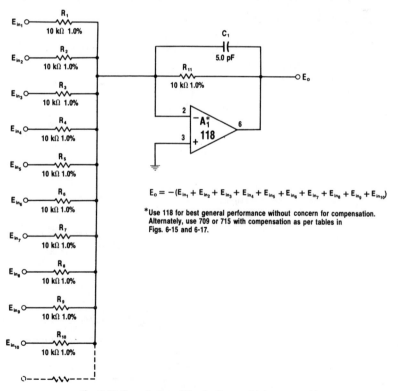

$$E_o = -(E_{in_1} + E_{in_2} + E_{in_3} + E_{in_4} + E_{in_5} + E_{in_6} + E_{in_7} + E_{in_8} + E_{in_9} + E_{in_{10}})$$

*Use 118 for best general performance without concern for compensation. Alternately, use 709 or 715 with compensation as per tables in Figs. 6-15 and 6-17.

Fig. 6-49. Summing amplifier (active combining network).

out cross talk or loss. This function is well suited for the summing amplifier (inverter), which is often referred to as an *active combining network*. A 10-input summing inverter configured for unity signal gain in each channel is shown in Fig. 6-49. This circuit uses 10-kΩ input resistances and a 10-kΩ feedback resistance. A 118 op amp is used because of its high gain-bandwidth product and fast slewing rate.

Channel isolation is an important performance parameter in a summing amplifier because it is undesirable for any signals to be coupled between adjacent channels. In general, for maximum isolation, the input resistances (R_i) should be high and the source impedances (R_s) low. Also, the feedback resistance (R_f) should be high, with high loop gain ($A_{vo}\beta$). In practice, summing amplifiers are often made unity gain where each individual input resistance equals the feedback resistance, so channel isolation must be optimized by controlling the source impedances or the loop gain.

The primary determinant of interchannel isolation is the nonzero summing-bus impedance presented by the virtual ground of the in-

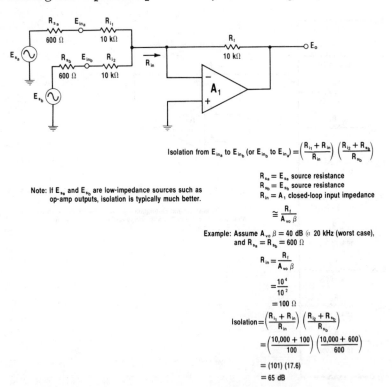

Isolation from E_{in_a} to E_{in_b} (or E_{in_b} to E_{in_a}) $= \left(\dfrac{R_{i_1} + R_{in}}{R_{in}}\right)\left(\dfrac{R_{i_2} + R_{s_b}}{R_{s_b}}\right)$

Note: If E_{s_a} and E_{s_b} are low-impedance sources such as op-amp outputs, isolation is typically much better.

$R_{s_a} = E_{s_a}$ source resistance
$R_{s_b} = E_{s_b}$ source resistance
$R_{in} = A_1$ closed-loop input impedance

$\cong \dfrac{R_f}{A_{vo}\beta}$

Example: Assume $A_{vo}\beta = 40$ dB (@ 20 kHz (worst case), and $R_{s_a} = R_{s_b} = 600$ Ω

$$R_{in} = \dfrac{R_f}{A_{vo}\beta}$$

$$= \dfrac{10^4}{10^2}$$

$$= 100 \text{ Ω}$$

Isolation $= \left(\dfrac{R_{i_1} + R_{in}}{R_{in}}\right)\left(\dfrac{R_{i_2} + R_{s_b}}{R_{s_b}}\right)$

$$= \left(\dfrac{10{,}000 + 100}{100}\right)\left(\dfrac{10{,}000 + 600}{600}\right)$$

$$= (101)(17.6)$$

$$= 65 \text{ dB}$$

Fig. 6-50. Method of calculating interchannel isolation for summing amplifier.

verter and, to a lesser extent, by the source impedances at the inputs. Fig. 6-50 illustrates the method of calculating interchannel isolation. There are two attenuations that a signal must undergo in order to leak from one channel to an adjacent channel. The first attenuation consists of R_i and R_{in}; the second consists of R_i and R_s. A typical example is calculated in Fig. 6-50.

The loop gain of the amplifier used will limit the attenuation due to a rise in R_{in} at the higher audio frequencies where the loop gain is lower. For a noise gain of 20 dB, such as in the 10-input summing amplifier of Fig. 6-49, a GBP of 20 MHz is required for 40 dB of loop gain at 20 kHz. In the example calculation in Fig. 6-50, the resulting cross talk is −65 dB at 20 kHz, which is quite reasonable.

It can be seen from this example calculation that if R_s is low, cross talk decreases. Therefore, by operating from low-impedance sources such as op-amp outputs, R_s is controlled and cross talk is reduced. In any case, the figures quoted are worst case, and cross talk decreases in proportion to the increase in loop gain at the lower frequencies. For this reason, a high GBP amplifier such as the 118 is recommended for summing-amplifier use. However, if a fixed number of inputs are used, a custom-compensated type such as the 709 or 715 can also be used, with compensation adjusted for the noise gain of the summing network (see the tables in Figs. 6-15 and 6-17).

The natural sign inversion of the summing amplifier may be a disadvantage for some applications. If so, this can be cancelled by an additional unity-gain inverter or by a transformer connected for phase inversion. Additional inputs are possible, of course, with no theoretical limit. Practical limits arise because of loop-gain limitations at high frequencies. In situations involving 20 or more inputs, a custom-compensated amplifier should be considered.

Stereo Pan-Pot Circuit

A common requirement in the audio recording process is a "pan pot," a control that can electrically position a single source of sound across the panorama from the left to the right stereo channels. The requirement for a panning circuit is that when positioned full left or full right, the gain from the input to the output is unity, and when positioned centrally (control midpoint), the gain from the input to each output is −3 dB.

A stereo pan-pot circuit is shown in Fig. 6-51. In this circuit, R_1 is a dual control with a linear taper, wired in reverse so that when R_{1_A} is at maximum, R_{1_B} is at minimum, and vice-versa. This allows the signal to be panned full right or full left. At the midpoint of R_1, the signal fed into each amplifier input resistor (R_4 and R_6) is 0.707 (−3 dB) of E_{in}, due to bridging resistors R_2 and R_3. A_1 and A_2 are unity-gain inverters, which can also be summing amplifiers when additional panning circuits are wired into their summing points. The selection guidelines for A_1 and A_2 are the same as for the summing amplifier of Fig. 6-49.

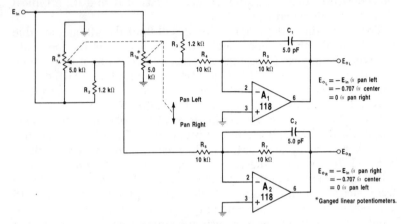

Fig. 6-51. Stereo pan-pot circuit.

Impedance Matching Techniques

In Section 6.3.2 on increased power output circuits using op amps, little attention was paid to matching the op-amp output impedance to the load. Usually, the extremely low characteristic output impedance of an op amp with heavy feedback is not a detriment, but rather is a great asset because it makes the output voltage quite independent of loading. There are, however, situations that require matched or controlled source impedances. The best examples of these are circuits that feed telephone distribution lines, and circuits that work into passive filters or equalizers designed for specific source impedances. In these situations, it is mandatory to provide a matched source impedance, typically 500 or 600 ohms.

The simplest method of impedance matching is the "brute-force" technique of a "build out" series resistance equal to the load impedance, as illustrated in Fig. 6-52A. In this circuit, A_1 and its associated components can be any op-amp feedback circuit; the only assumption made is that the output impedance of the op amp is much less than R_s and R_L, which, for typical load values, is reasonable. R_s is simply a dummy resistance that is equal in value to the load impedance, R_L. For complete isolation, an output transformer is used together with a coupling capacitor, C_o, to eliminate dc from the transformer primary.

The obvious disadvantage of this technique is that power is wasted in R_s, since R_s drops half the output voltage from A_1. This

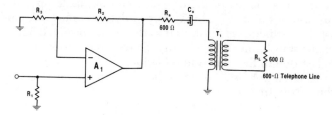

(A) Series resistance.

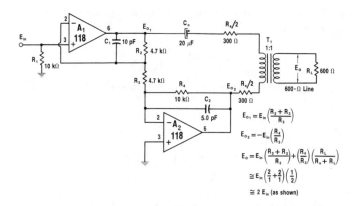

$$E_{o_1} = E_{in}\left(\frac{R_2 + R_3}{R_3}\right)$$

$$E_{o_2} = -E_{in}\left(\frac{R_4}{R_3}\right)$$

$$E_o = E_{in}\left(\frac{R_2 + R_3}{R_3}\right) + \left(\frac{R_4}{R_3}\right)\left(\frac{R_L}{R_s + R_L}\right)$$

$$\cong E_{in}\left(\frac{2}{1} + \frac{2}{1}\right)\left(\frac{1}{2}\right)$$

$$\cong 2 E_{in} \text{ (as shown)}$$

(B) Series resistance with differential drive.

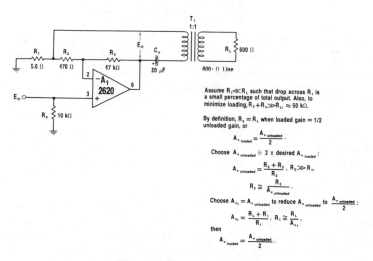

Assume $R_1 \ll R_L$ such that drop across R_1 is a small percentage of total output. Also, to minimize loading, $R_2 + R_3 \gg R_L$, ≈ 50 kΩ.

By definition, $R_s = R_L$ when loaded gain = 1/2 unloaded gain, or

$$A_{v\,loaded} = \frac{A_{v\,unloaded}}{2}.$$

Choose $A_{v\,unloaded}$ @ 2 x desired $A_{v\,loaded}$:

$$A_{v\,unloaded} = \frac{R_2 + R_3}{R_2}, R_3 \gg R_1,$$

$$R_2 \cong \frac{R_3}{A_{v\,unloaded}}.$$

Choose $A_{v_1} = A_{v\,unloaded}$ to reduce $A_{v\,unloaded}$ to $\frac{A_{v\,unloaded}}{2}$:

$$A_{v_1} = \frac{R_L + R_1}{R_1}, R_1 \cong \frac{R_L}{A_{v_1}},$$

then

$$A_{v\,loaded} = \frac{A_{v\,unloaded}}{2}.$$

(C) Impedance transformation.

Fig. 6-52. Impedance matching techniques.

is not serious in terms of gain (which can be made up), but it is serious in terms of overload margin and dynamic range. A modification of this technique is illustrated in the circuit of Fig. 6-52B, which drives the transformer differentially, thereby recovering the dynamic range lost due to the source termination.

In this circuit, A_1 is a voltage follower with a gain of $(R_2 + R_3)/R_2$; thus, its output, E_{o_1}, is

$$E_{o_1} = E_{in}\left(\frac{R_2 + R_3}{R_3}\right).$$

A_2 is an inverter that inverts the output of A_1, developing an output, E_{o_2}, which is

$$E_{o_2} = -E_{in}\left(\frac{R_4}{R_3}\right).$$

The signal applied to R_s, then, is the difference between E_{o_1} and E_{o_2}, or

$$E_{o_d} = E_{o_1} - E_{o_2}$$
$$= E_{in}\left(\frac{R_2 + R_3}{R_3}\right) + \left(\frac{R_4}{R_3}\right).$$

The output voltage, E_o, is the voltage seen after the termination, or across R_L (assuming T_1 is a 1:1 transfer):

$$E_o = E_{in}\left(\frac{R_2 + R_3}{R_3}\right) + \left(\frac{R_4}{R_3}\right)\left(\frac{R_L}{R_s + R_L}\right).$$

Both stages in the circuit of Fig. 6-52B are operated with similar noise gains, but this is not essential. The gain of A_1 can be used to vary the composite circuit gain without altering the balance between the two outputs if $R_2 + R_3$ is maintained equal to R_4. The absolute power-output capability of this circuit is limited by the 118s, but it can easily develop outputs of +15 dBm or more with negligible distortion (which is more than can be applied to a telephone line). In practice, the theoretical value of $R_s = R_L$ may require some slight downward adjustment if T_1 does not have negligibly small series resistance.

The preceding two methods of impedance matching are actually the same basic technique—the insertion of a fixed resistance in series with a low-impedance source to define the source impedance. A third method, shown in Fig. 6-52C, accomplishes impedance matching with considerably more finesse, using a combination of current and voltage feedback to improve efficiency. This circuit uses current feedback developed across a small resistance (R_1), which is in series with the load. This current feedback is combined with voltage feedback from R_2-R_3 in such a manner as to cause the circuit to act as an impedance equal to R_L, thus satisfying the matching requirement. Since the resistance (R_1) in series with the load can be low in value and "transformed" upward by feedback, this technique is most efficient, capable of delivering nearly the full output swing of the amplifier to the load.

The operation of this circuit is based on the fact that in any amplifier, when $R_s = R_L$, the loaded voltage gain is one-half that of the unloaded voltage gain. In Fig. 6-52C, the voltage feedback from R_2-R_3 defines the unloaded voltage gain; then an equal gain ratio, provided by $(R_1 + R_L)/R_1$, is made to reduce this gain by a factor of two, thus satisfying the requirement of matched impedance. The circuit is most efficient at higher gains where $R_1 \ll R_L$. Also, $R_2 + R_3$ should be $\gg R_L$ for minimum power loss. The relationships given are approximate and if exact figures for gain and source impedance are required, some trimming of R_1 may be necessary. The values shown yield a closed-loop gain of 34 dB matched to the 600-Ω line. Power output, of course, depends on the amplifier, and losses due to R_1 will be almost negligible at closed-loop gains of 20 dB or greater. Although any op amp can be used in this circuit, the 2620 offers the best choice of bandwidth with no external compensation required. If power output appreciably higher than +15 dBm is required, a booster should be used (see Section 6.3.2).

Transformerless, Balanced Transmission System

Standard audio interconnection techniques employ transformer coupling at both input and output, and balanced transmission lines for common-mode noise immunity. This system works very well, but for high-quality use, the transformer cost is appreciable. Fig. 6-53 illustrates a system that performs electronically the functions of output and input transformers, and also retains the noise-rejection property of balanced signal-line transmission.

The circuit of Fig. 6-53A forms the transmission end of the system and employs two 1556s as a follower and inverter, respectively. A_1 repeats the input signal, E_{in}, in low-impedance form at E_{o_1}, driving one side of the balanced line. Simultaneously, A_2 inverts E_{o_1}, creating E_{o_2}, which is a mirror image of E_{in}. E_{o_2} is applied to the opposite side of the balanced line. The total voltage across the line is then the difference of E_{o_1} and E_{o_2}, or $E_{o_1} - E_{o_2}$, which equals $2E_{in}$.

The 1556 was chosen for this application because of its low input current and fast slewing rate, plus the fact that it is internally compensated and thus easily applied. R_1 and R_2 are necessary to stabilize A_1 and A_2 in the presence of long, high-capacitance lines. This stage can apply up to ±20 V across the twisted pair with negligible distortion.

At the opposite end of the transmission line, the signal is received by the circuit of Fig. 6-53B. This circuit is a differential amplifier optimized for audio-frequency use. It converts the balanced line signal back to single-ended form, restored to its original level.

As discussed in Section 5.14 of Chapter 5 on instrumentation amplifiers, one of the drawbacks of the basic differential amplifier is the low input impedance, which causes common-mode errors when source impedances are unequal. In this case, however, the source impedance is quite low (and balanced), being essentially the dc resistance of the transmission line. Therefore, additional buffering is not required.

A 118 op amp was chosen for this application because of its excellent common-mode rejection at the higher audio frequencies, its high GBP, and its internal compensation. In order to realize high CMRR at the higher frequencies, the bridge resistances must be kept low enough to negate the effects of capacitive imbalance at the input terminals of A_1. Good circuit layout will also be helpful in minimizing this problem.

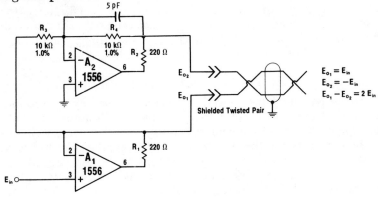

(A) Differential line driver.

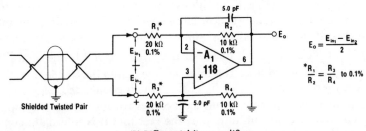

(B) Differential line amplifier.

Fig. 6-53. Transformerless, balanced transmission system.

As in any differential-amplifier configuration, an imbalance in the bridge components will ruin the CMRR, and the situation is even worse in low-gain configurations. In the circuit of Fig. 6-53B, if any one of the resistors is off by 0.1%, the CMRR will be 60 dB. With well-matched components, this circuit will have a CMRR of 80 dB or better over the entire audio range.

With regard to performance, this system can meet or exceed the performance of any system using the best available transformers. Frequency response is far in excess of transformer capability, as is linearity. Noise rejection should be as good as or better than a transformer system since the lines are held at a very low impedance by the line-driver circuit (Fig. 6-53A), which minimizes electrostatic coupling. Finally, the cost of the components for this system is below that of a high-quality transformer.

Precision VU Meter Amplifier

The almost universal method of monitoring audio signal levels is by means of a VU meter, a specialized voltmeter calibrated to read power in a 600-Ω circuit. Standard VU meters will read 0 VU when connected across a 600-Ω line at a level of 1.0 mW (0 dBm), which is an industry standard reference level. A VU meter is a specially designed meter with defined ballistic characteristics that are valid only when the meter is connected through its specified source impedance of 3600 Ω. It has an internal rectifier and, with the external resistor, is used as a passive device to monitor the level of 600-Ω lines. The total impedance of such a metering circuit is 7500 Ω which, although generally termed a bridging circuit, does introduce a small loss of a fraction of a decibel, in addition to a slight distortion of the signal, in a 600-Ω circuit.

The bridging error and distortion due to the meter impedance in shunt with the signal line can be virtually eliminated by the voltage-follower buffer circuit shown in Fig. 6-54. This circuit uses a 1556 op amp because of its low bias current, which allows it to work from megohm source resistances with low output offset. A 1.0-MΩ bias resistor (R_1) is used, which essentially constitutes the input impedance of the circuit. The only real need for R_1 is to prevent off-scale meter deflection in the absence of an input connection, such as is encountered in portable use. If the circuit is used as an integral part of a piece of equipment, R_1 can be eliminated.

Since the VU meter is actually a voltmeter calibrated to read power in a 600-Ω circuit, its use at other line impedances will necessitate recalibration. This is a relatively simple matter because most standard impedances are lower than 600 Ω. It involves rescaling the voltage for 1.0 mW at the lower impedance up to the 600-Ω voltage for 1.0 mW. In practice, this is done by adding a feedback network to provide the A_1 stage with a gain higher than unity, and does not compromise the input impedance to any significant extent. As noted in Fig. 6-54, the difference in voltage levels between the impedances is equal to the square root of the impedance ratio, and this defines the gain of the stage. Since this circuit is a measuring device, the scaling factor provided by R_3 and R_4 should be accurate; therefore, precision components should be used.

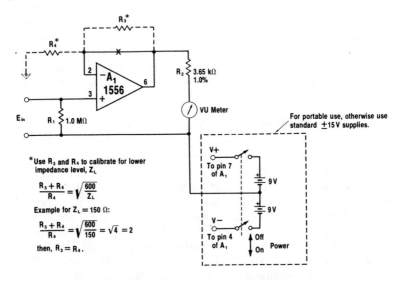

Fig. 6-54. Precision VU-meter amplifier.

The 1556 has a quiescent power-supply current of only a milliampere and works well at lower supply voltages; thus, operation from a pair of 9-V batteries is quite feasible. With this circuit, the accuracy of the indicated audio signal levels will be entirely a function of the quality of the VU meter used.

Phase Manipulation Circuits

Using op-amp circuit techniques, it is possible to alter the phase/frequency and amplitude characteristics of audio signals in a very precise and predictable manner. Phase-shifted and controlled stages are very useful tools when used in combination with other op-amp circuits.

Constant-Amplitude, Phase Lead/Lag Circuits. Two circuits that exemplify the simplicity of op-amp techniques in phase manipulation are shown in Fig. 6-55. These circuits are identical except for the positions of R_3 and C_1, which determine the lag or lead characteristics. The circuit of Fig. 6-55A operates as follows: R_3 and C_1

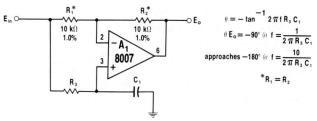

(A) Constant-amplitude lag circuit.

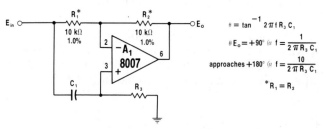

(B) Constant-amplitude lead circuit.

Fig. 6-55. Constant-amplitude, phase lead/lag circuits.

form a simple lag circuit with the output across C_1 applied to the reference input of A_1. The voltage across C_1 will lag E_{in} by 45° when $X_{C_1} = R_3$, or

$$f = \frac{1}{2\pi R_3 C_1} .$$

Because of zero differential-input voltage, the voltage across C_1 must also appear at the summing point through feedback. If $R_1 = R_2$, the phase angle of the output signal will be −90°, or twice the phase angle of the signal at the summing point, with an amplitude equal to E_{in}.

This circuit can be said to have a phase "gain" of $(R_1 + R_2)/R_1$, and it will increase the phase of the signal at the reference input. R_1 and R_2 may be used to adjust the phase of E_o if desired, but the output voltage will remain constant as the input frequency is varied only when $R_1 = R_2$.

The circuit of Fig. 6-55B is a mirror image of the circuit of Fig. 6-55A, achieved by interchanging C_1 and R_3. This circuit has the same gain properties as the circuit of Fig. 6-55A, but in this case the phase shift is a lead.

Perhaps the most useful function for these circuits is the generation of 90° leading or lagging signals for phase detectors and similar circuits. The networks are easily adjustable by varying either R_3 or C_1, and the constant-amplitude output can be a great convenience.

At a given output phase-angle setting, a continuously variable phase adjustment from zero to the output phase angle can be realized by simply connecting a potentiometer from the input to the output of either circuit. Virtually any op amp compensated for unity gain will work in this circuit, but a low-input-current, high-input-resistance type such as the 8007 will allow the widest range of R_3-C_1 values. The R_1-R_2 values are not critical but should be matched, so 10-kΩ, 1.0% values are suggested.

Linear-Feedback, Gain-Controlled Stages

A very useful feature of the op-amp feedback configuration is the fact that the feedback current is independent of the resistance through which it flows. This factor can be used to advantage to build precision gain-controlled stages, with the gain adjusted by means of a single resistance, as illustrated in Fig. 6-56.

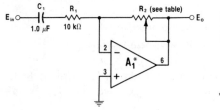

$E_o = -E_{in}\left(\dfrac{R_2}{R_1}\right)$

$R_{in} = R_1$

$f_{cL} = \dfrac{1}{2\pi R_1 C_1}$

Gain is linearly and continuously variable from 0, when $R_2 = 0$, to R_2/R_1, when $R_2 =$ maximum.

*A_1 must be compensated for unity gain; therefore, it should be a high f_t type if $R_{2(max)} / R_1 > 1$.

$R_{2(max)} / R_1$	R_2 (linear)	A_1 (suggested)
1	10 kΩ	118, 8007, 1556
10	100 kΩ	118

(A) Inverting amplifier.

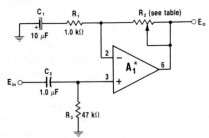

$E_o = E_{in}\left(\dfrac{R_1 + R_2}{R_1}\right)$

$R_{in} = R_3$

$f_{cL} = \dfrac{1}{2\pi R_1 C_1}$

Gain is linearly and continuously variable from 1, when $R_2 = 0$, to $(R_1 + R_2)/R_1$, when $R_2 =$ maximum.

*A_1 must be compensated for unity gain; therefore, it should be a high f_t type if $R_{2(max)}/R_1 > 1$.

$R_{2(max)} / R_1$	R_2 (linear)	A_1 (suggested)
2	1.0 kΩ	118, 8007, 1556
11	10 kΩ	118

(B) Noninverting amplifier.

Fig. 6-56. Linear-feedback, gain-controlled stages.

Fig. 6-56A is an inverting configuration in which feedback resistor R_2 is used to vary the gain. With R_1 and C_1 fixed in this circuit, the input current to the summing point will remain constant, as will the low-frequency, -3-dB rolloff point. R_2 permits adjustment of the inverting gain from zero when $R_2 = 0$, up to a maximum gain of R_2/R_1 when R_2 is at maximum resistance. Tabular values are given for maximum gains of 1 and 10.

The amplifier must be compensated for the lowest gain condition where $R_2 = 0$ and feedback is 100%; therefore, unity-gain compensation is necessary. If maximum gains much higher than unity are required, A_1 should be a wide-bandwidth, fast-slewing type, such as a 118, or a 2620 or 715 compensated for unity gain. This circuit can serve as a precision attenuator if R_2 is made a calibrated control, with the gain varying linearly with the total resistance of R_2.

A similar gain-controlled stage is possible with the noninverting configuration, as shown in Fig. 6-56B. Feedback resistor R_2 is also used in this circuit to vary the gain. A basic difference in this circuit is its minimum gain, which is unity when $R_2 = 0$. The circuit must also be compensated for unity gain due to 100% feedback when $R_2 = 0$. For this reason, a wide-bandwidth, fast-slewing device is preferred for A_1, as in the inverting circuit. Also as in the inverting circuit, gain adjustment does not affect the frequency response or the input impedance. The gain of this circuit will vary linearly with R_2 from a minimum of unity when $R_2 = 0$, up to a maximum gain of $(R_1 + R_2)/R_1$ when R_2 is at maximum resistance.

In both of these circuits, remote adjustment of gain is possible if feedback resistor R_2 is electronically adjustable. For example, if R_2 is a light-dependent resistor or other voltage- or current-dependent resistance, such possible uses as agc amplifiers, compression amplifiers, etc., are suggested.

REFERENCES

1. Al-Nasser, F. "Tables Speed Design of Low-Pass Active Filters." *EDN*, March 15, 1971.

2. *Application Note—Audio Operational Amplifier Model 2520*. Automated Processes, Inc., 1971.

3. *Applications Manual for Computing Amplifiers*. Philbrick Researches, Inc., Dedham, Mass., 1966.

4. Barna, A. *Operational Amplifiers*. John Wiley & Sons, Inc., New York, 1971.

5. Brokaw, A. P. "Simplify, 3-Pole Active Filter Design." *EDN*, December 15, 1970.

6. Clayton, G. B. *Operational Amplifiers*. Butterworth, Inc., Toronto, Ont., Canada, 1971.

7. Dobkin, R. C. *Feedforward Compensation Speeds Op Amp*. National Semiconductor LB-2, April 1969. National Semiconductor Corp., Santa Clara, Calif.

8. _____. *High Q Notch Filter*. National Semiconductor LB-5, April 1967. National Semiconductor Corp., Santa Clara, Calif.

9. _____. *LM118 Op Amp Slews 70 V/µs*. National Semiconductor LB-17, September 1971. National Semiconductor Corp., Santa Clara, Calif.

10. _____. *Op Amp Circuit Collection*. National Semiconductor Application Note AN-31, February 1970. National Semiconductor Corp., Santa Clara, Calif.

11. Doyle, N. P. *A Low-Noise Tape Preamplifier*. Fairchild Semiconductor Application Bulletin APP-180, September 1969. Fairchild Semiconductor, Mountain View, Calif.

12. _____. "Swift, Sure Design of Active Bandpass Filters." *EDN*, January 15, 1970.

13. Giles, J. N. *Fairchild Semiconductor LIC Handbook*. Fairchild Semiconductor, Mountain View, Calif., 1967.

14. Gittleman, R. "Applications of the Audio Operational Amplifier to Studio Use." *Journal of the AES*, Vol. 17, No. 3, June 1969.

15. Jung, W. G. "New IC Approach to Audio Power." *Broadcast Engineering*, October 1972.

16. _____. "Optimizing IC Op Amp Speed." *db, The Sound Engineering Magazine*, January 1973.

17. _____. "The Pitfalls of the General Purpose IC Operational Amplifier as Applied to Audio Signal Processing." *Journal of the AES*, Vol. 21, No. 9, November 1973.

18. Kesner, D. *A Simple Technique for Extending Op Amp Power Bandwidth*. Motorola Application Note AN-459, May 1971. Motorola Semiconductor Products, Inc., Phoenix, Ariz.

19. Kincaid, R. "RC Filter Design by the Numbers." *The Electronic Engineer*, October 1968.

20. Losmandy, B. J. "Operational Amplifier Applications for Audio Systems." *Journal of the AES*, Vol. 17, No. 1, January 1969.

21. Mitra, S. K. *Active Inductorless Filters*. IEEE Press, New York, 1971.

22. Ruchs, R. G. *High Power Audio Amplifiers With Short Circuit Protection*. Motorola Application Note AN-485, May 1970. Motorola Semiconductor Products, Inc., Phoenix, Ariz.

23. Sallen, R. P.; Key, E. L. "Practical Method of Designing RC Active Filters." *IRE Transactions*, Vol. CT-2, 1955.

24. Smith, J. I. *Modern Operational Circuit Design.* John Wiley & Sons, Inc., New York, 1971.

25. Tobey, G. E.; Graeme, J. G.; Huelsman, L. P. *Operational Amplifiers—Design and Applications.* Burr-Brown Research Corp., McGraw-Hill Book Co., New York, 1971.

26. Tremaine, H. M. *The Audio Cyclopedia,* 2nd ed., Howard W. Sams & Co., Inc., Indianapolis, 1969.

27. Van Aken, R. "Applying the 540 Power Driver." *Proceedings of Electronic Products Magazine LIC Seminar,* June 1972.

28. Vander Kooi, M. K. *Predicting Op Amp Slew Rate Limited Response.* National Semiconductor LB-19, August 1972. National Semiconductor Corp., Santa Clara, Calif.

29. Widlar, R. J. *Monolithic Operational Amplifiers—The Universal Linear Component.* National Semiconductor Application Note AN-4, April 1968. National Semiconductor Corp., Santa Clara, Calif.

7

Signal-Generation Circuits

This chapter deals with the generation, shaping, and control of various kinds of signal waveforms. It discusses the standard functions of integration, differentiation, amplitude control, and their application in various circuits. Also discussed are signal-generation circuits such as sine-wave oscillators; multivibrators; triangle, ramp, and sawtooth generators; pulse generators; voltage-controlled oscillators; and voltage-controlled timers. These circuits will involve both new material and much of the circuit knowledge gained in previous chapters.

7.1 THE INTEGRATOR AND THE DIFFERENTIATOR

Previously, we have seen how modifications of the basic inverting amplifier give rise to the integrator and the differentiator. Both of these circuits are based primarily on the relationship between voltage and current in a capacitor.

7.1.1 Integrator Basics

Fig. 7-1 illustrates the operation of an ideal integrator. If a constant current, I (amperes), is applied to capacitor C (farads), the voltage across the capacitor will rise linearly at a rate of

$$\frac{\Delta E}{\Delta t} = \frac{I}{C} \text{ volts per second.}$$

Thus, a current of 1.0 μA applied to a capacitor of 1.0 μF produces a rising voltage across the capacitor, and this change occurs at the rate of 1.0 V/s.

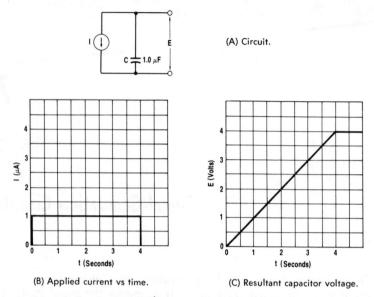

(A) Circuit.

(B) Applied current vs time.

(C) Resultant capacitor voltage.

Fig. 7-1. Dc current/voltage relationships for a capacitor.

In Fig. 7-1B, the 1.0-μA current is applied at time $t = 0$ and continues for a period of 4.0 seconds. At $t = 4$, the current is interrupted and the capacitor voltage (Fig. 7-1C) remains at the value accumulated up to that time (4.0 V). This mechanism is the basis for the op-amp integrator shown in Fig. 7-2. Capacitor C has one terminal at the summing point, the other at the output; thus, the capacitor voltage is also the output voltage. In effect, the op amp simulates an ideal current source, with one important difference—the output impedance of the op amp is low. So, while it provides a constant current drive to C, it simultaneously makes the voltage across the capacitor available at a low-impedance level.

The integrator output cannot be described by a simple algebraic relation; as we have seen, for a fixed (nonzero) input the output voltage changes at a rate determined by E_{in}, R, and C. Thus, the output voltage cannot be determined without also specifying the duration of time an input has been applied. If the output rate of change is expressed in terms of the feedback current, I_f, then

$$\frac{\Delta E_o}{\Delta t} = \frac{I_f}{C}$$

or

$$\Delta E_o = \frac{I_f}{C} \Delta t.$$

Since $I_f = I_{in}$ and, due to inversion,

$$\Delta E_o = \frac{-E_{in}}{RC}\, \Delta t,$$

after integration from 0 to t seconds,

$$E_o = \frac{-1}{RC}\int_0^t E_{in}\Delta t,$$

which is the output of the inverting integrator shown in Fig. 7-2. The 1/RC term of this expression is often called the integrator "gain," as it determines the slope of the output change. In the circuit shown, for example,

$$\frac{1}{RC} = \frac{1}{10^6 \times 10^{-6}} = 1.0,$$

so this time constant of 1.0 second produces a 1.0 V/s rate of change per volt of input. From this it can be seen that integrators make convenient circuits for the measurement of elapsed time—apply a known input to a calibrated integrator, and the voltage output can be read directly as a measure of elapsed time.

7.1.2 Realization of Practical Integrators

As may be noticed from the idealized integrator of Fig. 7-2, this configuration has an inherent drawback if E_{in} is left connected indefinitely: E_o will continue to rise until it reaches the saturation lim-

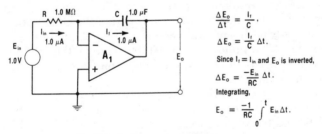

Fig. 7-2. Basic op-amp integrator.

its of A_1. This can again be appreciated by noting that the integrator is operating as an open-loop amplifier for dc inputs.

Integrators that allow operation in view of this limitation can take on various forms; for applications requiring precisely timed periods of integration, the circuits of Figs. 7-3 or 7-4 can be used. Both are sequentially operated integrators and have defined modes of operation. Since integration begins with whatever voltage is on the capac-

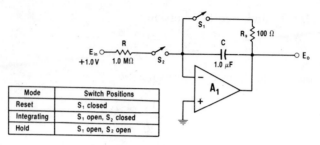

Mode	Switch Positions
Reset	S_1 closed
Integrating	S_1 open, S_2 closed
Hold	S_1 open, S_2 open

(A) Elementary test circuit.

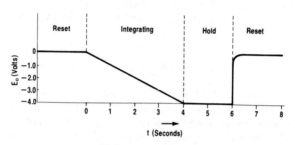

(B) Operating sequence.

Fig. 7-3. Integrator operation.

itor intially, the capacitor voltage must be reset to the desired value (usually zero) before each integration. Fig. 7-3B illustrates how this is done.

Switch S_1 is closed during the reset mode, discharging C through R_s. This leaves a residual voltage of zero. To begin the integration, S_1 is opened and S_2 closed. During this period the circuit operates as described previously and will charge C to a potential of -4 V in 4 seconds with the values shown. At the end of this period, S_2 is opened and the circuit "holds" the voltage on the capacitor for readout and subsequent processing.

An alternate form of the basic circuit is shown in Fig. 7-4. This circuit converts the reset cycle to an "initialize" cycle by the addition of R_1 and R_2. With S_1 closed (and S_2 open), R_1-R_2 and A_1 form an inverter, which charges C to an inverted multiple of the reference voltage. In this example the multiple is unity, thus C is initialized to $+4$ V. The integrating and hold modes are the same as before; the only difference is that C starts the integration with a $+4$-V potential. For example, a $+1$-V input will diminish the potential on C to zero in 4 seconds.

In either circuit, switches S_1 and S_2 can be relays or (more often) solid-state switches such as FETs, diodes, or bipolar transistors. The switching is directed externally by some form of control logic.

In many applications a simplified form of integrator can be used, as shown in Fig. 7-5. This differs from the ideal form of integrator by the addition of a dc "gain stop" resistor across C, reducing the integrator gain from the full open-loop value. The ratio of this shunt resistance to R should be as high as dc considerations allow so that ideal integrator behavior is not compromised. This form of integrator can be used successfully in such applications as square-wave to triangular-wave conversion.

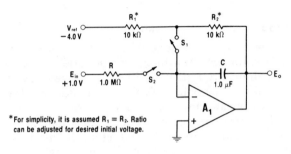

*For simplicity, it is assumed $R_1 = R_2$. Ratio can be adjusted for desired initial voltage.

(A) Test circuit.

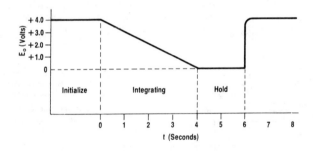

Mode	Switch Positions
Initialize	S_1 closed, S_2 open
Integrating	S_1 open, S_2 closed
Hold	S_1 open, S_2 open

(B) Operating sequence.

Fig. 7-4. Integrator with initial voltage applied.

The use of the integrator in its unmodified form (Fig. 7-2) is generally avoided because some means of introducing dc feedback must be used to stabilize the operating point and prevent saturation. However, this "classic" form of the integrator may sometimes appear as part of an overall feedback loop.

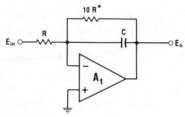

Fig. 7-5. "Continuous" integrator.

*Ratio of shunt resistance to R will determine integrator
accuracy. If possible (with dc stability), make shunt
resistance 100R or even 1000R.

7.1.3 Error Sources in the Integrator

Fig. 7-6 illustrates the sources of error that must be considered and minimized for optimum integrator performance. Capacitor C_t must be a high-quality type with a leakage current lower than the bias current of the amplifier. Typical examples are Teflon, polystyrene, polycarbonate, and mica types.

The amplifier must be compensated for unity gain and have good to excellent dc characteristics, depending on the maximum integration time. For long integration times, R_t and C_t will become large, which will reduce the integration current and make the error due to input bias current important. Any offset will be seen as an input current by the circuit and will be integrated along with the signal. Offset at the summing point can originate from either V_{io} or from $I_{ib} \times R_t$. V_{io} should be minimized by amplifier selection or nulling;

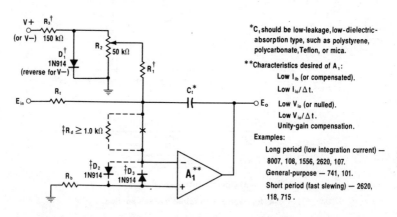

*C_t should be low-leakage, low-dielectric-
absorption type, such as polystyrene,
polycarbonate, Teflon, or mica.

**Characteristics desired of A_1:

    Low I_{ib} (or compensated).

    Low $I_{io}/\Delta t$.

    Low V_{io} (or nulled).

    Low $V_{io}/\Delta t$.

    Unity-gain compensation.

Examples:

    Long period (low integration current) —
    8007, 108, 1556, 2620, 107.

    General-purpose — 741, 101.

    Short period (fast slewing) — 2620,
    118, 715.

† R_1-R_3 and D_1 are optional, used to compensate I_{ib} of A_1.

$R_1 = \dfrac{0.6\,V}{2\,I_{ib}}$, $R_2 \leq 100\,k\Omega$ (not critical).

R_3 returned to V+ for npn-input amplifiers (usual case),
but to V— for pnp inputs.

Note: adjust R_2 for minimum output drift with
$E_{in} = 0$, after nulling V_{io}. If bias compensation
not used, set $R_b = R_t$.

†Use R_d if $C_t \geq 0.1\mu F$. Use D_2-D_3
for differential protection of A_1.

Fig. 7-6. Error sources and practical problems in the integrator.

I_{ib} can be minimized by choosing an op amp with high input imped-ance, such as a FET or super-β type. In some applications, I_{ib} can be compensated satisfactorily by using the method shown in Fig. 7-6.

Compensation of bias current is supplied by R_1, which provides a current to the summing point equal to the nominal bias current. This compensation is optimized by adjusting R_2 for minimal output drift with zero input voltage applied to R_t. The adjustment should be done after the input offset voltage has been nulled.

Diode D_1 derives a voltage source for the bias current compensa-tion and also provides some temperature tracking of the bias current. It has the further advantage of reducing sensitivity to supply-voltage changes. This compensation method works best with low-input-cur-rent bipolar amplifiers such as the type 108. (FET amplifiers do not generally require compensation.) In theory, bias current compen-sation can be applied to any amplifier, but it may not be necessary in many cases according to the circuit requirements. If this method is not used, it is still a good practice to include R_b, of a value nomi-nally equal to R_t.

Possible failure of the amplifier input stage is a problem in inte-grators, particularly if C_t is greater than about 0.1 μF. In such cases it is advisable to include a series resistance (R_d) to limit the dis-charge rate, and clamping diodes (D_2 and D_3) are recommended if the amplifier is unprotected differentially.

Integrators may also be required to operate at high speeds—for instance, in the generation of fast ramps and triangular waveforms. These applications require a high slew rate and a high f_t for the op amp but normally with less stringent dc requirements. Such applica-tions are satisfied by the high-speed types noted in Fig. 7-6.

7.1.4 The Differentiator

A natural companion to the integrator circuit is the differentiator. Like the integrator, it is best understood if viewed from the stand-point of the voltage/current relationships in the capacitive element, as illustrated in Fig. 7-7.

The integrator was used to show how the voltage across a capaci-tor rises linearly if the current in the capacitor is maintained con-stant. The reverse of this concept forms the basis of the differentia-tor. If a linear ramp of voltage is applied across a capacitor, the current in the capacitor will remain constant as long as the rate of change (slope) of the applied voltage is constant. Fig. 7-7A is the test circuit, and Fig. 7-7B is a graph of the voltage applied to the capacitor. The voltage across the capacitor rises at the rate of 1.0 V/s for 4 seconds. During this time, the current in the capacitor (Fig. 7-7C) is constant at 1.0 μA. This is nothing more than a re-statement of the basic relationship:

$$\frac{\Delta E}{\Delta t} = \frac{I}{C} \,,$$

which may be stated as

$$I = C\left(\frac{\Delta E}{\Delta t}\right).$$

Thus, in the example shown, a 1.0 V/s rate of change across the 1.0-μF capacitor results in a 1.0-μA current in the capacitor as shown in Fig. 7-7C.

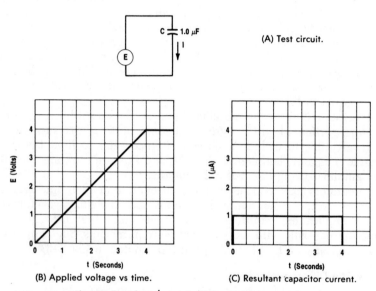

(A) Test circuit.

(B) Applied voltage vs time.

(C) Resultant capacitor current.

Fig. 7-7. Dc voltage/current relationships for a capacitor.

When the rate of voltage change across the capacitor falls to zero, the current in the capacitor also falls to zero. This is shown on the graph as the time beyond 4 seconds where $\Delta E = 0$ and $I = 0$.

In the operational differentiator of Fig. 7-8, capacitor C is the input element of the configuration and resistor R is the feedback element. As in the integrator, one terminal of the capacitor is held at ground potential by the summing point.

Input current I_{in} can be expressed in terms of C and E_{in} as

$$I_{in} = C\left(\frac{\Delta E_{in}}{\Delta t}\right),$$

and since $I_f = I_{in}$, we may substitute and add the sign inversion of A_1 to write an expression for E_o:

$$E_o = -I_f R = -I_{in} R,$$

which, when substituted for I_{in}, becomes

$$E_o = -RC\left(\frac{\Delta E_{in}}{\Delta t}\right).$$

Graphically, the differentiator action is illustrated by the sketches, which show the output to be an inverted product of the capacitor current (I_{in}) and R.

Since the differentiator responds only to changes in the input voltage (a capacitor will not carry current unless the applied voltage is changing), it will yield zero output voltage for a fixed (static) input voltage. The faster the input voltage changes, the greater will be the output voltage. In terms of frequency, the differentiator gives a rissing output voltage with increasing frequency, as would be expected from the decreasing input impedance due to the falling reactance of the capacitor.

In practical terms, the differentiator also has problems when applied in basic form (as in Fig. 7-8). The most apparent drawback is illustrated in Fig. 7-9. An earlier discussion of stability noted that, for stability to exist, the ideal $1/\beta$ curve must cross the open-loop gain curve with a net slope of less than -12 dB/octave. In Fig. 7-9A, it will be noted that the $1/\beta$ line intersects the gain curve at f_o, with a net slope between the curves of -12 dB/octave; thus, the charac-

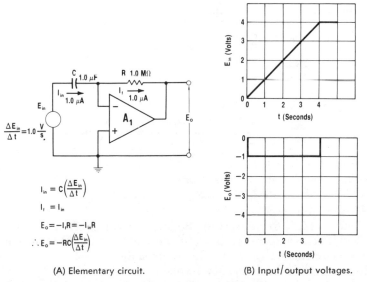

(A) Elementary circuit.

(B) Input/output voltages.

Fig. 7-8. Op-amp differentiator.

teristic is unstable. To make the $1/\beta$ line intersect the gain curve with a net slope of -6 dB/octave (required for stability), it must be modified to form the curve shown as $1/\beta'$. If f_o is the frequency at which the ideal $1/\beta$ curve intersected, a breakout must be introduced in the $1/\beta$ curve at f_1, where $f_1 = f_o/3.16$. This will cause the

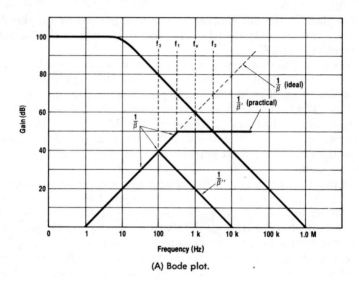

(A) Bode plot.

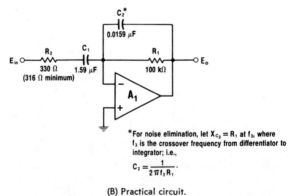

(B) Practical circuit.

Fig. 7-9. Stability conditions in the differentiator.

new curve ($1/\beta'$) to intersect the Bode plot at a frequency $f_2 = 3.16$ f_o. The $1/\beta'$ curve, therefore, has a full decade ($f_2 = f_1/10$) to assume a zero phase characteristic, which ensures stability.

To accomplish the frequency breakout, a resistive "stop" (R_2) is connected in series with C_1, as shown in Fig. 7-9B. The value of R_2

is chosen so that it is 3.16 times the reactance of C_1 at frequency f_o, or

$$R_2 = \frac{3.16}{2\pi f_o C_1} \, .$$

This gives the minimum value of R_2 required for stability, but in practice the next higher standard value is satisfactory. From the Bode plot it can be seen that such a modification results in little sacrifice of the useful dynamic range of the differentiator.

Another problem inherent in the differentiator is the 6-dB/octave rise in gain with increasing frequency. In practice, this effect greatly increases high-frequency noise, and in some cases, the noise may mask the desired signal if the signal has a small amplitude and is low in frequency. The noise problem can be dealt with by modifying the differentiator characteristic in another fashion.

If a modified curve $(1/\beta'')$ is introduced at frequency f_3, the high-frequency gain is reduced drastically from this frequency upward, while the differentiator characteristic remains unaltered below f_3. In actuality, a $1/\beta''$ characteristic produces a combination of differentiator and integrator action, with the crossover occurring at f_3.

To realize the $1/\beta''$ curve, C_2 is added across R_1, with C_2 chosen to be equal in reactance to R_1 at the crossover frequency, f_3, or

$$C_2 = \frac{1}{2\pi f_3 R_1} \, .$$

With this $1/\beta''$ curve, unity-gain stability is now required of A_1, whereas this was not necessarily so in the case of $1/\beta'$.

7.2 SINUSOIDAL OSCILLATORS

The most familiar waveform in electronics is the sine wave, and sine-wave signals of different frequencies are as fundamental to circuit work as dc supply potentials. Generating a sine wave is not hard in concept, as we have already seen by the ready tendency of op amps to oscillate when amplification is really the prime intent. This section concerns itself with the controlled form of sine-wave oscillator, having a defined and predictable frequency, amplitude, and in some cases, phase.

7.2.1 Wien-Bridge Oscillators

One of the most familiar types of sine-wave generators is the Wien-bridge circuit shown in Fig. 7-10. This circuit is a classic one in electronics and has been used since the days when it was realized in vacuum-tube versions. The Wien network, composed of R_1-C_1 and R_2-C_2, provides a positive feedback path around A_1, while R_3

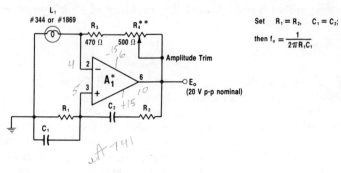

Set $R_1 = R_2$, $C_1 = C_2$;

then $f_o = \dfrac{1}{2\pi R_1 C_1}$

*Select A_1 according to operating
frequency and value of R_1:

$R_1 \geq 1.0$ MΩ — 8007, 1556, 108
$R_1 \leq 1.0$ MΩ — 118, 107, 741
$f_o \geq 1.0$ kHz — 118, 8007, 1556
$f_o \leq 1.0$ kHz — 107, 741, 8007, 108, 1556

* *Use R_4 to correct for lamp tolerance and
set output level, or fix $R_3 + R_4$ at 750 Ω.

Fig. 7-10. Wien-bridge oscillator.

and L_1 provide negative feedback. At some fundamental frequency, f_o, the overall phase shift is zero and transmission at this frequency is maximum in relation to all others. Positive feedback causes the circuit to oscillate at f_o, where

$$f_o = \frac{1}{2\pi R_1 C_1}$$

and $R_1 = R_2$, $C_1 = C_2$.

The attenuation of the Wien network at the frequency of oscillation is equal to 3. If the attenuation in the negative feedback path (R_3-L_1) is also 3, the bridge will be in balance and the differential input to A_1 will be small. It is this condition that must be maintained because, if the positive feedback is greater, oscillations will quickly build up until amplifier saturation is reached. On the other hand, if the negative feedback is greater, the oscillations die out. In a practical Wien-bridge oscillator, it is therefore necessary to provide some means of automatically balancing the feedback so that the amplitude of the oscillations can be regulated. In this state the purity of the output waveform will be at a maximum, as will the frequency stability. Another requisite is that the amplifier gain be large at the frequency of oscillation—the input error will then be small, which guarantees that the Wien network operates close to its natural frequency and is stable.

Any means of stabilizing the amplitude of a Wien-bridge oscillator must involve adjustment of the negative feedback divider to maintain the attenuation at 3. Typically, this can take the form of nonlinear elements: thermal types such as lamps or thermistors, nonlinear resistors, diode clippers, zener diodes, and so on. In Fig. 7-10, the nonlinear resistance of a lamp (L_1) is used to regulate the amount of negative feedback. L_1 responds to the average (not instantaneous) output level of A_1, adjusting its terminal resistance in inverse proportion. If the output level of A_1 rises, L_1 increases resistance, counteracting the rise. Similarly, a reduction in output results in a decrease of lamp resistance, stabilizing the oscillation level.

Lamp and thermistor stabilization schemes are popular ones, due mainly to their simplicity. They have several drawbacks, however, such as an inherent thermal time constant that limits usefulness to the lower frequencies.

The circuit of Fig. 7-10 is quite useful as a general-purpose Wien oscillator; with the appropriate amplifier, it can be used over a wide range of frequencies, and suggestions for choosing the amplifier are given in the notes. Resistors R_3-R_4 trim the negative feedback to accommodate lamp tolerances. If precise amplitude control or optimum stability for individual lamps is not necessary, let $R_3 + R_4 = 750 \, \Omega$. For frequency-tunable generators, either R_1-R_2 or C_1-C_2 can be ganged as a pair (with good tracking characteristics). If C_1-C_2 are selected as the tunable elements, large values for R_1-R_2 are required to cover the lower frequencies, which raises the network impedance. In such cases, C_1-C_2 should be in a shielded enclosure and stray capacitance to ground should be minimized for best results.

7.2.2 FET-Stabilized Wien Oscillator

Another popular method of achieving amplitude control is by using the variable channel resistance of a field-effect transistor. By sampling and rectifying the output voltage, a dc signal proportional to the output amplitude can be made to control the resistance of a FET. This technique works well within limits, but the channel resistance of the FET itself is nonlinear at high signal levels, and appreciable distortion can occur.

Fig. 7-11 is a Wien-bridge oscillator rearranged to effectively utilize the FET channel resistance as a gain control. In this circuit R_1-R_2 and C_1-C_2 again comprise the Wien network, but with the impedance of the legs scaled so that R_1-C_1 sees a voltage lower than R_2-C_2. This allows the voltage level at R_1-C_1 to be of lower amplitude. The circuit uses two amplifiers in the inverting mode; gain control is accomplished by FET Q_1, which is placed at the summing point of A_2 (a point of minimum voltage). Q_1 can then operate at a level low enough to make its distortion negligible. A_2 provides a

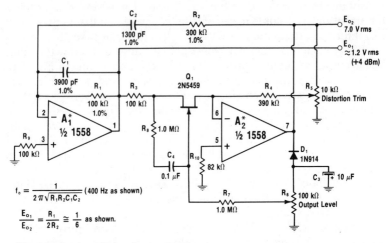

$$f_o = \frac{1}{2\pi\sqrt{R_1 R_2 C_1 C_2}} \text{ (400 Hz as shown)}$$

$$\frac{E_{o_1}}{E_{o_2}} = \frac{R_1}{2R_2} \cong \frac{1}{6} \text{ as shown.}$$

* A_1 and A_2 selected according to parameters , Fig. 7-10.

Fig. 7-11. Wien-bridge oscillator with FET stabilization.

nominal gain of 6, which is trimmed by R_5 so that Q_1 is operating in
the most linear portion of its characteristic.

The circuit has dual outputs available with two amplifiers; level
differences are determined by the Wien network (R_1-R_2). E_{o_1} will
have less residual distortion than E_{o_2} because it operates at a lower
level and is filtered by the Wien network prior to being controlled
by Q_1. The high output level of A_2 is sampled by R_6, which derives
the bias to control Q_1. This resistor can be used as an output-level
control to adjust output level linearly. R_5 is first trimmed for low
distortion, which is necessary due to differences among individual
FETs.

The amplifiers used should follow the guidelines set down for
Fig. 7-10. For general-purpose use, dual devices are obviously attractive. It should be noted that the equation for operating frequency is the general form, due to the difference in R_1-R_2 and C_1-C_2.
The ratio used in the bridge may be altered from that shown, if desired, but it should be appreciated that as R_2 increases above R_1,
stage A_2 must supply additional gain, thus making its distortion contribution more significant, particularly at high frequencies. The ratio
shown provides a good compromise between low-level operation of
Q_1 and minimal gain for the A_2 stage. When properly trimmed, the
oscillator has less than 0.05% distortion at both outputs with A_2
levels up to ±10 V p-p. When the oscillator is operated over a wide
range of frequencies, some adjustment of C_3 may be necessary at
low frequencies.

7.2.3 Quadrature (Sine/Cosine) Oscillator

In electronic systems a need often arises for two sine waves in quadrature, or with 90° of phase difference between them. This function is fulfilled by the oscillator of Fig. 7-12, which generates sine and cosine waveforms. The circuit is essentially two integrators in cascade with positive feedback. Because the phase shift of an integrator is 90°, outputs E_{o_1} and E_{o_2} differ in phase by 90°. Thus, with the loop oscillating, these outputs deliver sine and cosine waves.

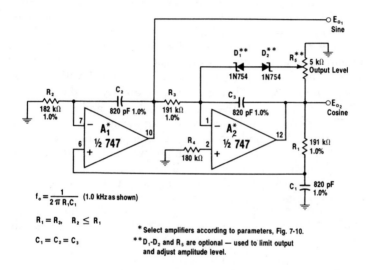

Fig. 7-12. Quadrature (sine/cosine) oscillator.

In theory, all resistances and capacitances are equal, but in practice, one resistance (typically R_2) is lowered slightly to ensure starting. The remaining timing components assume close tolerance values. With R_2 lowered slightly, the oscillations tend to grow in amplitude; if unchecked, they will stabilize at the saturation limits of A_2. To prevent this and to exercise predictable control on output amplitude, a limiting network, consisting of D_1-D_2 and R_5, is used around A_2. With D_1-D_2 directly across A_2, the outputs will stabilize at $\pm V_Z$. R_5 is used to set the output at any level above the zener limits of D_1-D_2.

The distortion of the output waveform is reasonably small, in the vicinity of 1.0%. The sine output terminal is lower in distortion than the cosine output because additional filtering of the sine signal occurs after limiting by D_1-D_2.

This circuit is useful where fixed-frequency sine waves in quadrature are needed. Because of the number of precision components in the loop, it does not adapt well to tuned applications. For general applications, dual op amps are convenient (as shown), but diverse applications should be governed by the considerations of Fig. 7-10.

7.3 MULTIVIBRATORS

7.3.1 Astable Multivibrator

Another op-amp oscillator circuit that must be termed a classic is the astable oscillator of Fig. 7-13A. This circuit, with minor modification, can be used with virtually any op amp and is useful over a very wide range of frequencies, limited only by the devices used. The output square wave can either be taken as the full saturated swing of the device (E_{o_1}) or it can be clamped with diodes for defined limits (E_{o_2}). The operating frequency is determined by R_t-C_t and the R_1-R_2 positive feedback network, and is relatively independent of supply voltages and output swing.

Operation is best understood by examining the time relationships in Fig. 7-13B. The circuit uses both positive and negative feedback, with regeneration supplied by the R_1-R_2 network and integration by the R_t-C_t network. The op amp compares the voltage output from these two points and changes states as their relative states change.

Assume the R_1-R_2 junction is initially at $+\beta V_Z$, which means the output is at $+V_Z$. The voltage across C_t (E_{C_t}) was previously at $-\beta V_Z$, but it is now charging toward $+V_Z$ through R_t (t_1). As E_{C_t} rises and reaches the potential of $+\beta V_Z$, the threshold potential of the amplifier is reached. Since E_{C_t} is applied to the ($-$) input, this positive rise causes the output to go negative. The negative-going output is immediately transmitted through R_2-R_1, and this positive feedback path causes the output to snap rapidly from positive to negative saturation. With E_{o_2} at $-V_Z$, E_{C_t} now begins to change toward this potential (t_2). The R_1-R_2 junction is now at $-\beta V_Z$, and as E_{C_t} decreases and crosses this potential, the circuit flips positive by regeneration, beginning a second cycle of oscillation (t_3); t_1 and t_2 comprise one period of the oscillation cycle, which is of duration T. Since β is a fixed fraction of V_Z (or $E_{o(sat)}$ if clamping is not used) and E_{C_t} is timed against V_Z and compared to βV_Z, V_Z is eliminated from the timing expression for symmetrical values of V_Z (or $E_{o(sat)}$). If t_1 and t_2 are the half-periods, the full period T is $t_1 + t_2$, which can be shown to be

$$T = 2R_t C_t \log_e \left(\frac{1 + \beta}{1 - \beta} \right).$$

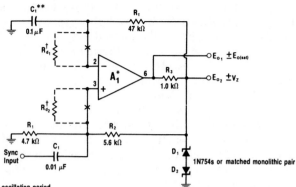

T = oscillation period

$$T = 2R_1C_1 \log_e\left(\frac{1+\beta}{1-\beta}\right),$$

where $\beta = \frac{R_1}{R_1+R_2}$.

If $\beta = 0.462$, $T = 2R_1C_1$,

$$f_o = \frac{1}{T} = \frac{1}{2R_1C_1} \quad \text{(100 Hz as shown)}$$

* Any op amp with required differential input rating.
  Suggestions:
   general-purpose — 101, 101A, 748
   vlf to medium hf — 2620
   hf — 715, 540, 709, 531

** C_1 should be returned to V+ for polarized capacitors.

† Use R_{d_1} - R_{d_2} for differential input protection, if
  necessary. Ideally, R_d values should be much
  greater than R_1 or $R_1 \parallel R_2$.

(A) Circuit.

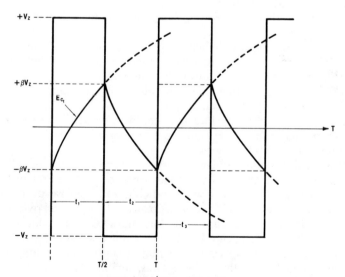

(B) Voltage/time relationships.

Fig. 7-13. Astable multivibrator.

This is the general expression for the period of the oscillator, from which it is apparent that the period (or frequency) can be controlled by either R_t, C_t, or β (R_1 and R_2).

It can also be seen that if the natural log factor on the right is made equal to unity, the log term will disappear, which considerably simplifies time calculations. If β is made equal to 0.462, this term becomes very close to unity, which allows the use of the simplified expression. In practice, R_1 and R_2 are chosen for a β of 0.462, then R_t and C_t are chosen from the simplified equation. It should be remembered that for low offset, R_t and $R_1 \parallel R_2$ should be chosen for minimum input offset error. It is, in fact, the low input offset of the op amp that lends the circuit its innate timing precision, for as long as V_{io} is much less than βV_z, the timing error due to amplifier offset will be negligible.

There are a few practical problems associated with this circuit that may or may not be significant, depending on the amplifier chosen. Since the function of the amplifier is essentially that of a comparator, performance is governed by many of the same considerations (see Chapter 5). The amplifier should not be frequency compensated, as compensation is not necessary for stability and it reduces high-frequency capability. The inputs to the amplifier are subjected to large differential voltages; therefore, protection is indicated for unprotected types, and internally clamped types such as the 108 and 118 will need a series resistance (R_d) to prevent excessive differential current flow—the resistance used should be much greater than either R_t or $R_1 \parallel R_2$ for minimum degradation of timing characteristics.

At low frequencies or when C_t becomes large, indicating use of a tantalum electrolytic type, two problems can occur. First, the capacitor must be polarized properly—this is satisfied by returning it to a supply voltage rather than ground, V+ usually being preferred. Also, C_t represents a potentially destructive element on switchoff because it looks directly into the amplifier input. For capacitance values greater than 0.1 μF, some series resistance to the ($-$) input is desired, usually 1 kΩ or greater.

Most of the above problems can be dealt with by the selection of the proper device or by the judicious use of protection. For instance, either the 101 or 748 would be a good choice for general-purpose use at frequencies below 100 kHz. The 2620 can be operated over an extremely wide range because of its low input current (which allows low frequencies) and wide bandwidth (which allows high frequencies). Generally, the op-amp types that are optimum for comparator use will work best in this circuit. Thus, for high-frequency use, the 715, 540, 709, and 531 work well; the very high uncompensated bandwidth of the 715 allows operation up to about 1 MHz. At these frequencies, stray capacitance should be minimized and resistances should be kept low. Also, transistor junction zeners work best for D_1-D_2 (see Chapter 5) and are recommended for the cleanest waveforms.

Note that if zener clamping is used to limit E_{o_2} to approximately ± 7 V and if β is set at less than 0.5, the differential input to A_1 will be less than the differential breakdown potential. This allows use of unprotected types without clamping, such as the 709 and 540. The 540, for instance, is very useful because it can deliver output currents of ± 100 mA.

If desired, this astable multivibrator can be easily synchronized by injecting pulses at the $(+)$ input through C_1. The circuit can be synchronized with either positive or negative pulses.

An example of a useful astable circuit application is shown in Fig. 7-14. This circuit is arranged for single-supply operation at 5 Hz. Input clamping and current protection are provided by D_1-D_2 and R_5, and circuit values are chosen to be generally uncritical of any op amp. Thus, virtually any device can be inserted into the socket for A_1 and given a quick functional check. D_3, an LED, provides an attention-getting 5-Hz flash rate that allows the checker to be used with no equipment other than power. Even battery operation is feasible, if desired, in which case R_8 can be increased to prolong battery life.

7.3.2 Monostable (One-Shot) Multivibrator

A modification of Fig. 7-13A yields a circuit that is stable in only one output state (monostable); this circuit is shown in Fig. 7-15.

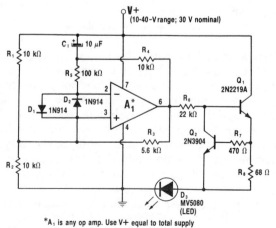

*A_1 is any op amp. Use V+ equal to total supply voltage — i.e., V+ = 30 V for ±15-V devices.

Fig. 7-14. Astable multivibrator for testing op amps (f ≅ 5 Hz).

The addition of D_1 across C_t clamps the $(-)$ input of the op amp at +0.6 V, which forces the amplifier to assume a defined output state. Since the positive feedback from R_1-R_2 can rise above this level, the output latches to the "high" state, or $+E_{o(sat)}$. Triggering is accomplished through D_2, which passes the differentiated negative input pulse at C_1-R_3 to the $(+)$ input. A negative input pulse that pulls the $(+)$ input below +0.6 V causes the output to flip to the negative output state, $-E_{o(sat)}$. This action is regenerative, and the output stays in the negative state because the $(-)$ input cannot immediately follow due to R_t-C_t. C_t then starts charging toward $-E_{o(sat)}$ through R_t.

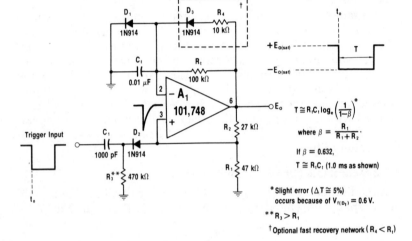

Fig. 7-15. Monostable multivibrator.

The voltage at the $(+)$ input at this time is $-\beta E_{o(sat)}$. As the voltage across C_t reaches this voltage, the amplifier flips positive once again, due to regeneration. The circuit does not completely recover, however, until C_t charges back up to +0.6 V, where D_1 clamps it in a static state. Because of this relatively long recharge cycle, the recovery time is poor, but it can be improved if desired by adding R_4-D_3, which provides a shorter time constant for recovery. The time of the output pulse width is determined by the initial capacitor voltage (+0.6 V) and by $-E_{o(sat)}$:

$$T = R_t C_t \log_e \left(\frac{-E_{o(sat)} - (V_{f(D_1)})}{-E_{o(sat)} - (\beta E_{o(sat)})} \right).$$

This is the complete, precise form of the equation, which in many situations can be simplified further. If $E_{o(sat)} \gg 0.6$ V, the initial capacitor charge can be assumed to be zero with slight error (about 5% for silicon diodes, half this figure for germanium). This yields a new equation,

$$T \cong R_t C_t \log_e \left(\frac{1}{1 - \beta} \right).$$

To simplify further: if β is made 0.632, the log term becomes equal to unity, or

$$T \cong R_t C_t.$$

The presence of D_1 also introduces a temperature coefficient of about $0.017\%/°C$, which should be considered in precise applications.

The triggering network of C_1-R_3 may need some alteration to suit different triggering requirements. R_3 should be greater than R_1 so that timing is not upset. Note that β determines the trigger sensitivity since it sets the voltage at the $(+)$ input.

In the example shown, R_t and C_t are chosen for a 1.0-ms pulse width, and β is set at 0.632 by R_1-R_2. As with the astable multivibrator on which this circuit is based, the timing period is independent of supplies, and zener clamping may be used at the output. Speed is not a prime feature of this circuit, so an uncompensated op amp should be used to optimize this factor. The 101 and 748 are good for pulse widths down to approximately 100 μs; below this, one of the faster types mentioned in Fig. 7-13A should be used. Input protection is a consideration in this circuit as in the astable circuit. The circuit can also be rearranged to deliver positive-going output pulses, if desired, by reversing D_1 and D_2 (and D_3 if used).

7.3.3 Bistable Multivibrator

The third general form of multivibrator, the bistable, is shown in Fig. 7-16. This circuit is essentially a comparator with ac input coupling through C_1-R_3 (see Chapter 5). Input sensitivity can be adjusted by altering β, since $\pm\beta E_{o(sat)}$ is the voltage required for triggering at the $(-)$ input.

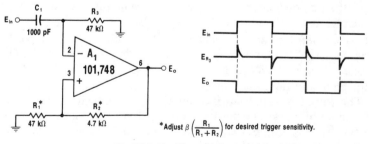

Fig. 7-16. Bistable multivibrator.

7.4 FUNCTION GENERATORS

As will soon be noted, many of the following circuits use voltage comparators in combination with integrators to generate time-dependent functions. To a large degree, many of these circuits will be limited primarily by the device used as a comparator. The response time and slew rate define the upper limit of usable speed; therefore, nearly all the devices recommended will be uncompensated types to take advantage of the greater potential speed. An optimum selection for a given application must be based on the performance of the op amp as a comparator. It is recommended that the performance of various devices as comparators (Chapter 5) be reviewed to keep the pertinent considerations in mind.

7.4.1 Basic Circuit

One of the most useful op-amp oscillator circuits is the triangle/square-wave function generator of Fig. 7-17A. This circuit, comprised of an "ideal" integrator (A_2) and a comparator with hystersis (A_1), simultaneously generates ultralinear triangle waveforms and symmetrical square waves. Operation over an extremely wide range of frequencies is possible using appropriate devices, from ultralow frequencies with periods measured in hours up to hundreds of kilohertz.

The circuit is best understood by regarding the timing diagram in Fig. 7-17B. Assume that the output of comparator A_1 has just switched to the high state and that E_{o_2} is at $+V_Z$ (breakdown voltage of D_1-D_2). The input to the integrator is then $+V_Z$, which means output E_{o_1} will integrate at a rate

$$\frac{E_{in}}{RC} = \frac{V_Z}{R_t C_t} \, V/s.$$

A_1 compares the sum of the voltages E_{o_1} and E_{o_2} against the ground reference on its $(-)$ input. As E_{o_1} ramps negative, the junction of R_1-R_2 decreases toward zero (t_1). When E_{o_1} crosses $-V_Z$ (or when E_{o_1} is equal and opposite to E_{o_2}), the voltage at the $(+)$ input of A_1 crosses zero and A_1 changes state rapidly, aided by positive feedback. E_{o_2} is now at $-V_Z$, and A_2 begins to integrate positive toward $+V_Z$ (t_2). When E_{o_1} crosses $+V_Z$, A_1 changes back to the high state and the cycle repeats.

The output voltage of A_1 is clamped at $\pm V_Z$, which determines the output amplitudes. The positive and negative ramp slopes are determined by $\pm V_Z$, R_t, and C_t, and are equal if the zener voltages are symmetrical (usually the case).

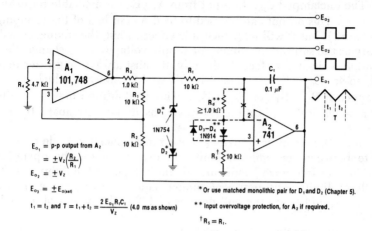

E_{o_1} = p-p output from A_2
$\quad = \pm V_z \left(\dfrac{R_2}{R_1} \right)$

$E_{o_2} = \pm V_z$

$E_{o_3} = \pm E_{o(sat)}$

$t_1 = t_2$ and $T = t_1 + t_2 = \dfrac{2 E_{o_1} R_1 C_1}{V_z}$ (4.0 ms as shown)

* Or use matched monolithic pair for D_1 and D_2 (Chapter 5).

** Input overvoltage protection, for A_2 if required.

† $R_5 = R_1$.

(A) Circuit.

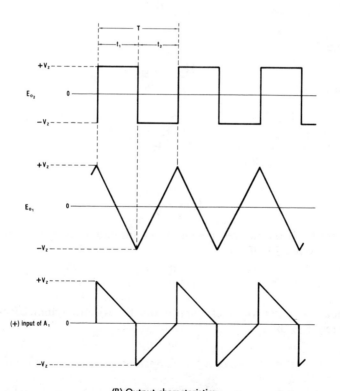

(B) Output characteristics.

Fig. 7-17. Function generator.

The unclamped direct output from A_1 (E_{o_3}) is available for external use. This output can be used to feed A_2 (in lieu of the clamping network), but it will introduce side effects. First, the frequency will vary as the saturation voltages or supply voltages of A_1 change. Second, if A_1 is used to feed A_2 directly, R_1 must always be greater than R_2 to set $E_{o_1} < E_{o_3}$. A_2 cannot be allowed to saturate, which would happen if $R_2 = R_1$ (or $E_{o_1} = E_{o_3}$). This modification may be useful for noncritical applications, however, as it does eliminate R_3 and D_1-D_2.

Since the circuit is actually a linear ramp generator made to oscillate between two voltage limits, an expression for the operating period (or frequency) must include both slopes of the ramp and the voltage limits. The pertinent timing data is shown in Fig. 7-17B, where t_1 and t_2 are the half-periods and T is the period of a single cycle.

The time for the first half-cycle is

$$t_1 = \frac{E_o \, t}{\Delta E_o}.$$

Since

$$\frac{\Delta E_o}{t} = \frac{E_{in}}{RC},$$

then

$$t_1 = \frac{E_o \, RC}{E_{in}}$$

or

$$t_1 = \frac{E_{o_1} R_t C_t}{V_Z},$$

where E_{o_1} is the desired peak-to-peak amplitude from A_2. Similarly, for the second half-cycle,

$$t_2 = \frac{E_{o_1} R_t C_t}{V_Z}.$$

Since the zener voltages (hence the times) are symmetrical, the period T is then

$$T = \frac{2E_{o_1} R_t C_t}{V_Z}.$$

This equation can be used in designing the circuit for specific times or specific output voltages. The output voltage (E_{o_1}) is scaled to V_Z

by a factor of 2:1; therefore, the relationship used to select R_1 and R_2 is

$$E_{o_1} = \frac{R_2}{R_1} 2 V_Z.$$

These points may be further illustrated in the example shown, which uses 1N754 zeners ($V_Z \cong \pm 7.5$ V). In Fig. 7-17A, $R_1 = R_2$, so the output is 15 volts peak-to-peak. The frequency is then $1/4R_tC_t$, or approximately 250 Hz.

Frequency can be varied without amplitude change by varying either R_t or C_t. R_t variation allows frequency change over many decades—limited at the low end by the bias current of A_2 and at the high end by the output current of A_2 or by its slew rate. C_t is most conveniently changed in decade steps, with low maximum values for reasons of economy. Obviously, as the stability of the frequency is directly proportional to R_t and C_t, they should be low-TC, close-tolerance types. Similarly, R_1-R_2 should be stable types for frequency and amplitude stability, and D_1-D_2 can be a low-TC monolithic zener combination (Chapter 5).

As always, amplifier selection plays an important role in performance. Since A_1 operates as a comparator, it should be an uncompensated type. However, a great many generators such as this are used at low frequencies, and the slewing rate of 741 types will introduce little error below 100 Hz. A_2 must be internally compensated; thus, the 741 is a good choice here for integration currents larger than its bias current. At ultralow frequencies where the integration current becomes very small, the 8007, 108, 1556, or 2620 will become more attractive. If extension of the low-frequency range is achieved by large C_t values, input protection precautions like those described for the integrator should be taken for A_2. At high frequencies the 741 becomes slew-rate limited; other types are better choices above a few kilohertz. Among these are the 531, 1556, 8007, 118, 2620, and 715. Further examples of selection rationale are demonstrated in the following circuits.

7.4.2 Modifications to the Basic Function Generator

The function generator of Fig. 7-17A not only is a versatile circuit in its own right, but it adapts readily to many extremely useful variations.

As discussed previously, the frequency of the function generator is controllable by varying either R_t or C_t. Variation of R_t is the simplest means of frequency change, but there is an alternate method that is attractive for other reasons. This circuit (Fig. 7-18) introduces a divider network, β, composed of R_5 and R_6, and placed between the clamping diodes and R_t. R_5 and R_6 vary the fraction of

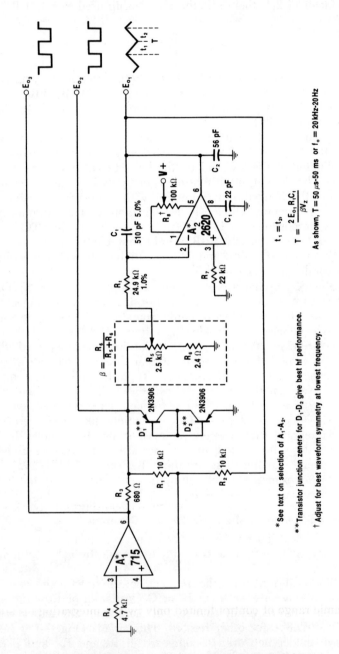

Fig. 7-18. Variable-frequency function generator (20 Hz-20 kHz).

$\pm V_Z$ that is fed to R_t; thus the input to the integrator in this circuit is $\pm\beta V_Z$. If the term βV_Z is substituted in the expression for t_1 and t_2, the new timing equation for T is

$$t_1 = t_2 = \frac{E_{o_1} R_t C_t}{\beta V_Z}$$

and

$$T = t_1 + t_2 = \frac{2E_{o_1} R_t C_t}{\beta V_Z} \, .$$

The use of R_5-R_6 represents a reduction in input current to A_2, the fraction being equal to β. Thus, similar to large values of R_t, it places a limitation on A_2 (in terms of input current) for very low frequencies. Dynamic range of frequency is optimized by selecting R_t such that when β is minimum the input current is still much greater than the bias current of A_2. Frequency variations of 1000:1 are relatively easy to achieve, and ratios of 10,000:1 are possible.

The reason behind the β voltage divider may already be obvious —the control of gain from unity to some fraction of the input can next be provided by an analog multiplier, as discussed in Chapter 5. Thus, if β (R_5 plus R_6) is replaced by a two-quadrant multiplier, the frequency may be made electronically variable, with a dynamic range proportional to the range of the multiplier.

In the example shown, the dynamic range is 3 decades; R_t and C_t are chosen for an upper frequency limit of 20 kHz, and the oscillator can be adjusted from 20 Hz to 20 kHz using R_5. A type 2620 is recommended for best high-frequency operation and low input current. A type 118 can also be used, but the dynamic range may be limited at low frequencies by its higher bias current (if so, bias compensation can be used). With both the 2620 and the 118, 20 kHz is not the upper limit of operation—they may be used up to 100 kHz or more. At such frequencies A_1 should also be very fast, hence the use of a 715 for this amplifier. A_2 should be offset nulled by adjusting for best symmetry at the lowest frequency of operation. If the frequency range is scaled downward, general-purpose types can be used for both A_1 and A_2, but nulling is still necessary if a 1000:1 frequency range is retained.

7.4.3 Function Generator With Independently Variable Slopes

Another modification to the basic function generator allows independent control of positive and negative slopes, both of which have a dynamic range of control limited only by the integrating op amp. With individual ramp control, the basic triangular output wave can be modified into a sawtooth waveform, either positive-going or negative-going.

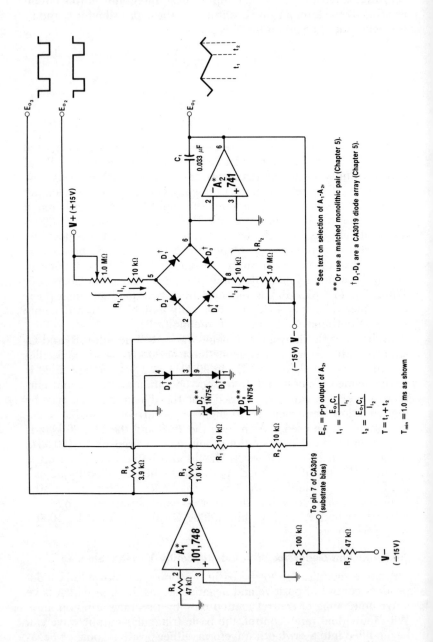

Fig. 7-19. Function generator with independently variable slopes.

The circuit shown in Fig. 7-19 uses a diode bridge at the summing point of integrator A_2, which acts as a current-mode gate under control of A_1. If the output of A_1 is high, D_1 and D_4 are switched on, causing R_{t_1} to inject current into the summing point from $V+$ through D_1. When the output of A_1 is low, D_2 and D_3 switch on and R_{t_2} conducts current from $V-$ to the summing point of A_2, thus controlling positive ramp slopes. If these currents are termed I_{i_1} and I_{i_2}, respectively, new expressions for the output slopes of A_2 can be written. If the negative slope has duration t_1 (Fig. 7-19) and the positive slope has duration t_2; then, for the negative slope,

$$\frac{\Delta E_o}{\Delta t} = \frac{I_{i_1}}{C_t},$$

or

$$t_1 = \frac{E_{o_1} C_t}{I_{i_1}},$$

where E_{o_1} is the desired peak-to-peak output swing from A_2. For the positive slope,

$$\frac{\Delta E_o}{\Delta t} = \frac{I_{i_2}}{C_t}$$

or

$$t_2 = \frac{E_{o_1} C_t}{I_{i_2}}$$

and

$$T = t_1 + t_2.$$

In practice, the control of I_{i_1} and I_{i_2} to vary ramp slopes can involve any of several methods: potentiometers for R_{t_1} and R_{t_2}, fixed resistors returned to variable voltages, or current sources. If R_{t_1} and R_{t_2} are potentiometers, the most stable method of control is a variable resistance to $V+$ or $V-$ because diodes D_1 and D_3 introduce some temperature dependence into I_{i_1} and I_{i_2}, and this variance is minimized when the voltage is high. Ideally, I_{i_1} and I_{i_2} are generated by constant-current sources such as those described in Chapter 4. If the current source is made voltage-controlled, it allows voltage control of either the wave period or, in the case of dual (complementary) current sources, the frequency at a constant duty cycle.

This circuit can also be used as a variable-period pulse generator with precise control of pulse width and frequency. A wide dynamic range of operation is available (many decades). C_t can be switch-selected for decade ranges, and R_{t_1} and R_{t_2} can be made calibrated potentiometers.

The considerations in this circuit differ little from the previous one. D_1-D_4 are ideally a matched diode bridge as shown. This has the bonus of allowing the use of "extra" diodes (D_5-D_6) as clamps for the input from A_1. R_5 is chosen so that it can supply adequate current to absorb I_{i_1} or I_{i_2} at their highest levels. Any excess current provided by R_5 is absorbed in the clamps, D_5-D_6. Amplifier selection is governed by the previous restrictions—the devices shown are for general-purpose use. R_{t_1}, R_{t_2}, and C_t in this circuit example are chosen to yield a minimum total period of 1.0 ms. R_{t_1} and R_{t_2} allow the period to be lengthened to a total of 100 ms. This circuit can

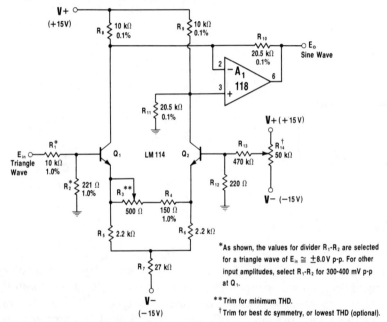

Fig. 7-20. Triangle to sine-wave converter.

serve as a useful source of adjustable ramp, triangular, pulse, and square waveforms.

7.4.4 Triangle to Sine-Wave Converter

The formation of sine waves in a function generator is normally a conversion process, one that synthesizes approximate sine curves from a triangular input wave. Many sine-wave generators use biased diodes to "round" and shape the peaks of triangle waves. The circuit of Fig. 7-20 is much simpler in concept, yet produces excellent results. It can be used with any triangle wave having constant amplitude and a 50% duty cycle.

The circuit uses a differential amplifier (A_1) and a matched transistor pair (Q_1-Q_2) with a controlled amount of emitter coupling. As has been previously described in the section on multipliers and instrumentation amplifiers (Chapter 5), an undegenerated, emitter-coupled amplifier is linear only for small signal levels. However, if operation is held to a region of controlled nonlinearity, an emitter-coupled pair can convert a linear input voltage such as a triangle wave into a good approximation of a sine-wave output. This is what Q_1-Q_2 of Fig. 7-20 accomplish, and A_1 converts the sinusoidal output current of Q_1-Q_2 to a buffered sine-wave output voltage.

Since this scheme involves precise control over the conduction of Q_1 and Q_2, it is critically dependent upon both the input amplitude and the degree of emitter coupling. R_1 and R_2 are chosen for approximately 300 to 400 mV p-p drive at Q_1. With levels in this range, R_3 can be set for a point of minimum output distortion. This is best done with a distortion analyzer, but an oscilloscope can also be used. Once R_3 is set, the input level must not change, or the distortion in the output will climb rapidly. For this reason, high-stability components are preferred for R_1-R_4; R_3 should preferably be a high-resolution trimmer, such as a 10-turn potentiometer.

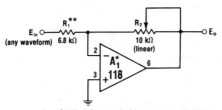

$E_o = \pm 10$V maximum, reducible to zero by adjusting R_1.

*Select for required bandwidth and slew rate. A_1 must be stable at unity gain.

**Trim if necessary for exact full-scale output desired.

Fig. 7-21. Buffer with feedback gain control.

Distortion is also affected to a smaller degree by the match of Q_1-Q_2. A matched transistor pair can be used without nulling and distortion will still be reasonably low ($\leq 1.0\%$). However, optimum performance is obtained by offset nulling or selection of a tightly controlled offset-voltage pair ($V_{io} < 0.5$ mV).

The differential to single-ended converter formed by A_1 is similar to others described previously; R_{10}-R_{11} may be used to scale the sine-wave output level. The values used in this example yield levels comparable to those of the triangular input waveforms. The op amp should be consistent with required speeds—a type 118 yields optimum performance in this regard.

7.4.5 Gain-Controlled Buffer Amplifier

Function generators can be very useful as laboratory tools, and the gain-controlled stage of Fig. 7-21 is a handy addition. The circuit gain is variable from zero to a maximum of R_2/R_1. Most of the function generators discussed have an output voltage $E_o = \pm V_Z$, which is about $\pm 7\text{-}8$ V. The ratio of R_2/R_1 shown scales this value continuously from zero to ± 10 V or so, and allows linear calibration of the output. Minimum rise and fall times are governed by the amplifier—a type 118 is recommended here. The output impedance remains low for any setting of R_2.

7.5 SAWTOOTH GENERATORS

One common circuit requirement is the sawtooth generator, frequently used to generate ramp voltages for timing purposes. The previous function generator with independent slope adjustments can be used to generate sawtooth waveforms, but circuit requirements often dictate a more specialized type of generator. The waveform itself can have either a linear or an exponential slope, depending on the application. Other variations are in the form of control: driven, triggered, free-running, or synchronized.

7.5.1 Basic Low-Frequency Sweep Generator

The sawtooth generator of Fig. 7-22 may be recognized as an integrator with clamping transistor Q_1 added, to reset the capacitor to zero at the end of each timing cycle. The circuit requires an external control voltage (E_c) to command the state of the ramp generator. If E_c is high, the circuit is in the hold mode. In this state R_1 holds Q_1 in saturation and R_3 is in parallel with C_t. This makes the output essentially zero, which establishes the output dc base line. The circuit will remain in this state indefinitely as long as E_c is high. When E_c is taken low, D_1 steers the current in R_1 away from Q_1 by reverse-biasing D_2 and D_3. This turns Q_1 off and also (importantly) prevents any "sneak path" current flow from the summing point, which would alter I_t.

With Q_1 off, the circuit begins to integrate at the rate of I_t/C_t volts per second. This rise continues until E_c again goes high, turning on Q_1 and discharging C_t. From this it may be seen that although R_t and C_t set the slope of the output waveform, the timing of the input control will determine the final end-point voltage. In designing this circuit for a specific application, the E_c timing characteristic must be known beforehand.

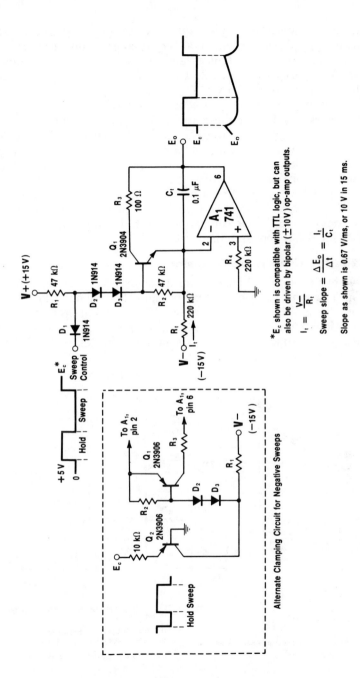

*E_c shown is compatible with TTL logic, but can also be driven by bipolar (±10 V) op-amp outputs.

$$I_1 = \frac{V-}{R_1}$$

$$\text{Sweep slope} = \frac{\Delta E_o}{\Delta t} = \frac{I_1}{C_1}$$

Slope as shown is 0.67 V/ms, or 10 V in 15 ms.

Alternate Clamping Circuit for Negative Sweeps

Fig. 7-22. Low-frequency sweep generator.

389

In the example shown, the values are chosen to be compatible with one typical requirement, a 60-Hz sweep generator for tv-raster vertical scan. Assuming a typical hold (retrace) interval of approximately 1.0 ms, R_t and C_t provide a slope of 10 V in 15 ms, the active portion of the vertical scan.

This sweep generator is best confined to low-frequency use, generally below 1 kHz. For these applications the 741 types are adequate. The circuit can be used at higher frequencies with a high-speed type, but a subsequent circuit shows an alternate form of sweep that allows the use of a low-frequency device for timing. Modification of this circuit for negative-going output waveforms is accomplished by substituting a pnp transistor for Q_1 and returning R_t to V+. A suitable drive voltage for the pnp transistor becomes more complicated if logic compatibility is to be preserved; one possibility for this is shown in the inset.

7.5.2 Fast Precision Sweep Generator

Due to slew-rate and bandwidth limitations, the sweep generator of Fig. 7-22 must use a high-speed op amp above about 1 kHz. The circuit of Fig. 7-23, however, produces fast sweeps of up to 30 V/μs using a low-frequency op amp. A_1 and Q_1 form a precision current source, I_t (Chapter 4), and Q_2 is a saturated switch that holds C_t

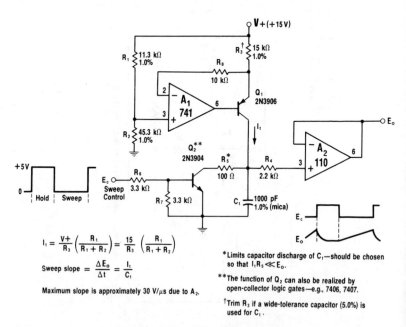

$$I_t = \frac{V+}{R_3}\left(\frac{R_1}{R_1 + R_2}\right) = \frac{15}{R_3}\left(\frac{R_1}{R_1 + R_2}\right)$$

$$\text{Sweep slope} = \frac{\Delta E_o}{\Delta t} = \frac{I_t}{C_t}$$

Maximum slope is approximately 30 V/μs due to A_2.

*Limits capacitor discharge of C_1—should be chosen so that $I_t R_5 \ll E_o$.

**The function of Q_2 can also be realized by open-collector logic gates—e.g., 7406, 7407.

†Trim R_3 if a wide-tolerance capacitor (5.0%) is used for C_1.

Fig. 7-23. Fast precision sweep generator.

near zero volts when E_c is high. When E_c falls low, Q_2 switches off and C_t begins to charge toward $+15$ V, forming a linear ramp with a slope of I_t/C_t (V/s). This voltage rise across C_t is buffered by A_2, a low-input-current, high-speed follower. The voltage E_o from A_2 represents the output from the generator, with timing according to E_c and slope set by I_t and C_t.

The key to higher speed is that A_1 does not see the high rate of voltage change—it is isolated by the collector of Q_1. Since Q_2 is a high-speed device, the real limitation on sweep speed is buffer A_2, which must be faster than the fastest trace (or retrace) of the saw-tooth voltage across C_t.

As shown, the circuit does not tax the speed capability of A_2 to any great extent except during the retrace interval. Retrace time is set by R_5 and C_t; R_5 is chosen for a compromise between the length of the retrace and the dc voltage drop due to I_t, since I_t-R_5 sets the baseline voltage of the circuit. Generally, R_5 values on the order of 100 Ω give satisfactory performance.

The values in this example are chosen as typical of a tv raster—a period of 63.5 μs, with approximately 50 μs active. Thus, E_o has a 0.2-V/μs rate of rise, or 10 V in 50 μs. The indicated values are precise, but R_3 may be trimmed to set the output slope. If independence of slope from the $+15$-V line is desired, R_1 may be changed to a 3-V zener or a higher-voltage zener with 3 V of reference voltage applied between $+15$ V and the $(+)$ input of A_1.

7.5.3 Long Period Timer

The two previous circuits are variations of the same type—i.e., driven sawtooth generators. The next circuit differs in that it responds to input triggers; after triggering it generates a single saw-tooth of prescribed duration, then returns to the standby state. It is similar to the monostable multivibrator, but in this case the timing ramp is buffered for external use. The circuit is also capable of extremely short recovery times, thus allowing immediate retriggering.

As shown in Fig. 7-24, this timer consists basically of a transistor switch (Q_1), a timing network (R_t-C_t), a buffer (A_1), and a comparator (A_2). The state of switch Q_1 is controlled by the comparator, which receives trigger pulses from an external source.

In the standby state, output E_{o_2} is high, clamped at $+V_z$ by D_1-D_2. This voltage holds Q_1 in the on state via R_6, and output E_{o_1} remains near zero volts. In this condition, the feedback path through R_1-R_2 scales the $+V_z$ voltage at E_{o_2} to $+V_zR_2(R_1 + R_2)$ at the $(+)$ input of A_2; for this example, the input voltage of A_2 is $+V_z/2$. Thus, a trigger pulse of $+(V_z/2 + V_f)$ volts at D_3 (or D_4) is required to overcome the bias on A_2, where V_f is the diode voltage drop. This positive pulse switches A_2 to the low state, which disables clamp

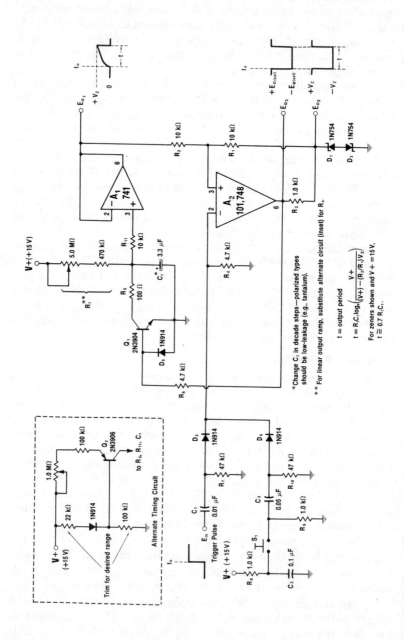

Fig. 7-24. Op-amp timer circuit.

Q_1. C_t then begins timing toward +15 V with a time constant of R_tC_t. The voltage at E_{o_1} required to reset A_2 will be $-(-V_ZR_2/R_1)$; in this case, simply $+V_Z$. When E_{o_1} reaches $+V_Z$, A_2 switches to the high state, shorting C_t and resetting the circuit to its standby state. The action is extremely fast due to the small time constant formed by R_5C_t and the fact that there is some regeneration for the reset mode (whereas none exists for the trigger mode). The circuit will thus respond almost instantly to a second trigger pulse after reset.

The timing equation for this circuit is dependent upon V+, zener voltage V_Z, and R_tC_t, according to

$$t = R_tC_t\log_e\left(\frac{V+}{(V+) - (R_2/R_1)V_Z}\right).$$

In the present example, V+ = 15 V, V_Z = 7.5 V, and $R_1 = R_2$, so the timing expression becomes

$$t = 0.7\ R_tC_t.$$

As shown, the circuit is suitable for timing periods of up to 10 seconds with R_t maximum, but larger values of C_t can be used for longer periods. R_t can also be increased, but there is an upper limit of about 5 MΩ in standard potentiometer values. C_t can be switch-selected for decade timing changes—good-quality capacitors should be used, such as tantalum electrolytics for large values or polycarbonate types for lower values. The 741 is a good choice for A_1 in general-purpose applications, but A_2 should be uncompensated to optimize its triggering capability. The push-button trigger circuit shown is designed to minimize the effects of switch bounce; S_1 triggers only on actuation, not on release.

The three circuit outputs consist of two timing gates from A_2, which are negative during the timing interval, and the sawtooth output, which rises exponentially toward $+V_Z$. Generally, for a timer the gate is the working output, but the sawtooth output may also be useful. If a linear sawtooth is desired, the alternate timing network in the inset can be used. It is designed to give the same times for a given value of C_t, and it has a comparable timing range.

7.5.4 Synchronized Sawtooth Oscillator

The sawtooth generators described thus far have been either driven or triggered types, both of which require an external oscillator for excitation. Drive sources for these circuits can be made from any of the astable oscillators described previously, but it is sometimes advantageous to make the sweep-generating functions part of the same circuit. An example of this is the sawtooth oscillator of Fig. 7-25, which is a source of both sawtooth and pulse waveforms, capable of being externally synchronized.

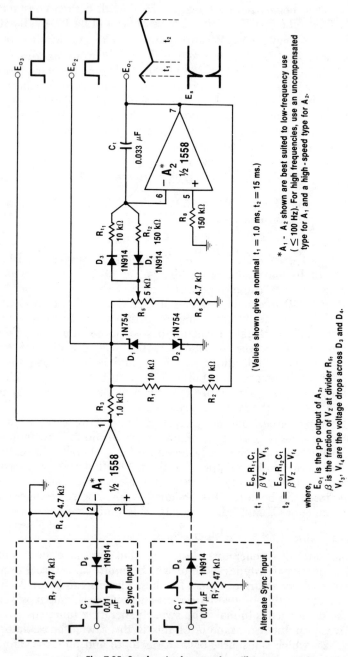

*A_1 - A_2 shown are best suited to low-frequency use
(≤ 100 Hz). For high frequencies, use an uncompensated
type for A_1 and a high-speed type for A_2.

(Values shown give a nominal $t_1 = 1.0$ ms, $t_2 = 15$ ms.)

$$t_1 = \frac{E_{o_1} R_{11} C_1}{\beta V_Z - V_{f_3}}$$

$$t_2 = \frac{E_{o_1} R_{12} C_1}{\beta V_Z - V_{f_4}}$$

where,

E_{o_1} is the p-p output of A_2,
β is the fraction of V_Z at divider R_5,
V_{f_3}, V_{f_4} are the voltage drops across D_3 and D_4.

Fig. 7-25. Synchronized sawtooth oscillator.

This circuit may be recognized as similar to the function generator of Fig. 7-17A, with suitable modifications for the sawtooth asymmetry, tunability, and synchronization. The use of D_3 and D_4 in series with R_{t_1} and R_{t_2} allows the negative and positive slopes to be set simply and independently. Tuning of the circuit is set by the variable-β network, R_5-R_6. If the negative output slope has duration t_1 and the positive slope has duration t_2, the design equations for these periods are

$$t_1 = \frac{E_{o_1} R_{t_1} C_t}{\beta V_z - V_{f_3}}$$

and

$$t_2 = \frac{E_{o_1} R_{t_2} C_t}{\beta V_z - V_{f_4}},$$

where V_{f_3} and V_{f_4} are the forward voltage drops of D_3 and D_4 respectively.

The circuit components here are chosen to be compatible with a 60-Hz sweep generator. R_{t_1} is set at $R_{t_2}/15$, yielding a trace/retrace ratio of 15 ($t_2 = 15$ ms and $t_1 = 1.0$ ms). R_5 provides a variation of 0.5:1 to allow tuning over a 2:1 range. In practice, frequency control R_5 is set for a natural frequency slightly lower than the incoming sync pulses. R_{t_1} and R_{t_2} may be altered to yield virtually any desired degree of asymmetry for various other applications.

The sync input, E_s, may be applied to either the $(-)$ or $(+)$ input of A_1, depending on the type of pulse available. Synchronization for either input occurs at the beginning of the t_1 interval.

Since this design example chosen is one of low frequency, an internally compensated amplifier may be used for A_1, such as the 741 (or 1558). As previously, three outputs are available: the sawtooth, E_{o_1}, and the two rectangular outputs, E_{o_2} and E_{o_3}. This circuit is a very useful one, and the substitution of high-speed op amps will allow its application over a wide range of frequencies.

7.6 VOLTAGE-CONTROLLED SIGNAL GENERATION AND MODULATION

An extension of basic op-amp circuit design is the adaptation to voltage control. Voltage-controlled functions and modulation techniques are extremely useful in instrumentation and control systems. By making some function of a periodic waveform vary according to another voltage, it is possible to transmit dc or low-frequency information as a modulated carrier, often with greater accuracy and greater convenience. This section examines basic op-amp techniques used to produce amplitude modulation, pulse-width modulation, and frequency modulation.

7.6.1 Pulse-Amplitude Modulator

A simple form of encoding a low-frequency signal on a carrier is by pulse-amplitude modulation, as in Fig. 7-26. This circuit processes a bipolar pulse carrier, E_c, by clamping its positive and negative excursions with diodes D_1 and D_2. D_2 clamps the negative peak of E_o to a voltage -0.6 V lower than the bias voltage of D_3, or zero

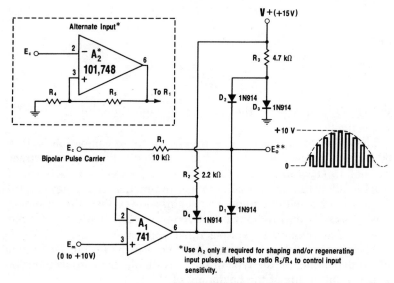

Fig. 7-26. Pulse-amplitude modulator.

volts, since the forward drops of D_2 and D_3 cancel. D_1 and D_4 perform a similar function for the positive peaks, clamping them to the voltage at the anode of D_4, which is E_m, provided by voltage follower A_1. The connection of D_1 and D_4 is arranged to cancel their forward drops and temperature coefficients, and to clamp E_o to E_m. Thus, as E_m varies from 0 to $+10$ V, the positive peaks of E_o vary in accordance, accomplishing amplitude modulation of the E_o pulses.

This circuit by nature has a high output impedance, essentially the value of R_1. A buffer may be required for low-impedance loads. The input voltage, E_c, should always be greater than the most positive peak of E_m for effective clamping. If E_c is small, some amplification may be necessary. This can be provided by a comparator such as A_2, which regenerates the input pulses to full amplitude with uniform rise and fall times.

As shown, the circuit responds to positive modulating voltages and delivers positive output pulses. For negative-going outputs, reverse all diodes, change the bias to -15 V, and let E_m vary from 0 V to -10 V. If minimum temperature drift of the clamping voltages is not required, the circuit can be simplified by wiring A_1 as a standard follower, with D_1 connected to its output and D_2 connected directly to ground.

7.6.2 Voltage-Controlled Monostable Circuit (Voltage to Pulse-Width Converter)

A monostable multivibrator that delivers an output pulse width proportional to an input voltage can be used as a pulse-width modulator (or voltage to pulse-width converter); Fig. 7-27 is such a circuit. The highly linear and precisely controlled ramp used to time the output pulse width is made available as an output. Hence, this circuit can also be used as a triggered voltage-controlled sweep generator. The circuit consists of two basic parts: a voltage-controlled integrator (A_1) and a threshold comparator (A_2). A_1 generates a voltage ramp with slope controlled by E_{in}, R_t, and C_t. A_2 controls the ramp-limit voltage. Pulse width t_c is determined by

$$t_c = \frac{E_{o_1} R_t C_t}{E_{in}} .$$

In the quiescent state, A_2 is high, holding Q_1 in saturation and clamping the output of A_1 at a voltage near ground. The circuit is stable in this state, since positive feedback from E_{o_2} holds the $(+)$ input of A_2 at $+V_Z R_1/R_2$, a voltage greater than the ground level on its $(-)$ input.

A negative trigger pulse at E_t greater than this bias will flip the comparator to the negative output state, which turns off Q_1 and starts a negative ramp of voltage from A_1. The output from A_1 decreases linearly with a slope of $R_t C_t / E_{in}$ volts per second. This voltage appears at the $(-)$ input of A_2, attenuated by a factor of $R_4/(R_4 + R_5)$. Furthermore, the negative threshold of A_2 is at $-V_Z R_1/(R_1 + R_2)$. Thus, if the ratios R_2/R_1 and R_5/R_4 are made equal, the comparator threshold voltage is simply $-V_Z$. When E_{o_1} crosses $-V_Z$, then, A_2 flips back to the positive (stable) state, which saturates Q_1, discharging C_t through R_8. This returns the circuit to its original state, ready for a second trigger pulse. The circuit has three outputs: the ramp output from A_1 (or E_{o_1}), and the two comparator outputs, E_{o_2} and E_{o_3}. As may be noted from the timing of E_{o_1}, the recovery time (t_r) of the ramp makes the total cycle time slightly in excess of t_c (the time duration of E_{o_2} and E_{o_3}). Controlling the recovery time of A_1 can involve either adjusting the simple RC time

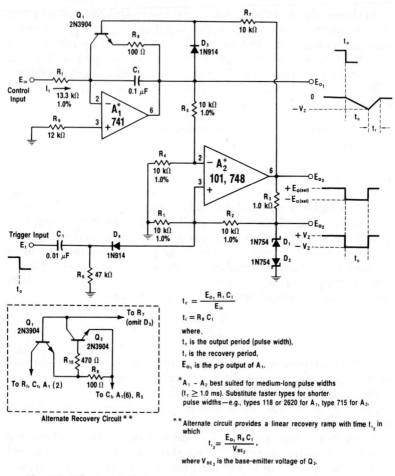

$$t_c = \frac{E_{o_1} R_1 C_1}{E_{in}}$$

$$t_r = R_5 C_1$$

where,

t_c is the output period (pulse width),

t_r is the recovery period,

E_{o_1} is the p-p output of A_1.

*$A_1 - A_2$ best suited for medium-long pulse widths ($t_c \geq 1.0$ ms). Substitute faster types for shorter pulse widths—e.g., types 118 or 2620 for A_1, type 715 for A_2.

**Alternate circuit provides a linear recovery ramp with time t_{r_2} in which

$$t_{r_2} = \frac{E_{o_1} R_8 C_1}{V_{BE_2}},$$

where V_{BE_2} is the base-emitter voltage of Q_2.

Fig. 7-27. Voltage-controlled monostable circuit (voltage to pulse-width converter).

constant of t_r, as shown, or if a more linear recovery ramp is desired, an alternate recovery circuit is given in the inset. This optional circuit uses transistor Q_2 to monitor the emitter current of Q_1 during capacitor discharge. The emitter current of Q_1 is maintained constant by Q_2, which provides a linear recovery ramp with time t_{r_2}, where

$$t_{r_2} = \frac{E_{o_1} R_8 C_t}{V_{BE_2}}$$

and V_{BE_2} is the base-emitter voltage of Q_2. In either discharge circuit, it is necessary to prevent possible base-emitter breakdown of

Q_1 due to the high p-p swing of E_{o_3} ($\pm E_{o(sat)}$). The basic circuit provides this through D_3. In the modified circuit, D_3 is unnecessary because the same function is provided by the base-collector junction of Q_2.

The circuit responds to positive input voltages at E_{in}. With E_{in} = +1.0 V, t_c is 10 ms, decreasing to 1.0 ms at E_{in} = +10 V. Longer times are possible by scaling R_t or C_t. For shorter pulse widths, a faster integrator should be used for A_1, such as a 118 or a compensated 2620. Also, A_2 should be speed-optimized for microsecond pulse widths; this can take the form of a 715 op amp and high-speed (transistor) diodes for D_1-D_2.

7.6.3 Voltage-Controlled Sawtooth/Pulse Generator (Voltage-to-Frequency Converter)

With some modification of the circuit just described, it can become an oscillating sawtooth/pulse generator, with period (or frequency) controlled by an external voltage. This circuit is shown in Fig. 7-28. A_1 is an integrator that generates a negative-going sawtooth waveform with slope determined by E_{in}, R_t, and C_t. A_2 is a threshold comparator, and Q_1 is a switch used to reset the ramp at the end of the negative sawtooth.

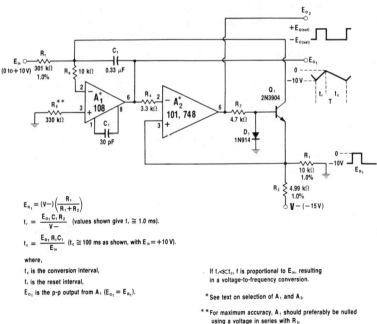

$$E_{R_1} = (V-)\left(\frac{R_1}{R_1+R_2}\right)$$

$$t_r = \frac{E_{o_1} C_1 R_2}{V-} \quad \text{(values shown give } t_r \cong 1.0 \text{ ms).}$$

$$t_c = \frac{E_{o_1} R_t C_1}{E_{in}} \quad (t_c \cong 100 \text{ ms as shown, with } E_{in} = +10 \text{ V).}$$

where,

t_c is the conversion interval,

t_r is the reset interval,

E_{o_1} is the p-p output from A_1 ($E_{o_1} = E_{R_1}$).

If $t_r \ll t_c$, f is proportional to E_{in}, resulting in a voltage-to-frequency conversion.

* See text on selection of A_1 and A_2.

** For maximum accuracy, A_1 should preferably be nulled using a voltage in series with R_5.

Fig. 7-28. Voltage-controlled pulse/sawtooth generator.

The circuit may be best understood if A_2 is assumed to be in a low state, with A_1 beginning a negative ramp. When A_2 is low, Q_1 will be off and its emitter will rest at the voltage set by divider R_1-R_2 (in this case, -10 V). This voltage sets the negative threshold of comparator A_2. The negative ramp interval, t_c, is

$$t_c = \frac{E_{o_1} R_t C_t}{E_{in}},$$

where E_{o_1} is the (p-p) output of A_1 (10 V).

As the output ramp of A_1 crosses -10 V, A_2 flips to the high state, driving Q_1 on. When initially turned on, Q_1 is clamped at its base by D_1; thus its emitter will initially rest at zero volts. The maximum current through Q_1 is set by the negative supply and by R_2, and this current is used to discharge C_t by extracting it from the summing point of A_1. The duration of the reset interval, t_r, is given by

$$t_r = \frac{E_{o_1} C_t R_2}{V-}.$$

The reset period ends when C_t is discharged to zero; A_2 then flips back to the low state, starting a new t_c period.

A previous equation shows that t_c is inversely proportional to E_{in}, thus the circuit can be used as a voltage-controlled sawtooth or pulse generator, where E_{in} controls the interval t_c for either E_{o_1} or E_{o_2}. The total period of the circuit is, of course, $T = t_r + t_c$. Since the pulse repetition frequency is $f_o = 1/T$, it can also be seen that if $t_r \ll t_c$, then $T \cong t_c$. This allows the circuit to be used as a voltage-to-frequency converter, in which case f_o is directly proportional to E_{in}.

The circuit shown has a reset interval of approximately 1.0 ms; t_c is 100 ms when E_{in} is $+10$ V. No offset null is shown on A_1 since the 108 is a low-offset device. However, if the circuit is to be used with a large dynamic range for E_{in} (i.e., if E_{in} can be very small), the input offset can contribute significant error. In such cases, offset can be nulled by introducing a small voltage at the $(+)$ input of A_1.

Higher-speed options for this circuit are possible, and these generally follow the considerations of Fig. 7-27. If a positive ramp output is desired, D_1 can be reversed, a pnp equivalent substituted for Q_1, and R_2 connected to $+15$ V. In this case, the circuit will respond to negative voltages at E_{in}.

REFERENCES

1. *Applications Manual for Computing Amplifiers.* Philbrick Researches, Inc., Dedham, Mass., 1966.

2. Clayton, G. B. *Operational Amplifiers.* Butterworth, Inc., Toronto, Ont., Canada, 1971.

3. Dobkin, R. C. *Op Amp Circuit Collection.* National Semiconductor Application Note AN-31, February 1970. National Semiconductor Corp., Santa Clara, Calif.

4. Giles, J. N. *Fairchild Semiconductor LIC Handbook.* Fairchild Semiconductor, Mountain View, Calif., 1967.

5. Miler, G. G. *A Simple Square-Triangle Waveform Generator.* Harris Semiconductor Application Note 510/A, October 1970. Harris Semiconductor, Melbourne, Fla.

6. Olson, H. "Use Diodes for Amplitude Control in 0.001 Hz Wien Bridge Oscillator." *Electronic Design,* April 1, 1972.

7. Routh, W. S. *An Applications Guide for Operational Amplifiers.* National Semiconductor Application Note AN-20, February 1969. National Semiconductor Corp., Santa Clara, Calif.

8. Smith, J. I. *Modern Operational Circuit Design.* John Wiley & Sons, Inc., New York, 1971.

9. Tobey, G. E.; Graeme, J. G.; Huelsman, L. P. *Operational Amplifiers—Design and Applications.* Burr-Brown Research Corp., McGraw-Hill Book Co., New York, 1971.

10. Widlar, R. J. *Drift Compensation Techniques for Integrated DC Amplifiers.* National Semiconductor Application Note AN-3, November 1967. National Semiconductor Corp., Santa Clara, Calif.

11. _____. *IC Op Amp Beats FETs on Input Current.* National Semiconductor Application Note AN-29, December 1969. National Semiconductor Corp., Santa Clara, Calif.

12. _____. *Monolithic Operational Amplifiers—The Universal Linear Component.* National Semiconductor Application Note AN-4, April 1968. National Semiconductor Corp., Santa Clara, Calif.

8

Unique Op-Amp Devices

This chapter explores the uses of a number of additional devices, those with characteristics that set them apart from previous amplifiers. Some are modified types of op amps and are applied by using the same general principles and axioms as before; others are totally unique, allowing applications not possible with standard op amps.

The unique devices, introduced briefly as Group V in Chapter 2, can be divided into three or four general categories. There are the programmable amplifiers, typified by the 4250 and 776, the 2400, and the 3080 and 3094. Of these, two additional classifications can be made. The 4250, 776, 3080, and 3094 are programmable in terms of quiescent power—the value of the programming current used can adjust various operating characteristics. Though all these types are similar in this respect, they differ in that the 4250 and 776 function as standard op amps, while the 3080 and 3094 are not, strictly speaking, true op amps. The latter two are operational transconductance amplifiers (OTAs), and this important distinction will be covered later.

Another variation is evident in the type 2400, an op amp that is programmable in a different sense: the programming current is used to select one of four differential-input stages, but the operating characteristics and quiescent current of each stage remain fixed.

The final category discussed is the CDA, or current-differencing amplifier. These are highly specialized amplifiers, not op amps at all by the strict definition; however, they are quite useful and, once understood, they can be applied with facility.

As in Chapter 5, a number of circuits presented in this chapter are modifications or adaptations of circuits obtained from manufacturers' data sheets. Figs. 8-51 through 8-53 originate from RCA application notes; Figs. 8-7, 8-9 through 8-11, 8-75 through 8-80, 8-86, and 8-87 are from material supplied by National Semiconductor.

8.1 PROGRAMMABLE OP AMPS

The 4250 and the 776 amplifiers can be described as both programmable characteristic amplifiers and as micropower amplifiers, for with their adjustable quiescent current they can be operated at very low standby power levels. Furthermore, both can be operated over a wide range of supply voltages (± 1.0 V to ± 18 V); they are highly suited to battery-operated systems, as well as to conventional power supplies.

8.1.1 The LM4250

A circuit diagram for the LM4250 is shown in Fig. 8-1. The pin arrangement and offset null are similar to the 741, and internal com-

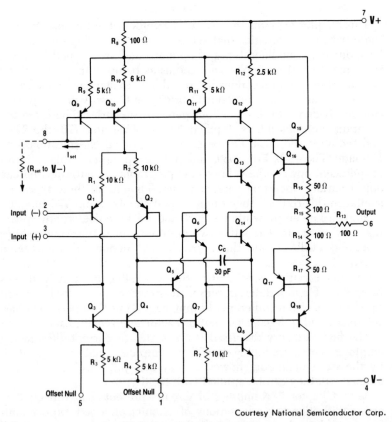

Courtesy National Semiconductor Corp.

Fig. 8-1. LM4250 schematic.

pensation is achieved with C_C, a 30-pF capacitor. In basic form this amplifier resembles the 741-101 combination since it incorporates a two-stage design.

The main feature of the LM4250 is the manner of biasing, which is accomplished by a single master bias terminal (pin 8). An external resistance from this terminal to V− (or to ground, in some instances) establishes an operating current in Q_9, called I_{set}. Q_{10}, Q_{11}, and Q_{12} are in parallel with Q_9, and they conduct currents proportional to I_{set}. Thus, it can be seen that I_{set} establishes the operating current for all stages of the circuit, and that variations in I_{set} will affect operating characteristics. The removal of I_{set} turns the amplifier off completely by removing current from the various stages, which has the same effect as removing power.

The key amplifier parameters governed by I_{set} are open-loop gain, gain-bandwidth, input bias current, input noise, slew rate, and standby (or quiescent) power. The dynamic range of I_{set} is specified from a maximum of 100 μA down to 100 nA. The low end of this range can be extended if desired, but operating parameters are specified only for I_{set} values greater than 100 nA.

8.1.2 The μA776

As shown in Fig. 8-2, the μA776 circuit resembles the LM4250, but with a few variations that can be significant in certain applications. Although schematically different, both amplifiers are functionally alike and their performance specifications are similar. They use the same pin configuration, are nulled identically, and may often be used interchangeably.

The major difference between the LM4250 and the μA776 is in the input stage. The LM4250 uses pnp transistors, Q_1-Q_2, as a simple differential pair. This gives rise to several advantages: a very constant β-versus-temperature curve, the ability to operate at common-mode voltages close to the V− supply (typically within 200 mV of V−), and a very low minimum supply voltage, ±1.0 V. The μA776, on the other hand, offers low input currents (for the same value of I_{set}) because of the higher β of npn types, but it has a greater bias current variation with temperature. The μA776 also has a common-mode input range that is 2 V_{BE} higher than the LM4250, due to the npn-pnp cascode arrangement, but with a slightly higher minimum supply voltage of ±1.2 V. These points should be considered in applications where interchangeability is a question.

8.1.3 General Characteristics, LM4250 and μA776

In many instances, programmability can make a single device perform the work of many. For example, at the upper limit of I_{set}, both the LM4250 and μA776 have characteristics similar to (or superior

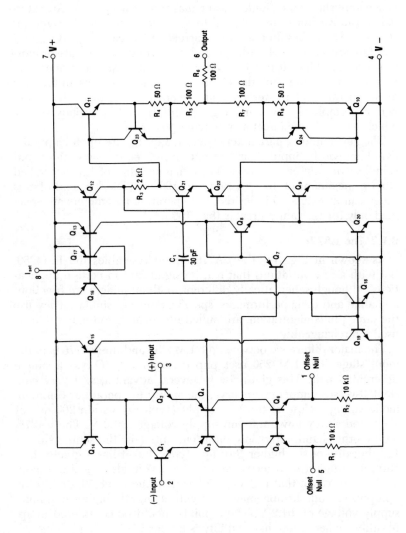

Courtesy Fairchild Semiconductor

Fig. 8-2. μA776 schematic.

to) the general-purpose 741. At lower I_{set} values, they can be used with input currents as low as 1-10 nA, thus placing them in the super-β class. Input offset voltages change very little over the total operating range of I_{set}, which is a great advantage. Finally, these amplifiers have an extremely wide range of operating voltage, ± 1.0 V to ± 18 V for the LM4250, and ± 1.2 V to ± 18 V for the μA776, to accommodate virtually any type of power supply, even a pair of 1.5-V flashlight cells. With programmable op amps, then, the user has a

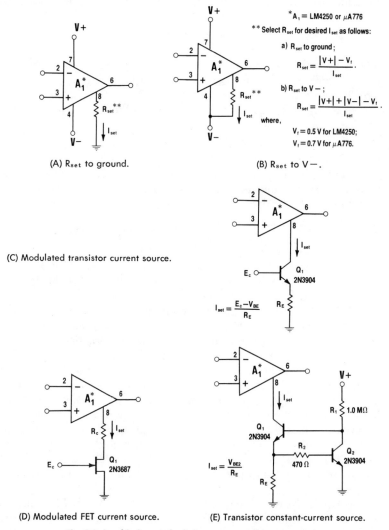

(A) R_{set} to ground.

(B) R_{set} to V−.

(C) Modulated transistor current source.

(D) Modulated FET current source.

(E) Transistor constant-current source.

Fig. 8-3. I_{set} biasing methods for programmable op amps.

great number of options for using the same stock device, and in most applications, the extra complexity needed to realize this versatility is just a single additional resistor.

Biasing Methods

The LM4250 and μA776 are biased identically, and several methods used to establish the I_{set} bias are illustrated in Fig. 8-3. The simplest and most direct method is a resistor, R_{set}, connected to ground. For a desired value of I_{set}, this resistance is determined by

$$R_{set} = \frac{|V+| - V_f}{I_{set}},$$

where V_f is the diode drop of the master bias transistor (0.5 V for the LM4250 and 0.7 V for the μA776). With low supply voltages, it may be more desirable to return R_{set} to V− instead of ground, as shown in Fig. 8-3B. The equation for R_{set} is then

$$R_{set} = \frac{|V+| + |V-| - V_f}{I_{set}}.$$

As an example, suppose the power supply used gives ±1.5 V and we want a resistor connected to V− (from pin 8) that will establish I_{set} at 1.0 μA for the LM4250:

$$R_{set} = \frac{+3.0 \text{ V} - 0.5 \text{ V}}{1.0 \times 10^{-6} \text{A}} = 2.5 \times 10^6 \ \Omega = 2.5 \text{ M}\Omega.$$

Under similar conditions, R_{set} would be slightly less (2.3 MΩ) for the μA776, and the R_{set} values would be smaller still if the resistors were returned to ground instead of V− (1.5 MΩ and 800 kΩ). For convenience, the manufacturers provide charts of R_{set} values for various values of I_{set} (see Fig. 8-4). These tables are calculated from the equation for R_{set} connected to V−, and, in practice, the closest standard resistance value should be used. For dynamic control of I_{set}, a modulated current source can be substituted for R_{set} as shown in Figs. 8-3C and 8-3D. Either of these circuits have the property of resisting changes in I_{set} due to supply voltage changes. Fig. 8-3C is a simple transistor current source that programs I_{set} according to the values of E_c and R_E. E_c can be used to vary I_{set} or to switch the amplifier on and off. Variations of this circuit include returning R_E to V− instead of to ground, and/or connecting the resistance to the collector side of Q_1 and operating Q_1 as a common-emitter saturated switch.

An extremely wide range of I_{set} variation is attainable with the FET current source of Fig. 8-3D. If the device shown for Q_1 is used, a change of 0.5 V in gate voltage will vary I_{set} over its full range.

V_s	I_{set}				
	$0.1\,\mu A$	$0.5\,\mu A$	$1.0\,\mu A$	$5\,\mu A$	$10\,\mu A$
± 1.5 V	25.6 MΩ	5.04 MΩ	2.5 MΩ	492 kΩ	244 kΩ
± 3.0 V	55.6 MΩ	11.0 MΩ	5.5 MΩ	1.09 MΩ	544 kΩ
± 6.0 V	116 MΩ	23.0 MΩ	11.5 MΩ	2.29 MΩ	1.14 MΩ
± 9.0 V	176 MΩ	35.0 MΩ	17.5 MΩ	3.49 MΩ	1.74 MΩ
±12.0 V	236 MΩ	47.0 MΩ	23.5 MΩ	4.69 MΩ	2.34 MΩ
± 15.0 V	296 MΩ	59.0 MΩ	29.5 MΩ	5.89 MΩ	2.94 MΩ

Courtesy National Semiconductor Corp.

(A) LM4250.

(B) μA776.

V_s	I_{set}	
	$1.5\,\mu A$	$15\,\mu A$
± 1.5 V	1.7 MΩ	170 kΩ
± 3.0 V	3.6 MΩ	360 kΩ
± 6.0 V	7.5 MΩ	750 kΩ
± 15 V	20 MΩ	2.0 MΩ

Courtesy Fairchild Semiconductor

Fig. 8-4. R_{set} for various I_{set} and V_s values.

Some series resistance (R_c) should be included to limit the maximum drain current through Q_1.

A circuit that programs a specific value of I_{set} and regulates it over a wide range of supply voltages is shown in Fig. 8-3E. Q_2 regulates the collecter current of Q_1 by sensing the voltage across R_E. Since I_{set} is ultimately regulated by the V_{BE} of Q_2, it will have the same temperature variance (approximately 0.3%/°C); with the low collector currents and "V_{BE} sensing" provided by Q_2, very low supply potentials can be used. The circuit shown can work with V+ potentials as low as +3.0 V, and a ±1.5-V power supply can be used if R_E and the emitter of Q_2 are returned to V− instead of to ground.

Programming for Desired Characteristics

The next consideration before applying the LM4250 or μA776 is the dependence of various operating parameters on I_{set}. The key parameters controlled by I_{set} are illustrated graphically in Figs. 8-5 and 8-6.

In terms of power consumption, the graph of supply current versus I_{set} shows that both amplifiers use essentially a constant idle current with varying supply voltage, as long as I_{set} is constant. For a given value of I_{set}, both have a quiescent current approximately 10 times the I_{set} value, with the LM4250 slightly better in this regard (lower current, thus lower power consumption).

Input bias current is also relatively unaffected by supply voltage when I_{set} is constant. As can be seen from comparing the graphs, the μA776 is significantly better in terms of input current for a given I_{set}, with an I_{ib} roughly five times smaller than that of the LM4250.

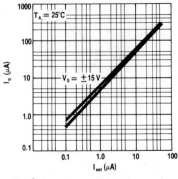

(A) Quiescent current vs set current.

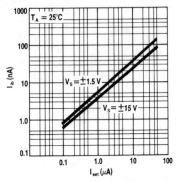

(B) Input bias current vs set current.

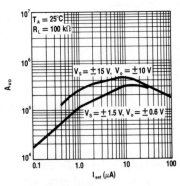

(C) Open-loop gain vs set current.

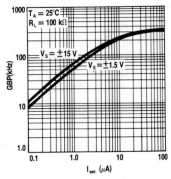

(D) Gain-bandwidth product vs set current.

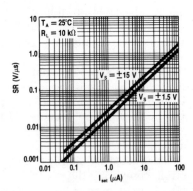

(E) Slew rate vs set current.

Courtesy National Semiconductor Corp.

Fig. 8-5. LM4250 characteristics for various I_{set} values.

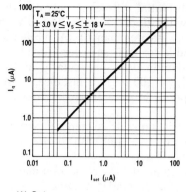

(A) Quiescent current vs set current.

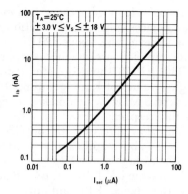

(B) Input bias current vs set current.

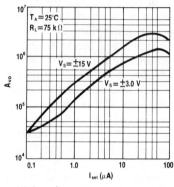

(C) Open-loop gain vs set current.

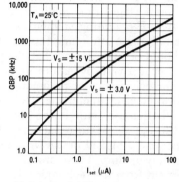

(D) Gain-bandwidth product vs set current.

(E) Slew rate vs set current.

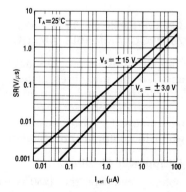

Courtesy Fairchild Semiconductor

Fig. 8-6. µA776 characteristics for various I_{set} values.

411

In open-loop gain there is a substantial difference between the two devices, plus some variation with supply voltage. The μA776 can achieve gains above 120 dB at I_{set} greater than 10 μA, while the two amplifiers are roughly comparable for gain at lower I_{set} values.

The μA776 shows greater gain-bandwidths, particularly at the higher values of I_{set}. Operating at $I_{set} = 100$ μA, for instance, it has an f_t of 5 MHz, which makes it superior to general-purpose devices in this respect.

The slew rate of both amplifiers is superior to general-purpose devices (above approximately 10 μA of I_{set}), and with the μA776 it can be as high as 5.0 V/μs (at $I_{set} = 100\mu$A).

While the LM4250 and μA776 are generally the same, one may be a better choice if the optimization of a particular parameter is desired. In addition to the I_{set}-dependent parameters, there is the consideration of supply voltage range. As noted previously, the LM4250 is slightly better in this regard because of the lower bias threshold of its input stage, thus allowing operation with supplies as low as ± 1.0 V. If operating voltage and power consumption must be kept to an absolute minimum, this can be a significant factor. In general, it should be appreciated that the programmability of either an LM-4250 or a μA776 by nature involves trade-offs and that optimizing I_{set} for one particular parameter may well sacrifice another desired performance characteristic. The most obvious of these trade-offs is a speed decrease with lower power, evidenced by both gain-band-width and slew-rate reductions. At a given I_{set}, the parameters of either the LM4250 or μA776 must be used in an error analysis as with any op amp. These procedures with programmable types are no different from the techniques used in previous chapters; in this case it just happens that there are an infinite set of conditions from which to choose!

8.2 APPLICATIONS OF TYPES 4250 AND 776 PROGRAMMABLE AMPLIFIERS

The applications of programmable amplifiers such as the types 4250 and 776 fall into three general classes: (1) micropower; (2) switched capability; and (3) modified standard applications, which utilize the variable characteristics to optimize one or more performance parameters. In this discussion, emphasis will be placed on the first two of these application categories.

8.2.1 Micropower Circuits

As noted previously, the 4250 is capable of operating from supplies as low as ± 1.0 V and is characterized at ± 1.5 V. With very low values of I_{set}, this makes it possible to have circuits with total power dissipations less than 1.0 μW. Since the typical shelf life of a 1.35-V mercury cell will not be affected by a power drain as high as 15 μW, it is entirely feasible to operate such circuits continuously without degradation of battery life.

The circuit of Fig. 8-7 is an example of extreme power economy; with a supply voltage of $V_S = \pm 1.0$ V, the total power consumption is only 500 nW. R_{set} is connected to ground rather than V− in this circuit. Amplifier current drain is about 200 nA from each side (400 nW) and R_{set} consumes approximately 50 nW, thus making the total less than 500 nW. This value is not in strict agreement with Fig. 8-5 because the current-voltage region here is beyond the point where the data is completely valid. In this case the curves are pessimistic, and actual power drain is less than the graphs of Fig. 8-5 would indicate.

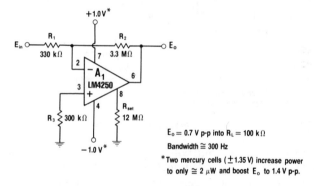

$E_o = 0.7$ V p-p into $R_L = 100$ kΩ
Bandwidth $\cong$ 300 Hz
*Two mercury cells (± 1.35 V) increase power to only $\cong 2$ μW and boost E_o to 1.4 V p-p.

Fig. 8-7. 500-nW amplifier.

Using standard 1.35-V mercury cells increases power consumption to only 1.0 μW and also increases E_o to 1.4 V p-p. If micropower circuits, such as those in Fig. 8-7, are set up with higher values of I_{set} (in order to approach the 15-μW-per-cell limit), appreciably better gain, bandwidth, and slew-rate properties can be realized with no appreciable sacrifice of battery life. For instance, drain can be increased to 11 μA per cell (corresponding to $I_{set} \cong 2.0$ μA) with appreciably greater speed (higher GBP and slew rate).

Other considerations of low-power operation are perhaps more obvious. Feedback resistances must be kept large to minimize their current drain, and in general any excessive loading is to be avoided. Feedback resistances in the megohm range present no problem with ultra-low-power operation since input currents are in the nanoamp region. By applying these considerations, virtually any of the standard op-amp configurations discussed earlier can be adapted to low-power versions.

8.2.2 Metering Circuits

Some extremely useful applications of battery-powered op amps are found in portable meter circuitry. Battery operation gives both portability and completely floating operation. The high gain, low bias current, and low offset voltage of the op amp allow precision dc measurements down to the nanoamp and millivolt regions.

A basic meter amplifier circuit is shown in Fig. 8-8. Amplifier A_1 is used as a current-to-voltage converter, and the input current, I_{in},

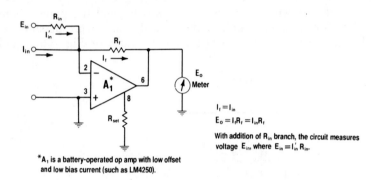

$$I_f = I_{in}$$
$$E_o = I_f R_f = I_{in} R_f$$

With addition of R_{in} branch, the circuit measures voltage E_{in}, where $E_{in} = I'_{in} R_{in}$.

*A_1 is a battery-operated op amp with low offset and low bias current (such as LM4250).

Fig. 8-8. Basic meter amplifier.

is converted to an output voltage, E_o, where $E_o = I_{in}R_f$. If A_1 is a low-power, battery-operated device such as the 4250, this conversion will be fairly accurate, generally more accurate than the meter movement used to read it. The offset null of A_1 can be used to minimize input offset voltage error, and if programmed for a low bias current, the amplifier can convert currents on the order of 100 nA with errors less than 1.0%. Voltages are measured by the addition of R_{in}, which converts the circuit to voltmeter operation.

A circuit that can be used as either a low-current ammeter or a voltmeter is shown in Fig. 8-9A. Here the 4250 is operated from a pair of 1.5-V flashlight cells and is programmed for an I_{set} of 100 nA. This provides input currents of less than 1.0 nA for low error due to bias current. R_1 adjusts the 50-μA meter movement for calibration, while R_2 nulls input offset voltage.

Resistor R_f' is used on the two lowest current ranges and the three lowest voltage ranges to compensate for bias current error in R_f. The floating input arrangement (when R_f' is used) may appear unusual at first glance since the path for input current is not obvious (the path is through R_f', the amplifier, and R_f). However, the input terminals are held at zero voltage difference, which is the ideal method of measuring current. When R_f' is used, the (+) input ref-

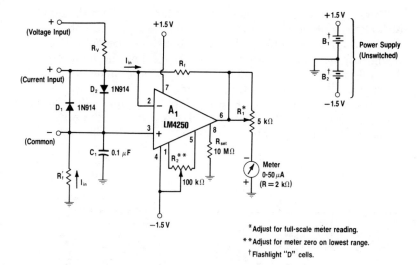

(A) Circuit schematic.

* Adjust for full-scale meter reading.
** Adjust for meter zero on lowest range.
† Flashlight "D" cells.

Resistance Values for DC Nano- and Microammeter

I (Full Scale)	R_f (Ω)	R_f' (Ω)
100 nA	1.5 M	1.5 M
500 nA	300 k	300 k
1.0 μA	300 k	0
5.0 μA	60 k	0
10 μA	30 k	0
50 μA	6.0 k	0
100 μA	3.0 k	0

Resistance Values for DC Voltmeter

V (Full Scale)	R_v (Ω)	R_f (Ω)	R_f' (Ω)
10 mV	100 k	1.5 M	1.5 M
100 mV	1.0 M	1.5M	1.5 M
1.0 V	10 M	1.5 M	1.5 M
10 V	10 M	300 k	0
100 V	10 M	30 k	0

(B) Values for various full-scale readings.

Fig. 8-9. Dc low-current ammeter and voltmeter.

erence terminal will assume a voltage of $-I_{in}R_f'$. Due to the zero input voltage differential, the $(-)$ input will also assume this potential. Since the currents in R_f and R_f' flow in opposite directions, the voltage at the output end of R_f (E_o) will be $I_{in}R_f$ volts lower than at the $(-)$ input. With $R_f' = R_f$, this in effect doubles the current, I_{in} through R_f, making the output voltage

$$E_o = 2I_{in}R_f$$

For values of $I_{in} \geqq 1.0$ μA, the bias current is a thousand times or more lower than I_{in}, and R_f' may be reduced to zero. Thereafter, changing R_f in steps (see Fig. 8-9B) allows currents up to 100 μA to be measured.

To read voltage inputs, the same circuit is used with the addition of R_V, a series input resistor used to scale the input current. The circuit behavior is essentially the same as before, the only difference being that R_V and the input voltage now define the input current. This allows voltages from 10 mV to 100 V to be metered using the resistance values indicated in Fig. 8-9B.

At currents higher than 100 μA, the power drain of the standard inverter becomes prohibitive, since $I_f = I_{in}$. An alternate metering arrangement for high currents is shown in Fig. 8-10. This circuit uses

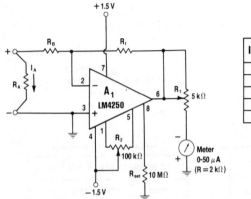

I (Full Scale)	$R_A(\Omega)$	$R_B(\Omega)$	$R_f(\Omega)$
1.0 mA	3.0	3.0 k	300 k
10 mA	0.3	3.0 k	300 k
100 mA	0.3	30 k	300 k
1.0 A	0.03	30 k	300 k
10 A	0.03	30 k	30 k

(A) Circuit schematic.   (B) Values for various full-scale readings.

Fig. 8-10. Dc ammeter.

shunt resistor R_A to generate voltages proportional to the current through it. The voltage is amplified at A_1 by a gain of R_f/R_B, and meter calibration and offset adjustments are the same as for Fig. 8-9A.

In all of these metering circuits the accuracy is directly proportional to the quality of the scaling resistances used. Therefore, R_B, R_A, R_f, and R_f' should be close-tolerance, stable types such as wire-wound resistors. Where appreciable power is dissipated as in R_V or R_A, consideration to resistor power ratings must also be given. In practice, the scaling resistors (Fig. 8-10B) will most likely be switch selected to set up the various functions and sensitivities. It is recommended that make-before-break (shorting) switches be used to avoid transients when the amplifier loop resistance is changed.

Another consideration is the availability of the very small resistances ($R_A \ll 1.0 \ \Omega$) needed for measuring large currents. A common method of manufacturing small values is to use strips of nichrome wire, bolted or clamped between two tie posts. As an example, if nichrome heating wire with a resistance of 8 Ω/ft is used, the length required to give 0.3 Ω is just under half an inch. Even lower resistances can be obtained by using small-diameter copper wire.

When making measurements of large currents, it is necessary to use connectors of sufficient size such that $R_{lead} \ll R_A$. Very thin leads may have resistances approaching the value of R_A. Fine calibration of the reading involves adjusting the wire length or the value of R_B while comparing the meter against a standard ammeter.

8.3 SWITCHED-MODE CIRCUITS

A number of circuit applications operate by making radical changes in I_{set}—either switching the amplifier from on to off or programming gross changes in amplifier characteristics. A few such applications will be covered in this section.

8.3.1 Sample/Hold

In Chapter 5, the sample/hold function and its basic requirements were discussed. Two of these requirements are a high slew rate (which determines acquisition time) and a low discharge rate for the storage capacitor. The circuit of Fig. 8-11 attacks these problems in an interesting fashion, programming a 776 between extreme I_{set} limits to obtain fast slewing for acquisition, and low input-bias current for a low discharge rate.

If E_s is high, both Q_1 and Q_2 are on and C_1 is charged to the value of E_{in} during the sample interval. Q_1 has a low ON resistance, and the source impedance of E_{in} is assumed to be low. Since E_s also turns on Q_2, this causes a 100-μA I_{set} to flow in R_3 which programs the 776 to

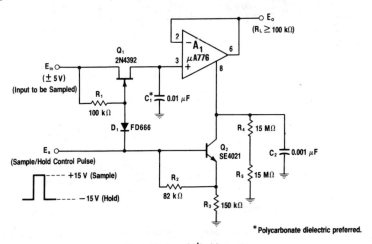

Fig. 8-11. Sample/hold circuit.

417

its highest speed. Thus, A_1 can follow E_{in} during the sample interval with a 5-V/μs slewing rate.

When E_s goes to the hold state, Q_1 and Q_2 are turned off and C_1 is isolated from E_{in}. With Q_2 off, A_1 reverts to a much lower I_{set} value, determined by R_4-R_5. This programs the 776 to have an I_{ib} less than 1.0 nA and minimizes the discharge rate of C_1 during the hold interval. Although the slewing rate of the 776 is reduced drastically by such a low value of I_{set}, this is immaterial during the hold state because E_o is unchanging. Q_2 is a low-leakage device used to minimize any leakage turn-on of the 776, which would raise the input bias current and increase droop during the hold interval.

8.3.2 Analog Multiplexers

The analog multiplexer, like the sample/hold function, is a standard analog circuit tool. It is used for a variety of purposes: signal commutation, gating, sampling, conditioning, scaling, sign alternation, etc.

"N"-Input, Single-Output Multiplexer

The circuit of Fig. 8-12 is a basic multiplexer using two 776 op amps as switched voltage followers. Only one of the amplifiers is

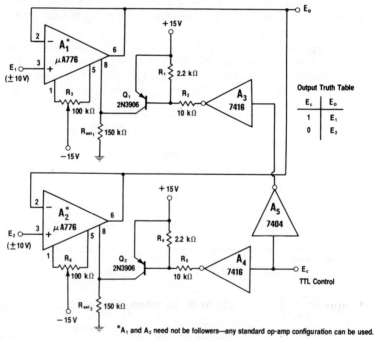

Fig. 8-12. Analog multiplexer.

permitted to be on at a given instant. This allows the outputs to be tied together in parallel. A virtue of this output bussing technique is the fact that the OFF amplifier always looks into a low impedance— that of the ON amplifier. This maximizes isolation since the amplifier with the ON state has a unity-gain, closed feedback loop around it and a characteristically low output impedance. The circuit shown can achieve isolations in excess of 80 dB at audio frequencies.

Stages A_1 and A_2 are connected as followers in order to optimize loading, linearity, and isolation. However, other op-amp configurations can also be used effectively—with gain insertion, sign changing, differential operation, and other features added. Both A_1 and A_2 are operated at their I_{set} limit to optimize bandwidth and slew rate. Individual channel offsets are available via R_3 and R_6.

The switching method in this circuit is somewhat unusual and is used for highest speed. Q_1 and Q_2 *shunt* the I_{set} current from R_{set_1} or R_{set_2} to turn their respective amplifiers off. This gives positive control of I_{set} without any concern for leakage, and it allows general-purpose transistors to be used. Since only one channel is allowed to be on at any time, an inverter is used between control inputs. The overall logic of output states is shown in the truth table.

This multiplexer is expandable to "N" inputs by adding additional op-amp outputs in parallel at E_o. Additional logic control will also be required, of course, and it must guarantee that only one of "N" channels is on at a given time. This function is easily satisfied by standard logic chips of the 7400 family.

Summing Multiplexer

A more general form of analog multiplexer is one that allows any or all inputs to be on at a given time. This can be accomplished with ON/OFF programming of a number of 776s and by combining the switched outputs at a summing inverter. One example of this technique is shown in Fig. 8-13. Amplifiers A_1-A_3 are voltage followers, programmed from ON to OFF by Q_1-Q_3 and A_5-A_7. When gated ON, the amplifiers have a 100-μA I_{set} and thus operate at maximum speed. The outputs are combined at a unity-gain summing inverter stage, A_4. A 101A feedforward connection is used here for the highest speed available with a general-purpose device. The scale factor for each channel is set by R_4/R_N, where $R_N = R_1, R_2, R_3, \ldots$ etc. An interesting feature of this multiplexer is the fact that the noise gain of stage A_4 is minimized when an input channel is switched off. Since A_1-A_3 appear as open circuits to R_1-R_3 when off, this maximizes the feedback to A_4 and reduces noise gain.

Stages A_1-A_3 can be offset nulled, if desired, to optimize dc accuracy (similar to Fig. 8-12); this process can also serve to null A_4 if the adjustment is made for zero offset at the output of A_4, with each stage—one through "N"—adjusted in sequence.

The circuit shown has a sign inversion due to A_4, which could be a disadvantage in some instances. This can be corrected (if necessary) by a second inverter following A_4, not by making A_1-A_3 inverters. Stages A_1-A_3 cannot use the inverting mode in this circuit because their input and output resistances would feed the OFF signal into R_1-R_3. With the logic shown, channels 1-3 are on when their respec-

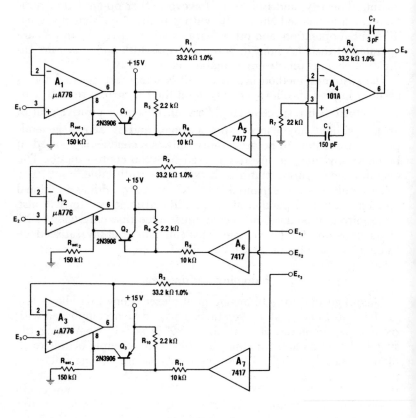

Output Truth Table

$E_{c_N}^*$	E_o
1	$-E_N \dfrac{R_4}{R_N}$
0	Off

*N is the ON channel (E_1, E_2, E_3, etc.)
Any or all inputs can be switched
ON simultaneously.

Fig. 8-13. Summing multiplexer.

tive control lines are in the "1" state. Additional channels can be added by connecting identical stages to the summing junction of A_4.

8.3.3 Binary-Weighted Amplifier With Programmable Gain

Many applications that involve interfacing with computers require programming of circuit variables by binary-coded digital inputs. A single programmable amplifier, such as the 4250 or 776, can be made to represent one control bit with two possible states (on and off). If the amplifiers are considered as switches, the number of possible switch states will be 2^n, where "n" is the number of "bits," or in this case, the number of amplifiers. Likewise, in a gain-controlled amplifier, the number of possible gain states will be 2^n; thus, two control stages yield four gain states, three yield eight states, four yield sixteen states, and so on.

Fig. 8-14A illustrates a circuit arranged for binary-coded digital control. This is somewhat similar to the summing multiplexer because it sums the output of a number of switched stages. However, unlike the multiplexer, this circuit adds additional input current to A_5, proportional to the common input voltage, E_{in}. As stages A_1-A_4 are turned on, there is a scaled decrease in the effective input resistance to A_5, thus increasing the gain of A_5 by steps.

R_1-R_4 constitute the input resistors to summer A_5. It will be noted that, beginning with R_1, each resistance is scaled to half that of the preceding, which has the effect of increasing the current in a sequence of 1, 2, 4, and 8, etc. It can be shown that for all possible states of the four control inputs, the current into the summing point of A_5 will follow a progression corresponding to the number represented by the binary inputs 2^0 to 2^3. Disregarding the effect of R_6 momentarily, it will be noted that with all bits off, the input current to A_5 is zero; with all bits on, it is maximum. The smallest increment of change is in the LSB (least significant bit) leg since R_1 is the highest resistance. Similarly, the largest increment of change is in the MSB (most significant bit) leg since R_4 is the smallest input resistance. From a gain of R_5/R_1 (with only LSB active), the gain can be changed in steps by a factor of $N-1$. In the example shown, $R_1 = R_5$, so the minimum (LSB) gain is unity and the maximum gain (with all bits on) is $(16-1)(R_5/R_1) = 15$. Similarly, if this were a 3-bit controller, the maximum gain, $A_{v_{max}}$, would be $A_{v_{max}} = (8-1)(R_5/R_1) = 7$.

From the truth table (Fig. 8-14B), it is evident that gain A_v changes from 0 to 15 in single steps as the digital word increases, for a total of 16 gain states. Some applications might require a minimum gain of unity rather than zero; the addition of R_6 around the switching networks of A_1-A_4 provides this. The gain change provided by

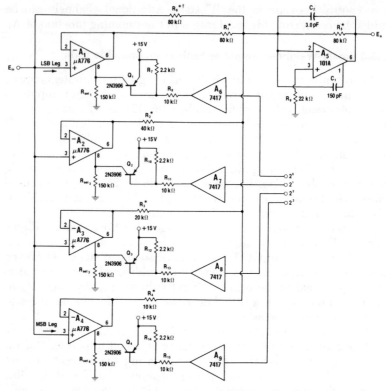

(A) Circuit schematic.

(LSB)			(MSB)		
2^0	2^1	2^2	2^3	A_v	A_v'
0	0	0	0	0	−1
1	0	0	0	−1	−2
0	1	0	0	−2	−3
1	1	0	0	−3	−4
0	0	1	0	−4	−5
1	0	1	0	−5	−6
0	1	1	0	−6	−7
1	1	1	0	−7	−8
0	0	0	1	−8	−9
1	0	0	1	−9	−10
0	1	0	1	−10	−11
1	1	0	1	−11	−12
0	0	1	1	−12	−13
1	0	1	1	−13	−14
0	1	1	1	−14	−15
1	1	1	1	−15	−16

(B) Output truth table.

Fig. 8-14. Logic-controlled amplifier with programmable gain.

A_1-A_4 is still the same; so, with R_6 the gain range is 1-16, indicated by A_v'.

Many interesting variations are possible with this circuit. For example, if the binary code is restricted to gain states from 0-9, it can be used as one digit of a BCD-programmed amplifier. The circuit shown is suitable for gains from 0-9 (or 1-10), but R_5 could also be raised to 800 kΩ for a range from 0-90 (or 10-100) in steps of 10. For best performance, the gain-scaling resistors, R_1-R_6, should preferably be a set with matched ratios and matched temperature coefficients.

8.4 FOUR-CHANNEL PROGRAMMABLE AMPLIFIER: THE HA-2400/2404/2405

The second type of programmable amplifier in the unique-devices group is the HA-2400, diagrammed in Fig. 8-15. As this figure shows, the device consists of four individual differential-input stages, any (or none) of which can be selected by an analog switch. The state of the analog switch is controlled by a decode/control section, which decodes the commands from the digital input lines. The two digital

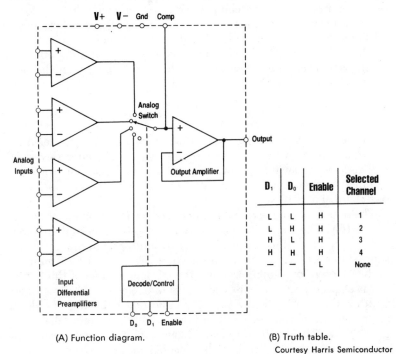

D_1	D_0	Enable	Selected Channel
L	L	H	1
L	H	H	2
H	L	H	3
H	H	H	4
—	—	L	None

(A) Function diagram.

(B) Truth table.

Courtesy Harris Semiconductor

Fig. 8-15. HA-2400 four-channel amplifier.

control lines, D_0 and D_1, control the four states of the analog switch. The third digital control line, ENABLE, switches the analog switch from on (high) to off (low). The logic of the D_0, D_1, and ENABLE inputs is shown in the truth table of Fig. 8-15B, and the logic inputs are compatible with DTL/TTL logic levels.

The input selected by the decode/control section is passed to a unity-gain output stage and appears at the output terminal. The input to this stage is a high-impedance point and is used with an external capacitor as a frequency-compensation node.

In effect, the selected input stage and the output stage of the HA-2400 operate to form four different op amps with a common output. (If considered as a single device, an op amp formed by this combination has characteristics that would place it in the high-frequency group.) Compensated for unity gain, the HA-2400 has an f_t of 8 MHz and a slew rate of 15 V/μs. At gains of 10 or greater, it requires no compensation and achieves a 40-MHz GBP with a 50-V/μs slew rate. Its dc characteristics are similar to or better than general-purpose devices: $V_{io} = 2.0$ mV, $I_{ib} = 50$ nA, $A_{vo} = 104$ dB, and it has a $\pm$10-V, or greater, input and output voltage range. Its switching characteristics are notable for both speed and degree of isolation. For instance, a switching operation from one channel to an adjacent channel is characterized by an initial 100-ns delay, then a slew-rate-limited rise to the level of the new channel. As an example, if Channel 1 is at -10 V, Channel 2 is at $+10$ V, and if unity-gain compensation is used (slew rate = SR = 15 V/μs), then the time required to reach the new level would be

$$\frac{\Delta E_o}{SR} = \frac{20 \text{ V}}{15 \text{ V}/\mu s} \cong 1.3 \ \mu s.$$

Since this is a worst-case solution, lower signal levels (smaller ΔE_o) or higher gains (a lighter compensation yields a greater slew rate) will reduce the switching time. In terms of isolation, an OFF input channel to the output is attenuated by 110 dB, measured with the OFF channel at $\pm$10 V.

The details of connecting and operating an HA-2400 are shown in Fig. 8-16A. The compensation capacitor, C_C, is connected from the compensation terminal (pin 12) to ac ground, preferably to the V+ supply pin as shown. In accordance with variations in gain for various closed-loop configurations, the minimum value of this capacitor is charted in Fig. 8-16B, which also indicates the resulting bandwidth and slew rate. There is a very important point that should be appreciated regarding C_C. Since it is a single capacitor that must provide stability for all four channel gains, the gain used in selecting a C_C value from Fig. 8-16B is the *lowest* gain of the four channels. This guarantees stability for all closed-loop settings.

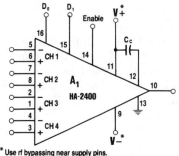

Gain		C_c pF	Bandwidth (Typical) (-3 dB), MHz	Slew Rate (Typical) V/μs
Noninverting	Inverting			
1	—	15	8.0	15
2	1	7	8.0	20
3	2	4	8.0	22
5	4	3	6.0	25
8	7	2	5.0	30
>10	>9	0	40 $\div$ Gain	50

* Use rf bypassing near supply pins.

(A) Schematic symbol.

(B) Minimum compensation values for various open-loop gains.

Courtesy Harris Semiconductor

Fig. 8-16. HA-2400 characteristics.

From the schematic, it is evident that the HA-2400 requires several additional pin connections for operation. Since it is a high-frequency device, good layout with rf bypassing is indicated. For clarity this is not shown on all subsequent circuits; nevertheless, it is strongly recommended in actual hookups. Lead lengths to C_C should be short and direct since the compensation point is a high-impedance node. Offset nulling, when necessary, is accomplished externally.

8.5 HA-2400 APPLICATIONS

The number of applications possible with this type of op amp is virtually unlimited. In addition to the four-input capability, many other possibilities stem from the wide frequency response of the HA-2400 and from the ability to optimize compensation externally. This section will treat not only "programmed variations" of previous circuits (to highlight the differences brought about by programming) but also some totally unique applications.

8.5.1 Multiplexers

Analog multiplexer applications using the HA-2400 are capable of unparalleled performance in terms of overall quality and simplicity. Furthermore, the flexibility of the operational multiplexer allows gain and sign inversion to be incorporated as a bonus.

Fig. 8-17 illustrates the general simplicity of a four-input noninverting multiplexer using the HA-2400. In this circuit, signal inputs E_1-E_4 are applied to the ($+$) inputs of channels 1-4, respectively. All channels are connected as voltage followers; thus, compensation capacitor C_1 has a value of 15 pF. The performance of the circuit can be appreciated by regarding the characteristics of the 2400 in the follower connection: channel isolation $\geq$100 dB, high input impedance, low output impedance, excellent output linearity at E_0 up to ± 10 V, and essentially zero TC and zero offset.

The four channels are selected in accordance with the truth table as shown, with the ENABLE input tied to +5 V. If fewer than four inputs are desired, the unused (+) terminals should be grounded, which will hold the output at zero when this channel is addressed. For instance, with a simple two-channel switch, ground E_3, E_4, and the D_1 control line and use E_1-E_2 with D_0 as control.

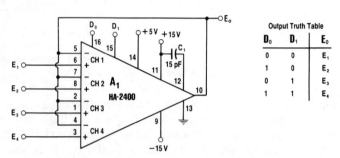

Output Truth Table

D_0	D_1	E_0
0	0	E_1
1	0	E_2
0	1	E_3
1	1	E_4

Fig. 8-17. Four-input noninverting multiplexer.

Eight-Input Multiplexer

As noted previously in discussions on multiplexers, many applications demand more than four input channels. For input expansion, two or more 2400s can be bussed together by connecting their compensation terminals. With only one of the devices enabled, this in effect removes the remaining amplifiers from the circuit. The output signal is taken from *one* of the amplifiers with feedback applied in conventional fashion to *all* inputs.

This is illustrated more clearly in Fig. 8-18, where A_1 and A_2 form an eight-input multiplexer for inputs E_1-E_8. As can be noted from the truth table and logic circuit, for the first four states A_1 is enabled, A_2 is disabled, and E_1-E_4 are multiplexed as in Fig. 8-17. In the second four states, $D_2 = 1$, A_1 is disabled and A_2 is enabled, thus multiplexing E_5-E_8. Considered as a unit with control lines D_0, D_1, and D_2, this circuit performs as a single eight-input multiplexer.

Since the compensation terminals are in parallel, only a single capacitor, C_1, is necessary for compensation of both amplifiers. No connection is made to the unused output terminal (pin 10 of A_2).

Expansion to a greater number of inputs is possible by connecting additional 2400s in a similar fashion, with extra logic to enable only the required four channels. For example, sixteen channels would require four amplifiers, and 2^4 states also imply four control lines or one in addition to those shown in Fig. 8-18.

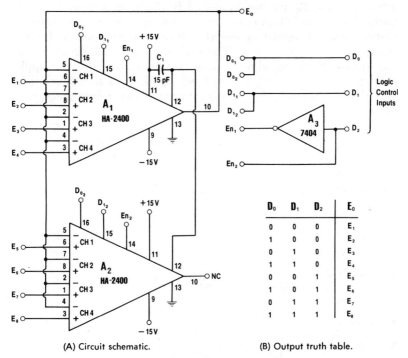

(A) Circuit schematic.

(B) Output truth table.

D_0	D_1	D_2	E_0
0	0	0	E_1
1	0	0	E_2
0	1	0	E_3
1	1	0	E_4
0	0	1	E_5
1	0	1	E_6
0	1	1	E_7
1	1	1	E_8

Fig. 8-18. Eight-input noninverting multiplexer.

Noninverting Multiplexer With Adjustable Scale Factor

Since the HA-2400 is an operational multiplexer, gain can be introduced in the channel-selection function. The circuit of Fig. 8-19A is exactly the same as Fig. 8-17 in terms of programming logic, but some input channels are connected for a gain greater than unity. Gain is calculated the same as for any op-amp noninverting stage, and the same error analysis techniques apply.

As shown here, Channel 1 is set up for unity gain, which dictates the value of compensation capacitor C_1. Bias compensation resistances may be used at the $(+)$ inputs for minimum dc offset. These values will be nominally equal to the equivalent resistance seen at the corresponding $(-)$ input. Note that the feedback resistances present a constant load at the amplifier output, regardless of the channel state. This is the general form of the circuit, with individual gain adjustments for each channel. Gain is calculated as in the standard noninverting stage:

$$A_v = \frac{R_{in} + R_f}{R_{in}},$$

where R_{in} and R_f are the input and feedback resistances for each particular channel. This circuit configuration is useful, for example, whenever input signals of differing levels are required to have a common level at the output. The individual feedback dividers provide a noninteracting adjustment of channel gains. For some applications, a common (tapped) feedback divider will suffice, which is considerably simpler, but it does sacrifice the independent gain adjustment.

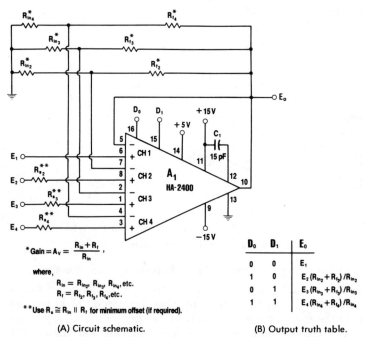

(A) Circuit schematic.

(B) Output truth table.

Fig. 8-19. Four-input multiplexer with adjustable scale factor.

Inverting Multiplexer With Adjustable Scale Factor

The HA-2400 is also easily arranged as an inverting multiplexer, as shown in Fig. 8-20A. In this circuit, the ON channel will have a gain of $-R_f/R_{in}$, where R_f and R_{in} are the feedback and input resistances, respectively, of that channel.

The loading of input and feedback resistances is different for this circuit than for the standard inverter due to the switching arrangement of the input channels. In fact, the summing point exists only for the ON channel and the three OFF junctions will move as E_1-E_4 and E_o vary. One effect of this is that the input resistance of a channel will vary from R_{in} when ON to $R_{in} + R_f$ when OFF. A more serious effect occurs when $R_{in} = 0$ (as in a current-to-voltage converter). In this case, the voltage rise at the $(-)$ input when OFF can be limited (if desirable) with a pair of back-to-back diodes from the $(-)$ input to common.

As shown, all the channel gains are unity, but any combination desired may be used. The gain accuracy, as with any feedback circuit, is determined by the loop gain and degree of precision of the resistors. C_1 is selected for optimum compensation, supplying a bandwidth of 8.0 MHz.

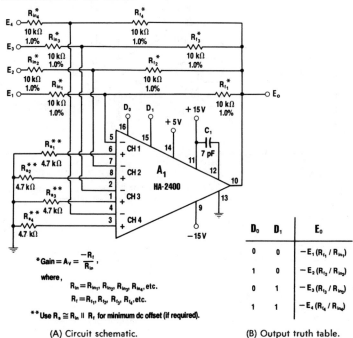

$$*\text{Gain} = A_v = \frac{-R_f}{R_{in}},$$

where,

$R_{in} = R_{in_1}, R_{in_2}, R_{in_3}, R_{in_4}, \text{etc.}$

$R_f = R_{f_1}, R_{f_2}, R_{f_3}, R_{f_4}, \text{etc.}$

**Use $R_s \cong R_{in} \parallel R_f$ for minimum dc offset (if required).

D_0	D_1	E_o
0	0	$-E_1 (R_{f_1} / R_{in_1})$
1	0	$-E_2 (R_{f_2} / R_{in_2})$
0	1	$-E_3 (R_{f_3} / R_{in_3})$
1	1	$-E_4 (R_{f_4} / R_{in_4})$

(A) Circuit schematic.   (B) Output truth table.

Fig. 8-20. Four-input inverting multiplexer with adjustable scale factor.

Although the previous circuits have illustrated multiplexers both as followers and as noninverting and inverting amplifiers, multiplexers can use other input configurations. In this fashion, differing input signal levels and sign changes can be normalized within a single multiplexer stage.

8.5.2 Programmable Attenuation and Amplification

The most useful applications of the HA-2400 are in programmable attenuation and amplification functions; several circuits to realize these functions are illustrated in Figs. 8-21 through 8-25.

Fig. 8-21A is a noninverting attenuator that is programmable between four states, with attenuation provided by the R_1-R_4 input divider. A_1 is connected as a follower to buffer the taps of R_1-R_4, delivering a precise replica of the attenuated signals at the output.

As shown, R_1-R_4 provide gains of 1, ½, ¼, and ⅛. These can be adjusted, of course, for any desired ratio, with an accuracy determined by the resistor tolerances. Although the R_1-R_4 divider is the

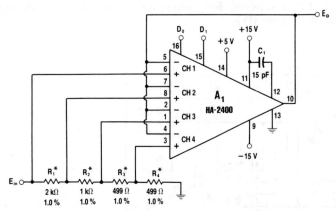

(A) Circuit schematic.

D_0	D_1	E_0
0	0	E_{in}
1	0	$E_{in}\left(\dfrac{R_2+R_3+R_4}{R_1+R_2+R_3+R_4}\right)$
0	1	$E_{in}\left(\dfrac{R_3+R_4}{R_1+R_2+R_3+R_4}\right)$
1	1	$E_{in}\left(\dfrac{R_4}{R_1+R_2+R_3+R_4}\right)$

(B) Output truth table.

Fig. 8-21. Noninverting four-state attenuator.

simplest form of attenuation, separate dividers for each channel can be used if independent adjustment is necessary. Extension to more than four states is possible by using the logic circuit of Fig. 8-18B. Programmable attenuation with inversion is also possible, and one method in which it may be accomplished was illustrated by the circuit of Fig. 8-20A with all inputs fed in parallel. This was the general form of inverting-mode programmable amplifier, allowing gain for each channel to be independently adjusted.

A simpler inverting attenuator than that of Fig. 8-20A is shown in Fig. 8-22A. In this circuit, R_1-R_5 form a tapped input-feedback divider. With the various input channels on, this technique shifts the summing point and the input/output ratio, changing the gain as the ratio R_f/R_{in} changes. Input resistance is at a minimum of R_1 when Channel 1 is on, and it reaches a maximum of $R_1 + R_2 + R_3 + R_4$ when Channel 4 is on. In the example shown, the gains are -1, $-\frac{1}{2}$, $-\frac{1}{4}$, and $-\frac{1}{8}$.

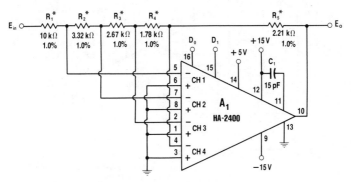

*As shown, R_1 - R_5 values yield gains of -1, $-\frac{1}{2}$, $-\frac{1}{4}$, and $-\frac{1}{8}$, with an accuracy of 1.0%.

(A) Circuit schematic.

D_0	D_1	E_o
0	0	$-E_{in}\left(\dfrac{R_2+R_3+R_4+R_5}{R_1}\right)$
1	0	$-E_{in}\left(\dfrac{R_3+R_4+R_5}{R_1+R_2}\right)$
0	1	$-E_{in}\left(\dfrac{R_4+R_5}{R_1+R_2+R_3}\right)$
1	1	$-E_{in}\left(\dfrac{R_5}{R_1+R_2+R_3+R_4}\right)$

(B) Output truth table.

Fig. 8-22. Inverting four-state attenuator.

Noninverting Four-State Amplifier

By placing a tapped voltage divider in a feedback loop as shown in Fig. 8-23A and by programming channels between the various taps, the net effect is a variable-β attenuator. The resulting gain is made to vary as an inverse of the attenuation, or as $1/\beta$, giving gains of $1/\beta_1$, $1/\beta_2$, $1/\beta_3$, and $1/\beta_4$.

The example shown uses the same network as that in Fig. 8-21A; thus, the gain function it provides is the reciprocal of these attenuating factors, or 1, 2, 4, and 8. Different gains, of course, are possible with different feedback attenuations. A separate circuit for inverting programmable gain is not shown, but it would resemble Fig. 8-20 or Fig. 8-22, with $R_f/R_{in} > 1$.

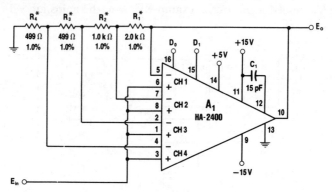

*As shown, R_1 - R_4 values yield gains of 1, 2, 4, and 8, with an accuracy of 1.0%.

(A) Circuit schematic.

D_0	D_1	E_0
0	0	E_{in}
1	0	$E_{in}\left(\dfrac{R_1+R_2+R_3+R_4}{R_2+R_3+R_4}\right)$
0	1	$E_{in}\left(\dfrac{R_1+R_2+R_3+R_4}{R_3+R_4}\right)$
1	1	$E_{in}\left(\dfrac{R_1+R_2+R_3+R_4}{R_4}\right)$

(B) Output truth table.

Fig. 8-23. Noninverting four-state amplifier.

Programmable Instrumentation Amplifier

An interesting use for the 2400 as a programmable attenuator is shown in Fig. 8-24. This circuit is actually an adaptation of the variable-gain instrumentation amplifier (see Chapter 5). A_2 provides a programmable attenuation factor of 0, 10, 20, or 30 dB; since this attenuation is in series with the feedback to A_1, it changes the β of A_1, thus changing the differential gain of the input stage.

Common-mode rejection is not degraded in this connection because R_6 still sees a low feedback impedance (A_2 in this case) and the bridge balance is not compromised. A_1 and the bridge compo-

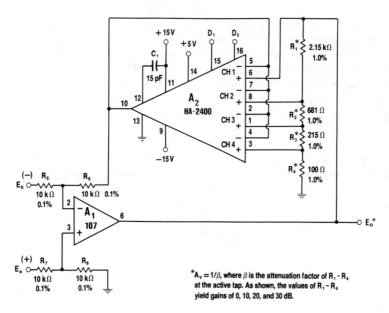

(A) Circuit schematic.

D_0	D_1	E_0
0	0	$E_a - E_b$
1	0	$(E_a - E_b)\left(\dfrac{R_1 + R_2 + R_3 + R_4}{R_2 + R_3 + R_4}\right)$
0	1	$(E_a - E_b)\left(\dfrac{R_1 + R_2 + R_3 + R_4}{R_3 + R_4}\right)$
1	1	$(E_a - E_b)\left(\dfrac{R_1 + R_2 + R_3 + R_4}{R_4}\right)$

(B) Output truth table.

Fig. 8-24. Instrumentation amplifier with programmable gain.

nents in this instance are more or less of general form, but the programmed feedback is also applicable to the more developed forms of the differential stage (detailed in Chapter 5). The circuit can be made to program gain at virtually any level (consistent with the loop gain of A_1) by rescaling R_1-R_4. More gain states can be added by expanding A_2 into multiple stages, as discussed in connection with Fig. 8-18.

Multistage Programmable Gain Amplifier

For situations that demand higher resolutions between gain states or a greater range of total gain change, multiple stages of programmed gain can be obtained by cascading two or more four-state circuits, as shown in Fig. 8-25A.

This circuit may be recognized as two programmed stages, each similar to the four-state amplifier of Fig. 8-23A. Operating together, the two stages, each with four gain states, yield 16 possible gain states. In general, if the minimum gain desired is 0 dB (or unity gain), the maximum gain span is given by

$$A_{v_{(max)}} = (N - 1) \Delta A_{v_N},$$

where N is the number of gain states and A_{v_N} is the increment of gain between states. This relationship must first be applied to both stages as a unit, to determine the basic gain increment, A_{v_N}. In the example of Fig. 8-25, $A_{v_{(max)}} = 45$ dB and $N = 16$; so

$$A_{v_N} = \frac{45}{15} = 3 \text{ dB.}$$

The first stage, A_1, supplies the smallest gain increments with four possible states; thus, the gain range of this stage, $A_{v_{1(max)}}$, spans 9 dB, or

$$A_{v_{1(max)}} = (N_1 - 1)\ 3 \text{ dB} = 9 \text{ dB.}$$

The second stage, A_2, can supply the remaining gain range with four states:

$$A_{v_{2(max)}} = 45 \text{ dB} - 9 \text{ dB} = 36 \text{ dB,}$$

and

$$A'_{v_N} = \frac{36}{3} = 12 \text{ dB.}$$

Thus, the available gains are 0, 3, 6, and 9 dB for A_1; and 0, 12, 24, and 36 dB for A_2.

From the truth table (Fig. 8-25B), note that the two stages are combined in a 4:1 "fine/coarse" relationship to supply the total gain required. For example, if the gain required is 6 dB, this is distributed between the stages as $6 + 0 = 6$ dB. If $A_v = 30$ dB, the gains combine as $6 + 24 = 30$ dB. This process can easily be extended with additional amplifiers to provide any desired increment—or total range—of gain.

Programmable Sign Changer

A specialized type of programmable amplifier is the sign changer, illustrated in Fig. 8-26. This type of circuit is confined to two-state operation, either inverting or noninverting.

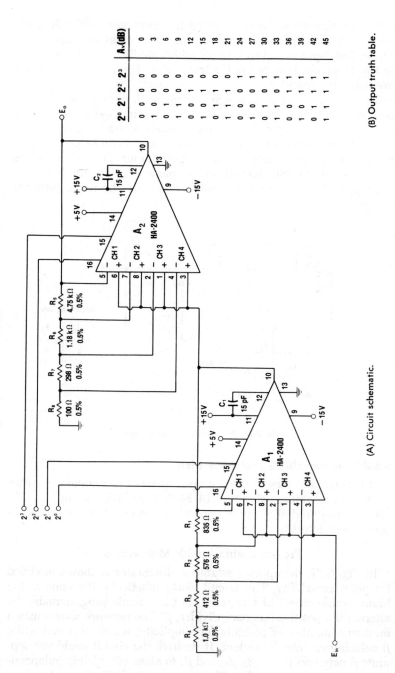

2^0	2^1	2^2	2^3	A_V(dB)
0	0	0	0	0
1	0	0	0	3
0	1	0	0	6
1	1	0	0	9
0	0	1	0	12
1	0	1	0	15
0	1	1	0	18
1	1	1	0	21
0	0	0	1	24
1	0	0	1	27
0	1	0	1	30
1	1	0	1	33
0	0	1	1	36
1	0	1	1	39
0	1	1	1	42
1	1	1	1	45

(B) Output truth table.

(A) Circuit schematic.

Fig. 8-25. Multistage amplifier with programmable gain.

435

The configuration shown is set up for unity gain, with Channel 1 wired as a voltage follower and Channel 2 wired as an inverter. The D_1 control input is tied to ground, which confines the programming to two channels, as shown in the truth table. The unused $(+)$ inputs are wired to ground.

This circuit is useful as a sign changer with digital control. If the controlling digital signal is derived from the input—for example, by using a zero-crossing detector (see Chapter 5)—the circuit can also be used as a precision full-wave rectifier, since it can be programmed to deliver a unipolar output with a bipolar input. The polarity of the full-wave output will depend on the phase of the control input in relation to E_{in}; therefore, the polarity can also be made programmable.

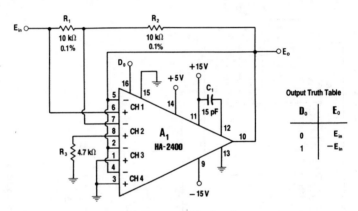

Fig. 8-26. Programmable sign changer.

8.5.3 Programmable Signal Generation

It is relatively easy to modify op-amp signal generation circuitry for programmability using the HA-2400. Very little (if any) modification is required of the fundamental design equations described in previous chapters.

Programmable Astable Multivibrator

In Fig. 8-27, the op-amp astable multivibrator is shown modified for programmability. This circuit works practically the same as the basic astable circuit of Chapter 7, but it is made programmable by altering the positive feedback divider, β. The network shown uses a minimum number of resistors for simplicity, which also makes the β calculations interdependent. If desired, the circuit could use separate β networks for $\beta_1, \beta_2, \beta_3,$ and β_4 to allow completely independent frequency settings. In either case, a single timing network is

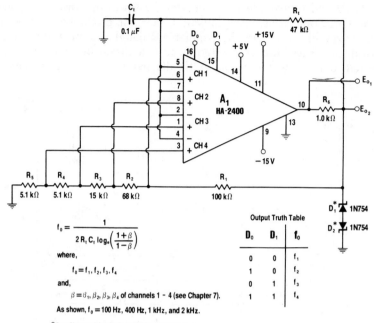

$$f_0 = \frac{1}{2 R_t C_t \log_e\left(\frac{1+\beta}{1-\beta}\right)}$$

where,

$$f_0 = f_1, f_2, f_3, f_4$$

and,

$\beta = \beta_1, \beta_2, \beta_3, \beta_4$ of channels 1 – 4 (see Chapter 7).

As shown, $f_0 = 100$ Hz, 400 Hz, 1 kHz, and 2 kHz.

*See Chapter 5 for diode clamping considerations.

Output Truth Table

D_0	D_1	f_0
0	0	f_1
1	0	f_2
0	1	f_3
1	1	f_4

Fig. 8-27. Programmable astable multivibrator.

used (R_tC_t). The HA-2400 is operated without compensation to maximize speed and allow operation at over 100 kHz. D_1-D_2 are shown as general-purpose zeners, but any of the previously described forms of clamping may be used.

As shown, four frequencies are available: 100, 400, 1000, and 2000 Hz. A useful application of this circuit would be as a frequency-shift keying (fsk) generator that can switch rapidly between two frequencies through digital control. Expansion to more than four frequencies involves simply connecting the compensation terminals of several devices together and using the ENABLE inputs as in Fig. 8-18. Any variations of the basic astable circuit, such as the monostable multivibrator, are also adaptable to programming by similar means.

Programmable Wien-Bridge Oscillator

The basic Wien-bridge oscillator can be programmed as shown in Fig. 8-28, which illustrates a circuit derived from the basic lamp-stabilized circuit of Chapter 7 (Fig. 7-10).

This circuit uses separate Wien networks for each frequency to be programmed, and it may be considered as four independent Wien oscillators with switch selection. Such a circuit is useful as a quickly settable and repeatable test oscillator for up to four fixed frequencies. One application example would be in the production testing of audio amplifiers, where the frequencies could represent the bandwidth points and the center frequency of a circuit that must be subjected to tests for gain, bandwidth, distortion, or other parameters.

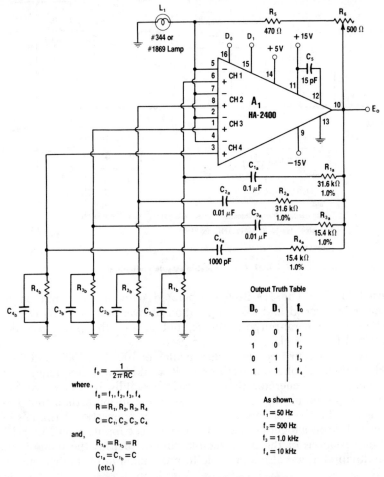

$$f_0 = \frac{1}{2\pi RC}$$

where,

$f_0 = f_1, f_2, f_3, f_4$
$R = R_1, R_2, R_3, R_4$
$C = C_1, C_2, C_3, C_4$

and,

$R_{1a} = R_{1b} = R$
$C_{1a} = C_{1b} = C$
(etc.)

Output Truth Table

D_0	D_1	f_0
0	0	f_1
1	0	f_2
0	1	f_3
1	1	f_4

As shown,
$f_1 = 50$ Hz
$f_2 = 500$ Hz
$f_3 = 1.0$ kHz
$f_4 = 10$ kHz

Fig. 8-28. Programmable Wien-bridge oscillator.

As shown, the frequencies are set up for 50, 500, 1000, and 10,000 Hz. A greater number of frequencies are available (for example, to check a filter circuit at many points) by using two or more 2400s, programmed as in Fig. 8-18. In any case, timing components should have close tolerances or accurate matching, to ensure balance and a stable amplitude.

8.5.4 Programmable Comparators

One use for which the HA-2400 is ideally suited is a selectable four-channel comparator. In the most general case, the four inputs are wired to compare four different sets of potentials, one value of which is routed to the output by the control inputs. Another asset of the device is the fact that the compensation terminal is at a potential close to that of the output and is a high-impedance node. It can easily be clamped by a pair of diodes, in a manner similar to the 101 clamping technique described in Chapter 5.

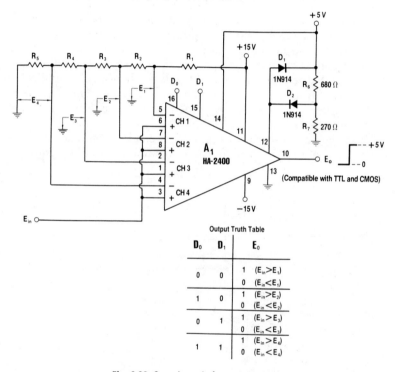

Output Truth Table

D_0	D_1	E_0	
0	0	1	$(E_{in} > E_1)$
		0	$(E_{in} < E_1)$
1	0	1	$(E_{in} > E_2)$
		0	$(E_{in} < E_2)$
0	1	1	$(E_{in} > E_3)$
		0	$(E_{in} < E_3)$
1	1	1	$(E_{in} > E_4)$
		0	$(E_{in} < E_4)$

Fig. 8-29. Scanning window comparator.

One version of the programmable comparator is shown in Fig. 8-29. Here the $(-)$ inputs are biased to voltages E_1-E_4, derived from a reference divider that can comprise any desired resistances. Thus, each input will have a slightly smaller comparison point than the next. Selection of inputs 1-4, then, constitutes a scanning process to determine where the input voltage is on the scale—i.e., between which two reference levels. The circuit is therefore a scanning window comparator. The comparison voltage could just as easily be made negative or be arranged for a low-to-high scanning sequence. Expansion to more than four levels is accomplished using two or more 2400s and additional control logic.

The clamping network on pin 12 confines the output between 0 and +5 V, making it logic-compatible. Clamping to other potentials involves designing the clamping network for a voltage between the positive supply limit on one end and 1.4 V more positive than the negative limit on the other end.

8.6 OPERATIONAL TRANSCONDUCTANCE AMPLIFIERS

The third type of unique op amp discussed in this chapter is the operational transconductance amplifier, or OTA. An OTA is like a standard op amp in many regards; in fact, many of the characteristics of the ideal op amp also apply to the OTA. However, the major difference that sets the device apart is its mechanism of amplification —like the transconductance amplifier, its voltage gain is $g_m R_L$. A better appreciation for this is gained by examining an equivalent circuit for the OTA.

From the circuit model of Fig. 8-30, it can be seen that the differential input of an OTA is identical to that of a standard op amp, and

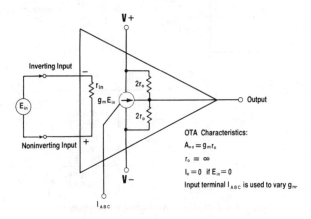

Fig. 8-30. Equivalent circuit for an OTA.

it operates in a similar fashion. The output, however, is entirely different. Whereas standard op amps are modeled as a voltage source in series with an output resistance, the OTA is modeled as a current source, $g_m E_{in}$, in parallel with the output resistance, r_o. In turn, r_o is modeled as two resistances of value $2r_o$, connected to V+ and V— since the output current is not referred to ground but may flow to either V+ or to V— as well. In the absence of feedback, I_o is independent of the voltage to which the output terminal is referred. This is another way of stating that the output impedance of an OTA is high, ideally infinite. The gain characteristic is determined by the product of g_m and the resistance shunting across the current generator, or $A_{vo} = g_m r_o$. Since r_o is ideally infinite, this makes the gain ideally infinite, as with a standard op amp. However, open-loop gain is reduced by external loading, unlike the standard op amp. With load R_L across the output, the gain becomes $g_m R_L$, which is the open-loop gain used in an error analysis. Also, an OTA ideally has zero input offset voltage, which means that the output *current* is zero if the differential-input *voltage* is zero. This is similar to the standard op amp, except that "output current" is substituted for "output voltage."

These basic differences in the characteristics of an OTA and a classical op amp can be summarized by stating that they are similar in input and open-loop gain characteristics. One achieves this end by a voltage-source output, while the other uses a current-source output. Thus, the open-loop gain of an OTA is directly dependent on output loading, but that of a regular op amp is not.

As noted from Fig. 8-30, there is another difference in the OTA: the additional terminal marked I_{ABC}. This terminal adjusts the transconductance of the device; it can also be used as a control of open-loop gain (and other characteristics, as will be seen later). To be precise, then, the device modeled in Fig. 8-30 is a *programmable* OTA if I_{ABC} is considered a programming input. However, the OTA's programming input terminal can also be used as a *signal* input. In practice, the I_{ABC} input is used either to establish an initial set of characteristics or to process input signals. Both applications will be illustrated in the examples that follow.

8.6.1 The CA3080

Of the basic OTA types considered in this section, the CA3080 most closely resembles the model of Fig. 8-30. As shown in the schematic (Fig. 8-31), the CA3080 uses no resistances whatever, only transistors and diodes. Transistor geometries and local feedback are used to control current gains within the circuit, and overall operating parameters are governed by the amplifier bias current (I_{ABC}) applied to pin 5. At the I_{ABC} terminal, diode D_1 and transistor Q_3 form a unity-gain current mirror. Since D_1 and Q_3 are matched, this causes I_{ABC} to be duplicated in the collector circuit of Q_3. Thus, the emitter current of the differential pair (Q_1-Q_2) is equal to I_{ABC}, and the operating parameters of Q_1-Q_2 are directly controllable by I_{ABC}, including input bias current, input resistance, and g_m. As may be recalled from the discussion of analog multipliers in Chapter 5, the emitter-current-controlled, differential amplifier is a natural two-quadrant multiplier. The forward transconductance, g_m, of such an amplifier is given by

$$g_m = \frac{q\alpha I_C}{2\kappa T} .$$

In the CA3080, $\alpha = 0.99$ and $I_C = I_{ABC}$. Therefore, at room temperature

$$g_m = 19.2 \, I_{ABC},$$

where g_m is in mmho and I_{ABC} is in mA. With this basic equation, the working g_m at any given value of I_{ABC} can be readily calculated.

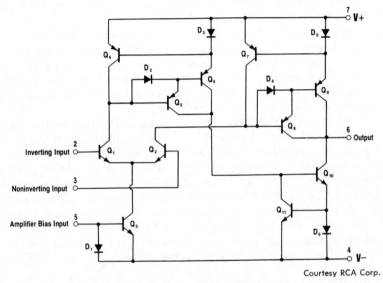

Courtesy RCA Corp.

Fig. 8-31. Schematic of CA3080/CA3080A.

The push-pull current outputs of the Q_1-Q_2 differential pair are applied to a pair of pnp current-mirror stages, Q_4-Q_6 and Q_7-Q_9. These stages have a unity current-transfer ratio but provide a signal inversion. The output of Q_5-Q_6 is further applied to a third (npn) current mirror, Q_{10}-Q_{11}. This stage inverts the signal from Q_1 again, after which the signal appears at the output in parallel with the output of Q_7-Q_9. The outputs of all these current-mirror stages are extremely high in impedance, thus imparting a very high output impedance to the circuit. The entire circuit operates class A; therefore, I_{ABC} programs the quiescent current of the circuit (nominally equal to $2 \, I_{ABC}$) and the peak output current, $\pm I_{ABC}$. Very little voltage swing is lost at either the input or output interface due to the current-mode biasing arrangement and the total absence of resistors.

Both the input pair and the output terminal of the CA3080 can operate at high common-mode potentials, typically within one or two diode drops of the supply potentials. Furthermore, operating parameters of the circuit can be considered essentially constant with varying supply voltage if I_{ABC} is maintained constant. (The supply-voltage range extends from ± 2 V to ± 18 V.)

The relationship of CA3080 operating characteristics to I_{ABC} is appreciated more readily by regarding Fig. 8-32. These ratings show a very linear relationship between I_{ABC} and a given parameter over at least four decades of I_{ABC}. In addition, input offset voltage (Fig. 8-32D) remains virtually unchanged over this same range for moderate temperature changes. The power dissipation for various supply voltages versus I_{ABC} is shown in Fig. 8-32H, which illustrates that the CA3080 can also operate in the micropower region.

8.6.2 The CA3094

Illustrated in Fig. 8-33 is the CA3094, a device also belonging to the OTA family but having the ability to operate as both an OTA and a conventional op amp. The CA3094 is similar to the CA3080, but it has an additional Darlington-connected output stage, Q_{12}-Q_{13}. Both the collector and emitter pins of Q_{13} are made available so that the device can be connected either to source (via pin 6) or to sink (via pin 8) load current through Q_{13}. Since either the emitter or collector of Q_{13} can be used as an output, the sense of polarity of the input terminals is dependent upon this connection, as indicated in the table. The normal OTA output (which is similar to the CA3080) is available at pin 1 and can be used as a frequency compensation point or for ON/OFF control of Q_{12}-Q_{13}. I_{ABC} is applied to pin 5, as in the CA3080, and the supply pins are standard. The CA3094 is flexible enough to be used as an OTA, a conventional op amp, or a gated, programmable power switch, since Q_{13} is rated at 100-mA average output current.

The I_{ABC}-dependent characteristics of the CA3094 and CA3080 are similar and generally follow the curves of Fig. 8-32. Due to the Q_{12}-Q_{13} output stage, however, the CA3094 has some additional characteristics involving the saturation and gain parameters of Q_{12}-Q_{13}. Q_{13} has a typical $V_{CE(sat)}$ of 400 mV at $I_C = 100$ mA, and the composite Q_{12}-Q_{13} stage has a β of 100,000 at 50 mA. This high value of gain can serve as a very effective buffer for the high impedance at pin 1, allowing a high overall voltage gain to be realized.

8.6.3 Frequency Compensation of OTAs

OTAs are unique in that their requirements for frequency compensation under closed-loop operation cannot be stated simply, because of the variable-gain characteristics. For both the CA3080 and

CA3094, the compensation connections for various closed-loop gains (at $I_{ABC} = 500\ \mu A$) are shown in Fig. 8-34 (A and B). Fig. 8-34C is a chart of the compensation values (R_C and C_C) for various closed-loop gains, Fig. 8-34D is the CA3094 open-loop (uncompensated) frequency response, and Fig. 8-34E is a chart of slew rate versus I_{ABC} at various values of C_C for both the CA3080 and CA3094.

In using the charts with these two amplifiers, there are a few points that should be kept in mind. First, the CA3094 is operated with the output stage as an emitter follower by using a resistor returned to V−. It is this circuit that is applicable as a standard (voltage output) op amp. The high β of the CA3094 Darlington output allows a dc open-loop gain of approximately 100 dB, with an uncompensated GBP of 300 MHz (Fig. 8-34D). Compensated for unity gain, the f_t of the CA3094 is on the order of 3 MHz.

Under certain conditions, the CA3080 will yield results similar to these since the voltage amplification mechanism of the two devices is the same. However, for the CA3080 to attain a high open-

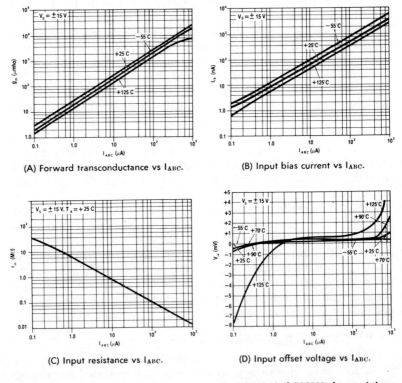

(A) Forward transconductance vs I_{ABC}.

(B) Input bias current vs I_{ABC}.

(C) Input resistance vs I_{ABC}.

(D) Input offset voltage vs I_{ABC}.

Fig. 8-32. Typical CA3080 characteristics as

loop gain, it must be buffered so that external loading does not reduce the product, $g_m R_L$. Buffering is, in fact, what the CA3094 provides internally with its Darlington stage, but the CA3080 can be operated similarly using an external buffer.

The frequency compensation components of Fig. 8-34A are valid for $I_{ABC} = 500$ μA, which is nearly a worst-case condition, since higher I_{ABC} values are not recommended. As noted from Fig. 8-34D, reduction of I_{ABC} reduces the GBP; so, at lower I_{ABC} settings the compensation capacitance shown for stability at 500 μA will actually be greater than necessary (i.e., overcompensation). If optimum speed is to be retained, C_C should be reduced in proportion to the I_{ABC} reduction.

Slew rate is another I_{ABC}-dependent parameter, since I_{ABC} directly determines the output current available to charge C_C. Slew rate for the CA3080 or CA3094 is simply I_{ABC}/C_C. For example, with either the CA3080 or the CA3094 operating at unity gain, the slew rate would be

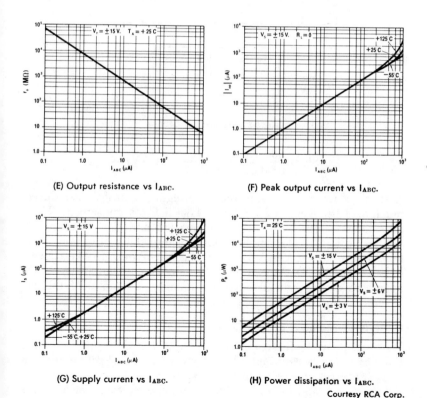

(E) Output resistance vs I_{ABC}.

(F) Peak output current vs I_{ABC}.

(G) Supply current vs I_{ABC}.

(H) Power dissipation vs I_{ABC}.

Courtesy RCA Corp.

a function of amplifier bias current (I_{ABC}).

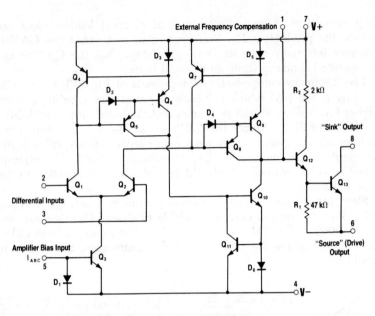

Output Mode	Output Terminal	Inputs	
		Inv.	Noninv.
"Source"	6	2	3
"Sink"	8	3	2

Fig. 8-33. Schematic of CA3094.

$$\text{SR} = \frac{500 \ \mu\text{A}}{1000 \ \text{pF}} = \frac{5 \times 10^{-4}}{10^{-9}} = 0.5 \ \text{V}/\mu\text{s}.$$

Thus, the slew rate will be increased at higher gains if C_C is reduced, but it will be decreased for lower I_{ABC} if C_C is unchanged. These considerations for frequency compensation and slew rate are not applicable to all OTA applications, because there are many situations where an OTA may be used uncompensated. Unlike conventional op amps, OTAs can even be operated as amplifiers in the open-loop mode with adequate dc stability. Examples of this are covered in the following applications.

8.6.4 Basic Methods of I_{ABC} Control

A final point of discussion before examining OTA applications is the technique for controlling I_{ABC}. Some examples of different forms of I_{ABC} control are shown in Fig. 8-35.

Figs. 8-35A and 8-35B are the simplest circuits, consisting of a single resistor (either to ground or to V+), with the current in the resistor establishing I_{ABC}. This method is similar to the basic I_{set} control method for the 4250 or 776, with the slight difference that the I_{ABC} input terminal is referred to V− in an OTA (whereas I_{set} is referenced to V+). This form of control is adequate if I_{ABC} will not be varied and if the supply voltage is constant. (See Fig. 8-3E for a method of supply-independent biasing which is also applicable to I_{ABC} control.)

In addition to those applications that require programming I_{ABC} for particular operating characteristics, OTAs are well suited for both gated and linear forms of I_{ABC} control to accomplish multiplexing, modulation, etc. Fig. 8-35C illustrates a simple logic-controlled OTA. An open-collector logic gate is used to steer current I_{ABC} either to Q_1 or to ground. When the gate output is high, I_{ABC} flows through Q_1 and biases A_1 on. When the gate output goes low, the current is diverted from Q_1 and A_1 is turned off. This circuit can be used at any I_{ABC} value within the rating of A_1, and I_{ABC} is not dependent upon the V− supply. The V+ supply can be any positive potential available.

For linear control of I_{ABC}, a means of generating a linear voltage-controlled current is necessary. Fig. 8-35D is an example where the emitter current of Q_2 is the difference of V+ and E_c. Q_1 provides temperature compensation for the V_{BE} variations of Q_2, thus making the output current relatively independent of temperature. Note that the output current of this stage is maximum when E_c is minimum and that it decreases as E_c approaches V+. This circuit is most appropriate for limited dynamic-range applications, with I_{ABC} variations of 40 dB or less for good linearity.

A very precise form of linear I_{ABC} control is the VCCS of Fig. 8-35E, which is explained in Chapter 4. This circuit generates an output current, $I_{ABC} = E_c/R_{ABC}$. For wide dynamic range, Q_1 must operate at low currents; this makes the input bias current of A_2 a consideration at $I_{ABC} \leq 500$ nA. For this reason an 8007 is shown, but a 108 (compensated) or a 1556 are also good choices. The offset of A_2 should be adjusted with E_c at a low level (< 100 mV) for the desired I_{ABC}. This forces I_{ABC} to be dependent on E_c only, with no error due to V_{io}, and optimizes the low-level linearity of I_{ABC}. With this circuit, dynamic ranges of four decades (80 dB) or more are possible, depending upon A_2. I_{ABC} is, of course, independent of both power supplies in this circuit. R_{ABC} should be a precision type for optimum performance.

Other forms of VCCS are possible as long as they satisfy the requirements of biasing for the I_{ABC} input, which is at a voltage potential one diode drop above the V− line (see Fig. 8-31). The clamping diode, D_1, is suggested for protection of Q_1 if E_c accidentally reverses polarity.

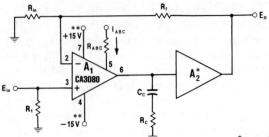

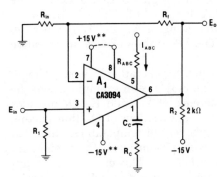

* To use the CA3080 as a conventional op amp, a unity-gain buffer (A_2) can be used at the output—such as a FET, Darlington pair, or other follower.

(A) CA3080 circuit showing compensation.

** In subsequent circuits, the supply terminals (pins 4 and 7) of the CA3080 and CA3094 are not shown if standard $\pm$15-V supplies are used. Pins 6 and 8 of the CA3094 (emitter and collector of Q_{13}) are always shown.

(B) CA3094 circuit showing compensation.

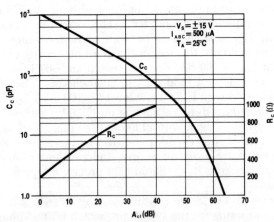

(C) Compensation values (R_C and C_C) vs closed-loop gain for the CA3080 and CA3094.

Fig. 8-34. Frequency compensation

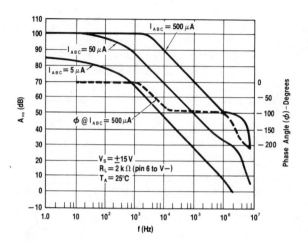

(D) CA3094 open-loop gain vs frequency.

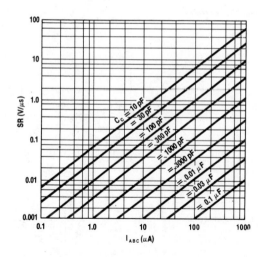

(E) Slew rate of CA3080 and CA3094 vs I_{ABC} and C_C.

of the CA3080 and CA3094.

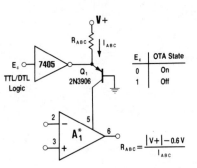

(A) R_ABC to ground.

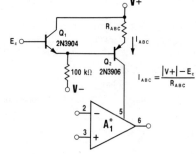

(B) R_ABC to V+.

(C) Gated TTL control.

(D) Linear control.

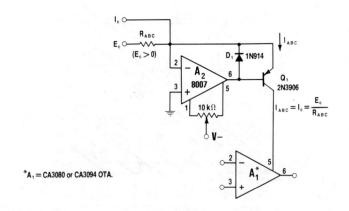

(E) Precision linear control.

Fig. 8-35. Methods of establishing I_{ABC}.

$$R_{ABC} = \frac{|V-| - 0.6\,V}{I_{ABC}}$$

$$R_{ABC} = \frac{|V+| + |V-| - 0.6\,V}{I_{ABC}}$$

E_c	OTA State
0	On
1	Off

$$R_{ABC} = \frac{|V+| - 0.6\,V}{I_{ABC}}$$

$$I_{ABC} = \frac{|V+| - E_c}{R_{ABC}}$$

$$I_{ABC} = I_c = \frac{E_c}{R_{ABC}}$$

*A_1 = CA3080 or CA3094 OTA.

8.7 OTA APPLICATIONS

This section discusses OTAs in various circuits, with special emphasis on applying the unique characteristics peculiar to these types.

8.7.1 Gain-Controlled Amplifiers

Since an OTA is an idealized differential amplifier with a single-ended output current, it follows that it is also an ideal two-quadrant transconductance multiplier, the basics of which were described in Chapter 5. It is usually much simpler to use an OTA for a multiplying function, however, as it contains much (all, in some applications) of the needed hardware. For voltage- or current-controlled amplification, it has already been shown that a two-quadrant muliplier is the best choice. This initial section discusses the advantages of OTAs and the considerations involved in using OTAs as gain-controlled amplifiers.

Basic Voltage-Controlled Amplifier (VCA)

The simplest form of circuit that utilizes the variable-gain property of an OTA is the VCA shown in Fig. 8-36. In this circuit a vari-

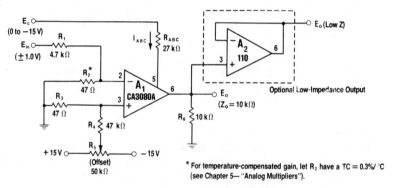

Fig. 8-36. Basic VCA using CA3080A.

able voltage at the E_c input varies the current in R_{ABC} and hence the g_m value of the 3080A. I_{ABC} is at its maximum of 500 μA when $E_c = 0$, and it is reduced as E_c approaches the V– potential (–15 V). (A 3080A is used because of its controlled characteristics with I_{ABC} variations.)

The output current of the 3080A develops a voltage across R_6 that constitutes the output voltage. Since the gain of an OTA is $g_m R_L$, a full-scale g_m of approximately 10 mmhos (times 10 kΩ) yields a voltage gain $A_v = (10^{-2})(10^4) = 100$. This, of course, assumes that any external parallel loading across R_6 is negligible.

The input voltage applied to A_1 is reduced by voltage divider R_1-R_2 for two reasons: to reduce the net gain of the circuit to unity and, more importantly, to reduce the input voltage applied to A_1. The natural transfer characteristic of a differential amplifier is linear only for small input amplitudes, and without correction it must be less than ± 10 mV for output distortion to be less than 1.0%. R_1 and R_2 form a 100:1 divider that scales a nominal ± 1-V signal to ± 10 mV at A_1 and satisfies this requirement. Larger input amplitudes can be used if greater output nonlinearity is tolerable, up to the point where output voltage is limited by $\pm I_{ABC} R_6$ volts, or ± 5 V as shown.

Since the amplifier gain is a direct function of g_m, g_m variations with temperature give it a $-0.3\%/{}^{\circ}C$ gain coefficient. This can be compensated by making the R_1-R_2 divider ratio vary with temperature at an equal and opposite rate, as discussed in Chapter 5. In practice, this would amount to making R_2 a series combination of Sensistor and low-TC resistor, with a net TC of $0.3\%/{}^{\circ}C$. The temperature coefficient of g_m should be considered in any OTA open-loop stage if good accuracy is expected.

Since input signals of ± 10 mV are not significantly greater than the possible input offset voltage of an OTA, offset voltage adjustment will normally be required. R_5 is adjusted for a zero dc output voltage at maximum gain.

For some applications, a disadvantage of this basic OTA gain control is its high output impedance, which is in fact the value used for R_6. Gain can be made independent of loading by following R_6 with a unity-gain, low-offset buffer such as a 110 (shown in the inset). This allows much higher gains to be realized because R_6 can assume values up to a megohm before the offset across R_6 becomes appreciable (due to bias current).

A second form of this basic circuit is illustrated in Fig. 8-37. This circuit is the same as Fig. 8-36, with the exception of the output circuit. Since the output of an OTA is a current source, a natural interface is a current-to-voltage converter. A_2 serves this function, producing an output voltage across R_6. For equivalent values of R_6, the output voltage in this case is identical to Fig. 8-36, with an additional sign inversion due to A_2. A_2 is shown as a general-purpose type in this example, but it can be any op amp that is compensated for unity gain. R_6 (and R_7) can be raised for greater gain, as previously, but if values beyond 100 kΩ are desired, a low-input-current amplifier should be considered for A_2, such as types 8007, 1556, or 108. A_2 adds an additional output offset voltage to E_o, which is equal to the unamplified V_{io} of A_2. For precise applications, then, offset nulling of A_2 should be considered in addition to offset nulling of the OTA.

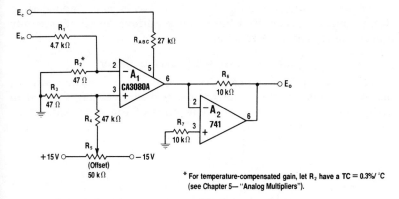

Fig. 8-37. VCA with current-to-voltage converter.

This basic circuit can also use a 3094 OTA, which has an internal buffer, allowing low-impedance outputs to be driven directly (Fig. 8-38). Here, R_6 and R_7 are used as load resistors for the OTA section of the 3094, and the voltage developed is buffered and taken from pin 6. R_8 serves as "pull-down" resistor for the emitter-follower output. Due to the voltage drop ($2 V_{BE}$) of the Darlington output stage, pin 6 will be biased 1.2 V below pin 1 (see schematic of 3094, Fig. 8-33). R_6-R_7 can be altered, if desired, to provide a bias voltage of +1.2 V at pin 1 and to cause the output to rest near zero volts. This does not alter the gain control mechanism of the OTA, and the load resistance at pin 1 is the parallel resistance of R_6-R_7. It should be noted that the circuit does not provide a precise dc base line because

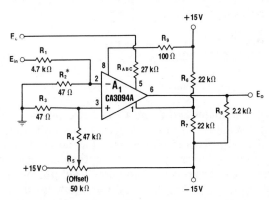

Fig. 8-38. VCA with CA3094 for buffered output.

of the temperature dependence of V_{BE}, but in many applications (for instance, if ac coupled) this is not important, and it can provide a much simplified VCA function.

Voltage-Controlled Mixer/Amplifier

OTA gain-controlled stages deliver a controlled output current; hence, they adapt quite readily to mixed or summed stages as shown in Fig. 8-39. This circuit is a modification of Fig. 8-37, with addi-

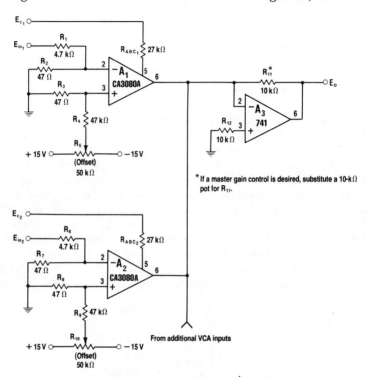

Fig. 8-39. Voltage-controlled mixer/amplifier.

tional VCA input stages and A_3 as a summing inverter. Scale factors for each input stage remain the same; so a composite output current is developed in R_{11}. This circuit is useful as an audio mixer for recording or public-address systems. Note that in such applications A_1 (or A_2, etc.) can be converted to a low-level preamp by applying the signal directly to the $(-)$ input, if the input signals are less than the ± 10-mV maximum mentioned previously. A composite gain control may be obtained by making R_{11} a linear rheostat, which will reduce all signals to zero together. The composite gain can also be made voltage controlled by using another VCA for this stage.

8.7.2 Improvements in Basic OTA Gain-Controlled Stages

Using OTAs as gain-controlled stages involves several points that should be considered for optimum performance. One of these—the variation in gain due to the temperature dependence of transconductance—has already been touched upon. Another is the limitation on linearity and dynamic range due to the differential-amplifier transfer characteristic. Finally, the I_{ABC} parameter must be considered in further detail if an extended range of linearity is to be achieved or if functions other than linear control are to be realized.

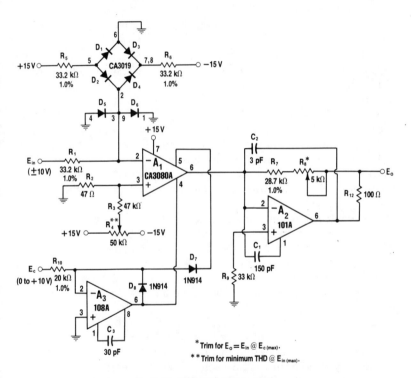

Fig. 8-40. High-performance VCA.

Fig. 8-40 is a highly developed form of VCA that incorporates a number of features to lend it greater precision.

As mentioned previously, the gain TC of a transconductance amplifier can be compensated by introducing an equal and opposite TC into the signal path. Chapter 5 (Fig. 5-67) also introduced another method, the generation of a linear transfer function by using an element within a feedback loop. Fig. 8-40 is an example of the latter

455

approach, but this circuit accomplishes linearity without adding active components.

The diode bridge, consisting of matched diodes D_1-D_4, is biased at a current value nominally equal to $I_{ABC(max)}$. With one side of the bridge (pin 6) grounded, the impedance looking into the opposite side (pin 2) is very low, essentially the diode dynamic impedance. If a linear current is fed into the bridge at this junction, the voltage developed will be the current/voltage characteristic of the bridge—identical to the differential-input voltage required for a linear output current. A current source to drive the bridge is very closely approximated by R_1, which converts the input voltage to a current that is absorbed in the bridge. The resultant voltage is applied to A_1 as an input voltage, automatically adjusting the drive as temperature varies.

With this technique the input to A_1 can be raised to about 100-mV p-p; compared to the previous 20 mV, this is a significant increase. With the values shown, input and output signal-handling range is ±10 V. Even at these output levels the distortion remains well below 1.0%, and at lower levels it falls to 0.1% or less. R_8 is a trim for unity gain at $I_{ABC(max)}$; R_4 is used to trim the input offset of A_1 for optimum linearity. The currents in R_5 and R_6 must be balanced for minimum voltage offset of the bridge—if this is not done, additional distortion will be generated due to the unbalanced transfer characteristic. Thus, R_5 and R_6 should have close tolerances and V+ and V− should track together.

The control current for A_1 is generated by a precision VCCS, which forces I_{ABC} to be linearly proportional to E_c. If other than a 108A type is used for A_3, it should be offset trimmed for calibration with E_c at +10 mV, or three decades below maximum. Operation over four decades or more is possible with a 3080A for A_1, but for I_{ABC} levels below 100 nA, A_3 should be an 8007 or a 108 to provide best tracking.

Another desirable form of I_{ABC} control is one that is exponentially related to the input control voltage, E_c. An antilog generator from Chapter 5 can be adapted to this purpose, giving an attenuation that changes by a factor of ten for each volt of change in E_c, or 20 dB/V. This arrangement offers a distinct advantage in audio mixers, for instance, where the attenuators are calibrated in dB units.

Amplitude Modulator

An amplitude modulator is a special case of the two-quadrant multiplier, arranged so that the modulating signal adds to and subtracts from a constant dc level and establishes an average carrier level (see Chapter 5). Fig. 8-41 is a simple example of an amplitude modulator using an OTA.

This circuit is similar to some circuits described previously, with two differences: load resistance R_8 is lowered to extend bandwidth and R_7 sets the static I_{ABC} current to 500 μA. This establishes a constant ±100-mV output carrier level with ±1.0 V of carrier input. C_1 and R_6 convert the modulating voltage, E_m, to a corresponding current added to the dc current in R_7; this, in effect, modulates I_{ABC}. With the values shown, ±10 V at the modulation input accomplishes 100% a-m. If desired, modulation sensitivity can be increased by decreasing the value of R_6.

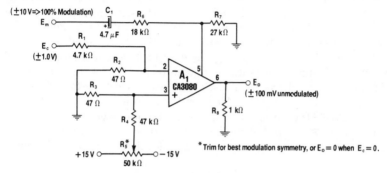

Fig. 8-41. Amplitude modulator.

Other schemes can be utilized for modulation of I_{ABC}, including dc coupling if necessary. The basic requirement is a static I_{ABC} that can be modulated between 2 I_{ABC} (positive peak) and 0 (negative peak). For best modulation symmetry, offset nulling of the OTA is recommended. This circuit is useful with carrier frequencies up to approximately 1 MHz. If desired, higher output levels are available by substituting a 3094 for the 3080 and increasing R_8. The 3094 output stage is then used as an emitter follower (similar to Fig. 8-38), furnishing a low output impedance.

AGC Amplifier

An interesting application of the OTA gain-control capability is illustrated in Fig. 8-42. This circuit is an OTA, automatic gain control (agc) amplifier, using a single 3094 as both a signal rectifier and a controlled gain stage.

With no signal applied, I_{ABC} is at a maximum set by V+ and R_5 + R_7. Output voltage is developed across R_8, the 3094 OTA-section load resistor. When signal is applied, output increases until the positive peaks reach a level of approximately 1.2 V. At this signal level, the 3094 output Darlington pair (see Fig. 8-33) begins to conduct since the emitter of Q_{13} (pin 6) is connected to ground. In essence, the conduction of Q_{13} is rectification of the pin 1 output level, and the Q_{13} current diverts some of the current from R_7. The current in Q_1 (or I_{ABC}) is correspondingly lowered, thus reducing the OTA gain. Further input increases cause further gain decreases; this regulates the output level at approximately 2×1.2 V p-p. The sensitivity of regulation is high; over the active dynamic range, the output changes only a few decibels. For the values shown, the circuit can control the output over about 30 dB of input variation. Distortion rises with increasing inputs because of the amplifier transfer characteristic, even though the output is held relatively constant. If desired, this could be corrected with the diode-input circuit of Fig. 8-40, but in basic form the circuit is best suited to input levels of about ± 10 mV as an operating center. Input offset is suggested for the 3094 to prevent an output base-line shift at low input levels. The rate of gain increase (from high-level input to low-level input) is set by the R_5-C_1 time constant, and C_1 can be altered for different times. This system is inherently a fast-attack, slow-decay system since Q_{13} can charge C_1 quickly, but C_1 must then discharge through R_5.

As shown, the circuit is best suited for low-level use, such as a microphone preamp that can be made to deliver a constant-level output. It can, of course, be used at higher levels with an input attenuator.

8.7.3 OTA Multiplexers

The variable g_m property of an OTA is useful not only in linearly controlled gain applications but also in switched-mode applications, such as multiplexers and gated amplifiers.

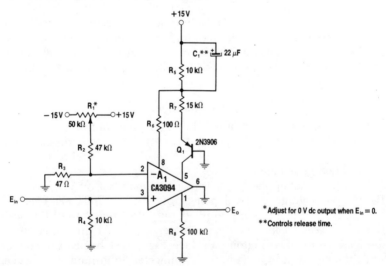

Fig. 8-42. OTA preamp with agc.

A basic, OTA two-channel multiplexer is shown in Fig. 8-43. This circuit programs a single OTA follower on, and the follower passes the signal to the output at unity gain. Both stages are operated with $I_{ABC} = 500 \ \mu A$ for the highest speed. Because only one channel is on at a given time, the outputs are simply bussed together, with common feedback. Thus, the compensation network, C_C-R_C, can be shared by the multiplex stages. The 10-kΩ resistors in series with the differential-input terminals of each stage prevent excessive differential-input current when that particular stage is in the off state. The control logic operates according to the truth table, and is TTL compatible.

With ±15-V supplies, the stage can handle ±5-V (or greater) input/output levels, but the same basic scheme can be used at lower supply levels—even battery-operated—due to the wide OTA supply range.

The circuit shown has a current output capability limited to $\pm I_{ABC}$; therefore, any load resistance used must be high enough so that the product ($I_{ABC}R_L$) is greater than $E_{in(max)}$. For $I_{ABC} = 500 \ \mu A$ and $E_{in} = \pm 10$ V, for instance, this implies an R_L value of 20 kΩ or greater.

For greater output drive, a combination 3080 and 3094 circuit can be used, as in Fig. 8-44. This allows the use of the 3094 output stage

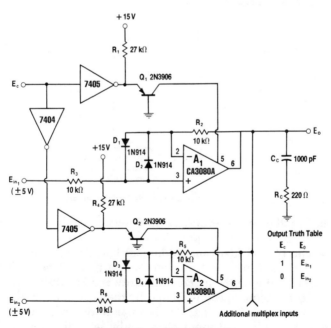

Fig. 8-43. Basic OTA multiplexer.

as an emitter follower, which increases the current output capability and removes the possibility of error due to loading.

This circuit is functionally identical to the 3080 circuit of Fig. 8-43 since the OTA outputs are bussed together at pin 1 of the 3094. Feedback is taken around the 3094 emitter follower, regardless of which channel is on. (The 3094 output stage can be operated independently of the OTA section.)

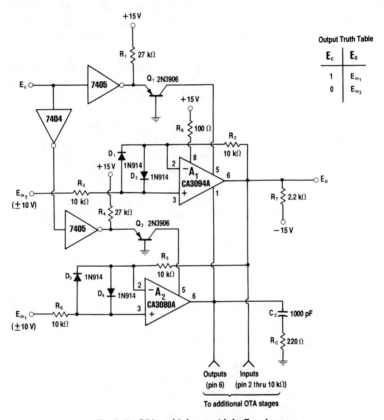

Fig. 8-44. OTA multiplexer with buffered output.

Either of the two previous multiplexers is easily expanded by bussing additional OTA input channels as shown, and by adding appropriate control logic and additional I_{ABC} drives. The performance of these multiplexers is excellent—on/off isolations of 80 dB or more, combined with the inherent linearity and low distortion of the follower connection. Speed is limited by the I_{ABC} value used and by C_C (approximately 0.5 V/μs as shown). If desired, gain can be added to the individual input channels by providing feedback attenuation. Due to the additional loading this represents on the output, it is most appropriate for Fig. 8-44.

Fig. 8-45 illustrates a type of multiplexer that is unique to the OTA— a summing multiplexer with the gain of each individual input channel also linearly controllable by an external voltage.

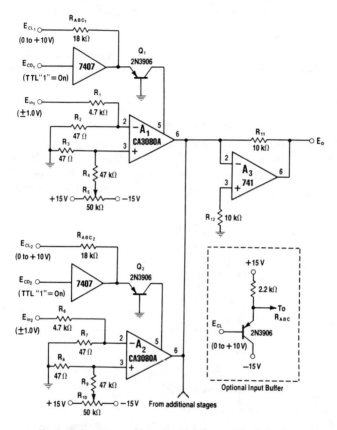

Fig. 8-45. Summing multiplexer with voltage-controlled gain.

This circuit is an adaptation of Fig. 8-39, the voltage-controlled mixer. A_1 and A_2 are gain-controlled input channels, summed at the A_3 output stage. A combination of linear and switched I_{ABC} control is used. With a "1" digital level at the E_{CD} inputs, Q_1 (or Q_2) is ON and conducts a current proportional to E_{CL}. With E_{CL} at +10 V, for example, I_{ABC} is at a maximum of 500 μA, yielding a net gain of unity for that channel. As E_{CL} is reduced, gain is reduced. E_{CD} can be used to switch the channel OFF, regardless of the E_{CL} level. Thus, the circuit is programmable in both a linear and a digital sense.

Like the previous circuits, this version is expandable by summing additional stages at the input to A_3. For precision or for a wide dynamic range of the E_{CL} inputs, the V_{BE} of Q_1 may be a limitation. Improved control of I_{ABC} can be obtained by using the optional input buffer (shown in the inset) which cancels the offset of Q_1. This provides a greater dynamic range of linear control as well as a high input resistance, with no sacrifice in logic control capability.

8.7.4 Waveform Generators

Because of the programmable output-current capability of an OTA, they are well suited to circuits requiring a controlled, constant current. Among these are function generators that operate on the principle of a constant current in a capacitor.

Basic OTA Function Generator

Fig. 8-46 illustrates a basic OTA function generator designed around a 3094. The I_{ABC} value is set by R_{ABC_1}. This current establishes the current applied to timing capacitor C_t. If a positive input is assumed at A_1, C_t will charge negatively toward V$-$ at the rate of

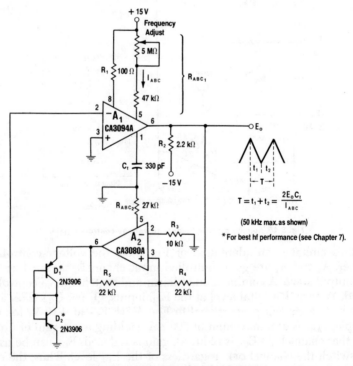

$$T = t_1 + t_2 = \frac{2E_0 C_t}{I_{ABC}}$$

(50 kHz max. as shown)

* For best hf performance (see Chapter 7).

Fig. 8-46. Basic OTA function generator.

I_{ABC} volts per second. The OTA output stage buffers the high-impedance node and presents a low-impedance replica of the C_t voltage at pin 6. A_2 is a control comparator with hysteresis, having trip levels set by its internal zener voltage and by R_4-R_5. A_2 changes state as E_0 crosses the comparison points, and reverses the relative input voltage to A_1. This causes the current in C_t to reverse, changing the output slope. The basic theory of this oscillating loop is the same as for those described previously in Chapter 7; the differences are only in the manner of implementation.

The 3094 used for A_1 accomplishes current-controlled integration and output buffering with a single device. The dynamic range of control is about 100:1 with this scheme, being limited at the low end by the idle current of the output stage. This current subtracts from the current in C_t, and, although small by virtue of the high Darlington current gain, it becomes significant at low I_{ABC} values. This has the effect of making the basic triangular waveform asymmetrical.

The circuit shown does not have a square-wave output to minimize the loading on A_2. If a high current output is desired from A_2, it can also be a 3094. (An example of this form is shown in a subsequent circuit.)

Many variations are possible with this function generator beyond the simple circuit shown. Frequency modulation of the output can be accomplished by summing a current at the I_{ABC} input of A_1. The circuit shown will operate in this fashion between 50 Hz and 50 kHz, but C_t can be switch selected for other ranges. The lower frequency limit is determined only by the small current drawn away from the timing capacitor. Reducing this error current with buffers can greatly extend the dynamic range, as shown in the next circuit.

High-Performance OTA Function Generator

A circuit optimized for low-timing-current error and wide dynamic range of control is shown in Fig. 8-47. This circuit uses an OTA to drive the classic form of function generator—an op-amp integrator that converts the input current (in this case $\pm I_{ABC}$) to a voltage ramp. A_1 is the current-controlled integrator, which delivers a timing current of $+I_{ABC}$ or $-I_{ABC}$ to A_2. A_2 is an 8007 (FET-input) op amp, which reduces the bias current error to around 2-3 pA. Assuming a 500-μA maximum value for I_{ABC} and a 500-pA usuable lower limit ($\cong 100\ I_{ib}$), the dynamic range is six decades. This range is highly dependent on the quality of A_4, the I_{ABC} control amplifier. The restrictions on I_{ib} that apply to A_2 also apply to A_4 since they handle the same current, I_{ABC}. Therefore, A_4 must be a device comparable in performance to A_2.

The input to A_4 can be either a current or a voltage, but a current drive will allow a greater dynamic range of control: as E_c reduces and approaches zero, the offset voltage and offset voltage drift of A_4 become increasingly significant. Offset voltage nulling is mandatory for a wide dynamic range of E_c and will allow about four decades of voltage control. A greater dynamic range, up to about six decades, is possible from a current-source input.

For smaller dynamic ranges, higher-input-current types such as a 108 or 1556 can be used for A_2 and A_4. Alternatively, even relatively high-current types such as the 741 can be used if bias current compensation is used at the summing points of A_2 and A_4 (see Chapter 7).

The considerations for selection of A_3 are generally from a speed standpoint. As shown, high-speed diodes and the maximum I_{ABC} are used with A_3. This yields a 50-kHz upper frequency limit, which is compatible with the 6-V/μs slew-rate limit of A_2. C_t can, of course, be changed for a different span of frequencies, as noted previously.

Variable-Period, Multifunction Generator

The basic current-controlled integration process using OTAs is adaptable to many forms of time-dependent functions beyond the basic sawtooth/square-wave function generator; Fig. 8-48 is one example.

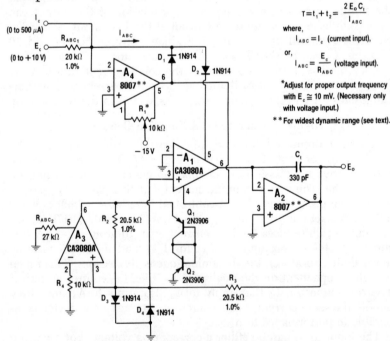

Fig. 8-47. Wide-range OTA function generator.

464

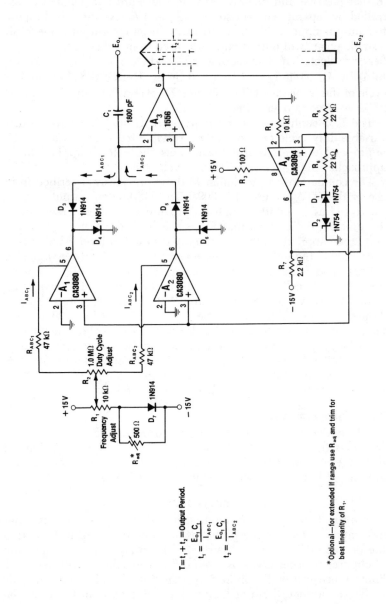

Fig. 8-48. Multifunction generator with triangle, sawtooth, pulse, and square-wave outputs.

$T = t_1 + t_2 = $ Output Period.

$$t_1 = \frac{E_{O_1} C_1}{I_{ABC_1}}$$

$$t_2 = \frac{E_{O_1} C_1}{I_{ABC_2}}$$

*Optional—for extended If range use R_{adj} and trim for best linearity of R_1.

This circuit is similar to the basic sawtooth integrator, differing in that positive and negative timing slopes are independently controlled by separate current sources, A_1 and A_2. A_1 controls the positive output slope, while A_2 controls the negative output slope. Only a single polarity of output current is used from either of these amplifiers, as selected by steering diodes D_3 and D_5. Thus, I_{ABC_1} is supplied to A_3 by A_1, while I_{ABC_2} is supplied by A_2. During the alternate OFF cycle of the respective OTAs, D_4 and D_6 clamp the outputs and minimize OFF/ON recovery time.

The I_{ABC} control network composed of R_1 and R_2 allows both a variable duty cycle (via R_2) and a variable frequency (via R_1). D_7 improves low-level control linearity as the voltage applied to R_2 approaches the I_{ABC} input-voltage level.

The comparator, A_4, is similar to those previously described in its use of the OTA section of a 3094. The Darlington output stage is connected as an emitter follower, providing a buffered rectangular wave at pin 6 (E_{o_2}). Output E_{o_2} is a bipolar waveform with a p-p amplitude approximately equal to $\pm V_Z$ shifted in level -1.2 volts.

As shown, the maximum square-wave frequency (R_2 centered) is 1.0 kHz and is adjusted by R_1 down to at least 10 Hz. A greater range can be realized by trimming the diode drop of D_7 with R_{adj} so that the D_7 voltage drop is nearer that of the OTA internal diode. At any frequency, the duty cycle can be adjusted for a 20:1 asymmetry, allowing sawtooth and pulse waveforms to be generated as well. With the values shown, minimum pulse (or ramp) width is 50 μs, limited by the slewing rate of A_3. Smaller values are possible if a 118 is substituted for A_3, but this may compromise the total range unless bias current compensation is used.

8.7.5 Signal Processing

Within the general realm of signal processing there are numerous functions that can use OTA characteristics to advantage. Many of these are not general or broad enough in scope to warrant separate groupings, but they deserve mention nevertheless.

Voltage Limiter

The function of op-amp limiting was discussed in various forms in Chapter 5. One of the problems often encountered in limiters is the degree of limiting, or "hardness." If an absolutely abrupt form of clipping is necessary, it is often difficult to achieve with feedback limiters because of the finite impedance of the elements typically used. An alternate form of limiter is possible with an OTA, as diagrammed in Fig. 8-49.

Since the output current of an OTA is limited to a maximum value of $\pm I_{ABC}$, the peak output voltage swing that it can deliver is the

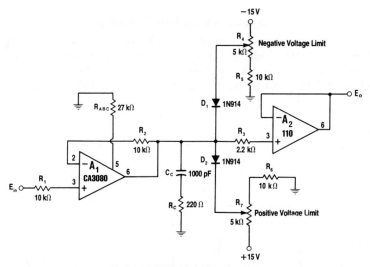

Fig. 8-49. OTA voltage limiter.

product of I_{ABC} and the load resistance. Thus, limiting will automatically occur if the load resistance is lowered below the value necessary to sustain full output. However, it is generally not desirable to simply lower R_L in a feedback stage since this reduces loop gain.

Another form of limiting can be used in which two diodes (D_1-D_2) are normally reverse biased at low levels. When either the positive or the negative output peaks from A_1 exceed the voltage limits set by R_4 and R_7, the diodes conduct and absorb the output current from A_1, limiting its voltage swing. This form of limiter requires a buffer, such as A_2, to maintain loop gain and ensure a constant limiting level with varying loads.

It should be noted that this limiter is absolute; once I_{max} has been exceeded, there can be no further output voltage change. The biased diodes are but one form of defining the signal swing; back-to-back zeners are another. Also, if temperature-independent limiting is desired, a precision clamp (described in Chapter 5) can be used. R_1 and R_2 are necessary to prevent excessive differential-input current to A_1 during limiting, and the stage must be compensated for the working gain. As shown, R_{ABC} sets the slew rate at maximum.

With ±15-V supplies, the stage can handle input/output levels of ±10 V or more, but the same basic scheme can be used at lower supply levels due to the wide OTA supply range.

The circuit has a current output capability limited to I_{ABC}; so the clamping network used must be designed to absorb I_{ABC} without appreciable voltage change.

Class-A "Totem-Pole" Amplifier

As noted previously, the 3094 can be operated with its output stage as a voltage buffer, which gives performance similar to a standard op amp. A simple pull-down resistor connected to V− allows the output stage to be used as a class-A emitter follower (see Fig.

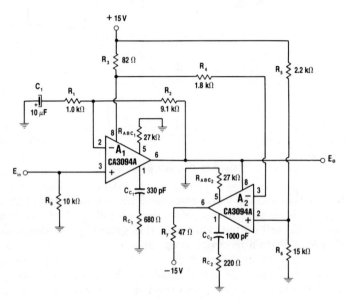

(A) Circuit schematic.

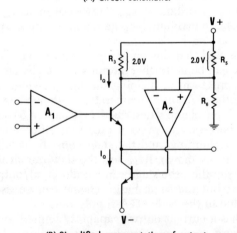

(B) Simplified representation of output.

Fig. 8-50. Class-A "totem-pole" amplifier.

8-34B). This resistor is, of course, the only path for negative output (sink) current. Consequently, if high peak currents are to be supplied, the pull-down resistor must be low, thus creating a substantial quiescent current in the output stage.

Excessive standby current can be eliminated by using a current source as a pull-down element, with the value of the current greater than the expected peak negative output current. A circuit using this principle is shown in Fig. 8-50A.

In this circuit, A_1 is an audio line amplifier with a gain of 20 dB, designed for an output capability of +20 dBm into 600 ohms. This output level requires a peak current of -18.2 mA; therefore, the pull-down current must be in excess of this value. A_2 supplies the negative current in this circuit, operating in a feedback loop around A_1 to control the quiescent current.

The A_2-A_1 output-stage combination form a "totem-pole" output— a configuration that has a characteristically low output impedance, even without overall feedback. R_5 and R_6 establish a reference voltage for A_2 (2.0 V) from V+ to the reference input. Since the $(-)$ input of A_2 will match this voltage, the drop across R_3 is maintained at 2.0 V, thus establishing the output current in A_1. This current is supplied by the output transistor of A_2, which drives A_1 as a cascode. This may be more obvious from the functional diagram of Fig. 8-50B. The voltage across R_5 will also be developed (by the feedback loop) across R_3; then R_3 establishes current I_Q.

The interesting point about the circuit is that I_Q remains constant, regardless of what happens in the feedback loop of A_1. Thus, the gain characteristics of A_1 are set independent of the A_2 loop, in conventional fashion. The feedback loop around A_2 is stabilized for unity gain by C_{C_2}-R_{C_2}. R_7 is selected to drop a voltage comparable to R_3. Generally the voltage drops across R_3 and R_7 should be minimized to allow maximum output swing.

This circuit is useful for virtually any linear amplifier employing the 3094 and can be easily scaled to other currents. As shown, A_1 and A_2 dissipate approximately 360 mW at $V_S = \pm 15$ V.

Sample and Hold

The sample/hold function is also well suited to OTA configurations; Fig. 8-51A illustrates this type of circuit. The 3080A is used as a gated voltage follower, with the output buffered by a 3N138 MOSFET. The extremely high FET-input resistance allows the full $g_m r_o$ product of the OTA to be realized, giving a high loop gain. The R_4-C_3 network serves the dual purpose of frequency compensation and storage of the sampled signal. When ON, this circuit follows the input with the precision that is normally expected of a voltage follower.

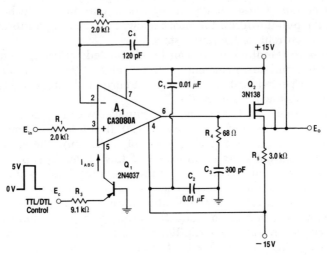

(A) Circuit schematic.

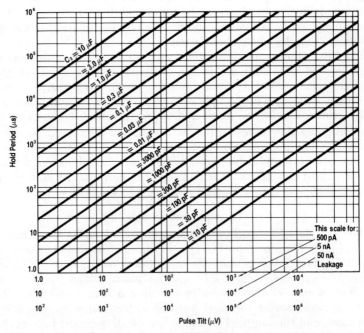

(B) Chart of sample/hold "tilt" as a function of storage capacitance and hold period.

Fig. 8-51. OTA sample/hold circuit.

When the digital sample command is removed, I_{ABC} is reduced to zero and the OTA is gated OFF. However, the charge on the phase compensation capacitor (C_3) is "held," and the MOSFET continues to present this buffered voltage to the output. The only path for discharge of the stored charge is by leakage through the FET gate or the OTA. Thus, the FET device and the 3080A (a low-leakage OTA) are used to minimize these currents. Typically the circuit can provide a discharge slope ("tilt" or "droop") of less than 1.0 mV/ms. A general relationship between storage capacitance, holding time, and tilt exists, as described basically in Chapter 5. The nomograph of Fig. 8-51B summarizes this relationship and can be used to predict the decay error for any time/leakage-current value.

A direct means of reducing the decay error is to increase the value of the storage capacitance. However, in this circuit the capacitor charging rate is limited by I_{ABC}; hence, this will be made at the expense of a lower slew rate, which determines how quickly the circuit can acquire a new sample after holding. The total acquisition time includes the slewing interval plus any subsequent ringing before the circuit has settled to a stable condition. In the circuit of Fig. 8-51A, transient response is optimized by capacitor C_4 and the acquisition time includes a 1.8-V/μs slewing interval plus 1.0 μs (or less) for settling.

For more modest requirements, where slew rate and tilt requirements are not stringent, a simple 3094 can be used to fulfill the sample/hold function by using its output buffer as an emitter follower. Error current can be controlled to some degree by the quiescent current of the emitter follower. A current of 1.0 mA, for instance, will yield a discharge current of about 100 nA. While this is much greater than the leakage current of the circuit in Fig. 8-51A, it may be adequate for many applications.

Comparators

As comparators, OTAs have some useful advantages in certain situations. For instance, they are adjustable in terms of input current, supply voltage, and slew rate. Also, the current output characteristics can make interfacing simple. Furthermore, the integral buffer of the 3094 allows loads of up to 100 mA (300 mA peak) to be driven. In the following general discussion, no details of different comparator configurations are given; for these the reader is referred to Chapter 5. Attention is directed here to the unique OTA characteristics that apply to comparator circuitry.

The most basic OTA comparator uses a 3080 as shown in Fig. 8-52A. Due to the wide OTA supply range, such a stage can be operated from 5-V digital supplies. A 3080 can interface directly with CMOS logic devices while retaining the full open-loop gain, thus making input sensitivity very high. Since it can be operated uncompensated, the slew rate is maximized and can be controlled directly via I_{ABC}; this is illustrated in Fig. 8-52B. Similarly, input current can be minimized by operating at low I_{ABC} values (see Fig. 8-32).

When operating from conventional supplies such as ±15 V, the OTA output swing can be clamped with biased diodes or zeners to define the voltage limits since I_{ABC} limits the output current.

Fig. 8-53A is a 3094 comparator with the output stage connected to source high-load currents at pin 6. Output pins 8 and 6 can be re-

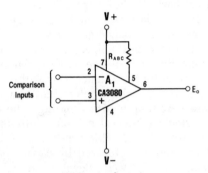

(A) Circuit schematic.

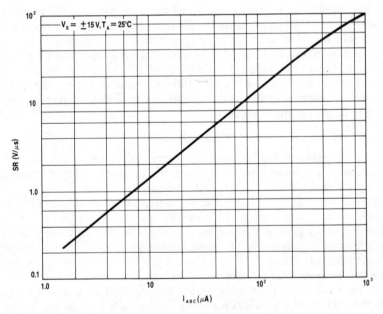

(B) Open-loop slew rate vs I_{ABC}.

Fig. 8-52. Basic OTA comparator.

ferred to supply potentials different from those of the input section—hence the different voltages shown. V_2^+ is used to define the positive output limit; e.g., +5 V for TTL logic. Pin 6 can then be returned either to ground or, if some sink current is necessary, to V_2^-. In this manner the end-point limits of the output swing can be set independently of V_1^+ and V_1^-. The input common-mode voltage range can in fact be much greater than at the output.

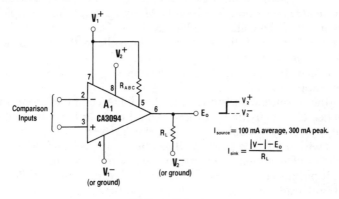

(A) Current-sourcing.

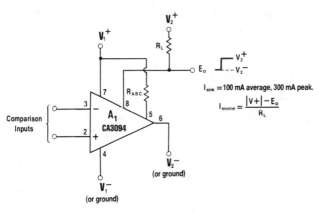

(B) Current-sinking.

Fig. 8-53. CA3094 comparators.

For current-sinking outputs (Fig. 8-53B), pin 8 is used with pin 6 tied to the desired negative limit, usually ground. The voltage at which the output will rest in its OFF state is defined by V_2^+. This configuration is very useful in interfacing with TTL systems. Typically it can drive 50 or more TTL input loads of 1.6 mA each.

8.8 CURRENT-DIFFERENCING AMPLIFIERS

The CDA was developed to meet a number of commercial/industrial requirements left unfilled by standard op amps. One of these is the requirement for operation from single-ended power supplies over a wide range of voltages, with little change in open-loop characteristics. Although standard op amps can sometimes be operated from single-ended supplies (see Chapter 6), their performance here is not ideal from several standpoints. Many op amps, for example, do not work at all at voltages as low as +5 V (logic supplies). Those that do will generally have a p-p output voltage that is drastically reduced from the power supply voltage. The CDA meets one requirement with its ability to operate from low-voltage, single-ended power supplies.

Another requirement is economy. The CDA combines modest performance characteristics with low overall cost. In keeping with this intent, currently available devices incorporate four individual amplifiers within a single package. The open-loop gain and other characteristics of each amplifier are somewhat reduced compared with general-purpose op amps such as the 741, but for many applications this slight trade-off can produce good performance and wide flexibility at minimum cost.

CDAs have a gain characteristic resembling those of standard op amps in some regards. While the full 100 dB or more of open-loop gain is not always necessary, a stable unity-gain frequency is required since the device is to be used with as few components as possible. Thus, the devices have a 6-dB/octave rolloff through unity gain, but open-loop gain may be less than 100 dB.

8.8.1 CDA Circuitry

A simple common-emitter amplifier, when loaded with a high collector resistance, can achieve gains as high as 60-70 dB with facility. This implies current-source loading, which not only imparts the high stage gain, but also allows the high peak-to-peak output voltage necessary to use the power supply voltage most efficiently. Supply-independent biasing can also be achieved, as seen from Fig. 8-54A where Q_1 is the common-emitter amplifier under discussion and Q_2 is its collector load. If the collector current of Q_2 is maintained constant for any value of V+ (by an internal regulation process, to be discussed shortly), the gain of Q_1 will not change with V+, nor will the input current. Thus, two major parameters are made supply-independent by the inclusion of Q_2. Also, if the base voltage bias of Q_2 is chosen to be very close to V+, the p-p swing available at Q_1 will be near the full supply voltage before Q_2 saturates. It remains only to buffer the high impedance at the collector of Q_1 so that low-

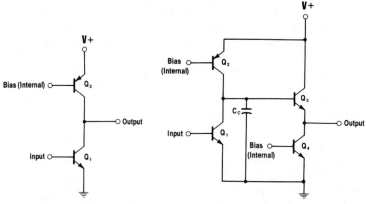

(A) High-gain, single-stage amplifier.   (B) Amplifier with output buffer added.

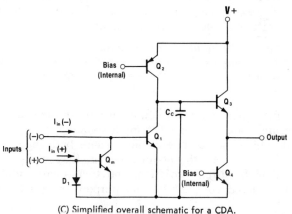

(C) Simplified overall schematic for a CDA.

Fig. 8-54. Basic CDA circuit.

impedance loads can be driven without loss of gain. This is accomplished by emitter-follower Q_3, with a class-A pull-down transistor, Q_4, as shown in Fig. 8-54B. The active pull-down element ensures optimum linearity without loss of output swing; it also provides a minimal quiescent current.

In essence, the buffered common-emitter stage just described is the basic structure of the voltage amplifier used in a CDA. This stage determines the open-loop gain, having a gain rolloff of 6 dB/octave introduced by compensation capacitor C_C. The buffered Q_1 gain stage has a low input current and a stable frequency response. At this point, compared to op-amp flexibility, the obvious omission is a differential-input capability; for as the circuit stands, it can only generate a signal inversion.

The differential-input capability requires one additional stage to provide both a noninverted signal output and also a simplified form of biasing, based on the current-differencing concept. This basic circuit, with a noninverting stage added, is shown in Fig. 8-54C. D_1 and Q_m form a current mirror, which inverts current $I_{in}(+)$ and provides a nominal gain of unity. Thus, for a given input current at the $(+)$ input, Q_m will extract an equal amount of current from the $(-)$ input terminal. The base current of Q_1 is typically in the 50-nA region and can be considered negligible with respect to current I_{in} $(-)$.

The input signal to amplifier Q_1 is therefore the *difference* of the currents, $I_{in}(+)$ and $I_{in}(-)$. With a negative-feedback, closed loop around the amplifier, it will work to minimize the current difference between $I_{in}(+)$ and $I_{in}(-)$; hence the term *current-differencing amplifier,* or CDA. Note that this is in direct contrast to the standard op amp, which operates to maintain the differential-input *voltage* at zero. In fact, we can modify the fundamental axioms of the standard op amp to state the conditions for the CDA:

1. *The differential-input current is zero.*
2. *With the loop closed, the total current into the $(-)$ input will be driven to be equal to the current into the $(+)$ or reference input.*

An axiom analogous to the "zero input current" of the ideal (voltage) op amp would state that the CDA input voltage is zero (a true current sink). This is not precisely true because both inputs will bias at $+V_{BE}$. However, near this nominal voltage they exhibit little voltage *change* with current variation, and their incremental voltage may be considered constant for the purpose of this approximate analysis.

The behavior of a CDA in closed-loop circuitry can be analyzed using these two axioms, just as standard op-amp circuitry is analyzed using its axioms of behavior. The differences in behavior of the CDA inputs should be understood from both a theoretical and a practical standpoint. Since the inputs are current nodes and do not "move" with changes in current, they should never be connected directly to a voltage source. However, advantage can readily be taken of the fact that the input terminals do not change in voltage; a simple series-input resistor to a source of voltage is all that is needed to define the input current. The action of *both* inputs is somewhat analogous to a summing point, and in fact they can be used as such.

A standard op amp is characterized by a common-mode input voltage range—the range of common input voltages over which the device operates within specification. By contrast, a CDA has a common-mode input *current* range—the range of currents over which the current mirror operates.

A more complete understanding of the functioning of the input stage can be taken from Fig. 8-55A, an equivalent circuit for a CDA.

Both input terminals are modeled as diodes to ground, D_1 at the (+) input and D_2 at the (−) input. Although in physical reality there is only one diode at the (+) input (D_1 of Fig. 8-54C), the behavior at the (−) input causes it to appear as a diode there, also.

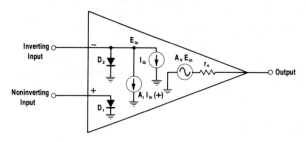

(A) Simplified equivalent circuit.

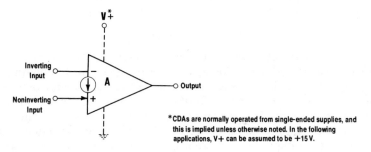

*CDAs are normally operated from single-ended supplies, and this is implied unless otherwise noted. In the following applications, V+ can be assumed to be +15 V.

(B) Schematic symbol.

Fig. 8-55. CDA operation.

The input current, $I_{in}(+)$, is mirrored at the (+) input and appears as a current source at the (−) input, $A_I I_{in}(+)$, where A_I is the current-mirror gain (nominally unity). Also appearing at the (−) input is the input bias current, I_{ib}.

E_{in}, the input voltage to the amplifier, appears only at the (−) input, although it may originate from either input. The output signal is $A_V E_{in}$, which appears behind r_o, the output resistance. In regard to the output stage, a CDA is no different in basic concept than a conventional op amp.

As noted from both the equivalent circuit and the schematic, only the (−) input terminal of a CDA has a requirement for input bias current. The current that is injected into the (+) input is considered a signal. Also, since the current mirror appears in shunt with the $(-)$ input terminal, its use is optional. For applications where it is not desirable, the current mirror can be effectively removed from the circuit by grounding the $(+)$ input terminal.

Since the input structure of a CDA is totally different from conventional op amps, the device warrants a different circuit symbol, shown in Fig. 8-55B. The general shape and input terminal placement is identical to the standard op amp, but a current-source symbol is added between the inputs to denote the mechanism of current differencing and the direction of conventional current flow. Also, the $(+)$ input has an arrow added to denote the injection of reference current into this terminal.

Unlike normal op amps, bipolar power supplies are not assumed to be the convention in CDA operation; single-supply operation is the standard method. In circuits that follow, the dotted connection shown is implied, unless shown otherwise.

8.8.2 CDA Devices

Having discussed some basic properties of the CDA, we can now examine representative devices, of which there are two primary examples: the MC3401/MC3301 and the LM3900/LM2900.

The MC3401/MC3301

The schematic of the MC3401 and MC3301 is shown in Fig. 8-56. This circuit includes four identical CDA circuits, plus the biasing to supply drive for the current sources. If we take an individual amplifier, the resemblance to Fig. 8-54C is apparent. Q_4, an added pnp buffer, reduces the loading on Q_1 by virtue of its current gain. No additional V_{BE} offset is introduced by Q_4, which would reduce output swing if an npn device were used. The Q_6-Q_7-Q_8 circuit is a regulator that programs the current source (Q_5) to a level of 200 μA. This, in turn, establishes the current in Q_1 at approximately 10 μA and sets the typical input bias current of Q_1 at 50 nA. Since Q_5 is referred to the V+ terminal, it sets the positive output swing at about $(V+) - V_{BE}$.

The current in Q_{10}, which determines the output sink current, is established by the 560-Ω resistor. The total output swing is typically only 1 volt less than the supply voltage, for any supply voltage within the device rating. Overall operating bias is furnished by the regulator made up of D_2-D_4, Q_8, and Q_6-Q_7. This circuit maintains open-loop characteristics relatively independent of operating supply voltage.

The 3.0-pF capacitor, C_1, compensates the open-loop response for a 6-dB/octave rolloff through unity gain. This capacitor and the source current available from Q_5 set the positive-going output slew

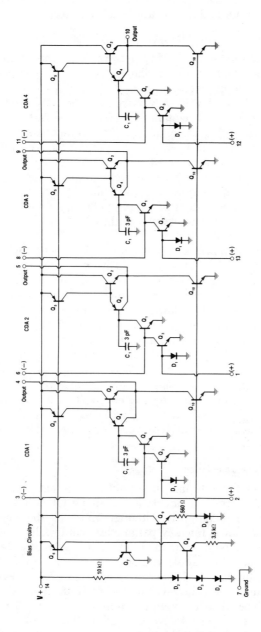

Courtesy Motorola Semiconductor Products, Inc.

Fig. 8-56. Schematic of a typical CDA (MC3401/MC3301).

479

rate of the circuit. The negative-going slew rate is determined by the sink current of Q_1 and can be appreciably faster.

The LM3900/LM2900

The schematic of the LM3900/LM2900 is shown in Fig. 8-57. These devices are basically similar to the MC3401/MC3301 and use the same pin configuration.

Although biasing levels are very similar, the LM3900/LM2900 use a different type of bias regulator that features a start/disconnect circuit, made up of Q_{20}, D_6, and Q_{30}. These components function only to start current flow in Q_3-D_5-D_8, and after Q_{29} is conducting, they are automatically disconnected. This isolates the current established in Q_{29}—and thus the amplifier current—from power suply changes and allows operation at low supply voltages. The current drain in this circuit is independent of supply voltage, an asset at high voltages where the power dissipation of the four amplifiers would otherwise be excessive.

A further difference is noted in the output stage, which uses an added pnp transistor (Q_{16}, Q_{19}, Q_{24}, or Q_{27}). This transistor is normally biased off for class-A operation and sink current is supplied only by the constant-current pull-down transistors. However, under large signal swings, the output stage can operate class B, driving this extra transistor to supply up to 40 mA of sink current. This condition will occur when load/sink current demands exceed the constant current (1.3 mA nominal) of the pull-down sources (Q_{31}, Q_{32}, Q_{34}, and Q_{35}).

For input protection against negative overdrive, a multiemitter transistor, Q_{21}, is used, having one emitter tied to each input terminal. The base bias applied to Q_{21} will cause these "diodes" to conduct at about -0.3 V and prevent input breakdown or parasitic action.

8.8.3 CDA Characteristics

Aside from the internal circuit differences just discussed, there are also differences in characteristics among CDA types. These are summarized in Table 8-1. Although most of the characteristics shown are similar, a few key parameters will usually govern the selection of one type over another. These are primarily the operating temperature and the supply voltage.

The MC3401 and LM3900 are rated from 0°C to +70°C (commercial grade), while the MC3301 and LM2900 operate from -40°C to +85°C. The MC3401 operates from supplies of +5 V to +18 V, and the MC3301 from +4 V to +28 V. Both the LM3900 and LM2900 operate from +4 V to +36 V. These are single-supply voltage ratings. CDAs can be operated from dual supplies if the total voltage range

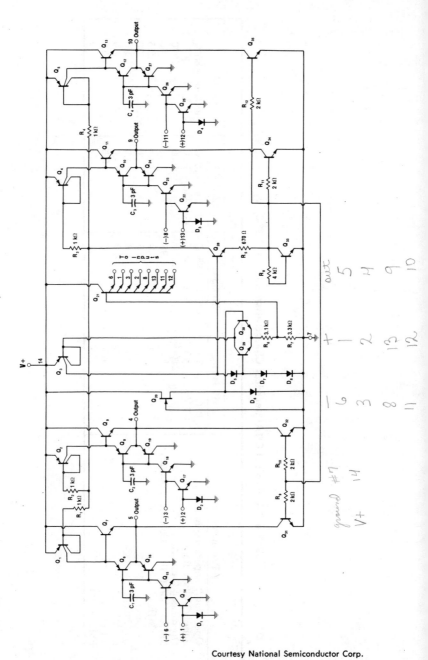

Courtesy National Semiconductor Corp.

Fig. 8-57. Schematic of LM3900/LM2900.

Table 8-1. Typical CDA Electrical Characteristics (T_A = 25°C, V_S = +15V)

Parameter	Device Type			
	MC3401	MC3301	LM3900	LM2900
Operating Temperature Range	0°C to +75°C	−40°C to +85°C	0°C to +70°C	−40°C to +85°C
Supply Voltage Range	+5 V to +18 V	+4 V to +28 V	+4 V to +36 V	+4 V to +36 V
Open-Loop Gain (A_{vo})	2000	2000	2800	2800
Mirror Gain (Mirror Current = 200 μA)	—	0.98	1.0	1.0
f_t (MHz)	5.0	4.0	2.5	2.5
I_{ib} (nA)	50	50	30	30
r_{in} (MΩ)	1.0	1.0	1.0	1.0
r_o (kΩ)	8.0	8.0	8.0	8.0
SR (V/μs)	0.6	0.6	0.5	0.5
PSRR (dB)	55	55	70	70

$(V+) + |V-|$ is within the device rating. Applications discussed in the section will generally be in terms of the basic devices, the MC-3401 and LM3900.

There are other differences between the devices: the LM3900/LM2900 types have about 9-dB higher open-loop gain, while the MC3401/MC3301 types have about twice the bandwidth. The gain and bandwidth characteristics of these CDAs are features that should be appreciated. Although the dc open-loop gain is small by comparison with general-purpose devices, there is more gain available at frequencies above about 1 kHz, as shown by Fig. 8-58. For the LM3900/LM2900 this difference is nearly 10 dB; for the MC-3401/MC3301 it is 12 to 14 dB. For optimization of audio-frequency loop gain, these CDA types can offer definite advantages over general-purpose op amps.

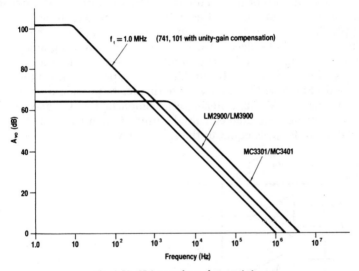

Fig. 8-58. CDA open-loop characteristics.

Before we depart into circuit discussions of CDAs, the functional diagram of Fig. 8-59 is presented. This diagram includes pinouts and supply terminals, and it can be used as a reference when working with the devices.

CDA Biasing

CDA biasing can take on several forms, as shown in Fig. 8-60. The simplest, most easily predictable form of bias using a CDA is via the current-mirror input, as shown in Fig. 8-60A. In this circuit, the current-mirror input is fed a reference current, I_1, which is given by

$$I_1 = \frac{(V+) - V_f}{R_b},$$

where V_f is the diode drop ($\cong 0.5$ V) of the mirror diode and R_b is the bias resistance. Since the current mirror and the CDA will act to maintain $I_2 = I_1$, resistor R_f has an identical current flowing in it. The CDA inputs are both at the same voltage ($+0.5$ V); so the output voltage can be readily determined from the ratio of R_f/R_b, or $E_{o(dc)} = V+ (R_f/R_b)$. Thus, when $R_b = 2R_f$,

$$E_{o(dc)} = V+ \left(\frac{R_f}{2R_f}\right) = \frac{V+}{2},$$

which biases the output at the supply midpoint, an optimum case for maximum undistorted swing. The output will be maintained at $V+/2$, regardless of the supply voltage.

A modified form of this technique is shown in Fig. 8-60B. Because the current-mirror bias of Fig. 8-60A is connected directly to the supply line, it will naturally couple any supply noise to the output. This noise could be decoupled by splitting R_b and using a capacitor from the midpoint of R_b to ground. However, if there are several stages, this method can be prohibitively expensive. An alternative method (Fig. 8-60B) uses a voltage divider to provide a fraction of $V+$, in this case $V+/2$. Filtering is accomplished by C_1, and the reference voltage generated can also be used at other stages. If R_b is set equal to R_f, $E_{o(dc)}$ is equal to the reference voltage.

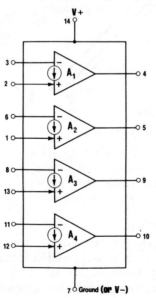

Fig. 8-59. Construction of quad CDAs and pin numbers (for MC3401/MC3301 and LM3900/LM2900).

484

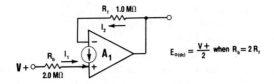

$E_{o(dc)} = \dfrac{V+}{2}$ when $R_b = 2R_f$

(A) Current-mirror biasing.

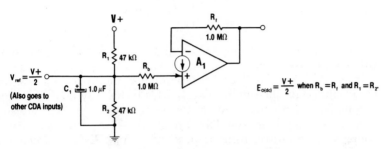

$E_{o(dc)} = \dfrac{V+}{2}$ when $R_b = R_f$ and $R_1 = R_2$.

(B) Current-mirror biasing with noise filtration.

(C) Current-mirror bias using dual supplies.

$E_{o(dc)} = 0\ V\ dc$

*Select R_b for a bias current I_b of 5 μA or more; i.e.,
$I_b \geq 100\, I_{ib}$.

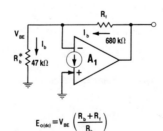

$E_{o(dc)} = V_{BE}\left(\dfrac{R_b + R_f}{R_b}\right)$

(D) V_{BE} multiplier biasing.

Fig. 8-60. CDA biasing techniques.

Biasing is even simpler when a CDA is used with dual supplies, as in Fig. 8-60C. Here R_b is set equal to R_f; so the output is automatically biased at ground level.

One general type of CDA biasing is termed "V_{BE} multiplier bias" since it uses V_{BE} of the $(-)$ input as the reference (Fig. 8-60D). The $(+)$ input is grounded, effectively removing the current mirror from the circuit. Resistors R_b and R_f are selected to provide the desired output voltage, according to

$$E_{o(dc)} = V_{BE}\left(\frac{R_b + R_f}{R_b}\right).$$

In the example shown, $V_{BE} = 0.5$ V and $E_{o(dc)} = 7.5$ V, the optimum value for a 15-V supply.

It should be noted that this type of bias multiplies V_{BE} by the noise gain established by R_b and R_f. This factor may be a limitation in some low-gain circuits due to the loss of loop gain; in such cases a current-mirror bias would be preferable. This technique is also temperature sensitive, being dependent on V_{BE}. Examples of these considerations will be covered in the applications section.

8.8.4 Basic CDA Amplifier Configurations

Like the standard op amp, the CDA has basic amplifying configurations such as noninverting, inverting, and differential stages. These configurations are best approached from the standpoint of ac amplification, for which the CDA is best suited.

Noninverting Amplifier

A CDA noninverting ac amplifier is shown in Fig. 8-61. This stage uses current-mirror bias in its simplest form, a resistor to V+. R_{in} is

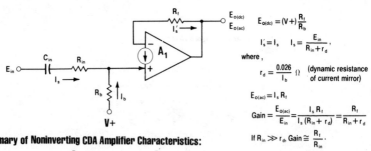

Summary of Noninverting CDA Amplifier Characteristics:

1) Gain $= A_V = \dfrac{R_f}{R_{in} + r_d}$; if $R_{in} \gg r_d$, $A_V \cong \dfrac{R_f}{R_{in}}$.

2) Input impedance $= R_{in} + r_d$.

3) Lower cutoff frequency $(-3$ dB$) = \dfrac{1}{2\pi R_{in} C_{in}}$.

Fig. 8-61 Noninverting ac amplifier using a CDA.

a series-input resistor, chosen for the desired stage gain. Since the current mirror appears as a virtual ground, the signal input current, I_s, is determined by E_{in} and R_{in} as

$$I_s = \frac{E_{in}}{R_{in} + r_d} \,,$$

where r_d is the dynamic resistance of the current mirror. This current modulates the dc bias current, I_b, thus modulating the composite mirror-input current. However, it is easier to visualize the gain mechanism if signal (I_s) and biasing (I_b) currents are considered separately. The current, I_s, appears inverted at the $(-)$ input. This current is inverted again to form I_s in R_f and is then converted to an output voltage, $E_{o(ac)}$, where $E_{o(ac)} = I_s R_f$.

Therefore, the stage gain is

$$A_v = \frac{E_{o(ac)}}{E_{in}} = \frac{I_s R_f}{I_s(R_{in} + r_d)} = \frac{R_f}{R_{in} + r_d} \,.$$

At room temperature, $r_d \cong 0.026/I_b$ Ω, and in most cases the value will be negligible compared with R_{in}. Thus, the stage gain can be approximated as

$$A_v \cong \frac{R_f}{R_{in}} \,.$$

A point to remember is that the current-mirror diode is a nonlinear impedance; therefore, current I_s will become more nonlinear as R_{in} approaches r_d. Practical solutions to the R_{in}-r_d relationship are taken up in the applications section.

$R_{in} + r_d$ constitute the input resistance of the stage, and when $R_{in} \gg r_d$, this simplifies to R_{in}. The lower frequency cutoff point (at -3 dB) is determined similar to the standard op-amp inverter:

$$f_c = \frac{1}{2\pi R_{in} C_{in}} \,.$$

There is a wide range of resistance possible for R_{in}-R_f, depending on the biasing and input impedance levels desired.

Inverting Amplifier

A basic CDA inverting amplifier is shown in Fig. 8-62, again using current-mirror bias. R_f will usually be set (nominally) at $R_b/2$, biasing the output to $V+/2$.

The generation of signal current in this stage is somewhat different than with the noninverting stage. The CDA amplifying mechanism will always work to maintain the current into the $(-)$ input equal to the mirror current (I_b). Thus, the presence of the closed loop causes the CDA to resist any changes in the net $(-)$ input current. A current injected through R_{in}, then, such as I_s, must be counteracted by an equal and opposite current through R_f. Although there is a current at the $(-)$ input, this current is constant and equal to the reference current, I_b. Therefore, the $(-)$ input behaves as a summing point, and the signal currents at R_{in} and R_f are equal. From this it

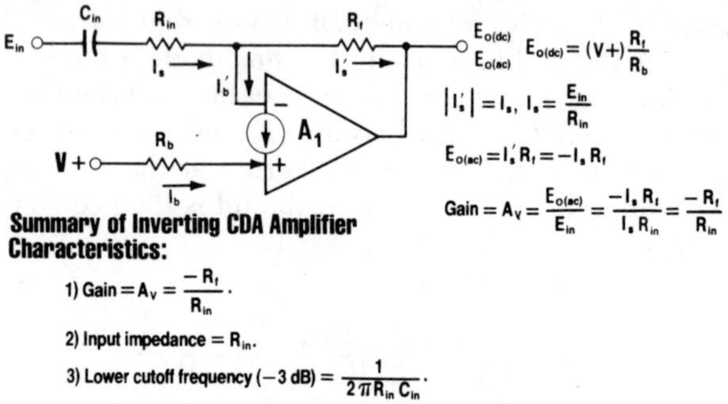

$$E_{o(dc)} = (V+)\frac{R_f}{R_b}$$

$$|I_s'| = I_s, \quad I_s = \frac{E_{in}}{R_{in}}$$

$$E_{o(ac)} = I_s' R_f = -I_s R_f$$

$$\text{Gain} = A_V = \frac{E_{o(ac)}}{E_{in}} = \frac{-I_s R_f}{I_s R_{in}} = \frac{-R_f}{R_{in}}$$

Summary of Inverting CDA Amplifier Characteristics:

1) Gain = $A_V = \dfrac{-R_f}{R_{in}}$.

2) Input impedance = R_{in}.

3) Lower cutoff frequency (-3 dB) = $\dfrac{1}{2\pi R_{in} C_{in}}$.

Fig. 8-62. Inverting ac amplifier using a CDA.

can be deduced that the ac voltage gain is the ratio of resistances R_f and R_{in}, with a sign change due to inversion. Or,

$$A_V = \frac{E_{o(ac)}}{E_{in}} = \frac{-I_s R_f}{I_s R_{in}} = \frac{-R_f}{R_{in}}.$$

The input resistance is equal to the value of R_{in}, and the lower cutoff frequency is determined by $R_{in} C_{in}$, as previously. The same general considerations apply to this stage as to the noninverting stage. Again, examples are treated in the applications section.

Differential Amplifier

The CDA differential amplifier configuration, shown in Fig. 8-63, is unique in that it does not require two pairs of matched resistors as does the op-amp differential amplifier. Like the op-amp differential amplifier, gain characteristics can be analyzed most easily by considering the response of the inputs separately, then combining the two resultant outputs. The gain characteristic for common-mode signals is different, however, and common-mode signal cancellation occurs through a different mechanism.

From Fig. 8-63, if $R_{in}' = R_{in}$, $E_{in_1} = E_{in_2}$, and $R_{in} \gg r_d$, it follows that $I_{s_1} = I_{s_2}$. If I_{s_1} and I_{s_2} are equal and if the mirror gain is unity, I_{s_1} will be inverted and appear at the $(-)$ input. Since $I_{s_1} = -I_{s_2}$, the two currents cancel and there is no differential current into the amplifier— i.e., the common-mode signal is rejected.

Cancellation is, of course, only as good as the adherence to unity gain and the matching of input currents. Good common-mode rejec-

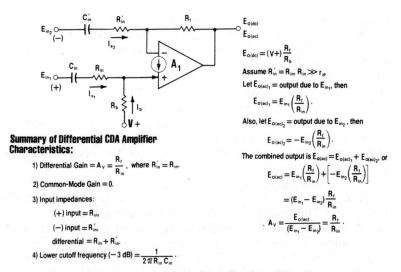

$$E_{o(dc)} = (V+)\frac{R_f}{R_b}$$

Assume $R_{in}' = R_{in}$, $R_{in} \gg r_d$.

Let $E_{o(ac)_1}$ = output due to E_{in_1}, then

$$E_{o(ac)_1} = E_{in_1}\left(\frac{R_f}{R_{in}}\right).$$

Also, let $E_{o(ac)_2}$ = output due to E_{in_2}, then

$$E_{o(ac)_2} = -E_{in_2}\left(\frac{R_f}{R_{in}}\right).$$

The combined output is $E_{o(ac)} = E_{o(ac)_1} + E_{o(ac)_2}$, or

$$E_{o(ac)} = E_{in_1}\left(\frac{R_f}{R_{in}}\right) + \left[-E_{in_2}\left(\frac{R_f}{R_{in}}\right)\right]$$

$$= (E_{in_1} - E_{in_2})\frac{R_f}{R_{in}}$$

$$A_v = \frac{E_{o(ac)}}{(E_{in_1} - E_{in_2})} = \frac{R_f}{R_{in}}.$$

Summary of Differential CDA Amplifier Characteristics:

1) Differential Gain $= A_v = \dfrac{R_f}{R_{in}}$, where $R_{in}' = R_{in}$.

2) Common-Mode Gain $= 0$.

3) Input impedances:

   (+) input $= R_{in}$,

   (−) input $= R_{in}'$,

   differential $= R_{in} + R_{in}'$.

4) Lower cutoff frequency (-3 dB) $= \dfrac{1}{2\pi R_{in} C_{in}}$.

Fig. 8-63. Differential ac amplifier using a CDA.

tion, therefore, requires that R_{in} be very high in relation to the mirror impedance, r_d. The input impedance of both inputs is the same as for noninverting and inverting stages; i.e., R_{in}. The differential-input impedance is $R_{in} + R_{in}'$, or $2R_{in}$. Similarly, the lower cutoff frequency is the same for each leg.

Although CDAs are best suited to ac use, this particular configuration can also be used for dc amplification by eliminating C_{in} and C_{in}'. As long as the common-mode input currents are within the dynamic range of the current mirror, it will respond only to the differential signals (E_{in_1} and E_{in_2}).

8.9 CDA APPLICATIONS

Unless otherwise noted, the circuitry discussed here can be used with any of the CDAs. Unlike other sections of the book, pin numbers are not necessarily shown because in most cases they can refer to any one of the four CDA circuits (see Fig. 8-59).

Ac amplifiers are, of course, the circuit configuration for which a CDA is primarily designed since a CDA uses a single-ended supply. All of the standard circuit configurations are realizable using CDAs, and in some cases there are advantages not found in the standard op-amp versions.

8.9.1 AC Amplifiers

Fig. 8-64 illustrates two practical versions of noninverting and inverting CDA amplifiers. The only difference between the two is the connection of R_1 and C_1; therefore, either circuit can use the same values, as shown in the table. For maximum, undistorted output swing, $R_3 = 2R_2$, but this relation can be relaxed for small output signals; that is, R_2 and R_3 can be 10% types such as 2.2-MΩ values. The R_1 values are shown tabulated for gains of 1, 10, and 100; intermediate values are readily calculated.

For the sake of simplicity, no output coupling capacitor is shown, although the output voltage does rest at a dc level of V+/2. Any dc blocking required will normally be provided by the input capacitor of a succeeding stage. For both of these stages, the input impedance is simply the value of R_1.

As noted in the figure, there is some deviation from the gain indicated at high noninverting gains, due to the current-mirror diode impedance. This becomes significant at low values of R_1 and should be evaluated by looking at Fig. 8-65. If r_d is not much less than R_1 at the mirror current used, some gain error will result, as well as some harmonic distortion. At 7.5 μA, r_d is 3500 Ω; therefore, the non-inverting signal gain will not be 100 for $R_1 = 10$ kΩ, but will be somewhat lower.

High Gain With High Input Impedance

A disadvantage of the basic CDA inverting and noninverting stages is the low value of input impedance that usually accompanies

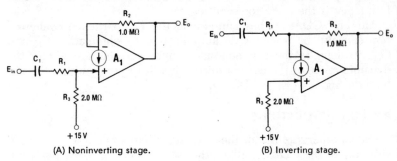

(A) Noninverting stage.   (B) Inverting stage.

GAIN	R_1^*	C_1^{**}
1	1.0 MΩ	0.01 μF
10	100 kΩ	0.1 μF
100	10 kΩ	1.0 μF

(C) Gain table.

* There will be some deviation from calculated gains with low values of R_1 in the noninverting stage, due to r_d.

** Values shown are for a −3-dB cutoff frequency of 15.9 Hz.

Fig. 8-64. Basic CDA gain stages.

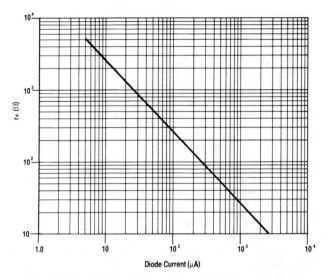

Fig. 8-65. Input diode impedance (r_d) vs mirror bias current (I_b).

high gain. This can be a disadvantage, both from the standpoint of loading on a preceding stage and also from the size of coupling capacitors required.

Fig. 8-66 is a circuit that provides both high gain and high input impedance in a single stage. The connection of $R_2 + R_5$, as far as dc is concerned, is nominally equal to $R_3/2$; thus, the output dc point is set at $V+/2$, as discussed previously. For ac signals, however, there is feedback attenuation established by R_4 and R_5. The gain provided by R_4 and R_5 is $(R_4 + R_5)/R_4$, which is the familiar $1/\beta$ expression. This gain is in addition to the gain established by the R_2/R_1 ratio. The composite gain, then, is their product, as shown.

The example uses a 1.0-MΩ resistor for R_1; thus, the R_2/R_1 ratio represents a loss, or a gain of one half. This is offset by R_4 and R_5, yielding a net gain of 20 dB. Although the stage shown is noninverting, this technique is just as applicable to the inverting stage, realized by moving R_1C_1 to the $(-)$ input. Gains different from that shown are achieved by choosing different values for R_4.

For noninverting stages, an additional virtue of this configuration is its linearity due to the high value of R_1 in relation to r_d. By contrast, a standard noninverting stage suffers in linearity at high gains because R_1 lowers, approaching r_d.

High Gain With Wide Bandwidth

If the basic noninverting stage of Fig. 8-64A is examined, it will be noted that there is no β network to attenuate the feedback signal.

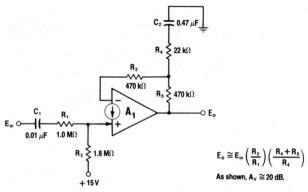

Fig. 8-66. High-gain amplifier with high input resistance.

This is due to the high output impedance of the current mirror, which causes β to be unity for all noninverting stages connected in this manner. In practice, it means that the full unity-gain bandwidth of the CDA device is available for virtually any operating gain. As an example, a 40-dB stage using CDAs can have a 3- to 4-MHz bandwidth. With a conventional gain-bandwidth relationship, this would require a GBP of 300-400 MHz (see Chapter 6). In the CDA inverting stage, R_{in} and R_f constitute a β network; therefore, the normal gain-bandwidth relationship holds. This is true also for noninverting stages using attenuation in the feedback path; Fig. 8-66 is one such example.

High Gain-Bandwidth Inverting Amplifier

While the single-stage CDA inverter has a closed-loop bandwidth that is inversely proportional to gain, it is also possible to design inverting configurations with high gain-bandwidth products, similar to the noninverting stage.

In Fig. 8-67, A_1 and A_2 form an inverting amplifier with a high GBP. The gain is provided by A_2, a noninverting stage with wide

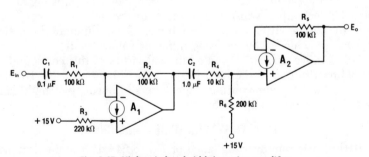

Fig. 8-67. High gain-bandwidth inverting amplifier.

bandwidth. A_1 is operated as a unity-gain inverter, which degrades the bandwidth of A_1 by only a factor of two. Thus, the overall circuit has a net bandwidth of half that of the devices used, with an overall voltage gain set by R_5 and R_4. In the configuration shown, $A_v \cong 10$.

Voltage Follower Variations

The connection for the CDA noninverting stage is unique in a number of other regards besides the bandwidth. These are described in the context of the follower circuit, shown in Fig. 8-68.

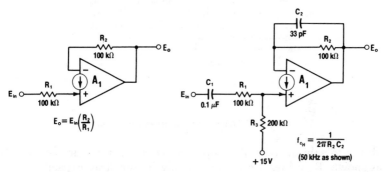

(A) Dc follower.   (B) Ac follower with high-frequency rolloff.

Fig. 8-68. CDA follower configurations.

This connection is the simplest form of CDA amplifier and is equally responsive to dc as well as ac. R_1 provides simultaneous bias current along with signal input current; in fact, the bias and signal currents are identical. With $R_1 = R_2$, the input voltage will be duplicated at the output.

The absolute values of R_1 and R_2 are not overly critical, and these can be scaled for higher input resistance if desired. With higher values of R_2 (say 1.0 MΩ), however, some bandwidth reduction will be noted because of the stray capacitance across R_2. With $R_2 = 1.0$ MΩ, this can occur at frequencies as low as 100 kHz. Lower R_2 values allow the full open-loop bandwidth to be realized, as long as the stray capacitive reactance is always greater than R_2.

There are also instances where advantage can be taken of the gain rolloff due to capacitive reactance. For instance, in Fig. 8-68B, a shunt capacitor (C_2) is purposely introduced across R_2 to cause the gain to be reduced 3 dB from unity at f_{c_H}, where

$$f_{c_H} = \frac{1}{2\pi R_2 C_2} .$$

With the values shown, the stage gain is down 3 dB at 50 kHz, and other cutoff values are possible by altering R_2 and C_2. The input shown is ac coupled, but feedback rolloff can obviously be used with the dc connection of Fig. 8-68A as well.

A more general form of a "gain-reduced follower" is the noninverting active attenuator shown in Fig. 8-69. This is also a circuit unique to the CDA. If R_1 is made greater than R_2, the gain is reduced below unity. Bias is controlled by the R_3/R_2 ratio, as previously. The gain here is 0.1 since $R_1 = 10\ R_2$. An incidental benefit of this circuit is the

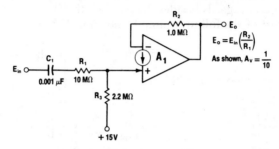

Fig. 8-69. Noninverting ac active attenuator.

ability to achieve very high input impedances—for example, 10 MΩ as shown. R_2 values are limited mainly by the stray capacitance effects mentioned previously. Since this is an active attenuator, the circuit output impedance is low.

Another circuit unique to the CDA is the noninverting summer, shown in Fig. 8-70. This circuit takes advantage of the low input impedance of the current mirror to combine a number of sources into a composite signal.

The diode impedance, r_d, is dependent on the mirror bias current (Fig. 8-65) and is 3.5 kΩ, as shown. As long as $R_1 \gg r_d$, mixing is accomplished with maximum isolation and good linearity. The gain for each channel is simply R_2/R_{1_a}, R_2/R_{1_b}, etc. Virtually any number of inputs can be accommodated with this configuration; the input impedance for each channel is the value used for R_1.

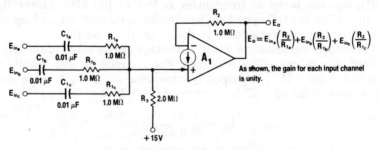

Fig. 8-70. Noninverting ac summer.

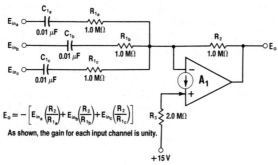

$$E_o = -\left[E_{in_a}\left(\frac{R_2}{R_{1_a}}\right) + E_{in_b}\left(\frac{R_2}{R_{1_b}}\right) + E_{in_c}\left(\frac{R_2}{R_{1_c}}\right)\right]$$

As shown, the gain for each input channel is unity.

Fig. 8-71. Inverting ac summer.

AC Inverting Summer

Since the inverting and noninverting CDA stages use very similar input networks, an inverting summer is achieved simply by moving the summing network to the ($-$) input, as in Fig. 8-71. The gain equations are the same as for the noninverting circuit except for sign inversion.

Differential Amplifier With High Input Impedance

As mentioned previously, the CDA differential amplifier requires high input resistances to realize good common-mode rejection. The differential amplifier depends upon the current mirror for common-mode rejection, so the current transfer linearity is also important—this again indicates the desirability of high input resistances to optimize these factors.

If gain is desired in addition to differential amplification with high input resistance, the circuit of Fig. 8-72 is useful. This circuit uses

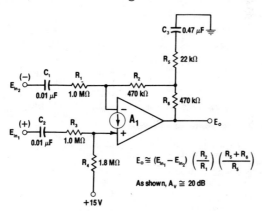

$$E_o \cong (E_{in_1} - E_{in_2})\left(\frac{R_2}{R_1}\right)\left(\frac{R_5 + R_6}{R_5}\right)$$

As shown, $A_v \cong 20$ dB

Fig. 8-72. Differential amplifier with high input impedance and gain.

high-value input resistances that would normally yield unity gain. R_5-C_3 attenuate the feedback, however, and provide gain (similar to Fig. 8-66). This preserves the high input impedance, linearity, and good common-mode rejection.

High-Level Output From CDAs

Like conventional op amps, CDAs are limited to a few milliamperes or less in the amount of output current they can deliver. However, for load impedances below 1.0 kΩ, or where appreciable power is to be delivered, buffer stages can be added to deliver any reasonable current level.

Fig. 8-73 is an example of such a buffer, a class AB push-pull circuit consisting of D_1, D_2, Q_1, and Q_2 with their associated components. Although shown with an inverting stage, this type of output is applicable to any CDA amplifier, with the qualifications noted.

The amplifier used must be compatible with the supply voltage and the output swing required. This, for instance, would indicate a 3900 for V+ = 36 V and a 3401 with V+ values up to 18 V. The transistors used for Q_1 and Q_2 should be compatible with the load current and supply voltage desired. The transistor types shown are satisfactory for the voltage listed and for loads down to 500 Ω.

Single-Ended to Push-Pull Converter

A pair of CDAs is handy for the conversion of a single-ended signal into equal but out-of-phase (or push-pull) voltages, as shown in Fig. 8-74.

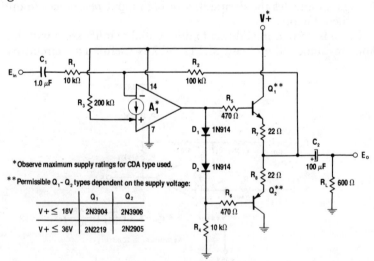

*Observe maximum supply ratings for CDA type used.

**Permissible Q_1 - Q_2 types dependent on the supply voltage:

	Q_1	Q_2
V+ ≤ 18V	2N3904	2N3906
V+ ≤ 36V	2N2219	2N2905

Fig. 8-73. Output buffer stage.

This circuit is simply a combination of inverting and noninverting unity-gain stages, with a common input. A single input capacitor (C_1) can be used because the dc potential on R_1 and R_4 is the same. Gain can be increased by lowering R_1 and R_4 or, for optimum linearity, by preceding A_1 and A_2 with a preamp stage.

8.9.2 Active Filters

As related in Chapter 6, some of the most useful applications of op amps involve the synthesis of filters with RC networks and an active block. Active filters that can be configured for current-mode inputs are even better suited for the CDA since the quad amplifiers

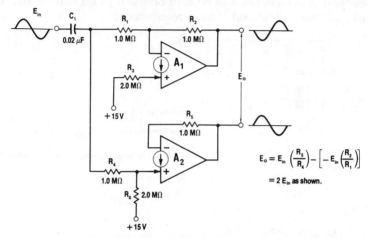

$$E_o = E_{in} \left(\frac{R_5}{R_4} \right) - \left[-E_{in} \left(\frac{R_2}{R_1} \right) \right]$$

$$= 2 E_{in} \text{ as shown.}$$

Fig. 8-74. Single-ended to push-pull converter.

can easily be made into multistage filters (a common requirement). The standard functions of low-pass, high-pass, bandpass, and notch filtering can all be realized with CDAs. The following circuits are representative of what can be accomplished with CDA active filters, but it should be realized that this discussion is by no means exhaustive. A complete discussion of active filters is beyond the scope of this section. The interested reader should consult the references listed, as well as the references in Chapter 6 on active filters.

A number of basic filter sections can be designed around a single CDA inverting stage. They are all second-order filters; thus, they provide cutoff rates of 12 dB per octave (40 dB per decade). As inverting stages, they normally provide a reversal of phase within the operating passband. They can all be designed for various gains and Q values, as well as various operating frequencies. With these single-stage filters, practical gains and Qs are confined to 10 or less for best performance, particularly at frequencies of 1.0 kHz or more.

Low-Pass Filters

A low-pass filter is illustrated in Fig. 8-75. In this circuit (as in others to follow), the design procedure is aided by some simplifications. For a given application, the circuit requirements will usually be stated in terms of the upper cutoff frequency, f_{c_H}, and the gain. The constant K sets the relation of C_1 and C_2. This simplifies the equations to those shown. The value of Q, unless otherwise dictated, is best set near unity, as this yields a minimum of peaking near the cutoff frequency. In the design procedure for this circuit, standard capacitor values are selected first, then the resistances are calculated. In general, resistances should be kept between 10 kΩ and 10 MΩ to satisfy output-loading and biasing requirements.

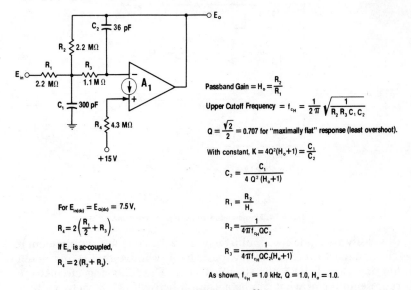

Passband Gain $= H_o = \dfrac{R_2}{R_1}$

Upper Cutoff Frequency $= f_{c_H} = \dfrac{1}{2\pi}\sqrt{\dfrac{1}{R_2 R_3 C_1 C_2}}$

$Q = \dfrac{\sqrt{2}}{2} = 0.707$ for "maximally flat" response (least overshoot).

With constant, $K = 4Q^2(H_o+1) = \dfrac{C_1}{C_2}$

$C_2 = \dfrac{C_1}{4\,Q^2\,(H_o+1)}$

$R_1 = \dfrac{R_2}{H_o}$

$R_2 = \dfrac{1}{4\pi f_{c_H}QC_2}$

$R_3 = \dfrac{1}{4\pi f_{c_H}QC_2(H_o+1)}$

As shown, $f_{c_H} = 1.0$ kHz, Q = 1.0, $H_o = 1.0$.

For $E_{in(dc)} = E_{o(dc)} = 7.5$ V,

$R_4 = 2\left(\dfrac{R_1}{2} + R_3\right).$

If E_{in} is ac-coupled,

$R_4 = 2(R_2 + R_3).$

Fig. 8-75. Low-pass active filter.

After the initial selection of C_1-C_2 values, the calculation of R_1-R_3 is relatively straightforward. R_2 is selected first, then R_1 (for gain), then R_3, by using the equations shown.

Bias resistance R_4 requires some special consideration if E_{in} is to be biased at a dc level of V+/2 (as from a CDA output). For this condition R_4 is calculated as $2(\frac{1}{2}R_1 + R_3)$. If E_{in} is ac coupled, the only dc path to the (−) input is through $R_2 + R_3$; so R_4 for this condition is simply twice $R_2 + R_3$.

In this example, f_{c_H} is 1.0 kHz, and the gain and Q are both unity. E_{in} is assumed to be biased at 7.5 V dc (or V+/2).

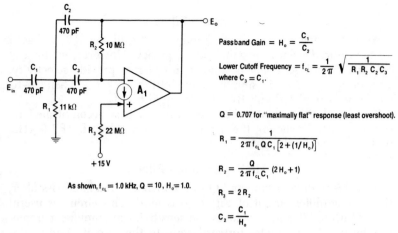

Passband Gain $= H_o = \dfrac{C_1}{C_2}$

Lower Cutoff Frequency $= f_{c_L} = \dfrac{1}{2\pi} \sqrt{\dfrac{1}{R_1\,R_2\,C_2\,C_3}}$

where $C_3 = C_1$.

$Q = 0.707$ for "maximally flat" response (least overshoot).

$R_1 = \dfrac{1}{2\pi f_{c_L} Q C_1 \left[2 + (1/H_o)\right]}$

$R_2 = \dfrac{Q}{2\pi f_{c_L} C_1}\,(2H_o + 1)$

$R_3 = 2R_2$

$C_2 = \dfrac{C_1}{H_o}$

As shown, $f_{c_L} = 1.0$ kHz, $Q = 10$, $H_o = 1.0$.

Fig. 8-76. High-pass active filter.

High-Pass Filter

An active high-pass filter is shown in Fig. 8-76. The biasing of this stage is simple because there is no dc path to the input. Gain is controlled by the ratio of C_1 to C_2. For simplicity, C_3 is made equal to C_1, which yields the cutoff frequency equation given.

Once the capacitor values are selected, the values of R_1 and R_2 are calculated. R_3 is simply $2R_2$ in order to bias $E_{o(dc)}$ at $V+/2$. For the values shown in this example, $f_{c_L} = 1.0$ kHz, $Q = 10$, and $H_o = 1$.

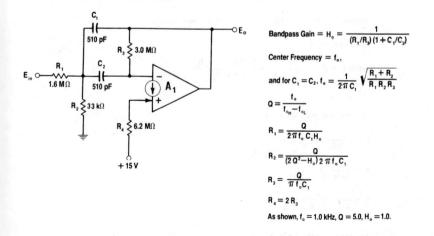

Bandpass Gain $= H_o = \dfrac{1}{(R_1/R_3)(1 + C_1/C_2)}$

Center Frequency $= f_o$,

and for $C_1 = C_2$, $f_o = \dfrac{1}{2\pi C_1} \sqrt{\dfrac{R_1 + R_2}{R_1\,R_2\,R_3}}$

$Q = \dfrac{f_o}{f_{c_H} - f_{c_L}}$

$R_1 = \dfrac{Q}{2\pi f_o\,C_1\,H_o}$

$R_2 = \dfrac{Q}{(2Q^2 - H_o)\,2\pi f_o\,C_1}$

$R_3 = \dfrac{Q}{\pi f_o\,C_1}$

$R_4 = 2R_3$

As shown, $f_o = 1.0$ kHz, $Q = 5.0$, $H_o = 1.0$.

Fig. 8-77. Bandpass active filter.

Bandpass Filter

As with previous circuits, the bandpass filter of Fig. 8-77 is based on the desired values for gain and frequency. However, in this circuit the Q will generally be higher in order to provide selectivity. The design process is simplified by letting $C_1 = C_2$. Then R_1-R_3 values are calculated and R_4 is made equal to $2R_3$.

Tuning of the circuit, when necessary, is best accomplished by trimming R_2. As shown, the nominal values yield an f_o of 1.0 kHz, with $Q = 5$ and unity gain.

High-Q Bandpass Filter

To achieve greater gain and Q simultaneously in a bandpass filter, the two-amplifier circuit of Fig. 8-78 is used. This circuit is useful for a Q up to 50, and it reduces the sensitivity to amplifier parameters by providing greater forward gain. In this circuit, A_1 operates

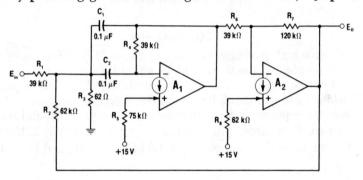

Bandpass Gain $= H_o = K\sqrt{Q}$, where K is typically between 1 and 10.

Center Frequency $= f_o$,

and for $C_1 = C_2$, $f_o = \dfrac{1}{2\pi C_1}\sqrt{\dfrac{R_3 R_6 + R_1 R_6 + R_1 R_3}{R_1 R_3 R_4 R_6}}$

$Q = \dfrac{f_o}{f_{c_H} - f_{c_L}}$

Let $R = R_1 = R_4 = R_6$, then $R_7 = KR$.

$R = \dfrac{Q}{2\pi f_o C_1}$ $R_5 = 2R_4$

                          $R_8 = 2(R_6 \parallel R_7)$

$R_2 = R\left(\dfrac{KQ}{2Q-1}\right)$

$R_3 = \dfrac{R}{Q^2 - 1 - 2/K + 1/KQ}$

As shown, $f_o = 1.0$ kHz, $Q = 25$, $H_o = 15$.

Fig. 8-78. High-Q bandpass filter.

somewhat as previously, but the added gain stage (A_2) provides controlled positive feedback. It also introduces an additional sign change so that the output signal is in phase with the input in this case.

The design procedure is begun with the requirements for f_o, gain, and Q. $C_1 = C_2$ (again, for simplicity), and R_1, R_4, R_6 are equal to "R." The constant K is established between 1 and 10. R_1, R_2, and R_3 are then chosen to satisfy the design requirements, and R_4 and R_8 are selected for proper biasing.

The example chosen is a 1.0-kHz filter with a gain of 15 (or 23 dB) and a Q of 25. This type of circuit is most useful for a fixed frequency, with constant gain and constant Q.

State Variable Filter

A circuit that provides a unique performance combination is the "state variable filter" of Fig. 8-79. This circuit has the ability to provide simultaneous bandpass, low-pass, and high-pass outputs. It is capable of a very high Q (100 or more) with excellent stability and low sensitivity to changes in the passive elements. The circuit can be used for high-Q bandpass filters or it can provide all three outputs at once. Furthermore, the addition of a fourth amplifier to sum the high-pass and low-pass outputs yields a notch filter.

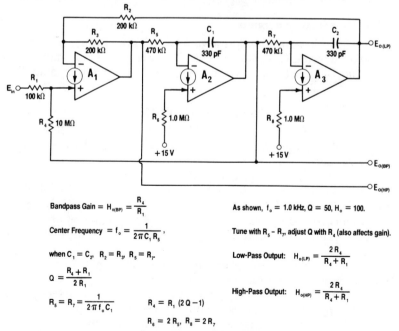

Bandpass Gain = $H_{o(BP)} = \dfrac{R_4}{R_1}$

As shown, $f_o = 1.0$ kHz, Q = 50, $H_o = 100$.

Center Frequency = $f_o = \dfrac{1}{2\pi C_1 R_5}$,

Tune with $R_5 - R_7$, adjust Q with R_4 (also affects gain).

when $C_1 = C_2$, $R_2 = R_3$, $R_5 = R_7$,

Low-Pass Output: $H_{o(LP)} = \dfrac{2R_4}{R_4 + R_1}$

$Q = \dfrac{R_4 + R_1}{2R_1}$

High-Pass Output: $H_{o(HP)} = \dfrac{2R_4}{R_4 + R_1}$

$R_5 = R_7 = \dfrac{1}{2\pi f_o C_1}$ $\qquad R_4 = R_1 (2Q - 1)$

$R_6 = 2R_5$, $R_8 = 2R_7$

Fig. 8-79. State variable filter.

As with the previous filters, several simplifying steps usually precede the design. The time constants of the two integrators, A_2-A_3, are made equal; so $R_5 = R_7$ and $C_1 = C_2$. Also, R_2 is set equal to R_3. As the design equations indicate, frequency is set by R_5-C_1 (and R_7-C_2). Gain and Q are set by R_4 and R_1 and are adjustable independently of the center frequency.

The biasing shown assumes $E_{in(dc)}$ to be +7.5-V dc. If E_{in} is ac coupled, an additional bias resistor with a value of $2(R_2 \parallel R_3) = 200$ kΩ will be required from the (+) input of A_1 to V+.

This filter is perhaps the best example of the value of active filter techniques. It can, for instance, provide a stable, high Q at very low frequencies where inductors are totally impractical. Yet the component values needed to realize these low frequencies are quite reasonable: e.g., changing C_1 and C_2 to 0.33 μF yields a 1.0-Hz filter with a Q of 50.

Active filters are one of the most frequent application areas for the CDA. In general, the performance extremes (gain and Q) are confined to the limits mentioned for good accuracy, due to the CDA gain and bandwidth limitations. This is not a serious drawback, however, since higher gains and higher Qs can be obtained with multistage filters (or with cascaded sections), thus taking advantage of the multiple-amplifier package.

8.9.3 Waveform Generators

As with standard op amps, a variety of waveform generators are possible by using CDAs. Some complex circuits are more attractive with the CDA version, however, because of the multiple-amplifier package.

Sine-Wave Oscillator

A low-distortion sine-wave oscillator using the four CDAs in a single package is shown in Fig. 8-80. As discussed in Chapter 7 (Section 7.2), one of the greatest design problems with a low-distortion sine-wave oscillator is regulating the amplitude. This circuit introduces a new means of gain control formed by A_1, a gain-controlled follower. R_1 forms the input resistance of the follower and diode D_2 acts as a current-steering element to control the signal input current to A_1. Control of the dc voltage applied to D_2 thus controls the gain of A_1.

A_2 and A_3 form a bandpass filter as described in Fig. 8-78. This section provides the high Q needed for waveform purity, and it also determines the oscillation frequency. A_4 is a differential detector and averager. Rectifier D_3 senses the output level and compares the rectified current to the reference current established by V_{ref} and R_{16}. C_4 provides the integration function, smoothing the voltage output

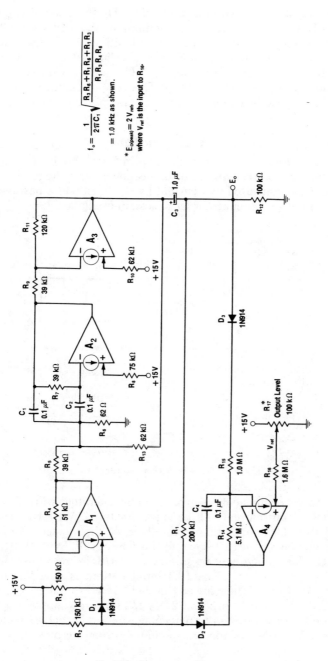

$$f_o = \frac{1}{2\pi C_1} \sqrt{\frac{R_3 R_6 + R_1 R_6 + R_1 R_3}{R_1 R_3 R_4 R_6}}$$

= 1.0 kHz as shown.

* $E_{o(peak)} = 2 V_{ref}$, where V_{ref} is the input to R_{16}.

Fig. 8-80. Sine-wave oscillator.

503

from A_4 to a suitable control potential for D_2. Variation of R_{17}, which controls V_{ref}, varies the output amplitude. V_{ref} will vary with the supply voltage, but it can be stabilized with zener diodes if desired.

For other frequencies, C_1-C_2 can be changed for coarse tuning and R_6 can be varied for trim. Both C_3 and C_4 will need upward adjustment for lower frequencies. This type of circuit is best suited as a stable, fixed-frequency source. It also provides good waveform purity (THD $\leqq 1.0\%$).

Astable Oscillator

A CDA astable oscillator is shown in Fig. 8-81. R_1 and C_1 form the timing components, and the exponential voltage developed across C_1 is converted to a current by R_2. R_4 provides positive feedback to the (+) input in order to sustain oscillation.

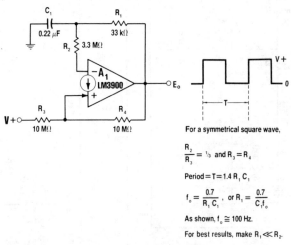

For a symmetrical square wave,

$$\frac{R_2}{R_3} = \frac{1}{3} \text{ and } R_3 = R_4$$

Period $= T = 1.4\,R_1\,C_1$

$$f_o = \frac{0.7}{R_1\,C_1}, \text{ or } R_1 = \frac{0.7}{C_1 f_o}$$

As shown, $f_o \cong 100$ Hz.

For best results, make $R_1 \ll R_2$.

Fig. 8-81. Astable oscillator.

With the components shown, it will be noted that when E_o is high, the (+) input current will be approximately $2(V+)/R_3$ (assuming $R_4 = R_3$). The upper timing threshold of the capacitor voltage is reached when a current equal to this flows in R_2. With R_2/R_4 equal to $1/3$, this voltage will be simply $2(V+)/3$. When C_1 reaches this voltage, E_o goes low. The (+) input current is now $V+/R_3$, and since $R_2/R_3 = 1/3$, the lower threshold is $V+/3$. Thus, the circuit oscillates between $V+/3$ and $2(V+)/3$ for any value of $V+$. Since the period is referenced to percentages of $V+$, it becomes independent of $V+$. The equation for period T is then simply

$$T = 1.4R_1C_1.$$

This circuit serves as a handy timing generator for any value of supply voltage. R_1 should be much less than R_2 for best results. Although any CDA will work, a 3900 will be more useful in driving low-resistance loads because of its greater current capability. At frequencies above a few kilohertz, particularly at high supply voltages, performance becomes limited by the CDA slew rate. The frequency shown is 100 Hz.

Pulse Generator

The astable oscillator can be easily modified for an asymmetrical duty cycle, which yields pulse waveforms as shown in Fig. 8-82.

In this circuit, the charge and discharge paths of timing capacitor C_1 are individually controlled by diodes D_1 and D_2. R_{1a} controls the charge rate of C_1 (period t_1), and R_{1b} controls the discharge rate (period t_2). R_{1a} and R_{1b} can be made into individual controls for variable pulse width and repetition rate. Or, if a constant frequency with variable duty cycle is desired, R_1 can be a single potentiometer with the tap to E_o and the ends to D_1 and D_2. Some minimum series resistance should be included, of course, to limit the range (and output current) of the amplifier.

As shown, the respective periods are 1.0 ms and 4.0 ms. The same general considerations for the CDA type and slew rate apply here as for the astable circuit.

Triangle/Square-Wave Oscillator

As a natural part of its oscillatory cycle, the astable oscillator generates an exponential timing wave (generally not a very useful

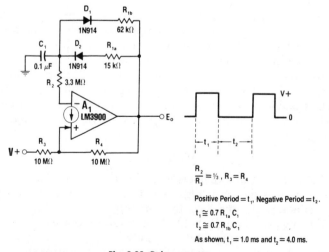

$$\frac{R_2}{R_3} = \frac{1}{3}, R_3 = R_4$$

Positive Period $= t_1$, Negative Period $= t_2$.

$t_1 \cong 0.7\,R_{1a}\,C_1$

$t_2 \cong 0.7\,R_{1b}\,C_1$

As shown, $t_1 = 1.0$ ms and $t_2 = 4.0$ ms.

Fig. 8-82. Pulse generator.

waveform in itself). One useful timing waveform, however, is the triangle, which can be generated by the circuit of Fig. 8-83.

This circuit is somewhat similar to the astable multivibrator since the square-wave-generating portion (A_2) is a similar comparator. In this case it senses the output of a linear ramp generator, A_1.

A_1 is a bidirectional integrator that charges and discharges C_1 with a constant current, thus generating a linear voltage ramp. The discharge current is set at $V+/R_1$. If $R_2 = R_1/2$, the charge current will be equal to this current since twice the ($-$) input current is applied to the ($+$) input; the result is an equal but opposite direction of current in C_1. The output voltage of A_1 is sensed by A_2, and the comparison points of A_2 are 2/3 V+ and 1/3 V+. Thus, the triangular output of A_1 is regulated at 1/3 V+ volts p-p.

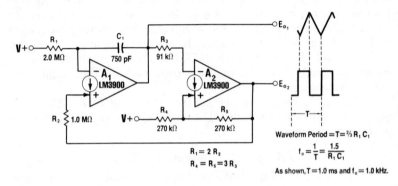

Fig. 8-83. Triangle/square-wave oscillator.

Again, since the timing is referenced to two currents proportional to V+, the timing period becomes supply independent. The period is $T = 2/3(R_1C_1)$ and the frequency is then $f_o = 1.5/R_1C_1$.

For best symmetry, choose $R_1 = 2R_2$, which will make the charge and discharge times nominally equal. The frequency of operation shown is 1.0 kHz, but this is readily changed by altering C_1, R_1, and R_2. The triangle peak-to-peak amplitude can be modified, if desired, by extending the comparator end points above 2/3 V+ and below 1/3 V+.

Basic Timer

A timing circuit that delivers a single output pulse and has external triggering is shown in Fig. 8-84. This circuit consists of a linear ramp generator, A_1, and a control flip-flop, A_2.

In the STANDBY state, R_4 holds A_2 in a low-output condition. Likewise, R_1 holds A_1 in a low state. A positive trigger arriving at its ($+$) input sets A_2 to the high state. With A_2 high, R_2 forces the net current in C_1 positive, thus beginning a positive output ramp. The timing ramp, E_{o_1}, builds up until the current in R_3 exceeds the upper threshold of A_2. This resets A_2, terminating the output pulse (of width "t") and returning A_2 to the STANDBY state. E_{o_1} ramps negative to 0 volts, whereupon the circuit is ready for another trigger. Note that this recovery time (negative E_{o_1} slope) is also equal to period "t."

The period is independent of V+, as before, and is simply

$$t = R_2 C_1.$$

The circuit shown has a timing period of 10 ms.

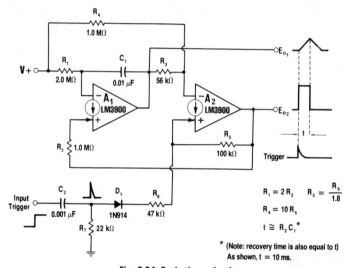

Fig. 8-84. Basic timer circuit.

General-Purpose Timer

A more general form of timer is shown in Fig. 8-85. With the addition of a third amplifier (A_3), this circuit eliminates the interdependence of R_1 and R_2, and makes the circuit more flexible.

In this circuit, when E_{o_2} is high, the charge time of C_1 is controlled by R_2. Thus,

$$t = \frac{R_2 C_1}{2}.$$

The circuit shown has a timing period of 15 ms. A_3 is an inverter that drives output E_{o_3}, the complement of E_{o_2}. R_1 controls the recovery time, t_r (or discharge time of C_1), according to

$$t_r = \frac{R_1 C_1}{2}.$$

With the separation of charge and discharge paths of C_1, the timing is much easier to control; that is, R_2 can be made variable for continuous control and C_1 can be switch-selected for range.

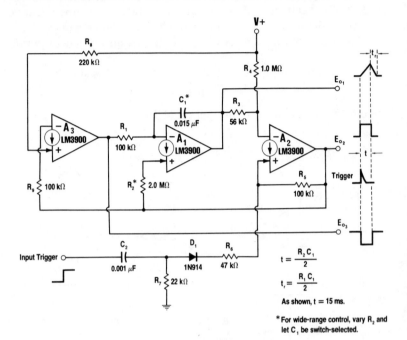

Fig. 8-85. General-purpose timer.

8.9.4 Logic Circuits

A useful property of the CDA is its ability to operate as a digital component—several standard logic elements can be constructed with CDAs. Although CDA performance is slow by modern standards, this is not a disadvantage in many applications, and it reduces the susceptibility of the circuit to noise. The wide supply range allows a choice of many different supply systems, and the high-output, low-input currents allow high fanouts to be achieved. Either the 3401 or 3900 can be used in logic functions, but the 3900 is preferred if operation at supply-voltage extremes is expected. It is also capable of sinking much greater output currents when overdriven at the $(-)$ input.

OR Gate

A CDA OR gate is illustrated in Fig. 8-86A. With a fixed bias current applied to the $(-)$ input through R_4, the output will be low if

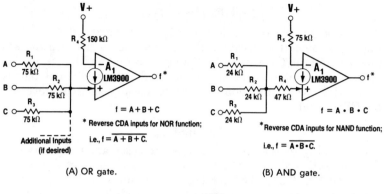

(A) OR gate.

(B) AND gate.

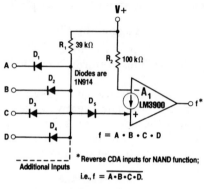

(C) High fan-in AND gate.

Fig. 8-86. Basic CDA logic circuits.

all inputs are low (near ground potential). If any input goes high (near V+), the current driven into the (+) input overrides the bias at the (−) input, forcing the output high. Any number of inputs can be combined by simply connecting additional input resistors. The circuit can also be converted to a NOR gate by reversing the connections to the (+) and (−) inputs.

Simple AND Gate

The AND function can be realized for a small number of inputs by the circuit in Fig. 8-86B. This works by summing three inputs through R_1-R_3, then applying the composite voltage to R_4. The resultant current is greater than that in R_5 if A, B, and C are all high; thus, the output is forced high. If any one is low, the (+) input current is less than the (−) input current and the output remains low. Reversing the CDA input terminals yields the inverted function, or a NAND gate.

High Fan-In AND Gate

For a logic AND function requiring many inputs, the circuit of Fig. 8-86C should be used. In this circuit, diodes perform the AND function and the CDA provides the logic current and buffering. Any number of inputs can be accommodated with additional diodes; again, the inverse function (NAND) is accomplished by reversing the CDA inputs.

R-S Flip-Flop

In digital systems an R-S flip-flop is often used as a temporary storage element. A single CDA can be used as a set/reset flip-flop, as shown in Fig. 8-87A. Positive feedback is supplied by R_4, causing the circuit to remain in the state of the *last* positive input pulse.

Toggle Flip-Flop

Another type of flip-flop is the toggle, which changes state on every other input pulse. This performs a divide-by-two function for the input frequency.

A CDA toggle flip-flop is shown in Fig. 8-87B. Differentiated pulses are applied to R_1-R_2. The negative edges have no effect, but positive edges trigger the side (A_1 or A_2) that is low at the time the pulse appears. This alternation occurs on every positive input, causing a division by two (see timing diagram).

Buffer Stage

Often a signal may need to be buffered or inverted. This is provided by the circuit of Fig. 8-87C, a simple buffer.

One-Shot Multivibrator

Another common digital component is the one-shot circuit, illustrated in Fig. 8-87D.

In this circuit, R_4 holds the output high in the STANDBY state. C_1 is then charged nearly to the V+ level through D_1. A negative input trigger forces the output low, and C_1 begins discharging through R_1. R_2 applies a decreasing current to the (−) input as C_1 discharges, and this current finally approaches the current in R_3. Since $R_2 = R_3/3$, the two input currents become equal when the voltage across C_1 is about V+/3. The output now switches high, returning the circuit to its STANDBY state. This recovery time is rapid since C_1 is recharged through the low impedance of D_1.

The pulse width is approximately equal to 1.1 R_1C_1, but some variation can be expected, particularly at low supply voltages. An advantage of this circuit is that pulse width can be programmed easily by using R_1 (one end of which is grounded). This resistance can be

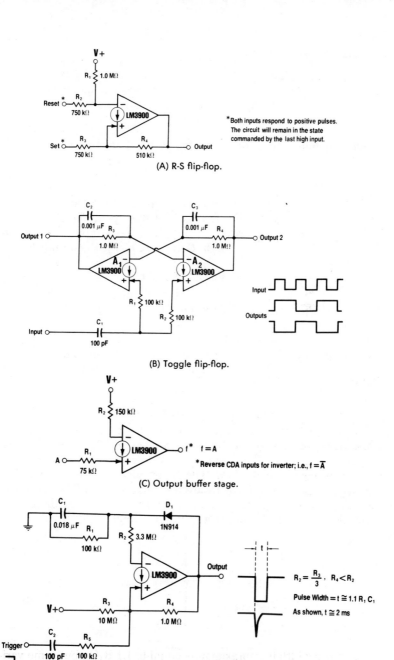

(A) R-S flip-flop.

*Both inputs respond to positive pulses. The circuit will remain in the state commanded by the last high input.

(B) Toggle flip-flop.

(C) Output buffer stage.

* Reverse CDA inputs for inverter; i.e., $f = \overline{A}$

$R_2 = \dfrac{R_3}{3}$, $R_4 < R_2$

Pulse Width = $t \cong 1.1\,R_1\,C_1$

As shown, $t \cong 2$ ms

(D) One-shot multivibrator.

Fig. 8-87. Additional CDA logic circuits.

Fig. 8-88. Basic CDA comparator.

either a potentiometer or else some form of manual or electronic switching.

8.9.5 Comparators

CDAs make extremely useful comparators as we have seen from sections of previous circuits. The basis of this operation is a comparison of the relative states of the $(+)$ and $(-)$ input currents. If $I(+) > I(-)$, the output is high. If $I(+) < I(-)$, the output is low.

Basic Comparator

A basic comparator is shown in Fig. 8-88. Input resistors R_1 and R_2 define the input currents. Thus (for $R_1 = R_2$), if $E_{in} > V_{ref}$, E_o is high; if $E_{in} < V_{ref}$, E_o is low.

It is only the *relative* state of the input currents that determines the output state. E_{in} and V_{ref} can be increased to very high voltages, where the only practical limitation is the power dissipation of R_1-R_2 and the maximum mirror current.

Comparator for Negative Voltages

The concept of relative-current comparison can be extended to allow negative voltages to be compared, as in Fig. 8-89. Here, R_1 and R_2 establish a common-mode bias current. Thus, V_{ref} and E_{in} can range to negative values. The input currents are compared as long as the currents in R_3 or R_4 are less than those in R_1 or R_2. With the values shown, V_{ref} and E_{in} can extend to -10 V, but there is no theoretical limit to the comparator input voltage.

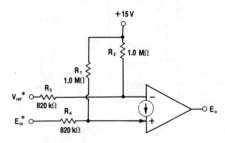

*As shown, V_{ref} and E_{in} can range to -10 V.

Fig. 8-89. CDA comparator for negative voltages.

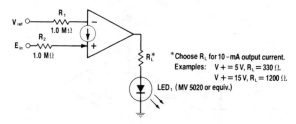

Fig. 8-90. CDA comparator with LED readout.

*Choose R_L for 10 -mA output current.
Examples: $V+ = 5$ V, $R_L = 330\ \Omega$.
$V+ = 15$ V, $R_L = 1200\ \Omega$.
LED_1 (MV 5020 or equiv.)

Comparator With LED Readout

Comparators are often used with visual readouts to indicate the relative state of the inputs being monitored. Fig. 8-90 is one example, having an LED to indicate $E_{in} > V_{ref}$.

A single LED can be driven with the 10-mA source current of a CDA. R_L is selected to limit the LED forward current, with typical values shown in the figure. The LED is on when $E_{in} > V_{ref}$, and the opposite condition ($E_{in} < V_{ref}$) can be indicated simply by reversing the CDA inputs.

Medium-Power Comparator

As mentioned previously, a 3900 is capable of sinking 30 mA or more when overdriven at the $(-)$ input terminal. This is used to advantage in Fig. 8-91 to drive medium-current loads such as lamps, several LEDs, or small relays. R_3 should be selected to provide 0.1 mA into the $(-)$ input of A_2.

Window Comparator

Two comparators can readily be connected in OR configurations to obtain a window comparator, as shown in Fig. 8-92.

Here R_1 and R_4 establish reference currents at the $(-)$ input of A_1 and the $(+)$ input of A_2. When E_{in} is low, so that the current in R_3 is less than that in R_4, A_2 goes high and the output is high. When

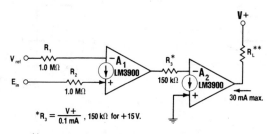

$$*R_3 = \frac{V+}{0.1\ mA},\ 150\ k\Omega\ for\ +15\ V.$$

$**R_L = 30\text{-mA}$ load (max), such as lamps, relays, or LEDs.

Fig. 8-91. Medium-power CDA comparator.

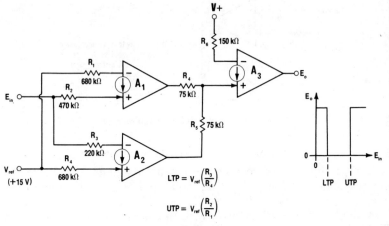

Fig. 8-92. CDA window comparator.

E_{in} causes the current in R_3 to be greater than in R_4, A_2 goes low. Then, as long as E_{in} is low enough that the current in R_2 is less than that in R_1, A_1 also remains low. In this region E_{in} is within its "window." When E_{in} causes the R_2 current to exceed the R_1 current, A_1 and the output are high. The circuit using A_3 is the same as the OR gate of Fig. 8-86A. In the example shown, the threshold voltages are established at 5 V and 10 V.

8.9.6 Comparators With Hysteresis

By adding feedback current to the current injected into the $(+)$ input, a comparator with hysteresis is formed, as illustrated in Fig. 8-93.

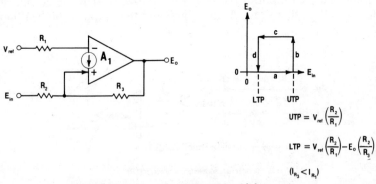

Fig. 8-93. Noninverting comparator with hysteresis.

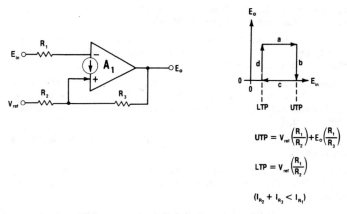

$$UTP = V_{ref}\left(\frac{R_1}{R_2}\right) + E_o\left(\frac{R_1}{R_3}\right)$$

$$LTP = V_{ref}\left(\frac{R_1}{R_2}\right)$$

$$(I_{R_2} + I_{R_3} < I_{R_1})$$

Fig. 8-94. Inverting comparator with hysteresis.

In this circuit, R_1 establishes the reference current applied to the $(-)$ input. With E_{in} rising from zero (segment a on the graph), some point will be reached where the current in R_2 equals that in R_1. At this upper trip point (UTP), the circuit switches to the high state, aided by feedback from R_3, and the result is seen as segment b in the graph. When E_{in} drops (segment c), it must reduce the current in R_2 to the point where the total current—through R_2 and R_3 into the $(+)$ input—again equals the reference current. This point is the lower trip point (LTP), and here the current reverts to its original output state (segment d).

A notable point about this circuit is that the (feedback) current in R_3 must always be less than that in R_1 (reference current); otherwise E_{in} will not be able to reach the LTP once the circuit has flipped high.

An inverting form of the comparator circuit is shown in Fig. 8-94. Here the reference current is set by R_2, and R_3 adds to this current.

The circuit output will initially be high with $E_{in} = 0$. As E_{in} increases (segment a), the $(-)$ and $(+)$ input currents become equal at the UTP and the output switches low. When E_{in} decreases and approaches the LTP (segment c), the current in R_1 equals that in R_2. At this point the circuit flips once again to its high output state (segment d). A necessary criterion for this circuit is that the net $(+)$ input current $(I_{R_2} + I_{R_3})$ be less than I_{R_1}; otherwise the UTP cannot be reached.

REFERENCES

1. Campbell, L. R.; Wittlinger, H. A. *Some Applications of a Programmable Power Switch/Amplifier*. RCA Application Note ICAN-6048, November 1972. RCA Solid State Div., Somerville, N. J.

2. Fredriksen, T. M. "Multiple-Function LICs." *Proceedings of Electronic Products Magazine LIC Seminar,* March 1973.

3. _____; Davis, W. F.; Zobel, D. W. "A New Current Differencing Single-Supply Operational Amplifier." *IEEE Journal of Solid State Circuits,* Vol. SC-6, No. 6, December 1971.

4. Fredriksen, T. M.; Howard, W. M.; Sleeth, R. S. *The LM3900—A New Current Differencing Quad of ± Input Amplifiers.* National Semiconductor Application Note AN-72, September 1972. National Semiconductor Corp., Santa Clara, Calif.

5. _____. "Use Current Mode IC Amplifiers." *Electronic Design,* January 18, 1973.

6. Hoover, M. V. "A Cornucopia of Linear ICs and Some of Their Applications." *Proceedings of Electronic Products Magazine LIC Seminar,* June 1972.

7. _____. *A Medley of Linear ICs and Some of Their Applications.* RCA Publication ST-4777A, January 1972. RCA Solid State Div., Somerville, N. J.

8. Jones, D. *The HA-2400 PRAM Four Channel Operational Amplifier.* Harris Semiconductor Application Note 514, February 1972. Harris Semiconductor, Melbourne, Fla.

9. Jung, W. G. "Automating the Audio Control Function, Part IV." *db, The Sound Engineering Magazine,* November 1972.

10. _____. "CDA—The New Current Differencing Amplifier." *Popular Electronics* including *Electronics World,* June 1973.

11. Kaplan, L.; Wittlinger, H. A. *An IC Operational Transconductance Amplifier (OTA) With Power Capability.* IEEE BTR-18, No. 3, August 1972. (RCA Publication ST-6077, RCA Solid State Div., Somerville, N.J.)

12. Mortensen, H. H. *A Fully Differential Input Voltage Amplifier.* National Semiconductor LB-20, December 1972. National Semiconductor Corp., Santa Clara, Calif.

13. Tobey, G. E.; Graeme, J. G.; Huelsman, L. P. *Operational Amplifiers—Design and Applications.* Burr-Brown Research Corp., McGraw-Hill Book Co., New York, 1971.

14. Vander Kooi, M. K. *The μA776—An Operational Amplifier With Programmable Gain, Bandwidth, Slew Rate, and Power Dissipation.* Fairchild Application Bulletin APP-218, June 1971. Fairchild Semiconductor, Mountain View, Calif.

15. _____; Cleveland, G. *Micropower Circuits Using the LM4250 Programmable Op Amp.* National Semiconductor Application Note AN-71, July 1972. National Semiconductor Corp., Santa Clara, Calif.

16. Wheatley, C. F.; Wittlinger, H. A. "OTA Obsoletes Op Amp." *Proceedings of the NEC,* December 1969. (RCA Publication ST-4159, RCA Solid State Div., Somerville, N. J.)

17. Wittlinger, H. A. *Applications of the CA3080 and CA3080A High-Performance Operational Transconductance Amplifiers.* RCA Application Note ICAN-6668, September 1971. RCA Solid State Div., Somerville, N. J.

III

APPENDIXES

APPENDIX A

Manufacturers' Data Sheets for General-Purpose Op Amps

This appendix includes catalog specification sheets for selected general-purpose op amps that will be useful in a large percentage of applications. These devices are well accepted as industry standards, and the data sheets reproduced here are those of the original manufacturers.

Space does not permit the inclusion of data sheets for the more-specialized devices; thus, it is suggested that the reader assemble catalog information for these types by writing the various manufacturers listed in Table A-1. These manufacturers are the original sources of the respective devices listed.

Table A-1. Original Source Manufacturers and Their Respective Devices

Manufacturer	Device
Fairchild Semiconductor Components Group Fairchild Camera and Instrument Corp. 464 Ellis Street Mountain View, CA 94040	μA709, μA709A, μA709C μA715, μA715C μA725, μA725A, μA725C μA741, μA741A, μA741C, μA741E μA747, μA747C μA748, μ748C μA776, μA776C
Harris Semiconductor A Division of Harris-Intertype Corp. P.O. Box 883 Melbourne, FL 32901	HA-2400, HA-2404, HA-2405 HA-2620, HA-2622, HA-2625
Intersil, Inc. 10900 N. Tantau Ave. Cupertino, CA 95014	8007M, 8007AM 8007C, 8007AC
Motorola Semiconductor Products, Inc. Technical Information Center P.O. Box 20912 Phoenix, AZ 85036	MC1536G, MC1436G, MC1436CG MC1537, MC1437 MC1556G, MC1456G, MC1456CG MC1558, MC1458, MC1458C MC3301P, MC3401P
National Semiconductor Corp. 2900 Semiconductor Drive Santa Clara, CA 95051	LM101, LM201, LM101A/LM201A, LM301A LM107/LM207, LM307 LM108/LM208, LM308, LM108A/ LM208A, LM308A LM110/LM210, LM310 LM118/LM218, LM318 LM2900, LM3900 LM4250/LM4250C
Raytheon Company Semiconductor Div. 350 Ellis Street Mountain View, CA 94042	RM4709, RM4709A, RC4709C
RCA Solid State Div. Linear Integrated Circuits Route 202 Somerville, NJ 08876	CA3080, CA3080A CA3094T, CA3094AT, CA3094BT
Signetics Corp. 811 East Arques Ave. Sunnyvale, CA 94086	SE531/NE531 SE540/NE540

µA709
HIGH PERFORMANCE OPERATIONAL AMPLIFIER
FAIRCHILD LINEAR INTEGRATED CIRCUITS

GENERAL DESCRIPTION – The µA709 is a monolithic High Gain Operational Amplifier constructed using the Fairchild Planar* epitaxial process. It features low offset, high input impedance, large input common mode range, high output swing under load and low power consumption. The device displays exceptional temperature stability and will operate over a wide range of supply voltages with little degradation of performance. The amplifier is intended for use in dc servo systems, high impedance analog computers, low level instrumentation applications and for the generation of special linear and nonlinear transfer functions.

ABSOLUTE MAXIMUM RATINGS

Supply Voltage	±18 V
Internal Power Dissipation (Note)	
Metal Can	500 mW
DIP	670 mW
Flatpak	570 mW
Differential Input Voltage	±5.0 V
Input Voltage	±10 V
Storage Temperature Range	
Metal Can, DIP, and Flatpak	−65°C to +150°C
Operating Temperature Range	
Military (709A and 709)	−55°C to +125°C
Commercial (709C)	0°C to +70°C
Lead Temperature	
Metal Can, DIP and Flatpak (Soldering 60 seconds)	300°C
Output Short Circuit Duration	5 seconds

NOTE
Rating applies to ambient temperature up to 70°C. Above 70°C ambient derate linearly at 6.3 mW/°C for Metal Can, 8.3 mW/°C for DIP and 7.1 mW/°C for the Flatpak.

EQUIVALENT CIRCUIT

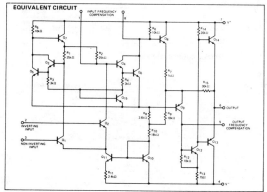

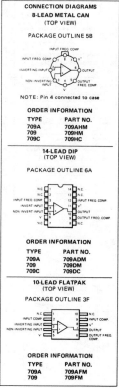

Courtesy Fairchild Semiconductor

521

709A

ELECTRICAL CHARACTERISTICS (T_A = +25°C, ±9 V ≤ V_S ≤ ±15 V unless otherwise specified)

PARAMETER (see definitions)		CONDITIONS	MIN.	TYP.	MAX.	UNITS
Input Offset Voltage		R_S ≤ 10 kΩ		0.6	2.0	mV
Input Offset Current				10	50	nA
Input Bias Current				100	200	nA
Input Resistance			350	700		kΩ
Output Resistance				150		Ω
Supply Current		V_S = ±15 V		2.5	3.6	mA
Power Consumption		V_S = ±15 V		75	108	mW
Transient Response	Risetime	V_S = ±15 V, V_{IN} = 20 mV, R_L = 2 kΩ, C_1 = 5 nF, R_1 = 1.5 kΩ, C_2 = 200 pF, R_2 = 50Ω C_L ≤ 100 pF			1.5	μs
	Overshoot				30	%

The following specifications apply for −55°C ≤ T_A ≤ +125°C:

PARAMETER	CONDITIONS	MIN.	TYP.	MAX.	UNITS
Input Offset Voltage	R_S ≤ 10 kΩ			3.0	mV
Average Temperature Coefficient of Input Offset Voltage	R_S = 50Ω, T_A = +25°C to +125°C		1.8	10	μV/°C
	R_S = 50Ω, T_A = +25°C to −55°C		1.8	10	μV/°C
	R_S = 10 kΩ, T_A = +25°C to +125°C		2.0	15	μV/°C
	R_S = 10 kΩ, T_A = +25°C to −55°C		4.8	25	μV/°C
Input Offset Current	T_A = +125°C		3.5	50	nA
	T_A = −55°C		40	250	nA
Average Temperature Coefficient of Input Offset Current	T_A = +25°C to +125°C		0.08	0.5	nA/°C
	T_A = +25°C to −55°C		0.45	2.8	nA/°C
Input Bias Current	T_A = −55°C		300	600	nA
Input Resistance	T_A = −55°C	85	170		kΩ
Input Voltage Range	V_S = ±15 V	±8.0			V
Common Mode Rejection Ratio	R_S ≤ 10 kΩ	80	110		dB
Supply Voltage Rejection Ratio	R_S ≤ 10 kΩ		40	100	μV/V
Large Signal Voltage Gain	V_S = ±15 V, R_L ≥ 2 kΩ, V_{OUT} = ±10 V	25,000		70,000	V/V
Output Voltage Swing	V_S = ±15 V, R_L ≥ 10 kΩ	±12	±14		V
	V_S = ±15 V, R_L ≥ 2 kΩ	±10	±13		V
Supply Current	T_A = +125°C, V_S = ±15 V		2.1	3.0	mA
	T_A = −55°C, V_S = ±15 V		2.7	4.5	mA
Power Consumption	T_A = +125°C, V_S = ±15 V		63	90	mW
	T_A = −55°C, V_S = ±15 V		81	135	mW

PERFORMANCE CURVES FOR 709A

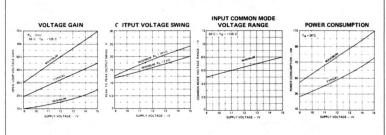

VOLTAGE GAIN OUTPUT VOLTAGE SWING INPUT COMMON MODE VOLTAGE RANGE POWER CONSUMPTION

709

ELECTRICAL CHARACTERISTICS (T_A = +25°C, ±9 V $\leq$ V_S $\leq$ ±15 V unless otherwise specified)

PARAMETER (see definitions)		CONDITIONS	MIN.	TYP.	MAX.	UNITS
Input Offset Voltage		$R_S \leq 10\,k\Omega$		1.0	5.0	mV
Input Offset Current				50	200	nA
Input Bias Current				200	500	nA
Input Resistance			150	400		kΩ
Output Resistance				150		Ω
Power Consumption		V_S = ±15 V		80	165	mW
Transient Response	Risetime	V_{IN} = 20 mV, R_L = 2 kΩ, C_1 = 5000 pF, R_1 = 1.5 kΩ, C_2 = 200 pF, R_2 = 50Ω		0.3	1.0	μs
	Overshoot	$C_L \leq 100$ pF		10	30	%

The following specifications apply for –55°C $\leq$ T_A $\leq$ +125°C:

PARAMETER		CONDITIONS	MIN.	TYP.	MAX.	UNITS
Input Offset Voltage		$R_S \leq 10\,k\Omega$			6.0	mV
Average Temperature Coefficient of Input Offset Voltage		$R_S = 50\Omega$		3.0		μV/°C
		$R_S \leq 10\,k\Omega$		6.0		μV/°C
Large Signal Voltage Gain		V_S = ±15 V, $R_L \geq 2\,k\Omega$, V_{OUT} = ±10 V	25,000	45,000	70,000	V/V
Output Voltage Swing		V_S = ±15 V, $R_L \geq 10\,k\Omega$	±12	±14		V
		V_S = ±15 V, $R_L \geq 2\,k\Omega$	±10	±13		V
Input Voltage Range		V_S = ±15 V	±8.0	±10		V
Common Mode Rejection Ratio		$R_S \leq 10\,k\Omega$	70	90		dB
Supply Voltage Rejection Ratio		$R_S \leq 10\,k\Omega$		25	150	μV/V
Input Offset Current		T_A = +125°C		20	200	nA
		T_A = –55°C		100	500	nA
Input Bias Current		T_A = –55°C		0.5	1.5	μA
Input Resistance			40	100		kΩ

PERFORMANCE CURVES FOR 709

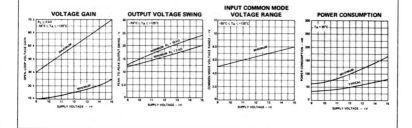

VOLTAGE GAIN OUTPUT VOLTAGE SWING INPUT COMMON MODE VOLTAGE RANGE POWER CONSUMPTION

Courtesy Fairchild Semiconductor

709C

ELECTRICAL CHARACTERISTICS (V_S = ±15 V, T_A = 25°C unless otherwise specified)

PARAMETER (see definitions)		CONDITIONS	MIN.	TYP.	MAX.	UNITS
Input Offset Voltage		$R_S \leq$ 10 kΩ, ±9 V $\leq V_S \leq$ ±15 V		2.0	7.5	mV
Input Offset Current				100	500	nA
Input Bias Current				0.3	1.5	μA
Input Resistance			50	250		kΩ
Output Resistance				150		Ω
Large Signal Voltage Gain		$R_L \geq$ 2 kΩ, V_{OUT} = ±10 V	15,000	45,000		V/V
Output Voltage Swing		$R_L \geq$ 10 kΩ	±12	±14		V
		$R_L \geq$ 2 kΩ	±10	±13		V
Input Voltage Range			±8.0	±10		V
Common Mode Rejection Ratio		$R_S \leq$ 10 kΩ	65	90		dB
Supply Voltage Rejection Ratio		$R_S \leq$ 10 kΩ		25	200	μV/V
Power Consumption				80	200	mW
Transient Response	Risetime	V_{IN} = 20 mV, R_L = 2 kΩ, C_1 = 5000 pF, R_1 = 1.5 kΩ, C_2 = 200 pF, R_2 = 50Ω $C_L \leq$ 100 pF		0.3		μs
	Overshoot			10		%

The following specifications apply for 0°C $\leq T_A \leq$ +70°C:

Input Offset Voltage		$R_S \leq$ 10 kΩ, ±9 V $\leq V_S \leq$ ±15 V			10	mV
Input Offset Current					750	nA
Input Bias Current					2.0	μA
Large Signal Voltage Gain		$R_L \geq$ 2 kΩ, V_{OUT} = ±10 V	12,000			V/V
Input Resistance			35			kΩ

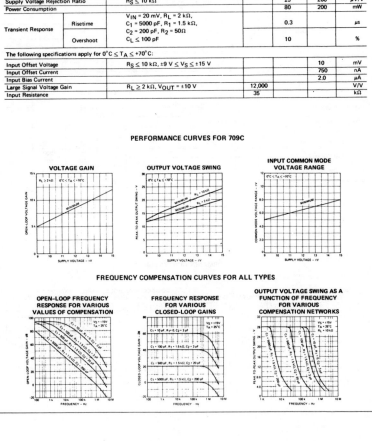

PERFORMANCE CURVES FOR 709C

VOLTAGE GAIN

OUTPUT VOLTAGE SWING

INPUT COMMON MODE VOLTAGE RANGE

FREQUENCY COMPENSATION CURVES FOR ALL TYPES

OPEN–LOOP FREQUENCY RESPONSE FOR VARIOUS VALUES OF COMPENSATION

FREQUENCY RESPONSE FOR VARIOUS CLOSED-LOOP GAINS

OUTPUT VOLTAGE SWING AS A FUNCTION OF FREQUENCY FOR VARIOUS COMPENSATION NETWORKS

Courtesy Fairchild Semiconductor

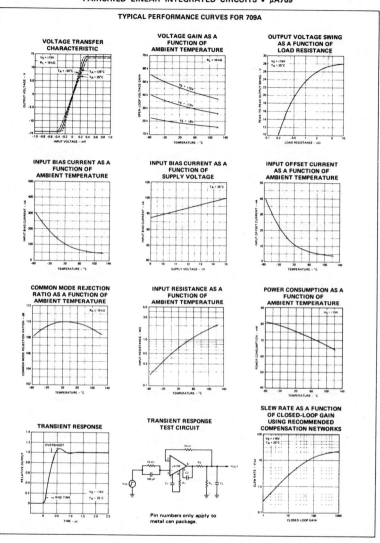

TYPICAL PERFORMANCE CURVES FOR 709A

Pin numbers only apply to
metal can package.

Courtesy Fairchild Semiconductor

TYPICAL PERFORMANCE CURVES FOR 709 AND 709C

**VOLTAGE TRANSFER
CHARACTERISTIC**

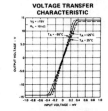

**INPUT BIAS CURRENT
AS A FUNCTION OF
AMBIENT TEMPERATURE**

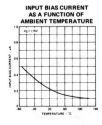

**INPUT OFFSET CURRENT
AS A FUNCTION OF
AMBIENT TEMPERATURE**

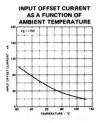

**INPUT RESISTANCE
AS A FUNCTION OF
AMBIENT TEMPERATURE**

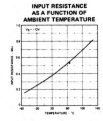

**POWER CONSUMPTION
AS A FUNCTION OF
AMBIENT TEMPERATURE**

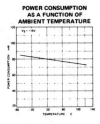

**INPUT BIAS CURRENT
AS A FUNCTION OF
SUPPLY VOLTAGE**

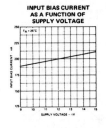

**OUTPUT VOLTAGE
SWING AS A FUNCTION OF
LOAD RESISTANCE**

**FREQUENCY COMPENSATION
CIRCUIT**

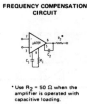

* Use R_2 = 50 Ω when the
amplifier is operated with
capacitive loading.

TRANSIENT RESPONSE

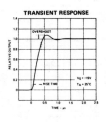

TYPICAL PERFORMANCE CURVES FOR 709 AND 709C

**FREQUENCY CHARACTERISTICS
AS A FUNCTION OF
SUPPLY VOLTAGE**

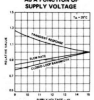

**FREQUENCY CHARACTERISTICS
AS A FUNCTION OF
AMBIENT TEMPERATURE**

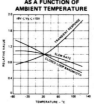

PROTECTION CIRCUITS

**OUTPUT SHORT-CIRCUIT
PROTECTION**

**INPUT BREAKDOWN
PROTECTION**

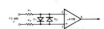

LATCH-UP PROTECTION

**SUPPLY OVERVOLTAGE
PROTECTION**

Pin numbers only apply to metal can package.

Courtesy Fairchild Semiconductor

527

µA741

FREQUENCY-COMPENSATED OPERATIONAL AMPLIFIER
FAIRCHILD LINEAR INTEGRATED CIRCUITS

GENERAL DESCRIPTION — The µA741 is a high performance monolithic Operational Amplifier constructed using the Fairchild Planar* epitaxial process. It is intended for a wide range of analog applications. High common mode voltage range and absence of "latch-up" tendencies make the µA741 ideal for use as a voltage follower. The high gain and wide range of operating voltage provides superior performance in integrator, summing amplifier, and general feedback applications.

- NO FREQUENCY COMPENSATION REQUIRED
- SHORT CIRCUIT PROTECTION
- OFFSET VOLTAGE NULL CAPABILITY
- LARGE COMMON-MODE AND DIFFERENTIAL VOLTAGE RANGES
- LOW POWER CONSUMPTION
- NO LATCH UP

ABSOLUTE MAXIMUM RATINGS

Supply Voltage	
Military (741)	±22 V
Commercial (741C)	±18 V
Internal Power Dissipation (Note 1)	
Metal Can	500 mW
DIP	670 mW
Mini DIP	310 mW
Flatpak	570 mW
Differential Input Voltage	±30 V
Input Voltage (Note 2)	±15 V
Storage Temperature Range	
Metal Can, DIP, and Flatpak	−65°C to +150°C
Mini DIP	−55°C to +125°C
Operating Temperature Range	
Military (741)	−55°C to +125°C
Commercial (741C)	0°C to +70°C
Lead Temperature (Soldering)	
Metal Can, DIP, and Flatpak (60 seconds)	300°C
Mini DIP (10 seconds)	260°C
Output Short Circuit Duration (Note 3)	Indefinite

EQUIVALENT CIRCUIT

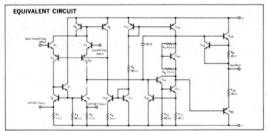

Notes on following pages.

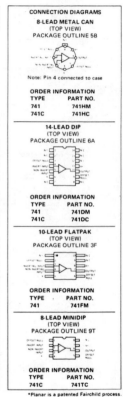

CONNECTION DIAGRAMS

8-LEAD METAL CAN
(TOP VIEW)
PACKAGE OUTLINE 5B

Note: Pin 4 connected to case

ORDER INFORMATION

TYPE	PART NO.
741	741HM
741C	741HC

14-LEAD DIP
(TOP VIEW)
PACKAGE OUTLINE 6A

ORDER INFORMATION

TYPE	PART NO.
741	741DM
741C	741DC

10-LEAD FLATPAK
(TOP VIEW)
PACKAGE OUTLINE 3F

ORDER INFORMATION

TYPE	PART NO.
741	741FM

8-LEAD MINIDIP
(TOP VIEW)
PACKAGE OUTLINE 9T

ORDER INFORMATION

TYPE	PART NO.
741C	741TC

*Planar is a patented Fairchild process.

Courtesy Fairchild Semiconductor

741

ELECTRICAL CHARACTERISTICS (V_S = ±15 V, T_A = 25°C unless otherwise specified)

PARAMETERS (see definitions)		CONDITIONS	MIN.	TYP.	MAX.	UNITS
Input Offset Voltage		$R_S \leqslant 10\ k\Omega$		1.0	5.0	mV
Input Offset Current				20	200	nA
Input Bias Current				80	500	nA
Input Resistance			0.3	2.0		MΩ
Input Capacitance				1.4		pF
Offset Voltage Adjustment Range				±15		mV
Large Signal Voltage Gain		$R_L \geqslant 2\ k\Omega$, V_{OUT} = ±10 V	50,000	200,000		
Output Resistance				75		Ω
Output Short Circuit Current				25		mA
Supply Current				1.7	2.8	mA
Power Consumption				50	85	mW
Transient Response (Unity Gain)	Risetime	V_{IN} = 20 mV, R_L = 2 kΩ, $C_L \leqslant$ 100 pF		0.3		μs
	Overshoot			5.0		%
Slew Rate		$R_L \geqslant 2\ k\Omega$		0.5		V/μs

The following specifications apply for −55°C ≤ T_A ≤ +125°C:

Input Offset Voltage		$R_S \leqslant 10\ k\Omega$		1.0	6.0	mV
Input Offset Current	T_A = +125°C			7.0	200	nA
	T_A = −55°C			85	500	nA
Input Bias Current	T_A = +125°C			0.03	0.5	μA
	T_A = −55°C			0.3	1.5	μA
Input Voltage Range			±12	±13		V
Common Mode Rejection Ratio		$R_S \leqslant 10\ k\Omega$	70	90		dB
Supply Voltage Rejection Ratio		$R_S \leqslant 10\ k\Omega$		30	150	μV/V
Large Signal Voltage Gain		$R_L \geqslant 2\ k\Omega$, V_{OUT} = ±10 V	25,000			
Output Voltage Swing		$R_L \geqslant 10\ k\Omega$	±12	±14		V
		$R_L \geqslant 2\ k\Omega$	±10	±13		V
Supply Current	T_A = +125°C			1.5	2.5	mA
	T_A = −55°C			2.0	3.3	mA
Power Consumption	T_A = +125°C			45	75	mW
	T_A = −55°C			60	100	mW

TYPICAL PERFORMANCE CURVES FOR 741

OPEN LOOP VOLTAGE GAIN AS A FUNCTION OF SUPPLY VOLTAGE
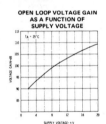

OUTPUT VOLTAGE SWING AS A FUNCTION OF SUPPLY VOLTAGE
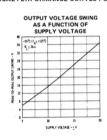

INPUT COMMON MODE VOLTAGE RANGE AS A FUNCTION OF SUPPLY VOLTAGE
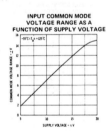

Courtesy Fairchild Semiconductor

741C

ELECTRICAL CHARACTERISTICS (V_S = ±15 V, T_A = 25°C unless otherwise specified)

PARAMETERS (see definitions)		CONDITIONS	MIN.	TYP.	MAX.	UNITS
Input Offset Voltage		$R_S \leqslant 10\ k\Omega$		2.0	6.0	mV
Input Offset Current				20	200	nA
Input Bias Current				80	500	nA
Input Resistance			0.3	2.0		MΩ
Input Capacitance				1.4		pF
Offset Voltage Adjustment Range				±15		mV
Input Voltage Range			±12	±13		V
Common Mode Rejection Ratio		$R_S \leqslant 10\ k\Omega$	70	90		dB
Supply Voltage Rejection Ratio		$R_S \leqslant 10\ k\Omega$		30	150	µV/V
Large Signal Voltage Gain		$R_L \geqslant 2\ k\Omega$, V_{OUT} = ±10 V	20,000	200,000		
Output Voltage Swing		$R_L \geqslant 10\ k\Omega$	±12	±14		V
		$R_L \geqslant 2\ k\Omega$	±10	±13		V
Output Resistance				75		Ω
Output Short Circuit Current				25		mA
Supply Current				1.7	2.8	mA
Power Consumption				50	85	mW
Transient Response (Unity Gain)	Risetime	V_{IN} = 20 mV, R_L = 2 kΩ, C_L ⩽ 100 pF		0.3		µs
	Overshoot			5.0		%
Slew Rate		$R_L \geqslant 2\ k\Omega$		0.5		V/µs

The following specifications apply for 0°C ⩽ T_A ⩽ +70°C:

Input Offset Voltage					7.5	mV
Input Offset Current					300	nA
Input Bias Current					800	nA
Large Signal Voltage Gain		$R_L \geqslant 2\ k\Omega$, V_{OUT} = ±10 V	15,000			
Output Voltage Swing		$R_L \geqslant 2\ k\Omega$	±10	±13		V

TYPICAL PERFORMANCE CURVES FOR 741C

OPEN LOOP VOLTAGE GAIN AS A FUNCTION OF SUPPLY VOLTAGE

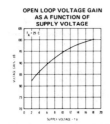

OUTPUT VOLTAGE SWING AS A FUNCTION OF SUPPLY VOLTAGE

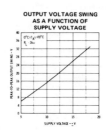

INPUT COMMON MODE VOLTAGE RANGE AS A FUNCTION OF SUPPLY VOLTAGE

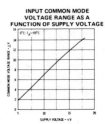

NOTES:
1. Rating applies to ambient temperatures up to 70°C. Above 70°C ambient derate linearly at 6.3 mW/°C for the Metal Can, 8.3 mW/°C for the DIP, 5.6 mW/°C for the Mini DIP and 7.1 mW/°C for the Flatpak.
2. For supply voltages less than ±15 V, the absolute maximum input voltage is equal to the supply voltage.
3. Short circuit may be to ground or either supply. Rating applies to +125°C case temperature or 75°C ambient temperature.

Courtesy Fairchild Semiconductor

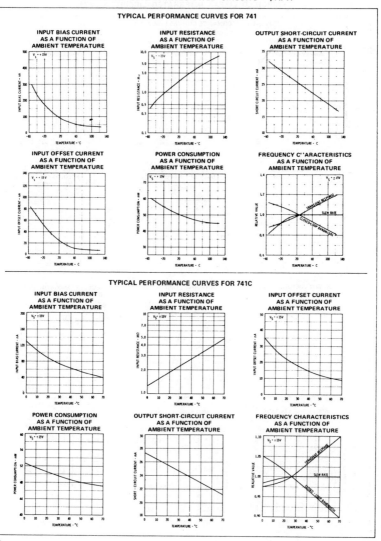

TYPICAL PERFORMANCE CURVES FOR 741

TYPICAL PERFORMANCE CURVES FOR 741C

Courtesy Fairchild Semiconductor

TYPICAL PERFORMANCE CURVES FOR 741 AND 741C (Cont'd)

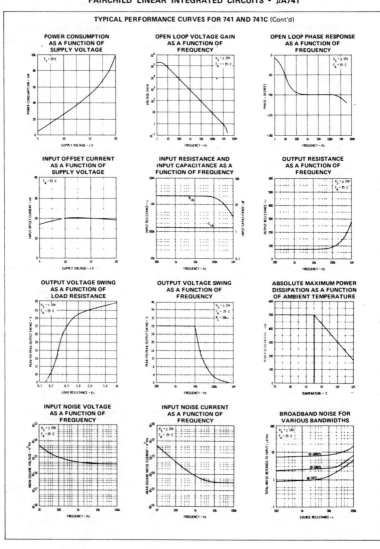

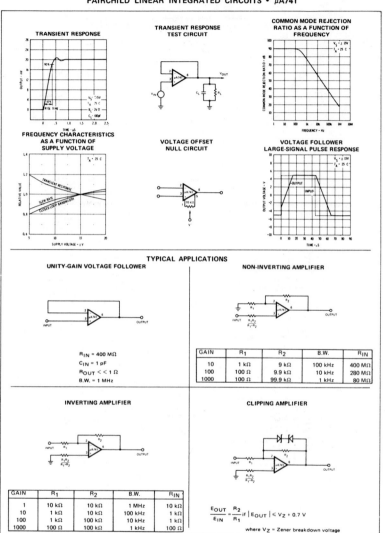

TYPICAL APPLICATIONS

UNITY-GAIN VOLTAGE FOLLOWER

R_{IN} = 400 MΩ
C_{IN} = 1 pF
R_{OUT} << 1 Ω
B.W. = 1 MHz

NON-INVERTING AMPLIFIER

GAIN	R_1	R_2	B.W.	R_{IN}
10	1 kΩ	9 kΩ	100 kHz	400 MΩ
100	100 Ω	9.9 kΩ	10 kHz	280 MΩ
1000	100 Ω	99.9 kΩ	1 kHz	80 MΩ

INVERTING AMPLIFIER

GAIN	R_1	R_2	B.W.	R_{IN}
1	10 kΩ	10 kΩ	1 MHz	10 kΩ
10	1 kΩ	10 kΩ	100 kHz	1 kΩ
100	1 kΩ	100 kΩ	10 kHz	1 kΩ
1000	100 Ω	100 kΩ	1 kHz	100 Ω

CLIPPING AMPLIFIER

$$\frac{E_{OUT}}{E_{IN}} = \frac{R_2}{R_1} \text{ if } |E_{OUT}| \leqslant V_Z + 0.7 \text{ V}$$

where V_Z = Zener breakdown voltage

Courtesy Fairchild Semiconductor

533

TYPICAL APPLICATIONS (Cont'd)

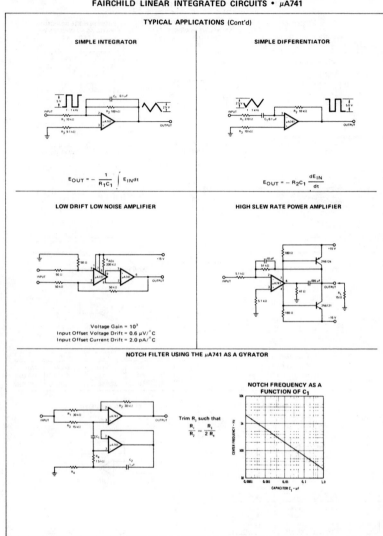

SIMPLE INTEGRATOR

$$E_{OUT} = -\frac{1}{R_1 C_1} \int E_{IN} dt$$

SIMPLE DIFFERENTIATOR

$$E_{OUT} = -R_2 C_1 \frac{dE_{IN}}{dt}$$

LOW DRIFT LOW NOISE AMPLIFIER

Voltage Gain = 10^3
Input Offset Voltage Drift = 0.6 μV/°C
Input Offset Current Drift = 2.0 pA/°C

HIGH SLEW RATE POWER AMPLIFIER

NOTCH FILTER USING THE μA741 AS A GYRATOR

Trim R_1 such that
$$\frac{R_1}{R_2} = \frac{R_3}{2 R_4}$$

NOTCH FREQUENCY AS A FUNCTION OF C_1

Courtesy Fairchild Semiconductor

µA741A • µA741E
FREQUENCY COMPENSATED OPERATIONAL AMPLIFIER
FAIRCHILD LINEAR INTEGRATED CIRCUITS

GENERAL DESCRIPTION — The µA741A and E are high performance monolithic Operational Amplifiers constructed using the Fairchild Planar* epitaxial process. They are intended for a wide range of analog applications. High common mode voltage range and absence of "latch-up" tendencies make the µA741A and E ideal for use as voltage followers. The high gain and wide range of operating voltage provides superior performance in integrator, summing amplifier, and general feedback applications. Electrical characteristics are identical to MIL-M-38510/10101.

- **NO FREQUENCY COMPENSATION REQUIRED**
- **SHORT-CIRCUIT PROTECTION**
- **OFFSET VOLTAGE NULL CAPABILITY**
- **LARGE COMMON-MODE AND DIFFERENTIAL VOLTAGE RANGES**
- **LOW POWER CONSUMPTION**
- **NO LATCH UP**

ABSOLUTE MAXIMUM RATINGS

Supply Voltage	±22V
Internal Power Dissipation (Note 1)	
Metal Can	500 mW
DIP	670 mW
Flatpak	570 mW
Differential Input Voltage	±30V
Input Voltage (Note 2)	±15V
Storage Temperature Range	−65°C to +150°C
Operating Temperature Range	
Military (741A)	−55°C to +125°C
Commercial (741E)	0°C to +70°C
Lead Temperature (Soldering, 60 seconds)	300°C
Output Short Circuit Duration (Note 3)	Indefinite

EQUIVALENT CIRCUIT

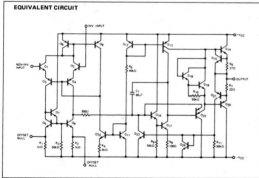

Notes on following pages.

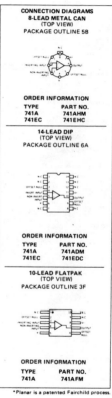

*Planar is a patented Fairchild process.

Courtesy Fairchild Semiconductor

741A

ELECTRICAL CHARACTERISTICS ($V_S = \pm 15V$, $T_A = 25^\circ C$ unless otherwise specified)

PARAMETERS (see definitions)		CONDITIONS	MIN.	TYP.	MAX.	UNITS
Input Offset Voltage		$R_S \leqslant 50\Omega$		0.8	3.0	mV
Average Input Offset Voltage Drift					15	μV/°C
Input Offset Current				3.0	30	nA
Average Input Offset Current Drift					0.5	nA/°C
Input Bias Current				30	80	nA
Power Supply Rejection Ratio		$V_S = +10, -20$; $V_S = +20, -10V$, $R_S = 50\Omega$		15	50	μV/V
Output Short Circuit Current			10	25	35	mA
Power Dissipation		$V_S = \pm 20V$		80	150	mW
Input Impedance		$V_S = \pm 20V$	1.0	6.0		MΩ
Large Signal Voltage Gain		$V_S = \pm 20V$, $R_L = 2k\Omega$, $V_{OUT} = \pm 15V$	50			V/mV
Transient Response	Rise Time			0.25	0.8	μs
(Unity Gain)	Overshoot			6.0	20	%
Bandwidth (Note 4)			.437	1.5		MHz
Slew Rate (Unity Gain)		$V_{IN} = \pm 10V$	0.3	0.7		V/μs
The following specifications apply for $-55^\circ C \leqslant T_A \leqslant +125^\circ C$						
Input Offset Voltage					4.0	mV
Input Offset Current					70	nA
Input Bias Current					210	nA
Common Mode Rejection Ratio		$V_S = \pm 20V$, $V_{IN} = \pm 15V$, $R_S = 50\Omega$	80	95		dB
Adjustment For Input Offset Voltage		$V_S = \pm 20V$	10			mV
Output Short Circuit Current			10		40	mA
Power Dissipation	$V_S = \pm 20V$	$-55^\circ C$			165	mW
		$+125^\circ C$			135	mW
Input Impedance		$V_S = \pm 20V$	0.5			MΩ
Output Voltage Swing	$V_S = \pm 20V$,	$R_L = 10k\Omega$	±16			V
		$R_L = 2k\Omega$	±15			V
Large Signal Voltage Gain		$V_S = \pm 20V$, $R_L = 2k\Omega$, $V_{OUT} = \pm 15V$	32			V/mV
		$V_S = \pm 5V$, $R_L = 2k\Omega$, $V_{OUT} = \pm 2$ V	10			V/mV

NOTES
1. Rating applies to ambient temperatures up to 70°C. Above 70°C ambient derate linearly at 6.3mW/°C for the Metal Can, 8.3mW/°C for the DIP and 7.1mW/°C for the Flatpak.
2. For supply voltages less than ±15V, t ie absolute maximum input voltage is equal to the supply voltage.
3. Short circuit may be to ground or either supply. Rating applies to +125°C case temperature or 75°C ambient temperature.
4. Calculated value from: $BW(MHz) = \dfrac{0.35}{\text{Rise Time } (\mu s)}$

741E

ELECTRICAL CHARACTERISTICS (V_S = ±15V, T_A = 25°C unless otherwise specified)

PARAMETERS (see definitions)		CONDITIONS	MIN.	TYP.	MAX.	UNITS
Input Offset Voltage		$R_S \leq 50\Omega$		0.8	3.0	mV
Average Input Offset Voltage Drift					15	μV/°C
Input Offset Current				3.0	30	nA
Average Input Offset Current Drift					0.5	nA/°C
Input Bias Current				30	80	nA
Power Supply Rejection Ratio		V_S = +10, −20; V_S = +20, −10V, R_S = 50Ω		15	50	μV/V
Output Short Circuit Current			10	25	35	mA
Power Dissipation		V_S = ±20V		80	150	mW
Input Impedance		V_S = ±20V	1.0	6.0		MΩ
Large Signal Voltage Gain		V_S = ±20V, R_L = 2kΩ, V_{OUT} = ±15V	50			V/mV
Transient Response (Unity Gain)	Rise Time			0.25	0.8	μs
	Overshoot			6.0	20	%
Bandwidth (Note 4)			.437	1.5		MHz
Slew Rate (Unity Gain)		V_{IN} = ±10V	0.3	0.7		V/μs
The following specifications apply for 0°C ≤ T_A ≤ 70°C						
Input Offset Voltage					4.0	mV
Input Offset Current					70	nA
Input Bias Current					210	nA
Common Mode Rejection Ratio		V_S = ±20V, V_{IN} = ±15V, R_S = 50Ω	80	95		dB
Adjustment For Input Offset Voltage		V_S = ±20V	10			mV
Output Short Circuit Current			10		40	mA
Power Dissipation		V_S = ±20V			150	mW
Input Impedance		V_S = ±20V	0.5			MΩ
Output Voltage Swing		V_S = ±20V, $R_L \geq 10k\Omega$	±16			V
		R_L = 2kΩ	±15			V
Large Signal Voltage Gain		V_S = ±20V, R_L = 2kΩ, V_{OUT} = ±15V	32			V/mV
		V_S = ±5V, R_L = 2kΩ, V_{OUT} = ±2 V	10			V/mV

**VOLTAGE OFFSET
NULL CIRCUIT**

**TRANSIENT RESPONSE
TEST CIRCUIT**

Courtesy Fairchild Semiconductor

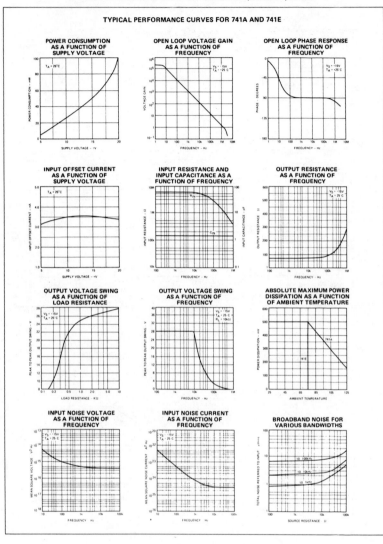

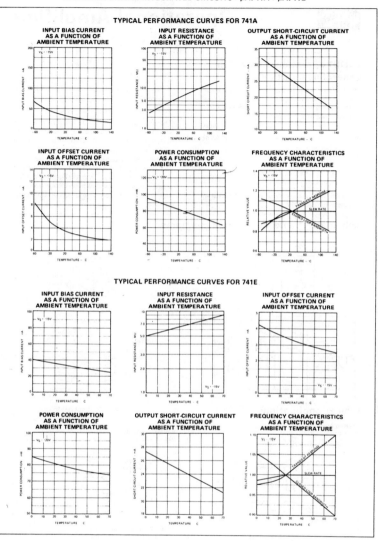

TYPICAL PERFORMANCE CURVES FOR 741A

TYPICAL PERFORMANCE CURVES FOR 741E

Courtesy Fairchild Semiconductor

Operational Amplifiers

LM101 operational amplifier general description

The LM101 is a general-purpose operational amplifier built on a single silicon chip. The resulting close match and tight thermal coupling gives low offsets and temperature drift as well as fast recovery from thermal transients. In addition, the device features:

- Frequency compensation with a single 30 pF capacitor

- Operation from ±5V to ±20V

- Low current drain: 1.8 mA at ±20V

- Continuous short-circuit protection

- Operation as a comparator with differential inputs as high as ±30V

- No latch-up when common mode range is exceeded

- Same pin configuration as the LM709.

The unity-gain compensation specified makes the circuit stable for all feedback configurations, even with capacitive loads. However, it is possible to optimize compensation for best high frequency performance at any gain. As a comparator, the output can be clamped at any desired level to make it compatible with logic circuits. Further, the low power dissipation permits high-voltage operation and simplifies packaging in full-temperature-range systems.

schematic** and connection diagrams

typical applications **

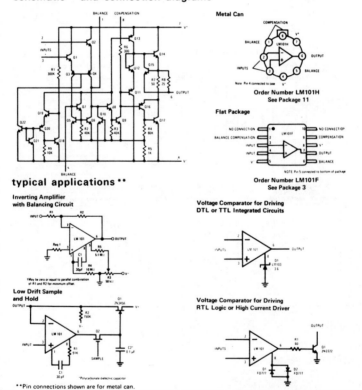

**Pin connections shown are for metal can.

Courtesy National Semiconductor Corp.

absolute maximum ratings

Supply Voltage	±22V
Power Dissipation (Note 1)	500 mW
Differential Input Voltage	±30V
Input Voltage (Note 2)	±15V
Output Short-Circuit Duration (Note 3)	Indefinite
Operating Temperature Range	$-55°C$ to $+125°C$
Storage Temperature Range	$-65°C$ to $+150°C$
Lead Temperature (Soldering, 60 sec)	$300°C$

electrical characteristics (note 4)

PARAMETER	CONDITIONS	MIN	TYP	MAX	UNITS
Input Offset Voltage	$T_A = 25°C$, $R_S \leq 10k\Omega$		1.0	5.0	mV
Input Offset Current	$T_A = 25°C$		40	200	nA
Input Bias Current	$T_A = 25°C$		120	500	nA
Input Resistance	$T_A = 25°C$	300	800		$k\Omega$
Supply Current	$T_A = 25°C$, $V_S = ±20V$		1.8	3.0	mA
Large Signal Voltage Gain	$T_A = 25°C$, $V_S = ±15V$ $V_{OUT} = ±10V$, $R_L \geq 2k\Omega$	50	160		V/mV
Input Offset Voltage	$R_S \leq 10k\Omega$			6.0	mV
Average Temperature Coefficient of Input Offset Voltage	$R_S \leq 50\Omega$		3.0		$\mu V/°C$
	$R_S \leq 10k\Omega$		6.0		$\mu V/°C$
Input Offset Current	$T_A = +125°C$ $T_A = -55°C$		10 100	200 500	nA nA
Input Bias Current	$T_A = -55°C$		0.28	1.5	μA
Supply Current	$T_A = +125°C$, $V_S = ±20V$		1.2	2.5	mA
Large Signal Voltage Gain	$V_S = ±15V$, $V_{OUT} = ±10V$ $R_L \geq 2k\Omega$	25			V/mV
Output Voltage Swing	$V_S = ±15V$, $R_L = 10k\Omega$ $R_L = 2k\Omega$	±12 ±10	±14 ±13		V V
Input Voltage Range	$V_S = ±15V$	±12			V
Common Mode Rejection Ratio	$R_S \leq 10k\Omega$	70	90		dB
Supply Voltage Rejection Ratio	$R_S \leq 10k\Omega$	70	90		dB

Note 1: For operating at elevated temperatures, the device must be derated based on a 150°C maximum junction temperature and a thermal resistance of 150°C/W junction to ambient or 45°C/W junction to case for the metal-can package. For the flat package, the derating is based on a thermal resistance of 185°C/W when mounted on a 1/16-inch-thick, epoxy-glass board with ten, 0.03-inch-wide, 2-ounce copper conductors (see curve).
Note 2: For supply voltages less than ±15V, the absolute maximum input voltage is equal to the supply voltage.
Note 3: Continuous short circuit is allowed for case temperatures to +125°C and ambient temperatures to +70°C.
Note 4: These specifications apply for $-55°C \leq T_A \leq 125°C$, ±5V, $\leq V_S \leq ±20V$ and C1 30 pF unless otherwise specified.

Courtesy National Semiconductor Corp.

guaranteed performance characteristics

typical performance characteristics

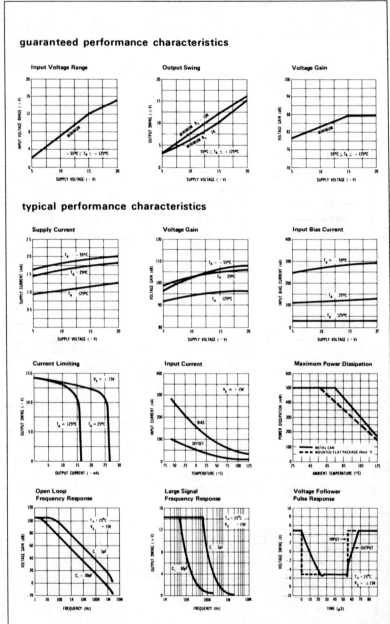

Operational Amplifiers

LM201

LM201 operational amplifier
general description

The LM201 is a general-purpose operational amplifier built on a single silicon chip. It is identical to the LM101 except that operation is specified over a 0 to 70°C temperature range. The device features:

- Frequency compensation with a single 30 pF capacitor
- Operation from ±5V to ±20V
- Low current drain: 1.8 mA at ±20V
- Continuous short-circuit protection
- Operation as a comparator with differential inputs as high as ±30V

- No latch-up when common mode range is exceeded
- LM709 lead configuration in metal cans and flat-packages.

The unity-gain compensation specified makes the circuit stable for all feedback configurations, even with capacitive loads. However, it is possible to optimize compensation for best high frequency performance at any gain. As a comparator, the output can be clamped at any desired level to make it compatible with logic circuits. Further, the low power dissipation permits high-voltage operation and simplifies packaging.

schematic** and connection diagrams

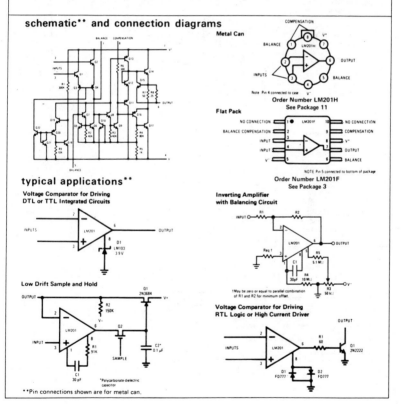

Courtesy National Semiconductor Corp.

absolute maximum ratings

Supply Voltage	±22V
Power Dissipation (Note 1)	250 mW
Differential Input Voltage	±30V
Input Voltage (Note 2)	±15V
Output Short-Circuit Duration (Note 3)	Indefinite
Operating Temperature Range	$0°C$ to $+70°C$
Storage Temperature Range	$-65°C$ to $+150°C$
Lead Temperature (Soldering, 10 sec)	$300°C$

electrical characteristics (note 4)

PARAMETER	CONDITIONS	MIN	TYP	MAX	UNITS
Input Offset Voltage	$T_A = 25°C$, $R_S \leq 10k\Omega$		2.0	7.5	mV
Input Offset Current	$T_A = 25°C$		100	500	nA
Input Bias Current	$T_A = 25°C$		0.25	1.5	μA
Input Resistance	$T_A = 25°C$	100	400		$k\Omega$
Supply Current	$T_A = 25°C$, $V_S = ±20V$		1.8	3.0	mA
Large Signal Voltage Gain	$T_A = 25°C$, $V_S = ±15V$ $V_{OUT} = ±10V$, $R_L \geq 2k\Omega$	20	150		V/mV
Input Offset Voltage	$R_S \leq 10k\Omega$			10	mV
Average Temperature Coefficient of Input Offset Voltage	$R_S \leq 50\Omega$ $R_S \leq 10k\Omega$		6 10		μV/$°$C μV/$°$C
Input Offset Current	$T_A = +70°C$ $T_A = 0°C$		50 150	400 750	nA nA
Input Bias Current	$T_A = 0°C$		0.32	2.0	μA
Large Signal Voltage Gain	$V_S = ±15V$, $V_{OUT} = ±10V$ $R_L \geq 2k\Omega$	15			V/mV
Output Voltage Swing	$V_S = ±15V$, $R_L = 10k\Omega$ $R_L = 2k\Omega$	±12 ±10	±14 ±13		V V
Input Voltage Range	$V_S = ±15V$	±12			V
Common Mode Rejection Ratio	$R_S \leq 10k\Omega$	65	90		dB
Supply Voltage Rejection Ratio	$R_S \leq 10k\Omega$	70	90		dB

Note 1: For operating at elevated temperatures, the device must be derated based on a $100°C$ maximum junction temperature and a thermal resistance of $150°C/W$ junction to ambient or $45°C/W$ junction to case for the metal-can package. For the flat package, the derating is based on a thermal resistance of $185°C/W$ when mounted on a 1/16-inch-thick, epoxy-glass board with ten, 0.03-inch-wide, 2-ounce copper conductors (see curve).
Note 2: For supply voltages less than ±15V, the absolute maximum input voltage is equal to the supply voltage.
Note 3: Continuous short circuit is allowed for case temperatures to $70°C$ and ambient temperatures to $55°C$.
Note 4: These specifications apply for $0°C \leq T_A \leq 70°C$, ±5V, $\leq V_S \leq$ ±20V and C1 = 30 pF unless otherwise specified.

Courtesy National Semiconductor Corp.

guaranteed performance characteristics

typical performance characteristics

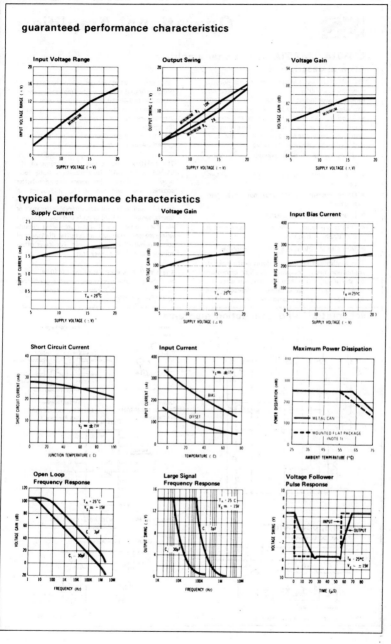

Courtesy National Semiconductor Corp.

Operational Amplifiers

LM101A/LM201A operational amplifier
general description

The LM101A and LM201A are general purpose operational amplifiers which feature improved performance over industry standards like the LM101 and the 709. Advanced processing techniques make possible an order of magnitude reduction in input currents, and a redesign of the biasing circuitry reduces the temperature drift of input current. Improved specifications include:

- Offset voltage 3 mV maximum over temperature
- Input current 100 nA maximum over temperature
- Offset current 20 nA maximum over temperature
- Guaranteed drift characteristics
- Offsets guaranteed over entire common mode and supply voltage ranges
- Slew rate of 10V/μs as a summing amplifier

This amplifier offers many features which make its application nearly foolproof: overload protection on the input and output, no latch-up when the common mode range is exceeded, freedom from oscillations and compensation with a single 30 pF

capacitor. It has advantages over internally compensated amplifiers in that the frequency compensation can be tailored to the particular application. For example, in low frequency circuits it can be overcompensated for increased stability margin. Or the compensation can be optimized to give more than a factor of ten improvement in high frequency performance for most applications.

The LM101A series offers the features of the LM101, which makes its application nearly foolproof. In addition, the device provides better accuracy and lower noise in high impedance circuitry. The low input currents also make it particularly well suited for long interval integrators or timers, sample and hold circuits and low frequency waveform generators. Further, replacing circuits where matched transistor pairs buffer the inputs of conventional IC op amps, it can give lower offset voltage and drift at a lower cost.

The LM201A is identical to the LM101A, except that the LM201A has its performance guaranteed over a $-25°C$ to $85°C$ temperature range, instead of $-55°C$ to $125°C$.

schematic** and connection diagrams

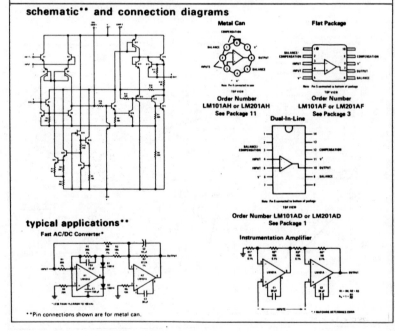

typical applications**

Fast AC/DC Converter*

**Pin connections shown are for metal can.

Courtesy National Semiconductor Corp.

absolute maximum ratings

Supply Voltage	±22V
Power Dissipation (Note 1)	500 mW
Differential Input Voltage	±30V
Input Voltage (Note 2)	±15V
Output Short-Circuit Duration (Note 3)	Indefinite
Operating Temperature Range LM101A	−55°C to 125°C
LM201A	−25°C to 85°C
Storage Temperature Range	−65°C to 150°C
Lead Temperature (Soldering, 10 sec)	300°C

electrical characteristics (Note 4)

PARAMETER	CONDITIONS	MIN	TYP	MAX	UNITS
Input Offset Voltage	$T_A = 25°C$, $R_S \leq 50\,k\Omega$		0.7	2.0	mV
Input Offset Current	$T_A = 25°C$		1.5	10	nA
Input Bias Current	$T_A = 25°C$		30	75	nA
Input Resistance	$T_A = 25°C$	1.5	4		MΩ
Supply Current	$T_A = 25°C$, $V_S = ±20V$		1.8	3.0	mA
Large Signal Voltage Gain	$T_A = 25°C$, $V_S = ±15V$ $V_{OUT} = ±10V$, $R_L \geq 2\,k\Omega$	50	160		V/mV
Input Offset Voltage	$R_S \leq 50\,k\Omega$			3.0	mV
Average Temperature Coefficient of Input Offset Voltage			3.0	15	μV/°C
Input Offset Current				20	nA
Average Temperature Coefficient of Input Offset Current	$25°C \leq T_A \leq 125°C$ $-55°C \leq T_A \leq 25°C$		0.01 0.02	0.1 0.2	nA/°C nA/°C
Input Bias Current				100	nA
Supply Current	$T_A = +125°C$, $V_S = ±20V$		1.2	2.5	mA
Large Signal Voltage Gain	$V_S = ±15V$, $V_{OUT} = ±10V$ $R_L \geq 2\,k\Omega$	25			V/mV
Output Voltage Swing	$V_S = ±15V$, $R_L = 10\,k\Omega$ $R_L = 2\,k\Omega$	±12 ±10	±14 ±13		V V
Input Voltage Range	$V_S = ±20V$	±15			V
Common Mode Rejection Ratio	$R_S \leq 50\,k\Omega$	80	96		dB
Supply Voltage Rejection Ratio	$R_S \leq 50\,k\Omega$	80	96		dB

Note 1: The maximum junction temperature of the LM101A is 150°C, while that of the LM201A is 100°C. For operating at elevated temperatures, devices in the TO-5 package must be derated based on a thermal resistance of 150°C/W, junction to ambient, or 45°C/W, junction to case. For the flat package, the derating is based on a thermal resistance of 185°C/W when mounted on a 1/16-inch-thick epoxy glass board with ten, 0.03-inch-wide, 2-ounce copper conductors. The thermal resistance of the dual-in-line package is 100°C/W, junction to ambient.

Note 2: For supply voltages less than ±15V, the absolute maximum input voltage is equal to the supply voltage.

Note 3: Continuous short circuit is allowed for case temperatures to +125°C and ambient temperatures to +75°C.

Note 4: These specifications apply for $±5V \leq V_S \leq ±20V$ and $-55°C \leq T_A \leq 125°C$, unless otherwise specified. With the LM201A, however, all temperature specifications are limited to $-25°C \leq T_A \leq 85°C$.

Courtesy National Semiconductor Corp.

guaranteed performance characteristics

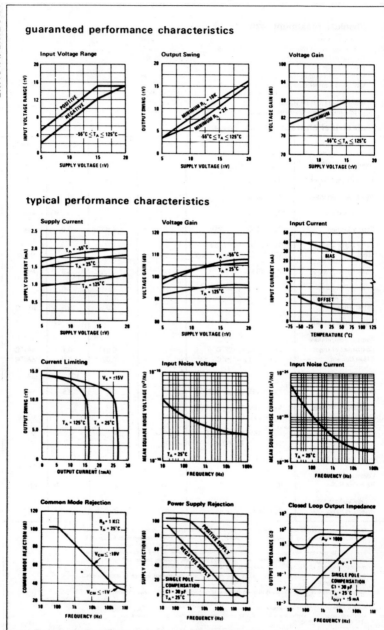

typical performance characteristics

compensation circuits**

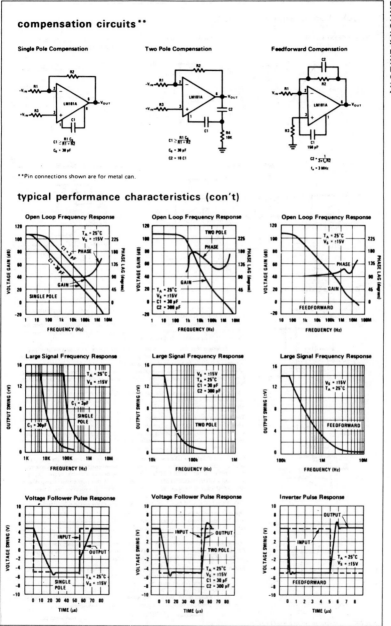

**Pin connections shown are for metal can.

typical performance characteristics (con't)

Courtesy National Semiconductor Corp.

typical applications ** (con't)

Variable Capacitance Multiplier

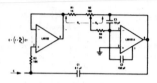

Simulated Inductor

Fast Inverting Amplifier With High Input Impedance

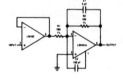

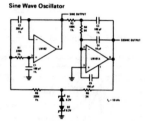

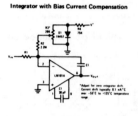

Inverting Amplifier with Balancing Circuit

Sine Wave Oscillator

Integrator with Bias Current Compensation

application hints**

Protecting Against Gross Fault Conditions

Although the LM101A is designed for trouble free operation, experience has indicated that it is wise to observe certain precautions given below to protect the devices from abnormal operating conditions. It might be pointed out that the advice given here is applicable to practically any IC op amp, although the exact reason why may differ with different devices.

When driving either input from a low-impedance source, a limiting resistor should be placed in series with the input lead to limit the peak instantaneous output current of the source to something less than 100 mA. This is especially important when the inputs go outside a piece of equipment where they could accidentally be connected to high voltage sources. Large capacitors on the input (greater than 0.1 μF) should be treated as a low source impedance and isolated with a resistor. Low impedance sources do not cause a problem unless their output voltage exceeds the supply voltage. However, the supplies go to zero when they are turned off, so the isolation is usually needed.

Compensating For Stray Input Capacitances Or Large Feedback Resistor

The output circuitry is protected against damage from shorts to ground. However, when the amplifier output is connected to a test point, it should be isolated by a limiting resistor, as test points frequently get shorted to bad places. Further, when the amplifier drives a load external to the equipment, it is also advisable to use some sort of limiting resistance to preclude mishaps.

Precautions should be taken to insure that the power supplies for the integrated circuit never become reversed—even under transient conditions. With reverse voltages greater than 1V, the IC will conduct excessive current, fuzing internal aluminum interconnects. If there is a possibility of this happening, clamp diodes with a high peak current rating should be installed on the supply lines. Reversal of the voltage between V^+ and V^- will always cause a problem, although reversals with respect to ground may also give difficulties in many circuits.

Isolating Large Capacitive Loads

The minimum values given for the frequency compensation capacitor are stable only for source resistances less than 10 kΩ, stray capacitances on the summing junction less than 5 pF and capacitive loads smaller than 100 pF. If any of these conditions are not met, it becomes necessary to overcompensate the amplifier with a larger compensation capacitor. Alternately, lead capacitors can be used in the feedback network to negate the effect of stray capacitance and large feedback resistors or an RC network can be added to isolate capacitive loads.

Although the LM101A is relatively unaffected by supply bypassing, this cannot be ignored altogether. Generally it is necessary to bypass the supplies to ground at least once on every circuit card, and more bypass points may be required if more than five amplifiers are used. When feed-forward compensation is employed, however, it is advisable to bypass the supply leads of each amplifier with low inductance capacitors because of the higher frequencies involved.

** Pin connections shown are for metal can.

Courtesy National Semiconductor Corp.

Operational Amplifiers

LM301A operational amplifier
general description

The LM301A is a general-purpose operational amplifier which features improved performance over the 709C and other popular amplifiers. Advanced processing techniques make possible an order of magnitude reduction in input currents, and a redesign of the biasing circuitry reduces the temperature drift of input current.

This amplifier offers many features which make its application nearly foolproof: overload protection on the input and output, no latch-up when the common mode range is exceeded, freedom from oscillations and compensation with a single 30 pF capacitor. It has advantages over internally compensated amplifiers in that the compensation can be tailored to the particular application. For

example, as a summing amplifier, slew rates of 10 V/μs and bandwidths of 10 MHz can be realized. In addition, the circuit can be used as a comparator with differential inputs up to ±30V; and the output can be clamped at any desired level to make it compatible with logic circuits.

The LM301A provides better accuracy and lower noise than its predecessors in high impedance circuitry. The low input currents also make it particularly well suited for long interval integrators or timers, sample and hold circuits and low frequency waveform generators. Further, replacing circuits where matched transistor pairs buffer the inputs of conventional IC op amps, it can give lower offset voltage and drift at reduced cost.

schematic** and connection diagrams

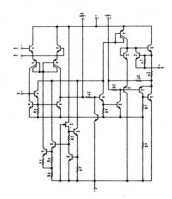

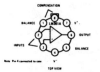

Order Number LM301AH
See Package 11

Order Number LM301AN
See Package 20

typical applications **

Integrator with Bias Current Compensation

Low Frequency Square Wave Generator

Voltage Comparator for Driving DTL or TTL Integrated Circuits

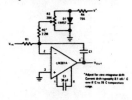

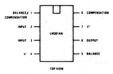

**Pin connections shown are for metal can.

Courtesy National Semiconductor Corp.

absolute maximum ratings

Supply Voltage	±18V
Power Dissipation (Note 1)	500 mW
Differential Input Voltage	±30V
Input Voltage (Note 2)	±15V
Output Short-Circuit Duration (Note 3)	Indefinite
Operating Temperature Range	0°C to 70°C
Storage Temperature Range	-65°C to 150°C
Lead Temperature (Soldering, 10 sec)	300°C

electrical characteristics (Note 4)

PARAMETER	CONDITIONS	MIN	TYP	MAX	UNITS
Input Offset Voltage	$T_A = 25^\circ$C, $R_S \leq 50$ kΩ		2.0	7.5	mV
Input Offset Current	$T_A = 25^\circ$C		3	50	nA
Input Bias Current	$T_A = 25^\circ$C		70	250	nA
Input Resistance	$T_A = 25^\circ$C	0.5	2		MΩ
Supply Current	$T_A = 25^\circ$C, $V_S = \pm15$V		1.8	3.0	mA
Large Signal Voltage Gain	$T_A = 25^\circ$C, $V_S = \pm15$V $V_{OUT} = \pm10$V, $R_L \geq 2$ kΩ	25	160		V/mV
Input Offset Voltage	$R_S \leq 50$ kΩ			10	mV
Average Temperature Coefficient of Input Offset Voltage			6.0	30	μV/$^\circ$C
Input Offset Current				70	nA
Average Temperature Coefficient of Input Offset Current	25°C $\leq T_A \leq 70^\circ$C 0°C $\leq T_A \leq 25^\circ$C		0.01 0.02	0.3 0.6	nA/$^\circ$C nA/$^\circ$C
Input Bias Current				300	nA
Large Signal Voltage Gain	$V_S = \pm15$V, $V_{OUT} = \pm10$V $R_L \geq 2$ kΩ	15			V/mV
Output Voltage Swing	$V_S = \pm15$V, $R_L = 10$ kΩ $R_L = 2$ kΩ	±12 ±10	±14 ±13		V V
Input Voltage Range	$V_S = \pm15$V	±12			V
Common Mode Rejection Ratio	$R_S \leq 50$ kΩ	70	90		dB
Supply Voltage Rejection Ratio	$R_S \leq 50$ kΩ	70	96		dB

Note 1: For operating at elevated temperatures, the device must be derated based on a 100°C maximum junction temperature and a thermal resistance of 150°C/W junction to ambient or 45°C/W junction to case.

Note 2: For supply voltages less than ±15V, the absolute maximum input voltage is equal to the supply voltage.

Note 3: Continuous short circuit is allowed for case temperatures to 70°C and ambient temperatures to 55°C.

Note 4: These specifications apply for 0°C $\leq T_A < 70^\circ$C, ±5V, $\leq V_S \leq \pm15$V and C1 = 30 pF unless otherwise specified.

Courtesy National Semiconductor Corp.

guaranteed performance characteristics

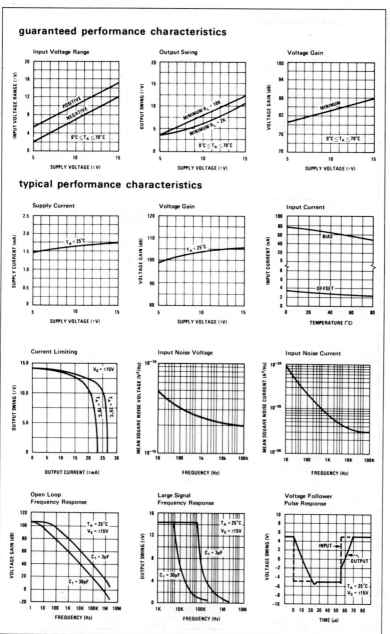

typical performance characteristics

Courtesy National Semiconductor Corp.

typical applications ** (con't)

Standard Compensation and
Offset Balancing Circuit

Fast Summing Amplifier

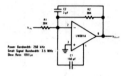

Fast Voltage Follower

Bilateral Current Source

**Pin connections shown are for metal can.

Courtesy National Semiconductor Corp.

APPENDIX B

Linear IC Cross-Reference Guide

As noted in Appendix A, the manufacturers of the devices listed in Table A-1 are the original sources of those devices. In addition, most manufacturers supply, or "second source," standard devices that are not of their own origin. The following cross-reference listings, furnished through the courtesy of the respective manufacturers, will be of assistance in correctly identifying a device by its alternate-source part number(s). If the device is listed as a "direct" or "pin-for-pin" replacement, it is an electrical and mechanical duplicate of the original. If, however, a device is listed as a "functional" equivalent, it is not necessarily a direct substitute mechanically or electrically in all details. In these cases, consult the manufacturer's data sheets in order to be assured of suitability. In all cases, alternate-source types should be qualified by in-circuit testing as a final verification of suitability.

MOTOROLA TO FAIRCHILD

MOTOROLA	FAIRCHILD DIRECT REPLACEMENT	FAIRCHILD FUNCTIONAL EQUIVALENT	MOTOROLA	FAIRCHILD DIRECT REPLACEMENT	FAIRCHILD FUNCTIONAL EQUIVALENT
MC943	SH2001		MC1529		μA730
MC1303		μA749C	MC1530		μA702
MC1304	μA732C		MC1531		μA702
MC1305		μA732C	MC1533		101
MC1307	μA767C		MC1535		μA749
MC1310		μA758C	MC1536		μA741
MC1326		μA746C	MC1537		μA749
MC1328		μA746C	MC1539		101
MC1339		μA749C	MC1540		7525
MC1350		μA757C	MC1541		7524
MC1351		3065	MC1543		7524
MC1352		μA757C	MC1545		μA733
MC1353		μA757C	MC1546		μA733
MC1355		3065	MC1550		μA757
MC1357	2136		MC1552		μA715
MC1358	3065		MC1553		μA715
MC1364	3064		MC1556		μA725
MC1370	μA780C		MC1558	1558	
MC1371	μA781C		MC1560		μA723
MC1410		μA733C	MC1561		μA723
MC1414		μA711C	MC1563		μA723
MC1420		μA733C	MC1566		μA723
MC1429		μA730C	MC1569		μA723
MC1430		μA702C	MC1580		9615
MC1431		μA702C	MC1582		9614
MC1433		301	MC1583		9615
MC1435		μA749C	MC1584		9615
MC1436		301	MC1590		μA757
MC1437		μA749C	MC1596	μA796	
MC1438		μA749C	MC1709	μA709	
MC1439		301	MC1710	μA710	
MC1440		7525	MC1711	μA711	
MC1441		7524	MC1712	μA702	
MC1445		μA733C	MC1723	μA723	
MC1446		μA733C	MC1741	μA741	
MC1456		μA725C	MC1748	μA748	
MC1458	1458		MC75107A	75107A	
MC1460		μA723C	MC75108A	75108A	
MC1461		μA723C	MC75109	75109	
MC1463		μA723C	MC75110	75110	
MC1466		μA723C	MC75325	75325	
MC1469		μA723C	MC55107A	55107A	
MC1488		9616C	MC55108A	55108A	
MC1489		9617C	MC55109	55109	
MC1496	μA796C		MC55110	55110	
MC1509		μA733	MFC4060		μA723
MC1510		μA733	MFC6010		μA703
MC1514		μA711	MFC8000		μA739
MC1519		μA733	MFC8001		μA739
MC1520		101	MFC8002		μA739
MC1525		μA730	MFC8030		μA703
MC1526		μA730	MFC8040		μA791

MOTOROLA TO FAIRCHILD (cont)

MOTOROLA	FAIRCHILD DIRECT REPLACEMENT	FAIRCHILD FUNCTIONAL EQUIVALENT
MFC8070		μA742
MLM101A	101A	
MLM105	105	
MLM107	107	
MLM109	109	
MLM201	201	
MLM205	205	
MLM207	207	
MLM209	209	
MLM301	301	
MLM305	305	
MLM307	307	
MLM309	309	

NATIONAL TO FAIRCHILD

NATIONAL	FAIRCHILD DIRECT REPLACEMENT	FAIRCHILD FUNCTIONAL EQUIVALENT	NATIONAL	FAIRCHILD DIRECT REPLACEMENT	FAIRCHILD FUNCTIONAL EQUIVALENT
DM7820		9615	LM111	111	
DM7820A		9615	LM112		μA776
DM7822		9617	LM118		μA772
DM7830		9614	LM119		μA760
DM7831		9614	LM120	μA78N00	
DM7832		9614	LM121		μA727
DM8820		9615	LM160	μA760	
DM8820A		9615	LM161		μA760
DM8822		9617	LM200		μA723C
DM8830		9614	LM201	201	
DM8831		9614	LM202	202	
DM8832		9614	LM204	204	
LH0002		μA791	LM205	205	
LH0002C		μA791C	LM206		μA710C
LH0020		μA725	LM207	207	
LH0020C		μA725C	LM208	208	
LH0021		μA791	LM208A	208A	
LH0021C		μA791C	LM209	209	
LH0041		μA791	LM210	210	
LH0041C		μA791C	LM211	211	
LH0042		μA740	LM216		μA740
LH0042C		μA740C	LM216A		μA740
LH0052		μA740	LM218		μA772
LH0052C		μA740C	LM219		μA760
LH101		107	LM219		μA760
LH201		207	LM300		μA723
LH2101A		101A	LM301A	301A	
LH2201A		201A	LM302	302	
LH2301A		301A	LM304	304	
LH2108		108	LM305	305	
LH2208		208	LM306		μA710C
LH2308		308	LM307	307	
LH2110		110	LM308	308	
LH2210		210	LM308A	308A	
LH2310		310	LM309	309	
LH2111		111	LM310	310	
LH2211		211	LM311	311	
LH2311		311	LM312		μA776C
LH24250		μA776	LM316		μA740C
LH24250C		μA776C	LM316A		μA740C
LM100		μA723	LM318		μA772C
LM101	101		LM320-05		μA78N05
LM101A	101A		LM340-05	μA7805C	
LM102	102		LM340-06	μA7806C	
LM104	104		LM340-08	μA7808C	
LM105	105		LM340-12	μA7812C	
LM106		μA760	LM340-15	μA7815C	
LM107	107		LM340-18	μA7818C	
LM108	108		LM340-24	μA7824C	
LM108A	108A		LM350	75325	
LM109	109		LM376	376	
LM110	110		LM709	μA709	

Courtesy Fairchild Semiconductor

NATIONAL TO FAIRCHILD (cont)

NATIONAL	FAIRCHILD DIRECT REPLACEMENT	FAIRCHILD FUNCTIONAL EQUIVALENT	NATIONAL	FAIRCHILD DIRECT REPLACEMENT	FAIRCHILD FUNCTIONAL EQUIVALENT
LM709A	μA709A		LM4250	μA776	
LM709C	μA709C		LM4250C	μA776C	
LM710	μA710		LM7520		7524
LM710C	μA710C		LM7521		7524
LM711	μA711		LM7522		7524
LM711C	μA711C		LM7523		7524
LM723	μA723		LM7524	7524	
LM723C	μA723C		LM7525	7525	
LM725	μA725		LM7528	7528	
LM725A	μA725A		LM7529	7529	
LM725C	μA725C		LM7534	7534	
LM733	μA733		LM7535	7535	7524
LM733C	μA733C		LM7538		7524
LH740A	μA740		LM7539		7524
LH740AC	μA740C		LM75325	75325	
LM741	μA741		LM75450A	75450A	
LM741C	μA741C		LM75451A	75451A	
LM747	μA747		LM75452	75452	
LM747C	μA747C		LM75453	75453	
LM748	μA748		LM75454	75454	
LM748C	μA748C		LMDAC-01		μA722
LM1488		9616	NH00011	SH2001	
LM1489		9617	NH00011CN	SH2002	
LM1489A		9617	NH00013	SH0013	
LM1414		μA711C	NH00016	SH2200	
LM1458	1458		NH00017	SH2200	
LM1514		μA711	NH00018	SH2200	
LM1558	1558				

RCA TO FAIRCHILD

RCA	FAIRCHILD DIRECT REPLACEMENT	FAIRCHILD FUNCTIONAL EQUIVALENT	RCA	FAIRCHILD DIRECT REPLACEMENT	FAIRCHILD FUNCTIONAL EQUIVALENT
CA3000		μA702	CA3046	3046	
CA3001		μA733	CA3047		μA709
CA3002		μA703	CA3048		μA749
CA3004		μA703	CA3048H		μA749
CA3005		μA703	CA3050		μA730
CA3006		μA703	CA3051		μA730
CA3007		μA716	CA3052		μA739
CA3008		μA702	CA3053		μA703
CA3008A		μA702	CA3054	3054	
CA3010		μA702	CA3058		μA742
CA3010A		μA702	CA3059		μA742
CA3011		μA753	CA3060A		μA739
CA3012		μA753	CA3060B		μA739
CA3013		μA753	CA3060		μA739
CA3014		μA753	CA3064	3064	
CA3015		μA702	CA3065	3065	
CA3015A		μA702	CA3066	3066	
CA3016		μA702	CA3067	3067	
CA3016A		μA702	CA3070	μA780	
CA3018	3018		CA3071	μA781	
CA3018A	3018A		CA3072	μA746	
CA3019	3019		CA3075	3075	
CA3021		μA757	CA3076	3076	
CA3022		μA757	CA3078		μA776
CA3023		μA757	CA3079		μA742
CA3026	3026		CA3085		μA723
CA3028		μA703	CA3085A		μA723
CA3028A		μA703	CA3085B		μA723
CA3029		μA702	CA3086	3086	
CA3029A		μA702	CA3088		μA720
CA3030		μA702	CA3089		3075
CA3030A		μA702	CA3090		μA758
CA3033		μA709	CA3091		μA795
CA3033A		μA709	CA3118		3018
CA3035		μA739	CA3118A		3018
CA3036	3036		CA3146		3046
CA3037		μA709	CA3146A		3046
CA3037A		μA709	CA3458	1458	
CA3038		μA709	CA3541		7524
CA3038A		μA709	CA3558	1558	
CA3039	3039		CA3741C	μA741C	
CA3040		μA733	CA3741	μA741	
CA3041		3065	CA3747C	μA747C	
CA3042		3065	CA3747	μA747	
CA3043		3065	CA3748C	μA748C	
CA3044	3064		CA3748	μA748	
CA3045	3045		CA6741	μA741	

Courtesy Fairchild Semiconductor

SIGNETICS TO FAIRCHILD

SIGNETICS	FAIRCHILD DIRECT REPLACEMENT	FAIRCHILD FUNCTIONAL EQUIVALENT	SIGNETICS	FAIRCHILD DIRECT† REPLACEMENT	FAIRCHILD FUNCTIONAL EQUIVALENT
501		μA733	5558	1458	
510		μA730	7520		7524
511		3045	7521		7524
515		μA730	7522		7524
516		μA740	7523		7524
518		μA711	7524	7524	
526		μA710	7525	7525	
527		μA760	75450		75450A
528		7524	75450A	75450A	
529		μA760	75451		75451A
531		μA715	75451A	75451A	
533		μA776	LM101	101	
536		μA740	LM107	107	
537		μA725	LM108	108	
550		μA723	LM109	109	
592		μA733	LM201	201	
μA709	μA709		LM207	207	
μA710	μA710		LM209	209	
μA711	μA711		LM301	301	
μA723	μA723		LM307	307	
μA733	μA733		LM308	308	
μA740	μA740		LM309	309	
μA741	μA741		8T13	8T13	
μA747	μA747		8T14	8T14	
μA748	μA748		8T23	8T23	
5556		μA776	8T24	8T24	

SPRAGUE TO FAIRCHILD

SPRAGUE	FAIRCHILD DIRECT REPLACEMENT	FAIRCHILD FUNCTIONAL EQUIVALENT	SPRAGUE	FAIRCHILD DIRECT REPLACEMENT	FAIRCHILD FUNCTIONAL EQUIVALENT
ULN2111	2136		ULN2128	μA767	
ULN2113		3065	ULN2129		3075
ULN2114	μA746		ULN2131	μA753	
ULN2120	μA732		ULN2136	2136	
ULN2121		μA767	ULN2165	3065	
ULN2122		μA732	ULX2205		μA706
ULN2124	μA780		ULX2211		μA704
ULN2126	μA739		ULX2275		μA705
ULN2127	μA781		ULX2277	μA705	

TEXAS INSTRUMENTS TO FAIRCHILD

T.I.	FAIRCHILD DIRECT REPLACEMENT	FAIRCHILD FUNCTIONAL EQUIVALENT	T.I.	FAIRCHILD DIRECT REPLACEMENT	FAIRCHILD FUNCTIONAL EQUIVALENT
SN52101A	101A	μA710	SN7521		7524
SN52107	107		SN7522		7524
SN52510		μA710	SN7523		7524
SN52558	1558		SN7524	7524	
SN52702	μA702		SN7525	7525	
SN52709	μA709		SN7526		7524
SN52709A	μA709A		SN7527		7524
SN52710	μA710		SN7528		7524
SN52711	μA711		SN7529		7524
SN52720		μA711	SN75100L		9615
SN52733	μA733		SN75107A	75107A	
SN52741	μA741		SN75108A	75108A	
SN52747	μA747		SN75109	75109	
SN52748	μA748		SN75110	75110	
SN52770		μA740	SN75114	9614C	
SN52771		μA740	SN75115	9615C	
SN52810		μA710	SN75150		9616C
SN52811		μA711	SN75152	9627C	
SN52820		μA734	SN75154		9617C
SN5510		μA733	SN75182		9615
SN5511		μA733	SN75183		9614
SN5512		μA733	SN75232	7534	
SN5514		μA733	SN75233	7525	
SN55107A	55107A		SN75234	75234	
SN55108A	55108A		SN75235	75235	
SN55109	55109		SN75238		7524
SN55110	55110		SN75239		7524
SN70024		μA706C	SN75324		75325
SN72301A	301		SN75325	75325	
SN72307	307		SN75326		75325
SN72400		μA723C	SN75327		75325
SN72510		μA710C	SN75450		75450A
SN72558	1458		SN75451		75451A
SN72702	μA702C		SN75452	75452	
SN72709	μA709C		SN75453	75453	
SN72710	μA710C		SN75454	75454	
SN72711	μA711C		SN75460	75460	
SN72720		μA711C	SN75461	75461	
SN72733	μA733C		SN75462	75462	
SN72741	μA747C		SN75463	75463	
SN72748	μA748C		SN75464	75464	
SN72770		μA740C	SN76001		μA706C
SN72771		μA740C	SN76003		μA706C
SN72810		μA710C	SN76005		μA706C
SN72811		μA711C	SN76010		μA706C
SN72820		μA734C	SN76013		μA706C
SN7510		μA733C	SN76050		μA706C
SN7511		μA733C	SN76104	μA732C	
SN7512		μA733C	SN76105		μA732C
SN7514		μA733C	SN76107	μA767C	
SN7520		7524	SN76110	μA767C	

Courtesy Fairchild Semiconductor

TEXAS INSTRUMENTS TO FAIRCHILD (cont)

T.I.	FAIRCHILD DIRECT REPLACEMENT	FAIRCHILD FUNCTIONAL EQUIVALENT
SN76131	µA739C	
SN76149	µA749C	
SN76177	µA705C	
SN76242	µA780C	
SN76243	µA781C	
SN76246	µA746C	
SN76266	3066	
SN76267	3067	
SN76350		µA720C
SN76550		µA723C
SN76552		µA723C
SN76553		µA723C
SN76564	3064	
SN76603	µA703C	
SN76619		µA703C
SN76630	µA786C	
SN76640		3065
SN76642		3075
SN76643	2136	
SN76660		3065
SN76665	3065	
SN76666	3066	
SN76670		3065
SN76675	3075	
SN76676	3076	
SN76680		3065

FAIRCHILD TO MOTOROLA

FAIRCHILD DEVICE NUMBER		MOTOROLA DIRECT EQUIVALENT	MOTOROLA FUNCTIONAL EQUIVALENT
DEVICE TYPE	ORDER CODE		
μA702	U3F 7702 312	MC1712F	
	U3F 7702 313	MC1712CF	
	U5B 7702 312	MC1712G	
	U5B 7702 393	MC1712CG	
	U6A 7702 312	MC1712L	
	U6A 7702 393	MC1712CL	
μA703	U5D 7703 312		MFC6010
	U5D 7703 393		MFC6010
	U5D 7703 394		MFC6010
μA709	U3F 7709 311	MC1709F	
	U3F 7709 312	MC1709F	
	U3F 7709 313	MC1709CF	
	U5B 7709 311	MC1709G	
	U5B 7709 312	MC1709G	
	U5B 7709 393	MC1709CG	
	U6A 7709 311	MC1709L	
	U6A 7709 312	MC1709L	
	U6A 7709 393	MC1709CL	
μA710	U3F 7710 312	MC1710F	
	U3F 7710 313	MC1710CF	
	U5B 7710 312	MC1710G	
	U5B 7710 393	MC1710CG	
	U6A 7710 312	MC1710L	
	U6A 7710 393	MC1710CL	
μA711	U3F 7711 312	MC1711F	
	U3F 7711 313	MC1711CF	
	U5F 7711 312	MC1711G	
	U5F 7711 393	MC1711CG	
	U6A 7711 312	MC1711L	
	U6A 7711 393	MC1711CL	
μA719	U5F 7719 312		MC1357
	U5F 7719 393		MC1357
μA723	U5R 7723 312	MC1723G	
	U5R 7723 393	MC1723CG	
	U6A 7723 312	MC1723L	
	U6A 7723 393	MC1723CL	
μA729	U6A 7729 394	MC1305P	
μA732	U6A 7732 394	MC1304P	
μA733	U3F 7733 312	MC1733F	
	U3F 7733 313	MC1733CF	
	U5F 7733 312	MC1733G	
	U5F 7733 393	MC1733CG	
	U6A 7733 312	MC1733L	
	U6A 7733 393	MC1733CL	
μA739	U6A 7739 312	MC1303P	
	U6A 7739 393	MC1303P	
μA741	U3F 7741 312	MC1741F	
	U3F 7741 313	MC1741CF	
	U5B 7741 312	MC1741G	
	U5B 7741 393	MC1741CG	
	U6A 7741 312	MC1741L	
	U6A 7741 393	MC1741CL	
	U6T 7741 393	MC1741CP2	
	U9T 7741 393	MC1741CP1	
μA746	U5E 7746 394		MC1328P
	U6A 7746 394	MC1328P	
μA747	U5F 7747 312		MC1558G
	U5F 7747 393		MC1458G
	U6W 7747 312		MC1558L
	U6W 7747 393		MC1558CL
	U7A 7747 312		MC1558L
	U7A 7747 393		MC1558CL

FAIRCHILD DEVICE NUMBER		MOTOROLA DIRECT EQUIVALENT	MOTOROLA FUNCTIONAL EQUIVALENT
DEVICE TYPE	ORDER CODE		
μA748	U3F 7748 312	MC1748F	
	U3F 7748 313	MC1748CF	
	U5B 7748 312	MC1748G	
	U5B 7748 393	MC1748CG	
	U6A 7748 312	MC1748L	
	U6A 7748 393	MC1748CL	
	U6T 7748 393	MC1748CP2	
	U9T 7748 393	MC1748CP1	
μA754	U5E 7754 393		MC1355P
	U6A 7754 394		MC1355P
μA757	U6A 7757 312		MC1350P
	U6A 7757 393		MC1350P
μA767	U6A 7780 394	MC1307P	
μA780	U6A 7781 394	MC1370P	
μA781	U6A 7795 312	MC1371P	
μA795	U6A 7795 312	MC1595L	
	U6A 7795 393	MC1595CL	
μA796	U5E 7796 312	MC1596G	
	U5E 7796 393	MC1596CG	
μA7524	U7B 7524 392	MC7524	
μA7525	U7B 7525 393	MC7524	
μA7805	UGH 7805 393	MC7805CP	
μA7806	UGH 7806 393	MC7806CP	
μA7808	UGH 7808 393	MC7808CP	
μA7812	UGH 7812 393	MC7812CP	
μA7815	UGH 7815 393	MC7815CP	
μA7818	UGH 7818 393	MC7818CP	
μA7824	UGH 7824 393	MC7824CP	
μA9614	U4L 9614 51X		MC1582L
	U4L 9614 59X		MC1582L
	U7B 9614 51X		MC1582L
	U7B 9614 59X		MC1582L
μA9615	U4L 9615 51X		MC1584L
	U4L 9615 59X		MC1584L
	U7B 9615 51X		MC1584L
	U7B 9615 59X		MC1584L
μA9620	U31 9620 51X		MC1580L
	U31 9620 59X		MC1580L
	U6A 9620 51X		MC1580L
	U6A 9620 59X		MC1580L
μA9621	U3I 9621 51X		MC1584L
	U3I 9621 59X		MC1584L
	U6A 9621 51X		MC1584L
	U6A 9621 59X		MC1584L
μA9622	U3I 9622 51X		MC1583
	U3I 9622 59X		MC1583
	U6A 9622 51X		MC1583
	U6A 9622 59X		MC1583
CA3064	CA 3064/5A	MC1364G	
CA3065	CA 3065/7F	MC1358PQ	
CA3075	CA 3075/	MC1375P	

Courtesy Motorola Semiconductor Products, Inc.

NATIONAL TO MOTOROLA

NATIONAL TYPE NUMBER	MOTOROLA DIRECT REPLACEMENT	MOTOROLA FUNCTIONAL EQUIVALENT	NATIONAL TYPE NUMBER	MOTOROLA DIRECT REPLACEMENT	MOTOROLA FUNCTIONAL EQUIVALENT
LH101F		MC1741F	LM710CN	MC1710CP	
LH101H		MC1741G	LM711H	MC1711G	
LH201H		MC1741G	LM711CH	MC1711CG	
LM100H		MC1723G	LM723D	MC1723L	
LM101H	MC1748G		LM723H	MC1723G	
LM101AH	MLM101AG		LM723CD	MC1723CL	
LM102H	MLM110G		LM723CH	MC1723CG	
LM104H	MLM104G		LM733D	MC1733L	
LM105H	MLM105G		LM733H	MC1733G	
LM106H		MC1710G	LM733CD	MC1733CL	
LM107H	MLM107G		LM733CH	MC1733CD	
LM108H		MC1556G	LM741D	MC1741L	
LM108AH		MC1556G	LM741F	MC1741F	
LM109K	MLM109K		LM741H	MC1741G	
LM110H	MLM110G		LM741CD	MC1741CL	
LM112H		MC1556G	LM741CH	MC1741CG	
LM118H		MC1539G	LM741CN	MC1741CP1	
LM200H		MC1723CG	LM741CN-14	MC1741CP2	
LM201H	MC1748CG		LM746N	MC1328P	
LM201AH	MLM201AG		LM747D	MC1747L	
LM202H	MLM210G		LM747CC	MC1747CL	
LM204H	MLM204G		LM748H	MC1748G	
LM205H	MLM205G		LM748CH	MC1748CG	
LM206G		MC1710CG	LM1303N	MC1303L	
LM207H	MLM207G		LM1304N	MC1304P	
LM208H		MC1456G	LM1305N	MC1305P	
LM209K	MLM209K		LM1310N	MC1310P	
LM210H	MLM210G		LM1307N	MC1307P	
LM212H		MC1456G	LM1351N	MC1351P	
LM218H		MC1439G			
LM300H		MC1723CG	LM1414J	MC1414L	
LM301AH	MLM301AG		LM1414N	MC1414L	
LM301AN	MLM301API		LM1458H	MC1458G	
LM302H	MLM310G		LM1458N	MC1458P1	
LM304H	MLM304G		LM1489J	MC1489L	
LM305H	MLM305G		LM1489AJ	MC1489AL	
LM306H		MC1710CG	LM1496H	MC1496G	
LM307H	MLM307G		LM1496N	MC1496L	
LM308H		MC1456G	LM1514J	MC1514L	
LM308AH		MC1456G	LM1558H	MC1558G	
LM309K	MLM309K		LM1596H	MC1596G	
LM310H	MLM310G		LM2111N	MC1357P	
LM312H		MC1456G	LM3064H	MC1364G	
LM318H		MC1439G	LM3064N	MC1364P	
			LM3065N	MC1358P	
LM350N		MC75450P			
LM351N	MC75453P		LM3067N		MC1328P
LM370H		MC1590G	LM3070N	MC1370P	
LM370N		MC1350P	LM3071N	MC1371P	
LM371H		MFC6010	LM3900N	MC3401P	
			LM3901N	MC3302P	
LM376N		MFC6030A	LM5520J		MC7520L
LM380N		MFC9020			
LM381N		MC1339P	LM5521J		MC7521L
LM382N		MC1339P	LM5523J		MC7523L
LM703LN		MFC6010	LM5525J		MC7525L
			LM5528J		MC7528L
LM709H	MC1709G		LM5529J		MC7529L
LM709CH	MC1709CG				
LM709CN	MC1709CP2		LM5534J		MC7534L
LM710H	MC1710G		LM5535J		MC7535L
LM710CH	MC1710CG		LM5538J		MC7538L
			LM5539J		MC7539L
			LM7520J	MC7520L	

Courtesy Motorola Semiconductor Products, In

NATIONAL TO MOTOROLA (cont)

NATIONAL TYPE NUMBER	MOTOROLA DIRECT REPLACEMENT	MOTOROLA FUNCTIONAL EQUIVALENT
LM7520N	MC7520L	
LM7521J	MC7521L	
LM7521N	ML7521L	
LM7522J	ML7522L	
LM7522N	MC7522L	
LM7523J	MC7523L	
LM7523N	MC7523L	
LM7524J	MC7524L	
LM7524N	MC7524L	
LM7525J	MC7525L	
LM7525N	MC7525L	
LM7528J	MC7528L	
LM7528N	MC7528L	
LM7529J	MC7529L	
LM7529N	MC7529L	
LM7534J	MC7534L	
LM7534N	MC7534L	
LM7535J	MC7535L	
LM7535N	MC7535L	
LM7538J	MC7538L	
LM7538N	MC7538L	
LM7539J	MC7539L	
LM7539N	MC7539L	
LM75450AN		MC75450P
LM75451AN		MC75451P
LM75452N	MC75452P	
LM75453N	MC75453P	

Courtesy Motorola Semiconductor Products, Inc.

RCA TO MOTOROLA

RCA DEVICE NUMBER	MOTOROLA DIRECT EQUIVALENT	MOTOROLA FUNCTIONAL EQUIVALENT	RCA DEVICE NUMBER	MOTOROLA DIRECT EQUIVALENT	MOTOROLA FUNCTIONAL EQUIVALENT
CA3000		MC1550G	CA3047A		MC1433L
CA3001		MC1550G	CA3048		MC3401P
CA3002		MC1550G	CA3052		MC1339P
CA3004		MC1550G	CA3053		MC1550G
CA3005		MC1550G	CA3055		MC1723G
CA3006		MC1550G	CA3056		MC1741CG
CA3007		MC1550G	CA3056A		MC1741G
CA3008		MC1709F	CA3058		MFC8070
CA3008A		MC1709F	CA3059		MFC8070
CA3010		MC1709G	CA3064	MC1364	
CA3010A		MC1709G	CA3065	MC1358	
CA3011		MC1590G	CA3066		MC1398P
CA3012		MC1590G	CA3067		MC1328P
CA3013		MC1355P	CA3070	MC1370P	
CA3014		MC1357P	CA3071	MC1371P	
CA3015		MC1709G	CA3072	MC1328P	
CA3015A		MC1709G	CA3075		MC1351P
CA3016		MC1709F	CA3076		MC1590G
CA3016A		MC1709F	CA3079		MFC8070
CA3020		MC1554G	CA3085		MC1723G
CA3020A		MC1554G	CA3085A		MC1723G
CA3021		MC1590G	CA3085B		MC1723G
CA3022		MC1590G	CA3090Q		MC1310P
CA3023		MC1590G	CA3741T		MC1741G
CA3028A		MC1550G	CA3741CT		MC1741CG
CA3028B		MC1550G			
CA3029		MC1709CP2			
CA3029A		MC1709CP2			
CA3030		MC1709CP2			
CA3030A		MC1709CP2			
CA3031	MC1712				
CA3032	MC1712L				
CA3033		MC1533L			
CA3033A		MC1533L			
CA3035		MC1352P			
CA3037		MC1709L			
CA3037A		MC1709L			
CA3038		MC1709L			
CA3038A		MC1709L			
CA3040		MC1510G			
CA3041		MC1351P			
CA3042		MC1357P			
CA3043		MC1357P			
CA3047		MC1433L			

Courtesy Motorola Semiconductor Products, Inc.

SIGNETICS TO MOTOROLA

SIGNETICS TYPE NUMBER	MOTOROLA DIRECT REPLACEMENT	MOTOROLA FUNCTIONAL EQUIVALENT	SIGNETICS TYPE NUMBER	MOTOROLA DIRECT REPLACEMENT	MOTOROLA FUNCTIONAL EQUIVALENT
NE501A		MC1733CL	N7523B	MC7523P	
NE501K		MC1733CG	N7524B	MC7524P	
NE510A		MFC8000P			
NE510J		MFC8000P	N7525B	MC7525P	
NE515A		MC1420G	SE501K		MC1733G
			SE510A		MFC8000P
NE515G		MC1520F	SE510J		MFC8000P
NE515K		MC1420G	SE515G		MC1520F
NE516A		MC1420G			
NE516G		MC1520F	SE515K		MC1520G
NE516K		MC1420G	SE516A		MC1520G
			SE516G		MC1520F
NE518A		MLM306G	SE516K		MC1520G
NE518G		MLM306G	SE518A		MLM106G
NE518K		MLM306G			
NE528B		MC1444L	SE518G		MLM106G
			SE518K		MLM106G
NE528E		MC1444L	SE528E		MC1544L
NE531G		MC1439G	SE528R		MC1544L
NE531T		MC1439G	SE531G		MC1539G
NE531V		MC1439PZ			
NE533G		MC1776CG	SE531T		MC1539G
			SE533G		MC1776G
NE533V		MC1776CG	SE533T		MC1776G
NE533T		MC1776CG	SE537G		MC1556G
NE537G		MC1456G	SE537T		MC1556G
NE537T		MC1456G			
PA239A	MC1339		SE540L		MFC8020A
			SE550L		MC1723G
NE540L		MFC8020A	S5556T	MC1556G	
NE550A		MFC6030A	S5558T	MC1558G	
NE550L		MC1723CG	S5558F	MC1558L	
N5070B	MC1370				
N5071A	MC1371		S5595F	MC1595L	
			S5596K	MC1596G	
N5072A	MC1328		S5596F	MC1596L	
N5111	MC1357.		S5709G	MC1709F	
N5556T	MC1456G		S5709T	MC1709G	
N5556V					
N5558V	MC1458P1	MC1456G	S5710T	MC1710G	
			S5711K	MC1711G	
N5558T	MC1458G		S5723T	MC1723G	
N5558F	MC1458L		S5733K	MC1733G	
N5595A	MC1495L		S5741T	MC1741G	
N5595F	MC1495L				
N5596A	MC1496L				
N5596K	MC1496G				
N5709A	MC1709CP2				
N5709G	MC1709CF				
N5709T	MC1709CG				
N5709V	MC1709CP1				
N5710A	MC1710CP				
N5710T	MC1710CG				
N5711A	MC1711CP				
N5711K	MC1711CG				
N5723A		MFC6030A			
N5723T	MC1723CG				
N5733K	MC1733CG				
N5741A	MC1741CP2				
N5741T	MC1741CG				
N5741V	MC1741CP1				
N5747A	MC1747CL				
N5747F	MC1747CL				
N5748A		MC1747CG			
N5748T	MC1748CG				
N7520B	MC7520P				
N7521B	MC7521P				
N7522B	MC7522P				

Courtesy Motorola Semiconductor Products, Inc.

T.I. TYPE NUMBER	MOTOROLA DIRECT REPLACEMENT	MOTOROLA FUNCTIONAL EQUIVALENT	T.I. TYPE NUMBER	MOTOROLA DIRECT REPLACEMENT	MOTOROLA FUNCTIONAL EQUIVALENT
SN5500F			SN55110J	MC55110L	
SN5510F	MC1510F		SN55325J	MC55325L	
SN5510L	MC1510G		SN56514L		MC1596G
SN5511F		MC1510F	SN72301AL	MLM301AG	
SN5511L		MC1510G	SN72301AN	MLM301AP1	
			SN72301AP	MLM301AP1	
SN5524J		MC7524L			
SN5525J		MC7524L	SN72306L	MLM306L	
SN5528J	MC5528L		SN72307L	MLM307G	
SN5529J	MC5529L		SN72558L	MC1458G	
SN5534J	MC5534L		SN72558P	MC1458P1	
			SN72702F	MC1712CF	
SN5535J	MC5535L				
SN5538J	MC5538L		SN72702L	MC1712CG	
SN5539J	MC5539L		SN72702N	MC1712CL	
SN7510F	MC1410F		SN72709L	MC1709CG	
SN7510L	MC1410G		SN72709N	MC1709CP2	
SN7511L		MC1410G			
			SN72709P	MC1709CP1	
SN7520J	MC7520S		SN72709S	MC1709CF	
SN7520N	MC7520L		SN72710J	MC1710CL	
SN7521J	MC7521L		SN72710L	MC1710CG	
SN7521N	MC7521L		SN72710N	MC1710CP2	
SN7522J	MC7522L				
			SN72710S	MC1710CF	
SN7522N	MC7522L		SN72711J	MC1711CL	
SN7523J	MC7523L		SN72711L	MC1711CG	
SN7523N	MC7523L		SN7271N	MC1711CP2	
SN7524J	MC7524L		SN72611S	MC1711CF	
SN7524N	MC7524L				
			SN72720N	MC1414L	
SN7525J	MC7525L		SN72733L	MC1733CG	
SN7525N	MC7525L		SN72733N	MC1733CL	
SN7528J	MC7528L		SN72741J	MC1741CL	
SN7528N	MC7528L		SN72741L	MC1741CG	
SN7529J	MC7529L				
			SN72741N	MC1741CP2	
SN7529N	MC7529L		SN72741P	MC1741CP1	
SN52101AL	MLM101AG		SN72741Z	MC1741CF	
SN52106L	MLM106G		SN72747J	MC1747CL	
SN52107L	MLM107G		SN72747N	MC1747CL	
SN52558L	MC1558G				
			SN72748L	MC1748CG	
SN52702F	MC1712F		SN72770L		MC1456G
SN52702L	MC1712G		SN72771L		MC1456G
SN52702N	MC1712L		SN75107J	MC75107L	
SN52702Z	MC1712F		SN75107N	MC75107L	
SN52709F	MC1709F				
			SN75108J	MC75108L	
SN52709L	MC1709G		SN75108N	MC75108L	
SN52710J	MC1710L		SN75109J	MC75109L	
SN52710L	MC1710G		SN75109N	MC75109L	
SN52710N	MC1710P		SN75110J	MC75110L	
SN52710S	MC1710F				
			SN75110N	MC75110L	
SN52711J	MC1711L		SN75150J		MC1488L
SN52711L	MC1711G		SN75150N		MC1488L
SN52711S	MC1711F		SN75154J		MC1489AL
SN52733J	MC1733G		SN75154N		MC1489AL
SN52741J	MC1741L				
			SN75234J		MC7534L
SN52741L	MC1741G		SN75235J		MC7535L
SN52741Z	MC1741F		SN75238J		MC7538L
SN52747J	MC1747L		SN75239J		MC7539L
SN52748J		MC1748G	SN75325J	MC75325L	
SN52748L	MC1748G				
			SN75450N	MC75450P2	
SN52770L		MC1556G	SN75450AN		MC75450P2
SN52771L		MC1556G	SN75451P	MC75451P	
SN55107J	MC55107L		SN75451AP		MC75451P
SN55108J	MC55108L				
SN55109J	MC55109L				

T.I. TYPE NUMBER	MOTOROLA DIRECT REPLACEMENT	MOTOROLA FUNCTIONAL EQUIVALENT
SN75452P	MC75452P	
SN75453P	MC75453P	
SN75454P	MC75454P	
SN76104N	MC1304P	
SN76105N	MC1305P	
SN76107N	MC1307P	
SN76242N	MC1370P	
SN76243N	MC1371P	
SN76246N	MC1328P	
SN76514L		MC1496G
SN76514N		MC1496L
SN76530P	MC1330P	
SN76564N	MC1364P	
SN76600P	MC1350P	
SN76642N	MC1350P	
SN76650N	MC1352P	
SN76651N	MC1351P	
SN76653N	MC1353P	
SN76665N	MC1358P	
SN76675N	MC1375P	

Courtesy Motorola Semiconductor Products, Inc.

FAIRCHILD DEVICE NUMBER	NATIONAL PIN-FOR-PIN EQUIVALENT	NATIONAL FUNCTIONAL EQUIVALENT
U3F7101311 (UA101AF)	LM101AF	
U3F7101333 (UA201AF)	LM201AF	
U3F7702312		LM101AF
U3F7702313		LM101AF
U3F7709311		LM709AH
U3F7709312		LM709H
U3F7709313		LM709H
U3F7710312		LM710AH
U3F7710313		LM710CH
U3F7711312		LM711H
U3F7711313		LM711H
U3F7733312		LM733H
U3F7733313		LM733H
U3F7741312	LM741F	
U3F7741313	LM741F	
U3F7748312	LM101AF	
U3F7748313	LM201AF	
U3I962051X		DM7820D
U3I962059X		DM8820N
U3I962151X		DM7830D
U3I962159X		DM8830N
U3I962251X		DM7820D
U3I962259X		DM8820N
U3M7722333		LMDAC-01
U3M7722334		LMDAC-01
U4L961451X		DM7830D
U4L961459X		DM8830N
U4L961551X		DM7820D
U4L961559X		DM8820N
U4L961651X		LM1488N
U4L961659X		LM1488N
U4L961751X		LM1489AN
U4L961759X		LM1489AN
U5A7064394 (UA3064)	LM3064H	
U5B7101312 (UA101H)	LM101H	
U5B7101311 (UA101AH)	LM101AH	
U5B7101333 (UA201AH)	LM201AH	
U5B7101392 (UA301AH)	LM301AH	
U5B7201393 (UA201H)	LM201H	
U5B7702312		LM101AH
U5B7702393		LM301AH
U5B7709311	LM709AH	
U5B7709312	LM709H	
U5B7709393	LM709CH	
U5B7710312	LM710AH	
U5B7710393	LM710CH	
U5B7716393		LM380N
U5B7730312		LM114AH
U5B7730393		LM114H
U5B7735312		LM4250H
U5B7735333		LM4250H
U5B7735393		LM4250CH
U5B7740312		LH740AH
U5B7740393		LH740AC
U5B7741312	LM741H	
U5B7741393	LM741CH	
U5B7748312	LM748H	
U5B7748393	LM748CH	
UEB7749394		LM1303N
U5B7776312	LM4250H	
U5B7776393	LM4250CH	
U5B7777312	LM101AH	
U5B7777393	LM301AH	
U5D7703312		LM703LH
U5D7703393	LM703LH	
U5E7064394 (UA3064)	LM3064H	
U5E7746394		LM746CN
U5E7754393		LM3065N
U5E7796312	LM1596H	
U5E7796393	LM1496H	
U5F7711312	LM711H	
U5F7711393	LM711CH	
U5F7715312		LM118H
U5F7715393		LM318H
U5F7719312		LM273H
U5F7719393		LM373H
U5F7733312	LM733H	
U5F7733393	LM733CH	
U5F7734312		LM111H
U5F7734393		LM311H
U5F7747312	LM747H	
U5F7747393	LM747CH	
U5R7723312	LM723H	
U5R7723393	LM723CH	
U5T7725311		LM725AH
U5T7725312		LM725H
U5T7725333		LM725H
U5T7725393		LM725CH
U5U7726312		LM114A
U5U7726323		LM114H
U5U7727312		LH1725H
U5U7727333		LH1725H
U5Z7703394		LM703LH
U6A7065394 (UA3065)	LM3065N	
U6A7101311 (UA101AD)	LM101AD	
U6A7101312 (UA101D)	LM101D	
U6A7101333 (UA201AD)	LM201AD	
U6A7101393 (UA301AD)	LM301AD	
U6A7201393 (UA201D)	LM201D	
U6A7702312		LM101AD
U6A7702393		LM301AD
U6A7709311		LM709AH
U6A7709312		LM709H
U6A7709393	LM709CN	
U6A7710312		LM710AH
U6A7710393	LM710CN	
U6A7711312		LM711H
U6A7711393	LM711CN	
U6A7715312		LM118D
U6A7715393		LM318D
U6A7723312	LM723D	
U6A7723393	LM723CD	
U6A7729394	LM1304N	
U6A7732394	LM1305N	
U6A7733312	LM733D	
U6A7733393	LM733CD	
U6A7739312		LM1303D
U6A7739393		LM1303N
U6A7741312	LM741D	
U6A7741393	LM741CN-14	
U6A7746394	LM746CN	
U6A7748312	LM101AD	
U6A7748393	LM301AD	
U6A7749312		LM1303N
U6A7749393		LM1303N
U6A7750312		LM111H
U6A7750393		LM311H
U6A7754394		LM3065N
U6A7757312		LM374H
U6A7757393		LM374H
U6A7760312	LM160J	
U6A7777312	LM101AD	

FAIRCHILD DEVICE NUMBER	NATIONAL PIN-FOR-PIN EQUIVALENT	NATIONAL FUNCTIONAL EQUIVALENT
U6A7767394		LM1304N
U6A7760393	LM360J	
U6A7777393	LM301AD	
U6A7781394	LM3071N	
U6A7784354		LM3065N
U6A962051X		DM7820D
U6A962059X		DM8820N
U6A962151X		DM7830D
U6A962159X		DM8830N
U6A962251X		DM7820D
U6A962259X		DM8820N
U6B7780394	LM3070N	
U6W7747312	LM747D	
U6W7747393	LM747CD	
U7A7747312	LM747D	
U7A7747393	LM747CD	
U7B7524392	LM7524J	
U7B7525393	LM7525J	
U7B7761391		LM7524J
U7B7761392	LM7524J	
U7B7761393	LM7525J	
U7B961551X		DM7820D
U7B961559X		DM8820N
U7B964451X		DH0011H
U7B961451X		DM7830D
U7B961459X		DM8830N
U7B961651X		LM1488N
U7B961659X		LM1488N
U7B961751X		LM1489AN
U7B961759X		LM1489AN
U7F7065394 [UA3065]	LM3065N	
U7F7784354		LM3065N
U9T7101393 [UA301AN]	LM301AN	
U9T7201393 [UA201T]	LM201N	
U9T7741393	LM741CN	
U9T7748393	LM748CN	
U9T7777393		LM301AN
UGH7805393	LM340K-05	
UGH7808393	LM340K-08	
UGH7812393	LM340K-12	
UGH7815393	LM340K-15	
UGH7818393	LM340K-18	
UGH7824393	LM340K-24	
UGJ7805393	LM340T-05	
UGJ7808393	LM340T-08	
UGJ7812393	LM340T-12	
UGJ7815393	LM340T-15	
UGJ7818393	LM340T-18	
UGJ7824393	LM340T-24	
UGJ7109312 [UA109K]	LM109K	
UGJ7109333 [UA209K]	LM209K	
UGJ7109393 [UA309K]	LM309K	
UXX7791312		LH0021K
UXX7791393		LH0021CK

Courtesy National Semiconductor Corp.

MOTOROLA TO NATIONAL

MOTOROLA DEVICE NUMBER	NATIONAL PIN-FOR-PIN EQUIVALENT	NATIONAL FUNCTIONAL EQUIVALENT	MOTOROLA DEVICE NUMBER	NATIONAL PIN-FOR-PIN EQUIVALENT	NATIONAL FUNCTIONAL EQUIVALENT
MC1303L		LM1303N	MC1489L	LM1489J	
MC1304P	LM1304N		MC1496G	LM1496H	
MC1305P	LM1305N		MC1496L	LM1496N	
MC1306P		LM380N	MC1509F		LM733H
MC1307P	LM1307N		MC1510F		LM733H
MC1326P		LM3067N	MC1510G		LM733H
MC1326PQ		LM3067N	MC1514L	LM1514J	
MC1328G		LM3067N	MC1519G		LM733H
MC1328P		LM3067N	MC1520F		LM733H
MC1328PQ		LM3067N	MC1520G		LM733H
MC1350P		LM703L	MC1530F		LM101AF
MC1351P	LM1351N		MC1530G		LM101AH
MC1358P		LM3065N	MC1531F		LM101AF
MC1358PQ		LM3065N	MC1531G		LM101AH
MC1380P		LM380N	MC1533F		LM101AF
MC1410G		LM733CH	MC1533G		LM101AH
MC1414L	LM1414J		MC1533L		LM101AD
MC1420G		LM733CH	MC1535F		LM1303N
MC1430F		LM301AF	MC1535G		LM1303N
MC1430G		LM301AH	MC1536G	LM1536H	
MC1430P		LM301AN	MC1537L		LM1458N-14
MC1431F		LM301AF	MC1538R		LH0002H
MC1431G		LM301AH	MC1539G		LM101AH
MC1431P		LM301AN	MC1539L		LM101AD
MC1433F		LM301AF	MC1504F		LM5524J
MC1433G		LM301AH	MC1540G		LM5524J
MC1433L		LM301AN	MC1540L		LM5524J
MC1435F		LM1303N	MC1541F		LM5524J
MC1435G		LM1303N	MC1541L		LM5524J
MC1435L		LM1303N	MC1550F		LM171H
MC1436CG	LM1436H		MC1550G		LM171H
MC1436G	LM1436H		MC1552G		LM733H
MC1437L		LM1458N-14	MC1553G		LM733H
MC1437P		LM1458N-14	MC1554G		LM380N
MC1438R		LH0002H	MC1556G		LM108H
MC1439G		LM301AH	MC1558G	LM1558H	
MC1439L		LM301AH	MC1558L	LM1558D	
MC1439P2		LM301AH	MC1560G		LM105H
MC1440F		LM7524J	MC1560R		LM105H
MC1440G		LM7524J	MC1561G		LM105H
MC1440L		LM7524J	MC1561R		LM105H
MC1441F		LM7524J	MC1563G		LM104H
MC1441L		LM7524J	MC1563R		LM104H
MC1454G		LM380H	MC1566L		LM104H
MC1456CG		LM308H	MC1569G		LM105H
MC1456G		LM308H	MC1569R		LM105H
MC1458CG	LM1458H		MC1580L		DM7831J
MC1458CL		LM1458N-14	MC1582L		DM7830J
MC1458CP1	LM1458N		MC1583L		DM7820J
MC1458CP2	LM1458N-14		MC1584L		DM7820AJ
MC1458G	LM1458H		MC1590G		LM170H
MC1458L		LM1458N-14	MC1596G	LM1596H	
MC1458P1	LM1458N		MC1596I		LM1596H
MC1458P2	LM1458N-14		MC1709CF		LM709CH
MC1460G		LM305H	MC1709CG	LM709CH	
MC1460R		LM305H	MC1709CL		LM709CN
MC1461G		LM305H	MC1709CP1	LM709CN	
MC1461R		LM305H	MC1709CP2		LM709CN
MC1463G		LM304H	MC1709F		LM709H
MC1463R		LM304H	MC1709G	LM709H	
MC1466L		LM304H	MC1709L		LM709H
MC1469G		LM305H	MC1710CF		LM710CH
MC1469R		LM305H	MC1710CG	LM710CH	
MC1488L	LM1488J		MC1710CL		LM710CH
MC1489AL	LM1489AJ		MC1710F		LM710H

MOTOROLA DEVICE NUMBER	NATIONAL PIN-FOR-PIN EQUIVALENT	NATIONAL FUNCTIONAL EQUIVALENT
MC1710G	LM710H	
MC1710L		LM710H
MC1711CF		LM711CH
MC1711CG	LM711CH	
MC1711CL		LM711CH
MC1711F		LM711H
MC1711G	LM711H	
MC1711L		LM711H
MC1712CF		LM733CH
MC1712CG		LM733CH
MC1712CL		LM733CH
MC1712F		LM733H
MC1712G		LM733H
MC1712L		LM733H
MC1723CG	LM723CH	
MC1723CL	LM723CD	
MC1723G	LM723H	
MC1723L	LM723D	
MC1733CG	LM733CH	
MC1733CL	LM733CD	
MC1733G	LM733H	
MC1733L	LM733D	
MC1741CF	LM741CF	
MC1741CG	LM741CH	
MC1741CL		LM741CH
MC1741CP1	LM741CN	
MC1741CP2	LM741CN-14	
MC1741F	LM741F	
MC1741G	LM741H	
MC1741L	LM741D	
MC1748CG	LM748CH	
MC1748G	LM748H	
MFC40000D		LM380N
MFC4010A		LM381N
MFC4050		LM380N
MFC4060		LM376N
MFC6010		LM2111N
MFC6030		LM376N
MFC6070		LM380N
MFC8000		LM703LN
MFC8001		LM703LN
MFC8002		LM703LN
MFC8010		LM380N
MFC8030		LM703LN
MFC8040		LM381N
MFC9020		LM380N
MLM101AG	LM101AH	
MLM105G	LM105H	
MLM107G	LM107H	
MLM109K	LM109K	
MLM201AG	LM201AH	
MLM205G	LM205H	
MLM207G	LM207H	
MLM209K	LM209K	
MLM301AG	LM301AH	
MLM305G	LM305H	
MLM307G	LM307H	
MLM309K	LM309K	

Courtesy National Semiconductor Corp.

SIGNETICS TO NATIONAL

SIGNETICS DEVICE NUMBER	NATIONAL PIN-FOR-PIN EQUIVALENT	NATIONAL FUNCTIONAL EQUIVALENT	SIGNETICS DEVICE NUMBER	NATIONAL PIN-FOR-PIN EQUIVALENT	NATIONAL FUNCTIONAL EQUIVALENT
N5201A		LM301AD	NE550L		LM723CH
N5307T	LM307H		NE555V	LM555CN	
N5308T	LM308H		NE555T	LM555CH	
N53A1T	LM301AH		NE565A	LM565CN	
N53A1V	LM301AN		NE565K	LM565CH	
N53A8T	LM308AH		NE566T	LM566CH	
N5556V		LM307N	NE566V	LM566CN	
N5558F	LM1458N		NE567T	LM567CH	
N5558T	LM1458H		NE567V	LM567CN	
N5596K	LM1496H		PA239A		LM381N
N5596K		LM1496N	S5101T	LM101H	
N5709A	LM709CN		S5107T	LM107H	
N5709T	LM709CH		S5108T	LM108H	
N5709V		LM709CN	S51A1T	LM101AH	
N5710A	LM710CN		S51A8T	LM108AH	
N5710T	LM710CH		S5556L		LM107H
N5711A	LM711CN		S5558T	LM1558H	
N5711K	LM711CH		S5596K	LM1596H	
N5723A	LM723CN		S5709T	LM709H	
N5723L	LM723CH		S5710T	LM710H	
N5733A	LM733CN		S5711K	LM711H	
N5733K	LM733CH		S5711T		LM711H
N5740T	LH740CH		S5723L	LM723H	
N5741A	LM741CN-14		S5733F	LM733D	
N5741T	LM741CH		S5733K	LM733H	
N5741V	LM741CN		S5740T	LM740H	
N5747A	LM747CH		S5741T	LM741H	
N5747F	LM747CD		S5747K	LM747H	
N5747K	LM747CH		S5748T	LM748H	
N5748A		LM748CH	SE501G		LM733H
N5748T	LM748CH		SE501K		LM733H
N5748V	LM748CN		SE510A		LM171H
N7520B	LM7520N		SE510J		LM171H
N7521B	LM7521N		SE515G		LM733H
N7522B	LM7522N		SE515K		LM733H
N7523B	LM7523N		SE518A		LM106H
N7524B	LM7524N		SE518G		LM106H
N7525B	LM7525N		SE518K		LM106H
NE501A		LM733CN	SE526A		LM106H
NE501G		LM733CH	SE526G		LM106H
NE501K		LM733CH	SE526K		LM106H
NE510A		LM371H	SE529K	LM161H	
NE510J		LM371H	SE531G		LM118H
NE515A		LM733CN	SE533G		LM4250CH
NE515G		LM733CH	SE533T		LM4250H
NE515K		LM733CH	SE537G		LM108H
NE518A		LM306H	SE537T		LM108H
NE518G		LM306H	SE540L		LH0021K
NE518K		LM306H	SE550L		LM723H
NE526A		LM306H	SE555T	LM555H	
NE526G		LM306H	SE555V	LM555N	
NE526K		LM306H	SE565K	LM565H	
NE529K	LM361H		SE566T	LM566H	
NE529A	LM361N		SE567T	LM567H	
NE531G		LM318H	SU536G		LM216H
NE531T		LM318H	SU536T		LM216H
NE531V		LM318H			
NE533G		LM4250CH			
NE533T		LM4250CH			
NE533V		LM4250CH			
NE536T		LM316H			
NE537G		LM308H			
NE537T		LM308H			
NE540L		LH0021CK			
NE550A		LM723CH			

TEXAS INSTRUMENTS DEVICE NUMBER	NATIONAL PIN-FOR-PIN EQUIVALENT	NATIONAL FUNCTIONAL EQUIVALENT	TEXAS INSTRUMENTS DEVICE NUMBER	NATIONAL PIN-FOR-PIN EQUIVALENT	NATIONAL FUNCTIONAL EQUIVALENT
SN5500F		LM5524J	SN52748Z		LM748H
SN5510F		LM733H	SN52770J		LM108D
SN5510L		LM733H	SN52770L		LM108H
SN5511F		LM733H	SN52770Z		LM108F
SN5511L		LM733H	SN52771J		LM112D
SN5524J	LM5524J		SN52771L		LM112H
SN5525J	LM5525J		SN52771Z		LM112F
SN7500F		LM7524J	SN55107J	LM55107J	
SN7501F		LM7524J	SN55108J	LM55108J	
SN7502F		LM7524J	SN55109J	LM55109J	
SN7510F		LM733CH	SN55110J	LM55110J	
SN7510L		LM733CH	SN55182J	DM7820AJ	
SN7511L		LM733CH	SN55183J	DM7830J	
SN7520J	LM7520J		SN56514L		LM1496H
SN7520N	LM7520N		SN72301AJ	LM301AD	
SN7521J	LM7521J		SN72301AL	LM301AH	
SN7521N	LM7521N		SN72301AN		LM301AN
SN7522J	LM7522J		SN72301AP	LM301AN	
SN7522N	LM7522N		SN72301AZ	LM301AF	
SN7523J	LM7523J		SN72307J	LM307D	
SN7523N	LM7523N		SN72307L	LM307H	
SN7524J	LM7524J		SN72307N	LM307N	
SN7524N	LM7524N		SN72307P		LM307H
SN7525J	LM7525J		SN72307Z	LM307F	
SN7525N	LM7525N		SN72558L	LM1458H	
SN7528J	LM7528J		SN72558P	LM1458N	
SN7528N	LM7528N		SN72702F		LM301AF
SN7529J	LM7529J		SN72702L		LM301AH
SN7529N	LM7529N		SN72702N		LM301AN
SN52101AJ	LM101AD		SN72709L	LM709CH	
SN52101AL	LM101AH		SN72709N	LM709CN	
SN52101AZ	LM101AF		SN72709P		LM709CN
SN52107J	LM107D		SN72709S		LM709CH
SN52107L	LM107H		SN72710J		LM710CN
SN52107Z	LM107F		SN72710L	LM710CH	
SN52558L	LM1558H		SN72710N	LM710CN	
SN52702AF		LM101AF	SN72710S		LM710CH
SN52702AL		LM101AH	SN72711J		LM711CN
SN52702AN		LM301AN	SN72711L	LM711CH	
SN52702F		LM101AF	SN72711N	LM711CN	
SN52702L		LM101AF	SN72811S		LM711CH
SN52702N		LM301AN	SN72720N	LM1414N	
SN52702Z		LM101AF	SN72733L	LM733CH	
SN52709AF		LM709AH	SN72733N	LM733CN	
SN52709AL	LM709AH		SN72741J	LM741CD	
SN52709AN		LM709AH	SN72741L	LM741CH	
SN52709F		LM709H	SN72741N	LM741CN-14	
SN52709L	LM709H		SN72741P	LM741CN	
SN52709N		LM709H	SN72741Z	LM741CF	
SN52710J		LM710H	SN72747J	LM747CD	
SN52710L	LM710H		SN72747N	LM747CN	
SN52710N		LM710H	SN72748N		LM748CN
SN52710S		LM710H	SN72748P	LM748CN	
SN52711J		LM711H	SN72748J		LM748CN
SN52711L	LM711H		SN72748L	LM748CH	
SN52711N		LM711H	SN72748Z		LM748H
SN52711S		LM711H	SN72770J		LM308D
SN52733L	LM733H		SN72770L		LM308H
SN52741J	LM741D		SN72770N		LM308H
SN52741L	LM741H		SN72770P		LM308H
SN52741Z	LM741F		SN72770Z		LM308F
SN52747J	LM747D		SN72771L		LM312H
SN52747Z	LM747F		SN72771N		LM312D
SN52748J		LM748H	SN72771P		LM312D
SN52748L	LM748H		SN72771Z		LM312F

TEXAS INSTRUMENTS DEVICE NUMBER	NATIONAL PIN-FOR-PIN EQUIVALENT	NATIONAL FUNCTIONAL EQUIVALENT
SN75100L		DM8820D
SN75107J	LM75107J	
SN75107N	LM75107N	
SN75108J	LM75108J	
SN75108N	LM75108N	
SN75109J	LM75109J	
SN75109N	LM75109N	
SN75110J	LM75110J	
SN75110N	LM75110N	
SN75150J		DM8830J
SN75150N		DM8830N
SN75105P		DM8830N
SN75182J	DM8820AJ	
SN75182N	DM8820AN	
SN75183J	DM8830J	
SN75183N	DM8830N	
SN75324J	LM75324J	
SN75324N	LM75324N	
SN75325J	LM75325J	
SN75325N	LM75325N	
SN75450N	LM75450N	
SN75450AN	LM75450N	
SN75451P	LM75451N	
SN75451AP	LM75451N	
SN75452P	LM75452N	
SN75453P	LM75453N	
SN75454P	LM75454N	
SN75460	LM75460N	
SN75461	LM75461N	
SN75462	LM75462N	
SN75463	LM75463N	
SN75464	LM75464N	
SN76514L		LM1496H
SN76514N		LM1496H

RCA DIRECT-REPLACEMENT GUIDE

Analog Devices Type No.	RCA Direct Replacement
AD741	CA741T
AD741C	CA741CT

Advanced Micro Devices Type No.	RCA Direct Replacement
AM101T	CA748T
AM201T	CA748T
AM741T	CA741T
AM741CT	CA741CT
AM747T	CA747T
AM747CT	CA747CT
AM748T	CA748T
AM748CT	CA748CT

Fairchild Semiconductor Type No.	RCA Direct Replacement
LM108H	CA108T
LM108AH	CA108AT
LM208H	CA208T
LM208AH	CA208AT
LM308H	CA308T
LM308AH	CA308AT
U5B7741312	CA741T
U5B7741393	CA741CT
U5B7748312	CA748T
U5B7748393	CA748CT
U5F7747312	CA747T
U5F7747393	CA747CT
U6A7746394 (μA746)	CA3072
U6B7780394 (μA780)	CA3070
U6A7781394 (μA781)	CA3071
741HC	CA741CT
741HM	CA741T
741TC	CA741S
746DC	CA3072
746PC	CA3072
748HC	CA748CT
748HM	CA748T
748TC	CA748CS
780DC	CA3070
780PC	CA3070
781DC	CA3071
781PC	CA3071

Intersil Type No.	RCA Direct Replacement
ICL-101-TY	CA748T
ICL-201-TY	CA748T
ICL-741-TY	CA741T
ICL-741C-TY	CA741CT
ICL-748-TY	CA748T
ICL-748C-TY	CA748CT
ICL-8101-PA	CA748S
ICL-8201-PA	CA748S
ICL-8741-PA	CA741S
ICL-8741C-PA	CA741CS
ICL-8748-PA	CA748S
ICL-8748C-PA	CA748CS

Motorola Semiconductor Type No.	RCA Direct Replacement
MC1328P2	CA3072
MC1357P	CA2111AE
MC1358P	CA3065
MC1441L	CA1541D
MC1458G	CA1458T
MC1458CP1	CA1458S
MC1541L	CA1541D
MC1558G	CA1558T

Motorola (Cont'd) Semiconductor Type No.	RCA Direct Replacement
MC1741G	CA741T
MC1741CG	CA741CT
MC1741CP1	CA741CS
MC1741P2	CA741S●
MC1741CP2	CA741CS●
MC1748G	CA748T
MC1748CG	CA748CT
MC3401P	CA3401E

National Semiconductor Type No.	RCA Direct Replacement
LM101H	CA748T
LM108H	CA108T
LM108AH	CA108AT
LM201H	CA748C
LM208H	CA208T
LM208AH	CA208AT
LM308H	CA308T
LM308AH	CA308AT
LM741H	CA741T
LM741CH	CA741CT
LM741CN	CA741CS
LM747H	CA747T
LM747CH	CA747CT
LM747CN	CA747CE
LM748H	CA748T
LM748CH	CA748CT
LM748CN	CA748CS
LM1458H	CA1458T
LM1458N	CA1458S
LM1558H	CA1558T
LM2111	CA2111AE

Precision Monolithic Type No.	RCA Direct Replacement
SSS108J	CA108T
SSS108AJ	CA108AT
SSS208J	CA208T
SSS208AJ	CA208AT
SSS308J	CA308T
SSS308AJ	CA308AT

Raytheon Type No.	RCA Direct Replacement
RC101TE	CA748T
RC741TE	CA741CT
RC748TE	CA748CT
RM101TE	CA748T
RM741TE	CA741T
RM748TE	CA748T
RM4558TE	CA1558T

Signetics Type No.	RCA Direct Replacement
N5558V	CA1458S
N5741T	CA741CT
N5741V	CA741CS
N5747A	CA747CE
N5748T	CA748CT
N5748V	CA748CS
S5558T	CA1558T
S5741T	CA741T
S5748T	CA748T

Silicon General Type No.	RCA Direct Replacement
SG101M	CA748S
SG101T	CA748T
SG108T	CA108T

Silicon (Cont'd) General Type No.	RCA Direct Replacement
SG108AT	CA108AT
SG201M	CA748CS
SG201T	CA748CT
SG208T	CA208AT
SG208AT	CA208AT
SG308T	CA308AT
SG308AT	CA308AT
SG741M	CA741S
SG741T	CA741T
SG741CM	CA741CS
SG741CT	CA741CT
SG747T	CA747T
SG747CT	CA747CT
SG748M	CA748S
SG748T	CA748T
SG748CM	CA748CS
SG748CT	CA748CT

Solitron Type No.	RCA Direct Replacement
UC4741	CA741T
UC4741C	CA741CT

Sprague Type No.	RCA Direct Replacement
ULN2111A	CA2111AE
ULN2114A	CA3072
ULN2124A	CA3070
ULN2127A	CA3071
ULN2741D	CA741T
ULN2747A	CA747CE
ULS2741D	CA741CT

Texas Instruments Type No.	RCA Direct Replacement
SN52108L	CA108T
SN52108AL	CA108AT
SN52558L	CA1558T
SN52558P	CA1558S
SN52741L	CA741T
SN52741P	CA741S
SN52747L	CA747T
SN52748L	CA748T
SN52748P	CA748S
SN72308L	CA308T
SN72308AL	CA308AT
SN72558L	CA1458T
SN72558P	CA1458S
SN72741L	CA741CT
SN72741P	CA741CS
SN72747	CA747CT
SN72748L	CA748CT
SN72748P	CA748CS
SN76242	CA3070
SN76243	CA3071
SN76246	CA3072
SN76266	CA3066
2N76267	CA3067
SN76564	CA3064
SN76665	CA3065

Index